FOURTH CANADIAN EDITION

ESSENTIALS OF MANAGING HUMAN RESOURCES

Eileen B. Stewart
British Columbia Institute of Technology

Monica Belcourt
Professor of Human Resources Management
York University

George W. Bohlander
Professor Emeritus of Management
Arizona State University

Scott A. Snell
Professor of Business Administration
Darden Graduate School of Business
University of Virginia

NELSON EDUCATION

NELSON / EDUCATION

Essentials of Managing Human Resources, Fourth Canadian Edition

by Eileen B. Stewart, Monica Belcourt, George W. Bohlander, and Scott A. Snell

Vice President and Editorial Director:
Evelyn Veitch

Editor-in-Chief, Higher Education:
Anne Williams

Acquisitions Editor:
Amie Plourde

Marketing Manager:
Kathaleen McCormick

Senior Development Editor:
Sandy Matos

Photo Researcher:
Kristiina Bowering

Permissions Coordinator:
Kristiina Bowering

Senior Content Production Manager:
Anne Nellis

Production Service:
Elm Street Publishing Services

Copy Editor:
Erin Moore

Proofreader:
Elm Street Publishing Services

Indexer:
Elm Street Publishing Services

Manufacturing Manager:
Joanne McNeil

Design Director:
Ken Phipps

Managing Designer:
Franca Amore

Interior Design:
Greg Devitt

Cover Design:
Johanna Liburd

Cover Image:
© Larry Williams/CORBIS

Compositor:
Integra Software Services Pvt. Ltd

Printer:
RR Donnelley–Willard

Library and Archives Canada Cataloguing in Publication

Essentials of managing human resources / Eileen Stewart . . . [et al.]. – 4th Canadian ed.

Includes index.
ISBN 978-0-17-650015-3

1. Personal management— Textbooks. I. Stewart, Eileen B., 1943-

HF5549.E85 2010 658.3
C2009-906075-2

ISBN-13: 978-0-17-650015-3
ISBN-10: 0-17-650015-4

Dedication

To my son and daughter-in-law, Jason Robertson and Andrea McLean, who are my inspiration, and to my many friends, who are always there for me.

Eileen Stewart

BRIEF CONTENTS

DETAILED CONTENTS

PART 2: ATTRACTING AND SELECTING PEOPLE FOR THE ORGANIZATION

PART 3: DEVELOPING PEOPLE IN THE ORGANIZATION

PART 4: EMPLOYEE RELATIONS

PREFACE

The third edition of *Essentials of Managing Human Resources* made reference to the major economic and political events in North America that escalated the need for improved organizational results and confidence of employees, consumers, and shareholders. However, with the economic recession that started in 2008, the need is even greater as we will continue to have skill shortages and intense competition.

These issues have once again reignited the need for organizations to focus on the people in the company: the company's "human resources." This book is written to help you understand the HR "language"—the processes and systems integral to the success of the people in the organizations, and therefore the success of the organization. For example, one of the more important systems in an organization is recruiting capable and skilled people.

This textbook builds on concepts you have learned or been introduced to in either a general management or a general organizational behaviour course. It is written for students who will become (or are) supervisors and line managers and HR professionals. Since the text covers the major human resources management processes and systems, it will provide a good overview if you are thinking about moving into the HR profession.

Essentials is a shorter and a more relevant book for general business students with simpler language. It is important, however, to remember that the field of HR has its own "jargon" or specialized language. Therefore, one of the goals of this book is to help you learn the terminology so that you can deal with HR issues in a more informed way.

Finally, this book is designed to cover all the materials you will need for a good general understanding of all the HR activities in a company, as well as your role in managing people.

WHAT'S NEW IN THE FOURTH EDITION

Building on the successes of the third edition, and incorporating suggestions from users of the text, the following changes have been made:

- Approximately 99% of the references have been updated with 95% since 2007
- An "Emerging Trends" feature in each chapter
- "In View" video clips at the end of each part, including a short description of the video and questions for discussion
- Updated HRM Close-Ups in each chapter
- Updated content in Chapter 1 to reflect the "Great Recession"
- Revised Chapter 5 to focus on systems model of learning
- Combined and streamlined former Chapters 10 and 11 (Labour Relations and Collective Bargaining and Administration) into one chapter (Chapter 10)
- New Chapter 11 on international human resources management
- New case study material in each chapter
- Additional websites within each chapter
- Additional examples in each chapter
- Data and information from the 2006 Census

FEATURES OF THE BOOK

Each chapter contains the following materials:

- **Learning outcomes** are listed at the beginning of each chapter, with reference icons indicating the objective within the chapter.
- **HRM Close-Up** chapter opening relates a story about a supervisor's experience in human resources management.

- **Manager's Toolkit** boxes contain tools and resources for handling HR matters, including tips for supervisors.
- **At Work with HRM** boxes feature real-world applications relating to a specific topic with critical thinking questions at the end.
- **HRM and the Law** boxes help explain the legal implications of HR.
- **Emerging Trends** boxes explain issues that are becoming more important.
- **Ethics in HRM** boxes highlight sensitive issues supervisors might face.
- **Key terms** appear in boldface and are defined in margin notes. The key terms are also listed at the end of the chapter and in the Glossary.
- **Figures with graphs** and **research information** appear throughout the chapters.
- **Illustrations** reinforce points and maintain reader interest.
- A **Summary** at the end of each chapter reinforces the learning objectives.
- A **Need to Know/Need to Understand** box at the end of each chapter helps to identify key topics.
- **Review Questions** and **Critical Thinking Questions** provide basic recall as well as stimulating critical thinking questions for discussion.
- **Developing Your Skills** contain both text-based and Web-based experiential exercises.
- Two **case studies** in each chapter present current HRM issues in real-life settings that allow for critical analysis.
- **Notes and References** are included for further research and information.

- **Website addresses** are provided throughout the text and are indicated with a computer symbol in the margin.
- A new feature called **In View** is included at the end of each part. This feature describes the CBC videos included on the book's accompanying DVD and asks key questions about the videos that can be related to the material studied within the text's subsequent section.

SUPPLEMENTARY MATERIALS

A complete package of teaching and learning support materials accompanies this text:

- An **Instructor's Resource CD (IRCD)** includes an **Instructor's Manual** designed to increase the effective use of the text. It will include chapter overviews, video guides, detailed lecture outlines, answers to the end-of-chapter material, and case solutions.
- The **IRCD** also includes a **Computerized Test Bank** and a **Test Bank** with a balance of true/false, multiple-choice, and essay-type questions. The test bank is cross-referenced with the learning objectives for fast and relevant testing.
- **PowerPoint Slides** created by the author for continuity are also available on the **IRCD**.
- A website: **www.stewart4Ce.nelson.com** In fact, one of the most comprehensive websites available in human resource management that includes test-yourself exercises and Web links divided by subject: In the News; Human Resources Associations; Statutes, Regulations, and Government Agencies; Career Development; and General Interest Links, concerning job analysis, recruitment, compensation, and health and safety.
- The best in CBC Videos is available on a DVD.

ACKNOWLEDGEMENTS

This fourth edition could not have happened without the hard work of many people, particularly the users of earlier editions. We are grateful to the supervisors and HR practitioners who have shared their stories and helped influence the thinking.

Thanks to people such as Lewisa Anciano, Teligence, and John Beckett, B.C. Maritime Employers Association for your contributions. And thanks also to those that provided guidance and support throughout—Mory Mosadegh and Deb Broznitsky.

Many thanks to Deborah Sanborn and to the featured individuals for their work on "HRM Close-Ups."

The efforts of the Nelson team were excellent. Thanks to Evelyn Veitch, Anne Williams, Jackie Wood, Amie Plourde, and Sandy Matos for their guidance, wisdom, and patience.

The authors and publisher also wish to thank those people who reviewed this project during its development in the first, second, and third editions and provided important insights and suggestions:

Dr. Holly Catalfamo, *Niagara College*
Cathy Fitzgerald, *Okanagan College*
Lisa Guglielmi, MEd, CHRP, *Seneca College*
John Hardisty, *Sheridan College*
Dave Inkster, *Red Deer College*
Tracey Kalimeris, *George Brown College*
Ruthanne Krant, *Georgian College*
Dale McGory, IPMA-CP, *College of the North Atlantic*
Jody Merritt, *St. Clair College of Applied Arts & Technology*
David Morrison, *Durham College*
Melanie Peacock, *Mount Royal College*
Carol Ann Samhaber, *Algonquin College*
Indira Somwaru, *Seneca College*
Kathryn Taft, *Capilano College*

Our greatest thanks go to our families, particularly this author's son, Jason Robertson and daughter-in-law, Andrea McLean. They have provided help, support, research, and encouragement that were most welcome for the project to succeed. And the previous authors' spouses—Michael Belcourt, Ronnie Bohlander, and Marybeth Snell—have also provided invaluable guidance and assistance. We are grateful to all of them for their enthusiasm and guidance.

Eileen B. Stewart
British Columbia Institute of Technology

Monica Belcourt
York University

George W. Bohlander
Arizona State University

Scott A. Snell
University of Virginia

ABOUT THE AUTHORS

Eileen B. Stewart

Eileen Stewart continues to teach part-time at the British Columbia Institute of Technology where she had been Program Head, Human Resource Management Programs for a number of years. She is a senior human resources professional with extensive experience in all areas of human resource management including labour relations in both the public and private sectors. As the HR executive, she has managed human resource units in several of British Columbia's large public-sector organizations. With a diverse background that includes mining, banking, education, and municipal government, Ms. Stewart has a strong overall business orientation.

After receiving a B.A. in economics and commerce from Simon Fraser University, British Columbia, she joined Teck Mining as its first personnel manager. She then moved to the British Columbia Institute of Technology where she specialized in labour relations. She obtained her senior management experience at BCIT as director of personnel and labour relations; the University of British Columbia, as director of human resources; and the City of Vancouver, as general manager of human resources.

While working full-time, Ms. Stewart completed her M.B.A. at Simon Fraser University. She currently teaches HRM courses at BCIT and continues to provide consulting services to private, public, and not-for-profit organizations.

Ms. Stewart is active in the HR community through her continued involvement with the B.C. Human Resources Management Association (BCHRMA), where she chairs the HR Leadership Forum. She also served on the executive of the BCHRMA for a number of years, including serving as President. In addition to her professional involvement, she chairs the Board of Directors of the Women's Health Research Institute and sits on the Board of Directors, B.C. Women's Hospital and Health Centre Foundation. Previously she was Chair of the Board of Directors, YWCA of Vancouver, and was its chair for two years.

Monica Belcourt

Monica Belcourt is a Full Professor of Human Resources Management at York University. Her research is grounded in the experience she gained as Director of Personnel for CP Rail, Director of Employee Development, National Film Board, and as a functional HR specialist for the federal government. Dr. Belcourt alternated working in Human Resources Management with graduate school, obtaining an M.A. in Psychology, an M.Ed. in Adult Education, and a Ph.D. in management. She also holds the designation of Certified Human Resource Professional. Dr. Belcourt has taught HRM at Concordia, UQUAM, McGill, and York, where she founded and manages the largest undergraduate program in HRM in Canada. She created Canada's first degrees in human resources management: B.HRM, B.HRM (honours), and a Masters in HRM (www.atkinson. yorku.ca/mhrm/).

As Director of the International Alliance for HR Research, Dr. Belcourt manages these programs: The Research Forum in the *Human Resources Professional*, the Applied Research Stream at the annual conference; the *HRM Research Quarterly*, the best theses (M.A. & Ph.D.) awards program, and a funding program for HR research (www.yorku.ca/hrresall/).

Dr. Belcourt is Series Editor for the ITP Nelson Canada Series in HRM, which includes eight texts to date: *Performance Management through Training and Development, Occupational Health and Safety, Human Resources Management Systems, Recruitment and Selection in Canada, Compensation in Canada, Strategic Human Resources Planning, Research, Measurement and Evaluation in HRM,* and *The Canadian Labour Market*. Additionally, she is the lead author of the best-selling book, *Managing Human Resources*, published by Nelson, from which this text is adapted.

Active in many professional associations and not-for-profit organizations, Dr. Belcourt was the President (2003–04) of the Human Resources Professionals Association of Ontario and serves on the national committee for HR certification, and is a past board member of CIBC Insurance and the Toronto French School. She is a frequent commentator on HRM issues for CTV, *Canada AM*, CBC, *The Globe and Mail, The Canadian HR Reporter,* and other media.

George W. Bohlander

George W. Bohlander is Professor Emeritus of Management at Arizona State University. He teaches undergraduate, graduate, and executive development programs in the field of human resources and labour relations. His areas of expertise include employment law, training and development, work teams, public policy, and labour relations. He is the recipient of six outstanding teaching awards at ASU and has received the Outstanding Undergraduate Teaching Excellence Award given by the College of Business at ASU. In 1996, Dr. Bohlander received the prestigious ASU Parents Association Professorship for his contributions to students and teaching.

Dr. Bolander is an active researcher and author. He has published over 40 articles and monographs covering various topics in the human resources area ranging from labour–management cooperation to team training. His articles appear in such academic and practitioner journals as *Labor Studies Journal, Personnel Administrator, Labor Law Journal, Journal of Collective Negotiations in the Public Sector, Public Personnel Management, National Productivity Review, Personnel,* and *Employee Relations Law Journal.*

Before beginning his teaching career, Dr. Bohlander served as personnel administrator for General Telephone Company of California. His duties included recruitment and selection, training and development, equal employment opportunity, and labour relations. He was very active in resolving employee grievances and in arbitration preparation. Dr. Bohlander continues to be a consultant to both public- and private-sector organizations, and he has worked with such organizations as the U.S. Postal Service, Kaiser Cement, McDonnell Douglas, Arizona Public Service, American Productivity Center, Rural Metro Corporation, and Del Webb. Dr. Bohlander is also an active labour arbitrator. He received his Ph.D. from the University of California at Los Angeles and his M.B.A. from the University of Southern California.

Scott A. Snell

Scott A. Snell is Professor of Business Administration at the Darden Graduate School of Business at the University of Virginia. During his career, Dr. Snell has taught courses in human resources management, principles of management, and strategic management to undergraduate, graduates, and executives. He is actively involved in executive education and serves as faculty director for Penn State's Strategic Leadership Program as well as faculty leader for programs in human resources, developing managerial effectiveness, and managing the global enterprise. In addition to his teaching duties, Dr. Snell also serves as director of research for Penn State's Institute for the Study of Organizational Effectiveness.

As an industry consultant, Professor Snell has worked with companies such as Arthur Andersen, AT&T, GE, IBM, and Shell Chemical to redesign human resource systems to cope with changes in the competitive environment. His specialization is the realignment of staffing, training, and reward systems to complement technology, quality, and other strategic initiatives. Recently, his work has centred on the development of human capital as a source of competitive advantage.

Dr. Snell's research has been published in the *Academy of Management Journal, Human Resource Management Review, Industrial Relations, Journal of Business Research, Journal of Management, Journal of Managerial Issues, Organizational Dynamics, Organizational Studies, Personnel Administrator, Strategic Management Journal,* and *Working Woman.* He is also co-author of *Management: The Competitive Edge,* with Thomas S. Bateman. In addition, Dr. Snell is on the editorial boards of *Journal of Managerial Issues, Digest of Management Research, Human Resource Management Review,* and *Academy of Management Journal.*

He holds a B.A. in psychology from Miami University, as well as M.B.A. and Ph.D. degrees in business administration from Michigan State University. His professional associations include the Strategic Management Society, Academy of Management, and the Society for Human Resource Management.

1

PART

HRM Challenges and the Legal Context

CHAPTER 1

THE CHALLENGES OF HRM

OUTCOMES

After studying this chapter, you should be able to

1. Define human resources management (HRM).

2. Identify the processes and activities of HRM.

3. Explain the importance of HRM to the line manager.

4. Explain the relationship between the line manager and the HR practitioner.

5. Describe current business challenges facing organizations and the impact on people in organizations.

6. Identify key demographic and employee concerns.

7. Describe the link between business strategy and strategic HRM.

OUTLINE

HRM CLOSE-UP

"I need to help people understand the important business issues before new ideas can be implemented, all the time being positive and supportive of their need and ability to contribute with fresh thinking."

Tania Goodine always felt she'd like to manage people and develop a team. At university, she chose an undergrad degree in psychology, studied marketing, and then completed her MBA. Though her first job was as a marketing officer, it wasn't long before Goodine would head up a team of her own and find herself doing two things she loves: marketing and people management.

At Libro Financial Group, a credit union with 300 employees throughout southwestern Ontario, Goodine's title is vice president, Brand. She has responsibility for the identity of the credit union—its reputation in the community, its advertising and marketing programs, and its communications to employees and members.

In contrast to her early days at Libro, Goodine must now get work done through other people. This means spending much of her day developing and coaching people, and helping to solve problems. "It's always worth it," she says, "Investing time with people, no matter how challenging the conversation, is always worth the time and effort."

"In a service business, all you have are your people," says Goodine. "They are earning business and keeping business. Therefore all the human resources processes and programs we have in place are critical to our success as a company."

Training at Libro is flexible and employees complete programs at their own pace. Embracing individual differences and developing people to their full potential is Goodine's goal. "I believe people want to do a good job and when they're not, there's almost always a legitimate reason. Sometimes it's simply a training issue. It's almost never that they're unwilling," she explains.

The newest employees sometimes provide the greatest challenges for Goodine. They come to the organization with fresh ideas and eagerness, and it can be a fine balance to harness an employee's energy without shutting the person down. "I need to help people understand the important business issues before new ideas can be implemented, all the time being positive and supportive of their need and ability to contribute with fresh thinking. Exploring social media is one example of that, where we work to establish business objectives and

Tania Goodine, vice president, Brand, Libro Financial Group. Courtesy of Tania Goodine.

guidelines to manage risk, and then I get out of the way of creative ideas!"

Libro has a prescribed performance management process involving regular feedback with staff. This means there are no surprises when it comes to evaluating how a person is doing in their job. "I also look for opportunities to have people hold a mirror up to themselves," Goodine explains. "When employees can see a behaviour themselves, it makes learning and development so much easier."

The most valuable advice Goodine received as a new manager was during a supervisory training session. A leader explained that everybody has a personal knapsack of things they carry around with them. It is therefore important to recognize individual differences and vary your style accordingly. Sometimes a manager needs to be more direct and sometimes a softer approach is needed. "Set the tone from day one," says Goodine. "To get trust, you have to give it. Take the time to know people and try to connect in a genuine way."

INTRODUCTION

As this textbook is being written, the world is in the middle of its most severe economic downturn since the Great Depression almost 80 years ago. This time period is now being called "The Great Recession."[1] While there is no clear track as to why this happened, it does seem that the financial system in the United States may have created the catalyst that then began to paralyze financial systems in other countries. And as money throughout the world became tighter, companies that needed large amounts of cash flow began to experience difficulty in paying bills. Further, problems in sectors that were already in difficulty, such as the auto industry, became even more pronounced. Analysts are predicting that the global economy could contract by as much as 3% in 2009.

Along with the global economic contraction, major countries have spent trillions of dollars (trillion has 12 zeros!) to stimulate their economies. Whether or not any of these interventions have worked is a matter of time. What does appear to be happening is a shift in the global geographic and political landscape. For example, there have been concerns that the European Union (discussed later) may start to dissolve. While westernized countries have dominated the global financial markets, this too may shift given the problems with the U.S. banking system. However, it is important to remember that the Canadian system is different and Canada seems to be handling the recession slightly better.

The information being presented to you, particularly relating to the legal framework of employment and the various HR processes, will be relevant no matter what is occurring in the economy. However, by the time you are reading this, the challenges facing organizations may have shifted. It will be important for you, your classmates, and your instructor to consider what is happening on the world stage as you read what is being presented here.

The managing of people in an organization remains key to the business agenda—perhaps even more so now. New phrases, such as "human capital" and "intellectual assets," have crept into business jargon to emphasize the value that the people in the organization have. As Tania Goodine says in the opening vignette, it is important to recognize the individual differences of each employee and to adapt her style accordingly. But what is human resources management (HRM) and why is it important?

Just for a moment, imagine an organization without people. No employees, no supervisors, no managers, executives, or owners. It's a pretty tough assignment. Without people, organizations would not exist. And while this idea may not be much of a revelation, it brings home the point that organizations are made up of people. Successful organizations are particularly good at bringing together different kinds of people to achieve a common purpose. This is the essence of human resources management. As students, you are the future of any organization—whether you become employees, supervisors, or managers.

WHAT IS HUMAN RESOURCES MANAGEMENT?

 Outcome 1

Human resources management (HRM)
An integrated set of processes, programs, and systems in an organization that focuses on the effective deployment and development of its employees

Human resources management is more than hiring, paying, and training people. **Human resources management (HRM)** is an integrated set of processes, programs, and systems in an organization that focuses on the effective deployment and development of its employees.

The word "employee" is also intended to cover contract workers, people from other organizations who are working on a project, or any other similar working relationship. This is indicative of the new workplace that is far more fluid and flexible than the workforce of 10 to 20 years ago.

Managers use a lot of words to describe the importance of people to their organizations. The term "human resources" implies that people are as important to the success of any business as other resources are, such as money, materials, machinery, and information.

WHAT ARE THE HRM PROCESSES AND ACTIVITIES?

 Outcome 2

Before there can be a discussion about why to study HRM, let's look at the various individual systems and processes that fit together. There are some very traditional activities as well as some new and emerging activities. You will also notice that this book is structured on the typical HR activities in an organization.

1. *Organizational, work, and job design*—determining what tasks need to be done, in what order, with what skills, and how individual tasks fit together in work units. For example, in the HRM Close-Up, Goodine has to ensure that the tasks are coordinated in a way to get the work done of her team.

2. *Planning*—ensuring that people in the organization are the right people with the right skills at the right time in the right place. In the HRM Close-Up, Goodine has to plan when it is necessary to add more staff.

3. *Recruitment and selection*—sourcing, attracting, and hiring the people with the necessary skills and background. Again, Goodine had to find and hire the people who can best represent the company and do the work as expected.

4. *Training and development*—providing the resources to assist employees in developing the necessary knowledge and skills to do their job today and in the future. Goodine indicated that training is in a flexible format and that she spends a good portion of each day coaching and helping staff develop to their full potential.

5. *Performance management*—ensuring that there are appropriate mechanisms in place to provide feedback to employees on a regular basis. For Goodine and Libro to ensure that the business objectives are being met, they provide regular feedback so that there are no surprises during review time.

6. *Compensation (pay and benefits)*—developing and administering pay and benefits programs that will attract and retain employees. Being in the financial services business, Libro will need to ensure that its compensation program can attract and retain the calibre of staff it desires.

7. *Occupational health and safety*—ensuring that the safety and health of employees are maintained. Goodine and others in the company need to ensure that the physical premises have a safe and healthy work environment.

8. *Employee and labour relations*—ensuring that there are positive and constructive relations between the employees and their supervisors or managers and/or union representatives. Goodine notes that part of her job is to recognize individual differences in staff and adjust her management style accordingly.

While the above lists the more traditional areas, a number of areas are emerging as the field of HR grows and responds to the concerns of both employees and employers. Some of these are (1) organizational development and learning (an extension of training and development); (2) high-performance work groups or teams (an extension of job design); (3) flexible work arrangements (ways to engage employees and address demographic issues); and (4) HRIS—human resource information (and management) systems. HRIS will be discussed more fully in this chapter's section under "Technology." These processes and activities and their relationship to the organization and the employees are shown in Figure 1.1.

WHY STUDY HUMAN RESOURCES MANAGEMENT?

Outcome 3

To work with people in any organization, it is important to understand human behaviour and be knowledgeable about the various systems and practices available to effectively use as well as build a skilled, knowledgeable, and motivated workforce. At the same time, managers must be aware of economic, technological, social, and legal issues that either help or hinder their ability to achieve organizational success. The line manager or supervisor is the key link between the employee and the organization. Therefore, the manager must have a thorough knowledge and understanding of contemporary HRM and how these practices influence the output of any organization. You are the managers and employees of tomorrow: studying HRM will help you understand your roles and responsibilities in helping to manage your company's people—its human resources.

In the process of managing human resources, increasing attention is being given to the individual needs of the employees. Organizations throughout North America have learned that "their best assets had legs."[2] Thus, this book will not only emphasize the importance of the contributions that HRM makes to the organization but will also show how, through good people management in an organization, the individual and our overall society are improved. Consider how you feel

FIGURE 1.1   Overall Framework for HR

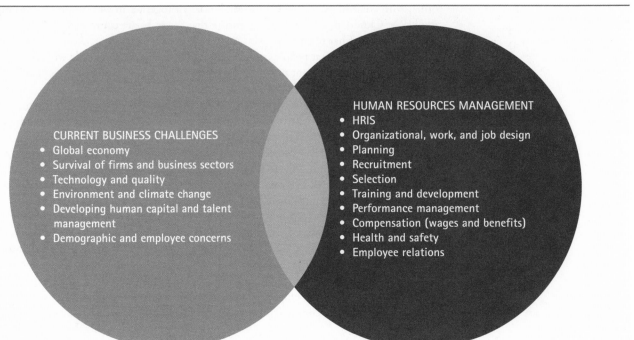

CURRENT BUSINESS CHALLENGES
- Global economy
- Survival of firms and business sectors
- Technology and quality
- Environment and climate change
- Developing human capital and talent management
- Demographic and employee concerns

HUMAN RESOURCES MANAGEMENT
- HRIS
- Organizational, work, and job design
- Planning
- Recruitment
- Selection
- Training and development
- Performance management
- Compensation (wages and benefits)
- Health and safety
- Employee relations

and behave if your work isn't enjoyable and you don't feel that you understand your role in the organization or that your work doesn't appear to be valued. You might respond in a variety of ways, including being unconcerned about a customer complaint. By acting in this way, you are not contributing to the success of the organization, which includes your own success. If enough people do this, our overall productive capacity as a society will decrease.

In addition, employees and the public at large are demanding that employers demonstrate greater social responsibility in managing their people. Complaints that some jobs are deadening the spirit and injuring the health of employees are not uncommon. Complaints of discrimination against women, visible minorities, the physically and mentally challenged, and the elderly with respect to hiring, training, advancement, and compensation are being levelled against some employers. Issues such as comparable pay for dissimilar work, the high cost of health benefits, daycare for children of employees, and alternative work schedules are ones that many employers must address as our workforce grows more diverse.

THE PARTNERSHIP OF LINE MANAGERS AND HR PROFESSIONALS

Role of the Line Manager

Managing people depends on effective supervisors and line managers. Although HR professionals may have responsibility for coordinating programs and policies pertaining to people-related issues, managers and employees themselves are ultimately responsible for making the organization successful. All line managers, in effect, are people managers—not the HR professional or HR unit. It is through the effective leadership of the line manager or supervisor that the talent or "intellectual capital" of the organization is enhanced. Remember that it is the line manager who directly interacts with the employees and is responsible for the effective contribution of those employees to the organization. In a recent survey of the world's most admired companies, it was noted that employees tend to trust information from their direct managers more than other managers and that these same direct managers have a huge influence on the reasons employees stay with the organization.[3] For example, when an organization wishes to place an increased emphasis on the growth and development of its people, it is the line manager who is front-and-centre in identifying the gaps in any skill sets. It is only then that the HR practitioner can offer some ways and means of bridging the gap.

It is also important to understand that the supervisor or manager has "line authority"—being directly responsible for the product or service. Unlike line managers who are directly responsible for a product or service, HR professionals are typically "staff"—people who help and support the line manager. HR professionals may have "functional authority"; that is, they have the legitimate authority in HR areas, such as recruitment strategies or developing organizational programs, to recognize employees. In today's organizations, most HR professionals no longer have total functional authority and are expected to provide advice and guidance to the line. However, there might be a situation that could have very serious consequences for the organization. In this case, the HR professional will be expected to provide advice in a strong and influential way ensuring that the line manager understands the impact on the organization prior to taking action.

Readers of this book will become line managers, supervisors, and employees as well as HR professionals. This text is oriented toward helping people manage people more effectively and understanding the various HR processes, whether they become first-line supervisors or HR professionals. Students now preparing for careers in organizations will find that the study of HRM provides a background that will be valuable in managerial and supervisory positions. Discussions concerning the role of the HR department can provide a better understanding of the functions performed by this department. A familiarity with HRM will help facilitate closer cooperation between HR professionals, whether they are part of the organization or are a contracted service, and will provide an opportunity to more fully use the expertise of HR professionals. For example, an HR professional can assist the supervisor in developing steps to improve the performance of a particular employee. The consequences for the supervisor of developing a poor approach could result in the employee either not improving the performance or the employee feeling unsupported or criticized by the supervisor's approach. In either situation, the primary objective of improving performance would not be achieved.

Role of the HR Professional

It is important for line managers to understand the role or function HR professionals play, whether these individuals are part of the organization or are external resources retained by the organization. HR practitioners are increasingly becoming more professional and are being trained with common bodies of knowledge and information. Besides knowing how to recruit and pay people appropriately, HR professionals need sound business knowledge, good problem-solving and influence skills, and personal credibility (trust and the ability to build personal relationships). The HR practitioner's primary role in today's organizations is to help equip the line manager with the best people practices so that the organization can be successful. HR professionals can provide service activities, such as recruiting and training. Further, they can be active in policy formulation and implementation in such areas as workplace harassment, healthy work environments, and change management. Lastly, an HR professional can be an employee advocate by listening to employee concerns and ensuring that the organization is aware of and responding to those concerns. HR professionals are expected to fulfill their role by actively involving others in the organization, particularly the supervisors and managers, in the development and design of HR programs.

For example, a company may want the HR professional to develop an overall recruitment approach to attract individuals with key skill sets. This approach would then generate a pool of applicants with the required skills. However, it would be the line manager who would actually select the best person from this pool.

Dave Ulrich,[4] a leading author on human resources practices, states that an HR professional must focus on delivering value to the various stakeholders in any organization—the line managers, the investors, and the employees.

Above all else, HR professionals must be able to integrate business skills, HR skills, and skills in helping employees handle change so that their organization can build and maintain a competitive advantage through its people.

In the highly competitive hospitality industry, it is important that hotel managers work closely with HR professionals to hire and retain capable employees.

The Sheraton Centre Toronto

The Ongoing Partnership

As we look at the competitive and social challenges facing human resources management in the next section of this chapter, it is important to reinforce the idea that managing people is not something that occurs in a back room or is done by HR professionals alone. Managing people is every manager's responsibility and obligation, and successful organizations are those that equip their line managers with a thorough understanding of good HRM practices—either through having an HR unit or retaining expertise when needed. The key is to find ways to develop and utilize the talents of employees so that they reach their greatest potential. If an organization has an HR unit, the HR professionals are there to provide guidance and assistance as internal consultants to the line manager or to help design and deliver programs and services to better equip employees, supervisors, and managers to contribute to organizational success. Even without an HR professional, the manager is still responsible for effective human resources management.

In organizations that have an HR unit, HR managers assume a greater role in top-management planning and decision making, a trend that reflects the growing awareness among executives that HRM can make important contributions to the success of an organization. And HR professionals have a critical role to play in facilitating the success of managers by leveraging best practices across the organization.[5] A recent study conducted by Watson Wyatt Worldwide indicated that an integrated approach to compensation and employee learning and development not only enabled organizations to retain their top performers, but that the financial performance of the organization was also increased.[6] For additional information on the studies conducted by Watson Wyatt in this area, access their website at **www.watsonwyatt.com**.

Let's reconsider the comments made by Goodine in the chapter's opening story. The organization has over 300 employees and also has an HR unit with an HR manager. But many smaller organizations often wonder at what point it should hire an HR professional? Frequently when an organization has 75 to 100 employees, the owners or senior management may decide that it would be best to have professional assistance. Figure 1.2 shows what the relationship between HR and other business units might be in a small organization.

Watson Wyatt Worldwide
www.watsonwyatt.com

FIGURE 1.2 Relationship of HR to Other Business Units

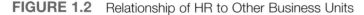

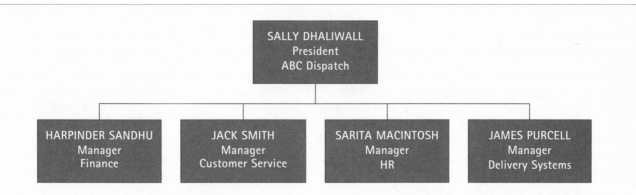

This means that if Jack needed to hire a customer service agent, he would work with Sarita in confirming the job requirements, identifying possible recruitment sources, doing the final interviewing, and making the decision on which candidate to hire. Sarita, on the other hand, would assist Jack as required, including the development of appropriate interview questions and conducting reference checks.

In a larger organization, the HR department may have several professionals to work with employees, supervisors, and managers. Frequently, a particular HR person might be assigned to Jack Smith and be the key contact for all HR services.

CURRENT BUSINESS CHALLENGES

**Conference Board
of Canada**
www.conferenceboard.ca

**Society for Human
Resource Management
(SHRM)**
www.shrm.org

**The Human Resource
Planning Society**
www.hrps.org/

Organizations, such as the Conference Board of Canada (**www.conferenceboard.ca**), the Society for Human Resource Management (**www.shrm.org**), and the Human Resource Planning Society (**www.hrps.org/**), conduct ongoing studies of the most important competitive trends and issues facing firms. As we go forward into a new global environment, some of the business challenges are considerably different than they were just a few years ago.

1. Global economy
2. Survival of firms and business sectors
3. Technology and quality
4. Responses to environment and climate change
5. Developing human capital and talent management
6. Demographic and employee concerns

Challenge 1: Global Economy

The Canadian economy is primarily built on exports, including those in natural resources such as oil, gas, mining, and forestry. Because of this, many Canadian companies have been involved in the global markets for years. As Canada has moved into other goods and services to export, many companies have created global operations or worked collaboratively with foreign companies to sell Canadian products. Canadian exports were valued at over $450 billion in late 2008.[7] This represents approximately 40% of Canada's gross domestic product (GDP).[8] At Work with HRM 1.1 provides insights about a number of Canadian companies who are successful in the global marketplace.

Perhaps one of the more dramatic changes for a Canadian company in the global marketplace has been Nortel Networks. At the beginning of the 21st century, it was the darling of the tech world—trading at a high of $124.50/share in 2000. However, the 114-year-old company went into bankruptcy in February 2009 and by late June 2009 had been delisted from the S&P/TSX composite index. Its assets are being sold off, unit by unit, with Nokia Siemens vying for two of its more significant units. Some analysts say that the company had been mismanaged for years and that it allowed competitors to become more prominent. Canada has lost one of the most admired research and development and telecom equipment manufacturers in the world.[9]

EMPLOYEES: THE KEY DRIVERS FOR GLOBAL SUCCESS

Organizations, such as Diamond and Schmitt, KELK, Les Industries Mailhot, and RWDI Inc., identify that their success in the global market is dependent on the skills and capabilities of their employees. All were honoured in early 2009 for being in the list of the top 50 Best Managed Companies in Canada. Diamond and Schmitt is an architectural firm that excels in innovation and design, as well as creating a non-hierarchal team that empowers everyone in the team to contribute their best. It is ranked by the Institute of British Architects as one of the top 100 international firms.

KELK, a firm that specializes in the design and manufacture of electronic measurement equipment for use in harsh conditions such as steel rolling mills, encourages its scientists, sales and administrative staff to be as innovative as possible to meet the needs of their worldwide clients. Headquartered in Toronto, it has encouraged its people through the same company guidelines for over 30 years.

Likewise, Les Industries Mailhot, a Quebec-based firm that manufactures hydraulic cylinders, attributes its success to its people. The company has grown from 35 to 350 employees in the last 20 years. The CEO delegates a great deal of responsibility to the managers and ensures that

they have the authority they need to achieve the agreed-to business goals. Its competitive advantage is that it has targeted recession-resistant clients such as snow and waste removal firms.

Lastly, RDWI is a Guelph, Ontario, environmental engineering firm whose successes include the world's tallest tower—Burj Dubai—and the glass platform overlooking the Grand Canyon. It has a unique niche where it shows clients how they can minimize the environmental impact of projects, including meeting or exceeding any regulations. It can only do this by having people who are interested and challenged, and have an entrepreneurial spirit. RDWI hires engineers that like to be on the cutting edge and then it ensures that the projects taken on provide the opportunities allowing them to come up with new ways of doing things.

CRITICAL THINKING QUESTIONS

1. What other businesses in your geographic area have a global marketplace?
2. What type of skills might their employees need to continue being a global player?

Source: Adapted from "Canada's 50 Best," Special Report, *National Post*, Monday, February 2, 2009.

Impact of Globalization

Globalization
Moving local or regional business into global marketplace

By partnering with firms in other regions of the world and using information technologies to coordinate distant parts of their businesses, companies, such as Bombardier, General Electric, and SNC Lavalin, have shown that their vision for the future is to offer customers "anything, anytime, anywhere" around the world. But **globalization** is not just something of interest to large firms. While estimates vary widely, 70 to 80% of the Canadian economy today is affected by international competition. This means, for a small distributor in Kamloops, British Columbia, or a small manufacturer in Alliston, Ontario, that the competition today is no longer the distributor or manufacturer in the next town or province. Trade agreements that allow a freer flow of goods and services mean that competitors may be located anywhere around the world. For example, Finning International, one of the world's largest dealers in Caterpillar heavy equipment, based in Vancouver, British Columbia, generates close to $6 billion, in annual revenue from its worldwide markets of which about 40% is from customer support, including equipment rentals.[10] In order to remain competitive, managers of today's organizations, both large and small, must ensure that they manage their human resources in the most productive, efficient, and effective way possible.

However, even with good people management, Canadian organizations are struggling. While Canada managed to avoid the recession for most of 2008, unfortunately being so tied-in to the global marketplace, the recession caught up with Canada in 2009. The economy shrank at an annualized rate of 3.4% at the end of 2008 and was predicted to shrink by another 1.2% in 2009.[11]

Effect of Globalization on HRM

When managers start to "go global," they have to balance a complicated set of issues related to different geographies, cultures, laws, and business practices. Human resources issues underlie each of these concerns and include such things as identifying capable expatriate managers who live and work overseas; designing training programs and development opportunities to enhance the managers' understanding of foreign cultures and work practices; and adjusting compensation plans to ensure that pay schemes are fair and equitable across individuals in different regions with different costs of living.

So, while managing across borders provides new and broader opportunities for organizations, it also represents a quantum leap in the complexity of human resources management. Whether you are working for a large multinational company or a small parts distributor, HRM in other countries has an impact on you. Chapter 11 focuses on international human resource management.

Challenge 2: Survival of Firms and Business Sectors

While the U.S. economy has been in a longer recession than Canada, the two economies are closely linked since approximately 75% of Canada's GDP is exported to the U.S.[12] As a result, many firms and certain sectors in North America have been impacted more than others. For example, Alberta has been very prosperous for a number of years due to the oil and gas production that has generated healthy revenues as commodities in the global economy continued to rise in price. However, when the price of crude oil went from a high of $147.50/barrel in July 2008 to a low of $35/barrel in February 2009 (a decrease of over 75%), Alberta was suddenly faced with a significant shortfall in oil royalties.[13]

And it isn't just the price of the natural resource on the world market, but it is also the price per share and therefore the value of the company that has also been impacted. It is important to reflect on the decline in the stock market from mid-2008 to early 2009. In that time period, the Toronto Stock Exchange went from a high of over 15,000 points to a low of approximately 7500 points—losing 50% of the value.[14] In addition to the problems in the stock market, the banking system in the U.S. has had trouble accessing funds and therefore companies have had trouble borrowing money to keep the operations going. Thus without sufficient cash flow, coupled with declining sales and revenue, has created situations where companies are in survival mode.

Oil and gas are not the only natural resources in Canada that are experiencing difficulties. Mining companies have seen their stock and mineral prices drop significantly. For example, Ontario-based Timminco Ltd., a global leader in the production of minerals with a specialty in very pure silicon, has seen its stock go from a high of $35.69 in June 2008 decline to $2.23 in March 2009. In addition, the demand for its silicon—which is used in solar energy installations—has plummeted. To survive, the company has curtailed its production for three months and has put any expansion plans on hold.[15]

In addition to oil, gas, and mining, the manufacturing sector, particularly in Ontario and Quebec, has seen rapid declines. Manufacturing sales decreased by 5.4% in the month of January 2009 alone—falling to its lowest level in almost 10 years.[16] And much of the decrease is attributable to the auto and auto parts industries. There is no doubt that the auto industry has suffered greatly in both Canada and the United States. And even with large economic stimulus dollars from both the Canadian and U.S. governments, there is grave concern as to how many of the current auto manufacturers will survive. The Canadian government is reluctant to provide additional money unless labour costs are reduced. Perhaps the automaker in the most difficulty is Chrysler who has been negotiating a buy-out from Fiat. However, to do this, it will still need operating dollars on a short-term basis. And to get any money from the government, labour costs must be reduced—which means getting CAW to agree to significant cost savings for both active and retired workers. The CAW agreed in late April 2009 to labour cost reductions that would result in $240 million savings per year for Chrysler Canada.[17] Further, on June 10, 2009, Fiat's buyout of Chrysler was completed, thereby giving the automaker an opportunity to become competitive once more.[18] At about the same time, Roger Penske, the billionaire owner of Penske Racing, the Indy car racing team, purchased the Saturn brand from GM.[19]

Managing Costs

Companies for a number of years have had pressures to lower costs and improve productivity to maximize efficiency. Labour costs are one of the largest expenditures of any organization, particularly in service and knowledge-intensive companies. Organizations have tried a number of approaches to lower costs, particularly labour costs. These include downsizing and outsourcing, each of which has a direct impact on HR policies and practices.

Downsizing is the planned elimination of jobs. The pain of downsizing and layoffs has been widespread throughout Canada, particularly in 2009. Bombardier, the Canadian maker of aircraft, cut 3000 jobs from its workforce due to the decline in orders for airplanes and airplane parts.[20] And with the bankruptcy of Nortel Networks, approximately 27,500 employees are being impacted. Some will be rehired as assets are sold but that does not minimize the dislocation and uncertainty for everyone.[21]

Virtually every major corporation within the country has undergone some cycle of downsizing. What is intriguing about the current economic climate is that there is a continual concern about a labour shortage as the Canadian economy recovers and therefore some companies are being particularly careful about how they reduce or eliminate work.

A number of lessons were learned in earlier downsizing situations and therefore organizations are being much more careful about where the operations are reduced. For a number of years, the general approach was to do an across-the-board reduction or eliminating individuals based on performance. However, through studies it has been demonstrated that it can take 6–18 months for a company to realize the savings from job cuts.[22] Therefore, without a well-designed downsizing approach, the company may find that the best and brightest have left.[23]

Organizations are attempting to be more creative in order to minimize the amount or type of downsizing. For example, Rogers Communication has informed staff that they can voluntarily move to four days with reduced pay. While it hadn't tried the idea before, it was felt to be a better alternative to layoff.[24] Other companies such as Ontario-based Lakeside Steel are laying everyone off for a very short period of time.[25] Some companies are also promoting job-sharing or encouraging people to take extended vacation without pay.[26] Again, attempting to minimize the impact on individuals while dealing with the current financial realities is in the longer term best interests of the organization and the people.

If jobs and people have to be eliminated, the manner in which it is done also has to be carefully planned. As much attention needs to be paid to those people who will still be employed as is the attention given to departing employees. It is the people who are still employed that will help the company recover from recessionary times and it is important that they feel that the company has treated everyone well. During these times it is important to have the CEO speak directly with the employees, answer questions, and be honest as to whether future cuts will have to be made.[27] Interestingly, social networking sites have forced some organizations to be more transparent and candid about downsizing so that bad things are not said about the company on personal blogs or personal networks such as Twitter.[28]

Outsourcing and Employee Leasing

Outsourcing simply means hiring someone outside the company or bringing in a company to perform tasks that could be done internally. Companies often hire the services of accounting firms, for example, to take care of financial services. Interest in outsourcing has been spurred by executives who want to focus their organization's activities on what they do best. Increasingly, activities such as maintenance, security, catering, and payroll are being outsourced in order to increase the organization's flexibility and to lower overhead costs. Sometimes there is a perception that people working for outsourcing firms are not paid well. This is not necessarily true—it depends on the service and/or products expected. For example, Infosys Technologies now handles such critical services as market research, copyediting, patent generation, and the drafting of legal documents and engineering plans.[29]

In economic uncertainty, considering outsourcing could be helpful in keeping the company going. For example, Telus recently opened its fourth call centre in Manila, hoping to tap into the large number of returning workers to the Philippines. In doing so, Telus will be better able to serve

Downsizing
The planned elimination of jobs

Outsourcing
Contracting outside the organization for work that was formerly done by internal employees. The small-business owner saves money, time, and resources by outsourcing tasks such as accounting and payroll.

its growing client base.[30] And many companies in India that provide such services believe strongly that not considering outsourcing where appropriate stops globalization.[31] However, since there is always a risk of doing this, here are some important things to examine:

1. What type of work is appropriate for outsourcing?
2. How will the service providers be evaluated?
3. What will be the structure of the arrangement—will it be in another country and what is the currency exchange rate?[32]

In some situations a large portion of a company is outsourced in order to create a new business. This occurred with both Hydro One Inc. (formerly Ontario Hydro) and BC Hydro where a number of their customer service areas were outsourced. As an alternative to layoffs and outsourcing, some companies are exploring the idea of employee leasing, where employees are let go and then hired by a leasing company that contracts back with the original company. The Bank of Montreal outsourced its human resources processing services (payroll and benefits administration, HR call centres, and employee records) to Exult, a company specializing in outsourcing, in a contract that saw the transfer of 100 BMO employees to Exult.

In addition to downsizing, outsourcing, and employee leasing, organizations are also making more use of contract workers and part-time workers as a way to contain costs. All of these are HRM concerns as managers work to ensure these individuals understand the mission of the organization and are actively engaged and committed to the organization.

Challenge 3: Technology and Quality

Advancements in technology have enabled organizations to improve processes (both production and administrative), reduce costs, and improve quality. With computer networks, unlimited amounts of data can be stored, accessed, and used in a variety of ways, from simple record keeping to controlling complex equipment. The effect is so dramatic that at a broader level, organizations are changing the way they do business. Use of the Internet to transact business has become so pervasive for both large and small companies that *e-commerce* is rapidly becoming the organizational challenge of the new millennium. Even following the "dot-com bust," in which many promising new Internet companies failed rapidly, the Web is transforming the way traditional brick-and-mortar companies do business. For example, a Montreal native who is working at Harvard University Medical School helped create an interactive online disease database that has revolutionized the way people find out about medical issues worldwide.[33] Organizations are connected via computer-mediated relationships, and they are giving rise to a new generation of "virtual" workers who work from home, hotels, their cars, or wherever their work takes them. The implications for HRM are at times mind-boggling.

It is hard to imagine that the Web is only 20 years old and yet the impact has been huge. For example: there are blogs and instant messaging through companies such as MSN; there are online communities where people can come together who share common interests; there is 24/7 news feeds; maps and directions, e-mail; and Google.[34] Can you remember when "to google" wasn't a verb! A recent study by Watson Wyatt Worldwide has identified that the successful search engine is the most used site on the Internet and it is allowing employees to contribute and drive change within the organization.[35] Further, it is important to remember the impact that the Internet has had on networking with the creation of social networks such as Facebook. According to recent statistics, almost 10% of a person's time is spent on social networking and blog sites.[36]

As a consequence, the skills necessary to be successful are different. For example, this text provides you with websites for additional information. You can access **www.jobfutures.ca** for information on trends in jobs and occupations, earnings, and work prospects in Canada. Likewise, some of you will get work after you finish school by posting your résumé online through **www.monster.ca**, **www.workopolis.com**, or **www.ca.manpower.com**, or by having your own home page with your résumé.

Figure 1.3 provides information about the skills that are important for contributing to innovation in the workplace.

Job Futures
www.jobfutures.ca

Monster.ca
www.monster.ca

Workopolis
www.workopolis.com

Manpower
www.ca.manpower.com

FIGURE 1.3   Innovation Skills

The Conference Board of Canada conducted a study to determine what organizations look for in order to produce new and improved porcesses, products, and services. Here is a partial list of what it found:

Creativity and continuous improvement skills—necessary to generate ideas
- Exploring options
- Being adaptable
- Asking questions
- Putting forward own ideas
- Demonstrating trust in other's ideas

Risk-taking skills—necessary for being entrepreneurial
- Being open to opportunities for change
- Assessing risk
- Encouraging others to bring new ideas forward
- Learning from your experiences
- Accepting failures

Relationship-building skills—necessary to develop relationships that support innovation
- Understanding and working within a group
- Engaging others to use their skills and knowledge
- Sharing information
- Encouraging others to speak freely
- Providing honest praise and constructive feedback

Implementation skills—necessary to turn ideas into processes, products, and services
- Accessing and applying knowledge
- Adapting to changing requirements
- Using the right tools and technologies
- Adopting a "can-do" attitude
- Tolerating mistakes when trying out new ideas

Source: Adapted from Conference Board of Canada Innovation Skills Profile (ISP) found at: http://www.conferenceboard.ca/topics/education/learning-tools/isp.aspx.

Influence of Technology in HRM

Human resources information system (HRIS)
A technology system that provides data for purposes of control and decision making

Information technology has, of course, changed the face of all business processes in Canada and abroad. Perhaps the most central use of technology in HRM is an organization's **human resources information system (HRIS)**. An HRIS provides data for purposes of control and decision making; in this sense it moves beyond simply storing and retrieving information to include broader applications, such as producing reports, forecasting HR needs, assisting in strategic planning and career and promotion planning, and evaluating HR policies and practices. These systems are designed as a resource to be used by the line manager and the HR practitioner to make the best decisions for the organization.

The impact of information technology (IT) within HR has been both pervasive and profound. IT allows firms to store and retrieve large amounts of information quickly and inexpensively. It also enables them to rapidly and accurately combine and reconfigure data to create new information and institutionalize organizational knowledge. With IT networks, managers can communicate more easily and selectively with others in remote parts of the world, thereby allowing for even better use of the information at their disposal. In that regard, IT can be a potent weapon for lowering administrative costs, increasing productivity, speeding response times, improving decision making, and enhancing service. It may also be vital for coordinating activities with parties external to the firm. Ultimately, IT can provide a data and communications platform that helps HR link and leverage the firm's human capital to achieve a competitive advantage.

IT influences HRM in three basic ways. The first is its operational impact; that is, automating routine activities, alleviating the administrative burden, reducing costs, and improving productivity

A person working in a pharmaceutical laboratory needs not only technical skills but also skills in working with others.

John A. Rizzo/Photodisc Green/Getty Images

internal to the HR function itself. The most frequent uses of IT in HRM include automating payroll processing, maintaining employee records, and administering benefits programs. Another new advance in this area is biometric time clocks that provide the highest level of security available.[37] In addition, other organization processes such as performance management and training/development can also be managed very effectively with the type of technology that is now available.[38]

The second way IT influences HR is by enhancing services to line managers and employees. Initially security was a big concern, particularly in relation to employees having access to their own information. However, since online security has improved so much, companies have created more and more applications of employee self-service. And in this way employees bypass HR and handle information about themselves directly. Examples of this are: accessing pay statements and updating personal information such as change of address.[39]

The third influence of IT on HR is the Internet as it has revolutionized our ability to access and use information. A growing number of companies, such as Canada Post, the City of Vancouver, Hewlett-Packard (Canada), and IBM Canada, are using the Internet to do everything from reading current job postings, to applying online, to creating "virtual" worlds for training and development purposes. Web 2.0 technology allows users to create a variety of interactive connections, including social networks, wikis, blogs, and podcasts.[40] Needless to say, an entire new vocabulary has evolved. Lastly, IT has a transformational impact by redefining the activities that HR undertakes. For example, Don Tapscott, a leading authority on business strategy and organizational transformation, states that the HR professional will change from simply executing HR processes and functions to being a leader for new models of talent and collaborative work.[41] Manager's Toolkit 1.1 provides helpful current website addresses for the supervisor or manager.

Quality

Meeting customer expectations is essential for any organization. In addition to focusing on internal management issues, managers must also meet customer requirements of quality, innovation, variety, and responsiveness. These standards often separate the winners from the losers in today's competitive world. How well does a company understand its customers' needs? How fast can it develop and get a new product to market? How effectively has it responded to special concerns? "Better, faster, cheaper"—these standards require organizations to constantly align their processes with customer needs. Management approaches such as quality management, Six Sigma, and

A GUIDE TO INTERNET SITES

The Internet offers managers and HR professionals a vast amount of resources for research, news, recruitment, and networking with people and organizations. Listed below are some Internet sites related to the HR field. Their addresses (URLs) are printed here for reference, but once you get started, it's easier to access the rest by following the links to related sites.

GENERAL HR SITES

www.workforce.com

This site posts articles regarding the latest trends and topics in human resources. It also provides links to HR specialist consultants.

www.hrreporter.com

An excellent Canadian resource for current news, information on the latest trends and practices, expert advice, experiences and insights from HR practitioners, research, and resources.

www.hronline.com

This site is an independent, Canadian information service devoted to human resources.

www.kickstarthr.com

This Canadian site provides all the necessary tools and strategies to attract and retain staff.

www.hrprosgateway.com

This is an excellent source of up-to-date human resources information, featuring online articles, discussion forums, and links to related sites.

SPECIALIZED SITES

www.canoshweb.org

Offers a variety of information regarding safety in the workplace, reports and statistics, and industry trends. This site also provides online access to the Workers' Compensation legislation in Canadian jurisdictions.

www.acjnet.org

The "Access to Justice Network" site provides online access to federal and provincial statutes and regulations, including a virtual courtroom.

www.statcan.gc.ca

The Statistics Canada site offers daily news updates, census information, and free tabular data on various aspects of the Canadian economy.

www.cchra.ca

This site provides information about membership in Canadian HR associations, information resources, links to relevant HR sites, and information about the HR professional designation, Certified Human Resources Professional (CHRP).

In addition to the above sites, this book's website, **www.stewart4Ce.nelson.com** provides useful and up-to-date website links to accompany this text.

process reengineering, provide comprehensive approaches to responding to customers. These have direct implications for HR: the requirement to hire staff that can work in teams, the necessity of having compensation systems that support quality objectives, and the need to have performance management systems that recognize the importance of customer satisfaction. The role that quality improvements play in the Canadian healthcare system is described in At Work with HRM 1.2.

The attention to quality started about 20 years ago with total quality management (TQM) and was based on a management philosophy that focused on understanding customer needs, doing things right the first time, and striving for continuous improvement. Pioneered by Deming, a number of studies have demonstrated the strong positive link between a focus on quality and higher customer satisfaction.[42] TQM is still practiced in many countries. For example, Tata Steel, a global steel company with operations in Asia, won the 2008 Deming Prize for Excellent in Total Quality Management.[43] Since continuous improvement was primarily incremental in its approach, organizations began to use the concept of re-engineering or business process improvement to redesign significant processes. The basic question asked was: "What are the steps necessary now to achieve the desired business outcome."[44]

Companies, such as Motorola, GE, and Home Depot, then adopted a more systematic approach to quality, called Six Sigma, which includes major changes in management philosophy

AT WORK **with HRM 1.2**

CONTINUOUS IMPROVEMENT

The National Quality Institute is a not-for-profit whose mission is to advance organizational excellence throughout Canada. It does this in a number of ways including a recognition program for having attained certain goals. A recent recipient of its Order of Excellence Award was Diversicare Canada Management Services, a long-term care and nursing home industry. Based in Ontario, the company manages 38 facilities in Ontario and Western Canada. Diversicare owns some facilities while the company only manages others. After a period of time, managers noticed that the quality in the different facilities varied great from one place to another. It was because of these variations that the company embarked upon a continuous improvement program.

In order to achieve consistency in quality, the company began using 16 indicators—such as number of falls in patients or number of workplace injuries. The company knew that the staff wanted to provide the very best patient care and therefore needed better systems. Along with the improvement initiatives, the managers also developed a "cheerleading" approach. Managers learned to lead, coach, and encourage employees to become involved with the quality programs.

Like any other change in any organization, the improvement program didn't blossom overnight. It took a number of years with some dedicated staff and managers to reach the turning point. But the company felt it was worth it when it achieved the NQI Order of Excellence.

CRITICAL THINKING QUESTION

Is use of any quality improvement initiatives another management fad to get more work out of people? Explain the reasons for your answer.

Sources: Adapted from Uyen Vu, "Quality Improvement Success Stories," *Canadian HR Reporter*, www.hrreporter.com/ArticleView.aspx?l=1&articleid=4729 (accessed March 17, 2009); "About Diversicare," www.diversicare.ca; and "Canada Awards for Excellence Recipients," National Quality Institute, www.nqi.ca (accessed March 19, 2009).

Six Sigma
A process used to translate customer needs into a set of optimal tasks that are performed in concert with one another

ISO 9000
Worldwide quality standards program

International Organization for Standards
www.iso.org

Benchmarking
Finding the best practices in other organizations that can be brought into a company to enhance performance

and HR programs. **Six Sigma** is a statistical method of translating a customer's needs into separate tasks and defining the best way to perform each task in concert with the others. In addition, using Six Sigma can guide a business toward innovative solutions by saving money on the various processes that then can be invested in innovative ideas.[45] And Six Sigma can be used for internal organizational processes that deal with internal "customers." For example, Six Sigma has been used in a number of North American organizations to create work environments that are healthier and safer.[46] What makes Six Sigma different from other quality efforts is that it catches mistakes before they happen. In a true Six Sigma environment, variation from standard is reduced to only 3.4 defects per million.[47]

In addition to TQM and Six Sigma, other organizations focus on the importance of quality through ISO 9000 and 14000 certification or benchmarking. **ISO 9000** is a worldwide approach to quality management standards that can cover both product design and product delivery. ISO 14000 focuses on standards for environmental management. Companies go through a certification process to demonstrate that they have achieved certain quality standards. Some of the Canadian companies certified include CAE Inc. (Quebec), Cloverdale Paint (British Columbia), Sea-Can Containers (Alberta), Global Upholstery (Ontario), and Johnston Industrial Plastics (Ontario). For more information on international quality standards, visit **www.iso.org**.

Benchmarking looks at the "best practices" in other companies, whether they are competitors or not. By looking at other companies, managers and employees can assess whether something could be used in their organization to improve overall performance. For example, Royal Bank is involved in benchmarking customer service practices with other financial institutions in North America.

Key to all of these techniques is good HR practices. One of the reasons that HR programs are so essential to programs such as Six Sigma is that they help balance two opposing forces. Six Sigma's focus on continuous improvement drives the system toward disequilibrium, while Six Sigma's focus on customers, management systems, and the like provide the restraining forces that keep the system together. HR practices help managers balance these two forces. This means that the manager plays

International Quality Systems Directory

www.iso.org

Standards Council of Canada

www.scc.ca

Quality Digest

www.qualitydigest.com

National Quality Institute

www.nqi.ca

The Baldrige National Quality Program

www.quality.nist.gov/

a key role in motivating employees to care about quality and helping the company foster a work environment that will allow employees to succeed in quality initiatives. Toyota is well known for the emphasis put on team work and the role the individual plays in quality assurance. And the approach that Toyota has pioneered has moved into the health care area. Provincial Health Services Authority in British Columbia has been using the Toyota-inspired model to make small changes that have resulted in huge reductions in patient wait times; shorter wait times mean improved patient safety. For example, at B.C. Cancer Agency, the time to see a specialist was reduced 83%.[48]

Visit the following sites for the most current information about quality initiatives: **www.iso. org**, **www.scc.ca**, **www.qualitydigest.com**, and **www.nqi.ca**.

Another approach to overall quality in an organization is The Baldrige Award for Performance Excellence, sponsored by the National Institute of Standards and Technology in the United States This award looks at excellence from a systems perspective with detailed criteria in the areas of leadership; strategic planning; customer focus; measurement and knowledge management; workforce focus; process management; and results. Companies as small as Mesa Products that manufactures devices that control metal corrosion on pipelines or companies as large as Boeing have been recipients.[49]

Before we leave the discussion on quality, there is some new research that suggests certain business processes might be better if they weren't standardized. As so often happens with great and new ideas, managers might go overboard and use the technique on everything. However, some output in variability may be better for organizational performance than not. For example, the Ritz-Carlton, a global hotel chain noted for its exceptional service, found that certain routines in creating a great guest experience actually weren't working. For example, staff always saying "good morning" felt stuffy in some situations. To make the interaction with guests seem more natural and spontaneous, the company changed one of its value statements to "I build strong relationships and create Ritz-Carlton guests for life." This change led to encouraging the employees to sense customers' needs and respond accordingly.[50]

Challenge 4: Environment and Climate Change

As the globe progresses further into the 21st century, more and more attention is being paid to the health of our planet. The world population is increasing, natural resources are declining, and the climate is changing. People are realizing that there might be finite limits to how much human kind can be sustained. With this, businesses are examining the threats and opportunities that are presented by these concerns.

Some of the threats are in the oil and gas industry where on one hand there is increased demand for its products but on the other hand a desire to reduce the world's reliance on fossil fuels for energy. Canada's economy has benefitted greatly from our ability to export our oil and gas on the global markets. Change to that would cause dislocation to both the employees and government revenues.

On the other hand, the public view of power generation has created potential opportunities for both hydro and solar power—creating new demand for cleaner energy. For example, Canadian Solar Inc. is a relatively new company that manufactures and custom-designs solar power systems.[51] And while Canada has a long history of using hydroelectric energy in certain provinces, there is more demand expected for "green power." BC Hydro in mid-2009 is expecting a number of proposals from small, independent producers to supply more and more clean power. Also, New Flyer Industries Inc., headquartered in Manitoba, was showcased as a green business that was expanding and hiring and thus helping with the economic recovery in North America. It received this high recognition due to its investment in future technology that is environmentally friendly.[52]

Besides the environment, climate change is also on businesses' agenda. AMEC, a global engineering company with offices throughout Canada indicates that more and more of its clients are looking for sustainability in engineering projects—from fossil-fuel emission reductions to structures that can handle more extreme weather.[53]

As new business opportunities are created, it also means that new jobs and careers will also be created. For example, some of the newer careers are environmental engineers and technologists, conservation biologists, and environmental communications. Also skills that have been acquired in traditional areas can be transferred to newer environmental jobs—such as people with skills in pipelines working in the newer geothermal heating and cooling systems industry.[54]

Challenge 5: Human Capital and Talent Management

Human capital
The individual's knowledge, skills, and abilities that have economic value to an organization

The idea that organizations "compete through people" highlights the fact that success increasingly depends on an organization's ability to manage "human capital." **Human capital** is an overall term used to describe the value of knowledge, skills, and capabilities that may not show up on a company's balance sheet but nevertheless have tremendous impact on an organization's performance. There is no doubt that the knowledge, skills, and abilities of people are becoming increasingly important—and perhaps even more so as the world recovers from the current recession.[55]

Human capital is intangible and elusive and cannot be managed the way organizations manage jobs, products, and technologies. One of the reasons for this is that employees, not the organization, own their own human capital. If valued employees leave a company, they take their human capital with them, and any investment the company has made in training and developing those people is lost. Once again, it is important to emphasize that the supervisor/manager is the link between the organization and the employees. Therefore, managers are key in helping the organization maintain and develop its human capital.

To build human capital in organizations, managers must begin to develop ways of ensuring superior knowledge, skills, and experience within their workforce and to find ways to distribute this "capital" throughout the organization. Staffing programs focus on identifying, recruiting, and hiring the best talent available. Training and development investments, particularly for managers to coach and mentor the staff, can improve the overall organizational performance.[56] In addition, employees need opportunities for development on the job. Therefore, managers have to do a good job of providing developmental assignments to employees and making certain that job duties and requirements are flexible enough to allow for growth and learning. To successfully develop people, supervisors and managers have to "let go."

Core competencies
A combination of knowledge, skills, and characteristics needed to effectively perform a role in an organization

Further, more and more organizations are recognizing that sets of knowledge capabilities—**core competencies**—are part of their human capital. These competencies are necessary in order to be different from their competition and provide ongoing value to their customers. For example, a core competency might be: *Focus on customer*: ability to make an effort to identify internal and external customers and understand what adds value for them; to create an environment that appreciates delivery of good customer service.

While many core competencies are similar from one organization to another, such as focus on customer or active listening skills, each organization will develop its own set and define the competency to fit the particular organization. Thus, it is the combination of competencies of all employees in that organization that makes it stand out from its competition.

Once competencies are identified, organizations have to find ways of using and improving the competencies that exist.[57] This has to go beyond the investment in employee development. Too often, employees have skills that go unused. Some of this can be achieved by moving high-potential employees into a different role in the organization that stretches them and builds specific competencies.[58] Efforts to empower employees and encourage their participation and involvement utilize the human capital available more fully. Bill Weldon, CEO of Johnson & Johnson, says it quite well: "one of the most important things we are doing is helping employees recognize that we're going to continue to invest in them and their development."[59]

Developmental assignments, particularly those involving teamwork, can also be a valuable way of facilitating knowledge exchange and mutual learning. Effective communications (whether face to face or through information technology) are instrumental in sharing knowledge and making it widely available throughout the organization. As Dave Ulrich noted, "Learning capability is *g* times *g*—a business's ability to *generate* new ideas multiplied by its adeptness at *generalizing* them throughout the company."[60] Gary Hamel, a leading authority on human resource practices and organizational performance recently stated:

> . . . challenge is to build an organization as human as the people who work there. Our adaptability make us human—we cross oceans for jobs; we go back to school; we can reinvent ourselves and invent things; we have stories. But our organizations are less adaptable. We utilize a technology of management from 100 years ago, invented to run people into automatons, not to get the best out of people . . . changing this is a business imperative.[61]

Talent management
Leveraging competencies to achieve high organizational performance

Leadership and Management Development Council
www.leadershipmanagement.bc.ca

As companies continue to focus on their human capital, the concept of **talent management** has evolved. This is concerned about leveraging the competencies in the organization by ensuring that the competencies are in the right places in the organization and then measuring the impact of those competencies against goals. Given the breadth of the concept, companies will look at various HR practices that have to be more clearly integrated than what might be found in many organizations. The HR practices that need to be considered to attract, keep, and engage employees are:

Leadership development
Succession planning
Career planning
Performance management
High-potential employee development
Learning and training
Competency management
Retention
Professional development[62]

For additional online resources that help small organizations develop their human capital, see **www.leadershipmanagement.bc.ca**.

Challenge 6: Demographic and Employee Concerns

In addition to the competitive challenges facing organizations, managers in general, and HR professionals in particular, need to be concerned about changes in the makeup and expectations of their employees. Some of these issues will be discussed here and others will be discussed in other chapters.

Among the most significant challenges to managers are the demographic changes occurring in Canada. You can find current information about the labour force through Statistics Canada (**www.statcan.gc.ca**). Because they affect the workforce of an employer, these changes—in employee background, age, gender, and education—are important topics for discussion.

Statistics Canada
www.statcan.gc.ca/

Diversity of Backgrounds

Canadian workers will continue to be a diverse group. According to the 2006 Census, immigrants represent almost 70% of labour force growth and with Canada being close to zero growth, it is predicted that the only population growth will be through immigration.[63] Most of the immigration is from Asia—a sharp contrast to immigration that occurred 40 years ago, primarily from European countries. Immigrants tend to settle in large urban areas such as Toronto, Montreal, and Vancouver. It is also predicted that in less than 10 years, approximately 50% of the population in Toronto and Vancouver will be visible minorities. Currently, visible minorities make up over 40% of Toronto's workforce.[64] The majority of immigrants coming to Canada are from China, South Asia, Korea, and the Arab countries. Aboriginals make up 3.8% of the population, and more than half are under 25 years of age.

To ensure that skilled immigrants have access to employment opportunities, a number of partnerships have developed such as the Toronto Region Immigrant Employment Council (TRIEC) or the Assisting Local Leaders with the Employment of Skilled Immigrants (ALLIES). The purpose of these agencies is to help immigrants overcome barriers, including how to have their professional qualifications assessed.[65]

The Aboriginal Human Resources Development Council of Canada
www.ahrdcc.com

Organizations are also looking at ways to make better use of the Aboriginal community, especially since this portion of the Canadian population has a high youth component—approximately 50% of the more than 1.2 million Aboriginal people are 0–24 years of age.[66] For additional information on the Aboriginal talent pool in your local community, visit **www.ahrdcc.com** (The Aboriginal Human Resources Development Council of Canada).

Generations at Work

The working-age population in Canada is becoming older—there are more individuals than ever before in the older age brackets (ages 45 to 64) and fewer individuals than ever in the younger brackets. The 45 to 64 age bracket increased to 38% of the Canadian population according to the

2006 Census, or over 12 million people. This age bracket accounted for virtually one-quarter of Canada's total population of just over 30 million in 2001, compared with only 20% in 1991. Data show that there are fewer young people entering the working-age population to replace individuals in the age group nearing retirement.[67]

The age distribution throughout the Canadian workforce means that there can be several generations working together—all with different values and expectations. For example, the Baby Boomers (born between 1946 and 1965) have a tendency to be competitive, optimistic, and respond well to hierarchy; Gen X (born between 1966 and 1979) are skeptical, independent, tend to be tech-savvy, career-oriented, and are less comfortable with hierarchy; Gen Y (born between 1980 and 1999) tend to be candid about participating in the workforce, want to take on responsibility quickly and are highly-educated. Gen Y, sometimes referred to as Millennials is the generation that grew up with computers, cellphones, CDs, DVDs, etc., were told by their parents that there were special, are energetic, and very achievement-oriented.[68] Further, younger workers sometimes feel as if they don't fit into the organization, particularly if they don't have the technological tools they grew up with—leading to a high level of dissatisfaction.[69] As a result, employers will need to be very vigilant about understanding the needs, wants, and values of the different age cohorts in their organization. Figure 1.4 provides a summary of the generational differences, including those individuals that are 65 but perhaps not retired yet.

Companies are responding in a number of ways to this demographic shift. More attention is being paid to the corporate culture and ensuring that staff fit well with the culture and the values of the organization. And culture is important as it does drive the performance and results of the company. Read Manager's Toolkit 1.2 to read about some of the other HR practices affected by an aging population.

FIGURE 1.4   How Generations Look at Work and Life

	Veterans	Baby Boomers	Generation X	Generation Y (Millennial)
Work ethic and values	Hard work Respect authority Sacrifice Duty before fun Adhere to rules	Workaholics Work efficiently Question authority	Eliminate the task Self-reliance Want structure and direction Skeptical	"What's next?" Multitasking Entrepreneurial Tolerant Goal oriented
Work is …	An obligation	An exciting adventure	A difficult challenge	A means to an end
Leadership style	Directive Command and control	Consensual Collegial	Everyone is the same Challenge others Ask why	Yet to be determined
Interactive style	Individual	Team player Loves to have meetings	Entrepreneur	Participative
Communications	Formal memo	In person	Direct Immediate	E-mail Voice mail
Feedback and rewards	No news is good news Satisfaction in a job well done	Don't appreciate it Money Title recognition	"Sorry to interrupt but how am I doing?" Freedom is the best reward	"Whenever I want it, at the push of a button" Meaningful work
Messages that motivate	"Your experience is respected"	"You are valued" "You are needed"	"Do it your way" "Forget the rules"	"You will work with other bright, creative people"
Work and family life	Not in this lifetime!	No balance Work to live	Balance	Balance

Source: Adapted from Sarah Dobson, "Passing the Knowledge Baton from One Generation to the Next," *Canadian HR Reporter*, October 20, 2008, www.hrreporter.com/ArticleView.aspx?l=1&articleid=6438 (accessed March 27, 2009).

MANAGER'S TOOLKIT **1.2**

OLD, BUT NOT OUT

The number of Canadians 55 and older is about 27% of the workforce, compared to 29% under 35, and 44% between 35 and 55. The average age of retirement is declining, from 65 in the early 70s to about 61 in 2003. By 2010, older workers will have higher education levels, more training, and more transferable skills, all of which will make them more employable. Many older workers want to continue to work after they retire, mostly because they enjoy work. It is also important to remember that mandatory retirement at age 65 has been virtually eliminated. And given the recent economic turmoil, as many as 1/3 may postpone retirement—which can be good with the continued skill shortage when the economy rebounds. Their ability to learn and adapt to new technologies does not differ from that of younger workers. However, they do want flexible arrangements, such as reduced hours, working part-time, work with less responsibility, special assignments, and consulting work. It is also important to ensure that if an older worker decides not to retire due to economic concerns that the person does not "retire on the job" and becomes less productive. Managers will need to pay close attention and be sure that the older workers continue to be engaged in what they are doing.

As employers face labour shortages in specific sectors such as health care, there will be more attempts to provide innovative HR programs to retain older workers. For example, the average age of retirement for a registered nurse is 57, so in an attempt to retain these experienced nurses, the Province of New Brunswick is introducing a phased-in retirement program. Nurses can reduce their work hours by about 50% and access their pension plans to supplement their incomes.

The economic problems have also seen older workers deciding to delay retirement. This is helping deal with a skilled labour shortage, but it also creating new challenges as employers accommodate those employees that are staying due to financial need.

Sources: Adapted from Jonathan Chevreau, "One in Three Postponing Retirement," *Financial Post,* January 30, 2009, FP3; Presentation by Christopher McHardy, "Mandatory Retirement in BC: The Beginning of the End!" May 11, 2007; Presentation by Dr. Gloria M. Gutman, "The End of Mandatory Retirement: Implications for Individuals and Organizations," May 11, 2007; Eric Beauchesne, "Recession Could Force Workers to Retire on the Job,'" *The Vancouver Sun,* January 9, 2009, B2; and Shannon Proudfoot, "Companies Shifting to an Older Workforce," *The Vancouver Sun,* April 20, 2009, B1.

Skills and Labour Shortage

With the aging of the workforce and fewer new entrants, there is a concern about shortages—and primarily for skilled workers. The current economic climate will improve and the shortages will be as problematic as it was before the recession. For example, the government of Saskatchewan is on a recruitment drive to get graduates from Ontario universities and colleges to relocate to Saskatchewan for at least seven years—and it is spending $20,000 per graduate as a cash inducement.[70] Unfortunately, some organizations feel that is just a matter of either doing more advertising or dedicating more people to recruitment activities. However, as was stated a few paragraphs ago, there are fewer new entrants due to fewer people being born.

To deal with these shortages, there are a number of things an employer can do, including providing more mentoring for Millennials, ensuring that the management style in the organization is suitable for both tech-savvy workers and with people who are not comfortable with change, and using a risk-management approach to recruitment—which means identifying whether current talent matches the company's future needs.[71] In addition, there is a great deal of pressure on colleges and apprenticeship training to increase graduates as approximately 42% of the skills shortage is in those types of occupations—technologists, medical technicians, plumbers, carpenters, etc.[72]

Part of the concern about a shortage of labour is that the current standard of living could decline with a lifeless economy and high inflation. A group of Canadian economists suggested that employers would also need to increase productivity with the existing labour base and perhaps even discourage people from retiring.[73] Provincial governments have another solution to minimize the skill shortages from one province to another. They have encouraged the removal of labour barriers such as those in which doctors and plumbers have to re-qualify individually in each province. There was an agreement in late 2008 that means anyone qualified in a profession or other regulated occupation could easily get work in another province without having to re-qualify.[74]

Gender Distribution of the Workforce

According to Statistics Canada 62% of labour force participants are women with an 83% participation rate in the 25–44 age bracket.[75] Employers are under constant pressure to ensure equality for women with respect to employment, advancement opportunities, and compensation. And since the rate is so high during women's child bearing years, employers also need to accommodate working mothers and fathers through parental leaves, part-time employment, flexible work schedules, job sharing, telecommuting, and childcare assistance. Employers are also finding that many working people are now faced with being caregivers to aging parents. Thus, the whole area of "dependant care" is creating issues in organizations that will require creative solutions. In addition, because more women are working, employers are more sensitive to the growing need for policies and procedures to eliminate sexual harassment in the workplace. Some organizations have special orientation programs to acquaint all personnel with the problem and to warn potential offenders of the consequences. Many employers are demanding that managers and supervisors enforce their sexual harassment policy vigorously.

Rising Levels of Education

The educational attainment of the Canadian labour force has steadily risen over the years. Not coincidentally, the most secure and fastest-growing sectors of employment over the past decade have been in those areas requiring higher levels of education. As organizations become more sophisticated and use more technology, there is less and less employment available for unskilled workers. The more education a person has, the greater the chances are of having work. The participation rate for those individuals with high school was 75% compared to 83% for university graduates. People with grade 3 or less have about a 45% participation rate.[76] What is also notable is that more and more people are combining school and work—over 60% of full-time students were also working and most were employed in retail, grocery stores, or food outlets.[77] Women make up over 60% of university and college graduates, are actively employed, and are primarily in the sales and service occupations.[78]

It is important to observe that while the educational level of the workforce has continued to rise, there is a widening gap between the educated and noneducated, leading to different types of work experiences. At the lower end of the educational spectrum, many employers are coping with individuals who are functionally illiterate—unable to read, write, calculate, or solve problems at a level that enables them to perform even the simplest technical tasks, such as reading an

As more and more employees strive to balance the demands of their jobs with the needs of their families, employers are responding by offering greater flexibility such as part-time work and parental leave.

Ryan McVey/Photodisc Green/Getty Images

operating manual or reading safety procedures. The topic of literacy will be discussed in more detail in Chapter 5 but it is important to know that 40% of the Canadian adult population lacks the basic literacy skills to meet everyday requirements in our society and that the employees with the lowest level of literacy skills are in manufacturing, construction, and the transportation industries.[79]

The Changing Nature of the Job

The era of the full-time ongoing job seems to have disappeared. Nearly half of all jobs created during the last two decades were nontraditional—that is, part-time, temporary, or contract work. As job security erodes, so do pension plans and health-care benefits, particularly for part-timers. About 20% of the working population work part-time and almost all do so voluntarily. Further, over 15% of Canadians are self-employed.[80] With the change in the traditional notion of "job," companies, however, do place high value on team-structured work and on projects. This also leads to new issues in creating effective HR processes.

Cultural Changes

The attitudes, beliefs, values, and customs of people in a society are an integral part of their culture. Naturally, their culture affects their behaviour on the job and the environment within the organization, influencing their reactions to work assignments, leadership styles, and reward systems. Like the external and internal environments of which it is a part, culture is undergoing continual change. HR processes and systems, therefore, must be adjusted to accommodate and integrate these changes.

Employee Rights

Over the past few decades, legislation has radically changed the rules for managing employees by granting them many specific rights. Among these are laws granting the right to equal employment opportunity, union representation if desired, a safe and healthy work environment, minimum working conditions (hours of work, wages, vacations, etc.), and privacy in the workplace.

Ethics

With the various business scandals that continue to plague North America, increased attention is being paid to business ethics. This topic will be explored more fully in Chapter 9; however, Ethics in HRM 1.1 describes employees' views of ethics.

Concern for Privacy

HR managers and their staffs, as well as line managers, generally recognize the importance of discretion in handling all types of information about employees. The *Personal Information Protection and Electronic Documents Act* (PIPEDA) is a federal law that deals with the collection, use, and disclosure of personal information (note that Quebec is the only province with similar laws, although Ontario and others have draft legislation in place). This law requires federally regulated organizations holding personal information on customers or employees to obtain their consent before it uses, collects, or discloses this information. Chapter 2 will describe more on privacy.

Changing Attitudes toward Work

Another well-established trend is for employees to define success in terms of personal self-expression and fulfillment of potential on the job. They are frequently less obsessed with the acquisition of wealth and now view life satisfaction as more likely to result from balancing the challenges and rewards of work with those of their personal lives. Though most people still enjoy work and want to excel at it, they tend to be focused on finding interesting work and may pursue multiple careers rather than being satisfied with just "having a job." People also appear to be seeking ways

ETHICS **in HRM 1.1**

LEADERS AND ETHICS

Walker Information, a firm that specializes in measuring employee and customer satisfaction, recently conducted a benchmark survey on ethics. There were some interesting results!

Only slightly more than half of the employees surveyed believed that the senior leaders in their organization had high personal integrity. Further, almost half of the employees felt there is pressure to cut corners and 1 in 12 employees had witnessed an ethical violation related to accounting in the past two years. Lastly, 1 in 3 employees believe that their company is not highly ethical.

And according to a study by the Conference Board of Canada, the CEO is considered to be the most important person in setting the tone for creating and maintaining an ethical culture. Employees judge the words and actions of CEOs when assessing if the organization is ethical.

Sources: Adapted from Marc Dirzin, "Five Years Later, Outrage Surfaces about Business Ethics," Walker Library, www.walkerinfo.com/knowledge-center/walker-library/article.asp?id=297&catid=9&pnum=1&ptitle=Ethics (accessed March 25, 2009); and Danielle Harder, "Ethics Start Right at the Top: Study," *Canadian HR Reporter*, October 22, 2007, www.hrreporter.com/ArticleView.aspx?l=1&articleid=5555 (accessed March 25, 2009).

of living that are less complicated but more meaningful. These new lifestyles cannot help but have an impact on the way employees are motivated and managed. Figure 1.5 outlines the job characteristics considered very important in the Canadian workforce of the 21st century.

Balancing Work and Family

Work and the family are connected in many subtle and not-so-subtle social, economic, and psychological ways. Because of the new forms that the family has taken—for example, the two-wage-earner and the single-parent family—work organizations find it necessary to provide employees with more family-friendly options. "Family friendly" is a broad term that may include flexible work

FIGURE 1.5 What Employees Want in Job Quality

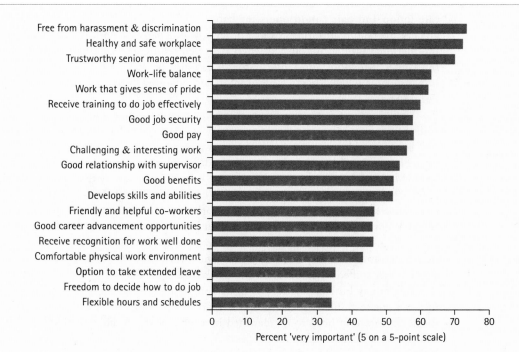

Source: Graham Lowe, "21st Century Job Quality: Achieving What Canadians Want," Canadian Policy Research Networks, September 2007.

schedules, daycare, part-time work, job sharing, parental leave, executive transfers, spousal involvement in career planning, assistance with family problems, and teleworking. Another emerging issue is that of eldercare. Many employees not only balance work and childcare but are also responsible for aging parents.

Ikea Canada is well-known for the type of flexibility it provides. The focus there is on results, rather than the time, and provides options for the employees to balance the various demands on their lives. Likewise, Kodak Graphic Communications Canada provides a culture where people are measured by what they contribute to the performance of the organization—not on what hours they work. In addition, teleworking can provide flexibility as well as reduce the requirements for office space as has been done at Bell Canada.[81]

For organizations to be successful in creating better balance for employees in their work and family lives, the culture and the managers must be clearly supportive and understanding. Companies have to accept that employees have commitments in life beyond those at work.[82]

BUSINESS STRATEGY AND STRATEGIC HUMAN RESOURCES MANAGEMENT

Outcome 7

As you can see, there are many challenges and issues facing supervisors and managers, as well as HR professionals, in today's business environment. In order to affectively manage these challenges, organizations develop a business strategy to enable it to achieve a high level of performance. The strategy helps the organization determine what business or businesses it will be in, why it exists, what its key goals are, and what actions it needs to take to realize those goals.

It is important to recognize the distinction between *corporate strategies* and *business strategies*. Corporate strategy deals with questions such as these: Should we be in business? What business should we be in? Corporate strategies are company-wide and focus on overall objectives, such as long-term survival and growth. There are two main types of corporate strategies: The first is a restructuring strategy, to ensure long-term survival, and under this option, we can find turnaround situations (Harmac Mill.), divestitures (the Gillett empire getting rid of the Montreal Canadiens), liquidation (Circuit City), and bankruptcy (Magna Entertainment).

The second corporate strategy is growth. Organizations can grow incrementally (by adding new products or new distribution networks). For example, Procter & Gamble added skin care lotion and hair conditioners for babies and began to distribute to drugstores as well as grocery stores. Organizations can gain new customers by expanding internationally as Finning International Ltd. accomplished when it started selling and renting Caterpillar equipment to the United Kingdom and Chile. Growth can also be achieved through mergers and acquisitions, such as when Rogers Communications acquired Fido and Best Buy Canada acquired Future Shop.

Unlike corporate strategy, business strategy focuses on one line of business and is concerned with the question "How should we compete?" Michael Porter has developed a classification system that helps us understand five ways in which a business unit can compete.[83] Let us illustrate his model by analyzing how hamburgers are sold. Restaurants can compete by being a low-cost provider (McDonald's); by trying to differentiate its products in a way that will attract a large number of buyers (e.g., Burger King introduces the Whopper); by being a best-cost provider through giving more value for the money (e.g., East Side Mario's sells hamburgers, but on a plate in an attractive environment); by focusing on a niche market based on lower cost to a select group of customers (e.g., offering fish burgers or vegetarian burgers); or by offering a niche product or service customized to the tastes of a very narrow market segment (de Bistro Moderne restaurant in Vancouver sells a hamburger stuffed with short ribs and black truffle, for $28).

Part of any business strategy is to be competitive. However, to be competitive, an organization needs to think about its people as part of its "competitive advantage." Thus, the people in the organization need to be managed in a manner that enables achievement of the business strategy.

While people have always been central to organizations, today's employees are critical in helping to build a firm's competitive advantage. Competitive advantage is a capacity or quality that an organization has that gives it an edge over its competition. The advantage could be productivity, price, quality, delivery, or service. Therefore, the focus of current HRM thinking and research is identifying and implementing people processes and systems that can make a particular firm stand out above the rest. Thus, the HR practices are expected to develop the employees' abilities and to motivate employees such that the organization is successful. There is also a body of knowledge that suggests these practices do not necessarily lead to the organizational results desired if these HR practices are not "strong" in the implementation and execution.[84] Therefore, for HR processes to lead to organizational success, the HR systems must be supported, used, and highly regarded. And this strategy identifies the role the line manager plays in, for example, management development.

An HR strategy aligned with the business strategy is particularly critical in organizations whose products or services rely upon the knowledge, skills, abilities, and competencies that are embedded in the employees—the knowledge workers. Research has confirmed that the better an organization makes use of the knowledge contained in all the people in the organization, the higher the financial performance of the organization.[85] As a result, the HR areas of recruitment, learning and development, and retention—or "talent management"—become crucial to the attainment of the business goals.

For example, companies such as CIBC are intentionally designed to increase the value that employees add to the bottom line and to customer satisfaction. It actively involves employees in day-to-day decisions, such as determining what specific steps can be taken to reduce customer complaints. Also, companies such as the Four Seasons Hotels invest a great deal to hire and train the best and brightest employees in order to gain advantage over their competitors.

Strategic human resources management
Identifying key HR processes and linking those to the overall business strategy

What then is the link between business strategies and strategic HRM? As stated earlier, **strategic human resources management** involves identifying key HR processes and linking those to the overall business strategy.[86] When one company buys another company, often the success of the new business revolves around how well the people side of the merger was handled. For example, as the Yellow Pages Group acquires companies or as occurred with the Telus/B.C. Tel merger, a review of the HR processes becomes part of the due diligence step so that potential risks can be identified and then aligned in the new organization.[87]

Organizations of all sizes, public or private, will undertake a set of HR practices that enhance the employees' contribution for organizational success—the success as defined by the business strategy. Thus, all managers play a tremendous role in developing and maintaining effective HR practices and assisting the organization in acquiring a competitive advantage. If a manager believes that employees must be carefully monitored, when the business strategy suggests that employees need to be empowered, then it is highly likely the business will not succeed. When a company (or a line manager) doesn't link the people processes and practices with the business objectives, the company may not be able to achieve the necessary competitive advantage.[88] For example, if a company wished to focus on providing superb customer service, then the company would have an employee selection process that hired people with those skills. Further, it might also have a training program that reinforced the expectations regarding customer service. And it would also have a performance appraisal system that rated how well the employee did in customer service. Or the company might decide that the focus on the customer needed to have full-time rather than part-time staff. This is exactly what Loblaw's did during the most critical part of the 2008 recession. It decided to improve its retention of staff, which had a direct impact on customer satisfaction, by converting as many as 10,000 part-time jobs into full-time.[89]

While "competing through people" may be a key theme for human resources management, the idea remains only a framework for action. On a day-to-day basis, managers frequently focus on specific business challenges and issues and may not always focus as critically on the people issues. You can see from Figure 1.1 that HRM helps blend many aspects of management–business pressures, such as technology and the global market, with the changing nature of the workforce. By balancing what are sometimes competing demands, HRM plays an important role in getting the most from employees for organizational success and providing a work environment that meets the employees' short- and long-term needs.

SUMMARY

1. Define human resources management (HRM).
   - Integrated set of processes, programs, and systems that focus on effective deployment and development of employees.

2. Identify the processes and activities of HRM.
   - Organizational, work, and job design
   - Planning
   - Recruitment and selection
   - Training and development
   - Performance management
   - Compensation—developing and administering pay and benefits programs that will attract and retain employees
   - Occupational health and safety
   - Employee and labour relations

3. Explain the importance of HRM to the line manager.
   - Line manager is key link between employee and organization.
   - Helps you understand roles and responsibilities in managing employees.
   - People have always been central to organizations, but their strategic importance is growing in today's knowledge-based industries.

4. Explain the relationship between the line manager and the HR practitioner.
   - Every manager's job is managing people.
   - Successful organizations equip their line managers with a thorough understanding of HRM.
   - HR professionals help the line manager be a good people manager by providing advice as well as direct services.
   - Combining expertise of HR professionals with the experience of line managers can develop and utilize the talents of employees to their greatest potential.

5. Describe current business challenges facing organizations and the impact on people in organizations.
   - Globalization is creating pressure for managers to effectively manage people.
   - Survival of firms and business sectors will focus on maximizing utilization of employees.
   - Technology has enabled organizations to focus on quality and customer.
   - Environment and climate change is creating both threats and opportunities.
   - Businesses are concerned about their human capital and talent management.

6. Identify key demographic and employee concerns.
   - There is a diverse and aging workforce with an increased participation of females.
   - There are different generations working side-by-side with differing values and expectations.
   - There will be a shortage of labour in the not too distant future.
   - The work landscape is changing with more part-time and self-employed people.
   - Employees have more rights.

7. Describe the link between business strategy and strategic HRM.
   - Business strategy involves formulation of company's mission, goals, and action plans.
   - Part of any business strategy is to be competitive; to be competitive, an organization needs to think about its people as part of its "competitive advantage."
   - Strategic HRM focuses on linking and aligning the HRM processes to the business strategy.
   - The HR processes and programs will reflect the particular strategy, such as growth.

NEED TO KNOW
- Definition of HRM
- Names of HR processes
- Definition of strategic human resources management
- Nature of employee expectations and concerns

NEED TO UNDERSTAND
- Impact of current business challenges on HRM
- Link of strategic HRM with business planning
- Role of line managers in responding effectively to the expectations and concerns of employees

KEY TERMS

benchmarking 17

core competencies 19

downsizing 12

globalization 10

human capital 19

human resources information system (HRIS) 14

human resources management (HRM) 4

ISO 9000 17

outsourcing 12

Six Sigma 17

strategic human resources management 27

talent management 20

REVIEW QUESTIONS

1. What is the definition of human resources management?
2. What are the eight HRM processes and activities?
3. How would you describe the relationship between the line manager and an HR professional?
4. What are the current business challenges facing Canadian organizations?
5. What is the important link between a business strategy and the HR strategy?

CRITICAL THINKING QUESTIONS

1. Your manufacturing company is considering the creation of another plant in South America. What are the major human resources management issues that need to be considered?
2. You are a supervisor in a fast-food restaurant. You have a very diverse customer base. What might be your HR concerns in attracting and retaining employees who can provide excellent customer service?
3. A number of jobs and careers are being created in the larger environmental arena—such as environmental educators, waste management and recycling, and environmental planning. Do you really believe that this is a new industry or is it a fad? Why or why not? Explain your reasoning.
4. The major utility company in your province has just announced that it is outsourcing its customer service functions. What reasons might have led to this decision?
5. What would be the human resources implications if Canada decided to change its immigration policy and significantly reduce the number of immigrants from all parts of the world?
6. List at least three pros and three cons of having a more diverse workforce. Is Canada in a better position to compete globally because of our diverse population?

DEVELOPING YOUR SKILLS

1. Working in groups of four to six students, identify what role the line manager would play and the HR professional would play in the following activities. Where would overlaps occur and where would any problems arise?
   a. Job design
   b. Recruitment and selection
   c. Training and development
   d. Performance management
   e. Pay and benefits
   f. Disciplinary matters
2. In groups of three to four students, prepare a list of both positive and negative experiences you've had as an employee. Once the list is generated, identify what HRM practice or activity might have improved the negative experiences, and what HRM practice contributed to the positive experiences.
3. Visit each of the websites listed in Manager's Toolkit 1.1. Identify two or three sites that would be useful to you in a supervisory role and give reasons for your choices. Working in groups of four to five students, share your information with each other. Discuss any sites the groups had in common.

4. Visit the following websites and determine which site would be more useful to you when looking for work. What if you were a supervisor? Write a one-page summary giving reasons why you chose the site(s).

   www.hrdc-drhc.gc.ca/
   www.monster.ca
   www.workplace.ca
   www.workinfonet.ca
   www.workopolis.com

5. Earlier in the chapter you were introduced to the idea that the skills required to be successful in today's organizations is different. To determine your skills, attitudes, and behaviours for contemporary organizations, access the Skills Credentialing Tool for Individuals through the Conference Board of Canada. Access the online tool at **www.conferenceboard. ca/topics/education/default.aspx** and follow the instructions.

Case Study   **1**

Planning for the Future

With the economic recession that started in Canada in late 2008, firms have focused more on reducing labour costs compared to the predicted skilled labour shortage. However, some companies such as Best Buy Canada are preparing for the economic recovery by actively engaging graduates. It is doing this by ensuring that there is a presence of Best Buy managers on various college and university campuses.

While many companies have reduced their campus recruiting, Best Buy is participating in career fairs and providing internships to current students. Best Buy feels that it is important for students to know who it is and what types of careers are possible. The company does presentations about the company during its participation in first-year student orientation at some campuses. In addition to building relationships with students, it also works closely with faculty in a variety of disciplines as well as working with university career centres. Rodney Bush, human resources manager, states, "The talent pipeline is something you always want to have your finger in because when the economy does pick up, we want to be in a position to capitalize on that."

For Best Buy, it is important to maintain the employer brand even if it doesn't have many openings at any particular point in time.

Source: Adapted from Derek Sankey, "By Tapping Young Talent, Companies Prepare for the Economic Recovery," *The Vancouver Sun*, March 28, 2009. Material reprinted with the express permission of: "CANWEST NEWS SERVICE", a CanWest Partnership.

Questions

1. What are the pros and cons of actively recruiting on campuses during a recession?
2. What would Best Buy want students to know about the company?
3. Does Best Buy recruit on your campus? What would you want to know if you spoke to a Best Buy representative?

Case Study  2

The Environment and Economics

What does the environment have to do with economics? Well, depending on who you ask, almost everything. As fossil fuels became more expensive in mid-2008, alternative energy sources (and the companies that developed and produced that energy) became more attractive. And as more people looked to things like solar and wind power, new businesses were created as were new jobs. Evidence of this can be found in many places.

Unilever, a large multinational organization, focuses on personal care and food products. One of its products is tea—19 billion bags a year of Lipton, Red Rose, and Salada. While there have been many critics of it as a company, its tea operations have received high praise. The reason: it has improved farming practices in Kenya that has been a benefit to the land and the workers. The focus is on sustainable production that combines environmental care and worker welfare—a holistic approach. Through these changes it is striving to source tea by sustainable means—and receive certification through the Rainforest Alliance. This will have a huge impact on the global tea industry as Unilever has 12% of the total market share. As world demand increases for sustainable products, the price will increase the international price of tea that in turn will improve the lives of the 2 million Kenyans who work in the tea sector.

Sources: Adapted from Vanessa Farquharson, "How Corporate Giant Unilever is Improving its Farming Practices, One Plantation at a Time," *National Post,* March 26, 2009; and "Time for a Green Bottom Line," *The Vancouver Sun,* March 28, 2009, J6.

Questions

1. Identify the opportunities and threats of businesses shifting to more environmentally friendly practices.
2. What HRM issues arise as businesses shift the way the products are manufactured?
3. Do you think more businesses ought to spend money on environmental improvements? Why or why not?

NOTES AND REFERENCES

1. Peter Goodspeed, "Global Mess Gives Birth to New Era," *National Post,* March 14, 2009, A12–13.
2. Howard Levitt, "Managers have Duty to Remain Loyal to Employer," *National Post,* November 12, 2008, FP15.
3. "What Makes the Most Admired Companies Great," presentation by Hay Group, Vancouver, June 2008.
4. Dave Ulrich and Wayne Brockbank, "The Premise of the HR Value," *The HR Value Proposition* (Boston: Harvard Business School Press, 2005).
5. *The Power of Integrated Reward and Talent Management2008/2009 Global Strategic Rewards Report and United States Findings,* Watson Wyatt, 2008.
6. "What Makes the Most Admired Companies Great," June 2008.
7. *Canadian International Merchandise Trade,* November 2008, Catalogue no. 65-001-X, Statistics Canada.
8. "Canada Trade Deficit Biggest on Record," Reuters Canada, March 13, 2009, http://ca.reuters.com/article/topNews/idCA-TRE52C2UY20090313 (accessed March 18, 2009).
9. James Bagnall, "Nortel's 114-year Dynasty Ends in Pieces," *Financial Post,* June 22, 2009, FP1; and Theresa Tedesco and Jamie Sturgeon, "Nortel: Cautionary Tale of a Former Canadian Titan," *Financial Post,* June 27, 2009, FP1.
10. "Fourth Quarter and Annual 2008 Results," Finning International, February 18, 2009.
11. Alia McMullen and Paul Vieira, "Canadian Economy Shrinks, Stock Market Tumbles," *The Vancouver Sun,* March 3, 2009, C1; and "IMF Slashes Canada's GDP Growth for 2009 and 2010," January 28, 2009, *CBCnews.ca,* www.cbc.ca/money/story/2009/01/28/imf-canada-growth.html?ref=rss (accessed March 18, 2009).

12. "Canada's Trade Deficit Biggest on Record," *Reuters Canada*, March 13, 2009.

13. Lionel Laurent, "OPEC Rises Above Price Pressures," *Forbes.com*, March 16, 2009, www.forbes.com/2009/03/16/oil-opec-saudi-markets-commodities-crude.html (accessed March 17, 2009).

14. "S&P/TSX Composite," *globeinvestor.com*, March 17, 2009, http://investdb.theglobeandmail.com/invest/investSQL/gx.index_today?pi_symbol=TSX-I&pi_action=.

15. Peter Koven, "Timminco Cuts to Survive," *Financial Post*, March 18, 2009, FP1.

16. "Monthly Survey of Manufacturing," January 2009, *The Daily*, Catalogue 11-001-XIE, Statistics Canada, March 17, 2009.

17. "CAW Reaches Tentative Agreement with Chrysler, Voting this Weekend," press release, www.newswire.ca/en/releases/archive/April2009/24/c5174.html (accessed June 27, 2009).

18. Nicolas Van Praet, "No Easy Road for Chrysler," *Financial Post*, June 11, 2009, FP1.

19. Nathan Vanderklippe, "Billionaire Penske Gets Deal for Saturn," *The Globe and Mail*, June 6, 2009, B5.

20. Scott Deveau, "Bombardier Cuts 3,000 jobs, Won't Rule Out More Reductions," *The Vancouver Sun*, April 3, 2009, C3.

21. Bert Hill, "Analysts Cast Doubt on Takeover of Nortel Assets," *The Vancouver Sun*, June 23, 2009, C2.

22. Robert I. Sutton, "What's the Best Strategy for Astrigo?" *Harvard Business Review*, March 2009, 40.

23. Madhav Murti, "Outsourcing Opportunities in Bad Economy," *Canadian HR Reporter*, January 26, 2009, www.hrreporter.com/ArticleView.aspx?l=1&articleid=6628 (accessed March 20, 2009).

24. Peter Tingling, "Layoffs: Deciding Who Stays and Who Goes," *National Post*, November 28, 2008, FE1.

25. Tavia Grant, "Not a Cure-all, But Creativity is Saving Some Jobs," *The Globe and Mail*, January 24, 2009, B15.

26. "Downsizing the Smart Way," *Financial Post*, February 4, 2009, FP4.

27. Howard Levitt, "Some Companies Look to Brighter Days for Staffing," *The Vancouver Sun*, February 18, 2009, D8.

28. Glen Korstrom, "Morale Can be Boosted Even during Job Cuts," *Business in Vancouver* 1005, no. 17 (January 27-February 2, 2009).

29. "Welcome to the Lay-it-Bare Layoff," *PeopleTalk*, Spring 2009, 10.

30. Joanne Lee-Young, "Telus Opens Fourth Call Centre in Manila," *The Vancouver Sun*, March 23, 2009, C1.

31. Heather Timmons, "Indian Outsourcing Here to Stay," *Financial Post*, June 4, 2009, FP7.

32. Karen Mazurkewich, "Outsourcing Moves Up to Key Services," *Financial Post*, April 25, 2008, FP1.

33. Thomas Jolicoeur, "Canadian Helped Create Interactive Disease Website," *The Vancouver Sun*, March 13, 2009, B3.

34. "20 Ways the Web Changed the World," *The Vancouver Sun*, March 13, 2009, B3.

35. Michael Rudnick and Wendy Kouba, "How the 'Google Effect' Is Transforming Employee Communications and Driving Employee Engagement," Watson Wyatt Worldwide, 2006.

36. "Networking Sites' Minutes Surge 63% in a Year," *The Vancouver Sun*, March 13, 2009, B8.

37. Ann Macaulay, "Better Payroll Tech Means Better Workflow, Savings," *Canadian HR Reporter*, June 18, 2007, 11.

38. Garry Priam, "Dollars and Sense," *PeopleTalk* 11, no. 4 (Winter 2008): 54–56.

39. Sarah Dobson, "Self-service Inevitable, but Buy-in a Challenge," *Canadian HR Reporter*, June 18, 2007, 9.

40. Sharon Boglari, "Point>Click>Connect," *PeopleTalk* 11, no. 4 (Winter 2008): 14–19.

41. Don Tapscott, "Winning in the Wiki-Workplace," *PeopleTalk* 11, no. 4 (Winter 2008): 58.

42. Enrique Claver and Juan José Tari, "Total Quality Management on Customers, People and Society Results and Quality Performance in SMEs," *Quality & Reliability Engineering International*.2, no. 24 (March 2008): 199–211.

43. "Tata Steel Wins Deming Award," *The Hindu*, October 8, 2008, 15.

44. Suresh Subramoniam, "Commanding the Internet Era," *Industrial Engineer*, October 2008, 44–48.

45. Angie Eichel, "Six Sigma, Innovation can Co-exist," *Canadian HR Reporter*, March 24, 2008, 23.

46. The term Six Sigma is a registered trademark of Motorola. It is based on the Greek letter sigma, used as a symbol of variation in a process (the standard deviation). For more information see Peter S. Pande, Robert P. Neuman, and Roland R. Cavanagh, *The Six Sigma Way: How GE, Motorola, and Other Top Companies Are Honing Their Performance* (New York: McGraw-Hill, 2000).

47. Jack B. ReVelle, "Six Sigma," *Professional Safety*, October 2004, 38–46.

48. Amy O'Brian, "Patients to Need Less Patience," *The Vancouver Sun*, March 21, 2009, A6.

49. "2009–2010 Criteria for Performance Excellence," Baldrige National Quality Program; Ryan C. Burge, "The Baldrige Journey," *Industrial Engineer*, February 2009, 40–44.

50. Joseph M. Hall and M. Eric Johnson, "When Should a Process Be Art, Not Science?" *Harvard Business Review*, March 2009, 58–65.

51. Peter Koven, "Shine is Off the Solar Power Industry," *Financial Post*, March 24, 2009, C4.

52. Scott Simpson, "Green Power Bids Flooding In to BC Hydro," *The Vancouver Sun*, November 25, 2008, D3; and Tara Perkins, "Hiring, Growing and Green: Meet the Poster Child for Stimulus," *The Globe and Mail*, March 20, 2009, B1.

53. Scott Simpson, "Latest Business Challenge is Climate Change," *The Vancouver Sun*, November 21, 2008, H3.

54. Greg McMillan, "The Greening of the Jobscape," *The Globe and Mail*, November 14, 2008, B7.

55. A. Kochetkova, "The Formation of Human Capital," *Russian Education and Society*.48, no.2 (February 2006): 5–16.

56. I-Ming Wang, Chich-Jen Shieh, Fu-Jin Wang, "Effect of Human Capital Investment on Organizational Performance," *Social Behavior and Personality: An International Journal* 36, no. 8 (2008): 1011–1022.

57. Farah Naqvi, "Competency Mapping and Managing Talent," *The Icfaian Journal of Management Research* VIII, no. 1 (2009): 85–94.

58. Judy Orr, "Job Rotations Give Future Leaders the Depth They Need," *Canadian HR Reporter*, January 30, 2006, www.hrreporter.com/ArticleView.aspx?l=1&articleid=4227 (accessed March 19, 2009).

59. Dave Ulrich, Steve Kerr, and Ron Ashkenas, *The GE Work-Out: How to Implement GE's Revolutionary Method for Busting Bureaucracy & Attacking Organizational Problems* (New York: McGraw-Hill Professional Publishing, 2002).

60. Geoff Colvin, "The World's Most Admired Companies 2009," *Fortune,* March 16, 2009, 78.

61. "Global Talent Management: Strategy, Risk and Execution," Mercer HR Symposium, September 8–9, 2008, Washington, D.C., www.mercer.com/flipbook/HR_Symposium/FINAL/hr_symposium.html (accessed March 19, 2009).

62. Pat Galagan, "Talent Management: What Is It, Who Owns It, and Why Should You Care?" *T-D,* May 2008, 40–44. Source: TRAINING & DEVELOPMENT by Galagan, Pat. Copyright 2008 by AMERICAN SOCIETY FOR TRAINING AND DEVELOPMENT (VA). Reproduced with permission of AMERICAN SOCIETY FOR TRAINING AND DEVELOPMENT (VA) in the format Textbook via Copyright Clearance Center.

63. *Canadian Demographics at a Glance,* Catalogue no. 91-003-0X, Statistics Canada, January 2008, 5.

64. Canada's Ethnocultural Mosaic 2006 Census, Catalogue no. 97-562-X, Statistics Canada, 29.

65. Shannon Klie, "Immigrant Employment Model Goes National," *Canadian HR Reporter,* October 22, 2007, 3.

66. CBC News, "2006 Census Release, Aboriginal Peoples," www.cbc.ca/news/interactives/cp-aboriginal-census/ (accessed March 21, 2009).

67. *Canadian Demographics at a Glance,* 25.

68. Presentation at B.C.I.T. during Professional Development Day, March 2007; and Donna Nebenzahl, "Managing the Employee Demographic Gap," *The Vancouver Sun,* March 14, 2009, I2.

69. Derek Abma, "Canadians have Trouble Fitting in at Work: Survey," *The Vancouver Sun,* October 22, 2008, F5.

70. Michael McKiernan, "Ontario Grads Offered $20K to Head West," *National Post,* March 24, 2009, A9.

71. Sharon Boglari, "HR Heads in the Sand: Is Your Workplace Truly Prepared for Your Labour Needs of Tomorrow?" *PeopleTalk,* Fall 2007, 12–15.

72. Eric Beauchesne, "Skills Shortage to Worsen," *National Post,* April 23, 2008, WK4; Brian Morton, "Trades Opportunities in the Spotlight at Trading Up Fair," *The Vancouver Sun Working,* April 12, 2008, E1; and Brian Morton, "Plenty of Jobs in Tourism Sector," *The Vancouver Sun,* November 7, 2008, H4.

73. John Morrissy, "Future Labour Shortages Could Invite Social Unrest: Report," *The Vancouver Sun,* January 7, 2009, www.vancouversun.com/business/fp/Future+labour+shortages+could+invite+social+unrest+report/1152125/story.html (accessed January 8, 2008).

74. Justine Hunter, "Provincial Labour Barriers to Fall," *The Globe and Mail,* December 6, 2008, A4.

75. "Canada, Labour Force and Participation Rates by Sex and Age Group," Statistics Canada, www40.statcan.gc.ca/l01/cst01/labor05-eng.htm (accessed March 24, 2009).

76. "The Canadian Labour Market at a Glance," Statistics Canada, January 30, 2009, 54.

77. "The Canadian Labour Market at a Glance," 56.

78. "University Degrees, Diplomas and Certificates Awarded," *The Daily,* Statistics Canada, March 11, 2009; and "The Canadian Labour Market at a Glance," 52.

79. Workplace Literacy, www.workplaceliteracy.ca/ (accessed March 25, 2009).

80. "The Canadian Labour Market at a Glance," 44 and 59.

81. Kira Vermond, "Punching In on the Variable Close," *The Globe and Mail,* March 22, 2008, B14; Peter Browne, "Teleworking is Here to Stay," *National Post,* April 2, 2008, WK4; and Daryl-Lynn Carlson, "A Picture of Life Balance," *National Post,* October 22, 2008, WK2.

82. Ellen Ernst Kossek and Leslie B. Hammer, "Supervisor Work-Life Training Gets Results," *Harvard Business Review,* November 2008, 36; Kathleen M. Lingle, "Work-Life Means Business," *PeopleTalk,* Spring 2009, 26–27; and Laurent M. Lapierre, "The Art of Balance Work and Family Life," *Financial Post,* March 17, 2009, FP11.

83. Michael E. Porter, *On Competition* (Boston, Massachusetts: Harvard Business Press, 2008).

84. David E. Bowen and Cheri Ostroff, "Understanding HRM—Firm Performance Linkages: The Role of the 'Strength' of the HRM System," *The Academy of Management Review* 29, no. 2 (April 2004): 203–221.

85. Matthew Guthridge, Asmus B. Komm, and Emily Lawson, "Making Talent a Strategic Priority," *The McKinley Quarterly,* January 2008, 48–59.

86. Allan R. Cohen and David L. Bradford, "Building a New Partnership," *Resources in the 21st Century* (Hoboken, N.J.: John Wiley & Sons, Inc., 2003): 135–142.

87. Uyen Vu, "HR's Role in Mergers, Acquisitions," *Canadian HR Reporter,* December 4, 2006, www.hrreporter.com/ArticleView.aspx?l=1&articleid=4861 (accessed March 27, 2009).

88. Bowen and Ostroff, "Understanding HRM–First Performance Linkages."

89. Shannon Klie, "Part-Times Could Go Full Time at Grocery Giant," *Canadian HR Reporter,* March 23, 2009, 1.

CHAPTER 2

THE LEGAL FRAMEWORK OF HRM

OUTCOMES

After studying this chapter, you should be able to

1 Explain the impact of laws on the behaviour and actions of supervisors and managers.

2 Discuss the legal framework of HRM in Canada.

3 Explain and describe discrimination and harassment in the workplace.

4 Describe the line manager's role in creating a work environment that is free from harassment and discrimination.

5 Identify the general types of employment laws in Canada.

6 Explain and describe the difference between employment equity and pay equity.

7 Describe the differences between diversity and employment equity.

OUTLINE

HRM CLOSE-UP

"The lack of exposure to human resource realities can blind side you."

Launched in 1996, Outpost has carved a niche for itself in the travel magazine business. Adventure travel is its focus and the journalists write about off-the-beaten-track excursions to interesting and unusual places.

For the magazine's editorial director and publisher, most of today is spent reviewing a story about a 75-kilometre trail hike on Vancouver Island, calling potential advertisers, and finalizing a deal with a tour company for coveted back cover advertising space. But Matt Robinson must also set aside time for human resources management because his responsibilities cover all aspects of the magazine's operation.

Though admittedly a 'hands-off' manager, Matt does acknowledge that a good 15% of his time is spent interacting with the people who work for him. "We are small and therefore have to be nimble with staffing," explains Robinson. "The people who work for us are often part-time contract, freelance, or casual and we also manage up to 12 student interns from colleges and universities annually."

Managing interns may seem straightforward but there are things a manager has to be aware of when accepting interns. Robinson describes the legal considerations to do with workers' compensation, saying that if a magazine compensates an intern during their unpaid internship, that payment, though intended to show appreciation for the work, may interfere with that student's school insurance coverage, transferring liability back to the company. "Small companies with nominal staff wouldn't necessarily know about this," commented Robinson. "It's hard to stay on top of all the legalities of human resources. It's best to read up a little here and there so that you have the knowledge you need to avoid legal issues in the future."

Robinson has sought legal advice from time to time for help with tasks like drawing up contracts. He says that other responsibilities related to managing people are fairly obvious, like maintaining a safe office environment, providing staff the proper tools to do their jobs, and ensuring everyone has time for a proper lunch. He also cautions that "the lack of exposure to human resource realities can blind side you."

Years ago, Robinson had an issue with an employee using a company computer inappropriately during work time. Although the laws are not entirely defined regarding use of the Internet during work hours, it is important to inform staff of company policies related to personal blogging, signing on to Facebook,

Matt Robinson. Courtesy of Matthew Robinson

texting, and twittering during business hours. It is also important to let staff know that the company Web administrator has access to company electronic mail and that copies of that mail are saved as standard business practice.

Hiring the right person for the right job can be the best way to avoid legal problems down the road. "We're all salespeople," says Robinson, "especially in a job interview. It can take 60 days to start seeing things in terms of an employee's work performance." Doing research, asking for references, and spending quality time checking those references will pay off in the long run. "Be careful also about giving recommendations for past employees," he adds, "because that can come back to haunt you as well!"

For new people managers, Robinson has some solid advice: "Take the time to know something about human resources. It may be true that the strongest irons are forged in the hottest fires but an HR issue can be a fire that's a little too hot!" He acknowledges that entrepreneurs are at the highest risk because they want to get things done quickly and are not in the practice of prevention. "You want to offer a fair day's pay for a fair day's work and have fun doing it, but the proper parameters have to be there."

INTRODUCTION

As the HRM Close-Up shows, there is no doubt that employment laws affect line managers and what they are expected to do to successfully manage the people they are responsible for. Laws have been written to protect the employer and the employees; these laws reflect the values of society and in some situations laws have been enacted because of poor management practices. Therefore, it is important for supervisors to understand the legal context in which they have to operate. Managers, supervisors, and employees can no longer behave and act in certain ways without severe consequences. When managers ignore the legal aspects of HRM, they risk incurring costly and time-consuming litigation, negative public attitudes, and damage to organization morale.

And some of the laws address not just legal issues; the issues can also be emotional. For example, human rights legislation is paramount over other laws and concerns all individuals regardless of their gender, race, religion, age, marital status, disability, family status, sexual orientation, national origin, colour, or position in an organization. All employees, including supervisors and managers, should be aware of their personal biases and how these attitudes can influence their dealings with each other. It should be emphasized that whether the supervisor unintentionally or intentionally acts a certain way, the supervisor is responsible for any illegal actions. Being ignorant of the law is not a valid excuse. As Matt Robinson indicates, entrepreneurs are at the highest risk as they want to get things done quickly. This chapter will focus on the various employment laws at both the federal and provincial levels that affect how a manager practises human resources management.

Beyond legislation, there is also an expectation in today's society that treating employees in certain ways is just "good business." Thus, the concept of diversity management in a multicultural society has become part of business simply because it makes good business sense. It is important to remember that we have gone beyond what is required by law in our human resources management practices.

THE LEGAL FRAMEWORK OF HRM

Canada has two distinct sets of legislation: federal and provincial. Federal laws apply to everyone who resides in Canada. For example, everyone must pay income taxes. Other laws are handled at the provincial level. For example, the provinces are responsible for determining who can get a driver's licence. While this chapter will discuss specific employment laws, other kinds of laws, such as common law (our body of law that is developed as a result of judicial decisions), contract law (the laws that relate to legal and binding agreements, such as the purchase of a car), and government regulations (called statutory law), can also have an impact on HR. For example, common law establishes the basic employee–employer relationship of trust. Contract law governs a person engaged in a fee-for-service activity for a company. Statutory law creates employment conditions, such as providing minimum wages or holidays with pay (e.g., Canada Day on July 1).

Federal legislation applies to only about 10% of Canadian workers who are employed by the federal government departments and agencies, Crown corporations, and other businesses and industries under federal jurisdiction, such as banks, airlines, railway companies, and insurance and communications companies. Examples of these companies are CIBC, Scotiabank, Air Canada, WestJet, Bell, and CBC.

In addition, each province and territory has its own legislation that covers employment standards, human rights, labour relations, and worker health and safety. Companies covered under provincial legislation would include the corner 7 Eleven, the local McDonald's, and others such as Canadian Tire and Walmart. Although there is a great deal of similarity across provinces and territories, there are some notable variations in minimum wage and vacation entitlement, for example. Also, some aspects of human rights legislation differ from one jurisdiction to another. Some provinces and territories have employment equity legislation, and others do not. For example, Ontario and Quebec have stringent pay equity legislation. However, in Alberta and British Columbia, there is no such legislation. Therefore any pay equity adjustments are the decision of the organization.

Although both Employment Insurance (EI) and the Canada Pension Plan (CPP) are regulated by federal law, all employers and employees are covered, not just federal employees. EI provides for wage payment should you lose your job, and CPP provides for a small pension when you retire. Quebec has its own pension plan, which is similar to the Canada Pension Plan. Changes to EI over the last several years have had an impact on human resource practices in organizations. For example, compassionate care leave is available for employees where they can take up to six weeks off (with partial pay) to care for a family member who is gravely ill or at risk of dying.[1] Also, recently there was a recommendation from the EI advisory program that parental benefits offered under the EI program ought to be extended to 18 months.[2]

Federal Employment Laws

Canada Labour Code

laws.justice.gc.ca/en/L-2/
index.html

**Canadian Human
Rights Act**

laws.justice.gc.ca/
en/h-6/31147.html

For companies that are federally regulated, there are two basic employment laws: the **Canada Labour Code** and the **Canadian Human Rights Act**. The Labour Code covers basic employment conditions, labour relations, and health and safety in the federal sector. This law is administered by the Canada Industrial Relations Board.

Like the Labour Code, the Canadian Human Rights Act applies to all federal government departments and agencies, Crown corporations, and businesses and industries under federal jurisdiction, such as banks, airlines, railway companies, and insurance and communications companies. It is administered by the Canadian Human Rights Commission, which makes decisions on complaints involving discrimination and harassment. The concept of a certain level of basic human rights is part of the very fabric of Canadian society. And it is an area that is constantly expanding. For example, in mid-2008, the legislation was changed to ensure that Canada's Aboriginal people had full access to the human rights system.[3]

Of increasing concern for managers and HR professionals is privacy legislation. There are two primary laws—one that applies to only federally regulated companies (e.g., banks, airlines, etc.) and one that extends the federal legislation to provinces and businesses within the provinces. These laws are the **Personal Information Protection and Electronic Documents Act (PIPEDA)** and provincial legislation called the Personal Information Privacy Act (PIPA). These acts have a direct influence on how companies and managers handle employee information and the rights of employees regarding this information. Both acts enhance the protection granted to employees on their personal information that a company retains. Organizations can only use the information (such as social insurance number) for its intended purpose (to remit premiums to the Canada Pension Plan). Organizations can no longer collect personal information without disclosing the full use to employees. Further, organizations must seek written permission from the employee to disclose personal information. For example, if you want to get a car loan, your employer is obliged to seek your written authorization to disclose your pay to the lending agency.

**Personal Information
Protection and Electronic
Documents Act (PIPEDA)**

laws.justice.gc.ca/en/P-
8.6/92607.html

These acts have been most noted in the monitoring of e-mails and website visits of employees while at the worksite. More information on this will be covered in Chapter 9, Management Rights, Employee Rights, and Discipline.

As businesses look outside of Canada for new employees, organizations have become more familiar with the Immigration and Refugee Protection Act when they wish to recruit and hire people who are not citizens or permanent residents of Canada. This will be discussed in Chapter 4, Human Resource Planning, Recruitment, and Selection.

Provincial Employment Legislation

Each province and territory has relatively similar legislation that provides certain rights and guarantees regarding employment. For example, each province has maximum limits regarding hours per day or hours per week that a person can work before the organization is obliged to pay overtime wages. Similarly, the health and safety of workers are also covered by provincial legislation. In addition, provinces and territories have legislation dealing with human rights and legislation that covers unions and their relationships with employers. In the following sections, you will get information about these major types of employment laws whether they are provincial or federal. Figure 2.1 provides a summary of the various federal and provincial employment laws referred to in the previous two sections.

FIGURE 2.1   Major Employment Laws in Canada

Jurisdiction	Basic Employment Conditions	Labour Legislation	Occupational Health and Safety and Workers' Compensation	Human Rights
Federal	Canada Labour Code	Canada Labour Code	Canada Labour Code	Canadian Human Rights Act
Alberta	Employment Standards Code	Labour Relations Code	Occupational Health and Safety Code	Human Rights Citizenship and Multiculturalism Act
British Columbia	British Columbia Employment Standards Act	Labour Relations Code	Workers' Compensation Act	Human Rights Code
Manitoba	Employment Standards Code	Labour Relations Act	Workplace Safety and Health Act	Human Rights Code
New Brunswick	Employment Standards Act	Industrial Relations Act	Occupational Health and Safety Act	Human Rights Act
Newfoundland and Labrador	Labour Standards Act	Labour Relations Act	Occupational Health and Safety Act	Human Rights Code
Nova Scotia	Labour Standards Code	Industrial Standards Act	Occupational Health and Safety Act	Human Rights Act
Nunavut	Public Service Act	Public Service Act	Safety Act/Workers' Compensation Act	Canadian Human Rights Act
Ontario	Employment Standards Act	Labour Relations Act, 1995	Occupational Health and Safety Act/Workplace Safety and Insurance Act	Human Rights Code
Prince Edward Island	Employment Standards Act	Labour Act	Occupational Health and Safety Act	Human Rights Act
Quebec	Act Respecting Labour Standards	Labour Code	Act Respecting Occupational Health and Safety	Quebec Charter of Human Rights and Freedoms
Saskatchewan	Labour Standards Act	Trade Union Act	Occupational Health and Safety Act	Saskatchewan Human Rights Code

Note: Websites for legislation can be found in the Appendix at the end of this chapter.

HUMAN RIGHTS LEGISLATION

The legislation that has had the most far-reaching impact on employment conditions has been in the area of human rights. Although the original human rights legislation was at the federal level, all provinces have enacted similar laws. The basic foundation of human rights legislation is that every person has an equal opportunity and should not be discriminated against on the grounds of race, ethnic or national origin, colour, religion, age, sex, disability, or family or marital status.[4] And until 2008, "age" was defined to be the ages between 19 and 65 in most jurisdictions. However, most jurisdictions eliminated the "65," which means that in most cases the notion of "mandatory retirement" would now be illegal. In order to still have a mandatory retirement policy, the organization would have to demonstrate that it was a BFOR (bona fide occupational requirement).[5] The concept of BFOR will be discussed later in this chapter.

Human rights legislation is enforced through human rights commissions (or tribunals). Since human rights legislation is paramount over other employment laws, the decisions of these commissions and tribunals have a huge influence over all types of employment issues. Importantly, commission decisions have changed expectations regarding the proper treatment of employees. Thus, organizations now have higher standards to meet. It is useful also to remember that complaints can be started by a customer against an employee.[6]

Since this legislation has had a profound effect on the employment landscape, the latter part of this chapter will discuss the impact of the legislation in more detail. Websites for accessing the legislation can be found in the Appendix at the end of this chapter.

Discrimination

Outcome 3

The essence of human rights legislation is to prohibit discrimination on the basis of race, religion, gender, age, national or ethnic origin, disability, or family or marital status. The majority of provincial human rights legislation also covers sexual orientation. Figure 2.2 provides a partial listing of prohibited grounds of discrimination in employment for federal, provincial, and territorial jurisdictions. Note that some jurisdictions include pardoned convictions (e.g., federal, British Columbia, Ontario, and Quebec) and records of criminal convictions (British Columbia, Quebec, Prince Edward Island, and the Yukon Territory) as prohibited grounds. A person's political beliefs are protected in some jurisdictions such as British Columbia, Manitoba, Quebec, and Prince Edward Island. The complete list of prohibited grounds can be found at the Canadian Human Rights Commission in its publications link (**www.chrc-ccdp.ca**).

Many employment barriers are hidden, unintentionally, in the rules and procedures that organizations use in their various human resources management practices. These barriers, referred to as **systemic discrimination**, have prevented the progress of these designated groups. Inequity can result if these barriers discourage individuals based on their membership in certain groups rather than on their ability to do a job that the employer needs done. An example of systemic discrimination would occur when an employer's workforce represents one group in our society and the company recruits new employees by posting job vacancies within the company or by word of mouth

Systemic discrimination
The exclusion of members of certain groups through the application of employment policies or practices based on criteria that are not job-related

---

FIGURE 2.2   A Partial List of Prohibited Grounds of Discrimination in Employment

This partial list provides comparative information on the prohibited grounds of discrimination covered by federal, provincial, and territorial human rights legislation in Canada. In some instances, prohibited grounds for employment differ from those for the provision of services. The complete list can be found through the Canadian Human Rights Commission.

Prohibited Ground	Jurisdiction	Comments
Race or colour		
Employment	all jurisdictions	
Provision of Service	all jurisdictions	
Religion		
Employment	all jurisdictions	Yukon's Act reads "religion or creed, or religious belief, religious association or religious activity"
Provision of Service	all jurisdictions	Yukon's Act reads "religion or creed, or religious belief, religious association or religious activity"
Physical or mental disability		
Employment	all jurisdictions	Quebec uses the phrase "handicap or use of any means to palliate a handicap"
Provision of Service	all jurisdictions	Quebec uses the phrase "handicap or use of any means to palliate a handicap"
Dependence on alcohol or drugs		
Employment	all except Yukon and Northwest Territories	Policy to accept complaints in British Columbia, Alberta, Saskatchewan, Manitoba, Ontario, New Brunswick and Prince Edward Island
		Included in "handicap" ground in Quebec
		Provisions dependence only in New Brunswick and Nova Scotia
Provision of Service	all except Yukon, Northwest Territories and Quebec	Previous dependence only in New Brunswick and Nova Scotia Included in "handicap" ground in Quebec

Source: Canadian Human Rights Commission, "Prohibited Ground of Employment Discrimination by Jurisdiction." http://www.chrc-ccdp.ca/pdf/prohibit_en.pdf. Reproduced with the permission of the Ministry of Public Works and Government Services, 2009.

among the employees. This recruitment strategy is likely to generate a candidate similar to those in the current workforce, thereby unintentionally discriminating against other groups of workers in the labour market. A better approach might be to vary recruitment methods by contacting outside agencies and organizations.

Bona fide occupational qualification (BFOQ)
A justifiable reason for discrimination based on business reasons of safety or effectiveness

Employers may be permitted to discriminate if employment qualifications are based on a **bona fide occupational qualification (BFOQ)** or bona fide occupational requirement (BFOR). For example, airlines retire pilots at age 60.[7] A BFOQ is justified if the employer can establish its necessity for business operations. Business necessity is a practice that includes the safe and efficient operation of an organization. In other words, differential treatment is not discrimination if there is a justifiable reason. However, it should be pointed out that it is difficult for many employers to establish legitimate BFOQs. Therefore, a supervisor will probably be asked to carefully examine job requirements and demonstrate that a certain characteristic is absolutely essential. For example, the federal government has been allowed to hire only women as guards in prisons for women; however, a retail store specializing in women's fashions would not be allowed to hire only women. Frequently, the HR professional and the line manager would work together to review job requirements to determine if the qualifications met the BFOQ requirement. For recruitment and hiring purposes, it is important that job requirements not create a discriminatory situation. Likewise, even the process of hiring can be considered discriminatory if inappropriate questions are asked. This area will be discussed more fully in Chapter 4.

This partial list provides comparative information on the prohibited grounds of discrimination covered by federal, provincial and territorial human rights legislation in Canada. In some instances, prohibited grounds for employment different from those for the provision of services. The complete list can be found through the Canadian Human Rights Commission.

Most of the decisions made by the Supreme Court of Canada, human rights tribunals, and arbitrations have looked at whether the discrimination was "intentional" or "unintentional." Intentional discrimination is very clear and direct, such as a requirement that only males five feet nine inches and taller could apply for a certain job. On the other hand, some discriminatory employment situations were unintentional. An example of unintentional discrimination is the requirement that a firefighter be able to run a certain distance within a fixed amount of time.

A Supreme Court decision several years ago changed this approach from previous court decisions.[8] The case involved a female forest firefighter in British Columbia who was terminated after performing successfully on the job for three years. As a consequence of a coroner's report, new fitness standards had been instituted requiring that all firefighters be able to run 2.5 km in 11 minutes. The person failed the standard on four attempts and was terminated, even though she had been doing the work successfully. The Court decided that the test was discriminatory since females have a lower aerobic capacity than males and would therefore not be able to meet the standard. The decision went on to establish a new approach to BFOQ that will require employers to demonstrate that it is impossible to accommodate individuals discriminated against without undue hardship. This means that whatever the standard is, it must provide for individual accommodation, if possible.

Reasonable accommodation
Attempt by employers to adjust the working conditions and employment practices of employees to prevent discrimination

Another concept that has arisen from human rights decisions is that of reasonable accommodation. **Reasonable accommodation** involves adjusting employment policies and practices so that no individual is denied benefits, is disadvantaged with respect to employment opportunities, or is blocked from carrying out the essential components of a job because of race, colour, disability, or any of the other prohibited grounds of discrimination. This also means that as new prohibited grounds are added to any human rights legislation, these too would be eligible for reasonable accommodation. For example, "religion" is a prohibited ground and as such, it is quite possible that an employee could ask to wear a specific article of clothing (such as a head covering) that is required by the religion.[9] Specifically, an employer needs to thoroughly consider methods by which the employee's characteristic (family status, gender, disability, etc.) can be accommodated in the workplace, including whether the specific tasks can be organized in a way to deal with the characteristic.[10] For example, if someone does not have the necessary degree of hand-eye coordination to do detailed electronics work, the employer may be obliged to reconfigure the tasks so that the person can do the work. Whether an employer can accommodate the work to fit the individual needs is ultimately a decision made by human rights tribunals. Ethics in HRM 2.1 describes what happens with reasonable accommodation when the definition of "disability" is expanded.

It is no longer acceptable for employers to simply assume that all employees will "fit in" no matter what their special needs. Employers must find the means to alter systems to meet the needs of their employees as long as this does not cause "undue hardship to the employer." However, undue hardship may be something different for a small organization compared with a large organization. For example, it may be a hardship for a small firm to modify a washroom to accommodate a person in a wheelchair. However, it may be reasonable to expect a large organization, with its own building, to renovate or install a washroom that can accommodate a wheelchair.

Reasonable accommodation may include redesigning job duties; adjusting work schedules; providing technical, financial, and human support services; and upgrading facilities. The City of Toronto developed award-winning facilities in its Barrier Free Access program, which was designed to allow people with disabilities accessible passage throughout city facilities. There are several Canadian not-for-profit organizations that support and encourage employment opportunities for people with disabilities. Among those are The Neil Squire Foundation (**www.neilsquire.ca**) and Abilities (**www.abilities.ca**). While many employers tend to think of accommodation in terms of physical disabilities, it is important to remember that the duty to accommodate includes all the prohibited grounds of discrimination, including mental illness. Therefore, it is important that employers carefully listen to any employee who says that they are "stressed." It may be that the individual has a mental illness or disorder.[11] Organizations such as Mental Health Works (**www.mentalhealthworks.ca/**) can provide advice and guidance regarding workplace issues.

Reasonable accommodation benefits all employees. The provision of allowances for childcare expenses when employees take company-sponsored courses not only removes a barrier that blocks many women but also may assist any employee with sole parenting responsibilities. The flexible work schedules adopted by some companies in northern Canada benefit First Nations employees who are prepared to work unusual hours in exchange for significant breaks away from the worksite in order to take part in traditional hunting and fishing activities. Many other employees also benefit from these flexible work schedules. Further, with the cultural and religious diversity of the Canadian population, more and more employers are being asked for accommodation for a person

Neil Squire Foundation
www.neilsquire.ca

Abilities Magazine
www.abilities.ca/

Mental Health Works
www.mentalhealthworks.ca/

ETHICS in HRM 2.1

EXPANDING DEFINITIONS

In mid-2007, the Canadian Human Rights Commission added "environmental sensitivities" to the definition of disability. By doing so, employers will now be required to potentially accommodate any employee who may be sensitive to their working environment. The specific case that created the expanded definition involved an office worker in Alberta. This individual's physician validated that the person demonstrated extreme sensitivities to chemicals associated with recent renovations of the office space. Initially the employer allowed the person to be absent due to health reasons while ways to accommodate the situation were sought. The employer also asked the physician to inspect the office space and the

person's work tasks and to make recommendations for accommodation.

After several weeks, the employer requested that the employee return to work. The employee refused to do so as none of the physician's recommendations had been implemented. The Alberta Court of Appeal eventually heard the complaint. In its decision, the court stated that while the company had attempted to accommodate and had asked that the physician make recommendations, by not implementing any of the recommendations the company did not really attempt to solve the problem.

Are there circumstances where an employer would not follow requested recommendations?

Source: "Being Sensitive to Employees' Environmental Sensitivities," *Canadian HR Reporter,* September 22, 2008.

Businesses today are actively seeking skilled and capable people with physical challenges.

Keith Brofsky/Photodisc Green/Getty Images

to take the day off to celebrate important religious days of their faith.[12] At Work with HRM 2.1 provides two accommodation cases that were decided by the courts.

Reverse Discrimination

Reverse discrimination
Giving preference to members of certain groups such that others feel they are the subjects of discrimination

In pursuing initiatives to avoid discrimination, employers may be accused of **reverse discrimination**, or giving preference to members of certain groups such that others feel they are being discriminated against. For example, if a company feels that it has too few women employees, it may take active steps to hire more women. However, by hiring more women, the company may hire fewer men, opening itself to criticisms that it is discriminating against men. When these charges occur, organizations are caught between attempting to correct past discriminatory practices and handling present complaints that they are being unfair. If an organization is required to comply with any type of employment equity legislation (discussed later), it can be quite legal to discriminate and hire certain individuals.

In some cases, organizations may identify the need to hire a certain proportion of people from specific groups, such as visible minorities. While these organizations may state that they wish to find a larger pool of qualified applicants from a particular group, the organizations may in fact create a type of quota system for hiring. If it is perceived that there are hard numbers attached to hiring, then it is easy for individuals not in a targeted group to feel that they are being discriminated against. Charges of reverse discrimination have occurred in the fire and police services as those organizations try to achieve a workforce that is more reflective of the residents in their communities.

Harassment

Outcome 4

Harassment
Any unwanted physical or verbal conduct that offends or humiliates the individual

Besides prohibiting discrimination, human rights legislation also prohibits **harassment.** Some provinces protect only against sexual harassment, while other provinces prohibit any type of workplace harassment. Harassment is any unwanted physical or verbal conduct that offends or humiliates a person.[13] Harassment can take many forms and can be one incident or several incidents. It is not acceptable, for instance, for one co-worker to strike another, and it is not acceptable to make personal comments that are offensive to the other person. When dealing with harassment in the workplace, a manager needs to ask whether a "reasonable person" would consider a certain behaviour or action as harassment. If the answer is yes, then the supervisor is expected to act accordingly. It is interesting to note that what is considered harassment in today's workplace, was sometimes considered acceptable behaviour not long ago. For example, it was acceptable at one point to call someone a name that reflected the person's ethnic background.

AT WORK **with HRM 2.1**

THE DUTY TO ACCOMMODATE

- An employee at Hydro-Quebec was terminated after missing 1000 days of work over a seven-year period. The union representing the employee claimed that the individual suffered from a mental illness and therefore ought to have been accommodated. The Supreme Court of Canada ruled that the employer's duty to accommodate ends when there is no reasonable chance that the employee could fulfill their basic obligations of work. The company had produced evidence from medical experts that indicated the employee's attendance would not improve and therefore even with accommodation the employee would not be productive. The termination was upheld.

- The Canadian Human Rights Tribunal found that Canada Post failed to accommodate a mail carrier with autism. For over 15 years the employee had a good work record with no discipline issues and eventually requested accommodation. Since people with autism dislike change, the employee was allowed to keep the same delivery route, start work earlier, and sort mail differently. Occasionally, the employee came to work with cuts on the arm that was not noted until the autism was identified. At that point, other employees expressed concerns about their safety and over time created a work environment that was negative and created undue workplace stress for the autistic employee. Eventually the employee launched a human rights complaint that included a statement that the management did little to educate the other employees about autism nor did management try to improve the negative work environment. The tribunal concluded that Canada Post treated the employee poorly and insensitively to the needs of an autistic person.

CRITICAL THINKING QUESTION
Do you think these were appropriate decisions? Why or why not?

Sources: Janice Tibbetts, "Decision Limits Duty of Employers to Accommodate Sick Employees," *The Vancouver Sun*, July 18, 2008, A6; and Jeffrey R. Smith, "Canada Post Fails to Deliver Accommodation," *Canadian HR Reporter,* November 17, 2008, 5.

HRM and the law 2.1

HARASSMENT CAN BE COSTLY

In 2008, a case between a trainee and the RCMP was decided by the Canadian Human Rights Tribunal that cost the RCMP approximately $200,000. The specifics of the case involved an individual who entered the training academy but whose training contract was terminated several months later. The trainee claimed that this was the result of three months of harassment and discrimination. The trainee was of Persian descent and was ridiculed for wearing a religious pendant and for using a signature that showed a Persian style. Furthermore, the trainee stated that the instructor was hostile, verbally abusive, leading to an inability of the trainee to develop and demonstrate the necessary skills. Countering these statements of the trainee, the RCMP indicated that the contract had been terminated through legitimate performance evaluations and that the trainee's contract was terminated, as the standards expected by the training academy were not being met and that there was some question of the person's mental stability. The RCMP went on to indicate that the person would not be eligible to re-enroll in a future training session. Through testimony and evidence, the tribunal concluded that the complaint was legitimate and the RCMP did not provide a satisfactory explanation that one or more of the prohibited grounds were not factors in the termination. The tribunal did go on to conclude that while discrimination might have occurred, harassment did not. Given the length of time since the incident (almost 10 years), the tribunal ordered not only compensation amounting to over two years of salary and benefits as a constable but also ordered that the person be offered re-enrolment in the training academy.

What do you think of the decision? Why?

Sources: Extract from Canadian Human Rights Commission, *Ali Tahmourpour, Complainant-and-Royal Canadian Mounted Police* April 16, 2008, www.chrt-tcdp.gc.ca/search/view_html.asp?doid=897&lg=_e&isruling=0 (retrieved January 7, 2009).

While for some time discussions of harassment have focused on sexual harassment, in the last several years the focus has been on general harassment in the workplace. Specifically, organizations have developed policy statements and guidelines for dealing with harassment in the workplace.

The Canadian Human Rights Commission defines harassment as follows:

> Harassment is any unwanted physical or verbal conduct that offends or humiliates you. Such conduct can interfere with your ability to do a job or obtain a service. Harassment is a type of discrimination. It can take many forms, such as
>
> - threats, intimidation, or verbal abuse;
> - unwelcome remarks or jokes about subjects like your race, religion, disability or age;
> - displaying sexist, racist, or other offensive pictures or posters;
> - sexually suggestive remarks or gestures;
> - inappropriate physical contact, such as touching, patting, pinching, or punching;
> - physical assault, including sexual assault.
>
> Harassment will be considered to have taken place if a reasonable person ought to have known that the behaviour was unwelcome.[14]

What this means for supervisors is that they are expected to work with employees to ensure they are behaving and acting in an acceptable fashion. For example, HRM and the Law 2.1 describes the impact of a harassment complaint at the RCMP. And while supervisors are expected to handle things a certain way, employees are also expected not to harass.

A company's policies on harassment must be broad. For example, Ceridian Canada, a firm in Markham, Ontario, has a clear policy through its company values that is a great tool in preventing harassment. It has identified prohibited behaviours in creating a culture of respect as well as consequences of such behaviour.[15]

In another example, Seneca College's discrimination and harassment policy states:

> It is the Policy of Seneca College that all employees and students have a right to work and study in an environment that asserts the personal worth and dignity of each individual.
>
> In order to achieve this objective, Seneca College will not tolerate any form of discrimination and/or harassment in its employment, educational, accommodation or business dealings. Every member of the College community has the right to file a complaint of discrimination/harassment.[16]

Its policy defines harassment as:

> Engaging in a course of vexatious comments or conduct related to one or more of the prohibited grounds that is known or might reasonably be known to be unwelcome/unwanted, offensive, intimidating, hostile, or inappropriate, which adversely affects the employment or academic status of the individual.[17]

Seneca's policy is very far-reaching as it applies to students, faculty and staff, and visitors to the campus as well as corporations and vendors who do business with the college.

For harassment policies to succeed, confidentiality is necessary, and so is a method for filing complaints. Without organizational commitment to zero tolerance of harassment, such policies are meaningless. It is also important to remember that harassment is against the law. As the Province of Saskatchewan reminds employers:

> If you violate the *Code* you could be liable for the harm caused by discrimination.[18]

Manager's Toolkit 2.1 presents some suggestions for an effective harassment policy.[19]

The concepts of harassment in the workplace are being broadened to include psychological harassment, such as bullying. Psychological harassment can create a poisoned worked environment and is based on grounds other than those prohibited in human rights legislation. While some jurisdictions have enacted legislation prohibiting psychological harassment, such as Quebec, other jurisdictions such as the federal government and Ontario have not been successful. However, as of October 1, 2008, Saskatchewan incorporated psychological harassment into its health and safety legislation.[20]

GUIDELINES FOR HAVING AN EFFECTIVE ANTI-HARASSMENT ENVIRONMENT

1. Develop a written policy explaining what harassment is and the employer's commitment to a harassment-free work environment.

2. Have a statement of duties of everyone involved—employer, managers, supervisors, and employees.

3. Have clear procedures in place for complaints.

4. Create an outline of how a complaint will be handled, including confidentiality, and what will happen at conclusion of investigation.

5. Identify consequences for any employee who exhibits the prohibited behaviours or actions, and anyone who files a false complaint.

6. Communicate the policy to everyone and provide ongoing education and training.

Additional resources from the various human rights commissions are available at the following websites:

- www.albertahumanrights.ab.ca (Province of Alberta)
- www.bchrt.bc.ca/ (Province of British Columbia)
- www.gov.mb.ca/hrc (Province of Manitoba)
- www.ohrc.on.ca (Province of Ontario)
- www.shrc.gov.sk.ca/ (Province of Saskatchewan)

Adapted from Michael Fitzgibbon, "Fighting harassment in the workplace," *Canadian HR Reporter*, October 22, 2007, 25–30.

Canadian Human Rights Commission (CHRC)

www.chrc-ccdp.ca

Enforcement of Human Rights Legislation

The federal government and each province and territory have a commission or similar agency to deal with complaints concerning discriminatory practices covered by legislation. For example, the Canadian Human Rights Commission (CHRC) (**www.chrc-ccdp.ca**) deals with complaints from those employees and businesses covered by the Canadian Human Rights Act. These commissions can act on their own if they feel there are sufficient grounds for a finding of discrimination. The agencies also have the ability to interpret the act. Figure 2.3 presents a flowchart of the process used

FIGURE 2.3   Canadian Human Rights Commission Disputes Resolution Process

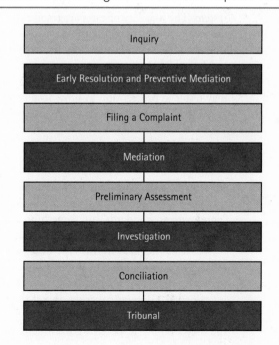

Source: Canadian Human Rights Commission "Overview-Resolving Disputes: Dispute Resolution Process" URL: http://www.chrc-ccdp.ca/disputeresolution_reglementdifferends/drp_prd-en.asp Author/Organization: Canadian Human Rights Commission Reproduced with the permission of the Ministry of Public Works and Government Services, 2009.

at CHRC to resolve complaints. You will note that the process includes a very early step of resolution and preventive mediation. Other human rights commissions operate in a similar fashion. The steps are as follows:

1. Inquiry—Individual contacts the CHRC about launching a complaint and the CHRC determines if the allegations fall within its jurisdiction.
2. Early Resolution and Preventive Mediation—A CHRC representative determines if it is the correct agency and if so, encourages the parties to seek resolution by using its trained specialists in mediation.
3. Filing a Complaint—If the matter hasn't been resolved in Step 2, and if the individual wishes to pursue the matter, a complaint is filed. The CHRC can decide to deal with the complaint or it can be dismissed. If the CHRC will hear the complaint, a review is done to determine if mediation would work.
4. Mediation—Specialists are assigned by the CHRC to assist the parties in finding a mediated solution. This is a voluntary and confidential step.
5. Preliminary Assessment—If the parties are not willing to be involved in mediation (or if mediation is not appropriate), the complaint is referred to the Investigation Division to determine next steps. This stage of the process can once again include mediation or a decision to have a full investigation.
6. Investigation—An investigation, including any documents and other evidence, is gathered; a report is then prepared of the analysis of the information along with a recommendation as to the further handling of the case that is submitted to the commissioner. The commission can dismiss the case, refer it to conciliation, or refer to the tribunal for a final and binding decision. For example, AZ Bus Tours was recently ordered to compensate an employee over $15,000 for lost wages as well as $3,000 for pain and suffering. The employee stated that a documented medical condition had not been accommodated and certain shifts were not being assigned. The tribunal concluded that the person had been discriminated against due to a disability.[21]

Any person who obstructs an investigation or a tribunal, or fails to comply with the terms of a settlement, can be found guilty of an offence that may be punishable by a fine and/or jail sentence. If the guilty party is an employer or an employee organization, the fine might be as high as $50,000 and up to $5,000 for individuals.[22]

Provincial human rights laws are enforced in a similar manner to that used in the federal system. The majority of cases are resolved at the investigation stage. If no agreement can be reached, the case is presented to the province's human rights commission. The members of the commission study the evidence and then submit a report to the minister in charge of administering human rights legislation. The minister may appoint an independent board of inquiry, which has similar powers to a tribunal at the federal level. Failure to comply with the remedies prescribed by the board of inquiry may result in prosecution in provincial court. Individuals may be fined between $500 and $1,000, and organizations or groups between $1,000 and $10,000. These levies may vary across provinces.

EMPLOYMENT STANDARDS LEGISLATION

Outcome 5

All federal, provincial, and territorial jurisdictions have passed employment standards laws specifying the minimum obligations of employers. The names of the laws usually include the words "employment standards" or something similar. However, the minimum obligations for federal companies are covered under the Canada Labour Code.

Usually included in this type of legislation are items such as hours of work, minimum wages, overtime pay, vacation pay, public holidays, and who is covered by the legislation. Standards vary between provinces. In Manitoba, for instance, "domestic workers" are covered. However, a person is defined as a domestic worker only if the person works more than 24 hours per week for a family doing cooking, cleaning, and childcare, for the entire family. The legislation also typically reflects the views of the respective government with regard to their social policy. For example, British Columbia's legislation provides the right for a person to take a limited number of days off to tend to childcare needs. Other jurisdictions, such as Ontario, have no such provision. In British Columbia, the legislation provides nine statutory holidays; in Ontario, there are only eight. There

Ontario Employment Standards

www.labour.gov.on.ca/

Manitoba Employment Standards

www.gov.mb.ca/labour/
standards/

New Brunswick Employment Standards

www.gnb.ca/0308/
index-e.asp

is usually a separate branch or agency that administers and interprets the legislation for both employers and employees. All the websites are listed in the Appendix at the end of this chapter but you can look at several of the following: **www.labour.gov.on.ca/**, **www.gov.mb.ca/labour/ standards/**, and **www.gnb.ca/0308/index-e.asp.**

This is important legislation as it applies to all employers, whether they are unionized or not. And because it specifies minimum obligations of employers, every employer—large and small— needs to be aware of the legislation. It is particularly important during difficult economic times that employers take note of their legal obligations. For example, in Ontario, pregnant employees and employees on parental leave are protected by both the ESA and human rights legislation, in relation to termination or layoff.[23]

The legislation is administered by an agency or commission that both interprets and enforces the law. For example, if employees feel that they are not receiving the right amount of vacation pay, they can contact the agency and find out what the right amount should be. If they are getting the wrong amount, then the agency can contact the employer and start an investigation.

LABOUR RELATIONS LEGISLATION

Labour relations legislation governs both the process by which a trade union acquires bargaining rights and the procedures by which trade unions and employers engage in collective bargaining. In some jurisdictions, such as Ontario, the legislation (Labour Relations Act, 1995) applies primarily to workplaces in the private sector but also to certain parts of the public sector (municipal workers, hospital employees, school boards, etc.). Ontario also has separate legislation for certain types of employers in the public sector, such as hospitals and Crown corporations.[24] However, in other jurisdictions, such as British Columbia, the legislation can apply to any workplace—whether it is in the public or private sector. Labour relations legislation only applies to unionized employees and to employers with unionized employees. Currently, approximately 5.7 million employees (or 31% of the workforce) in Canada belong to a union, primarily in the public sector (61%) with only 20% of the unionized workers are in the commercial sector.[25]

Labour relations legislation is usually administered through an agency called the Labour Relations Board, which is responsible for administering and enforcing the legislation. This board makes decisions on a variety of complaints from either a union or an employer. An employer might complain about the location of a trade union's picket or union members might complain that the union has not fairly represented them. The people making these decisions are hired by the board and are usually lawyers or have some type of legal training.

More information on labour relations legislation will be covered in Chapter 10.

HEALTH AND SAFETY LEGISLATION AND WORKERS' COMPENSATION

As you will see later in this book, the health and safety of employees is a responsibility of employers. This responsibility is governed by legislation that describes the expected standards for health and safety in the workplace, as well as outlining the role and involvement of employees in health and safety. Recent changes to this type of legislation have not only increased responsibility for employers, but have also placed more onus for a healthy and safe work environment on employees.[26] Violations of health and safety statutes are administered through a government agency, frequently called the Workers' Compensation Board. As part of the legislation, workers can receive a monetary payment if they are injured at work. Thus the employer is responsible not only for the health and safety of the workplace but also for financial compensation if the worker is injured on the job.

Additional information on health and safety legislation will be covered in Chapter 8.

Construction workers must adhere to strict guidelines in order to meet workplace safety regulations.

Photodisc Collection/Getty Images

EMPLOYMENT AND PAY EQUITY

Outcome 6

Central to Canada's economic growth and prosperity in a highly competitive global marketplace will be a barrier-free environment in which all Canadians can fully explore and develop their career potential. Labour force statistics, described in Chapter 1, indicate changing patterns of immigration, the rising labour force participation rates of women, and an aging population with a proportionately higher incidence of disabilities. Women, visible minorities, First Nations, and people with disabilities make up over 60% of Canada's labour force, and their numbers continue to rise. These designated-group members entering Canada's labour pool constitute a vital resource, and their full participation in the workplace will be fundamental to an organization's ability to understand and respond to the needs of a rapidly changing marketplace.

Employment Equity

Employment equity
A distinct Canadian process for achieving equality in all aspects of employment

Equity by definition means fairness or impartiality. In a legal sense, it means justice based on the concepts of ethics and fairness and a system of jurisprudence administered by courts and designed primarily to decrease the rigidity of common law. The implementation of **employment equity** has involved the establishment of policies and practices designed to ensure equitable representation in the workforce and to redress past discriminations as they relate to employment and employment practices.

The Law on Employment Equity

The Employment Equity Act requires that the federal government, federal agencies, and Crown corporations with 100 employees or more and that are regulated under the Canada Labour Code must implement employment equity and report on their results. Some of the companies that are covered by the Employment Equity Act are the Royal Bank, Rogers Foods Ltd., General Electric Canada, Brinks Canada Limited, Toronto Port Authority, and Canadian Wheat Board.[27] Under the act the employer is required to develop plans to better represent certain designated groups (women, First Nations people, visible minorities, and people with disabilities). In creating the plan, the employer must identify and remove any employment barriers, such as a keyboarding test for jobs in which no keyboarding is required. Further, the plan must have a timetable for achieving these changes. While this law does not extend to the provinces, the federal government, through its Federal Contractors Program, expects organizations that do business with the federal government to implement employment equity principles.

While there are no specific provincial acts pertaining to employment equity, the concept of employment equity is rooted in federal and provincial employment standards legislation, human rights codes, and the Canadian Charter of Rights and Freedoms. Employment equity involves the identification and removal of systemic barriers to employment opportunities that adversely affect designated groups, women, visible minorities, First Nations people, and people with disabilities. Employment equity also involves the implementation of special measures and reasonable accommodation (which was discussed earlier under "Discrimination").

Designated groups
Women, visible minorities, First Nations peoples, and persons with disabilities who have been disadvantaged in employment

The legislation identified four **designated groups** in Canada that had not received equitable treatment in employment: women, First Nations peoples, visible minorities, and people with disabilities faced significant but different disadvantages in employment. Some of the disadvantages included high unemployment, occupational segregation, pay inequities, and limited opportunities for career progress. While there has been progress, some of the original concerns have not been advanced very far.

While women represent 47% of the people employed,[28] employment for women tends to be concentrated in retail trade, banking, education, and health care (77%). On the other hand, while women represent approximately half of workforce participants, only 7% hold managerial positions.[29] Women tend to be underrepresented in trades, manufacturing, and construction, but they are close to being equally represented (3.5%) with men (2.5%) in recreation and sports jobs.[30]

While the number of First Nations people is about 3.7%[31] of the population, the numbers of young Aboriginal workers will increase, and in western Canada they will account for a substantial portion of labour market growth. However, many First Nations people face major employment barriers, which may be compounded by low educational achievement and lack of job experience, as well as language and cultural barriers. In urban centres, many First Nations workers are concentrated in low-paying, unstable employment. Economic self-sufficiency and participation in the economy are seen as essential to First Nations development. At Work with HRM 2.2 describes the success of Nasittuq Corporation in assisting First Nations people to become an integral part of its workforce.

AT WORK **with HRM 2.2**

EMPLOYMENT EQUITY SUCCESS STORY

Human Resources Development Canada recognized Nasittuq Corporation as its "success story" in 2007. Nasittuq is an agency, with headquarters in Ottawa, which operates and maintains the North Warning System of radar that detects airborne threats to North America. Its facilities are primarily in northern Ontario, which means that it operates in areas with high populations of Aboriginal peoples.

The creative ways in which it has demonstrated its commitment to hiring and advancement of Aboriginals is:

- Creating partnerships in communities where it does business and by participating in community events, raising awareness about Nasittuq as an employer.

- Advertising for job openings in publications that target Aboriginal communities.

- Having a specialized on-the-job training program that matches the training to the exact needs of the trainee.

- Creating a development program that is a combination of academic studies and on-the-job training that leads to certification of technical skills.

- Providing annual scholarship awards to encourage Aboriginal students to pursue more advanced education.

The company believes it has been successful through an active and visible commitment to employment equity by extensive information on its internal website and by requiring each employee each year to sign a document indicating that they understand the company's employment equity values. Further, the company places emphasis on work-life balance and focuses on each employee's individual needs.

CRITICAL THINKING QUESTIONS

1. What has the company you are working for (or recently worked for) done to assist visible minorities, people with disabilities, and First Nations people in getting hired?
2. Is there more that they could do?

Source: Adapted from Human Resources and Social Development Canada, *Employment Equity Act: Annual Report 2007*: 29-31.

Visible-minority groups vary in their labour force profiles and in their regional distributions. Toronto and Vancouver have large visible-minority populations. Studies have shown that Latin Americans and Southeast Asians experience lower-than-average incomes, higher rates of unemployment, and reduced access to job interviews, even for those persons with the same qualifications as other candidates. Systemic barriers that have a negative employment impact on visible minorities can include culturally biased aptitude tests, lack of recognition of foreign credentials, and excessive levels of language requirements. Recent statistics indicate that although visible minorities, 84% of whom are immigrants, possess higher educational achievements, they also have the highest unemployment rates and tend to work in jobs with low skill requirements.[32]

Of the employable people with disabilities, only about 51% are actively participating in the workforce.[33] People with disabilities face attitudinal barriers, physical demands that are unrelated to actual job requirements, and inadequate access to the technical and human support systems that would make productive employment possible. The employment experiences of people with disabilities are also dependent on the extent of the limitations, as perceived by the person. In most cases, people with minor limitations do not experience as many barriers as those with more extreme limitations.[34]

As mentioned earlier in the chapter, these employment practices can unintentionally preclude certain segments of our population from employment opportunities. Manager's Toolkit 2.2 gives examples of suggested solutions to systemic barriers.

Benefits of Employment Equity

Employment equity makes good business sense since it contributes to the bottom line by broadening the base of qualified individuals for employment, training, and promotions, and by helping employers to avoid costly human rights complaints. Most provinces now have an active approach to ensuring there is appropriate representation in their workforces. Some of these initiatives can include career and mentoring programs for the designated groups.[35] Likewise, organizations such as Atlantic Tractors and Equipment in Nova Scotia and New Brunswick find that through employment equity initiatives they are able to attract young women to work for them.

Human Resources and Social Development Canada administers the federal Employment Equity Act and as part of that administration recognizes organizations that have made special efforts to achieve a workforce that is representative of our population. In the Annual Reports produced each year, a "success story" such as that described in At Work with HRM 2.2 is highlighted. As stated by Ivan Warwyk, president of Nasittuq Corporation, "Every employee is made aware of the organization's support for employment equity and belief in equitable treatment of all employees. Is it just an initiative, or is it part of how we conduct our daily business? A good part of it starts with me as the manager, and how it trickles down throughout the organization."[36]

MANAGER'S TOOLKIT **2.2**

EXAMPLES OF EMPLOYMENT PRACTICES

1. *Word-of-mouth recruiting.* While this is a common form of making job opportunities known to family and friends, this can be an effective tool for sourcing designated group members if the information is shared widely and to a variety of different communities.

2. *Job requirements.* Employers that require Canadian experience may be eliminating visible minorities, particularly recent immigrants. It is important to review the experience required and determine if having previous work in a Canadian environment is necessary for job success.

3. *Training and development.* It is important to review the organization's approach to training of its employees. Training opportunities that are linked to seniority, wage levels, and type of work could limit the participation of designated group members.

Source: *Guidelines for the Employment Equity Act and Regulations: Guideline 6: Employment Systems Review,* Human Resources and Social Development Canada, Labour Program.

First Nations University is a unique university in Canada that focuses on the educational needs of First Nations people.

Courtesy of First Nations University of Canada

Human Resources and Social Development Canada (HRSDC)

www.hrsdc.gc.ca/

For additional information on the Employment Equity Act, visit HRDC's website at **www. hrsdc.gc.ca/**.

Pay Equity

As a result of a 1978 amendment to the Canadian Human Rights Act, pay equity became law. Federal pay equity law makes it illegal for federally regulated employers to discriminate against individuals on the basis of job content. The focus of pay equity legislation is to narrow the wage gap between men and women, on the basis that women's work historically has been undervalued and therefore underpaid relative to work primarily done by men. For example, the average salary of males who worked full-time in 2008 was $49,441, compared with $41,371 for women.[37] Currently, eight provinces and the Yukon Territory have policies dealing with pay equity. Recently, the Province of New Brunswick have created a "wage gap action plan" with the goal of reducing the gap to 10%.[38]

Pay equity
The practice of equal pay for work of equal value

Pay equity means equal pay for work of equal value and is based on two principles. The first is equal pay for equal work. Equal pay for equal work means that if a woman and a man are doing substantially the same work for the same organization or company, they must receive the same wage unless the difference in pay is due to seniority, temporary training assignment, or merit.[39] Equal pay for equal work is regulated through basic employment conditions legislation, usually called an Employment Standards Act.

The second principle of pay equity is equal pay for work that may be comparable in value to the organization. Pay equity compares the value of and pay of different jobs. This means that male and female workers must be paid the same wage rate for jobs of comparable value, such as a nurse (historically female-dominated work) to an electrician (historically male-dominated).

Implementation of pay equity is based on comparing jobs performed mostly by women with jobs performed mostly by males. Comparisons require the use of a gender neutral job comparison system to evaluate the jobs in the organization.[40] The value of the work is based on the skills and effort required, the responsibilities of the job, and the conditions under which the work is performed. It is important to remember that the comparisons are made on job content, not on the performance of the employee. The comparison must be done in such a way that the characteristics of "male" jobs, such as manual skills of a machinery repairperson, are valued fairly in comparison with the characteristics of "female" jobs, such as the dexterity skills of a typist.[41] For example,

under pay equity, Canadian National Railways would need to compare the work of an accounts payable clerk with that of a person who repaired the train cars. Under provincial pay equity legislation in Ontario, the City of Toronto would compare the work of a clerk in the building department with that of a person repairing city roads.

The federal pay equity legislation applies to the workforce under its jurisdiction and covers all organizations regardless of number of employees. The federal pay equity system is complaint-based, meaning that complaints can be raised by an employee, a group of employees, or a union.[42]

In Ontario the legislation covers public- and private-sector employers with 10 or more employees. Like the federal legislation, Ontario's legislation is complaint-based. There is no pay equity legislation in either Alberta or British Columbia.

For more information on pay equity, check the following websites:

- www.payequity.gov.on.ca/index_pec.html
- www.chrc-ccdp.ca
- www.gov.ns.ca/lwd/payequity/

Even though there have been recent changes in some of the employment legislation described in these sections, changes will continue to be made as the Canadian social values change. See Emerging Trends 2.1 for things to watch.

EMERGING TRENDS 2.1

There have been several recent significant court decisions that may impact the rights of both employees and employers. Here are a few items to consider:

1. **Medical notes from doctors.** For years, employers have had to accept one-line notes from doctors about the medical condition of an employee. In most situations, employees were disadvantaged as the employers did not have good information about the health (or disability) of an employee and made decisions based on what they had. In a Supreme Court of Canada decision in 2008, the courts determined that an employee could be evaluated by a doctor of the firm's choosing.

2. **Accommodation.** The need to accommodate disabilities extended to permitting lengthy absences. However, another Supreme Court decision ruled that the employer could eventually terminate the employee if the company could not accommodate the person on a long-term basis.

3. **Non-performers.** If an employee is not performing as expected, an alternative may be to demote the person. If the pay is not changed substantially and the demotion is done in a caring fashion, courts are

not as sympathetic as they once were to claims of "constructive dismissal."

4. **Use of "contractors."** In a recent Ontario Court of Appeal, it determined that the person who was designated a "contractor" was in fact a full-time employee. The person did not work for any other organization and the nature of the work and the control of the work arrangement was strictly at the determination of the employer.

5. **Use of Internet to access legal assistance.** More and more court cases, as well as tribunal decisions such as human rights tribunals, can be accessed through the Internet. Such access allows both employers and employees to seek assistance when dealing with any employment law.

6. **Use and misuse of technology.** There have been more court cases involving employee blogs as they can divulge confidential and sensitive information. Also there are situations where the language is offensive and the information inaccurate. In addition, employers may need to consider how accessible they want employees to be with PDAs as constant use could attract overtime claims.

Source: Adapted from Howard Levitt, "Workplace Law: Recent Judgments a Sign of the Times," *The Vancouver Sun,* January 10, 2009, 15.

DIVERSITY

Outcome 7

Diversity management
The optimization of an organization's multicultural workforce in order to reach business objectives

Managing diversity goes beyond Canadian employment equity legislation's four designated groups in addressing the need to create a fair work environment. The terms "diversity management" and "employment equity" are often used interchangeably, but there are differences. **Diversity management** is voluntary; employment equity is not. Managing diversity is a broader, more inclusive concept encompassing such factors as religion, personality, lifestyle, and education. By managing diversity, organizations can improve overall business performance through better decisions.[43]

According to the most recent (2006) Statistics Canada census, over 16% of our total population is classified "visible minority."[44] In this context, diversity management is not merely a legal obligation but rather a business requirement for company success. Diversity is also not just about racial and cultural background—it is about accepting and understanding differences. One of the more progressive firms is CAE, a Montreal-based company that specializes in pilot simulation and other similar technologies. Since the company does business in about 80 different countries, talented people with the right skills are necessary for business success.[45] Further, organizations such as CN, Bank of Montreal, and L'Oréal are pioneers in the diversity movement. See At Work with HRM 2.3 for a fuller description of the work L'Oréal Canada is doing in the diversity arena.

Statistics show that the ethnocultural profile of Canada has been changing since the 1960s and will continue to change dramatically over the next 20 years. It has been estimated that by the year 2017 visible minorities will account for 20% of the Canadian population.[46] The top five nonofficial languages (i.e., neither French nor English) spoken by Canadians in 2001 were, in ranked order, Chinese, Italian, German, Polish, and Spanish.[47]

CEOs in Canada recognize the importance of diversity in their overall business strategy. As Canadian companies expand into the global marketplace, having employees from different countries can help with both contacts in those countries as well as understanding what the customers in those countries want.[48] Deloitte, a professional services company with expertise in accounting and finance, has created a position of Chief Diversity Officer whose role is to ensure that the diversity strategy is linked to the business strategy. As Jane Allen, the CDO

AT WORK with HRM 2.3

L'ORÉAL CANADA

L'Oréal Canada prides itself in listening to its staff and ensuring that its workforce of 56 different nationalities is key to business success. This feature is cited as one of the reasons L'Oréal Canada was named in the Top 100 Employers in Canada in 2008. Martial Lalancette, vice president of HR oversees the various HR processes that helps create a welcoming environment.

"The origin of our product is innovation and creativity. Creating teams of people from different backgrounds leads to better creativity and innovation because they all bring different perspectives and ideas. Our head office is the United Nations of L'Oréal." However, diversity within the company goes beyond a person's home country. It includes different generations. "We realized that the origin of a lot of our communication problems concerned the X and Y and baby boomer generations," said Lalancette. To work on this problem, the company created an intergenerational training program and since its launch two years ago, it has

become one of the most popular training programs at the company.

"Specifically with the new generations, the X and the Y generation, their expectation is not necessarily more salary or more benefits, it's much more about flexibility and the opportunity to learn. We hire employees for a career, not only for a job. We have to support them to develop their capacity," remarked Lalancette.

One of the other programs that has made L'Oréal successful is a 100% top-up for the first 17 weeks of maternity leave. This has enabled its female employees to focus on the new birth and not worry about a loss of income while on maternity leave.

CRITICAL THINKING QUESTION

Can you think of other initiatives organizations can use to help create a positive work environment that supports diversity?

states, "Our only business is the talent of our people. We don't manufacture anything, we don't sell products—we sell our people. If we don't have the very best people, then we won't be able to grow our business."[49]

While CEOs may recognize the importance of diversity, there are still ample examples of immigrants struggling to gain employment opportunities in their chosen field of study or experience. Studies done by Statistics Canada indicate that there is a gap in the employment rate for immigrants compared to Canadian born and that the gap is widening.[50] Therefore, there is a continuing need to create programs and other ways to tap into a vital and talented component of our population and maximize the country's human capital.

It is important to remember that in Canada, diversity also includes First Nations people. Alberta-Pacific Forest Industries Inc. recently won an award for its philosophy of trying to help communities help themselves by creating employment opportunities and Aboriginal apprenticeships.[51] Another example of diversity success is described in At Work with HRM 2.4 showcasing the business successes of a particular First Nations group in the interior of B.C.

AT WORK with HRM 2.4

BUSINESS SUCCESS FOR FIRST NATIONS

Chief Clarence Louie is very proud of the successes his community has achieved. As Chief and Administrator of the Osoyoos Indian Band and C.E.O. of Osoyoos Indian Band Development Corporation, he has provided leadership and vision for the Band to excel in a number of enterprises. He has been recognized with numerous awards, the most recent being in 2007 where he was named Chairman of the National Aboriginal Economic Development Board.

During the last 25 years the Band has created a large and successful business enterprise on the Band's 32,000 acres of land. The Band businesses include Nk'Mip vineyards, Nk'Mip Gas & Convenience Store, Nk'Mip construction, Oliver Readi Mix , Nk'Mip Golf Course, Nk'Mip Campground & RV Park, the first Aboriginal winery in North America—Nk'Mip Cellars and Nk'Mip Desert Cultural Centre—an eco-cultural centre that promotes Okanagan Native heritage and culture. The Band's development corporation is 25% owner in Spirit Ridge Vineyard Resort and Spa which is currently expanding from 94 rooms to an additional 132 room unit including a restaurant, spa and conference centre. The Band also has a minority interest in Mt. Baldy Ski Resort.

The variety of businesses provides the Band with numerous jobs and countless career opportunities for its members. The Osoyoos Indian Band prides itself in having low unemployment rates, a healthy economic outlook and the potential for more business development. Chief Louie is a strong believer in helping individuals with their education and expanding their areas of interest.

He also has a vision of developing his community into one of the greatest First Nations communities of North America.

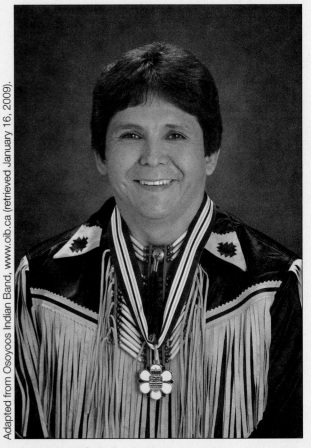

Adapted from Osoyoos Indian Band, www.oib.ca (retrieved January 16, 2009).

Chief Clarence Louie

Source: Adapted from Osoyoos Indian Band, www.oib.ca (retrieved January 16, 2009).

Creating an Environment for Success

Transforming an organizational culture into one that embraces diversity can be a complex and lengthy process. Diversity initiatives should be taken slowly so that everyone can understand that this change is an evolutionary process and that expectations should be realistic.

Leadership is one of the most important variables in an organization's ability to successfully incorporate the value of diversity into its business strategy. Good management is key to creating a workplace that values all employees and the talents and skills that they bring.[52]

As part of its commitment to its staff and its clients, Deloitte (mentioned above) ensures that diversity and inclusion are part of the organizational DNA.[53] Likewise, Scotiabank believes that having a diverse workforce means that it is better able to meet its customers' needs.[54]

Diversity is more than just ethnic and cultural background. At Work with HRM 2.5 describes how diversity is the soul of the business at Teligence.

Organizations seeking to incorporate the value of diversity into their corporate philosophies must adopt appropriate internally and externally focused communications. For example, a variety of municipalities and health-care agencies provide important information in a number of different languages.[55]

Training is essential to the success of diversity implementation. A number of companies, including Suncor Energy and Connaught Laboratories, have created a variety of different diversity training initiatives, including the one at Suncor called "We love the winter." This is specifically designed to help new immigrants, many from warm-climate countries, adjust to extremely cold winters in Fort McMurray, Alberta.[56] Cultural etiquette is an important aspect of diversity training that aims to explain the differences, or diversity, in people. For example, Farm Credit Canada (one

---

AT WORK **with HRM 2.5**

DIVERSITY: IN OUR SOUL

"Diversity is in our soul," says Lewisa Anciano, vice president of human resources for Teligence. "We are a model for the world as the newer generations in the workforce want to be open and be themselves—whoever they are. We like quirky people."

Teligence, a high-tech Canadian-owned company based in Vancouver, develops and delivers enhanced voice-enabled services for social networking and entertainment in North America. It is the largest company in the social chat business, now at 2300 people from just four only 15 years ago.

There are no diversity programs and yet everyone is comfortable with each other. People can speak their own language at work. It is a company that tends to attract immigrants as it is strictly performance-driven with no requirements about having previous Canadian work experience. With a true belief in people, and tied to its business strategy, the company also functions as advocates in the community. As Lewisa states, "People need a place to be safe to express who they are. We are that company. We find that people are open and honest during interviews and tell us who they are—whether it is gender

orientation or country of origin." People know that they can be themselves at Teligence without judgment. And diversity is more than just about ethnicity—it is about everyone being unique. The company is about performance and results—not what your background is. People are valued for contributing to the success of the company. "Much of this can be attributed to Teligence CEO and founder, Rob Madigan and his younger brother John (and executive director). Both truly embrace diversity and are advocates for hiring the right people for our culture."

With a business that provides technical know-how for telephone chat lines, it is important that the company has employees that understand the market. "While there is no conscious business strategy to have an eclectic workforce, it is just who we are."

CRITICAL THINKING QUESTIONS

1. What are the similarities between L'Oréal (At Work with HRM 2.3) and Teligence in relation to their diversity initiatives?

2. Which are the diversity initiatives at L'Oréal work at Teligence? Why or why not?

Source: Interview with Lewisa Anciano, February 2009.

of the 50 Best Employers in Canada) explicitly defines the behaviours expected from employees and board members toward each other and the customers.[57]

An added advantage of establishing a diversity initiative is its impact on employee retention. Keeping well-qualified and skilled employees is an important goal, considering the amount of resources, both in time and money, spent on recruiting and hiring new employees. The Yukon Government, through its public service commission, uses diversity initiatives to also fulfill its land claims obligations and help the territory grow and prosper.[58]

When establishing diversity initiatives, an overall review of policies and employment practices must be considered. The use of an employee attitude survey may prove beneficial in finding areas of systemic or perceived discrimination. The success indicators used most often by Canadian organizations are changes in staff attitudes, increases in promotions for minority employees, reduction in turnover of minority employees, reduction in number of harassment suits, improved recruitment statistics for minorities, and improvements in productivity. A final element in achieving success in the implementation of diversity initiatives is to monitor progress and provide qualitative and quantitative evidence of change.[59]

Measuring management's performance with regard to diversity initiatives will instill those values in the minds of all employees and demonstrate that valuing diversity is part of day-to-day business. Key to achieving success in diversity objectives is setting an example and creating an atmosphere that respects and values differences. Canadian organizations have recognized the competitive advantage gained by embracing diversity within their business strategies. Businesses have recognized that with a global economy and worldwide customers, it is important to have a workforce that understands people in other countries.[60]

SUMMARY

1. Explain the impact of laws on the behaviour and actions of supervisors and managers.
   - Accepted practices and behaviours of supervisors and managers toward their employees are governed through a variety of employment legislation at both the provincial and federal levels.
   - Various laws establish certain minimum requirements regarding working conditions as well as providing protection of basic human rights.

2. Discuss the legal framework of HRM in Canada.
   - There are two distinct sets of legislation—federal and provincial.
   - The Canadian Charter of Rights and Freedoms is the cornerstone of contemporary employment legislation.

3. Explain and describe discrimination and harassment in the workplace.
   - Discrimination is denying someone something because of race, ethnic background, marital status, or other prohibited grounds under human rights legislation.
   - Harassment is any behaviour that demeans, humiliates, or embarrasses a person.
   - Discrimination and harassment are illegal under human rights legislation.

4. Describe the line manager's role in creating a work environment that is free from harassment and discrimination.
   - Supervisor or manager needs to ensure that unacceptable behaviours are dealt with.
   - Supervisor is expected to work with employees to ensure that they are behaving and acting in an acceptable fashion.
   - Line manager is key link in creating an appropriate work environment.

5. Identify the general types of employment laws in Canada.
   - Employment standards legislation describes the basic obligations of employers.
   - Labour legislation governs both the process by which a trade union acquires bargaining rights and the procedures by which trade unions and employers engage in collective bargaining.
   - Health, safety, and workers' compensation legislation describes the expected standards for health and safety in the workplace and the impact if an employee is injured.

- Human rights legislation prohibits discrimination on the basis of such areas as race, ethnic origin, marital status, and gender.
- Human rights legislation is paramount over other employment laws.
- Human rights legislation also protects individuals from all types of harassment.

6. Explain and describe the difference between employment equity and pay equity.
   - Employment equity refers to the employment of individuals in a fair and unbiased manner.
   - Four groups in Canada (women, visible minorities, First Nations peoples, and people with disabilities) have been designated as those needing help to fix past wrongs.
   - The federal government and some provinces have legislation to help achieve a more equitable workforce.
   - Pay equity means equal pay for work of equal value.
   - Pay equity examines job content and compares dissimilar work in an organization.

7. Describe the differences between diversity and employment equity.
   - Managing diversity not only incorporates but also goes beyond employment equity.
   - The goal of diversity management is to make optimal use of an organization's multicultural workforce in order to realize strategic business advantages.

NEED TO KNOW

- Relationship of Charter of Rights and Freedoms to employment laws
- Names of employment laws and what they do
- Definition of harassment and discrimination
- Purpose and definition of employment and pay equity
- Definition of diversity

NEED TO UNDERSTAND

- Impact of legislation on managerial actions
- Relationship of bona fide occupational requirements to discrimination
- Impact of reasonable accommodation on managerial action
- Relationship of managerial behaviours to harassment and discrimination
- Impact of employment practices and managerial decisions on fair employment opportunities
- The link between diversity and business strategy

KEY TERMS

bona fide occupational qualification (BFOQ) 40

designated groups 49

diversity management 53

employment equity 48

harassment 42

pay equity 51

reasonable accommodation 40

reverse discrimination 42

systemic discrimination 39

REVIEW QUESTIONS

1. What are three employment laws in your province? Provide examples.
2. Which of the laws described pertain to providing minimum standards in relation to hours of work before overtime pay is required?
3. How would you react to a comment that a company discriminates against women by having a height requirement to do certain types of work?
4. Explain why employment equity is needed in organizations. What are the arguments for and against it?
5. Describe the purpose of the Employment Equity Act and discuss some of its provisions.
6. Describe the process involved in implementing an employment equity plan. How would you evaluate its success?
7. Define pay equity and discuss how it is related to discrimination.
8. Describe the ways in which an organization can optimize the use of a multicultural workforce.

CRITICAL THINKING QUESTIONS

1. Assume you are a person who is less than 1.5 m tall. You apply for work where there is occasional shelving of merchandise. The top shelf is 2.5 m from the ground and the merchandise weighs 10 kg. Can the company justify a BFOR? If so, what is it?
2. Here are some myths about employment equity:
   - It leads to hiring unqualified workers.
   - It causes an overnight change in the workforce makeup.
   - It's a plan that would make Calgary's workforce look like Toronto's.
   - This program lays off white males to make room for designated group members.
   - It's a program mainly for racial minorities.
   - Employers who implement the plan can destroy hard-won seniority provisions that protect all workers.
   - It's the end of hiring for white males.

   In groups, determine if group members share these beliefs. Go to the website of the Canadian Human Rights Commission (**www.chrc-ccdp.ca/publications/ee_faq_ee-en.asp**), review "Frequently Asked Questions," and compare your answers.
3. You have recently been hired to work in a small retail operation. The owner wants your help in developing a work environment that celebrates diversity. What would you suggest?
4. A friend of yours has heard you are taking a human resources course and wants some help. Your friend is a single parent with three children under the age of seven. The bus schedule has just changed and your friend won't be able to get the children to school and daycare and still be on time for work. Is this a case for reasonable accommodation?
5. Can you legally discriminate against the following:
   a. A person with a poor driving record for a bus driver position?
   b. A non-Baptist for the position of secretary in a Baptist private school?
   c. A person who is colour-blind for an electrician position?
   d. A person whose religious beliefs prevent them from working Saturday at a retail store?
   e. A person with a criminal record for a position of cashier?
   f. A person in a wheelchair for a server in a restaurant?
6. After receiving several complaints of sexual harassment, the senior manager of a city library decides to establish a sexual-harassment policy. What should be included in the policy? How should it be implemented?
7. "Discrimination against older persons does not generate the same degree of moral outrage as other forms of discrimination." Do you agree? To learn more about age discrimination and why mandatory retirement has all but been eliminated, read the full text of the Ontario Human Rights Commission's submission to the Ministry of Labour on mandatory retirement (**www.ohrc.on.ca/en/resources/submissions/ MandatoryRetirement**).

DEVELOPING YOUR SKILLS

1. Over the last several years, the problem of harassment has captured the attention of all managers and employees. While it is widely known that harassment is both unethical and illegal, the incidents of harassment continue to plague business. Unfortunately, when these cases arise, they cause morale problems among employees, embarrassment to the organization, and costly legal damages. Consequently, all managers and supervisors play a central role in preventing harassment. It is important that managers understand the definition of harassment, who is covered by harassment guidelines, and how to prevent its occurrence.
   a. Working in teams of five or six members, develop an outline for an anti-harassment training program. Assume that the organization has 1500 employees who work with both internal and external customers.

As a minimum your training outline should consider (1) who should attend the training sessions, (2) the content outline for the training program (the list of materials your team wants to teach), (3) specific examples to illustrate the training materials, and (4) how to investigate harassment complaints.

    b. Present your training outline to other class members.

2. Contact your student services office, or the human resources department where you work, and determine if it has a discrimination policy. If there is one, review the policy, including the manner in which it is enforced, and write a one-page analysis of how useful it is. If there is no policy, write a one-page summary indicating what the employer might do if there was a complaint about discrimination.

3. On an individual basis, identify which of the following statements are true and which are false:
   a. Most people with disabilities do not require special work arrangements.
   b The real problem for people with disabilities is holding a job, not getting one.
   c. Employees with disabilities tend to have more accidents than other employees.
   d. People with the most severe impairments are likely to be at the top in job performance.
   e. Turnover tends to be higher among employees with disabilities than among other employees.
   f. Employees with disabilities are less likely to have a record of absenteeism.
   g. Other employees tend to respond negatively when accommodations (e.g., wheelchair ramps) are made for employees with disabilities.

   Working in groups of three to five students, share your individual responses. Review the correct answers (based on statistical evidence) at the end of the chapter (page 64). For each item you answered incorrectly, ask yourself, "Where did I get that idea?" Discuss any incorrect answers including why you gave the answer you did.

   The Canadian Council on Rehabilitation and Work shares knowledge and attempts to influence attitudes for equitable employment for people with disabilities; visit their website at **www.ccrw.org**.

4. Using any search engine, conduct a search using the phrase "sexual harassment" or the word "discrimination." Note the number of matches. Review the first 10 matches and determine if these would be a helpful resource site. Prepare a one- to two-page summary of the results of your search, indicating whether the sites were useful.

5. Access the websites of the employment laws in your province and review the home page of each and at least one other link. Identify which site would be the most helpful to you as an employee. Prepare a one- to two-page summary describing which site was useful and why.

6. By using the websites of at least three provincial employment standards laws, determine the minimum wage for each of those provinces. Are they higher or lower than the minimum wage in your province?

7. With reference to the employment standards legislation in your province, determine the following:
   a. Minimum wage
   b. Overtime hours and payment
   c. Paid holidays
   d. Maternity/parental leave

Case Study 1

But Was It Harassment?

Bill Smith, plant superintendent in a commercial laundry, was in his office reviewing a handwritten note that had just arrived. He was both surprised and concerned about the contents. The note indicated that Bob Jones had been making comments of a sexual nature to several of the female staff. What was disturbing about this was that Bob was Bill's best supervisor and had been involved in a relationship with one of the plant staff. Bill decided that he must investigate the allegation.

Bill decided to meet with Bob and bring the matter to his attention. During the meeting, Bob got very angry and accused his former girlfriend of spreading rumours. When pressed further, Bob confirmed that he had been joking with one of the junior secretaries and said that he would help her get a new computer if she treated him nicely. Bob also confirmed that while he knows the company has a policy about this sort of thing, he wasn't sure exactly what was expected.

After meeting with Bob, Bill decided that the company needed to have a training program on harassment and discrimination. As part of the training, Bill suggested a role-play exercise to explore workplace behaviours that might be construed as harassment. All supervisors in the plant were expected to attend.

Several days after the training, Bill got a phone call from one of his top production people. She expressed concern that Bob had just put up a calendar in his office that showed a scantily clad girl. The worker said that she approached Bob and asked him to remove the calendar as it didn't seem to comply with what was described in the training. She then described how Bob laughed and said, "Who cares about that kind of stuff? This is just some phase we are going through, and it will fade out soon." Bill also discovered that Bob had left the training session before it was over.

Questions

1. Are these two incidents harassment? Why or why not?
2. Who is more responsible for this situation—Bob or Bill?
3. If you were Bill, what would you do now?

Case Study 2

Developing New Job Requirements

Jesse Wong, owner/operator of a commercial and residential cleaning business, has been very concerned about the high incidence of back injuries and accidents involving cleaning solutions. The company employs approximately 300 people with the following profile:

65% female
35% male
30% who immigrated to Canada within the last year
80% with English as a second language

The company has been very successful, with revenues growing on a yearly basis, particularly in the commercial sector. Currently, the typical job duties include vacuuming floors; emptying trash and recycling containers, some of which are quite heavy; dusting furniture; mopping floors; disinfecting and cleaning bathroom and kitchen fixtures; waxing floors and furniture; and the occasional window washing.

In a meeting with the company's human resources practitioner, Jesse expresses a desire to change the skill requirements for all new employees. He feels that if the skills are different, the company will be able to reduce the accident and injury rates. His proposal for the skills level is

a. able to read and speak English to a grade 8 level,
b. able to lift 25 kg, and
c. able to handle chemicals safely.

During the discussions, the HR person expresses some concern about whether these new skill requirements would be considered *bona fide occupational qualifications*. There have been a number of recent complaints to the provincial human rights agency from employees at other cleaning companies when those companies changed the skill requirements. While the human rights agency hadn't made any decisions yet, the complaints revolved around English speaking and reading levels and lifting heavy objects.

Questions

1. What would you say to Jesse to explain the concept of BFOQ?
2. In your understanding of BFOQ, would any of these skill requirements stand up to a challenge? If so, why? If not, why not?
3. What would you say to Jesse about his proposal?

APPENDIX

WEBSITES FOR EMPLOYMENT LEGISLATION

1. Federal Government
   - Canada Labour Code: laws.justice.gc.ca/en/L-2
   - Canadian Human Rights Act: laws.justice.gc.ca/en/showdoc/cs/H-6/
2. Province of Alberta
   - Employment Standards Code: www.qp.gov.ab.ca/documents/acts/E09.cfm
   - Labour Relations Code: www.qp.gov.ab.ca/documents/Acts/L01.cfm?frm_isbn=9780779734757
   - Occupational Health and Safety Act: employment.alberta.ca/cps/rde/xchg/hre/hs.xsl/307.html
   - Human Rights, Citizenship and Multiculturalism Act: www.albertahumanrights.ab.ca/
3. Province of British Columbia
   - Employment Standards Act: www.bclaws.ca/Recon/document/freeside/-- e --/employment standards act rsbc 1996 c. 113/00_96113_01.xml
   - Labour Relations Code: www.bclaws.ca/Recon/document/freeside/-- l --/labour relations code rsbc 1996 c. 244/00_96244_01.xml
   - Workers' Compensation Act: www.bclaws.ca/Recon/document/freeside/-- w --/workers compensation act rsbc 1996 c. 492/00_act/96492_00.htm
   - Human Rights Code: www.bchrt.bc.ca/human_rights_code/default.htm
4. Province of Manitoba
   - Employment Standards Act: www.gov.mb.ca/labour/standards/index.html
   - Labour Relations Act: web2.gov.mb.ca/laws/statutes/ccsm/l010e.php
   - Workplace Safety and Health Act: www.safemanitoba.com/
   - Human Rights Code: web2.gov.mb.ca/laws/statutes/ccsm/h175e.php
5. Province of New Brunswick
   - Employment Standards Act: www.gnb.ca/0308/002-e.asp
   - Industrial Relations Act: www.gnb.ca/0110/index-e.asp
   - Occupational Health and Safety Act: www.worksafenb.ca/index_e.asp
   - Human Rights Code: www.gnb.ca/0062/deplinks/ENG/PSE.htm (to download copy of legislation)
6. Province of Newfoundland and Labrador: all statutes are accessible through www.assembly.nl.ca/ with links to each law
7. Province of Nova Scotia: all statutes are accessible through www.gov.ns.ca/legislature/legc/ with links to each law
8. Province of Ontario: all statutes are accessible through www.e-laws.gov.on.ca/navigation?file=home&lang=en with links to each law
9. Province of Prince Edward Island: electronic versions of the legislation can be accessed by downloading PDF files from www.gov.pe.ca/law/statutes/index.php3

10. Province of Quebec: all statutes are accessible through www2.publicationsduquebec.gouv. qc.ca/home.php with links to each law

11. Province of Saskatchewan: electronic versions of the legislation can be accessed by downloading PDF files from www.publications.gov.sk.ca/deplist.cfm?d=1&c=42&cl=5#O

12. Government of Nunavut: all statutes are accessible through www.justice.gov.nu.ca/apps/authoring/dspPage.aspx?page=CURRENT%20CONSOLIDATIONS%20OF%20ACTS%20AND%20REGULATIONS&letter=* with links to each law.

Video Feature

PART 1—IN VIEW

1. "Family Trouble" (02:16)

A new study funded by Health Canada found that many Canadians are dealing with work stress by delaying having children, having fewer children, or deciding not to have any. Canadians from Toronto share their decisions about work and family life.

2. "Operation Harassment" (16:11)

This is the story of a police officer, a promotion, and what became the career from hell. Ken Smith is an RCMP officer in New Brunswick. And his promotion was the last good thing that happened to him at work. After that, it became a blur of harassment, secrets, and surveillance, all directed against him.

3. "Dress Code" (04:08)

It wasn't long ago that talking about the office conjured up images with a suit and tie and pen and paper. But the Canadian workplace has been evolving. It's affecting everything from how jobs are done, to where they are, even what we wear on the job. Deborah Goble reports on office dress codes.

4. "Homework" (02:50)

Conway Fraser reports on working from home.

5. "Chief Louie" (11:05)

With so much poverty in so many First Nations communities across the country, one Chief offers Native Canadians some pretty blunt advice—simply work harder. Chief Clarence Louie wants First Nations communities to take their economic future into their own hands. He should know. His band owns and runs several successful businesses.

6. "Reasonable Accommodation" (11:13)

There is a growing debate in this country about the direction of multiculturalism and about what it means to be Canadian. What should new immigrants do to fit in? What is 'reasonable accommodation?' The issue is so thorny in Quebec that the provincial government is holding public hearings. This week, the commission is hearing from the people of the small town of Herouxville, where much of the controversy in that province first began.

QUESTIONS

1. What techniques do you use to minimize stress? How effective are they?

2. What are your feelings about working from home? About what you can wear to work?

3. What are the biggest HR challenges facing organizations in your city and/or province?

4. Is there more that provinces and the federal government can do to assist First Nations communities to improve their economic lives? What suggestions do you have?

5. Should there be more legislation to protect employees? Why or why not?

6. What else can employers do to ensure that harassment doesn't occur in the workplace?

NOTES AND REFERENCES

1. Service Canada, "Employment Insurance Compassionate Care Benefits," www.hrsdc.gc.ca/eng/ei/types/compassionate_care.shtml (accessed January 12, 2009).

2. Gloria Galloway, "EI Extension had Ottawa," *The Globe and Mail,* March 22, 2008, A10.

3. "Canadian Human Rights Commission Applauds Passage of C-21 through Commons," News Room, Canadian Human Rights Commission, May 29, 2008, www.chrc-ccdp.ca/media_room/news_releases-en.asp?id=472 (accessed November 17, 2008).

4. *Canadian Human Rights Act*, Section 2, Purpose of Act, October 23, 2008, http://laws.justice.gc.ca/en/ShowFullDoc/cs/H-6///en (accessed November 17, 2008).

5. Kirsten Hume, "Grey Areas in End of Mandatory Retirement," *Canadian HR Reporter,* March 10, 2008, 5.

6. David Wylie, "Comedian Faces Human Rights Charges," *National Post,* June 26, 2008, A8.

7. Jeffrey R. Smith, "Air Canada Pilots' Challenge to Mandatory Retirement Shot Down," *Canadian HR Reporter,* September 21, 2007, www.hrreporter.com/ArticleView.aspx?l=1&articleid=5471 (accessed June 6, 2009)..

8. Canadian Human Rights Commission, "Bona Fide Occupational Requirements and Bona Fide Justifications under the Canadian Human Rights Act: The Implications of Meiorin and Grismer,"April 17, 2007, www.chrc-ccdp.ca/discrimination/occupational-en.asp#implications (accessed January 5, 2009).

9. "What is Duty to Accommodate?" Canadian Human Rights Commission, www.chrc-ccdp.ca/preventing_discrimination/duty_obligation-en.asp (accessed June 6, 2009) .

10. Jeffrey R. Smith, "Canada Post Fails to Deliver Accommodation," *Canadian HR Reporter,* November17, 2008, 5.

11. "Defining the Employer's Duty to Accommodate the Stress of Work and Family Life," reference materials acquired during a seminar sponsored by Fasken Martineau, Vancouver, B.C., May 5, 2006.

12. Suzanne McFarlane, "The Separation of Church and Work," *Canadian HR Reporter,* July 16, 2007, 17.

13. Definition of harassment, Canadian Human Rights Commission, www.chrc-ccdp.ca/discrimination/what_is_it-en.asp (accessed January 7, 2009).

14. "Discrimination and Harassment," www.chrc-ccdp.ca/discrimination/what_is_it-en.asp (accessed January 7, 2009). Source: Overview-Resolving Disputes: Discrimination and Harassment URL: http://www.chrc-ccdp.ca/discrimination/what_is_it-en.asp Author/Organization: Canadian Human Rights Commission. Reproduced with the permission of the Ministry of Public Works and Government Services, 2009.

15. Jeffrey R. Smith, "Employers: Don't Let Workplace Harassment Catch You Off Guard," *Canadian HR Reporter,* October 22, 2007, 29.

16. Seneca College, Human Resources, Resolution, Equity and Diversity Centre, "Discrimination and Harassment Policy and Procedures," www.senecac.on.ca/policies/dh.html (accessed January 7, 2009). Source: Seneca College, Human Resources, Resolution, Equity and Diversity Centre, "Discrimination and Harassment Policy and Procedures," http://www.senecac.on.ca/policies/dh.html (retrieved January 7, 2009).

17. Ibid.

18. Saskatchewan Human Rights Commission, "A Guide to Human Rights for Employers," www.shrc.gov.sk.ca/publications.html/ (accessed January 7, 2009).

19. Adapted from Michael Fitzgibbon, "Fighting Harassment in the Workplace," *Canadian HR Reporter,* October 22, 2007, 25-30.

20. Stuart Rudner, "Psychological Harassment Hurts Employees, Productivity," *Canadian HR Reporter,* October 22, 2007, 31.

21. *Barbara Tanzos, Complainant-and-AZ Bus Tours Inc.* (2007), T832/8203, www.chrt-tcdp.gc.ca/search/view_html.asp?doid=858&lg=_e&isruling=0 (accessed January 9, 2009).

22. Canadian Human Rights Act, paragraphs 53 and 54.

23. Shannon Klie, "Poor Economy No Excuse for Discrimination," *Canadian HR Reporter,* May 18, 2009, 1.

24. Ontario Ministry of Labour, "Legislation and Regulations," www.labour.gov.on.ca/english/about/leg/index.html (accessed January 8, 2009).

25. "Diverging Trends in Unionization," Statistics Canada, www.statcan.gc.ca/bsolc/olc-cel/olc-cel?lang=eng &catno=75-001-X20051047827 (accessed January 9, 2009); and "Labour Force Participation Rates," Statistics Canada, www40.statcan.gc.ca/l01/cst01/labor05-eng.htm (accessed January 9, 2009).

26. For more detailed information on changes to health and safety legislation, refer to the discussion papers from British Columbia ("Protecting Young Workers"), www.worksafebc.ca/publications/reports/focus_reports/Default.asp; and Ontario ("Tougher Occupational Exposure Limits To Protect Workers") www.labour.gov.on.ca/english/hs/.

27. Labour Program, *Employment Equity Act: Annual Report 2007,* Human Resources and Skills Development Canada, www.hrsdc.gc.ca/eng/labour/publications/equality/annual_reports/2007/page00.shtml (pdf format, accessed January 9, 2009).

28. "Labour Force Participation Rates by Sex and Age Group," Statistics Canada, www40.statcan.gc.ca/l01/cst01/labor05-eng.htm (accessed January 9, 2009).

29. Statistics Canada, "CANSIM Table 282-00108, Labour Force Survey Estimates (LFS), by National Occupational Classification for Statistics (NOC-S) and Sex (2007)," estat.statcan.gc.ca/cgi-win/CNSMCGI.EXE (accessed January 9, 2009).

30. Ibid.

31. Statistics Canada, "Aboriginal Identity Population, 2006 Census," www12.statcan.gc.ca/english/census06/data/highlights/Aboriginal/pages/Page.cfm?Lang=E&Geo=PR&Code=01&Table=1&Data=Count&Sex=1&Age=1&StartRec=1&Sort=2&Display=Page (accessed January 9, 2009).

32. Diane Galarneau and René Morisette, *Immigrants' Education and Required Job Skills,* Statistics Canada, www.statcan.gc.ca/pub/75-001-x/2008112/pdf/10766-eng.pdf (PDF Version, 152 kb) (accessed January 9, 2009).

33. Statistics Canada, *Participation and Activity Limitation Survey of 2006: Labour Force Experience of People with Disabilities in Canada* www.statcan.gc.ca/pub/89-628-x/89-628-x2008007-eng.htm (accessed January 10, 2009).

34. Ibid.

35. "Employment Equity," Manitoba Civil Service Commission, www.gov.mb.ca/csc/employment/emplequity.html (accessed January 10, 2009).

36. Labour Program, *Employment Equity Act: Annual Report 2007*, Human Resources and Skills Development Canada, www.hrsdc.gc.ca/eng/labour/publications/equality/annual_reports/2007/page00.shtml (pdf format, accessed January 9, 2009): 31.

37. Statistics Canada, "Average Hourly Wages of Employees by Selected Characteristics and Profession," www40.statcan.gc.ca/l01/cst01/labr69a-eng.htm (accessed January 10, 2009).

38. Shannon Klie, "New Brunswick Closing Gender Wage Gap," *Canadian HR Reporter,* June 18, 2007, 6.

39. Ontario Pay Equity Commission, "Guideline #12—Permissible Differences in Compensation," www.payequity.gov.on.ca/peo/english/guidelines/ge_12.html (accessed January 10, 2009).

40. Ontario Pay Equity Commission, "Guideline #9—Gender Neutral Job Comparison," www.payequity.gov.on.ca/peo/english/guidelines/ge_9.html (accessed January 10, 2009).

41. Ibid.

42. "Complaints by Individuals" and "Complaints by Groups," http://laws.justice.gc.ca/en/h-6/sor-86-1082 (accessed January 10, 2009).

43. Mark Schoeff, Jr., "Diversity's Strategic Role," *Workforce Management,* January 4, 2008, 5.

44. Statistics Canada, *Canada's Ethnocultural Mosaic, 2006 Census,* 97-562-X (downloaded in pdf format, January 12, 2009), 12.

45. Shannon Klie, "Top 20 Firms Know Value of Immigrants," *Canadian HR Reporter,* March 10, 2008, 1.

46. Statistics Canada, *Canada's Ethnocultural Mosaic, 2006 Census,* 13.

47. Statistics Canada, "Population by Mother Tongue (2006 Census), www40.statcan.gc.ca/l01/cst01/demo11a-eng.htm (accessed January 12, 2009).

48. Alexandra Lopez-Pacheo, "How Can Diversity Help Business," *The National Post,* November 17, 2008, FP7.

49. Shannon Klie, "Hail the New Chief," *Canadian HR Reporter,* July 14, 2008, www.hrreporter.com/ArticleView.aspx?l=1&articleid=6203 (accessed January 12, 2009).

50. "Canada's Immigrant Labour Market," *The Daily,* May 13, 2008, www.statcan.gc.ca/daily-quotidien/080513/dq080513a-eng.htm (accessed June 6, 2009).

51. Derek Sankey, "Forest Company Keys into Aboriginal Workforce," *The Vancouver Sun,* April 5, 2008, E2.

52. Rosemary Barnes, "Encouraging Diversity Key to Success," *The Globe and Mail,* September 11, 2004, B13.

53. Deloitte, www.deloitte.com/dtt/section_node/0,1042,sid%253D202561,00.html (accessed January 12, 2009).

54. Shannon Klie, "Top Employers Know Diversity is 'Good Business'," *Canadian HR Reporter,* May 5, 2008, www.hrreporter.com/ArticleView.aspx?l=1&articleid=6040 (accessed January 12, 2009).

55. *Current,* a publication by the Vancouver Coastal Health Authority and notices sent to residents of the City of Vancouver.

56. Danielle Harder, "Diversity Broadly Defined at Suncor Energy," *Canadian HR Reporter,* August 5, 2008, www.hrreporter.com/ArticleView.aspx?l=1&articleid=6039 (accessed January 12, 2009).

57. Farm Credit Canada, "Cultural Practices," www.fcc-fac.ca/en/AboutUs/Profile/culturalpractices_e.asp (accessed January 12, 2009).

58. Public Service Commission, "Diversity in Government," www.psc.gov.yk.ca/diversity/index.html (accessed January 12, 2009).

59. Shannon Klie, "Top Employers Know Diversity is 'Good Business'."

60. Lesley Young, "Diversity Drives KPMG to Top," *Canadian HR Reporter,* March 24, 2008, www.hrreporter.com/ArticleView.aspx?l=1&articleid=5920 (accessed January 12, 2009).

ANSWERS TO DEVELOPING YOUR SKILLS, QUESTION 3

a. True
b. False
c. False
d. True
e. False
f. True
g. False

PART 2

Attracting and Selecting People for the Organization

CHAPTER 3

DEFINING AND DESIGNING THE WORK

OUTCOMES

After studying this chapter, you should be able to

1 Explain the supervisor's role in defining and designing work.

2 Discuss the relationship between job requirements and HRM processes.

3 Explain the relationship between job analysis and a job description.

4 Define and describe the sections in a job description.

5 Describe the uses of information gained from job analysis.

6 Define employee contribution and describe the relationship of job design to employee contributions.

7 Discuss the different types of work designs to increase employee contribution.

OUTLINE

HRM CLOSE-UP

Dawn Mucci, founder and President of The Lice Squad, Ontario and her team. Courtesy of Dawn Mucci.

"If you don't know what your strengths and weaknesses are, how do you formulate a plan?"

"I was wearing a lot of hats and realized I had to start putting those hats on other people's heads!" says Dawn Mucci, founder and president of The Lice Squad. A rather odd comment from someone who spends her day advising kids not to share hats, hair accessories, or other head gear in order to prevent the spread of pediculus humanus capitas—human head lice.

Realizing the need to help frantic families deal with this very common pest, Mucci set up shop in 2001 with a desk, phone, and computer. She fielded calls, provided in-home head lice removal service, and screened school children. It wasn't long before she needed a team of on-call contractors to handle client service. Four years later, the first full-time hire was an office manager.

"What I needed was a carbon copy of me," Mucci comments, "I had a long list of duties but needed to allocate more of my time on training, selling franchises, and developing the company."

When the demand grew for her proprietary non-pesticide head lice product and high quality nit comb, Mucci's next hire was a product distribution manager. Following that, was a bookkeeper—a position she describes as the most important one mainly because accounting was not one of her core strengths.

Mucci knows her company is going to continue to grow but rather than ramp up staff and wait for the business, she waits for business volume to warrant new positions. And, she tends to hire part-time at the outset. This strategy has worked well for her and makes good business sense. "I can't spend money on salaries until there's a job that is going to bring in revenue, increase sales, or create goodwill for the company," she explains.

Contracted positions also help to fill in the gaps. Jobs like Web development, information technology, and graphics design have definite ebbs and flows so shorter term contracts work best for Mucci.

The Lice Squad's office employees have written job descriptions so that they understand what has to be accomplished each work day. Mucci admits to being an easy-going boss and appreciates employees setting their own goals. "I make sure we all share the overall goal of the company," Mucci explains, "but I like my staff to seek out opportunities themselves and show initiative. I also expect learning curves as well as the odd ruffle!"

Running a relatively small operation that is growing and developing requires flexibility and compromise. Jobs at The Lice Squad can change depending on the person in the job. Mucci appreciates feedback and input. "Since I am now less focused on the day to day details, my office manager is often the one to suggest things that could be done better."

And for Mucci, hiring the right person is critical. "Everyone has skills—tasks they are good at doing. But if they are not passionate about the work at hand, it doesn't matter what skill level they bring to the job."

And with a business that revolves around head lice, making sure the hat fits is an ongoing challenge. Mucci is on a mission to rid the world of head lice—and that's a job description you won't find anywhere else.

INTRODUCTION

Just as The Lice Squad has evolved and Mucci had to determine who was going to do what, other organizations are looking at how work is arranged to make them more competitive.

Organizations are transforming themselves in an attempt to become more effective. Companies like Karo, a Calgary-based branding agency are paying attention to the structure and culture of their organizations. Karo practices what it preaches by creating "tribes" within its organization—smaller, and more interconnected to deliver results to its clients.[1] There is emphasis on smaller scale, less hierarchy, fewer layers, and more decentralized work units. As organizations reshape themselves, managers want employees to operate more independently and flexibly to meet customer demands. To do this, managers require that decisions be made by the people who are closest to the information and who are directly involved in the product or service delivered. The objective is to develop jobs and basic work units that are adaptable enough to thrive in a world of high-speed change.

This chapter will discuss how jobs can be designed to best contribute to the objectives of the organization and at the same time satisfy the needs of employees who perform them. You will learn about the role of the line manager in defining and designing work and the terminology used in the workplace that describes how jobs are defined. Several innovative job design and employee contribution techniques that increase job satisfaction while improving organizational performance are discussed. Teamwork and the characteristics of successful teams are highlighted. The chapter concludes by briefly discussing the importance of integrating other HR processes to strengthen employee contributions.

THE LINE MANAGER'S ROLE IN DEFINING WORK

Outcome 1

The line manager or supervisor is the primary individual who determines what tasks and activities need to be performed, and in what order, to reach the company's goals or objectives. Therefore, it is critical that the line manager understand what steps need to occur to maximize organizational performance. The line manager will take an active role in determining what skills and abilities are needed to successfully perform the work. The line manager is the most knowledgeable person about the work to be done and the skills necessary to do the work. Therefore, the line manager will play an integral role in developing and/or writing a job description.

RELATIONSHIP OF JOB REQUIREMENTS AND HRM PROCESSES

Outcome 2

Job
A group of related activities and duties

Position
Specific duties and responsibilities performed by only one employee

Work
Tasks or activities that need to be completed

A number of HRM processes, such as recruitment or training, make use of information about the work or job. A **job** consists of a group of related activities and duties. Ideally, the duties of a job should consist of natural units of work that are similar and related. They should be clear and distinct from those of other jobs to minimize misunderstanding and conflict among employees and to enable employees to recognize what is expected of them. For some jobs, several employees may be required, each of whom will occupy a separate position. A **position** consists of the specific duties and responsibilities performed by only one employee. In a city library, for example, four employees (four positions) may be involved in reference work, but all of them have only one job (reference librarian).

In many ways, the words "job" and "position" are relics of the industrial age. As organizations need to be more flexible and adaptable and utilize their people resources well for a competitive advantage, managers also need to think in terms of "work." By thinking of "**work**," employers have more flexibility to define what needs to be done and when and to change employee assignments on a short-term basis. You will recall from Chapter 1 that you were introduced to the concept of "competencies"—characteristics or behaviours that are necessary for successful work performance in an organization. Competencies become very important when focusing on "work" compared to job. Instead of organizations focusing on job descriptions, companies will use "work profiles" or "contract work" to describe the work to be done. Further, the concept of "roles" is also linked to competencies. Your "role" is the part you play in the organization, and it will have certain expected behaviours. For example, your role as a customer service representative includes active listening as an expected behaviour. You will continue to see more references to work and work processes, project management, tasks and task analysis rather than "job."

Whether thinking in terms of "job" or "work," a manager needs to describe what tasks need to be done, in what order, the skills a person needs to successfully perform the work requirements, and the role a person plays in the company. This is the essence of organizational success. For all HR processes you will need to have this type of information.

Job Analysis

Job analysis
Process of obtaining information about jobs by determining the duties, tasks, or activities and the skills, knowledge, and abilities associated with the jobs

Job analysis is sometimes called the cornerstone of HRM because the information it collects serves so many HRM processes. **Job analysis** is the process of obtaining information about jobs (or work) by determining what the duties, tasks, or activities of those jobs are and the necessary skills, knowledge, training, and abilities to perform the work successfully. The procedure involves undertaking a systematic approach to gathering specific job information, such as equipment used, individual tasks performed, and skills needed. When completed, job analysis results in a written report (job description) summarizing the information obtained from the analysis of 20 or 30 individual job tasks or activities.[2] The ultimate purpose of job analysis is to improve organizational performance and productivity. Figure 3.1 illustrates how job analysis is done and what the information is used for.

Job analysis is concerned with objective and verifiable information about the actual requirements of a job (compared to "job design" that reflects subjective opinions about the ideal requirements of the job). The outcome of a job analysis is a written job description. It should be as accurate as possible if it is to be of value to those who make HRM decisions. These decisions may involve any of the HR processes—from recruitment to termination of employees. Job analysis is not done in a vacuum: it is important that the organization's goals and strategies be known and understood. Without the organizational context or an understanding of the organization as a whole, the requirements identified may not reflect foreseeable future requirements.

Job analysis is typically undertaken by trained HR people; however, it can also be done by a line manager who has good analytical abilities and writing skills. The HR professional can provide assistance to the manager in gathering the relevant information by ensuring that appropriate questions are asked and that the job is not inflated. It is also valuable to have the person doing the work (and the supervisor or team leader) review the data gathered to ensure it is accurate and complete.

Job data can be collected through interviews (asking questions, such as "What duties do you perform every day?" or "What tools do you use to complete these duties?"), questionnaires (forms that ask you to write down tasks performed, purpose of job, equipment, and materials used, etc.), observation of someone doing the work, an employee log (a diary of work activities during a specified period of time), or any combination of these methods. Review the Manager's Toolkit 3.1 for some sample questions that could be either in an interview or on a questionnaire.

Frequently, in larger organizations a uniform approach is used to collect the data, such as asking people to fill out a questionnaire that requests only a list of work activities. Ethics in HRM 3.1 describes what can happen if a job is inflated.

For links to a variety of resources on writing job descriptions and conducting a job analysis, go to **www.hrgopher.com/** and click the link "Job Descriptions" or **www.job-analysis.net/**

HR Gopher
www.hrgopher.com/

Job-Analysis.Net work
www.job-analysis.net/

Job Descriptions

Job description
A document that lists the tasks, duties, and responsibilities of a job to be performed along with the skills, knowledge, and abilities, or competencies needed to successfully perform the work

Once all the information on a particular job has been collected, it is organized into a **job description**—a written document. This description includes the types of duties or responsibilities, and the skills, knowledge, and abilities, or competencies (job specifications) needed to successfully perform the work. Since there is no standard format for job descriptions, they tend to vary in appearance and content from one organization to another. However, the typical headings are the following:

1. Job title
   Provides an indication of what the duties might be or the nature of the work. For example, the title might be "night supervisor," "salesperson," "lab assistant," or "team leader."

FIGURE 3.1 The Process of Job Analysis

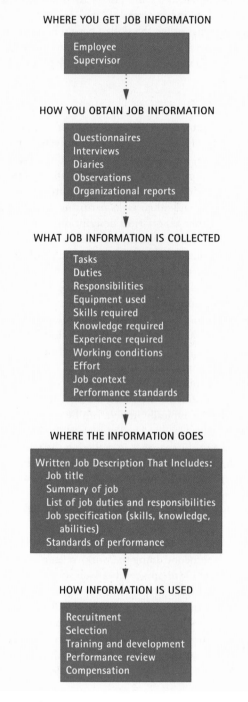

2. Summary of job

   Two to three sentences describing the overall purpose of the job; it answers the question "Why does this job exist?"

3. List of duties and responsibilities

   Individual statements, usually listed in order of importance, of the key duties and responsibilities; you would expect to see between 10 and 15 statements.

4. Job specification

   Two to three sentences describing the knowledge, skills, and abilities.

5. Date

   It is important to date the job description so that there is a time reference. The organization needs to think about the currency of the information when it is used for a variety of HR processes.

JOB ANALYSIS QUESTIONS

Here are some sample questions when conducting a job analysis for a clerical job.

1. In a brief statement (three to four sentences), describe the basic purpose of your position. Do it in a way that answers "Why does my position exist?"

2. What are the most important responsibilities of your position, and how much time do you spend on each of these? Please list each main responsibility in order of importance. Start each statement with an action verb; some examples are "provides," "determines," "verifies."

3. What are the key tasks for each of the above responsibilities? What percentage of your time each month do you spend on each task?

4. What are the physical surroundings and/or hazards of your position? (This can include travel, exposure, danger, environmental risks, etc.)

5. Describe the mental and/or physical effort you expend in performing your work. For example, do you have long periods of intense concentration? Do you keyboard for long periods of time? Is there a lot of routine? Is the position physically demanding? Please include the frequency of the effort.

6. What are the knowledge and basic skills required to successfully fulfill the responsibilities?

7. Describe two or three of the more difficult problems you must solve to get your job done. Include situations that are a constant challenge as well as situations that require judgment and time to consider alternative solutions before problems can be resolved.

Sometimes organizations might indicate that the employee's or job incumbent name ought to be included. This is neither relevant nor appropriate as the description is of the job, not the person.

Job specifications
Statement of the needed knowledge, skills, and abilities of the person who is to perform the position. The different duties and responsibilities performed by only one employee

The specific skills, knowledge, and abilities that are required to successfully perform the job become the **job specifications**. Skills relevant to a job can include education and experience, specialized training, and specific abilities, such as manual dexterity. If there are any physical demands to the job, such as walking long distances or reaching high shelves, these would also be part of the job specifications. Many organizations now view job specifications as including "employability" skills and knowledge, such as problem-solving abilities. For a more complete list of employability skills, see Figure 5.2 in Chapter 5.

The Manager's Toolkit 3.2 provides an example of a job description for the manager of retail operations at a sports arena. Note that this particular job description includes specific HR responsibilities, as noted in the first section under "People Management." This sample job description

INFLATING THE JOB

At some point in your working life, you will be asked to describe your job, perhaps when being interviewed by a job analyst or by answering questions on a form. Most employees have a reasonable expectation that their answers will affect their lives in significant ways. The information obtained may be used to reclassify the job to either a higher or lower pay level. Most employees believe that standards of performance may change, and the employer will expect them to work faster or to do more,

although that is not the goal of job analysis. As a result of these beliefs and expectations, employees have a vested interest in "inflating" their job descriptions, by making the job sound very important and very difficult. Thus, night clerks in hotels become auditors and receptionists become administrators. Making a job sound more important than it is may reflect an employee's sincere belief in the significance of his or her contribution, or it may be an attempt to lobby for higher pay.

SAMPLE JOB DESCRIPTION

Position: Manager, Retail Operations
Reports to: Director, Retail Operations
Date: February 2010

SUMMARY

The manager, retail operations, is responsible for all aspects of retail operations for game nights and events. The manager ensures the store, booths, and kiosks are staffed with well-trained sales and service professionals and are visually attractive with appropriate merchandise for the customer environment. While staff development, sales, and service are primary focus areas, administrative activities such as payroll and scheduling are also part of this role.

ESSENTIAL DUTIES AND RESPONSIBILITIES

People Management

1. Recruit, train, motivate, and develop a professional and knowledgeable part-time and on-call service and sales workforce.
2. Coach and communicate with employees in a fair and consistent manner (i.e., mentoring sessions, performance evaluations).
3. Work closely with senior retail management and human resources regarding disciplinary and other sensitive employee issues.
4. Identify and implement employee recognition and incentive programs.
5. Ensure staff are trained in all key areas of the business.

Business Management

1. Ensure selling areas are open for business on time and are clean and visually attractive.
2. Identify opportunities for increasing revenue.
3. Create sales and promotional programs.
4. Work with marketing staff regarding event details, such as expected attendance levels, merchandise deals, internal and external event contacts.
5. Produce sales reports.

Administration

1. Schedule staff in a fair and consistent manner.
2. Input payroll information into payroll time-management system.
3. Monitor payroll against budget and sales.
4. Develop and maintain an employee manual.

Required Experience and Qualifications (Job Specifications)

1. Four to six years' retail experience, with at least two years' supervisory experience.
2. Degree or diploma in business administration or related field.
3. Excellent leadership skills with the ability to coach, mentor, and motivate a sales service team.
4. Excellent communication, interpersonal, and problem-solving skills.
5. A solid understanding of the business and customer environment.
6. Must be able to identify and implement new business opportunities and promotions.
7. Flexible and adaptable.
8. Computer literate with a working knowledge of MS Word, MS Excel, point-of-sale software, and electronic mail systems.
9. Must be able to work evenings and weekends.

Standards of Performance

1. Meets on a weekly basis with all staff to review sales results.
2. Orients new staff during the first shift on customer-service requirements.
3. Meets or exceeds monthly sales targets.
4. Submits sales within 24 hours of each event.
5. Trains staff on any new procedures within one week.
6. Keeps customer satisfaction levels at 80% or above.

includes both job duties and job specifications and should satisfy most of the job information needs of managers who must recruit, interview, and orient a new employee. While this job description does not have any signature lines, many job descriptions will have a place for the supervisor (and/or HR person) to sign and date as an indication that the information in the document is accurate and complete as of the date on the description.

Job descriptions are of value to both the employees and the employer. From the employees' standpoint, job descriptions that include standards of performance can be used to help them learn their job duties and to remind them of the results they are expected to achieve.

Problems with Job Descriptions

While many managers consider job descriptions a valuable tool for performing HRM activities, several problems are frequently associated with these documents, including the following:

1. If they are poorly written, using vague rather than specific terms, they provide little guidance to the jobholder (e.g., "other duties as assigned").
2. They are sometimes not updated as job duties or specifications change.
3. They may violate the law by containing specifications not related to job success (e.g., "must be single between the ages of 25 and 35").
4. They can limit the scope of activities of the jobholder.
5. They do not contain standards of performance, which are essential for selecting, training, evaluating, and rewarding jobholders.
6. They can be the basis for conflict, including union grievances, when expected behaviours are not included.

Writing Clear and Specific Job Descriptions

When writing a job description, it is essential to use statements that are concise, direct, and simply worded. Unnecessary words or phrases should be eliminated. Typically, the sentences that describe job duties begin with a present-tense and action-oriented verb, with the implied subject of the sentence being the employee performing the job. An example for an accounting clerk for a small company might read: "Deposits cheques on a daily basis" or "Prepares month-end financial statements by the 10th of the following month." (Note that these two statements include performance standards.) The term "occasionally" is used to describe those duties that are performed once in a while. The term "may" is used in connection with those duties that are performed only by some workers on the job. Other examples of action-oriented, present-tense verbs include "coordinates," "handles," "researches," "conducts," "generates," and "evaluates." You can also get a list of verbs used in job descriptions at **www.job-analysis.net/.**

Even when set forth in writing, job descriptions and specifications can still be vague. To the alarm of many employers, however, today's legal environment has created what might be called an "age of specifics." Human rights legislation requires that the specific performance requirements of a job be based on valid job-related criteria. Decisions that involve either job applicants or employees and are based on criteria that are vague or not job-related are increasingly being challenged successfully. Managers of small businesses, where employees may perform many different job tasks, must be particularly concerned about writing specific job descriptions. Or in a very small business, such as Aquinox Pharmaceuticals Inc. in British Columbia, the focus is not so much on writing a job description but identifying the core activities and then describing the attributes needed to be successful.[3]

When preparing job descriptions, managers must be aware of human rights legislation. Written job descriptions must match the requirements of the job. Position descriptions may need to be altered to meet reasonable accommodation. Reasonable accommodation is used most frequently to match religious or disability needs although any prohibited ground for discrimination under human rights legislation would have to be considered for reasonable accommodation. The 2008 case *Jim Smith and Canadian National Railway* made it clear that reasonable accommodation for physical disability and family status reasons is valid.[4] Job descriptions written to match the needs for reasonable accommodation reduce the risk of discrimination. The goal is to match and accommodate human capabilities to job requirements. For example, if the job requires the jobholder to read extremely fine print, to climb ladders, or to memorize stock codes, these physical and mental requirements should be stated within the job description.

Human rights legislation requires that specific job requirements be based on valid job-related criteria. For example, pilots must have a certain level of eyesight.

J. Luke/PhotoLink/Getty Images

Standards of Performance

Standards of performance
Set out the expected results of the job

This is the section least likely to be included in a job description; however, it often provides the most valuable data for both the manager and employee. **Standards of performance** set out the expected results of the job—what you are expected to accomplish, as well as how much and how fast. Look again at the sample job description above—it has several performance standards. From the employer's standpoint, written job descriptions can serve as a basis for minimizing the misunderstandings that occur between managers and their subordinates concerning job requirements. They also establish management's right to take corrective action when the duties covered by the job description are not performed as required by performance standards.

JOB ANALYSIS IN A CHANGING ENVIRONMENT

The traditional approach to job analysis assumes a static job environment and large organizations in which jobs remain relatively stable even though incumbents who might hold these jobs perform them differently. Here, jobs can be meaningfully defined in terms of tasks, duties, processes, and behaviours necessary for job success. This assumption, unfortunately, discounts technological advances that are often so accelerated that jobs, as they are defined today, may be obsolete tomorrow and the very notion of an "employer" could change dramatically.[5]

Furthermore, downsizing, the adoption of teams, the demands of small organizations, or the need to respond to global change can alter the nature of jobs and the requirements of individuals needed to successfully perform them. For organizations using "virtual" jobs or "virtual" teams, there is a shift away from narrow job specifications and descriptions to a world where the work is "dejobbed" and emphasis is placed on the distribution of work.[6] In a dynamic environment where job demands rapidly change, job analysis data can quickly become inaccurate, and outdated job analysis information can hinder an organization's ability to adapt to change. Likewise, large organizations can find that the job information is outdated if it is not regularly reviewed and adjusted as needs change.

For organizations that operate in a fast-moving environment, several novel approaches to job analysis may accommodate needed change. First, managers might adopt a future-oriented approach to job analysis where managers have a clear view of how jobs should be restructured to meet future organizational requirements. Second, organizations might adopt a competency-based approach to job analysis in which emphasis is placed on characteristics or behaviours of successful performers rather than on standard job duties and tasks and so on. As was described in Chapter 1,

Determining the tasks to be done often involves seeking input from the people who actually do the work.

Jon Riley/Getty Images

these competencies would match the organization's culture and strategy and might include things such as interpersonal communication skills, decision-making ability, conflict resolution skills, adaptability, and self-motivation.[7] This technique of job analysis serves to enhance a culture of focus on the customer and continuous improvement since organizational effectiveness is the goal. Neither of these two approaches is without concerns, including the ability of managers to predict future job needs accurately, and the need for job analysis to comply with human rights legislation. A third and perhaps more practical method might be to have a "living job description" that is updated as the job changes. The line manager and employee would then ensure that substantial changes in duties, responsibilities, skills, and other work characteristics are documented on an ongoing basis. A type of "living job description" is a behavioural job description: one that describes how the work is to be done and what results are expected. Often these descriptions also describe typical issues and problems that may occur and the results that can be expected in dealing with the issues. By doing this, the manager and employee can also establish standards of performance.

In order to have the "right people with the right skills at the right time," contemporary managers must take the time to think about the work and the skills required to do the work. Organizational success depends on capable people. Managers want to be sure that they have the correct number of employees and the correct skills mix. Clearly identifying the work duties and the skills needed to perform the work can help managers achieve that objective. It is important to remember that the purpose of identifying who does what is for the purpose of bringing all the talent together, mobilizing that talent for organizational success.[8]

USES OF INFORMATION FROM JOB ANALYSIS

Outcome 5

As stated earlier in the chapter, a variety of HRM processes make use of the output of job analysis: recruitment, selection, legal issues, training and development, performance reviews, and compensation. These are discussed below.

Recruitment

Recruitment is the process of locating and encouraging potential applicants to apply for job openings. Because job specifications establish the qualifications required of applicants for a job opening, they serve an essential role in the recruiting function as they define "who" will be successful doing the job and provide a basis for attracting qualified applicants.

Selection

After you have located individuals who are interested in working for you, you must now hire someone. Selection is the process of choosing the individual who has the relevant qualifications and who can best perform the job. Therefore, a manager will use the information on the job description as a basis to compare the skills and abilities of each applicant.

Legal Issues

In the past, job specifications used as a basis for selection sometimes bore little relation to the duties identified in the job description. Many examples can be cited of job requirements that do not match the actual duties of a job: the requirement that applicants for a labourer's job have a high school diploma; the requirement that firefighters be at least six feet tall; the requirement that applicants for the job of truck driver be male. These kinds of job specifications serve to discriminate against members of certain designated groups, many of whom have been excluded from these jobs.

Given changes to our society and the various employment laws, employers must be able to show that the job specifications used in selecting employees for a particular job relate specifically to the duties of that job. Because line managers usually help define the job specifications, they must ensure that the job requirements recruit the best candidate and do not discriminate. Managers must be careful to ensure that they do not hire employees on the basis of "individualized" job requirements that satisfy personal whims but bear little relation to successful job performance. Read HRM and the Law 3.1 to understand more about the legal implications of inappropriate job requirements.

Training and Development

Any discrepancies between the knowledge, skills, and abilities (referred to as KSAs) demonstrated by a jobholder and the requirements contained in the description and specification for that job provide clues to training needs. Also, if the job specification section contains competencies (such as "focuses on customer" or "demonstrates excellent customer service skills"), these competencies could provide the basis for training. As line managers are often responsible for training the new employee, accurate job specifications and descriptions are essential. Also, as career development is often a concern for both the manager and the employee, the formal qualification requirements set forth in higher-level jobs serve to indicate how much more training and development are needed for employees to advance to those jobs.

HRM and the law 3.1

JOB REQUIREMENTS THAT DISCRIMINATE

In 2007, charges of discrimination were confirmed against the Blue Heron Charity Casino in Ontario for its decision to hire a man for a housekeeping position instead of a woman who had already been working part-time. The casino indicated that only men could clean men's washrooms and that it had sufficient number of women to clean the women's washrooms. While the Ontario Human Rights Tribunal acknowledged that the male gender for cleaning men's washrooms was appropriate, it did determine that cleaning washrooms was only one component of a housekeeper's job and that the casino could have accommodated the woman housekeeper. The casino was ordered to pay $10,000 in general damages as well as wage loss for a period of 18 months.[9]

In 2008 a B.C. case involved the termination of a paramedic who was unable to perform a manual pulse-taking due to nerve damage in the employee's hands. The question before the Human Rights Tribunal was whether the need to manually take a person's pulse was a bona fide occupational requirement (BFOR). The second question was, if the requirement was bona fide, could the person have been accommodated? While the Ambulance Service in B.C. had initially accommodated the employee by assigning the person to driving duties, on a longer-term basis the Ambulance Service needed paramedics to perform all their duties and not just drive. Through evidence, it was demonstrated that taking a person's pulse manually was a BFOR and that to accommodate the employee would be an undue hardship.[10]

Job analysis can be used to determine the type of training required to perform the job.

Photodisc Collection/Getty Images

Performance Reviews

The requirements contained in the job description provide the criteria for evaluating the performance of the jobholder. Evaluating an employee's performance is a major responsibility of the line manager. The results of the performance evaluation may reveal, however, that certain requirements established for a job are not completely valid. For example, the job description may require an employee to keyboard at the rate of 60 words per minute (wpm), but the performance review may determine that 30 wpm is satisfactory. As already stressed, these criteria must be specific and job-related. If the criteria used to evaluate employee performance are vague and not job-related, employers may find themselves being charged with unfair discrimination. Evaluating employees fairly and objectively requires standards of performance that determine how the job should be done—how fast, how well, how timely, and so on. A recent case of discrimination due to gender was dismissed as the Canadian Human Rights Tribunal determined that the performance review conducted to determine "merit" during a downsizing exercise was appropriate.[11]

Compensation

Job descriptions are often used solely for compensation purposes. In determining the rate at which a job is paid, the relative worth of the job is one of the most important factors. This worth (*pay rate*) is based on what the job demands of an employee in skill, effort, and responsibility, as well as on the conditions and hazards under which the work is performed. Systems that measure the worth of jobs are called *job evaluation systems* (see Chapter 7). Job descriptions and job specifications are used as sources of information in evaluating jobs. Often these job evaluation systems are designed by the HR department. Ultimately, however, it is the line manager who makes pay decisions based on performance relative to the standards of performance that have been established.

DESIGNING THE JOB

Outcome 6

Job design
Process of defining and organizing tasks, roles, and other processes to achieve employee goals and organizational effectiveness

An outgrowth of job analysis, **job design** is the process of defining and arranging tasks, roles, and other processes to achieve employee goals and organizational effectiveness. For example, organizations engaged in continuous improvement or process re-engineering may revamp their jobs in order to eliminate unnecessary job tasks or find better ways of performing work.[12] Job design should facilitate the achievement of organizational objectives and at the same time recognize the capabilities and needs of those who are to perform the job. Well-designed jobs can assist in helping an organization be successful. Job design can also include job rotation (in which people move from one job to another to learn new tasks), job enlargement (in which a person's job expands in the types of tasks he or she is expected to perform), and job enrichment (in which a person's job takes on higher-order responsibilities).

As Figure 3.2 illustrates, job design is a combination of four basic considerations: (1) the organizational objectives the job was created to fulfill; (2) industrial engineering considerations, including ways to make the job technologically efficient; (3) ergonomic concerns, including workers' physical and mental capabilities; and (4) employee contributions. Employee contributions are reflected in the participation of employees in making job improvements or enhancing operational decisions.

Job Design and Job Characteristics

Job characteristics model
An approach to job design that recognizes the link between motivational factors and components of the job to achieve improved work performance and job satisfaction

Job design studies explored a new field when behavioural scientists focused on various job dimensions that would improve simultaneously the efficiency of organizations and the job satisfaction of employees. The **job characteristics model** proposes that three psychological states of a jobholder result in improved work performance, internal motivation, and lower absenteeism and turnover. The motivated, satisfied, and productive employee is one who (1) experiences meaningfulness of the work performed, (2) experiences responsibility for work outcomes, and (3) has knowledge of the results of the work performed. When these three psychological states are achieved, the employee is more strongly motivated to continue doing the job well.

There are five job characteristics in this model:

1. *Skill variety.* The degree to which a job entails a variety of different activities, which demand the use of a number of different skills and talents by the jobholder.
2. *Task identity.* The degree to which the job requires completion of a whole and identifiable piece of work—that is, doing a job from beginning to end with a visible outcome.
3. *Task significance.* The degree to which the job has a substantial impact on the lives or work of other people, whether in the immediate organization or in the external environment.
4. *Autonomy.* The degree to which the job provides substantial freedom, independence, and discretion to the individual in scheduling the work and in determining the procedures to be used in carrying it out.
5. *Feedback.* The degree to which carrying out the work activities required by the job results in the individual being given direct and clear information about the effectiveness of his or her performance.

FIGURE 3.2   Basis for Job Design

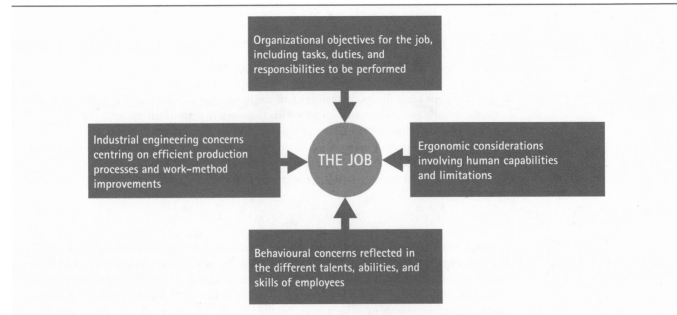

The job characteristics model seems to work best when certain conditions are met. One of these conditions is that employees must have the psychological desire for the autonomy, variety, responsibility, and challenge of enriched jobs. When this personal characteristic is absent, employees may resist the job redesign effort. A study within Toyota determined that when production lines were streamlined and the work characteristics of job autonomy, skill utilization, and participating in decision-making were reduced and/or eliminated that there was a negative outcome on production.[13] Also, job redesign efforts almost always fail when employees lack the physical or mental skills, abilities, or education needed to perform the job. Forcing enriched jobs on individuals who lack these traits can result in frustrated employees.

Designing Work for Group Contributions

Although a variety of group techniques have been developed to involve employees more fully in their organizations, all these techniques have two characteristics in common—enhancing collaboration and increasing synergy. By increasing the degree of collaboration in the work environment, these techniques can improve work processes and organizational decision-making. By increasing group synergy, they underline the adage that the contributions of two or more employees are greater than the sum of their individual efforts. Research has shown that working in a group setting strengthens employee commitment to an organization's goals, increases employee acceptance of decisions, and encourages a cooperative approach to workplace tasks. Further research has demonstrated that group work design must also create task challenges to the group and take into consideration the social routines of a group.[14] Two collaborative techniques are discussed below: employee empowerment and employee teams.

Role of Management

Leadership issues arise at several levels when employees are involved in decision making. At both the executive and management levels, there needs to be clear support for employee involvement and teams as there may be changes required in processes and actions to support this new way of doing business. For many years, managers and supervisors have played the role of decision maker. Thus, organizations will need to redefine the role of supervisor when employees are participating more in the operations of the company. As stated by Judi Hess, managing director for Kodak Canada, "Decisions within the company are based on a process of inclusion. We get input from stakeholders and make decisions in consensus. A lot of people might say decisions take longer and that's probably correct. But what matters is the time to implement decision. Decisions can be made very quickly but not implemented because the divisions or stakeholders don't buy into them."[15]

Therefore, when designing work for either individual or group contributions, it is critical that the organization be very clear on what is expected of managers and supervisors and the skills necessary to be successful. Further, the organization needs to carefully consider its overall design and structure. Research has demonstrated that the organizational structure is the key determinant of behaviours in the organization.[16] This means that if the organization wants a more committed and engaged workforce, then the way in which it is structured—who reports to whom and who makes decisions—will greatly influence the effectiveness of the leaders.

Organizations such as American Express and Reebok International have found that the success of employee involvement depends on first changing the roles of managers and team leaders. With fewer layers of management and a focus on team-based organizations, the role of managers and supervisors is substantially different. Managers are expected to be open to suggestions, actively support two-way communication, and encourage risk-taking.[17] Rather than autocratically imposing their demands on employees and closely watching to make sure that the workers comply, managers share responsibility for decision making with employees. Typically, the term "manager" has been replaced by "team leader." In a growing number of cases, leadership is shared among team members. Kodak, for example, rotates team leaders at various stages in team development. Alternatively, different individuals can assume functional leadership roles when their particular expertise is needed most.

A clear example of the role senior managers play in creating an involved organization is described in At Work with HRM 3.1.

Employee empowerment: leveraging the full capabilities of all employees. This group is working on a way to improve their product delivery system.

Photodisc/Getty Images

Employee Empowerment

Outcome 7

Employee empowerment
Granting employees power to initiate change, thereby encouraging them to take charge of what they do

Job enrichment, job characteristics, and creating work groups are specific ways that managers or supervisors can follow to formally change the jobs of employees. A less structured method is to allow employees to initiate their own job changes through the concept of empowerment. **Employee empowerment** is a technique for involving employees in their work through a process of inclusion. Empowerment encourages employees to become innovators and managers of their own work, and involves them in their jobs in ways that give them more control. Empowerment has been defined as "pushing down decision-making responsibility to those close to internal and external customers."

While defining empowerment can become the first step to achieving it, in order for empowerment to grow and thrive, organizations must encourage these conditions:

- *Participation.* Employees must be encouraged to take control of their work tasks. Employees, in turn, must care about improving their work process and interpersonal work relationships.
- *Innovation.* The environment must be receptive to people with innovative ideas and must encourage people to explore new paths and to take reasonable risks at reasonable costs. An empowered environment is created when curiosity is as highly regarded as technical expertise.
- *Access to information.* Employees must have access to a wide range of information. Involved individuals make decisions about what kind of information they need to perform their jobs.
- *Accountability.* Empowerment does not involve being able to do whatever you want. Empowered employees should be held accountable for their behaviour toward others. They must produce agreed-upon results, achieve credibility, and operate with a positive approach.

Additionally, employee empowerment succeeds when the culture of the organization is open and receptive to change. An organization's culture is created largely through the philosophies of senior managers and their leadership traits and behaviours. In an empowered organization, effective leadership is exemplified by managers who are honest, caring, and receptive to new ideas, and who treat employees with dignity and respect and as partners in organizational success. Further, for empowerment to work, it must be aligned directly with the strategy of the organization and individual accountability throughout the entire enterprise.[18]

AT WORK with HRM 3.1

BEST EMPLOYER

Would you like to work for the #1 company? "Yes" is the answer most of us would give. EllisDon, an Ontario-based construction company, earned this distinction for two years in a row for 2007 and 2008 in the *Report on Business* magazine's "Top 50 Companies." But what led to that honour?

According to *ROB*, it is employers who go out of their way to meet the needs of their employees. For example, EllisDon has a practice of encouraging employees to tackle projects with autonomy. Brian Waltham, vice president for Southwestern Ontario states: "When you come to work here, you are given authority to do things the way you want right off the bat. At some other businesses, you do not control your own destiny. Managers actively work to ensure that staff have the resources to do their jobs as expected

and challenge employees to grow in their jobs. In addition, the company hires people who excel in this type of work environment.

Other workplace elements that put certain employers ahead of others include aligning employees' values with organizational values, fostering an environment of integrity and respect, and displaying ethical conduct. This requires hard work and thinking out of the box.

Check out *Report on Business* magazine **(business. theglobeandmail.com/)** for current information on the Top 50 Companies.

CRITICAL THINKING QUESTION

What would your company need to do to "go out of its way to meet the needs of the employees"?

Sources: Adapted from *50 Best Employers in Canada Offer Flexibility, Demonstrate Integrity, According to Hewitt Associates,* www.hewittassociates.com/Intl/NA/en-US/AboutHewitt/Newsroom/PressReleaseDetail.aspx?cid=4662; "50 Best Employers in Canada," *Report on Business*; and "EllisDon Repeats as No. 1 Employer," www.ellisdon.com/news/?i=136 (retrieved January 17, 2009).

American Society for Quality (ASQ)
www.asq.org

Hewitt
www.hewitt.com

However, some organizations will have difficulty instilling the concept of empowerment as managers are sometimes unwilling to give up power or actually give employees the authority to make decisions. For more information on how to encourage employee empowerment, access the resources and information at the American Society for Quality (**www.asq.org/**)

Manager's Toolkit 3.3 gives some additional examples of employee empowerment.

Employee Engagement

A concept resulting from employee empowerment is that of employee engagement—the employee who is committed and dedicated to the organization—where the organization has truly captured the total person in achieving organizational outcomes. A recent study by Hewitt (**www.hewitt.com**), a worldwide human resources outsourcing and consulting firm, found that employee engagement levels at high-growth companies exceed those of lower-growth companies by more than 20%. The study also suggests that higher-growth organizations focus more energy and attention on employee engagement than their counterparts. In addition, the study found that high-performing companies typically have better communication about career paths and opportunities for personal growth, and managers who are more focused on helping employees meet career goals. Employees at rapidly growing organizations are 18% more likely to feel that there are sufficient opportunities to obtain the skills necessary for advancement, 16% more likely to feel that they have a chance to improve their skills, and 16% more likely to know what skills they need to develop in order to advance.[19]

Canada Post has taken great steps to create an engaged workforce—very different from earlier days where there was much conflict between the managers and the employees.[20] The first step towards engagement was to ensure that employees knew of its key priorities and what role the employees contributed to its success. It created a variety of different ways for employees to make suggestions, including the creation of a president's website where employees can ask questions and get answers. The next step was to help employees understand the customer and understand that Canada Post was no longer a monopoly. This is done through communications and helping employees link their work to customer needs.

EXAMPLES OF EMPLOYEE EMPOWERMENT

Many types of organizations have successfully empowered their employees. Examples include such diverse companies as DuPont, Walmart, Costco, and Home Depot. Empowered employees have made improvements in product and service quality, reduced costs, increased productivity, and modified or, in some cases, designed products.

- D.L.G.L. Ltd., a Quebec-based information systems company, is run by an operational committee that is composed of employees who have 20 years or more of employment with the company.

- Aecon, a Toronto-based international construction company, creates a learning environment that encourages innovation and continuous

improvement. It provides a minimum of 32 hours of training per year to support on-going skills development.

- Ikea, a furniture retailer, where staff are listened to, encouraged, and supported as part of its shared value system. Staff are empowered to remove damaged goods without checking with a supervisor.

- Suncor has taken a fun approach to employee meetings to shift its culture from reactionary to being proactive in addressing safety issues and improving operational performance. The meetings include speeches, videos, and a question-and-answer session. One of the more creative ideas was a fake newscast from 100 years in the future.

Sources: Adapted from Richard Yerema, "The Top 100," Macleans, www.macleans.ca/business/companies/article.jsp?content=20081001_99175_991 75 (accessed January 17, 2009; "Corporate Culture Built on Happiness," National Post, August 18, 2008, 8; "True Stories," www.ikea.com/ms/en_CA/ jobs/true_stories/ingeborg/index.html (accessed June 6, 2009); Shannon Klie, "Dawning of a New Day at Suncor," Canadian HR Reporter, October 22, 2007, 21; and "Information on Working at Aecon," http://careers.aecon.com/studentsgraduates.aspx (accessed June 6, 2009).

To achieve a high level of employee engagement, it is critical that the leadership practices focus on these key areas:

Ensuring consistency and clarity of any and all communications;
Creating a hopeful future—making employees feel good about their work and opportunities;
Investing in talent development;
Displaying a high commitment to performance and supporting employees to achieve their goals.[21]

Research has demonstrated that there are several key elements of engagement that include a complete understanding of the types of people who will be successful in the organization over the long term; an employee experience that conveys and reinforces the values of the organization to potential and existing employees; and an orientation that honestly represents all elements of what it is really like to work in that organization.[22]

But why do employees want to be engaged? A further study by Towers Perrin, a global professional services company, describes the various drivers for employee engagement. Among the various drivers is the desire for learning and development opportunities as well as the organization's social responsibility. For others, see Figure 3.3.

Further, engagement leads to less frustration at work thereby creating greater impact at the work level that becomes increasingly important during a tough economic situation. Engagement also means that the managers need to pay careful attention to the work structures so that employees feel that they are working smart and efficiently.[23]

Employee Teams

During the past decade perhaps one of the more radical changes to how work is done is the introduction of **employee teams**. Employee teams are a logical outgrowth of employee involvement, the philosophy of empowerment, and employee engagement. While many definitions of teams exist, we define an employee team as a group of employees working together toward a common purpose,

Towers Perrin
www.towersperrin.com

Employee teams
An employee-contributions technique in which work functions are structured for groups rather than for individuals, and team members are given discretion in matters traditionally considered management prerogatives, such as process improvements, product or service development, and individual work assignments

FIGURE 3.3   Top Drivers of Attractions, Retention, and Engagement

Top Attraction Drivers	Top Retention Drivers	Top Engagement Drivers
Competitive base pay	Organization's reputation as a great place to work	Senior management sincerely interested in employee well-being
Career advancement opportunities	Satisfaction with the organization's people decisions	Improved my skills and capabilities over the last year
Challenging work	Good relationship with supervisor	Organization's reputation for social responsibility
Convenient work location	Understand potential career track within organization	Input into decision making in my department
Flexible schedule	Ability to balance my work/personal life	Organization quickly resolves customer concerns
Learning and development opportunities	Fairly compensated compared to others doing similar work in my organization	Set high personal standards
Vacation/paid time off	Work in environment where new ideas are encouraged	Have excellent career advancement opportunities
Reputation of the organization as a good employer	Competitive training	Enjoy challenging work assignments that broaden skills
Reasonable workload	Input into decision making in my department	Good relationship with supervisor
Organization's financial health	Organization's reputation for social responsibility	Organization encourages innovative thinking

Source: Towers Perrin, *2007-2008 Global Workforce Study.*

whose members have complementary skills, the work of the members is mutually dependent, and the group has discretion over tasks performed. Furthermore, teams seek to make members of the work group share responsibility for their group's performance. Inherent in the concept of employee teams is that employees, not managers, are in the best position to contribute to workplace improvements. With work teams, managers accept the notion that the group is the logical work unit, and then apply resources to resolve organizational problems and concerns, including quality improvement.[24] Teamwork also embraces the concept of synergy. Synergy occurs when the interaction and outcome of team members is greater than the sum of their individual efforts.[25]

Teams can operate in a variety of structures, each with different strategic purposes or functional activities. Figure 3.4 describes common team forms. One form, self-directed teams, also called *autonomous work groups* or *self-managed teams*, consists of employees who are accountable for a "whole" work process or segment that delivers a product or service to an internal or external customer. For example, teams at Lauralco aluminum smelter in Deschambault, Quebec, were given responsibility for health and safety, and in the first year, reduced accident frequency rates by half, and after seven years by 80%. Team members acquire multiple skills that enable them to perform a variety of job tasks. Activities within a self-directed team can include quality improvement, oversight of maintenance schedules, and logistics.[26]

To compete in national and international markets, managers have formed **virtual teams**.[27] **Virtual teams** use advanced computer and telecommunications technology to link team members who are geographically dispersed—often worldwide.[28] Management may form a cross-functional team (see Figure 3.4) to develop a new pharmaceutical drug and have the team operate in a virtual environment to achieve its goal. Virtual teams provide new opportunities for training, product development, and product market analysis. Importantly, virtual teams provide access to previously unavailable expertise and enhance cross-functional interactions.[29] However, while the benefits of virtual teams are many, they are not without their problems.

Virtual teams
A team with widely dispersed members linked together through computer and telecommunications technology

FIGURE 3.4　Forms of Employee Teams

Cross-functional Teams
A group staffed with a mix of specialists (e.g., marketing, production, engineering) and formed to accomplish a specific objective. Cross-functional teams are based on assigned rather than voluntary membership.

Project Teams
A group formed specifically to design a new product or service. Members are assigned by management on the basis of their ability to contribute to success. The group normally disbands after task completion.

Self-directed Teams
Groups of highly trained individuals performing a set of interdependent job tasks within a natural work unit. Team members use consensus decision making to perform work duties, solve problems, or deal with internal or external customers.

Task Force Teams
A task force is formed by management to immediately resolve a major problem. The group is responsible for developing a long-term plan for problem resolution that may include a charge for implementing the solution proposed.

Process-improvement Teams
A group made up of experienced people from different departments or functions and charged with improving quality, decreasing waste, or enhancing productivity in processes that affect all departments or functions involved. Team members are normally appointed by management.

Virtual Teams
A group, usually from a mix of specialty areas that uses technology so that the teams can operate across time, space, and physical boundaries.

Regardless of the structure or purpose of the team, here are a few of the characteristics that have been identified in successful teams:

- Commitment to shared goals and objectives
- Consensus decision-making
- Open and honest communication
- Shared leadership
- Climate of cooperation, collaboration, trust, and support
- Valuing of individual for their diversity
- Recognition of conflict and its positive resolution

Unfortunately, not all teams succeed or operate to their full potential. Therefore, in adopting the work team concept, organizations must address several issues that could present obstacles to effective team function, including authoritarian leadership, aggressive communication styles, faulty equipment, and repetitive, boring work.[30] For example, new team members must be retrained to work outside their primary functional areas, and compensation systems must be constructed to reward individuals for team accomplishments. Since team membership demands more general skills, and since it moves an employee out of the historical career path, new career paths to general management must be created from the team experience. Finally, as the team members become capable of carrying out functions, such as strategic planning, that were previously restricted to higher levels of management, managers must be prepared to utilize their newfound expertise.

Another difficulty with work teams is that they alter the traditional manager–employee relationship. Managers often find it hard to adapt to the role of leader rather than supervisor and sometimes feel threatened by the growing power of the team and the need to hand over authority.[31] Furthermore, some employees may have difficulty adapting to a role that includes traditional supervisory responsibilities.

It is important for line managers to understand employee empowerment, employee involvement, and employee teams as they will be asked to help create and support these types of work relationships. And since such arrangements can change the role of line managers, they need to be comfortable with and accepting of the changes. Increasingly, the role of the line manager is to find ways to help, support, and expand employee involvement within the company. Without the manager's support and encouragement in creating employee involvement opportunities, there is little chance that such initiatives will succeed.

For information about what might be in the future for job/work design, read Emerging Trends 3.1.

EMERGING TRENDS **3.1**

1. **Work design.** Managers and supervisors will need to focus on ensuring that the work (or job) is designed in a way that motivates employees. Employees want work that is meaningful and that has an impact on the organization. Gen X and Gen Y employees want more involvement in the organization and want to see the results of their efforts.

2. **Employee engagement.** Organizations will continually be challenged in engaging their employees while ensuring that there is a work-life balance, particularly for the Gen X, Y, and Millennium generations. The organization must be seen to be a winner and to have leaders who are admired. Given the present difficult economic times, managers at all levels must communicate continually. And some organizations believe that employee engagement helps when there are economic downturns that present challenges and necessitate sacrifices. A number of studies have also correlated strong customer satisfaction with employee engagement.

3. **Increasing use of competencies.** As work becomes more fluid, organizations will incorporate the core competencies for success in each job. These competencies will be the skills, knowledge, abilities, and behaviours that lead to desired results and will help in doing the "right work at the right time the right way." This will also help in ensuring that managers design work in such a way that the results of each person leads to organizational success.

4. **The emergence of "job architecture."** As organizations change and evolve, there will be certain critical points that require a business-led view of the structure of the organization. By using a job architecture model, the roles, skills, and careers of the individuals can be effectively managed and the various HR processes can be more clearly integrated.

Sources: Adapted from Dr. Vince Molinaro and Dr. David Weiss, "Driving Employee Engagement," The Banff Leadership Centre, www.banffleadership.com (accessed January 19, 2009); "The Importance of Employee Engagement," *VisionMonday*, December 15, 2008, 32-33; Sarah Dobson, "Building a Sustainable Culture," *Canadian HR Reporter*, October 20, 2008, www.hrreporter.com/ArticleView.aspx?l=1&articleid=6427 (accessed March 22, 2009); Darin Phillips, "Identifying Critical Job Competencies," *Fast Company*, August 4, 2008, www.fastcompany.com/discussion-topic/identifying-critical-job-competencies (accessed March 22, 2009); and "Job Architecture—The Key to Good Organizational Health," Watson Wyatt Ltd., March 2009.

SUMMARY

1. Explain the supervisor's role in defining and designing work.
   - Line manager or supervisor is the primary individual who determines what work needs to be done.
   - Line manager takes an active role in determining what skills and abilities are needed to successfully perform the work.

2. Discuss the relationship between job requirements and HRM processes.
   - HRM processes, such as recruitment or training, make use of information about the work or job.
   - A job consists of a group of related activities and duties.
   - A position consists of the specific duties and responsibilities performed by only one employee.

3. Explain the relationship between job analysis and a job description.
   - Job analysis is the process of obtaining information about jobs (or work) by determining what the duties, tasks, or activities are.
   - The outcome is a job description—a written document that contains a number of elements.
   - A job description is a written description listing the types of duties and the skills (job specifications) needed to successfully perform the work.

4. Define and describe the sections in a job description.
   - Job title—indication of what the duties might be or the nature of the work.
   - Summary of job—two to three sentences describing the overall purpose of the job.
   - List of duties and responsibilities—statements of the key duties and responsibilities.
   - Job specifications—statement of the needed knowledge, skills, and abilities or competencies of the person who is to perform the work.

5. Describe the uses of information gained from job analysis.
   - Job specifications establish the qualifications required of applicants for a job opening and play an essential role in the recruiting function.
   - Information on the job description is used as a basis for comparing the skills and abilities of each applicant in the selection process.
   - Managers must be careful to ensure that they do not hire employees on the basis of "individualized" job requirements that satisfy personal whims but bear little relation to successful job performance.
   - Requirements contained in the job description and specifications provide clues to training needs.
   - The pay of a job is based on what the job demands in skill, effort, and responsibility, as well as the conditions and hazards under which the work is performed.

6. Define employee contribution and describe the relationship of job design to employee contributions.
   - Job design is the process of defining and arranging tasks, roles, and other processes to achieve the employee's goals and organizational effectiveness.
   - Employee contribution is the degree to which employees are involved in making critical work-process or organizational decisions.
   - Job design can enhance or take away from the employee's ability to participate in decision making.

7. Discuss the different types of work designs to increase employee contribution.
   - Employee empowerment is a method of involving employees in their work and encouraging them to take charge of what they do.
   - Employee involvement groups are groups of five to 10 employees doing similar or related work who meet together regularly to identify, analyze, and suggest solutions to shared problems.
   - Employee teams are groups of employees who assume a greater role in the production or service process.

NEED TO KNOW

- Definition of job analysis, job description, job specification, and standards of performance
- Definition of employee contribution
- Definition of employee involvement, employee empowerment, and employee engagement.

NEED TO UNDERSTAND

- Relationship of job requirements to recruitment, selection, training, performance evaluation, and compensation
- Relationship between job analysis, job descriptions, job specifications, and standards of performance
- Role of line manager in designing job for maximum employee contributions.
- Ways to encourage employee involvement

KEY TERMS

employee empowerment 80

employee teams 82

job 68

job analysis 69

job characteristics model 78

job description 69

job design 77

job specifications 71

position 68

standards of performance 74

virtual teams 83

work 68

REVIEW QUESTIONS

1. Explain the difference between job analysis and job description.
2. List the problems associated with a written job description.
3. Describe the way in which information from job analysis is used.
4. What are the types of employee and group contribution?
5. What are the different forms of team?

CRITICAL THINKING QUESTIONS

1. You have just been hired as a customer service representative at a branch of a very large bank. The branch manager is considering creating a non-traditional work schedule for everyone. The manager has asked for your advice about what to consider to ensure its success—and the continued strong performance of the branch. What would you say?
2. Assume you are a new supervisor in a hotel and you've been asked to prepare a job description for room attendant. What would you include as five key duties and what would you list as three key skills? Would you involve the current cashier in the preparation of the job description? Why?
3. You are working for a company that has recently created a number of work teams. Your boss has been assigned to head up one of the teams. What advice would you give so that the team and your boss create a high-performing team?
4. You are working for a new recreational resort that has no written job descriptions. From your observation it appears that many of the employees are not always sure what to do, and sometimes there is overlap in tasks and activities between employees. What arguments would you use to convince your boss to develop written job descriptions?
5. You are a small business owner in the catering business. What might be some of the work design issues you would need to consider to recruit and keep top performers?
6. How often should a job description be reviewed and/or revised? Why?
7. What methods would you use to collect job information for the following jobs:
   a. Production employee
   b. Police officer
   c. Customer service representative (answering telephone enquiries)
   d. College teacher

DEVELOPING YOUR SKILLS

1. In groups of four to five students, identify the job specifications (knowledge, skills, and abilities) for the position of college instructor. (You will have approximately 20 minutes to complete the exercise.) Each group will then present its findings to the rest of the class. Discuss and compare the requirements and develop a single list of job specifications.
2. Working in groups of three to four students, identify what the group believes are successful characteristics of groups. Prepare a list of seven to eight significant characteristics that the group agrees upon. Share the results with the rest of the class.
3. Working in groups of four to five students, identify the tasks of a customer service person in a retail clothing store. How could the work be redesigned to keep employees and minimize turnover?
4. Access the Web page of the National Occupation Classification system that is managed by Human Resources and Social Development (**www.hrsdc.gc.ca**). Click the link on "Career Planning" and then click "National Occupational Classification." Search through the various job titles and find a job description that interests you. Prepare a one- to two-page summary describing the key duties and skills, and explain what training and experience you would need in order to be hired.
5. Each student will access the HRIM Mall website (**www.hrimmall.com**) and click "HR Resource" link and then the "Job Descriptions" link. Once you are into the site, pick a job description, download it, and print it. Using the printed job description, assess the content from a legal-compliance perspective. Bring the job description and evaluation to class. Your instructor will ask you to share your results with each other.

Case Study  1

Job Analysis and Hiring Decisions at Ovania Chemical Company

Background

Ovania Chemical Corporation is a specialty chemical producer of polyethylene terephthalate (PET) thermoplastic resins primarily used to make containers for soft drinks and bottled water, as well as packaging for food and pharmaceutical products. Though smaller than other chemical producers that produce globally, in recent years, advances in technology have altered the nature of chemical production, and like other firms in the industry, Ovania Chemical is taking steps to modernize its facilities. Not surprisingly, these technological changes have been accompanied by redesign in employee jobs. In fact, over the last three years, there have been drastic changes in both the number and the kinds of jobs being performed by employees. The latest change in one of its plants involves the job transformations of the system analyzer position.

The System Analyzer

Because chemical production involves highly integrated process technologies, someone must monitor all of the individual components simultaneously. The system analyzer is primarily responsible for this monitoring function. It is one of the most prestigious non-managerial jobs in the entire plant, and its importance is likely to grow.

Formerly the position was classified as that of a semiskilled maintenance technician, but as the plant has become more automated, the requirements for the system analyzer job have become much more extensive. Knowledge of pneumatics, hydraulics, information technology, programming, and electrical wiring are all increasingly critical aspects of this job. As these up-skilling trends continue, the three people who currently hold the position admit that they will be incapable of performing adequately in the future. It is estimated that within two years, the tasks, duties, and responsibilities of the system analyzer will have changed by more than 70%. For these reasons, management decided to recruit and select three new people for the rapidly transforming position.

Job Analysis and New Position Analysis

The plant manager, the HR manager, and two senior engineers worked with external consultants to conduct a job analysis for the new position of system analyzer. Although they had to project into the future regarding the specific nature of the job, they collectively felt they had created an accurate depiction of the requirements for someone who would occupy the position. Figure 3-5 shows a list of the major performance dimensions of the job and a subsample of specific tasks characteristic of each dimension.

From this list of tasks, the committee then delineated a set of personal qualities required for anyone who would hold the system analyzer position. These qualities included the 12 abilities shown in Figure 3-6. The numbers beside each ability indicate the tasks (see Figure 3-5) to which it is related. The abilities marked with an asterisk (*) were considered by the committee to be "critical."

Because of the two-year lead time before the newly transformed position would be put in place, the committee was very careful not to include in the selection battery any skills or knowledge that could reasonably be trained within that two-year period. Only aptitude or ability factors were incorporated into the selection process, rather than achievement tests.

Questions

1. How would you conduct a job analysis for a job that does not yet exist?
2. Given the significant shift of tasks and responsibilities in this case, would you have involved the existing employees in conducting the job analysis? Why or why not?
3. Do you think the company will need to do another job analysis after two years? Why or why not?

FIGURE 3.5 Performance Dimensions (Duties and Tasks)

Maintaining Spares and Supplies
1. Anticipates future need for parts and supplies and orders them.
2. Stocks parts and supplies in an orderly fashion.
3. Maintains and calibrates test equipment.

Troubleshooting
4. Applies calibration standards to verify operation by subjecting the system to known standards.
5. Decides whether the problem is in the sensor, in the processor, in the process stream, and/or in the sample system.
6. Use troubleshooting guides in system manuals to determine the problem area.
7. Uses test equipment to diagnose the problem.
8. Makes a general visual inspection of the analyzer system as a first troubleshooting step.
9. Replaces components such as printed circuit boards and sensors to see if the problem can be alleviated.

Handling Revisions and New Installations
10. Makes minor piping changes such as size, routing, and additional filters.
11. Makes minor electrical changes such as installing switches and wires and making terminal changes.
12. Uses common pipefitting tools.
13. Uses common electrical tools.
14. Reads installation drawings.

Record Keeping
15. Maintains system files showing the historical record of work on each system.
16. Maintains loop files that show the application of the system.
17. Updates piping and instrument drawings if any changes are made.
18. Maintains Environmental Protection Agency records and logbooks.
19. Disassembles analyzers to perform repairs onsite or back in the shop.
20. Replaces damaged parts such as filters, electronic components, light source, lenses, sensors, and valves.
21. Uses diagnostic equipment such as oscilloscopes, ohmmeters, and decade boxes.
22. Tests and calibrates repaired equipment to ensure that it works properly.
23. Reads and follows written procedures from manuals.

Routine Maintenance
24. Observes indicators on systems to ensure proper operation.
25. Adds reagents to systems.
26. Decides whether the lab results or the system is correct regarding results (resolves discrepancies between lab and analyzer results).
27. Performs calibrations.

FIGURE 3.6 Abilities and Tasks

Numbers represent tasks cited in Figure 3.5. Asterisks indicate abilities considered critical by the committee.

Skills	Task Numbers
*Finger dexterity	3, 4, 7, 9, 10, 11, 12, 13, 19, 20, 21, 22, 25, 27
*Mechanical comprehension	3, 5, 6, 8, 9, 10, 12, 13, 7, 14, 19, 20, 22, 23, 24, 27, 11, 17
*Numerical ability	11, 3, 4, 24, 10, 21, 12, 13, 14, 27
*Spatial ability	2, 4, 5, 9, 10, 11, 14, 19, 20
*Visual pursuit	3, 4, 5, 6, 7, 8, 9, 10, 11, 14, 16, 17, 19, 20, 21, 22, 27
*Detection	2, 3, 5, 6, 8, 9, 10, 14, 19, 20, 23, 7

(Continued)

Oral comprehension	1, 2, 5, 6, 26, 7, 8, 9, 19, 21, 25
Written comprehension	1, 15, 16, 17, 18
Deductive reasoning	1, 5, 3, 6, 7, 8, 9, 10, 11, 19, 21, 20, 22, 2, 26, 27
Inductive reasoning	1, 3, 5, 6, 7, 8, 9, 10, 11, 19, 21, 20, 22, 2, 26, 27
Reading comprehension	3, 6, 14, 7, 22, 23, 21, 9, 27
Reading scales and tables	3, 4, 7, 8, 9, 21, 23, 24, 27, 2, 6, 14

Case Study 2

Revitalizing Your Workspace

Air Miles, the consumer rewards company, recently relocated its headquarters in North York to Toronto. In the preparation, designing, and planning, it decided that it wanted workspace that would incorporate several of its key themes for its staff. These themes were health and well-being and employee engagement. In making the move, the company contemplated that as many as 10% of the staff might not make the move. However, what they experienced was less than 1%. As Bryan Pearson, president and CEO of Air Miles stated, "It is a testament to the design of the building and the facilities provided."

The new facility includes ergonomic furniture, more windows, and an on-site fitness facility. The company acknowledges that it didn't want to cut certain costs as it knew that what it was doing is making an investment in its employees. It knew that if employees were healthier, they would be more productive and would be happier and more motivated. To engage employees in the process, Air Miles began communicating its intentions 15 months before the move. In addition, staff were encouraged to provide input on size of space, design of space, etc. The employees would be moving into a slightly smaller space and a more open environment. Air Miles is thrilled as the staff are now highly energized and engaged, with more interaction and socialization between everyone. And even with the open concept, the noise level is lower than in the old environment. It seems that people are more respectful and considerate of each other. As Bryan concludes, "You need to know what kind of environment you want to create for your staff and how you want to treat them."

Source: Adapted from Sarah Dobson, "Getting Workspace into Shape," *Canadian HR Reporter*, January 12, 2009, www.hrreporter.com/ArticleView.aspx?l=1&articleid=6598 (retrieved March 22, 2009).

Questions

1. What arguments could be advanced both for and against involving employees in the redesign of office space?
2. Empowerment and engagement is mainly a motivational tool. Do you think the new offices will continue to keep employees engaged? What more might Air Miles have to do?
3. How might a manager in the former location react to managing in a more open environment?

NOTES AND REFERENCES

1. "Tribes are What Matter Now," May 6, 2009, www.karo.com/news/ideas/2009/05/06/TribesAreWhatMatterNow.aspx (accessed June 6, 2009).

2. Richard Henderson, *Compensation Management in a Knowledge-Based World*, 10thed. (Englewood Cliffs, N.J.: Prentice Hall, 2006).

3. Interview with Aquinox Business Analyst, Jason Robertson, February 2009.

4. J. Grant Sinclair, *Jim Smith and Canadian Human Rights Commission and Canadian National Railway* [Indexed as *Jim Smith v. Canadian National Railway*], file no. T939/5904, British Columbia, May 9, 2008, www.chrt-tcdp.gc.ca/search/view_html.asp?doid=901&lg=_e&isruling=0 (accessed January 16, 2009).

5. Robert Hof, "The End of Work as You Know It," *Business Week,* August 20, 2007, www.businessweek.com/magazine/content/07_34/b4047426.htm (accessed January 16, 2009).

6. Ibid.

7. Erich P. Prien, Kristin O. Prien, and Louis G. Gamble, "Perspectives on Non conventional Job Analysis Methodologies," *Journal of Business and Psychology* 18, no. 3 (Spring 2004): 337.

8. Uyen Vu, "Redesigning Org Chart to Mobilize Talent," *Canadian HR Reporter,* June 16, 2008, www.hrreporter.com/ArticleView.aspx?l=1&articleid=6152#Redesigning (accessed January 16, 2009).

9. *Seguin v. Great Blue Heron Charity Casino (2007),* 61 C.H.R.R. D/293, 2007 HRTO 33, Canadian Human Rights Reporter, www.chn-hr-reporter.ca (accessed January 17, 2009).

10. *Cassidy v. Emergency and Health Services Comm. (No. 2) (2008),* CHRR Doc. 08-195, 2008 BCHRT 125, Canadian Human Rights Reporter, www.chn-hr-reporter.ca (accessed January 17, 2009).

11. *Sosnowski v. Canada (Public Works and Government Services) (2005),* 56 C.H.R.R. D/108, 2005 CHRT 47, www.chn-hr-reporter.ca (accessed January 19, 2009).

12. Gail L. Rein, "Feel It—A Method for Achieving Sustainable Process Changes," *Business Horizons* 47, no. 3 (May/June 2004): 75–81.

13. Sharon K. Parker, "Longitudinal Effects of Lead Production on Employee Outcomes and the Mediating Role of Work Characteristics," *Journal of Applied Psychology* 88, no. 4 (2003): 620-634.

14. Annika Lantz and Agneta Brav, "Job Design for Learning in Work Groups," *Journal of Workplace Learning* 19, no. 5 (2007): 269-285.

15. Daryl-Lynn Carlson, "A Picture of Life Balance," *National Post,* October 22, 2008, WK2.

16. Sheila M. Puffer, "Changing Organizational Structures: An Interview with Rosebeth Moss Kanter," *The Academy of Management Executive* 18, no. 2 (May 2004): 96–105.

17. David Crisp, "Leadership Values Evolving," *Canadian HR Reporter*, September 8, 2008, www.hrreporter.com/ArticleView.aspx?l=1&articleid=6314 (accessed January 17, 2009).

18. Dr. Manoj K. Sharma and Gurvinder Kaur, "Employee Empowerment: A Conceptual Analysis," *The Journal of Global Business Issues* 2, no. 2 (Summer/Fall 2008): 7-12.

19. http://was4.hewitt.com/hewitt/resource/newsroom/pressrel/2004/05-18-04.htm (accessed October 30, 2004).

20. John Driscoll, "Canada Post Focuses on Employee Engagement," *News,* www.axiomnews.ca/NewsArchives/2006/March/March28.htm (accessed June 6, 2009).

21. Andrew Bell, "Ask Our Expert: Global Leadership and Engagement," Hewitt & Associates, www.hewittassociates.com/Intl/NA/en-US/KnowledgeCenter/ArticlesReports/ArticleDetail.aspx?cid=3680&tid=47 (accessed January 17, 2009).

22. Tamara J. Erickson and Lynda Gratton, "What It Means to Work Here," *Harvard Business Review,* March 2007, 104-112.

23. Mark Royal and Rebecca Masson, "Employee Engagement in Tough Times," Webcast sponsored by Hay Group, February 3, 2009.

24. "Employee Teams Make Progress Improving Quality," *The Chrysler TIMES,* September 26, 2008, www.thescoop-cg.com/2008/09/26/employee-teams-make-progress-improving-quality/ (accessed January 18, 2009).

25. Alden M. Hayashi, "Building Better Teams," *Sloan Management Review* 45, no. 2 (Winter 2004): 5.

26. Simone Kauffeld, "Self-directed Work Groups and Team Competence," *Journal of Occupational and Organizational Psychology* 79 (2006): 1-21.

27. Michael Hansen, "Virtual Teams That Work: Creating Conditions for Virtual Team Effectiveness," *Personal Psychology* 57, no. 1 (Spring 2004): 243.

28. Natalia Levina and Emmanuelle Vaast, "Innovating or Doing as Told? Status Differences and Overlapping Boundaries in Offshore Collaboration," *MIS Quarterly* 32, no. 2 (June 2008): 307-332.

29. Stacie A. Furst, Martha Reeves, Benson Rosen, and Richard S. Blackburn, "Managing the Life Cycle of Virtual Teams," *Academy of Management Executive* 18, no. 2 (May 2004): 6.

30. Mark Gorkin, "Key Components of a Dangerously Dysfunctional Work Environment," *Workforce Management,* www.workforce.com/archive/feature/22/22/18/223747.php (accessed January 18, 2009).

31. Edward de Bono and Robert Heller, "Team Management: True Leadership and Teamwork," *Thinking Managers,* July 8, 2006 www.thinkingmanagers.com/management/team-management.php (accessed January 18, 2009).

CHAPTER 4

HUMAN RESOURCE PLANNING, RECRUITMENT, AND SELECTION

OUTCOMES

After studying this chapter, you should be able to

1. Discuss the steps in human resource planning.

2. Describe the relationship between planning, recruiting, and selecting people to work with the organization.

3. Explain the advantages and disadvantages of recruiting from within the organization.

4. Explain the advantages and disadvantages of external recruitment.

5. Explain the objectives of the selection process.

6. Describe the typical steps in the selection process.

7. Identify the various sources of information used for selection decisions.

8. Discuss the different approaches to conducting an employment interview.

9. Explain the value of different types of employment tests.

OUTLINE

HRM CLOSE-UP

"I really hire for attitude and train for skills, placing less emphasis on credentials and more on the person."

Sean Frisky, owner of Ground Effects Environmental Services. **Courtesy of Sean Frisky**

Sean Frisky is fond of dirt and contamination. The more dirt, the messier the spill, the more complex the contaminant, the better—better for the niche service he offers in the field of contaminant clean-up.

Frisky was a university engineering student and was in the midst of a co-op work term at an oil and gas refinery in Saskatchewan when he observed an unreliable and poorly designed piece of machinery. He envisioned a new design with fewer moving parts and better run-times. His innovative thinking and determination to respond to a market that was just waking up to the need for environmental care and clean-up led to the business he runs today called Ground Effects Environmental Services.

Based in Regina, Saskatchewan, Frisky's team of engineers, millwrights, welders, electricians, drillers, field technicians, office administrators, and skilled labourers has together created dozens of new technologies used in the methodologies and the manufacturing of equipment used to clean up contaminants. Over the years, his company has moved into more sophisticated and complicated products and the workforce now includes specialists such as microbiologists and geologists.

Frisky worked alone for the first two years as he developed his business in his home garage. His first hires included an engineer, a field technician, and an office administrator. "Our approach is to let the market drive our need to add staff, rather than ramping up in order to accommodate something we think is on the horizon," explains Frisky. As his business grows, Frisky often sees the need for another level of staff. For instance, when he found himself with four welders on staff, it made sense to hire a welder foreperson to help manage the area. And one of his latest hires is a chief financial officer that he describes as "a beautiful thing—freeing my time to focus on new markets and developing technology."

Frisky feels lucky that he has been able to recruit primarily within the province where he operates his business. He has had many good referrals from current employees who recommend family and friends. Frisky is responsive but careful at the same time. "These people are acquainted with the company and come in understanding our approach to work and they often fit the mould. But you do have to exercise some caution."

Typically, Frisky uses newspaper and Internet advertising to post positions. When interviewing potential employees, he finds that most candidates have anticipated the questions he's going to ask and have prepared what they know to be the right answers. He therefore tries to get to know the individual's personality and asks questions to understand how they would react in certain situations. "I really hire for attitude and train for skills, placing less emphasis on credentials and more on the person," comments Frisky.

Finding people who work well on the team is also a priority. "I use the analogy of a hockey team. We can't all be Wayne Gretzkys, but if we are diligent, hard-working, and really focus on all of our strengths, we can have a strong team," Frisky explains. As the company expands and the number of employees grows, he has been able to start hiring from within. "The best guy is usually the one who knows the ropes and it's great to be able to recognize employees with a promotion or a new challenge. It's one of the key benefits of being part of a growing company."

INTRODUCTION

In earlier chapters we stressed that the structure of an organization and the design of the work within it affect the organization's ability to reach its objectives. These objectives, however, can be achieved only through the efforts of people. It is essential that work within the organization is done by people who are qualified to do the work. To achieve this, defining the core competencies for any work is critical to the recruitment and selection processes. And this starts with the line manager, who is also encouraged to think about current and future people requirements. Sean Frisky clearly understands the importance of planning and finding the right person for his company. He uses a variety of ways to find (recruit) and then pick (select) the people who have the attitudes desired to make the firm successful. And it is important that this process supports both operational and strategic planning.

Employment recruiting and selection continue to be one of the top concerns of all levels of management within an organization. Despite the economic challenges of the last couple of years, almost all organizations are finding it increasingly difficult to secure qualified applicants to fill job openings. According to recent studies, most employers have entered a period in which jobs ranging from the unskilled to the professional and highly technical are harder to staff; this condition is not likely to improve in the near future.[1] No longer can managers rely solely upon unsolicited applications to fill openings nor can they be sloppy in making hiring decisions. This chapter will discuss the process of planning for staffing requirements, and then finding, attracting, and selecting applicants.

HUMAN RESOURCE PLANNING

You will recall from Chapter 1 that a company becomes competitive by means of its people. Therefore, it is essential that an organization look strategically at its people and the skills they require to accomplish the strategic and operational goals of the organization.

But what is meant by "strategic"? While strategy has many definitions, we will use the one you might have learned in a management course. Strategic plans tend to be broader in scope, longer in time frames (two to three years), provide overall direction, and apply to the entire organization. Basically, a company's strategy lies in determining its key goals and the actions it needs to take to achieve those goals. Strategic HRM, as noted in Chapter 1, includes all the HR policies, processes, and practices that help the company achieve those goals through its employees. Therefore, it is important that the line manager link the goals of the company to the skills of the people employed.

In linking goals to skills, the line manager will need to anticipate the current and future needs of the company and develop the road map to get there. What the manager is really doing is ensuring that the people with the right skills for the present and for future organizational growth.[2] This is called **human resource planning.** Human resource planning is a process to ensure that the people required to run the company are being used as effectively as possible, where and when they are needed, in order to accomplish the organization's goals. Depending on the organization, the process might also be called manpower planning or employment planning. No matter which phrase is used, the purpose is still the same: to have the right people with the right skills in the right jobs at the right time. Given the economic uncertainty, organizations sometimes may want to ignore this. However, it is even more important in difficult financial circumstances to ensure that they have the appropriate staff to achieve success in both the short term and into the future.[3]

Human resource planning
Process that the people required to run the company are being used as effectively as possible, where and when they are needed, in order to accomplish the organization's goals

Linking HR Planning to Strategic Planning

Organizations will undertake strategic planning where major objectives are identified and comprehensive plans are developed to achieve the objectives. Because strategic planning involves the allocation of resources, including the people resources of the organization, HR planning is aligned to ensure the objectives are met. And from the overall organizational objectives, divisions and/or departments will also set objectives that support the attainment of organizational objectives. Thus, the line manager will need to make plans not only for business objectives but plans for the necessary staffing resources. For example, if the organization has strategically decided to enter a new market, it needs to ensure that it has the people with the right skill sets to gain a foothold in that market. Consequently, the HR plan must have an activity that assesses the skill of current employees and possibly a recruitment activity that attracts new employees with the necessary skills.

Likewise, through HR planning, all HR processes, systems, and practices can be aligned to the overall business strategy. In doing this, the organization ensures that it has the people capabilities to adjust to changes in the environment. One area of strategic HR planning that is receiving much attention is succession planning. Organizations are concerned about developing leaders for the future and are focusing efforts on training and development programs so that the leaders have the competencies necessary that can keep pace with the direction of the organization.[4] In the best companies, such as Fairmont Hotels, BMO, and IBM, there is virtually no distinction between strategic planning and HR planning; the planning cycles are the same and HR issues are seen as inherent in the management of the business. Northern Lights Health Region in Alberta, serving a population base of over 100,000 people, decided that it had to increase its staff by 10% to 15% each year in order to meet the demands of an increasing population base. To do this, workforce simulations were created to test various options to ensure that the staff planning strategy fit the overall strategy of the health region.[5]

Importance of Planning for Staffing Needs

Why is it important for the line manager to be involved in human resource planning? Consider these facts about the Canadian labour force:

- In 2009, over 17 million Canadians were in the labour force out of a population of about 33.5 million. The workforce is aging—over 15% of the workforce is 55 or older.
- The manufacturing sector, particularly in Ontario and Quebec, continue to shrink and as a result, there are many fewer jobs for machine operators, steel fabricators, parts assemblers, and inspectors.
- Around 21% of the Canadian workforce was born in another country.
- Labour shortages are predicted for retail, construction, and health sectors.
- Today, 34% of workers are part-time or self-employed. Five percent of Canadians hold two or more jobs. The number of self-employed is around 15% of total employment.[6]

These dramatic shifts in the composition of the labour force require that managers become more involved in planning their staffing needs, since such changes affect not only employee recruitment but also methods of employee selection, training, compensation, and motivation. To illustrate the impact of changes in the workforce, companies, such as Akita, Precision Drilling Corporation, and Ensign Resource Services, have actively sought women and immigrants to move into Canada's drilling industry.[7] Without doing their own workforce planning, they would not have known there was a problem. An organization may incur several intangible costs as a result of inadequate or no people planning. For example, inadequate planning can cause vacancies to remain unfilled. The resulting loss in efficiency can be costly, particularly when lead-time is required to train replacements. Situations also may occur in which employees are laid off in one department while applicants are hired for similar jobs in another department.

Realistically, planning occurs more systematically in medium and larger organizations. Small, entrepreneurial organizations tend to approach HR staffing needs on a more short-term basis. For example, Alpha Safety, a company that provides safety services in remote locations in western Canada, including the Arctic, has less than 100 employees with only 15 full-time employees. Given the nature of the work with some of the shifts for medics as long as 65 days, the company needs to keep a close eye on how employees are feeling about the work and the working conditions. To replace staff is difficult and very time-consuming. To help ensure there are staff when needed, part of the HR plan is to constantly source for new medics.[8]

Another example of the importance of workforce planning is at Sorin Group Canada—a company in British Columbia that manufactures a tissue heart valve. It is the only Canadian company that does this and it is beginning to supply the valves to the United States. The nature of the work requires specialized technicians that hand-suture the valve that is quite small—measured in millimetres. Sorin plans on a year-by-year basis depending on the demand for the valve. Since it is in such a niche market, it has also focused on succession planning as a way to ensure that the capabilities of the people are ready when needed.[9]

Statistics Canada provides a variety of different reports that can be helpful in HR planning. The "Population Pyramid" website at **www.statcan.gc.ca/kits-trousses/animat/edu06a_0000-eng.htm** is animated to demonstrate the changes in population from which organizations can determine their own trends in relation to their staffing needs.

Statistics Canada
Population Pyramids

www.statcan.gc.ca/
kits-trousses/animat/
edu06a_0000-eng.htm

A research scientist has knowledge and company-specific skills that are directly linked to the company's strategy.

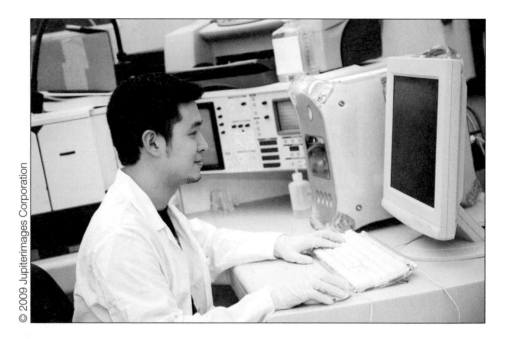

© 2009 Jupiterimages Corporation

Outcome 1

Trend analysis
Quantitative approach to forecasting labour demand on an organizational index

Management forecasts
Opinions and judgments of supervisors or managers and others that are knowledgeable about the organization's future employment needs

Staffing table
Graphic representations of organizational jobs along with the numbers of employees currently occupying those jobs and future employment needs

Markov analysis
Method for tracking the pattern of employee movements through various jobs

Skills inventory
Information about the education, experiences, skills, etc. of staff

HR Planning Approaches

Since the overall outcome of HR planning is to have the right people with the right skills at the right time in the right job, there is a need to forecast the demand for employees. Forecasting can be done through quantitative approaches, such as a **trend analysis,** or through qualitative approaches, such as **management forecasts.**

A trend analysis will forecast employment requirements on some type of organizational index, such as sales or units of production. Previous years' experiences will be analyzed and projections will be made for the future. In management forecasts, the opinions and judgments of people who are knowledgeable about the organization's future needs will develop scenarios that can be used for planning purposes.

Besides forecasting the demand for employees, an organization will also need to look at the supply of employees. This includes looking both internally, in the organization, and externally, to the larger labour market. Two techniques to assess the internal supply are **staffing tables** and **Markov analysis.** Staffing tables are graphic representations of all organizational jobs, along with the numbers of employees currently occupying those jobs (and perhaps also future employment requirements derived from demand forecasts). Markov analysis shows the percentage (and actual number) of employees who remain in each job from one year to the next, as well as the proportions of those who are promoted, demoted, or transferred, or who leave the organization. While staffing tables and Markov analysis focus on numbers of employees, another technique focuses on the skill mix or **skills inventory.** When assessing the organization's supply, organizations will identify the key skills or core competencies necessary for organizational success. Without knowing the core competencies required for business success, the other HR processes may not be successful. All other HR needs are based on the identified competencies of employees to ensure good organizational performance. Organizations such as Hewlett-Packard and DuPont Canada use HR information and enterprise systems to assist in this task. Figure 4.1 describes the steps in the planning process.

Results of HR Planning

The outcome of HR planning is to achieve a useable balance between the demand for and supply of employees. It is here that organizations can see the results of good HR planning. The demand for and supply of labour is very much a function of the economic environment. For example, with the worldwide recession starting in 2008, many organizations found that they had to modify their plans and did not need as many people. However, educational institutions were still graduating students (high school, college and university) who were looking for employment.[10]

FIGURE 4.1 The HR Planning Steps

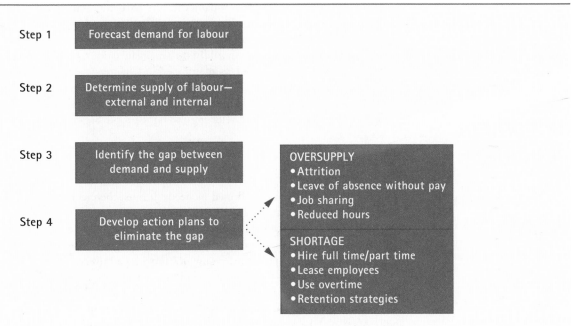

But HR planning is not a guarantee that there might not come a time when the organization has too many employees for its immediate or long-term needs. This can be the result of severe economic conditions as mentioned in Chapter 1 or major company collapses, such as Nortel Networks' bankruptcy in 2009. In either case, a company may be faced with terminating or laying off employees. However, there are other ways that an organization can balance its employee complement without having to terminate people or hire more staff.

Ways to Deal with an Oversupply of Labour

Some organizations have decided that since employees are key to its success, any need to reduce employee numbers would be done by attrition. Attrition is the natural departure of employees through people quitting, retiring, or dying. Usually organizations can estimate how many people leave and for what reasons. Therefore, an organization may be able to avoid downsizing because it knows that people will leave.

Not all attrition is good. If too many people leave—high turnover—it can cost the company more money than intended. Replacing an employee is a costly and time-consuming activity. It is currently estimated that the costs of turnover can be as high as two times the annual compensation, particularly in high-demand skill areas.[11] One of the more serious business issues of the 21st century has been the concern with retaining key employees.

If the organization can predict that the excess supply of employees is more short-term, it may suggest that some employees take a leave of absence (without pay), that they job-share, reduce working hours (and pay), or the organization can redeploy people to units that have a need. Generally speaking, most organizations do not stop hiring just because of economic pressures. Frequently, it may mean that there are too many people in one area of the business and not enough in another area. By utilizing a number of strategies an organization can minimize the need to terminate employees.

Ways to Deal with Shortages of Labour

Even though human resource planning frequently focuses on the surplus of employees, currently much of the attention has been on projected labour shortages—particularly in certain occupations and/or industries. Further, the need for additional employees may be short-term or temporary, and, therefore, the organization will not want to hire for the longer term. Therefore, the organization may request that employees work extra hours, such as during peak periods.

As mentioned in Chapter 1, the number of part-time employees has increased a great deal. Therefore, it is not unusual for companies to hire part-time staff to cover for absences of regular, full-time employees. Likewise, organizations will utilize the services of a temporary employment agency to acquire short-term staff, particularly in areas where a certain type of expertise is required, such as software programmers. In addition, an organization could increase the use of overtime, enhance retention strategies, and, as mentioned in Chapter 1, employees could be leased.

For more information on HR planning, see The HRM Guide at **www.hrmguide.net/canada/**.

Once a manager knows what work is to be done and the skills required to do the work successfully, the task of finding and selecting the right people begins.

The HRM Guide

www.hrmguide.net/canada/

RECRUITMENT

 Outcome **2**

Recruitment
The process of locating and encouraging potential applicants to apply for jobs

Once an organization has determined its needs, it must then recruit potential employees. The line manager, together with available HR professionals, will identify where a company might look for these candidates. **Recruitment** is the process of locating and encouraging potential applicants to apply for existing or anticipated job openings. The purpose of recruitment is to have a large pool of potentially qualified applicants. Figure 4.2 provides an overview of the recruitment process.

This process informs the applicants about the qualifications required to perform the job and the career opportunities the organization can offer its employees. Whether or not a particular job vacancy will be filled by someone within the organization or from outside will, of course, depend on the availability of people, the organization's HR practices, and the requirements of the job to be staffed.

One of the biggest challenges for organizations is to continue the recruitment process even during difficult economic times. As mentioned in the section on HR planning, and in Chapter 1 regarding the business environment and demographics, there is still a shortage of people with certain skill sets for certain types of industries. Therefore, it is important to focus on employee retention as well as focusing on accessing new talent. And given the demographics of the workforce, from people who are choosing not to retire to those just coming out of school, it is important to understand what employees are wanting to keep them in the organization through building a better workplace that makes people want to stay.[12]

In some cases there is a need for the organization to consider its "branding" from a future employer perspective. For those of you who have not had a course in marketing, "branding" refers to

FIGURE 4.2   The Recruitment Process

the need to have a total and holistic approach to how the marketplace sees the company and/or products. There is a desire to have a uniform image come into the consumer's mind when the company or product is visible. Many companies are now transferring the concept of "branding" to its employment framework—to have a uniform image come into prospective employees' minds (and existing employees) when the company name is mentioned. By using a branding approach to all aspects of employment, contemporary organizations can create an opportunity to retain their key talent.

Recruiting Within the Organization

Outcome 3

Most public sector organizations, and many private sector organizations, try to follow a policy of filling job vacancies above the entry-level position through promotions and transfers. By filling vacancies in this way, an organization can capitalize on the investment it has made in recruiting, selecting, training, and developing its current employees. Promotion-from-within policies at CIBC and Canada Mortgage and Housing Corporation have contributed to the companies' overall growth and success.

Advantages of Recruiting from Within

Promotion serves to reward employees for past performance and is intended to encourage them to continue their efforts. Promoting from within makes use of the people who already know the organization and the contribution they have made. It also gives other employees reason to anticipate that similar efforts by them will lead to promotion, thus improving morale within the organization. This is particularly true for members of designated groups who have encountered difficulties in finding employment and have often faced even greater difficulty in advancing within an organization. Most organizations have integrated promotion policies as an essential part of their employment equity programs.

Transfers can also serve to protect employees from layoff or to broaden their job experiences. This becomes more noticeable as organizations become flatter with fewer layers between the frontline employees and the executives. Furthermore, the transferred employee's familiarity with the organization and its operations can eliminate the orientation and training costs that recruitment from the outside would entail. Most important, the transferee's performance record is likely to be a more accurate predictor of the candidate's success than the data gained about outside applicants.

Methods of Locating Qualified Internal Job Candidates

The effective use of internal sources requires a system for locating qualified job candidates and for enabling those who consider themselves qualified to apply for the opening. Qualified job candidates within the organization can be located by using computerized record systems, and by internal job postings.

By filling job vacancies from within, organizations can capitalize on investments made in developing current employees.

Keith Brofsky/Photodisc Green/Getty Images

HRIS

HUMAN RESOURCE INFORMATION SYSTEMS Information technology has made it possible for organizations to create databases that contain the complete records and qualifications of each employee within an organization. Combined with increasingly user-friendly search engines, managers can access this information and identify potential candidates for available jobs. Organizations have developed résumé-tracking systems that allow managers to query an online database of résumés. Companies such as Oracle and SAP Canada are leaders in developing technology for staffing and skills management. Similar to the skills inventories mentioned earlier, these information systems allow an organization to rapidly screen its entire workforce to locate suitable candidates to fill an internal opening. These data can also be used to predict the career paths of employees and to anticipate when and where promotion opportunities may arise. Since the value of the data depends on its being kept up to date, the systems typically include provisions for recording changes in employee qualifications and job placements as they occur.[13]

SUCCESSION PLANNING It is quite likely that many organizations have done some succession planning—the process of identifying, developing, and tracking key employees for future promotions. Therefore, when a job opening occurs in a particular part of the organization, it might make use of the succession plan and put the employee into the vacancy. Succession plans rely upon the organization identifying its long-term goals, outlining the competencies required to achieve those goals, and making sure the employee is developed in order to assume other roles and take on other responsibilities.

INTERNAL JOB POSTING Organizations may advertise about job openings through a process referred to as **internal job posting.** In the past, this process has consisted largely of posting vacancy notices on company employment boards in an HR department or common area, such as lunchroom. In addition, internal advertising can also be done through a company's intranet, e-mails, or other types of internal memos, and company newsletters. Increasingly, companies such as Xerox are developing computerized job posting systems and maintaining voluntary lists of employees looking for upgraded positions. As part of the overall approach to assessing internal staff and their skill sets, organizations will use technology, including Web-based solutions, to determine if any staff have the necessary skills for a certain role.[14]

Internal job posting can provide many benefits to an organization. However, these benefits may not be realized unless employees believe the process is being administered fairly. Furthermore, it is more effective when internal job posting is part of a career development program in which employees are made aware of opportunities available to them within the organization. For example, the organization may provide new employees with literature on job progression that describes the lines of job advancement, training requirements for each job, and skills and abilities needed as they move up the job-progression ladder.

Internal job posting
Method of communicating information about job openings

Limitations of Recruiting from Within

Sometimes certain jobs that require specialized training and experience cannot be filled from within the organization and must be filled from the outside. This is especially common in small organizations. Also, for certain openings it may be necessary to hire individuals from the outside who have gained the knowledge and expertise required for these jobs from another employer.

Even though the company may encourage that job openings be filled from within the organization, potential candidates from the outside should be considered in order to prevent the inbreeding of ideas and attitudes. Applicants hired from the outside, particularly for certain technical and managerial positions, can be a source of new ideas and may bring with them the latest knowledge acquired from their previous employers. Indeed, excessive reliance on internal sources can create the risk of "employee cloning." Furthermore, it is not uncommon for firms in competitive fields, such as high technology or retailing, to attempt to gain secrets and managerial talent from competitors by hiring away their employees.

Recruiting Outside the Organization

Frequently, organizations will decide to fill positions by bringing people in from outside the organization. Thus, when a mid-level manager of the organization leaves, a chain reaction of promotions may subsequently occur. This creates other openings throughout the organization. The question, therefore, is not whether to bring people into the organization, but rather at which level they are to be brought in.

Usually, external recruitment is organized and coordinated by an HR department with the line manager frequently giving suggestions about where to recruit, such as an ad in a newspaper or professional journal. However, if there is no HR department, the line manager will perform this function. These people need to be aware of such things as labour market conditions and where to recruit.

In the past few years, organizations such as Barrick Gold, Espresso, and Porche Cars Canada have brought in outsiders to be their new CEOs. In fact, a very high percentage of Fortune 500 companies who replace their CEOs do so by hiring executives from outside their companies. In many of these cases, hiring someone from the outside is seen as bringing in new ideas, different styles, and new energy.[15]

Advantages and Disadvantages of External Recruitment

Like recruiting from within, external recruitment has advantages and disadvantages. One advantage of bringing someone in from outside the organization is that the individual brings certain unique skills that the company needs now. Likewise, it is possible to bring in people with a variety of different experiences and perspectives.

A disadvantage to external recruitment is the lack of solid information about the person's performance on the job. That information is available only through second-hand sources, such as what the applicant volunteers and what references might say. Also, the person may not know the industry or organization, necessitating more extensive orientation and training. Further, there may be constraints in the organization, such as salary levels, that prevent the organization from accessing a large pool of applicants. In addition, there are usually significant costs associated with external recruitment. These costs include the amount of time, the cost of advertising (sometimes as much as $9,000 per newspaper), and the cost of familiarizing the person with the organization. Lastly, there may be legislative requirements, such as employment equity, which lead to certain applicant pools.

The Labour Market

Labour market
Area from which applicants are recruited

The **labour market,** or the area from which applicants are recruited, will vary with the type of position to be filled and the amount of compensation to be paid. Recruitment for executives and technical personnel who require a high degree of knowledge and skill may be national or even international in scope. Most colleges and universities, for example, conduct national employment searches to fill top administrative positions. Recruitment for jobs that require relatively little skill, however, may encompass only a small geographic area. The reluctance of people to relocate may cause them to turn down offers of employment, thereby eliminating them from employment consideration beyond the local labour market.

The condition of the labour market may also help to determine which recruiting sources an organization will use. During periods of high unemployment, organizations may be able to maintain an adequate supply of qualified applicants from unsolicited résumés alone. A tight labour market, one with low unemployment, may force the employer to advertise heavily and/or seek assistance from local employment agencies. How successful an organization has been in reaching its employment equity goals may be still another factor in determining the sources from which to recruit. Typically, an employer at any given time will find it necessary to utilize several recruitment sources.[16]

For a number of years, Canada has relied on immigration to assist in meeting the demand for labour. While other countries may be reducing the number of immigrants, Canada has set a target for 2009 the same as 2008.[17] In addition, the department responsible for immigration, Citizenship and Immigration Canada, has worked with businesses to create processes that are more responsive to labour market shortfalls. Some of the occupations that are highly recruited for in other countries are: health care workers and skilled trades.[18] These changes are intended to allow applicants into Canada that have the skills that are in short-supply. As mentioned in Chapter 1, Canada has an aging population with insufficient younger workers to fill the work requirements in the future. Further, as more and more individuals become part of a global talent pool, companies will seek a number of ways to recruit beyond one's home country.

Outside Sources of Recruitment

The outside sources from which employers recruit will vary with the type of position to be filled. A software developer, for example, is not likely to be recruited from the same source as a retail service person. Trade schools can provide applicants for entry-level positions, though these recruitment sources are not as useful when highly skilled employees are needed. Networking, referrals from previous and existing staff, information from customers/clients, and being involved in the community are a few ways that organizations seek people outside the organization. A variety of new and creative recruitment approaches is emerging, including Web-based social networks such as MySpace, Facebook, LinkedIn, and Twitter. For example, LinkedIn (**www.linkedin.com**) recently expanded its site to support corporate recruiters including company information that the company can configure to match the particular job opening.[19]

Some of the major outside sources of recruitment are described below.

LinkedIn
www.linkedin.com

MySpace
www.myspace.com

Facebook
www.facebook.com

Twitter
twitter.com

ADVERTISEMENTS One of the frequent methods of attracting applicants is through advertisements. Although websites, newspapers, and trade journals are the media used most often, radio, television, billboards, posters, and e-mail are also used. Advertising has the advantage of reaching a large audience of possible applicants. Some degree of selectivity can be achieved by using newspapers and journals directed toward a particular group of readers. Professional journals, trade journals, and publications of unions and nonprofit organizations fall into this category.

As Manager's Toolkit 4.1 illustrates, the preparation of recruiting advertisements requires creativity in developing design and message content. Well-written advertisements highlight the major assets of the position while showing the responsiveness of the organization to the job and career needs of the applicants. Among the information typically included in advertisements is a statement that the recruiting organization is an equal-opportunity employer.

Human Resources and Skills Development Canada
www.hrsdc.gc.ca

Canada's Human Resources and Skills Development (HRSDC) branches (**www.hrsdc.gc.ca**) are responsible for administering the Employment Insurance program and can be found in most communities. Individuals who become unemployed must register at one of these offices and be available for "suitable employment" in order to receive their weekly employment insurance cheques. Consequently, public employment agencies are able to refer to employers with job openings those applicants with the required skills who are available for employment. Applicants for jobs can access the Employment Telemessage system via the telephone, or review online information at the centre itself. There is also a national job bank that lists information about jobs across the country.

In addition, HRSDC provides assistance to employers in approving special work permits to enable people from other countries to move to Canada for employment. While approvals of special permits have become more difficult during the recession, Canada still has a shortage of skilled workers in long haul trucking, doctors, nurses, and certain medical technologists such as lab and x-ray.[20]

Jobserve
www.jobserve.ca

Monster
www.monster.ca

Workopolis
www.workopolis.ca

INTERNET The Internet is the most commonly used search tactic by job seekers; 60% of Canadians with Internet access have gone online in search of a job. Both companies and applicants find the approach cheaper, faster, and potentially more effective. At Work with HRM 4.1 describes how Jobserve links companies with people who have the necessary skills.

Further, many companies use their websites to announce job openings. For example, Wal-Mart Canada posts detailed information about job openings at its website. Likewise, WestJet and CIBC actively use their company websites to encourage people to consider working for them. Canadian recruiting sites include Monster.ca (**www.monster.ca**), Workopolis (**www.workopolis.ca**), NiceJob (**www.nicejob.ca**), and working.com (**www.working.com**), a site that provides information about job opportunities listed in the major Canadian newspapers. In addition, Human Resources and Skills Development Canada (HRSDC) has a virtual library of career and employment information (**www.jobbank.gc.ca**).

NiceJob
www.nicejob.ca

working.com
working.com

HRSDC Job Bank
www.jobbank.gc.ca

Employers claim that the Internet is faster (with some job applicants responding within 30 minutes of the job posting); that it generates higher-quality candidates; and that it is cheaper (by as much as 80%) than traditional advertising media. An Internet posting can be as low as $50 per month compared to a newspaper ad of $6,000 per day, with Monster and Workopolis being about $750 per job posting. According to a SHRM (Society for Human Resource Management) study, checking postings on the Internet is the most commonly used search tactic by job seekers

Source: Courtesy of Spectra Energy Transmission

and 9 out of 10 recruiters use the Internet to get the word out about new positions.[21] For example, Monster has over 10 million visitors per month.[22] Both companies and job seekers find the approach is cheaper, faster, and potentially more effective. Estimates are that there are more than 4000 websites where applicants can submit their employment backgrounds and potential employers can check for qualified candidates. A capability like this can help companies find the people with the competencies that are required in today's dynamic business environment.

There is also a need to prepare Internet advertisements in a careful way so that the website does attract the qualified people you are seeking. Manager's Toolkit 4.2 provides tips for creating such a website. But having a Web-based ad is not sufficient. The organization must also have the means to easily and quickly process the number of applications that can come from this tool. To help organizations screen

AT WORK **with HRM 4.1**

JOBSERVE.CA

Jobserve was Canada's first online job site and it helps link job seekers with jobs that match their needs and skills. According to the company, the process is fast and effective, and very, very simple for those with little time to pursue jobs.

The job seeker searches for career opportunities by category (such as advertising) and then by location (such as Alberta-all cities). All available positions are then listed for that location. Once the job seeker finds the appropriate position(s), the person applies with some basic information online and then uploads both a cover letter and résumé. Recruiting companies post jobs, listing skills required. Very sophisticated software matches job seekers to the posted opportunities. Within minutes of a company posting a job, the application-matching software sends a notification by e-mail to the job seekers whose profiles match it, giving a detailed job description, salary, etc. The job seeker can reply by e-mail or by an internal messaging system.

In addition, the site can also provide instant messaging to job seekers.

Jobserve.ca prides itself in having technology that can get the match of the right candidate with the right job. It has over 220,000 postings each month with over 1 million résumés on file. And employers can search the résumé database at any time they wish. The service is free for job seekers, but the companies pay a fee based on the number of jobs advertised.

Jobserve is a Canadian company with job opportunities posted for the U.K., Australia, and the U.S.

CRITICAL THINKING QUESTIONS

1. What do you think is making Internet recruiting so popular?

2. What are the potential problems that can happen with Internet recruiting?

large amounts of information from online sources, companies have integrated front-end career websites with their own databases.[23] This type of software can pull the right data from all candidates and organize the data that makes the review of the applicants more efficient. In addition, résumés are stored and the software is sophisticated enough to connect candidates directly to the hiring manager. Some of the technology in use, particularly in larger organizations, enables the job application to be moved electronically from one step to another, thus ensuring that a good candidate isn't lost due to lengthy delays.

Companies, such as Finning International and Hydro One, and organizations, such as the federal government and the Government of Ontario, use the Internet to attract people. Employers indicate that the reason is to increase the opportunity to attract the people with the right skill sets for their organizations.

MANAGER'S TOOLKIT **4.2**

DEVELOPING EFFECTIVE WEBSITE ADVERTISEMENTS

1. Design a creative job advertisement. Work as hard building the "employer" brand as you do the product brand.

2. Market the company—don't sell a job. Talk about the vision and the opportunities and provide an overview of the company.

3. Use familiar job titles.

4. Create job information that talks about what the employee will be doing and the potential for the future.

5. Link your site to other sites, anything from career sites and trade sites to game sites—anywhere your potential employee might surf.

6. Once candidates have entered your employment site, let them join forums or connect with an employee similar to them. Give them a reason to return.

7. Use a video link to create a virtual tour of the work site and other employees.

Sources: Adapted from Antonio da Luz, "Video Enhances Online Job Ads," *Canadian HR Reporter*, November 2, 2008; and Rick Milgram, "Getting the Most Out of Online Job Ads," *Canadian HR Reporter*, www.hrreporter.com (accessed January 22, 2009).

EMPLOYMENT AGENCIES Employment agencies, including executive search firms and temporary employment agencies, attempt to match applicants with the specific needs of a company. A fee is charged to the employer for services that are tailored to the employer. By law, job seekers cannot be charged for helping in finding work. It is common for such agencies to specialize in serving a specific occupational area, such as office staff or technical computer people. Private agencies usually focus on clerical, technical, and junior–middle management whereas executive search firms tend to focus on senior and executive management. These agencies may charge an employer 25 to 30% of the annual salary if they find a candidate who gets hired. Since these agencies differ in the services they offer, job seekers would be wise to take the time to find a recruiter who is knowledgeable, experienced, and professional. When talking with potential recruiters, individuals should discuss openly their philosophies and practices with regard to recruiting strategies, including advertising, in-house recruiting, screening procedures, and costs for these efforts.

Executive search firms (also called "headhunters") are employment agencies that typically focus on senior-level and executive-level managerial positions. The search tends to be very focused to that specific employer. The fees charged by the agencies to the employer may range from 30 to 40% of the annual salary for the position to be filled. The employer pays this fee.

As noted earlier, it is an increasingly common occurrence to bring in new chief executive officers (CEOs) from outside the organization. A large number of these new CEOs are placed in those positions through the services of an executive search firm. Since high-calibre executives are in short supply, a significant number of the nation's largest corporations, including the Government of Alberta and Memorial University, use executive search firms to fill their top positions.

Agencies that provide temporary employees is one of the fastest-growing recruitment sources. Companies such as Imperial Oil Ltd., International Forest Products, and SaskTel use temporary employees extensively. "Temps" are typically used for short-term assignments or to help when managers cannot justify hiring a full-time employee, such as for vacation fill-ins, for peak work periods, or during an employee's parental or sick leave.

Increasingly, temps are being employed to fill positions once staffed by permanent employees. At Hydro-Québec, for example, "long-term temporaries" have replaced permanent hires as a staffing practice. Employees are hired for one- to three-year terms. This practice is growing because temporaries can be laid off quickly, and with less cost, when work lessens. The use of temporaries thus becomes a viable way to maintain proper staffing levels. Also, the employment costs of temporaries can often be lower than those of permanent employees because temps are usually not provided with benefits and can be dismissed without the need to file employment insurance claims.

The drawbacks of contract employees are that their commitment to the company is lower than that of full-time employees, and they may take confidential information to their next employer, possibly a competitor.

Check out the websites of Angus One Professional Recruiters (**www.angusone.com**), Olsten Staffing Services (**www.olsten.com**), Korn/Ferry International (**www.kornferry.com**), and Manpower, one of Canada's largest temporary agencies (**www.manpower.ca**) to find out more about employment agencies.

Angus One Professional Recruiters
www.angusone.com

Olsten Staffing Services
www.olsten.com

Korn/Ferry International
www.kornferry.com

Manpower
www.manpower.ca

EDUCATIONAL INSTITUTIONS Educational institutions are a source of young applicants with formal training but relatively little full-time work experience. High schools are usually a source of employees for clerical and blue-collar jobs. Community colleges, with their various types of specialized training, can provide candidates for technical jobs. These institutions can also be a source of applicants for a variety of white-collar jobs, including those in the sales and retail fields. Some management-trainee jobs are also staffed from this source. Humber College in Etobicoke, Ontario, and the BC Institute of Technology offer a Human Resource Management post-diploma program. For technical and managerial positions, universities are generally the primary source. It is important for employers to be aware of what attracts students to employers. A survey was commissioned by nine larger employers that asked about 20,000 students from nearly every Canadian university and college about the factors they considered in choosing full-time employment. The top ranked factor was "opportunities for advancement" with #2 being "good people to work with."[24] Recently, a Canadian-wide accounting firm during its campus recruiting took a unique approach and merely asked students "what they want."[25]

OPEN HOUSES AND JOB FAIRS Organizations may also use open houses and job fairs to recruit new employees—particularly if the organization is expanding or is looking for particular types of skills. For example, with the shortage of skilled trades, an organization might participate in a job fair at an educational institution that graduates tradespeople. Or the organization might have an open house where potential applicants are encouraged to visit the company and see what might be available. Seasonal resort operations such as Whistler/Blackcomb in British Columbia use open houses at the start of each ski season as a way to attract people with a variety of skills. A recent innovative approach to job fairs was the creation of a "virtual" national career fair in June 2009. Sponsored by Shell Canada and Equitek, the fair was presented by **working.com** and enabled participants to have a virtual chat with employers, submit a résumé in real time, and to read articles from career experts.[26]

EMPLOYEE REFERRALS The recruitment efforts of an organization can be aided by employee referrals or recommendations made by current employees. Managers have found that the quality of employee-referred applicants is normally quite high, since employees are generally hesitant to recommend individuals who might not perform well. The effectiveness of this recruitment effort can be increased by paying commissions to employees when they make a successful "recruitment sale." A creative approach to referrals is through Bohire (**bohire.com**), a Web-based referral community. While it is a job board, people cannot apply directly. People refer other people to the jobs posted. And there is a cash payment to the referee by the employer if the person referred is hired.[27] Other types of incentives include paid time off and travel.[28] An organization, however, needs to ensure in utilizing employee referrals that it is not creating a situation of systemic discrimination.

UNSOLICITED APPLICATIONS AND RÉSUMÉS Many employers receive unsolicited applications and résumés from individuals who may or may not be good prospects for employment.[29] Even though the percentage of acceptable applicants from this source may not be high, it is a source that cannot be ignored. Many job search strategies suggest that individuals use this method to introduce themselves to organizations that are of interest to them.[30]

Good public relations dictate that any person contacting an organization for a job be treated with courtesy and respect. If there is no possibility of employment in the organization at present or in the future, the applicant should be tactfully and frankly informed of this fact.

PROFESSIONAL ORGANIZATIONS Many professional organizations and societies offer a placement service to members as one of their benefits. Listings of members seeking employment may be advertised in their journals or publicized at their national meetings. A placement

Johnson & Johnson uses job fairs as a way to attract applicants.

CP Photo/AP Photo/Mel Evans

centre is usually established at national meetings for the mutual benefit of employers and job seekers.

UNIONS If a company is unionized and has employees that belong to labour unions, those unions can be a principal source of applicants for blue-collar (such as welders, electricians, plumbers) and some professional jobs. Some unions, such as those in the maritime, printing, and construction industries, maintain hiring halls that can provide a supply of applicants, particularly for short-term needs. Employers wishing to use this recruitment source should contact their local union for employer eligibility requirements and applicant availability.

RECRUITMENT FOR DIVERSITY As organizations continue to have a diverse workforce, employers will often focus on attracting potential staff in communities of different ethnic and cultural backgrounds. Those employers that fall under the federal employment equity legislation (see Chapter 2) are expected to have a recruitment program that focuses on the designated groups of women, visible minorities, people with disabilities, and First Nations People. While Canada does not have a quota system (compared to the U.S.), under employment equity legislation, there is an expectation that over time those organizations that fall under the legislation have a workforce that is reflective of the general population of Canada.

As indicated in a recent study of the S&P 500 over the last five years, companies that aggressively sought and supported a diverse workforce outperformed the other companies in the study. According to Rajesh Subramaniam, CEO of FedEx Canada, "We have a tendency to reject what is different. And at the time, we need what is different. Because what is different is the only way we can grow. Sameness is suicide in the business world—particularly now as we operate in the global economy."[31] Therefore, it will be important for line managers and supervisors to be knowledgeable about and supportive of their organization's objective to have employees with diverse ethnic and cultural backgrounds. Managers may also be actively involved in recruitment "outreach" programs, where they speak at ethnic community centres to let people know about employment opportunities with their company. Other avenues for recruiting designated groups include ethnic community newspapers and TV stations. Maple Leaf Sports and Entertainment recently extended itself into the South Asian community by ensuring that hockey games were broadcast in Punjabi.[32]

A particularly effective organization in bridging the immigrant gap is the Toronto Region Immigrant Employment Council (TRIEC) (**www.triec.ca/**). It is an innovative partnership between employers, unions, post-secondary institutions, other community organizations, and government. The organization came into existence in 2003 when the city identified that to have well-settled and satisfied immigrants, it was necessary to have successful employment opportunities. The mission of the organization is to create and facilitate solutions to better the integration of immigrants into the regional workforce.[33] It is unique in that it doesn't work directly with immigrants but provides a collaborative approach to engaging the various parties that can help immigrants get settled, find work, and succeed in Canada.

There are also a number of organizations that help new immigrants, people with disabilities, and First Nations people find work. These are good sources for employers to find potential employees.

Other similar organizations include: MOSAIC (**www.mosaicbc.com**), Costi Immigrant Services (**www.costi.org/**), Diversity World (**www.diversityworld.com**), Canadian Abilities Foundation (**www.abilities.ca**), Aboriginal Skills and Employment Partnership (**www.hrsdc.gc.ca/eng/employment/aboriginal_training/index.shtml**), and Nation Talk (**www.nationtalk.ca/**).

TRIEC
www.triec.ca/

MOSAIC
www.mosaicbc.com

Costi Immigrant Services
www.costi.org/

Diversity World
www.diversityworld.com

Canadian Abilities Foundation
www.abilities.ca

Aboriginal Skills and Employment Partnership
www.hrsdc.gc.ca/eng/employment/aboriginal_training/index.shtml

Nation Talk
www.nationtalk.ca

SELECTION

Outcome 5

Once the recruitment process has yielded applicants whose qualifications appear to fit the organization's requirements, you then must assess those qualifications and make a decision on whom to hire—which individual or individuals will perform best on the job. It is usually the line manager's responsibility to make the final selection decision. If there is an HR department, it will usually play a supporting role by arranging interviews, doing reference checking, administering employment tests, and so on. However, if there is no HR professional to help, the line manager needs to know these steps and their importance.

Matching People and Jobs

Selection
The process of choosing individuals who have relevant qualifications and who will best perform on the job to fill existing or projected job openings

Making hiring decisions is not a scientific process, and, therefore, it cannot be structured to achieve perfect results. However, by being systematic in the selection process, there is a greater possibility of having staff that can do the work and achieve the goals of the organization.[34] **Selection** is the process of choosing individuals who have relevant qualifications to fill existing or projected job openings. Those responsible for making selection decisions should have adequate information on which to base their decisions. Information about the jobs to be filled, and as much relevant information as possible about the applicants themselves, is essential for making sound decisions. The objective is to have information that will predict job performance of the candidate in the organization.

Prior to the selection process, it is important to reconfirm the necessary knowledge, skills, and abilities for the job. As mentioned in Chapter 3, these job requirements are identified through job analysis. Managers can then use selection methods, such as interviews, references, psychological tests, and the like, to assess the applicant's competencies and match these against the requirements of the job and the needs of the organization.[35]

Ordinarily, managers are well acquainted with the requirements pertaining to skills, physical demands, and other factors for jobs in their respective departments. If the interview step includes professionals from the HR department, the HR professional will need to maintain a close liaison with the various departments to become thoroughly familiar with the jobs and competencies needed to perform them.

The Selection Process

Outcome 6

In most organizations, selection is a continuous process. Turnover inevitably occurs, leaving vacancies to be filled by applicants from inside or outside the organization or by individuals whose qualifications have been assessed previously. In some situations, organizations will have a waiting list of applicants who can be called when permanent or temporary positions become available.

The number of steps in the selection process and their sequence will vary, not only with the organization but also with the type and level of jobs to be filled. Each step should be evaluated on its contribution. The steps that typically make up the selection process are shown in Figure 4.3. Not all applicants will go through all these steps. Some may be rejected after a review of their application form or résumé, or after a preliminary interview.

As shown in Figure 4.3, organizations use several different means to obtain information about applicants. These include application forms and résumés, interviews, tests, and reference checks. Regardless of the method used, it is essential that it conform to accepted ethical standards, including privacy and confidentiality, as well as legal requirements. Above all, it is essential that the information obtained be sufficiently reliable and valid.

FIGURE 4.3   Steps in the Selection Process

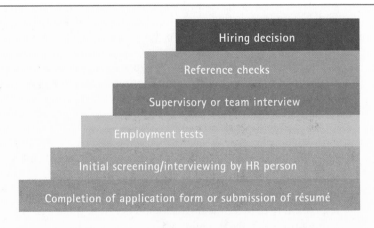

Note: Steps may vary. An applicant may be rejected after any step in the process.

Obtaining Reliable and Valid Information

The degree to which interviews, tests, and other selection procedures yield comparable data over a period of time is known as **reliability.** For example, unless interviewers judge the capabilities of a group of applicants to be the same today as they did yesterday, their judgments are unreliable (i.e., unstable). Likewise, a test that gives widely different scores when it is administered to the same individual a few days apart is unreliable.

In addition to having reliable information pertaining to a person's suitability for a job, the information must be as valid as possible. **Validity** refers to what a test or other selection procedure measures and how well it measures it. In the context of employee selection, validity is essentially an indicator of the extent to which data from a procedure (interview or test, for example) predict job performance. However, whether something is valid depends upon the selection tool's overall reliability. Therefore, whatever selection procedures or tools are used—whether an interview or an employment test—they must be both reliable and valid in order to provide useful information about predicting the applicant's performance in the organization. And the procedure or tool used may need to be modified (or not used) or the results carefully evaluated due to cultural differences. For example, companies that screen job applicants for values will not get good information about a person's overall capability to perform the job successfully; the best overall predictor for job performance (and training success) is the person's general mental abilities.[36]

Sources of Information about Job Candidates

Outcome 7

Many sources of information are used to provide as reliable and valid a picture as possible of an applicant's potential for success on the job. This section looks at the usefulness of application forms and résumés, reference checks, employment tests, and interviews.

Application Forms and Résumés

Most organizations require application forms to be completed because they provide a fairly quick and systematic means of obtaining a variety of information about the applicant. Application forms serve several purposes:

- They provide information for deciding whether an applicant meets the minimum requirements for experience, education, and so on.
- They provide a basis for questions the interviewer will ask about the applicant's background.
- They also offer sources for reference checks. For certain jobs, a short application form is appropriate.

As mentioned in the section on Internet sourcing, many organizations no longer are using paper applications and are having you apply for work directly online. In some cases there is an electronic application and in other cases you merely send your résumé to an e-mail address.

Individuals frequently exaggerate or overstate their qualifications on a résumé. However, the consequences of falsifying information on applications and résumés are frequently severe, such as termination. But candidates not only exaggerate; in a tight labour market, candidates sometimes delete advanced qualifications, as described in Ethics in HRM 4.1. Other cases highlight the importance of integrity in job applications. Some observers estimate that at least 33% of applicants "stretch" the truth on their résumés. Ethics in HRM 4.1 also describes these situations. Depending on the nature of the work or the organization, a person may be expected to fill out a questionnaire seeking very specific information to determine the person's fit to that organization.[37]

Résumés are prepared by the applicant and provide job-related information about the job seeker. A résumé will usually contain sections on work experience, education, volunteer activities, and personal interests. In preparing and presenting résumés, applicants can display their creativity in how they present themselves.

Students can practice reading and analyzing résumés online at these sites:

- www.pongoresume.com
- www.cecs.uwaterloo.ca/manual
- www.careermag.com
- jobstar.org/tools/resume/index.php

Reliability
The degree to which interviews, tests, and other selection procedures yield comparable data over time and alternative measures

Validity
How well a test or selection procedure measures a person's attributes

Pongo Résumé
www.pongoresume.com

University of Waterloo
www.cecs.uwaterloo.ca/manual

Career Magazine
www.careermag.com

JobStar
jobstar.org/tools/resume/index.php

ETHICS in HRM 4.1

WRITING IT WRONG

Most candidates for white-collar jobs prepare a résumé and submit it to prospective employers. They also complete the application form, answering questions required by employers for comparison purposes. Some recruitment agencies noticed during the last recession that résumé padding increased. Applicants were "stretching" the dates of their employment, misleading employers about the nature of their duties, and misrepresenting their salaries. While you are writing a résumé, adding three months to your previous employment, saying you were a night auditor instead of clerk, and adding $950 to your last salary seem like relatively harmless lies.

What are the facts? Studies of "creative" résumé writing indicate that about 30% of résumés report incorrect dates, 11% misrepresent reasons for leaving, and others exaggerate education attainments or omit criminal records. The probability is that about two-thirds of employers check references. Some former employers give only dates of employment and previous salary ranges.

Most organizations require you to sign a statement saying that the information you supply is true, and that if it is not you will be dismissed. Some cases of résumé padding have been heavily publicized. A Toronto Stock Exchange manager was dismissed for lying about having a master's degree. A Member of Parliament listed an ILB on his résumé, which normally stands for International Baccalaureate of Law, but which he claimed stood for Incomplete Baccalaureate of Law. In one heart-wrenching case, a person who was ready to retire was found to have lied about his age decades earlier to get a job. On discovery, he was dismissed and lost his pension. In another case, a Canadian businessman was sentenced to eight months in jail in New Zealand for lying on his résumé, by listing false qualifications, such as an MBA.

In a labour market where there are too many people chasing too few jobs, candidates will also lie on their résumés, but do so by dropping experience and educational qualifications. This practice, called "stripping," is used because job seekers are ready to take any job in order to survive or to hold them over until the jobs they really want are available.

Many managers remain unclear about the questions they can ask on an application form. While most know they should steer clear of such issues as age, race, marital status, and sexual orientation, other issues are less clear. The following are some suggestions for putting together an application form:

- *Application date.* The applicant should date the application. This helps managers know when the form was completed and gives them an idea of the time limit (for example, one year) that the form should be on file.
- *Educational background.* The applicant should also provide grade school, high school, college, and university attendance—but not the dates attended, since that can be connected with age.
- *Experience.* Virtually any questions that focus on work experience related to the job are permissible.
- *Arrests and criminal convictions.* Questions about arrests, convictions, and criminal records are to be avoided. If bonding is a requirement, ask if the individual can be bonded.
- *Country of citizenship.* Such questions are not permitted. It is allowable to ask if the person is legally entitled to work in Canada.
- *References.* It is both permissible and advisable that the names, addresses, and phone numbers of references be provided. (References are covered in more detail below.)
- *Disabilities.* Employers should avoid asking applicants if they have physical disabilities or health problems, if they have ever received psychiatric care or have been hospitalized, or if they have received workers' compensation.

Look at Emerging Trends 4.1 for the latest techniques used in developing resumes.

The Employment Interview

Traditionally, the employment interview has played a very important role in the selection process—so much so that it is rare to find an instance where an employee is hired without some sort of interview. Depending on the type of job, applicants may be interviewed by one person, by members of a work

EMERGING TRENDS **4.1**

1. *Video résumés.* With the evolution of so many different technologies, job seekers, especially those in creative fields, are using video technology to present their résumés. While there can be a number of legal issues associated with this for the potential employer, it has had some appeal for certain organizations.

2. *Use of keywords.* Companies that use sophisticated software to match a person's résumé to the opportunities within the organization will frequently screen or use "keywords" in the matching process. The technology behind this is very similar to that used by students when doing an electronic data base or Google search.

3. *Increased use of social networks.* More and more job seekers are using their contacts on social networks to get both recommendations and to post their résumés. Likewise, many organizations will search the various social network sites to gather information about applicants.

Sources: Adapted from "Résumés Redefined," CareerBuilder.com, www.careerbuilder.com/Article/CB-977-Cover-Letters-and-Resumes-R%C3%A9sum%C3%A9s-Redefined/?ArticleID=977 (accessed January 28, 2009); "Video Résumés Work," CV.TV; and "LinkedIn Beefing Up Recruiting Tools," *Workforce Management,* January 9, 2009.

team, or by other individuals in the organization. While researchers have raised some doubts about its validity, the interview remains a mainstay of selection because (1) it is especially practical when there are only a small number of applicants; (2) it serves other purposes, such as public relations; and (3) interviewers maintain great faith and confidence in their judgments. Nevertheless, the interview can be plagued by problems of subjectivity and personal bias. In such cases, some interviewers' judgments are more valid than those of others in the evaluation of applicants. Remember, the purpose of the interview is to gather relevant information to determine if the candidate has the skills, abilities, and knowledge to be successful on the job in the organization. However, it is also critical that the interview questions are based on the work requirements (as determined through the job analysis) and specific knowledge required for the job. Further, the interviewer needs to have been appropriately trained to ensure that the interview is conducted in a professional and business-like manner.[38]

Interviewing Methods

Employment or selection interviews differ according to the methods used to obtain information and to find out an applicant's attitudes, feelings, and behaviours. Organizations have a variety of methods to choose from. Further, depending on the number of interviews, more than one method may be used.

ONE-ON-ONE Most often, the first face-to-face interview occurs between the applicant and an interviewer. The interviewer could be an HR professional or a supervisor. Questions are asked and observations are made of both the interviewer and the applicant. The structure of the questions could be behavioural description interview (BDI), situational, or non-directive. (The different types of questions are explained below.)

PANEL OR GROUP INTERVIEW This type of interview involves a panel of interviewers who question and observe a single candidate. In a typical **panel** (or **group) interview**, the candidate meets with several interviewers who take turns asking questions. After the interview, the interviewers pool their observations to reach a consensus about the suitability of the candidate. It is reported that when people work together as a team, it is particularly useful to have some of the team members form the interview panel as much more in-depth questions can be asked of the candidates.[39] During the interview, the panel may use structured questions, situational questions, BDI questions, or a combination of all three.

TELEPHONE INTERVIEW Generally, organizations are doing more interviews today than they have done in the past. Much of this is caused by the need to make a better hire decision than in the past. Companies have assessed that a poor decision can be very costly and want to minimize the costs.

Panel interview
An interview in which a board of interviewers questions and observes a single candidate

Therefore, many companies use a telephone interview as the first interview in the screening process. This interview can be conducted by someone from the company, or with the advent of technology, companies can use software where applicants are asked to respond to questions by touching a keypad.

INTERNET-BASED INTERVIEW The increased use of technology has not only helped in creating a way to recruit job applicants, technology has also enabled organizations to pre-screen or assess applicants online. A growing number of organizations have been using online assessment tools to help with the interview process. Some companies will assess online using the GMA (general mental ability) tool or personality profiles. Sometimes the candidates are asked to answer a series of multiple-choice questions tailored to the job. These answers are compared either with an ideal profile or with the profiles developed on the basis of other candidates' responses. Using computer-based technology can also assist in filtering out unqualified candidates. Depending on the company and software in use, a computer interview conducted in conjunction with online tests can measure everything from contradictory responses to time delays related to answering to the applicants' keyboarding skills. For example, Wal-Mart uses this type of technology when screening for cashiers, stockers, and customer service representatives.[40]

In addition to the benefits of objectivity, some research evidence suggests that applicants may be less likely to engage in "impression management" in computerized interviews than in face-to-face interviews. Using such technology is typically at the initial stages of the interview process.[41]

Types of Interview Questions

Regardless of the type of interview method used, questions must be asked of the applicant. In addition, for an interview to be reliable, the questions must be stated in such a way that the same questions are asked of each applicant. The questions can be very specific to get specific answers (structured) or they can be less structured where very broad and open-ended questions are asked. Listed below are the types of interview questions typically used.

STRUCTURED QUESTIONS Since the objective of an interview is to gather data for making a decision, companies will look at the interview process as an investment and therefore create structured questions to determine if the person has the competencies to do the work.[42] Because a structured question is based on job requirements and an established set of answers against which applicant responses can be rated, they provide a more consistent basis for evaluating job candidates. Structured questions are more likely to provide the type of information needed for making sound decisions. They also help to reduce the possibility of legal charges of discrimination. Employers must be aware that any interview is highly vulnerable to legal attack and that more challenges (human rights and grievances) in this area can be expected in the future. The two main types of structured questions are discussed below.

Behavioural description interview (BDI)

Question about what a person actually did in a given situation

The leading type of interview question being used is a **behavioural description interview (BDI).** A BDI question focuses on real work incidents, not hypothetical situations as a situational interview question does. The BDI format asks job applicants what they actually did in a given situation. For example, to assess a potential manager's ability to handle a problem employee, an interviewer might ask, "Tell me about the last time you disciplined an employee." Or the format might be this sequence:

1. Describe a situation when you disciplined an employee.
2. What was the action taken?
3. What were the results?

Manager's Toolkit 4.3 provides an example of a BDI question and approach for interviewing someone for a front-desk position in a hotel.

Such an approach to interviewing is based on solid research that past performance is the best predictor of future performance. You will notice that with this type of interview, the questions can produce a variety of responses. The interviewer usually will clarify or ask further questions to get the necessary information. Many more organizations are using BDI questions to better assess the applicant's ability to perform successfully in the organization's environment. If you have recently looked for work, you may have encountered BDI questions.

This type of interview question is being used more for a number of reasons:

MANAGER'S TOOLKIT **4.3**

SAMPLE BDI INTERVIEW QUESTION

You are being considered for work in our hotel. As we encounter difficult situations with our customers, please describe a time you had to tell a customer that there was no reservation for a room. What action did you take? What were the results?

Some additional clarification might be gained from the following questions:

Was there any aspect of your decision that you were uncertain about?

Did the customer have information that you didn't have?

Could anyone overhear the customer?

What decision did you finally make?

1. Questions are based on the job requirements directly related to the skills necessary.
2. Answers are more easily rated against established criteria.
3. Minimizes bias on the part of interviewers.[43]

Situational question
Question in which an applicant is given a hypothetical incident and asked how he or she would respond to it

Another variation of a structured question is called a **situational question.** With this type of question, an applicant is given a hypothetical incident and asked to respond to it. The applicant's response is then evaluated relative to pre-established benchmark standards. Interestingly, many organizations are using situational questions to select new college graduates. Manager's Toolkit 4.4 shows a sample situational question used to select systems analysts at a chemical plant.

UNSTRUCTURED QUESTIONS These types of questions are broad and open-ended and allows the candidate to talk freely with little interruption from the interviewer. For example, an interviewer might ask: "Tell me more about your experiences on your last job." Through these questions, the applicant is allowed a great deal of latitude in guiding the discussions. Generally, the nondirective interviewer listens carefully and does not argue, interrupt, or change the subject abruptly. The interviewer also uses follow-up questions to allow the applicant to elaborate, makes only brief responses, and allows pauses in the conversation; the pausing technique is the most difficult for the beginning interviewer to master. There are some recruitment specialists that believe that an interview that is more conversational can provide better insight into who the person is.[44]

WHICH TYPE OF QUESTIONS TO USE? The greater freedom afforded to the applicant in the nondirective interview is particularly valuable in bringing to the interviewer's attention any information, attitudes, or feelings that may often be concealed by more structured questioning.

MANAGER'S TOOLKIT **4.4**

SAMPLE SITUATIONAL INTERVIEW QUESTION

QUESTION:

It is the night before your scheduled vacation. You are all packed and ready to go. Just before you get into bed, you receive a phone call from the plant. A problem has arisen that only you can handle. You are asked to come in to take care of things. What would you do in this situation?

RECORD ANSWER:

_____

_____

_____

SCORING GUIDE:

Good: "I would go in to work and make certain that everything is okay. Then I would go on vacation."

Good: "There are no problems that only I can handle. I would make certain that someone qualified was there to handle things."

Fair: "I would try to find someone else to deal with the problem."

Poor: "I would go on vacation."

However, because the applicant determines the course of the interview and no set procedure is followed, little information that comes from these interviews enables interviewers to cross-check agreement with other interviewers.

Thus the reliability and validity of the nondirective interview may be expected to be minimal. Based on experiences in hiring, it is probably a better approach to use both types of questions—structured to get good information about skills and competencies to do the work, and unstructured to help in determining the candidate's fit in the organization.[45]

Guidelines for Employment Interviewers

Studies on the employment interview tend to look at questions such as "What traits can be assessed in the interview?" and "How do interviewers reach their decisions?" The purpose of the studies is to assess how an interview can be structured to improve the overall process. Manager's Toolkit 4.5 presents some of the major findings of these studies. It shows that information is available that can be used to increase the validity of interviews.

Training has been shown to dramatically improve the competence of interviewers. If not done on a continuing basis, training should at least be done periodically for managers, supervisors, and HR representatives who conduct interviews. Interviewer training programs should include practice interviews conducted under guidance. Some variation in technique is only natural. However, the following list presents 10 ground rules for employment interviews that are commonly accepted and supported by research findings.

1. *Establish an interview plan.* Determine the areas and specific questions to be covered. Review job requirements, application or résumé data, test scores, and other available information before seeing the applicant.
2. *Establish and maintain rapport.* This is accomplished by greeting the applicant pleasantly, by explaining the purpose of the interview, by displaying sincere interest in the applicant, and by listening carefully.
3. *Be an active listener.* Strive to understand, comprehend, and gain insight into what is only suggested or implied. A good listener's mind is alert, and facial expressions and posture usually reflect this fact.

MANAGER'S TOOLKIT 4.5

MAJOR FINDINGS FROM RESEARCH STUDIES ON THE INTERVIEW

1. Structured interviews are more reliable than unstructured interviews.

2. Interviewers are influenced more by unfavourable than by favourable information.

3. Inter-rater reliability is increased when there is a greater amount of information about the job to be filled.

4. A bias is established early in the interview, and this tends to be followed by either a favourable or an unfavourable decision.

5. Intelligence is the trait most validly estimated by an interview, but the interview information adds nothing to test data.

6. Interviewers can explain why they feel an applicant is likely to be an unsatisfactory employee but not why the applicant may be satisfactory.

7. Factual written data seem to be more important than physical appearance in determining judgments. This increases with interviewing experience.

8. An interviewee is given a more extreme evaluation (positive/negative) when preceded by an interviewee of opposing value (positive/negative).

9. Interpersonal skills and motivation are probably best evaluated by the interview.

10. Allowing the applicant time to talk makes rapid first impressions less likely and provides a larger behaviour sample.

11. Nonverbal as well as verbal interactions influence decisions.

12. Experienced interviewers rank applicants in the same order, although they differ in the proportion that they will accept. Experienced interviewers tend to be more selective than less experienced ones.

4. *Pay attention to nonverbal cues.* An applicant's facial expressions, gestures, body position, and movements often provide clues to that person's attitudes and feelings. Interviewers should be aware of what they themselves are communicating nonverbally. However, be cautious as to your interpretation of nonverbal cues as there are some cultures, such as First Nations, that are more comfortable with silence.

5. *Provide information as freely and honestly as possible.* Answer the applicant's questions fully and frankly. Present a realistic picture of the job.

6. *Use questions effectively.* To obtain a truthful answer, questions should be phrased as objectively as possible, giving no indication of what response is desired.

7. *Separate facts from inferences.* During the interview, record factual information. Later, record inferences or interpretations of the facts. Compare inferences with those of other interviewers.

8. *Recognize biases and stereotypes.* One typical bias is for interviewers to consider strangers who have interests, experiences, and backgrounds similar to their own to be more acceptable. Stereotyping involves forming generalized opinions of how people of a given gender, race, or ethnic background appear, think, feel, and act. Also, interviewers will sometimes rate one competency very high, such as leadership, and assume that all other competencies are equally as high (halo effect). Likewise, an interviewer may consider all competencies average even though there is evidence of either poor or excellent job performance (central tendency).

9. *Control the course of the interview.* Stick to the interview plan. Provide the applicant with ample opportunity to talk, but maintain control of the situation in order to gather the information required.

10. *Standardize the questions asked.* To increase reliability and avoid discrimination, ask the same questions of all applicants for a particular job. Keep careful notes; record facts, impressions, and any relevant information, including what was told to the applicant. As noted earlier, structured questions and preparation are good ways of ensuring your get the information you are seeking.

Employers have found it advisable to provide interviewers with instructions on how to avoid potentially discriminatory questions in their interviews. The examples of appropriate and inappropriate questions shown in Figure 4.4 may serve as guidelines for application forms as well as pre-employment interviews. Complete guidelines may be developed from current information

FIGURE 4.4 Appropriate and Inappropriate Interview Questions

	Appropriate Questions	**Inappropriate Questions**
National or ethnic origin	Are you legally entitled to work in Canada?	Where were you born?
Age	Have you reached the minimum or maximum age for work, as defined by the law?	How old are you?
Sex	How would you like to be referred to during the interview?	What are your childcare arrangements?
Marital status	As travel is part of the requirement of our position, would you foresee any problems meeting this obligation?	What does your spouse do for a living? Is there travel involved? Who takes care of the children when you are away?
Disabilities	Do you have any conditions that could affect your ability to do the job?	Do you use drugs or alcohol?
Height and weight	(Ask nothing.)	How tall are you? How much do you weigh?
Address	What is your address?	What were your addresses outside Canada?
Religion	Would you be able to work the following schedules?	What are your religious beliefs?
Criminal record	Our job requires that our employees be bonded.	Are you bondable? Have you ever been arrested?
Affiliations	As an engineer, are you a member of the engineering society?	What religious associations do you belong to?

Canadian Human Rights Commission

www.chrc-ccdp.gc.ca

available from the office of the Canadian Human Rights Commission (or check the website at **www.chrc-ccdp.gc.ca**). Once the individual is hired, the information needed but not asked in the interview may be obtained if there is a valid need for it and if it does not lead to discrimination.

As a final helpful hint for interviews, applicants need to be provided with all aspects of the job, both desirable and undesirable (called a realistic job preview), so that the applicants may self-select out of the selection process if they feel they would not be satisfied with the job. This helps avoid production losses and costs associated with low job satisfaction that can result in the person leaving the organization.

Employment Tests

An employment test is an objective and standardized way to assess a person's KSAs, competencies, and other characteristics in relation to other individuals.[46] When an organization decides to use a particular employment test, it is critical that the attribute or skill being tested is used in the work. For example, if someone's keyboarding skills are tested and yet the job doesn't have any tasks that require keyboarding, it would be inappropriate to use that test. Again, the purpose of tests is to gather additional information on the candidate so that job performance in the organization can be predicted.

More and more organizations are using tests as part of the information-gathering activity on applicants.[47] While over 65% of employers use some type of employment testing, there is still some concern about legal challenges to the validity of the tests.[48] Therefore it is important to ensure the tests used match the needs of the organization.[49]

Types of Employment Tests

Outcome 9

Achievement tests
Measures of what a person knows or can do right now

Aptitude tests
Measures of a person's capacity to learn or acquire skills

Employment tests may be classified in different ways. Generally, they are viewed as measuring either **aptitude** (capacity to learn or acquire skills) or **achievement** (what a person knows or can do right now).

COGNITIVE ABILITY TESTS   Cognitive ability tests measure mental capabilities, such as general intelligence, verbal fluency, numerical ability, and reasoning ability. A variety of paper-and-pencil tests measure cognitive abilities, including the General Aptitude Test Battery (GATB), the Graduate Management Aptitude Test (GMAT), and the Bennett Mechanical Comprehension Test. Figure 4.5 shows some items that could be used to measure different cognitive abilities.

Although cognitive ability tests can be developed to measure very specialized areas such as reading comprehension and spatial relations, many experts believe that the validity of cognitive ability tests simply reflects their connection to general intelligence. Measures of general mental abilities have been shown to be good predictors of performance, as well as ability to be trained, across a wide variety of jobs.[50]

PERSONALITY AND INTEREST INVENTORIES   Whereas cognitive ability tests measure a person's mental capacity, personality tests measure personal characteristics such as extroversion, agreeableness, and openness to experience. While the ability for such tests to predict job performance has been quite low, recent research indicates that if using personality tests are only useful if the employer knows what kinds of personality traits are needed.[51] Personality tests can be problematic if they inadvertently discriminate against individuals who would otherwise perform effectively. Therefore, it is generally not recommended that personality tests be used for background information when selecting employees.

EMOTIONAL INTELLIGENCE   One of the newer, and somewhat debated, type of employment tests is one that measures the emotional intelligence of the applicant. Emotional intelligence has many definitions but the one most commonly used describes it as a composite of emotional reasoning abilities: perceiving, understanding, and regulating emotions.[52] This concept has become so popular that it is usually just referred to as EI. However, whether or not this is something that can be measured and then used for prediction on job performance is still being studied.[53] Further, there is recent debate, even among the original authors of EI, as to whether it is a unique ability or an eclectic mix of positive traits.[54]

Some employers use tests, such as keyboarding, to provide additional information for making a selection decision.

Alexandre Zveiger, www.photobank.ch/Shutterstock

FIGURE 4.5 Sample Measures of Cognitive Ability

Verbal	1. What is the meaning of the word "surreptitious"?

    a. covert   c. lively

    b. winding   d. sweet

2. How is the noun clause used in the following sentence? "I hope that I can learn this game."

    a. subject   c. direct object

    b. predicate nominative   d. object of the preposition

Quantitative 3. Divide 50 by 0.5 and add 5. What is the result?

    a. 25   c. 95

    b. 30   d. 105

4. What is the value of 144^2?

    a. 12   c. 288

    b. 72   d. 20736

Reasoning 5. _____ is to boat as snow is to _____ .

    a. Sail, ski   c. Water, ski

    b. Water, winter   d. Engine, water

6. Two women played 5 games of chess. Each woman won the same number of games, yet there were no ties. How can this be?

    a. There was a forfeit.   c. They played different people.

    b. One player cheated.   d. One game is still in progress.

Mechanical 7. If gear A and gear C are both turning counterclockwise, what is happening to gear B?

    a. It is turning counterclockwise.   c. It remains stationary.

    b. It is turning clockwise.   d. The whole system will jam.

A   B   C

Answers: 1. a, 2. c, 3. d, 4. d, 5. c, 6. c, 7. b

PHYSICAL ABILITY TESTS In addition to learning about a job candidate's mental capabilities, employers may need to assess a person's physical abilities as well. Particularly for demanding and potentially dangerous jobs like those held by firefighters and police officers, physical abilities such as strength and endurance tend to be good predictors of performance on the job but possibly also of ability to minimize injuries on the job.[55] A physical ability test is not the same as a medical exam. Some organizations may still require a medical exam prior to actually starting employment to ensure there is no medical condition that could preclude the employee from successfully performing the work. However, many organizations are no longer doing medical exams due to privacy issues or potential challenges of discrimination.

JOB SAMPLE TESTS Job sample tests, or work sample tests, require the applicant to perform tasks that are actually a part of the work required on the job. Like job knowledge tests, job sample tests are constructed from a carefully developed outline that experts agree includes the major job functions; the tests are thus considered content-valid. They are often used to measure skills for office and clerical jobs. Job sample tests have also been devised for many diverse jobs: a map-reading test for traffic control officers, a lathe test for machine operators, a complex coordination test for pilots, an in-basket test for managers, a group discussion test for supervisors, a judgment and decision-making test for administrators, to name a few.

SUBSTANCE ABUSE (DRUG AND ALCOHOL) TESTING The Canadian Human Rights Commission and some of its provincial counterparts have issued policies on employment-related drug testing. Generally speaking, an employer in Canada, compared to its U.S. counterparts, cannot do random substance abuse testing, even in safety-sensitive work environments, unless it is part of a negotiated rehabilitation program.[56] Addiction to drugs or alcohol is considered a disability, and the employer is to be guided by legislation and by practices such as workplace accommodation. For example, Canadian National Railway recently lost an arbitration regarding the dismissal of one of its employees. The employee had been terminated after a random drug test demonstrated that he had been using marijuana. There was no evidence to directly link the use of marijuana on a Saturday to the employee being impaired on Tuesday when the employee started work for that week.[57]

If the employer has established that drug testing is job-related—typically, this involves safety issues—the candidate must be informed that job offers are conditional on the successful passing of a drug test and that this test will be required during the course of employment. The employer then has the right to demand a medical examination. If an employee refuses, he or she can be dismissed. One of the more significant agreements on substance abuse testing was reached between the Construction Labour Relations Association and Council of British Columbia Building Trades in 2008. The agreement allows employers to do mandatory testing of all employees involved in workplace accidents or near misses, or when there's a reasonable suspicion of on-the-job impairment. Further, if an applicant agrees, pre-employment drug testing can occur.[58]

To comply with legal issues in Canada, any policies in relation to substance abuse testing must have a clear and legitimate purpose. As well, the policies must be administered in a reasonable manner, including being respectful of the employee's privacy rights.[59]

Reference Checks

Organizations use both the mail and the telephone to check references. But while references are commonly used to screen and select employees, they have not proved successful for predicting employee performance. Written letters of reference are notoriously inflated, and this limits their validity. Generally, telephone checks are preferable because they save time and provide for greater candour. At Intuit, the Edmonton, Alberta, software company that produces Quicken, managerial applicants are asked to provide between five and nine references that are then called and asked specific job-related questions.

An employer has no legal obligation to provide a former employee with a reference. To avoid liability, many employers are providing a perfunctory letter of reference, which supplies only the name, employment dates, last position with the company, and final salary. It is important for employers to be understanding of the handling of reference information so that the employer does not violate privacy laws.[60] However, inadequate reference checking can contribute to high turnover, employee

Certain jobs require people who can cope with potentially dangerous situations. The aftermath of this Alberta tornado put workers to the test.

CP PHOTO/Red Deer Advocate/Randy Fiedler

theft, and white-collar crime. By using sources in addition to former employers, organizations can obtain valuable information about an applicant's character and habits. Telephone interviews are most effective and one key question that is particularly effective in screening is to ask: "Would you rehire this employee?" Some employers prefer to outsource reference checking to professional firms, such as Intelysis Employment Screening Services in Toronto, Ontario, to get as accurate information as possible. Garda, a security firm headquartered in Montreal indicated that of the 130,000 annual employment references, about 12% of the applicants were not truthful about their education.[61]

Those individuals supplying references must do so in a responsible manner without making statements that are damaging or cannot be substantiated. To aid employers in ensuring appropriate reference checks are done, the National Association of Professional Background Screeners (**www.napbs.com**) was formed to create and promote standards when screening job applicants.[62]

Inadequate reference checking can contribute to high turnover or difficulties with the employee. Further, organizations could face legal liability issues if inadequate reference checks were done (see Chapter 9). Remember, the reference check is to get relevant information to predict whether the person will be a good match with the organization and is capable of performing the work successfully. Manager's Toolkit 4.6 provides some sample questions to use when doing reference checks.

w w w

National Association of Professional Background Screeners

www.napbs.com

MANAGER'S TOOLKIT **4.6**

SAMPLE REFERENCE CHECK QUESTIONS

1. How long has the person been employed in your organization?

2. Describe their attendance pattern.

3. What are the person's strengths?

4. What are some areas the person needs to develop?

5. Would you rehire?

6. Describe the person's ability to work with others or in a team.

Reaching a Selection Decision

While all of the steps in the selection process are important, the most critical step is the decision to accept or reject applicants. Because of the cost of placing new employees on the payroll, the short probationary period in many organizations, and human rights considerations, the final decision must be as sound as possible. Thus it requires systematic consideration of all the relevant information about applicants. It is common to use summary forms and checklists to ensure that all the pertinent information has been included in the evaluation of applicants.

Summarizing Information about Applicants

Fundamentally, an employer is interested in what an applicant both can do and will do. An evaluation of candidates on the basis of assembled information should focus on these two factors, as shown in Figure 4.6. The "can-do" factors include knowledge and skills, as well as the aptitude (the potential) for acquiring new knowledge and skills. The "will-do" factors include motivation, interests, and other personality characteristics. Both factors are essential to successful performance on the job. The employee who has the ability (can do) but is not motivated to use it (will not do) is little better than the employee who lacks the necessary ability.

Specific criteria must be established under the various factors, especially for the "can-do" factors. For example, if a person is being hired as a call-centre agent, one of the abilities might be to "input data quickly on a computerized system." In most call-centre environments, there are performance standards regarding the amount of time it would take to input the average call-centre information. The standard would also identify extremely poor performance. This would then be a specific level below which an applicant would not be deemed suitable for the job.

A useful approach to ensuring the criteria is appropriate and conforms to legal requirements is the OUCH test: Objective, Uniform in application, Consistent in effect, Has job relatedness.

Making a selection decision is no different than making any other type of management decision: identifying criteria and weighting of the criteria needs to be done. For practice on this, see the exercise at the end of this chapter in "Developing Your Skills."

It is much easier to measure what individuals can do than what they will do. The can-do factors are readily evident from test scores and verified information. What the individual will do can only be inferred. Responses to interview and application-form questions may be used as a basis for obtaining information for making inferences about what an individual will do.

Decision Strategy

The strategy used for making personnel decisions for one category of jobs may differ from that used for another category. The strategy for selecting managerial and executive personnel, for example, will differ from that used in selecting clerical and technical personnel. While many factors are to be considered in hiring decisions, the following are some of the questions that managers must consider:

1. Should the individuals be hired according to their highest potential or according to the existing needs of the organization?
2. At what grade or wage level should the individual be started?
3. Should initial selection be concerned primarily with an ideal match of the employee to the job, or should potential for advancement in the organization be considered?
4. To what extent should those who are not qualified but are qualifiable be considered?

FIGURE 4.6   "Can-Do" and "Will-Do" Factors in Selection

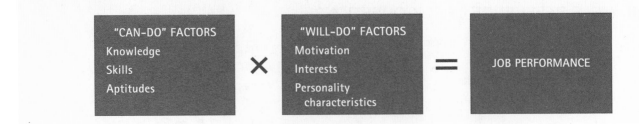

HRM and the law 4.1

LEGAL IMPLICATIONS OF HIRING PROCESS

When making a hiring decision, managers must ensure that facts are used when assessing qualifications. In a case between the National Bank of Canada and an applicant, it was determined by the Canadian Human Rights Commission that this was not done.

Specifically, an applicant who identified herself as a transgendered individual applied for part-time work in the bank's call centre, TelNat. TelNat continually recruited new staff as it had a 20 to 30% turnover rate. During the initial application review stage, the TelNat staff noted that the applicant had a broad and varied background—including a law degree and an MBA, and had had a successful career as a management consultant. All of her work and education, however, had occurred as a male. The applicant indicated during the interview that she wished to reorient her life and career. She also

wished a prospective employer to know the full background and provided information to TelNat representatives on how other large North American financial institutions had developed policies and practices for hiring such individuals.

The various stages of the screening process went well, including three interviews, until the call-centre manager made a final decision. At that point, a decision was made that the person lacked experience in customer sales and service. The commission in analyzing the facts of the information determined that she had extensive background in customer sales and service. Further, notes on the résumé by TelNat indicated that it agreed she had the necessary background.

The commission concluded that the applicant had not been hired based on sex.

Source: Canadian Human Rights Tribunal, Tribunal canadien des droits de la personne Micheline Montreuil, Complainant, and Canadian Human Rights Commission, and National Bank of Canada, 2004 CHRT 72004/02/05.

---

5. Should overqualified individuals be considered?
6. What effect will a decision have on meeting employment equity plans and diversity considerations?

The Final Decision

The line manager makes the decision as to who gets hired. Therefore, it is important that the manager understand the importance of the steps necessary to make a good decision. In large organizations, notifying applicants of the decision and making job offers is often the responsibility of the HR department. This department will confirm the details of the job, working arrangements, wages, and so on, and specify a deadline by which the applicant must reach a decision. In smaller organizations without an HR practitioner, the manager will notify the candidates. Therefore, if there is an HR department, it is valuable to forge a strong partnership with HR in order to gain their valuable technical and legal assistance.

To better understand the implications of a poor hiring process, read HRM and the Law 4.1.

SUMMARY

1. Discuss the steps in human resource planning.
   - Forecast demand for labour in the organization.
   - Determine the supply of labour—both external and internal to the organization.
   - Identify the gap between demand and supply.
   - Develop action plans to close or eliminate the gap.

2. Describe the relationship between planning, recruiting, and selecting people to work with the organization.
   - As organizations plan for their future, supervisors and managers at all levels must play an active role in planning for future people requirements.
   - It is critical that the organization have the right number and type of employees available to implement a chosen business plan.
   - Managers play a key role in planning for the human resources necessary to achieve the business plan.

3. Explain the advantages and disadvantages of recruiting from within the organization.
   - By recruiting from within, an organization can capitalize on previous investments made in recruiting, selecting, training, and developing its current employees.
   - Internal promotions can reward employees for past performance and send a signal to other employees that their future efforts will pay off.
   - A disadvantage can be the inbreeding of ideas and attitudes.
4. Explain the advantages and disadvantages of external recruitment.
   - External recruitment can bring in new ideas and acquire people with specialized skills.
   - Constraints on the organization, such as a legislated employment equity plan, may lead to a different pool of applicants than what the manager may want.
5. Explain the objectives of the selection process.
   - The selection process attempts to get the right person with the right skills at the right time in the right job.
6. Describe the typical steps in the selection process.
   - Typical steps start with the receipt of an application form, then an initial interview, possible employment tests, an interview with the supervisor, reference checks, and then a hiring decision.
7. Identify the various sources of information used for selection decisions.
   - Interviews
   - Application forms or résumés
   - References
   - Employment tests
8. Discuss the different approaches to conducting an employment interview.
   - Unstructured, wherein the interviewer is free to pursue whatever approach and sequence of topics might seem appropriate.
   - Structured, wherein each applicant receives the same set of questions, which have pre-established answers.
   - Situational, in which candidates are asked about hypothetical situations and how they would handle them.
   - Behavioural descriptions of previous work experiences.
   - Interviews can be conducted by a single individual, a panel, or via a computer interface.
9. Explain the value of different types of employment tests.
   - More objective than the interview.
   - Can provide a broader sampling of behaviour and skills.

NEED TO KNOW

- Purpose of human resource planning
- Definition of recruitment
- Various recruitment sources
- Definition and purpose of selection
- Typical steps in selection process
- Types of interview methods

NEED TO UNDERSTAND

- Advantages and disadvantages of internal or external recruitment
- Use of tests and interviews in selection decision
- Applications and interview questions in relation to human rights legislation
- Importance of good decision making in hiring

KEY TERMS

achievement tests 116

aptitude tests 116

behavioural description interview (BDI) 112

human resource planning 94

internal job posting 100

labour market 101

management forecasts 96

Markov analysis 96

panel interview 111

recruitment 98

reliability 109

selection 108

situational question 113

skills inventory 96

staffing table 96

trend analysis 96

validity 109

REVIEW QUESTIONS

1. Distinguish between the quantitative and qualitative approaches to forecasting human resource requirements.
2. What are the comparative advantages and disadvantages of filling openings from internal sources? From external sources?
3. If you were looking to hire for the following jobs, where might you recruit? (List both internal and external sources.)
   - Data entry clerk
   - Computer technician
   - Supervisor for retail store
   - Welder
   - Pharmacist
   - Plumber
4. Discuss some of the employment problems faced by members of the designated groups.
5. What are some of the problems that arise in checking references furnished by job applicants? Are there any solutions to these problems?
6. What characteristics do job knowledge tests and job sample tests have that often make them more acceptable to the examinees than other types of tests?
7. Personality tests, like other tests used in employee selection, have been under attack for several decades. What are some of the reasons applicants find personality tests objectionable? On what basis could their use for selection purposes be justified?
8. Compare briefly the major types of employment interviews described in this chapter. Which type would you prefer to conduct? Why?

CRITICAL THINKING QUESTIONS

1. You have recently applied for work at a large accounting firm as a junior accounting clerk. Part of the screening process will include a panel interview with the people you would be working with. What questions do you think they will ask you? What questions would you ask of them?
2. You are starting your own company and need the following positions filled:
   - Receptionist
   - Salespeople
   - Information technology people

   Identify two or three key job requirements for each position and then develop the selection criteria for each requirement. What selection tools or techniques would you use to assess each criterion?
3. You have just been asked to assist in hiring a new administrative assistant for a medium-sized manufacturing company. However, before starting the process, the owner of the company wants to know how much time it will take and what the cost will be. Estimate the number of staff hours and how many dollars that might be spent on this hiring.
4. Identify the steps that were used to hire you for a job that you either have now or had recently. What steps, if any, do you feel ought to have been included?

DEVELOPING YOUR SKILLS

jobsearchtech.com
jobsearchtech.com

careeronestop
www.acinet.org

1. Working in small groups of five or six, develop an advertisement for an instructor in your college. Ensure that you identify the skills, knowledge, and abilities required. Debrief with the entire class, share results, and identify common themes.
2. Working in groups of four to five students, list three recent times you have been interviewed. Working with this list, identify the type of interview conducted. Determine if the interview was valid and whether or not it was effective in attracting you to work for the organization.
3. Access **jobsearchtech.com** and click on the link "Writing Résumés." Pick one of the related links with sample résumés. Review the sample résumé and then prepare your résumé. Bring

your résumé to class and then working in pairs, critique each other's and identify what is similar and what is different in the formatting of each. Share your findings with the rest of the class.

4. Access **www.acinet.org/** and click on the link "Career Exploration." Identify at least three careers (be as specific as you can) that might interest you. Prepare a one- to two-page summary explaining why each career is interesting to you. Also explain how useful each website was in helping you explore those possible careers.

Case Study 1

Clean Up the "Resu-mess"

Plantronics Inc., a communications headset manufacturer, and Southern Company, an energy firm, both needed to hire engineers and those engineers needed to understand electricity. However, each company was looking for two very different types of candidates.

Plantronics wants engineers who can design the electronics for audio equipment. Southern, on the other hand, wants engineers to run nuclear, coal, natural gas, and hydroelectric power plants. Both companies have one problem in common: each has too many applicants to weed through.

Southern has 26,000 employees and to maintain the required staffing levels, it must hire more than 2000 full-time employees each year. But to do this, staff have to sort through more than 100,000 applicants. It was using online recruiting but the process wasn't automated. Candidates sent an e-mail to a generic address with the job requisition code in the subject line. If the code was missing, the résumé could get lost. However, other problems included candidates applying for every available job and résumés not listing the key information necessary such as needing experience on a particular type of equipment.

To make the screening process more efficient, Southern retained a vendor that provided electronic recruiting, applicant tracking, and staffing analysis. The vendor is also the one used by Plantronics. When applicants apply for a job on either Plantronics's or Southern's website and click on the jobs link, it takes them to the vendor's server, although there is nothing to indicate to applicants that they are going to a different site. There they can set up an account based on their education, job preferences, location, and so on and search for open positions. Applicants can also sign-up to receive e-mail alerts when jobs that meet their criteria become available in the future. Southern reports that 60% of its job candidates come through this feature.

The biggest advantage, however, is not in finding applicants, but in narrowing down which ones the company should pursue. There is not sufficient staff to read through hundreds of applications for a position. To simplify this, both Plantronics and Southern use the software's testing functions to prescreen candidates.

Screening questions are developed that can take several forms: yes/no, true/false, multiple choice, etc. Answers can be assigned different weights and certain answers can also automatically include or exclude the applicants who are not qualified. Plantronics uses, on average, 17 questions for each position.

When Southern started using the recruitment module, it screened out only 40% of the applicants. By refining the questions, the company has increased that to 65%. Plantronics sometimes screens out as many as 95%.

Questions

1. What competitive advantages do you see in using online screening tools to screen applicants?
2. Do you see any drawbacks associated with using an external system, and, if so, how might they be addressed?

Case Study 2

Aptitude Tests at an Electronics Corporation

An electronics plant in Midland, Ontario, has begun using aptitude tests as part of its selection process. Before they will be considered for new job openings and for promotions, new candidates must pass eight different aptitude tests. One test for manual dexterity requires applicants to move small metal pegs from holes on one side of a board to holes on the other side as fast as they can. In another test, employees are shown pictures of two cows—one white and the other spotted—and asked, "Which cow would be easier to see from an airplane?"

The company's employees see no relationship between their jobs and the cow test; they also find it humiliating to have to move pegs on a board in order to qualify for jobs they have been doing for years. In one testing session, 80% of employees failed. The price of failure is exclusion from higher-paying and more desirable jobs. Even more shameful is the fact that people with less seniority and little plant experience are passing the aptitude tests.

The dispute is deeply rooted. The union feels that the tests are allowing management to replace experienced workers with new hires who work for less pay. The fact that test results are almost always confidential has led to suspicions that the results are being manipulated in some way. After seeing their colleagues fail the tests, some workers are so discouraged that they don't even try for new jobs or promotions. Other changes that have been introduced along with the tests include 12-hour rotating shifts, the "flexible" replacement of workers, and new computerized inspection systems.

Management defends the testing, claiming that new plants and new work methods require aptitudes such as problem solving and flexible thinking. These skills are not usually associated with the stereotype of the senior blue-collar worker. In the past, young people had no need to even graduate from high school if there was a plant in town offering big paycheques for manual labour. The tests that have been introduced discriminate against older workers with less formal education. In demand today are employees who can do many jobs, solve problems, make decisions, provide creative solutions, and function effectively as part of an empowered work team.

Source: Reprinted by permission of the author Megan Terepocki.

Questions

1. Do you see any problems with the way the company's testing program is being managed? Discuss.
2. Suggest how the program might be modified.
3. The union is fighting to eliminate the testing. On what grounds could the union base its arguments?
4. If an employee files a complaint with the Ontario Human Rights Commission on the grounds that the test discriminated against him as an older worker, what kinds of information will have to be gathered to determine the validity of the claim?

Video Feature

PART 2—IN VIEW

1. "DOCTOR RECRUITMENT" (02:52)

There is a doctor shortage in Canada. Many cities and towns use recruiters to lure doctors to their community. This is an inside look at the job of a family physician recruiter.

2. "HIRING WARS" (06:02)

With a shortage of skilled workers, Canada isn't the only country that is looking to other countries to bring in employees. This provides an indication of what the U.S. offers to entice Canadians to move.

3. "TRUTH & CONSEQUENCES" (21:00)

Employers continue to look for a variety of ways to match applicants to the work requirements. This is an inside look at what some companies are considering.

QUESTIONS

1. What kind of organization or work environment do you want to work in?

2. Does it surprise you that physician recruiting is similar to other types of recruitment techniques? Why?

3. If people feel that they have the necessary skills yet are unable to find work, what other factors may explain this?

4. If you were a manager in an emerging industry (e.g., high tech), what techniques or tools would you use to recruit skilled workers?

5. If you are looking to change jobs, what resources could you use to let employers know of your qualifications?

NOTES AND REFERENCES

1. Workshop presented by Towers Perrin, "What Does the Talent Have to Say?" February 28, 2006; Corporate Leadership Council, "Attracting and Retaining Critical Talent Segments," 2006; and "Short Circuiting Labour Supply," *Canadian HR Reporter*, December 15, 2008, www.hrreporter.com/ArticleView. aspx?l=1&articleid=6560 (accessed January 21, 2009).

2. "Value-Adding and Survival Tactics for HR Professionals," *HR Focus*, January 2009, S1–2.

3. Hedley Lawson, Jr., "Into The Storm: Managing Your Business in a Financial Crisis," *Vision Monday*, December 15, 2008, 32.

4. Lynn Johnston, "Employees Put High Prices on Learning, Development," *Canadian HR Reporter*, November 3, 2008, www.hrreporter.com/ArticleView.aspx?l=1&articleid=6457 (accessed January 21, 2009).

5. Shannon Klie, "Guesses Just Don't Cut It Anymore," *Canadian HR Reporter*, March 24, 2008, 10.

6. Statistics Canada, "Canada's Changing Labour Force, 2006 Census: Overview," www12.statcan.ca/english/census06/analysis/labour/ov-cclf-01.cfm; "Occupational—National Occupational Classification for Statistics 2006" 97-564-XWE2006005, www.statcan.gc.ca/bsolc/olc-cel/olc-cel?catno=97-564-X2006005&lang=eng; and "Employment by Age, Sex, Type of Work, Class of Worker," www40.statcan.gc.ca/l01/cst01/labr66a-eng.htm (accessed January 21, 2009).

7. "Bridging the Oilpatch Labour Gap," *Financial Post*, March 16, 2004, FP8.

8. Lesley Young, "Alpha Safety a Leader with Personal Touch," *Canadian HR Reporter*, August 13, 2007, 9.

9. Sarah Dobson, "Pumping Up People Supply to Build Heart Valves," *Canadian HR Reporter*, February 23, 2009, 16.

10. News report on Global National TV, January 21, 2009.

11. Uyen Vu, "What's the Real Cost of Turnover?" *Canadian HR Reporter*, July 14, 2008, www.hrreporter.com/ArticleView.aspx?l=1&articleid=6213 (accessed January 22, 2009).

12. Lynn Carlson, "Competitive Concessions," *Financial Post*, March 26, 2008, WK2.

13. Interested readers can check out the websites of these companies at www.oracle.com/applications/peoplesoft-enterprise.html and www.sap.com/canada/index.epx.

14. David Burlington, "Unified Talent Management: The Platform Is the Service," *Workforce Management*, www.workforce.com/ (accessed January 22, 2009).

15. "Wishing Upon a Star: Hiring a CEO from Inside the Company Versus Going Outside," *Workforce Management*, www.workforce.com/archive/article/23/98/98.php?ht= (accessed January 22, 2009).

16. Michelle V. Rafter, "Special Report: Talent Acquisition—The Culture Connection," *Workforce Management*, www.workforce.com/archive/feature/25/65/45/index.php?ht= (accessed January 22, 2009).

17. "Canada Expects Up to 265,000 New Immigrants in 2009," *Canadian HR Reporter*, www.hrreporter.com/ArticleView.aspx?l=1&articleid=6550 (accessed January 22, 2009).

18. Ibid.

19. "LinkedIn Beefing Up Recruiting Tools," *Workforce Management*, January 9, 2009, www.workforce.com/section/00/article/26/08/38.php (accessed January 22, 2009).

20. Jeevyn Dhaliwal, "Employment Related Immigration," presentation February 24, 2009, Vancouver, BC.

21. George Bohlander and Scott Snell, *Managing Human Resources* (Mason, OH: South-Western Cengage Learning, 2007), 183.

22. Ibid.

23. Alice Snell, "Using Technology in Sourcing Talent," *Canadian HR Reporter*, January 29, 2007, www.hrreporter.com/ArticleView.aspx?l=1&articleid=4960 (accessed January 26, 2009).

24. Graham Donald, "People and Opportunities the Biggest Draw for Students," *Canadian HR Reporter,* April 25, 2005, 9.

25. Shannon Klie, "Firm Asks Students: What do You Want?" *Canadian HR Reporter,* www.hrreporter.com/ArticleView. aspx?l=1&articleid=6052 (accessed January 26, 2009).

26. "Working.com Virtual Career Fair," *The Vancouver Sun,* June 11, 2009, B8.

27. Uyen Vu, "Job Board Offers Cash for Referrals," *Canadian HR Reporter,* www.hrreporter.com/ArticleView. aspx?l=1&articleid=6158 (accessed January 26, 2009).

28. Jacques Gaumond, "Relying on Your Employees' Eye for Talent," *Canadian HR Reporter,* www.hrreporter.com/ArticleView. aspx?l=1&articleid=4559 (accessed January 26, 2009).

29. For additional sources on writing résumés, see BC Jobs.ca; Employment Ontario, "Resume Writing," www.edu.gov.on.ca/ eng/career/resume.html; Monster.ca; Rosanne Lurie, *Killer Cover Letters and Resumes!* (Wetfeet.com, Inc NetLibrary 2003); and Susan Britton Whitcomb, *Resume Magic* (Jist Works, 2006).

30. "Job Search Strategies," www.sasknetwork.gov.sk.ca/html/ JobSeekers/lookingforwork/searchstrategies.htm (accessed January 26, 2009); Career and Employment Services, University of Manitoba, "Job Search Strategies," www.umanitoba.ca/stu-dent/employment/media/job_search_workbook.pdf (pdf format downloaded January 26, 2009); and other similar resources on job search techniques.

31. Uyen Vu, "FedEx Holds Managers Accountable for Diversity," *Canadian HR Reporter,* November 8, 2004, 3.

32. Marina Jiménez, "Scoring Points with Newer Canadians," *The Globe and Mail,* March 13, 2009, L1.

33. "About Us," TRIEC, www.triec.ca/about/TRIEC (accessed June 10, 2009).

34. Frances X. Frei, "The Four Things a Service Business Must Get Right," *Harvard Business Review,* April 2008, 70–80.

35. Farah Naqvi, "Competency Mapping and Managing Talent," *Journal of Management Research* VIII, no. 1 (2009): 85–94.

36. Cristina Bertua, Neil Anderson, and Jesús F. Salgado, "The Predictive Validity of Cognitive Ability Tests: A UK Meta-analysis," *Journal of Occupational and Organization Psychology* 78 (2005): 387–409.

37. James Taranto "Tell Us Everything," *Wall Street Journal,* November 13, 2008, http://online.wsj.com (accessed January 28, 2009).

38. Bob Joseph, "Change in Approach Makes All the Difference," *Canadian HR Reporter,* www.hrreporter.com/ArticleView. aspx?l=1&articleid=6569 (accessed January 28, 2009).

39. Joel Koppelman, "Building the Team," *Smart Leaders,* December 2008, 11.

40. Nita Wilmott, "Interviewing Styles: Tips for Interview Approaches," About.com:Human Resources, humanresources. about.com/cs/selectionstaffing/a/interviews.htm (accessed January 30, 2009).

41. Ibid.

42. John Olmstead, "Predict Future Success with Structured Interviews," *Nursing Management,* March 2007, 52–53.

43. Shannon Klie, "Biases Creep into Interviews," *Canadian HR Reporter,* www.hrreporter.com/ArticleView. aspx?l=1&articleid=6012 (accessed January 30, 2009).

44. Ann Macaulay, "Don't Let Processes Get in the Way of a Good Hire, and Other Lessons," Canadian HR Reporter, June 6, 2005, 17.

45. Olmstead, "Predict Future Success with Structured Interviews."

46. For additional resources on employment testing, see Dan Biddle, *Adverse Impact and Test Validation: A Practitioner's Guide to Valid and Defensible Employment Testing,* 2nd ed. (Hampshire, U.K.: Gower Publishing Limited, 2006); Thomas P. Hogan, *Psychological Testing: A Practical Introduction,* 2nd ed. (New Jersey: John Wiley & Sons Ltd., 2007).

47. Chris Piotrowski and Terry Armstrong, "Current Recruitment and Selection Practices: A National Survey of Fortune 1000 Firms," North American Journal of Psychology 8, no. 3 (2006): 489–496.

48. Lauren J. Katunich, "Pre-Employment Psychological and Personality Testing," Fair Employment Guidelines 603 (New York, NY: Aspen Publishers, August 2005).

49. Ann Macaulay, "Finding Psychometrics that Pass the Test," *Canadian HR Reporter,* March 27, 2006, 10.

50. Kevin R. Murphy, Brian E. Cronin, and Anita P. Tam "Controversy and Consensus Regarding the Use of Cognitive Ability Testing in Organizations," *Journal of Applied Psychology* 88, no. 4 (2003): 660–671; Cristina Berua, Neil Anderson, and Jesùs F. Salgado, "The Predictive Validity of Cognitive Ability Tests;" and Kenneth G. Brown, Huy Le, and Frank L. Schmidt, "Specific Aptitude Theory Revisited: Is there Incremental Validity for Training Performance?" *International Journal of Selection and Assessment* 14, no. 2 (June 2006): 87–100.

51. Shannon Klie, "A Recruiter's Dream: Fake-proof Personality Test," *Canadian HR Reporter,* November 3, 2008, 1.

52. Laura Thi Lam and Susan L. Kirby, "Is Emotional Intelligence an Advantage? An Exploration of the Impact of Emotional and General Intelligence on Individual Performance," *The Journal of Social Psychology* 142, no. 1 (2002): 133–143.

53. Moshe Zeidner, Gerald Matthews, and Richard D. Roberts, "Emotional Intelligence in the Workplace: A Critical Review," *Applied Psychology: An International Review* 53, no. 3 (2004): 371–399.

54. John D. Mayer, Peter Salovey, and David R. Caruso, "Emotional Intelligence: New Ability or Eclectic Traits?" *American Psychologist* 63, no. 6 (September 2008): 503–517.

55. M. S. Sothmann, D. L. Gebhardt, T. A. Baker, G. M. Kastellos, and V. A. Sheppard, "Performance Requirements of Physically Strenuous Occupations: Validating Minimum Standards for Muscular Strength and Endurance," *Ergonomics* 47, no. 8 (June 22, 2004): 864–875.

56. Lorna Harris, "Pushing 'Borders' of Drug Testing," *Canadian HR Reporter,* December 1, 2008, 5.

57. Jeffrey R. Smith, "Positive Drug Test Not Cause for Dismissal," *Canadian HR Reporter,* November 3, 2008, www. hrreporter.com/ArticleView.aspx?l=1&articleid=6469 (accessed February 1, 2009).

58. "Mandatory Drug Tests for B.C. Construction Workers," *Canadian HR Reporter,* August 21, 2008, www.hrreporter.com/ ArticleView.aspx?l=1&articleid=6290 (accessed February 1, 2009).

59. Janice Rubin and Sharaf Sultan, "Drug and Alcohol Testing: Where Are We Now?" *Canadian HR Reporter,* March 9, 2009, 15.

60. Anthony Moffatt, "The Danger of Digging Too Deep," *Canadian HR Reporter,* August 11, 2008, www.hrreporter.com/ArticleView. aspx?l=1&articleid=6261 (accessed February 1, 2009).

61. Shannon Klie, "Weeding Out the Fakes," *Canadian HR Reporter,* May 7, 2007, www.hrreporter.com/ArticleView. aspx?l=1&articleid=5182 (accessed January 31, 2009).

62. Nancy Dunne, "Screeners Wanted," *Financial Post,* May 3, 2004, FE5.

PART 3

Developing People in the Organization

5

ORIENTATION, TRAINING, AND DEVELOPMENT

OUTCOMES

After studying this chapter, you should be able to

1 Discuss the systems approach to training and development.

2 Describe the components of a training-needs assessment.

3 Identify the principles of learning and how they facilitate training.

4 Identify the types of training and development methods used for all levels of employees.

5 List some of the characteristics of an effective orientation process.

6 Describe the special training programs that are currently popular.

7 Explain how a career development program integrates individual and organizational needs.

8 Discuss specialized career development needs.

OUTLINE

HRM CLOSE-UP

"Managers must give their employees time to learn the things they need to know."

Francisco Del Cueto has a cool job. As Chief Technology Officer, he oversees 25 people who develop animation software for feature films, television, and the Internet. Winner of the 2005 Primetime Emmy Engineering Award, Toon Boom Animation of Montreal has been in business for more than a decade and has clients all over the world.

Originally, the company bought USAnimation, a high-end 2D animation software that has now been phased out and replaced by the Harmony Solution. Toon Boom invested significantly in research and development to bring this enterprise solution to its current level of quality and efficiency. Today, Toon Boom offers both consumer level animation software used by children, animation hobbyists, creative professionals, and schools, plus it offers higher-end professional level software used by both small and large studios and independent filmmakers.

Like many companies, Toon Boom uses in-house training as part of its orientation program for staff. This is where software developers, technical support experts, technical writers, and client service representatives learn about animation production and the animation software the company sells. Del Cueto finds that experienced staff make the best educators. "These people are our 'demo artists' and regularly give demonstrations for clients," he explains. "They make very effective teachers for fellow staff."

Training and development in the tech industry brings unique challenges. "There is constant change with clients always looking for products that are easy-to-use, faster, cheaper, and offer more performance," says Del Cueto. Software developers must keep up with new technology including new versions of the operating system and new computer hardware. The company finds that external classes, even at universities, are often not advanced enough for the company's needs. "But luckily," says Del Cueto, "our developers tend to be self-learners who prefer reading a manual and practicing on a computer." Because of this, Toon Boom has a budget for books. "We also find that visits to client

Francisco Del Cueto, Chief Technology Officer, Toon Boom Animation Inc., Montreal. Courtesy of Francisco Del Cueto, Toon Boom Animation Inc.

sites prove to be very instructive since developers can see how the technology is actually used in the context of a real production," he adds.

Depending on the case, Toon Boom may allow employees to take one training class a year during business hours. Subject to management approval, the company may also reimburse up to $300 per year if the course is completed successfully.

One big challenge Toon Boom faced was adapting their animation software to a Mac platform. "People really wanted to use all our products on the Mac but we didn't have the expertise in-house," explains Del Cueto. "So we hired an instructor to teach the developers and allowed them time to become adept at it. The developers then became the in-house experts and held a seminar to teach other staff." As it turned out, the group approach to learning was highly effective: "This kind of learning is also a team-building exercise. When people learn the same thing at the same time, they tend to exchange what they learn."

In terms of identifying the type of training needed, Del Cueto takes his cues from the developers, technical writers, technical support experts, and service reps. He lets them tell him what training they need and how best to do it. "We go from bottom to top, definitely," he says, adding that, "managers must give their employees *time* to learn the things they need to know."

INTRODUCTION

Orientation
Formal process of familiarizing new employees with the organization, their jobs, and their work unit and embedding organizational values, beliefs, and accepted behaviours

Training
The acquisition of skills, behaviours, and abilities to perform current work

Development
The acquisition of skills, behaviours, and abilities to perform future work or to solve an organizational problem

The ability for an organization to ensure its people continue to learn, grow, and develop has become critical to business success. As we noted in Chapter 1, organizations often compete on competencies—the core sets of knowledge and expertise that give them an edge over their competitors. Frequently, organizations refer to "intellectual capital," which is the combination of the "human capital" (the competencies) and the organizational support that enables the human capital to flourish.[1] Further, as individuals learn (i.e., the human capital increases), the organization has the potential to learn. It is only through individuals that the organization gains knowledge.[2] **Orientation**, **training**, and **development** play a central role in enabling, nurturing, and strengthening the human capital in the organization. As will be discussed in this chapter, it is critical that organizations approach their orientation, training, and development needs in a systematic way so that there is a clear linkage to the organizations' strategic direction. In addition, rapidly changing technologies require that employees continuously hone their knowledge, skills, and abilities (KSAs), or "competencies," to cope with new processes and systems. A carefully designed program can also be a key lever in attracting and retaining the key competencies that will keep the organization's competitive advantage. As Francisco Del Cueto describes in the HRM Close-Up, his company is providing more training so that the company remains competitive. Jobs that require little skill are rapidly being replaced by jobs that require technical, interpersonal, and problem-solving skills. And, as described, the business world is constantly changing, requiring improved skills and abilities. The manager/supervisor plays a key role in ensuring that the training and development efforts are appropriate and reinforced for the individuals for whom they are responsible. Without the managers' involvement, organizational growth, success, and sustainability could be at risk. Other trends toward empowerment, total-quality management, teamwork, and international business make it necessary for managers as well as employees to develop the skills that will enable them to handle new and more demanding assignments.

APPROACH TO ORIENTATION, TRAINING, AND DEVELOPMENT

 Outcome **1**

Since the primary goal of orientation, training, and development is to contribute to the organization's overall goals, orientation, training, and development programs should be structured with an eye to organizational goals and strategies. Unfortunately, many organizations never make the connection between their strategic objectives and their training programs. Instead, fads, fashions, or "whatever the competition is doing" can sometimes be the main drivers of an organization's training agenda. As a result, much of an organization's investment can be wasted—training programs are often misdirected, poorly designed, inadequately evaluated—and these problems directly affect organizational performance.

To make certain that investments in orientation, training, and development have the maximum impact on individual and organizational performance, a systems approach to training should be used. The systems approach involves four phases: (1) needs assessment, (2) program design, (3) training delivery, and (4) evaluation of training. While the word "training" will be used in the discussion on the systems approach, all elements refer to orientation and development as well. Figure 5.1 is a useful model when designing the training programs. Each of the components of the systems approach will be discussed further in this chapter.

THE SCOPE OF ORIENTATION, TRAINING, AND DEVELOPMENT

Many new employees come equipped with most of the skills and capabilities needed to start work. Others may require extensive training before they are ready to make much of a contribution to the organization. All employees need some type of training and development on an ongoing basis to maintain effective performance or to adjust to new ways of work.

The term "training" is often used casually to describe any effort initiated by an organization to foster learning among its members. However, many experts make a distinction between training

FIGURE 5.1   Systems Model of Training

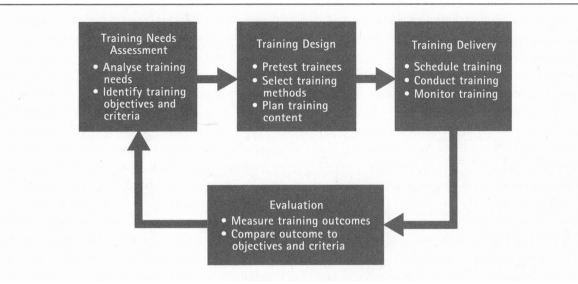

and development. Training tends to be more focused and oriented toward acquiring skills, behaviours, and abilities to perform current work, while development tends to be oriented more toward acquiring skills, behaviours, and abilities to perform future work or to solve an organizational problem. These terms tend to be combined into a single phrase—"training and development"—to recognize the combination of activities used by organizations to increase the abilities and capabilities of their employees.

Lastly, you often hear the word "learning." Learning refers to an ongoing change in behaviour and thinking—which is ultimately the goal of training and development.

The primary reason that organizations train new employees is to bring their KSAs up to the level required for satisfactory performance. As these employees continue on the job, additional training and development provide opportunities for them to acquire new knowledge and skills. As a result of this training, employees may be even more effective on the job and may be able to perform other jobs in other areas or at higher levels. To understand the importance of training in today's business environment, Figure 5.2 lists the skills that many employers seek.

Conference Board of Canada

www.conferenceboard.ca

Investments in Training

According to a Conference Board of Canada survey, Canadian businesses spend about $852 per employee each year on formal training and this amount has remained fairly stagnant for several years.[3] Overall, the average expenditure in Canada on training and development was 1.8% of payroll, and organizations annually provided about 25 hours of training per employee—a decrease of 10% since 2005.[4] However, organizations that make the 50 Best Employers in Canada list tend to place a much higher value on the continued learning and development of their employees. For example, Scotiabank in 2009 was ranked #20 on the Best Employers in Canada list while at the same time was #14 on Training's top 125.[5] Ethics in HRM 5.1 describes the debate surrounding decisions to force organizations to provide training and to force employees to take training. While it can be debated as to whether employees ought to be forced to take training, organizations that are listed on *Fortune's* 100 Best Companies to Work For continue to place high value on growth and learning and strongly encourage employees to study.[6]

In addition to formal training, more than $180 billion is spent on informal instruction that goes on every day in organizations everywhere. More and more organizations are also providing training on an "as need" basis and ensuring that it is linked to actual work experiences. For example, team training would be done as part of a team project that might be designing a new product. The types of training range from computer application skills to customer service.

FIGURE 5.2 Workplace Skills and Capabilities

Employees want to know what employers are looking for today in skill sets. The Conference Board of Canada researched this topic and has prepared the following broad list. While all employers do not look for all of these skills, many employers look for many of these skills.

Fundamental Skills

- Read and understand information presented in different forms (e.g., words, graphs)
- Write and speak so that others understand
- Use relevant knowledge and skills (scientific, technological) to explain and clarify
- Identify the root cause of a problem
- Evaluate solutions to make a decision
- Use numbers to complete tasks, such as making estimates and verifying calculations
- Manage information by locating, gathering, and organizing information using appropriate technology and systems

Personal Management Skills

- Be flexible and adaptable
- Be honest and ethical
- Be responsible for setting goals
- Be able to work safely
- Demonstrate positive attitudes and behaviours, such as dealing with people with honesty and integrity
- Be willing to keep learning

Teamwork Skills

- Understand and contribute to the organization's goals
- Understand and work within the dynamics of the group
- Plan and make decisions with others and support the outcomes
- Respect the thoughts and opinions of others
- Adapt to changing requirements
- Understand the role of conflict in group dynamics and resolve as appropriate

Source: Adapted from Employability Skills 2000+ PDF 2000 E/F (Ottawa: The Conference Board of Canada, 2000, pdf file). Reprinted with permission of The Conference Board of Canada.

A question always asked by organizations is: "Will training improve organizational performance?" The answer is an unqualified yes, even in difficult economic times. A review in 2008 conducted by the ASTD (American Society for Training and Development) concluded the following:

- While there is no enterprise-wide moratorium on training, there is a greater scrutiny on the training expenditures.
- Compared to earlier economic downturns, organizations are much more supportive of continuing with some training as those organizations believe it is worthwhile.
- Training that has a direct financial return will take precedence over certain types of development, such as for soft skills.
- Training can improve employee engagement, which in turn can reduce turnover.[7]

For training to be effective, it is important that employers provide strong support—whether it is paying for the training or encouraging people to increase their skill sets. Currently about 1/3 of the Canadian workforce participates in job-related training.[8]

A study conducted in late 2008 by the Hay Group indicated that in recessionary times it is even more important to provide growth and development opportunities for employees. Organizations may lose the commitment of their employees that will directly effect the financial performance of the organization. Therefore, if training dollars need to be cut, do so in a surgical fashion and determine where the dollars are best spent.[9]

ETHICS in HRM 5.1

MANDATORY OR VOLUNTARY?

There is only one payroll training tax in North America. The Quebec government program that forces employers to spend 1% of payroll on training may not have the intended consequences of increasing training investments in employees. Using data from a Statistics Canada survey, Alan Saks of the University of Toronto and Robert Haccoun of the Université de Montréal matched Quebec employers with Ontario employers and found that there were no differences in amounts spent on training. The paperwork is so cumbersome that many employers prefer to pay the 1% tax rather than go through the thick guidebooks necessary to report the training.

If there is little effect gained by forcing employers to provide training, are there benefits forcing employees to attend training? The answer is not clear: some studies report some slight benefits in outcomes (such as improved job performance) when employees voluntarily attend courses; other studies see no differences.

For years, there has been legislated training, most notably in the health and safety field. Every province requires that employees have been trained on the safe handling of potentially hazardous materials or conditions in the workplace. And this includes offices that use printers and copying machines. Further, under workplace health and safety legislation, an employer can be fined or have its insurance rates increased if employees are not trained.

What about the organizations that want to create a positive work environment with a diverse workforce? Diversity is not just about ethnicity; it is about differences in people, whether they are disabled, First Nations, or gay. For example, organizations such as the Ontario Public Service, HSBC Canada, Enbridge Inc., and Boeing Canada Technology Ltd. have developed very extensive training programs to create an inclusive workforce. Employees are expected to attend the training offerings and behave accordingly in the workplace. It is through these initiatives that organizations such as those listed are deemed to be progressive employers. These employers want to create an inclusive workforce to ensure that the organizations can succeed in their business objectives. Very few employers in Canada do not sell their services and/or products to a homogeneous client group. Therefore, the more diverse the workforce, the more likely the customer needs are understood.

CRITICAL THINKING QUESTIONS

1. Do you think mandatory training is right? Why or why not?
2. How would you react if your employer wanted you to participate in a training program that you thought was a waste of time? Why?

Sources: K. Harding, "A Taxing Way to Train Staff," *The Globe and Mail*, June 4, 2003, C1; D. Brown, "Legislated Training, Questionable Results," *Canadian HR Reporter* 15, no. 9 (May 6, 2002): 1; and Margaret Jetelina and Simona Siad, "Changing the Face of Canadian Business," canadianimmigrant.ca, www.canadianimmigrant.ca/careers/article/765 (accessed February 3, 2009).

SYSTEMATIC ORIENTATION, TRAINING, AND DEVELOPMENT

As mentioned earlier in the chapter, the model shown in Figure 5.1 allows organizations to identify what is needed for employee and organizational performance. Each of these components will be discussed in detail.

Phase 1: Conducting the Needs Assessment

Outcome 2

Managers and HR professionals should stay alert to the kinds of training that are needed, where they are needed, who needs them, and which methods will best deliver increased abilities to employees. If workers consistently fail to achieve productivity objectives, this might be a signal that training is needed. Likewise, if organizations receive an excessive number of customer complaints, this too might suggest inadequate training. To make certain that training is timely and focused on priority issues, and that training is the right solution for the concern, managers should approach a needs assessment systematically. You can also think of this as trying to identify the actual training problem. The needs assessment can occur at the organizational level (examining the environment

Determining the specific training needs of individuals helps determine their abilities before entering a training program.

Adam Crowley/Photodisc Green/Getty Images

and strategy of the company to see where training emphasis ought to occur); the task level (reviewing the activities of the work to determine the competencies needed); and the person level (reviewing which employees need training.)

A needs assessment can be done by asking (and answering) four questions:

1. How important is this issue to the success of the organization? If it is important, then proceed to answer the next three questions: Questions 2, 3, and 4.
2. What competencies or knowledge, skills, and abilities do employees *need*?
3. What competencies or knowledge, skills, and abilities do the employees currently *have*?
4. What is the gap between the desired (need) and the actual (have)?

Once answers have been determined, then specific action plans can be developed to address the gap. For example, since the September 11, 2001 attacks, training of airport security personnel has increased substantially. It has also increased for flight crews of airlines, employees in the transportation industry, workers in nuclear power plants, and even security staff at theme parks.

Manager's Toolkit 5.1 provides some suggestions for a simple approach to identifying training needs.

Other training issues tend to revolve around the strategic initiatives of an organization. Mergers and acquisitions, for example, frequently require that employees take on new roles and responsibilities and adjust to new cultures and ways of conducting business. Nowhere is this more prevalent than in grooming new leaders within organizations. Other issues, such as technological change, globalization, re-engineering, and total quality management, all influence the way work is done and the types of skills needed to do it. Still other concerns may be more tactical but no less important in their impact on training. Organizational restructuring, downsizing, empowerment, and teamwork, for example, have immediate training requirements. Finally, trends in the workforce itself have an impact on training needs. As we mentioned in Chapter 1, employees increasingly value self-development and personal growth, and with this has come an enormous desire for learning. At the same time, as older workers may decide to postpone retirement, training will need to be done for a variety of different generations. Because no company in the private sector can count on stable employment levels, organizations as diverse as Inco and Boeing are facing situations in which they need to prepare the next generations of employees as the current groups approach retirement.

CONDUCTING A TRAINING NEEDS ASSESSMENT

This approach is relatively simple and will take about one to two hours.

1. Gather together a group of people with similar jobs into a room with white boards and/or flip charts; have another individual (not part of the group) to act as facilitator.

2. Individually, ask each person to write down their 10 specific training needs. Be sure that the need is specific—such as "how to give feedback to colleagues" and not general like "team building."

3. Individually, each person will tell the whole group what the 10 training needs are. The facilitator will list each need on the white board. Do not list any duplicates. (Note: The facilitator may need to ask clarifying questions to ensure that it is a duplicate.)

4. The group will use some type of voting process to determine the top five training needs. This can be done by giving each participant 10 sticky dots and asking that they vote for no more than three training needs but putting one or more dots by the need. The needs with the most dots would then be the highest-rated ones.

5. Depending on the organization, the group could determine how the training needs will be implemented or the facilitator could use a brainstorming process to identify goals or outcomes for the top five training needs.

6. The facilitator will ensure that notes are taken of the session and that the top one or two needs of each person are recorded. This can be useful for the supervisor to work one-on-one with the employee to build appropriate training opportunities into the employee's performance plan.

It is important that the supervisor or manager be knowledgeable about the organization's needs, the requirements of the work, and the capabilities of the person in order to assess that training is the right solution. Training efforts (and dollars) can be wasted if the supervisor has not adequately determined whether training is appropriate. The question to ask here is "If Joe receives more training on how to handle customer complaints, will his performance improve?" If performance issues are due to ability problems, training may likely be a good intervention. However, if performance issues are due to poor motivation or factors outside an employee's control, training may not be the answer. Ultimately, managers have to sit down with employees to talk about areas for improvement so that they can jointly determine the training and developmental approaches that will have maximum benefit.[10]

Phase 2: Designing the Training Program

Once the training needs have been determined, the next step is to design (or buy) appropriate training programs. The success of training programs depends on more than the organization's ability to identify training needs. Success hinges on taking the information gained from the needs analysis and utilizing it to design first-rate training programs. Experts believe that training design should focus on at least four related issues: (1) instructional objectives, (2) trainee readiness and motivation, (3) principles of learning, and (4) characteristics of instructors.

Instructional Objectives

As a result of conducting organization, task, and person analyses, managers will have a more complete picture of the company's training needs. On the basis of this information, they can more formally state the desired outcomes of training through written **instructional objectives.** Generally, instructional objectives describe the desired outcomes of the training: the skills and knowledge the company wants people to have and the behaviours employees should acquire and/or change.

Instructional objectives
Desired outcomes of a training program

For example, a stated objective for one training program might be "Employees trained in team methods will be able to demonstrate the following skills within six months: Problem-solving, conflict resolution, and effective team meetings."

Frequently, managers will seek external resources to design the training program and write the learning objectives. However, this is done with the help and guidance of the manager. Therefore, it is important for managers to be able to describe what they want the person to do or how they want the person to act after completing a training program.

Trainee Readiness and Motivation

Trainee readiness

The consideration of a trainee's maturity and experience when assessing him or her

Two preconditions for learning affect the success of those who are to receive training: readiness and motivation. **Trainee readiness** refers to both maturity and experience factors in the trainee's background. Prospective trainees should be screened to determine that they have the background knowledge and the skills necessary to absorb what will be presented to them. The other precondition for learning is trainee motivation. For optimum learning to take place, trainees must recognize the need for new knowledge or skills, and they must maintain a desire to learn as training progresses. By focusing on the trainees themselves rather than on the trainer or training topic, managers can create a training environment that is conducive to learning. Six strategies can be essential:

1. Use positive reinforcement.
2. Eliminate threats and punishment.
3. Be flexible.
4. Have participants set personal goals.
5. Design interesting instruction.
6. Break down physical and psychological obstacles to learning.

While most employees are motivated by certain common needs, they differ from one another in the relative importance of these needs at any given time. Training objectives that are clearly related to trainees' individual needs will increase the motivation of employees to succeed in training programs. Again, the manager plays a vital role in ensuring that the training is suitable for the person and that the person is ready to take on the training initiative.

Principles of Learning

Outcome 3

As we move from needs assessment and instructional objectives to employee readiness and motivation, we are shifting from a focus on the organization to a focus on employees. Ultimately, training has to build a bridge between employees and the organization. One important step in this transition is giving full consideration to the psychological principles of learning, that is, the characteristics of training programs that help employees grasp new material, make sense of it in their own lives, and transfer it back to the job.

Because the success or failure of a training program is frequently related to certain principles of learning, managers as well as employees should understand that different training methods or techniques vary in the extent to which they utilize these principles. When investing in effective and efficient training programs, it is important that they incorporate the following principles of learning (see Figure 5.3):

GOAL SETTING It is important that the goals and objectives for the training are clear.

INDIVIDUAL DIFFERENCES People learn at different rates and in different ways.

ACTIVE PRACTICE AND REPETITION Trainees should be given frequent opportunity to practice their job tasks in the way that they will ultimately be expected to perform them.

WHOLE-VERSUS-PART LEARNING Most jobs and tasks can be broken down into parts that lend themselves to further analysis. Determining the most effective manner for completing each part then provides a basis for giving specific instruction.

FIGURE 5.3 Principles of Learning

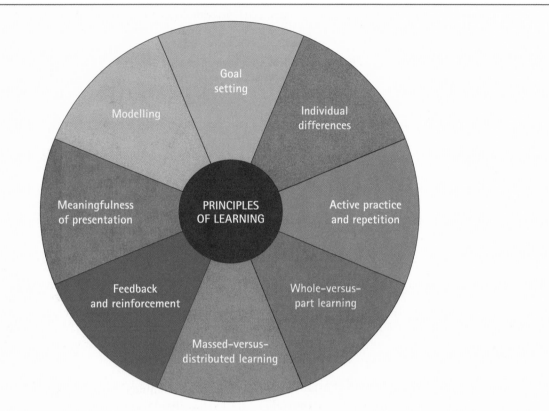

MASSED-VERSUS-DISTRIBUTED LEARNING Another factor that determines the effectiveness of training is the amount of time devoted to practice in one session. Should trainees be given training in 5 two-hour periods or in 10 one-hour periods? It has been found in most cases that spacing out the training will result in faster learning and longer retention.

FEEDBACK AND REINFORCEMENT Can any learning occur without feedback? Some feedback comes from self-monitoring while other feedback comes from trainers, fellow trainees, and the like. As an employee's training progresses, feedback serves two related purposes: (1) knowledge of results, and (2) motivation.

MEANINGFULNESS OF PRESENTATION The material to be learned must be presented in as meaningful a manner as possible so that the trainees can connect the training with things that are already familiar to them.

MODELLING The old saying "A picture is worth a thousand words" applies to training. Quite simply, we learn by watching.

Behaviour modification
Technique that if behaviour is rewarded it will be exhibited more frequently in the future

In recent years some work organizations have used **behaviour modification.** This technique operates on the principle that behaviour that is rewarded—positively reinforced—will be exhibited more frequently in the future, whereas behaviour that is penalized or unrewarded will decrease in frequency. For example, in safety training it is possible to identify "safe" behavioural profiles—that is, actions that ensure fewer accidents—as well as unsafe profiles. As a follow-up to training, or as part of the training itself, managers can use relatively simple rewards to encourage and maintain desired behaviour. It is important to use some type of incentive to reinforce the desired behaviour.[11]

Characteristics of Trainers

The success of any training activity will depend in large part on the skills and personal characteristics of those responsible for conducting the training. Good trainers, whether staff persons or line managers, need to be knowledgeable about the subject, be well-prepared, have good communication skills, and be enthusiastic with a sense of humour.

Phase 3: Implementing the Training Program

Despite the importance of needs assessment, instructional objectives, principles of learning, and the like, choices regarding instructional methods are where "the rubber meets the road" in implementing a training program. A major consideration in choosing among various training methods is determining which ones are appropriate for the KSAs to be learned. For example, if the material is mostly factual, methods such as lecture, classroom, or programmed instruction may be fine. However, if the training involves a large behavioural component, other methods, such as on-the-job training, simulation, or interactive video training, might work better.[12]

Training and Development Methods

Outcome 4

A wide variety of methods are available for training and developing employees at all levels. Some of the methods have a long history of usage. Newer methods have emerged over the years as the result of a greater understanding of human behaviour, particularly in the areas of learning, motivation, and interpersonal relationships. More recently, technological advances, especially in computer hardware and software, have resulted in training devices that in many instances are more effective and economical than the traditional training methods.

On-the-job training (OJT)
Method by which employees are given hands-on experience with instructions from their supervisor or other trainer

ON-THE-JOB TRAINING The most common method used for training employees is **on-the-job training (OJT).** OJT has the advantage of providing hands-on experience under normal working conditions and an opportunity for the trainer—a manager or senior employee—to build good relationships with new employees. Further, during economic slowdowns, OJT is viewed by some to be potentially the most cost effective means of facilitating learning in the workplace.[13]

Although all types of organizations use it, OJT is often one of the most poorly implemented training methods. Three common drawbacks include (1) the lack of a well-structured training environment, (2) poor training skills of managers, and (3) the absence of well-defined job performance criteria. To overcome these problems, training experts suggest the following:

1. Develop realistic goals and/or measures for each OJT area.
2. Plan a specific training schedule for each trainee, including set periods for evaluation and feedback.
3. Help managers to establish a non-threatening atmosphere conducive to learning.
4. Ensure that there are mechanisms to monitor and evaluate training programs.[14]

Manager's Toolkit 5.2 shows the basic steps of an OJT program. The following are other types of training approaches:

Apprenticeship training
System of training in which a worker entering the skilled trades is given thorough instruction and experience, both on and off the job, in the practical and theoretical aspects of the work

APPRENTICESHIP TRAINING **Apprenticeship training** is used extensively where individuals entering an industry, particularly in the skilled trades, such as machinist, laboratory technician, or electrician, are given thorough instruction and experience, both on and off the job, in the practical and theoretical aspects of the work. Many former fishermen left the declining East Coast fishery to join in a seafarers' training program funded by several companies, the federal government, and the Nova Scotia government to learn new skills working in the engine rooms of larger vessels. Magna International, the auto parts giant, pays students $8 to $15 per hour to train as millwrights and tool and die makers. Learning is offered variously in shops, laboratories, and classrooms. Recently, employers in the oil industry in Alberta have started to establish an apprenticeship approach to ensure that oil-patch workers have the appropriate training. With advanced technology, high-school dropouts and drifters won't provide the necessary skills to ensure quality work. In September 2008, Finning Canada and NAIT further enhanced the program that trains qualified apprentices specifically for the Caterpillar Dealer Service Technician program. This will provide the hundreds of heavy equipment technologists needed over the next several years.[15]

MANAGER'S TOOLKIT **5.2**

THE PROPER WAY TO DO ON-THE-JOB TRAINING

P   *Prepare.* Decide what employees need to be taught. Identify the best sequence or steps for training. Decide how best to demonstrate these steps. Have materials, resources, and equipment ready.

R   *Reassure.* Put each employee at ease. Learn about his or her prior experience, and adjust accordingly. Try to get the employee interested, relaxed, and motivated to learn.

O   *Orient.* Show the employee the correct way to do the job. Explain why it's done this way. Discuss how it relates to other jobs. Let him or her ask lots of questions.

P   *Perform.* When employees are ready, let them try the job themselves. Give them an opportunity to practice the job and guide them through rough spots. Provide help and assistance at first, then less as they continue.

E   *Evaluate.* Check the employees' performance, and question them on how, why, when, and where they should do something. Correct errors, repeat instructions.

R   *Reinforce and Review.* Provide praise and encouragement, and give feedback about how the employee is doing. Continue the conversation and express confidence in his or her doing the job.

Cooperative training
Training program that combines practical on-the-job experience with formal education

Internship programs
Programs jointly sponsored by colleges, universities, and other organizations that offer students the opportunity to gain real-life experience while allowing them to find out how they will perform in work organizations

COOPERATIVE TRAINING AND INTERNSHIP PROGRAMS Similar to apprenticeships, **cooperative training** and **internship programs** combine practical on-the-job experience with formal education. Typically, co-op programs are offered at universities where students work for an entire semester as part of their education. While they don't get course credit, they do graduate with an indication that they have been involved in a co-op program. This gives them the ability to demonstrate to prospective employers that they have work experience. The pioneer in co-op education is the University of Waterloo, but there are now co-op programs throughout Canada. Syncrude Canada, Harley-Davidson, and Canadian Microelectronics Corporation are among the many companies that have formed partnerships with education. Further, organizations benefit by getting student-employees with new ideas, energy, and eagerness to accomplish their assignments. Humber College in Toronto, British Columbia Institute of Technology (BCIT) in Burnaby, and many other colleges allow students to earn college credits on the basis of successful job performance and fulfillment of established program requirements.

CLASSROOM INSTRUCTION Classroom instruction enables the maximum number of trainees to be handled by the minimum number of instructors. This method lends itself particularly to training in areas where information can be presented in lectures, demonstrations, films, and videotapes or through computer instruction. Where it is not possible to obtain videotapes, audiotapes can be very valuable.

A special type of classroom facility is used in vestibule training. Trainees are given instruction in the operation of equipment like that found in operating departments. The emphasis is on instruction. For example, a check-out clerk in a supermarket first learns how to use the cash register.

SELF-DIRECTED LEARNING Self-directed learning occurs when individuals work at their own pace at programmed instruction. This typically involves the use of books, manuals, or computers to break down subject matter content into highly organized, logical sequences that demand continuous response on the part of the trainee.

AUDIO-VISUAL Audio-visual methods are used to teach the skills and procedures required for a number of jobs. An example would be golf and tennis coaches using video or camcorders so that their students can see their mistakes. Video-conferencing has also been successful in connecting First Nations communities in remote areas so that they can learn from each other.[16]

SIMULATION Simulation is used when it is either impractical or unwise to train employees on the actual equipment used on the job. An obvious example is training employees to operate aircraft, spacecraft, and other highly technical and expensive equipment. The simulation method provides realism in equipment and its operation. For example, before the launch of its first edition, the *National Post* used simulations to train a new workforce by requiring them to produce a mock newspaper with real content and headlines.

E-LEARNING The simpler, audiovisual, programmed, and computer-oriented training methods just discussed are evolving into what trainers today describe as e-learning. **E-learning** covers a wide variety of applications such as Web-based and computer-based training (CBT) and virtual classrooms. It includes delivery of content via the Internet, intranets and extranets, audiotape, videotape, satellite and broadcast interactive TV, DVD, and CD-ROM. E-learning makes it possible to provide drill and practice, problem solving, simulation, gaming forms of instruction, and certain very sophisticated forms of individualized instruction in a way that's more engaging for learners than traditional classroom instruction. It is also cheaper for employers to administer because, in many instances, it can be delivered directly via the employees' computer. Companies are engaging in more e-learning than ever before and are reporting that they are saving anywhere from 30 to 70% of their training costs.[17] Further, according to Industry Canada (**www.ic.gc.ca**), 98% of employees stated that e-learning helped them reach their own personal development goals and 83% of employees stated that e-learning increased their productivity.[18] In addition, there are systems available that can track the progress of learners. For example, go to **www.webct.com** and **www.desire2learn.com** to see how e-learning systems are used in educational institutions to track student progress.

E-learning also allows employees to search through a virtual sea of information in order to customize their own learning in their own time and space. More companies are demanding access to individual training components for employees to use when and where they need them. This helps alleviate the boredom trainees can experience during full-blow training courses, and employees are more likely to retain the information when they can immediately put it to use. It is also important to ensure that the culture of the organization supports and encourages e-learning. As the well-known e-learning educator, Marc Rosenberg states, "With a good learning culture in place, the first apparent benefits are higher employee satisfaction, morale and—probably—retention. Employees are more motivated and more inclined to do a good job when they feel their ideas are heard, when they can share and be recognized for what they know, when other people are available to help them, when they learn from mistakes rather than being punished.[19] Cisco, a hardware, software, and service company that focuses on Internet solutions, actively uses online technology to help its clients learn and connect, thereby increasing organizational performance.[20]

Although e-learning systems can be very sophisticated, they need not be overly expensive. Many e-learning training programs use existing applications employees are familiar with such as PowerPoint, Word, and Adobe Acrobat and convert them into Flash programs so that they can be easily viewed online with any Web browser. Web-based training can also be revised rapidly, thereby providing continuously updated training material. This not only makes it easier and cheaper to revise training curricula, but also saves travel and classroom costs. When combined with other communications technology such as e-mail, teleconferencing, videoconferencing, and groupware, Web-based training can be even more effective.

One catch to learning is that it requires some planning so that both employees on-site, connecting through high-speed corporate Internet connections, and employees off-site, with wireless modems or other slow connections, are able to access the training material. To cope with this limitation, companies frequently supply their off-site staff with CDs and DVDs containing the same training material employees on-site are able to download.

A review of training media can be found at Training Media Review (**www.tmreview.com**). This is a good resource for managers who want to find out about current effective training approaches.

ON-THE-JOB EXPERIENCES On-the-job experiences present managers with the opportunities to perform under pressure and to learn from their mistakes. Such experiences are some of the most powerful and commonly used techniques. However, just as on-the-job training for first-level employees can be problematic if not well planned, on-the-job management development should be well organized, supervised, and challenging to the participants. Methods of providing on-the-job experience include the following:

E-learning
Learning that takes place through electronic media

Industry Canada
www.ic.gc.ca

WebCT
www.webct.com

Desire2Learn
www.desire2learn.com

Training Media Review
www.tmreview.com

Mentors—Peer Resources
www.mentors.ca

Canadian businesses are increasing their training budgets in efforts to increase employee effectiveness. Computers and Web-based training are exploding.

© China Images / Alamy

a. *Coaching* involves a continuing flow of instructions, comments, and suggestions from the manager to the subordinate.

b. *Mentoring* usually involves an informal relationship in which an executive coaches, advises, and encourages a more junior employee. Some organizations have formal mentorship programs in which someone being considered for upward movement is assigned to another employee in the organization. A good mentor will focus on goals, opportunities, expectations, and standards and assist people in fulfilling their potential.[21]

c. *Understudy assignments* groom an individual to take over a manager's job by helping the individual gain experience in handling important functions of the job.

d. *Job rotation* provides, through a variety of work experiences, the broadened knowledge and understanding required to manage more effectively.

e. *Lateral transfer* involves horizontal movement through different departments, along with upward movement in the organization.

f. *Special projects* and *junior boards* provide an opportunity for individuals to become involved in the study of current organizational problems and in planning and decision-making activities.

g. *Action learning* gives managers release time to work full-time on projects with others in the organization. In some cases, action learning is combined with classroom instruction, discussions, and conferences.

h. *Staff meetings* enable participants to become more familiar with problems and events occurring outside their immediate areas by exposing them to the ideas and thinking of other managers.

i. *Planned career progressions* utilize all these different methods to provide employees with the training and development necessary to progress through a series of jobs requiring higher and higher levels of knowledge and/or skills.

The Canadian Federation of Independent Businesses (CFIB) report that the most effective form of training for businesses of fewer than 50 employees is on-the-job coaching.[22]

SEMINARS AND CONFERENCES Seminars and conferences are useful for bringing groups of people together for training and development. In management development, seminars and conferences can be used to communicate ideas, policies, or procedures, but they are also good for raising points of debate or discussing issues (usually with the help of a qualified leader) that have no set

answers or resolutions. In this regard, seminars and conferences are often used when attitude change is a goal. Check out **www.amanet.org** for a variety of conferences geared toward managers.

CASE STUDIES Case studies use documented examples, which may have been developed from the actual experiences of participants in their own organizations. Cases help managers learn how to analyze (take apart) and synthesize (put together) facts, become conscious of the many variables on which management decisions are based, and, in general, improve their decision-making skills.

This textbook uses case studies as a way for students, with the help of the instructor, to better understand and integrate the information covered in each chapter.

MANAGEMENT GAMES Management games are valuable for bringing a hypothetical situation to life and provide experiential learning. Many games have been designed for general use. For example, TD Bank uses a simulation called Desert Kings to encourage more open communication, to increase levels of team performance, and to increase commitment to both internal and external customer service. L'Oréal uses it to put the employee in the role of a general manager of a fictitious cosmetics company and to determine the profitability as the game progresses.[23]

ROLE PLAYING Role playing consists of assuming the attitudes and behaviour—that is, playing the role—of others, often a supervisor and a subordinate who are involved in a particular problem. By acting out another's position, participants in the role playing can improve their ability to understand and cope with others. Role playing can also help participants learn how to counsel others by helping them see situations from a different point of view. Role playing is used widely in training health-care professionals to be empathic and sensitive to the concerns of patients. It is also used widely in training managers to handle employee issues relating to absenteeism, performance appraisal, and conflict situations. At the end of this chapter, Developing Your Skills provides an opportunity for students to practice role playing.

Phase 4: Evaluating the Training Program

Training, like any other HRM process, should be evaluated to determine its effectiveness. A variety of methods are available to assess the extent to which training and development programs improve learning, affect behaviour on the job, and have an impact on the bottom-line performance of an organization. Unfortunately, few organizations adequately evaluate their training programs. In many ways, this goes beyond poor management; it is poor business practice. Given the substantial monetary stake that organizations have in training, it would seem prudent that managers would want to maximize the return on that investment.

There are four basic methods to evaluate training: (1) reactions, (2) learning, (3) behaviour, and (4) results. Some of these are easier to measure than others, but each is important in that it provides different information about the success of the programs. The combination of these can give a total picture of the training program in order to help the organization determine if business results are improving, and for managers to decide where problem areas lie, what to change about the program, and whether to continue with a program.[24]

At Work with HRM 5.1 provides an example of how a Saskatchewan company uses all four ways to evaluate its training.

Method 1: Reactions

One of the simplest and most common approaches to training evaluation is assessing participant reactions. Happy trainees will be more likely to want to focus on training principles and to utilize the information on the job. However, participants can do more than say whether they liked a program or not. They can give insights into the content and techniques they found most useful. They can critique the instructors or make suggestions about participant interactions, feedback, and the like.

While evaluation methods based on reactions are improving, too many conclusions about training effectiveness are still based on broad satisfaction measures that lack specific feedback. Furthermore, it should be noted that positive reactions are no guarantee that the training has been successful. It may be easy to collect glowing comments from trainees, but gratifying as this

AT WORK **with HRM 5.1**

A CLASSIC FOUR-LEVEL EVALUATION

CONEXUS is the largest credit union in Saskatchewan with assets of $1.1 billion. According to Gayle Johnson, CHRP, EVP Human Resources and Corporate Secretary, its training and development budget for its 465 employees is 6% of payroll. Three percemt is spent on university education, and the other 3% is spent on training. Its largest training program is one that develops financial service representatives (their title is to be changed to "relationship managers"). The training consists of several steps and each is measured.

In-house and classroom-based modules teach content, such as computer literacy, cash duties, and introduction to CONEXUS's products and services, and progresses through to more advanced training, such as consumer lending practices, estates, and minimal mortgage lending. Each three- to five-day module is followed by a work period of three to 12 months, so that employees can apply their knowledge. The four levels of measurement of the effectiveness of training are as follows:

1. *Reaction*: "Smile sheets" are completed by each participant at the end of the classroom training, asking questions such as "What did you get from this session?"

2. *Comprehensive Review*: Exams are given after each module and the results are fed back to the employees and managers.

3. *Employee Performance Competencies*: Every job family has a number of job-specific competencies, and managers are asked to rate the participants on these performance competencies. The changes in ratings are tracked.

4. *Results*: These vary by module. For example, after the cash-lending module, the performance tracked would be the number of call-outs to customers and the number of sales.

CRITICAL THINKING QUESTIONS

1. If the annual payroll for CONEXUS is $18,750,000, what is the annual dollar amount budgeted for training and development?

2. Are there other ways that CONEXUS could use to ensure that the training and development expenditures are worthwhile?

information is to management, it may not be useful to the organization unless it somehow translates into improved behaviour and job performance.

Method 2: Learning

Beyond what participants *think* about the training, it might be a good idea to see whether they actually learned anything. Testing knowledge and skills before a training program gives a baseline standard on trainees that can be measured again after training to determine improvement. This also means that whatever the person is learning must be used at work. For example, if a person were learning new software and the software hasn't been installed, the person's inability to perform is a result of resources, not that learning didn't take place.[25]

Method 3: Behaviour

Much of what is learned in a training program never gets used back on the job. It's not that the training was necessarily ineffective. In fact, on measures of employee reactions and learning, the program might score quite high. But for several reasons, trainees may not demonstrate behaviour change back on the job. **Transfer of training** (also called "transfer of learning") refers to the effective application of principles learned to what is required on the job. While it may not be necessary to measure the extent of the behaviour change, it is important for the supervisor to expect the behaviour change and to reinforce the changes.

Ultimately, the success or failure of any training is whether or not there has been a transfer of that training. To maximize the transfer, managers can take several approaches:

1. Feature identical elements of the job in the actual training.
2. Focus on general principles that can be adapted to fit situations in the work environment.
3. Establish a climate for transfer with the manager being supportive and ensuring that the employee uses the new skills.[26]

Transfer of training
Effective application of principles learned to what is required on the job

FIGURE 5.4   Measuring the Costs/Benefits of Training

In assessing the value of training (or learning), organizations will look at the costs and benefits of training and assign a dollar value. The typical costs included are:

- Trainer's salary/cost
- Trainees' salary/wages
- Materials for training
- Expenses for trainers/trainees (travel, etc.)
- Cost of facilities and equipment
- Lost productivity (opportunity cost)

The benefits include:

- Increase in productivity
- Decrease in errors
- Decrease in turnover
- Behaviour changes
- Improved safety record

For example, a revised safety training program may have the following costs: trainer time ($10,000); trainees' time ($20,000); materials ($5,000), and facilities ($1,000) for a total of $36,000. It was estimated that the training would cover two years and during that time, the company would save $50,000 in workers' compensation insurance and other related safety infractions. Therefore, the benefits outweigh the costs of revising the program.

Method 4: Results

Both the people responsible for training and the managers are under continual pressure to show that their programs produce "bottom-line" results. Most organizations measure their training in terms of its return on investment (ROI). This is even more so during economic downturns. Organizations want to know that the training has increased business results, whether it is profit, customer satisfaction, or decreased costs.[27] Figure 5.4 provides an example of the costs and benefits of a training program and how to calculate the ROI. TD Bank Financial Group takes ROI very seriously. It has a unit whose responsibility is to measure the value of the bank's training investment, about $50 million a year.[28] Manager's Toolkit 5.3 provides an update on a special project in Canada to better measure training results as well as some resources to determine the ROI.

Increasingly, organizations with sophisticated training systems look to training to support long-term strategy and change more than they look for short-term financial returns from their investments. For example, WestJet sees that its investment in training will support its strategic direction and reach the goal of being one of the top 5 airlines in the world by 2016.[29]

As training and development are increasingly viewed from a strategic standpoint, there is heightened interest in benchmarking developmental services and practices against those of recognized leaders in industry. While no single model for exact benchmarking exists, the simplest models are based on the late W. Edwards Deming's classic four-step process. The four-step process advocates that managers do the following:

1. *Plan.* Conduct a self-audit to define internal processes and measurements; decide on areas to be benchmarked; and choose the comparison organization.
2. *Do.* Collect data through surveys, interviews, site visits, and/or historical records.
3. *Check.* Analyze data to discover performance gaps and communicate findings and suggested improvements to management.
4. *Act.* Establish goals, implement specific changes, monitor progress, and redefine benchmarks as a continuous-improvement process.

Benchmarking
Process of measuring one's own services and practices against the recognized leaders in order to identify areas for improvement

To use **benchmarking** successfully, managers must clearly define the measures of competency and performance and must objectively assess the current situation and identify areas for improvement.

RETURN ON TRAINING INVESTMENT

Organizations spend a considerable amount on training each year. In 2008, approximately $56.2 million was spent in North America. However, with the economic challenges, organizations want to be sure that value is received from the training. This has led to an innovative project sponsored by Human Resources and Social Development Canada (HRSDC) and undertaken by the Canadian Society of Training and Development. The purpose of the project is to have organizations determine the business impact of the training as the training is being developed, not after the training has been done. The project, called "Investing in People," is designing tools and methods for monitoring and assessing the effectiveness of the training as it is being implemented. And the focus of the monitoring is to determine the change in business results. The Business Development Bank of Canada, which spends about 5% of its payroll on training, is participating to demonstrate how appropriate training can improve business outcomes.

Previously, the Conference Board of Canada determined that there was a positive relationship between formal training expenditures and performance indicators, such as employee productivity and company profitability. The "Investing in People" project will provide additional ways to evaluate training. In the meantime, a useful tool for developing Return on Training Investment (ROTI) can be found at the website of FutureEd Inc. (www.futured.com/audited/returned.htm).

Sources: Adapted from S. Dobson, "Project Connects Dots between T&D, Profit," *Canadian HR Reporter,* April 21, 2008, www.hrreporter.com/ArticleView.aspx?l=1&articleid=6010 (accessed February 7, 2009); and "2008 Industry Report," *Training,* November/December 2008, Vol. 45 Issue 9, 16–34.

American Society of Training and Development
www.astd.org

Canadian Society for Training and Development
www.cstd.ca

The American Society for Training and Development (ASTD) and its Institute for Workplace Learning have established a project that allows organizations to measure and benchmark training and development activities against each other. This benchmarking forum, which shares findings from over 800 companies, compares data on training costs, staffing, administration, design, development, and delivery of training programs. Not only do initiatives such as these help organizations evaluate their training programs, but the process serves as a feedback loop to reinitiate needs assessment and design of future training.[30]

Other helpful articles and publications on training and development can be found through the Canadian Society for Training and Development at **www.cstd.ca**.

Orientation

Orientation is a very particular type of training. The first objective in the orientation process is to get new employees off to a good start. This is generally accomplished through a formal orientation program. Orientation is the formal process of familiarizing new employees with the organization, their job, and their work unit and embedding organizational values, beliefs, and accepted behaviours. The benefit for new employees is that it allows them to get "in sync" so that they become productive members of the organization. Orientation is a process—not a one-day event. Further, it is important to remember that orientation is a socialization process, and that how employees are treated when they first join the organization makes a huge impact on their views of their supervisors, managers, and the organization.

Benefits of Orientation

In some organizations a formal new-hire orientation process is almost nonexistent or, when it does exist, is performed in a casual manner. Some readers may remember showing up the first day on a new job, being told to work, and receiving no instructions, introductions, or support. This is unfortunate, since a number of practical and cost-effective benefits can be derived from conducting a well-run orientation. Benefits frequently reported by employers include the following:

1. Lower turnover
2. Increased productivity

Video-streams and video-conferencing are frequently used in remote locations to orient new employees.

Thomas Northcut/Riser/Getty Images

3. Improved employee morale
4. Lower recruiting and training costs
5. Facilitation of learning
6. Reduction of the new employee's anxiety

The more time and effort an organization devotes to making new employees feel welcome, the more likely they are to identify with the organization and become valuable members of it. Further, with an effective orientation process, employees can become productive more quickly as well as helping the employees build a solid foundation for future success.[31] Unlike training, which emphasizes the "what" and "how," orientation stresses the "why." It is designed to develop in employees a particular attitude about the work they will be doing and their role in the organization. It defines the philosophy behind the rules and provides a framework for their work in that organization.

Continuous Process

Since an organization is faced with ever-changing conditions, its plans, policies, and procedures must change with these conditions. Unless current employees are kept up to date with these changes, they may find themselves embarrassingly unaware of activities to which new employees are being oriented. While the discussion that follows focuses primarily on the needs of new employees, it is important that all employees be continually reoriented to changing conditions. Many companies are using intranets (internal websites) and online orientation modules to keep new and current employees up to date. For an example of online orientation, check out **onlineorientation.com/** (Deliver the Promise Complete Online Orientation).

Online Orientation Program

onlineorientation.com/

Cooperative Endeavour

For a well-integrated orientation process, cooperation between line and staff is essential. The HR department is ordinarily responsible for coordinating orientation activities and for providing new employees with information about conditions of employment, pay, benefits, and other areas not directly under a supervisor's direction. However, the supervisor has the most important role in the orientation process. New employees are interested primarily in what their supervisor says and does and what their new co-workers are like. Before the arrival of a new employee, the supervisor should inform the work group that a new worker is joining the unit. It is also common practice for supervisors or other managerial personnel to recruit co-workers to serve as volunteer "sponsors" or "buddies" for incoming employees. In addition to providing practical help to newcomers, this approach conveys an emphasis on teamwork.

Careful Planning

An orientation process can make an immediate and lasting impression on an employee that can mean the difference between the employee's success and failure at work. Thus, careful planning—with emphasis on goals, topics to be covered, and methods of organizing and presenting them—is essential. Successful orientation processes emphasize the individual's needs for information, understanding, and a feeling of belonging.

To avoid overlooking items that are important to employees, many organizations devise checklists for use by those responsible for conducting the orientation. Orientation information can also be printed and given to the new employee. Companies are also beginning to use their intranets to make the information more readily available to their employees. The Manager's Toolkit 5.4 suggests items to include in an orientation checklist for supervisors. Orientation should focus on matters of immediate concern, such as important aspects of the job and organizational behaviour expectations (e.g., attendance and safety). Since orientation focuses on helping the new employee become familiar, comfortable, and productive, it is important not to overwhelm or provide too much information at one time. At Work with HRM 5.2 describes how Intuit Canada approaches the orientation process.

Those planning an orientation process should take into account the anxiety employees feel during their first few days on the job. It is natural to experience some anxiety, but if employees are too anxious, training costs, turnover, absenteeism, and even production costs may increase. Early in the orientation, steps should be taken to reduce the anxiety level of new employees. This anxiety reduction can be accomplished by establishing specific times in which the supervisor will be available for questions or coaching. Furthermore, reassuring newcomers that the performance levels they are observing among their co-workers will be attained within a predetermined time frame, based on experiences with other newcomers, can decrease anxiety. This reassurance is particularly important for employees with limited work experience who are learning new skills. In addition, if the organization has a number of new immigrants, the time period for the employee to feel comfortable and part of the organization can take years. A recent study at the University of Calgary identified that part of the orientation process for new immigrants needed to include close contacts with people in the community and people at work.[32] Such connections not only helped the immigrants understand the work place better, but the overall Canadian culture.

And of course, like other training initiatives, the orientation process would also need to be evaluated to ensure it is meeting organizational outcomes. For additional information and tips about planning an orientation, read the article entitled "A Quick Guide to Employee Orientation" at **www.work911.com/articles/orient.htm**.

W W W

Work 911

www.work911.com/articles/
orient.htm

SUPERVISORY ORIENTATION CHECKLIST

1. A formal greeting, including introduction to colleagues

2. Explanation of job procedures, duties, and responsibilities

3. Training to be received (when and why)

4. Supervisor and organization expectations regarding attendance and behaviour norms

5. Job standards and production and service levels

6. Performance appraisal criteria, including estimated time frame to achieve peak performance

7. Conditions of employment, including hours of work, pay periods, and overtime requirements

8. Organization and work unit rules, regulations, and policies

9. Overview of health and safety expectations, as well as when specific training will occur

10. Those to notify or turn to if problems or questions arise

11. Chain of command for reporting purposes

12. An overall explanation of the organization's operation and purpose

13. A review of the organizational chart or structure indicating departments and work flow

14. Offers of help and encouragement, including a specific time each week (in the early stages of employment) for questions or coaching

AT WORK **with HRM 5.2**

WOWING THE NEW HIRE

Intuit Canada, headquartered in Edmonton, Alberta, is a leading developer of financial software, including personal finance management, small business accounting, and tax preparation, with products, such as Quicken. Intuit is a top employer; in 2008, it was ranked the top employer in its industry for the fourth year in a row by *Fortune* magazine. What makes Intuit special is its success in a highly competitive industry. There are many factors, but evidence of its success is its low attrition rate of 3%, which is remarkable in a sector where the average turnover is 20%. Ninety-four percent of its employees report that Intuit is a "great place to work," according to their annual surveys.

Intuit is very careful about the first few days of a new employee's work life. There are too many stories about employees in other organizations showing up very excited about their new job, only to discover that no one remembers they are hired, supplies and offices are not ready, and the reporting manager is absent. Intuit is committed to wowing the candidate—now employee—on the first day. Upon arriving at work, new employees are greeted by name by the receptionist who gives them a stainless steel coffee mug engraved with their name. The hiring manager is called and arrives promptly. He knows the candidate and takes him to the workstation, showing him the computer, telephone, and office supplies. The next step is to introduce the new employee to colleagues and other team members and a "buddy" who has volunteered to guide the new employee and answer all questions for the next three weeks. New employees often struggle with simple questions, such as how does the photocopier work? Do most people bring their lunches to work? Next, the IT person arrives and helps set up voice mail, e-mail, Internet access, etc. Intuit considers it vital that when the new employee goes home that night, he should be able to answer the universal question "How was your first day on the job?" with "Wow, am I ever glad that I took this job!"

This informal orientation is completed by a formal session, in which information about the strategy, vision, plans, and history, including war stories and all the successes, is shared. A key part of this session is a discussion of Intuit values. At the end of the first week, and again at the end of the first month, feedback about the new employee's experiences is solicited on what worked, what was frustrating, and how the orientation can be improved.

CRITICAL THINKING QUESTIONS

1. What else might Intuit do to ensure that the orientation process is successful?
2. How does the orientation process at Intuit compare with an orientation process you experienced at your last job?

Sources: M. Belcourt and S. Taggar, "Making Government the Best Place to Work: Building Commitment," IPAC, New Directions Series 8 2002; and "America's Most Admired Companies 2008", *Fortune,* March 17, 2008.

SPECIAL TOPICS IN TRAINING AND DEVELOPMENT

While this chapter has focused almost exclusively on the processes underlying a systems model of training (needs assessment, principles of learning, implementation methods, evaluation), it may be useful to discuss some of the more popular topics that are covered in these training programs. As noted in Figure 5.2, there is a wide variety of skills and capabilities required in today's workplace. In addition to the training that addresses the competencies associated with a particular job, many employers develop training programs to meet the needs of a broader base of employees. This section summarizes some of these programs, including orientation, basic skills training, team training, and diversity training.

Basic Skills Training

The Canadian Council on Learning finds that almost one-half of Canadian adults and 42% of working-age Canadians are below the internationally accepted literacy standard for functioning in today's world.[33] Experts define an illiterate individual as one having a sixth-grade education or less. Working adults who improve their literacy skills gain better pay and more promotions and are employed for longer periods of time. Employers launch literacy training in order to improve productivity. Dofasco Steel in Ontario provides not only training in basic English and computer-related skills, but also advanced computer courses and business writing.[34]

These figures have important implications for society at large and for organizations that must work around these skill deficiencies. Never has this been truer, given tight labour markets on the one hand, and increasing skill requirements (related to advances in technology) on the other. Basic skills have become essential occupational qualifications, having profound implications for product quality, customer service, internal efficiency, and workplace and environmental safety. In the last several years, the number of businesses that require a high-level of knowledge has grown by almost 80%.[35] According to the ABC Canada Literacy Foundation, 15% of adult Canadians have serious problems dealing with any printed documents.[36] Canadian employers report that the top five skills they need in employees today are the ability to

- read and understand information
- listen, ask questions, and understand
- work in teams
- assess situations and identify problems
- share information orally and work with others

But grown-ups don't learn the way kids do, so many of the traditional basic skills training techniques are not successful with adults. To implement a successful program in basic and remedial skills, managers should do the following:

1. Explain to employees why and how the training will help them in their jobs.
2. Relate the training to the employees' goals.
3. Respect and consider participant experiences, and use these as a resource.
4. Use a task-centred or problem-centred approach so that participants "learn by doing."
5. Give feedback on progress toward meeting learning objectives.

At Work with HRM 5.3 provides additional information about what some other organizations are doing to improve workplace literacy.

AT WORK **with HRM 5.3**

WORKPLACE LITERACY SUCCESSES

There are a variety of success stories in Canada dealing with workplace literacy. The City of Moncton, with a workforce of over 600 employees, determined that grade 12 was a minimum requirement. However, many of its employees had been hired prior to that requirement and through a needs' assessment the City determined that there needed to be upgrading for many of its employees. The City discovered that writing, basic math, reading, and computer skills were needed at a level higher than some of its employees had. To bridge the gap, specialized training programs were developed. The result: employees have enhanced their basic computer skills; can better communicate ideas; have increased mobility within the municipality; and some have earned their grade 12 diploma.

Vecima Networks, a small electronics manufacturer in Victoria, B.C., identified that the real issue for its training focus was on the employees who actually work the assembly lines. Since many of the people on the assembly lines were high school dropouts or in low-skilled jobs, more than technical training was required. Employees stated that they didn't understand the engineers' instructions even when written in very basic language. To improve the situation, Vecima partnered with community resources and not-for-profits to design and deliver the literacy workshops for $50,000. The company feels that by this investment, it has improved its productivity as well as enhanced the overall skill level of its employees.

CRITICAL THINKING QUESTION

Do you think companies ought to investment in basic literacy training? Explain your reasoning.

Sources: Adapted from "CEOs Talk about Training & Development," *Canadian HR Reporter*, May 19, 2008, www.hrreporter.com/ArticleView.aspx?l=1&articleid=6082 (accessed February 8, 2009); and Conference Board of Canada, "Workplace Literacy Mini Case Study."

Team Training

As discussed in Chapter 3, organizations rely on teams to attain strategic and operational goals. Whether the team is an air crew, a research team, or a manufacturing or service unit, the contributions of the individual members of the team are not only a function of the skills and capabilities (competencies) of each individual but also of the interaction of the team members. To give an example of how important this can be to an organization, Dofasco had 6700 employees participate in four-day workshops on interpersonal and group skills over a three-year period. The company wanted all its employees to learn to work with each other in new and different ways.

Teamwork skills fall under two broad categories: task-related and team-related. In addition, new research suggests that successful teams develop a "shared mental model" of the task and can work more efficiently in actually working on the task.[37] Teamwork skills that characterize effective teams are shown in Figure 5.5. They include both task tools and techniques, and interpersonal skills. Teams need to evaluate themselves periodically to ensure that the goal(s) is being achieved and that there are no concerns about interpersonal relationships.[38]

Managers who want to design team training for their organization should keep the following points in mind:

1. Team building is a difficult and comprehensive process. Since many new teams are under pressure to produce, there is little time for training. Everything cannot be covered in a 24-hour blitz. Team training works best when it is provided over time and parallels team development.
2. Team development is not always a linear sequence of "forming, storming, norming, and performing." Training initiatives can help a team work through each of these stages, but managers must be aware that lapses can occur.
3. Additional training is required to assimilate new members. Large membership changes may result in teams reverting to a previous developmental stage.
4. Skills need to be acquired through practice and reviewing the performance of the teams.[39]

FIGURE 5.5   Team Skills

Task Tools/Techniques	Interpersonal skills
• Ability to use meeting time effectively	• Ability to communicate with team members and be open and honest
• Ability to problem-solve	• Ability to handle and resolve conflict
• Ability to brainstorm	• Ability to create climate of trust
• Ability to use decision-making tools	• Understanding how to establish norms
• Ability to identify and set goals	• Ability to handle difficult team members
• Ability to present ideas	• Ability to draw upon diversity within team
• Ability to evaluate progress of task	• Understanding stages of team development (forming, storming, norming, performing)
• Ability to project plan and manage tasks	• Ability to deal with team issues
• Ability to be creative and innovative	• Understanding ways to surface tension
	• Ability to assess team's performance
	• Ability to collaborate

Sources: Adapted from Judith A. Ross, "Make Your Good Team Great," *Harvard Business Review*, December 2008, 3–5; "Teaming Up," *Financial Planning*, November 2008, 33–34; and Terri A. Fredrick, "Facilitating Better Teamwork: Analyzing the Challenges and Strategies of Classroom-based Collaboration," *Business Communications Quarterly*, Volume 71, Number 4, December 2008, 439–455.

Employees are more diverse and expect to be involved in decision making.

© 2009 Jupiterimages Corporation

HRM and the law 5.1

TRAINING: DISCRIMINATION HAS ORGANIZATIONAL IMPLICATIONS

The complainant worked for the federal government and wished to be promoted from a technical position to a management position. Over a number of years the complainant had been provided with a variety of different training opportunities for management positions. The complainant took advantage of the training but did not participate in a formal career advancement program. Various performance reviews indicated that there had been formal training and experience in management systems but that no visible career advancement had been possible. Prior to the launching of the complaint, the employee had been told that promotions to a senior management level position were not possible without recent line management experience. There had also been an earlier tribunal decision that identified the biases of senior managers towards visible minorities—these managers felt visible minorities as culturally different and were not considered suitable for managerial positions.

Through the human rights hearing, it was determined that the complainant had not been provided appropriate assistance from the employer to actually acquire the management experience required for senior management positions. In the earlier human rights complaint, the tribunal determined that people who had had temporary assignments to managerial positions were more likely to get the promotion than those employees who were not. While the employee had been provided with some temporary assignment to a management position, these assignments were not systematic and were not frequent. The tribunal noted that to become a manager in the federal government a person needed management training and management experience.

Given the earlier incident with the same department of the government, the Canadian Human Rights Tribunal did determine that the complainant had been discriminated against due to race and ethnic background and ordered a lump-sum payment for lost wages, plus an additional $4,000 for special compensation in recognition of the poor way in which the employee was treated.

Source: *Shiv Chopra v. Health Canada*, http://chrt-tcdp.gc.ca/aspinc/search/vhtml-eng.asp?doid=619&lg=_e&isruling=1 or http://chrt-tcdp.gc.ca/aspinc/search/vhtml-eng.asp?doid=259&lg=_e&isruling=0. Canadian Human Rights Tribunal (CHRT), 2007. Reproduced with the permission of the Minister of Public Works and Government Services, 2009.

Diversity Training

Many large organizations sponsor some sort of diversity training. This emphasis is sparked by an awareness of the varied demographics of the workforce, the challenges of employment equity, the dynamics of stereotyping, the changing values of the workforce, and the potential competitive payoffs from bringing different people together for a common purpose.

There are basically two types of diversity training: (1) awareness building, which helps employees appreciate the benefits of diversity, and (2) skill building, which provides the capabilities necessary for working with people who are different. For example, a skill-building diversity program might teach managers how to conduct performance reviews with people from different cultures or teach male supervisors how to coach female employees toward better career opportunities. When designing a diversity training program it is important to take a systems approach (similar to that mentioned at the beginning of this chapter) and ensure that the existing policies, practices and procedures are examined for anything that might be hampering diversity.[40]

To understand the implications of training and diversity, read HRM and the Law 5.1.

CAREER DEVELOPMENT—INDIVIDUAL AND ORGANIZATIONAL NEEDS

Outcome 7

Career development programs, with their greater emphasis on the individual, introduce a personalized aspect to the term "development." Most training and development programs have a career development component. Most career development programs should be viewed as a dynamic process that attempts to meet the needs of managers, their employees, and the organization.

Career planning, on the other hand, is a systematic approach where you would assess your values, interests, abilities, goals, and identify the path(s) you would need to take to realize your career goals. It would then be through career development programs that you would journey along the career path.

Ultimately, in today's organizations, individuals are responsible for initiating their own career planning. It is up to individuals to identify their knowledge, skills, abilities, interests, and values and seek out information about career options in order to set goals and develop career plans. Managers should encourage employees to take responsibility for their own careers, by offering continuing assistance in the form of feedback on individual performance and making available information about the organization, the job, and career opportunities that might be of interest.

The organization should be responsible for supplying information about its mission, policies, and plans and for providing support for employee self-assessment, training, and development. Significant career growth can occur when individual initiative combines with organizational opportunity. Career development programs benefit managers by giving them increased skill in managing their own careers, greater retention of valued employees, increased understanding of the organization, and enhanced reputations as people developers. Some organizations make use of leadership career development programs. Enbridge, an Alberta-based company in the energy transportation and distribution business, changed the way in which it provided leadership development. For a number of years it sent a few executives each year to Queen's University for a three-week residential program. However, in assessing ways to maximize the training budget, the organization decided it could provide leadership training to a larger number of employees by custom-developing a program that could be delivered in-house. By changing the approach to delivery, Enbridge is now able to offer a leadership development program to 130 employees each year instead of five.[41] For more information about the types of programs available for leadership development, visit the website of The Banff Centre at **www.banffcentre.ca** and the Center for Creative Leadership at **www.ccl.org**.

As shown in Figure 5.6, organizational needs should be linked with individual career needs in a way that joins personal effectiveness and satisfaction of employees with the achievement of the organization's strategic objectives.

Center for Creative Leadership
www.ccl.org

The Banff Centre
www.banffcentre.ca

Creating Favourable Conditions

While a career development program requires many special processes and techniques, some basic conditions must be present if it is to be successful. These conditions create favourable conditions for the program.

FIGURE 5.6 Balancing Individual and Organizational Needs

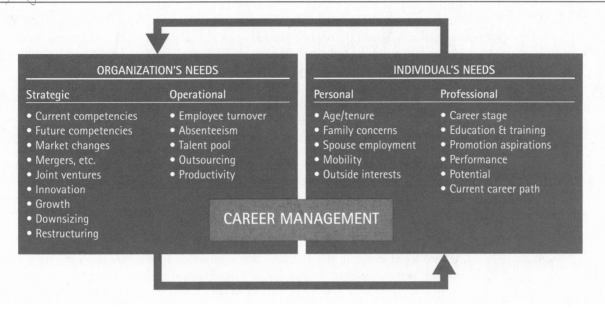

Management Support

If career development is to succeed, it must receive the complete support of top management. The system should reflect the goals and culture of the organization, and the people philosophy should be woven throughout. A people philosophy can provide employees with a clear set of expectations and directions for their own career development. For a program to be effective, managerial staff at all levels must be trained in the fundamentals of job design, performance appraisal, career planning, and coaching.

Goal Setting

Before individuals can engage in meaningful career planning, they must not only have an awareness of the organization's philosophy but also a clear understanding of the organization's more immediate goals. Otherwise, they may plan for personal change and growth without knowing if or how their own goals match those of the organization. For example, if the technology of a business is changing and new skills are needed, will the organization retrain to meet this need or hire new talent? Is there growth, stability, or decline in the number of employees needed? How will turnover affect this need? Answers to these kinds of questions are essential to the support of individual career planning.

Changes in HRM Practices

To ensure that its career development program will be effective, an organization may need to alter its current HRM practices. For example, a practice of job rotation can counteract obsolescence and maintain employee flexibility. Another practice that can aid development involves job transfers and promotions. A **transfer** is the placement of an employee in another job for which the duties, responsibilities, status, and remuneration are approximately equal to those of the previous job (or work requirements). A transfer may require the employee to change work group, workplace, work shift, or organizational unit; it may even necessitate moving to another geographic area. Transfers make it possible for an organization to place its employees in jobs where there is a greater need for their services and where they can acquire new knowledge and skills. A downward transfer, or demotion, moves an individual into a lower-level job that can provide developmental opportunities, but such a move is usually considered unfavourably by the individual who is demoted.

Transfer

Placement of an individual in another job for which the duties, responsibilities, status, and remuneration are approximately equal to those of the previous job

Promotion
Change of assignment to a job at a higher level in the organization

A **promotion** is a change of assignment to a job at a higher level in the organization. The new job (or work) normally provides an increase in pay and status and demands more skill or carries more responsibility. Promotions enable an organization to utilize the skills and abilities of its staff more effectively, and the opportunity to gain a promotion serves as an incentive for good performance. The two principal criteria for determining promotions are merit and seniority. Often the problem is to determine how much consideration to give to each factor.

As organizations continue to change, including their structure and number of employees, the ability to promote people as part of career development is becoming more difficult. The issues of balancing work and family, mentioned in Chapter 1, can become paramount when considering a promotion. Organizations are using "transfer" or "job rotation" more frequently. For example, Trojan Technologies, an Ontario-based company that designs, manufactures, and sells ultraviolet disinfection systems for water treatment, frequently moves employees across the organization. With a constantly changing environment, Trojan found that it was useful to expand the knowledge of its staff and to give technically trained staff an opportunity to better understand the business.[42]

Specialized Development Needs

Outcome **8**

As mentioned earlier in this chapter, "development" is a long-term approach for acquiring and utilizing new skills. Since the purpose of a development program is to give employees enhanced capabilities, there are a number of ways in which this can occur. The responsibility to develop the talent lies with all managers in the organization—not just the person's immediate supervisor or team leader.

Mentoring

When one talks with men and women about their employment experiences, it is common to hear them mention individuals at work who influenced them. They frequently refer to immediate managers who were especially helpful as career developers. But they also mention others at higher levels in the organization who provided guidance and support to them in the development of their careers. These managers (and executives) who coach, advise, and encourage less experienced employees are called **mentors.**

Mentors
Managers who coach, advise, and encourage less experienced employees

Generally, the mentor initiates the relationship, but sometimes an employee will approach a potential mentor for advice. Most mentoring relationships develop over time on an informal basis. However, many organizations emphasize formal mentoring plans that assign a mentor to those employees considered for upward movement in the organization. A good mentorship is a reciprocal relationship—with both the mentee and the mentor learning from each other.[43]

It is important to remember that a mentor relationship is a very personal one. Here are some tips to make the relationship successful:

1. *Mentoring is a personal interaction.* This is not a relationship that can be forced. It is a relationship that both people want to have.
2. *Being a mentor isn't for everyone.* Some people have a genuine interest in sharing their experiences with others while others are reluctant to give of themselves. You can't force someone to be a mentor.
3. *Make use of work assignments and challenges.* Using work assignments as a basis for discussion can assist in making the advice real and relevant, and creating a teachable moment.
4. *Mentoring is a two-way street.* Mentees have to be willing to be mentored; forcing someone into a formal mentoring program won't work.
5. *Be clear on expectations.* It is important, particularly at the early stages of mentoring, to be clear on what is expected of each other and when.[44]

Manager's Toolkit 5.5 provides guidelines for some of the qualities an individual should look for in a mentor.

Organizations with formal mentoring programs include Shell International, Sun Microsystems, Johnson & Johnson, and the Bank of Montreal. Alternatively, given the importance of the issue, a number of mentoring organizations have begun to spring up. When done well, the mentoring process is beneficial for both the mentee and the mentor. A new form of mentoring, sponsored by

Mentoring helps people at all levels in the organization develop their special skills and talents.

Larry Lilac / Alamy

Society for Canadian Women in Science and Technology

www.scwist.ca

National Mentoring Partnership

www.mentoring.org

Women's Enterprise Centre

www.womensenterprise.ca

the Ms. Foundation for Women, provides an opportunity for both girls and boys, 8 to 18 years old, to spend a day with parents or friends on the job. The program is designed to give young people more attention and to provide them with career role models. American Express, Chevron, and Estée Lauder Companies participate in this program.

Not surprisingly, mentoring is also being done electronically. E-mentoring brings experienced business professionals together with individuals needing advice and guidance. Even though participants in e-mentoring typically never meet in person, many form long-lasting e-mail connections that tend to be very beneficial. Still, most participants see these connections as supplements to—rather than substitutes for—in-person mentors.

There are a number of resources for mentoring. A few examples include the following:

Society for Canadian Women in Science and Technology (SCWIST) is an association that has assembled thousands of women in technology fields who act as online mentors to visitors to its website.

National Mentoring Partnership is an online site for a variety of different resources for mentors and mentees, including information about how to find a mentor.

Women's Enterprise Centre is an organization that encourages, helps, and supports women in B.C. who want to own, operate, and grow their own business.

MANAGER'S TOOLKIT 5.5

MENTOR GUIDELINES

Successful mentoring is built on a common understanding of interests and "ground rules." Here are some to consider before establishing a mentor–mentee relationship:

1. Formalize the expectations with a written agreement that outlines the behaviours of each person.

2. Understand that either party can withdraw from the relationship at any time, and it is not necessary to provide an explanation.

3. All documents exchanged, such as company plans or résumés, will be treated as confidential.

4. The mentor cannot be solicited for a job. Doing so is grounds for breaking the relationship.

5. Respect each other's time. Arrive on time and prepared with a list of questions or topics to be discussed.

6. Provide feedback honestly. For example, the mentee could state, "This is not the kind of information I need at this stage" or the mentor might advise, "You should not skip meetings just because they are tedious; it is an important part of this company's culture to be visible at these meetings."

Specialized Career Development for a Diverse Workforce

Today, some organizations offer extensive career development programs geared to special groups, such as women, minorities, youth, and/or dual-career couples. For example, male managers have traditionally had an informal network of interpersonal relationships that has provided a means for senior (male) members of the organization to pass along news of advancement opportunities and other career tips to junior (male) members. Women have typically been left outside this network, lacking role models to serve as mentors. To combat their difficulty in advancing to management positions, women in several organizations have developed their own women's networks. At the Bank of Montreal, a women's network serves as a system for encouraging and fostering women's career development and for sharing information, experiences, and insights.

Another example is an organization actively creating conditions that recognize and reward performance on the basis of objective, nondiscriminatory criteria. Many organizations are taking the position that their employees should reflect the communities in which they function. At the Bank of Montreal, each manager is required to set diversity targets.

Keeping a Career in Perspective

It is important in any training and development program to keep everything in perspective. While work is a very important part of someone's life, it is only a part. Organizations want people who maintain an appropriate balance between their work life and their personal life, and therefore can continue to grow and develop for personal satisfaction and success for the organization.

Some of the other areas of life that must be considered are the following:

1. Off-the-job interests can provide a break from the demands of a career while allowing employees to gain satisfaction from non-work-related activities.
2. Family life can be negatively affected if the organization does not provide recognition of a person's life outside of work. Conflict between work and family may arise over such issues as number of hours worked per week, the need to relocate for career advancement, and the amount of overtime that may be required.
3. Planning for retirement is an important consideration given the aging workforce. Many companies are now providing pre-retirement programs to allow an employee to be productive in the organization while minimizing problems that can arise in the retirement years.
4. Dual-career families are a factor in the contemporary business world. Therefore, career development and progress may need to take the goals of the partner into consideration.

As mentioned in Chapter 1, the workforce of today is very different than the workforce of yesterday. The organization may have as many as four generational cohorts—each with their own view and expectations about career development. Therefore, it will be important to maintain a balanced perspective on career development and to structure opportunities to fit the needs of both the diverse employee base and the organization.[45]

Emerging Trends 5.1 provides some additional information about what is on the horizon in relation to orientation, training and development.

EMERGING TRENDS **5.1**

1. *Increased use of Web-based and other e-learning.* As organizations continue to focus on getting optimum results from training dollars spent, and as e-learning systems evolve, more organizations will make use of online and other type of electronic learning resources.

2. *More partnerships between companies and educational institutions.* With an anticipated skilled labour shortage in the future, companies will work directly with post-secondary institutions to provide scholarships and awards to students that fit their needs. For example, EnCana Corporation recently established

awards for the top third and fourth year students in disciplines related to energy and the environment.

3. ***Using more than one training method.*** There is a shift to creating a blended approach to training delivery where experiential and e-learning works in conjunction with classroom discussions. The purpose is to keep the learner engaged and able to use the learnings quickly on the job. Simulations and games are being used more.

4. ***Increased attention to talent management.*** The concept of training and development is evolving into the concept of "talent management." It is looking at the people in the organization as "talent," and then creating a plan to have the people at the appropriate skill level when needed while recognizing that there is no longer a culture of lifetime employment.

Sources: Extracted from Peter Cappelli, "Talent Management for the Twenty-First Century," *Harvard Business Review,* March 2008, 74–81; Derek Sankey, "Oilpatch Looks to Build Future Workforce," *National Post,* April 15, 2008, SR7; "Executives Value Real-World Perspectives," *Canadian HR Reporter,* July 16, 2007, 15; and Shannon Klie, "The Coaching Executive," *Canadian HR Reporter,* July 16, 2007, 13.

SUMMARY

1. Discuss the systems approach to training and development.
   - Training and development need to be linked to the organization's goals and objectives.
   - A systems approach to training and development creates this link.
   - A systems approach consists of five phases: needs analysis, training program design, implementation, evaluation, and transfer to work environment.

2. Describe the components of a training-needs assessment.
   - Contributes to the organization's overall goals.
   - Involves four phases: needs assessment, program design, implementation, evaluation

3. Identify the principles of learning and how they facilitate training.
   - Goal setting.
   - Meaningfulness of presentation.
   - Modelling.
   - Individual differences.
   - Active practice and repetition.
   - Feedback.
   - Rewards and reinforcement.

4. Identify the types of training and development methods used for all levels of employees.
   - On-the-job.
   - Apprenticeship.
   - Cooperative and internship programs.
   - Computer-based.
   - Seminars and conferences.
   - Role playing and management games.

5. List some of the characteristics of an effective orientation process.
   - Familiarizing new employees with the organization, their job, and their work unit.
   - Embedding organizational values, beliefs, and accepted behaviours.
   - Active involvement and participation from the supervisor.

6. Describe the special training programs that are currently popular.
   - Basic skills training (such as literacy) where people learn basic reading and math.
   - Team work where people learn new behaviours and skills to work in teams.
   - Diversity where people develop an appreciation of the benefits of diversity.

7. Explain how a career development program integrates individual and organizational needs.
   • It blends employee effectiveness and satisfaction with the achievement of the organization's strategic objectives.
   • HRM practices must fit so that both individual and organization needs can be achieved.
8. Discuss specialized career development needs.
   • Mentoring programs where more senior individuals coach and encourage more junior staff.
   • Specialized career programs for diverse workforce where the organization gears the development to special groups, such as women, youth, etc.

NEED TO KNOW

• Definition of orientation, training, development, and learning
• Definition of employee involvement and empowerment
• Variety of training methods
• Ways to reinforce training in the work environment
• Basic approaches to development

NEED TO UNDERSTAND

• Importance of the line manager in identifying training needs
• Relationship of orientation to organizational performance
• Importance of ensuring appropriate method is used to enhance learning
• Role supervisor or line manager plays in helping the trainee use the new skills and behaviours
• Organizational and individual responsibility in a person's development

KEY TERMS

apprenticeship training 140
behaviour modification 139
benchmarking 146
cooperative training 141
development 132
e-learning 142

instructional objectives 137
internship programs 141
mentors 156
on-the-job training (OJT) 140
orientation 132
promotion 156

trainee readiness 138
training 132
transfer 155
transfer of training 145

REVIEW QUESTIONS

1. Describe the steps in developing a training and development program.
2. Describe and define the principles of learning.
3. What are the various methods for training and development?
4. Describe five task-related skills for teams and five interpersonal skills.
5. Explain mentoring.
6. List the four issues in evaluating training programs and describe why each is important.
7. What are the benefits of a well-designed orientation process?
8. Give some reasons for the trend toward increased emphasis on career development programs.

CRITICAL THINKING QUESTIONS

1. Your employer has approached you to assume a supervisory role. While this flatters you, you are also concerned about your ability to carry out the role successfully. What type of training or development might you want to help you succeed?
2. Sally was recently hired as a cashier for a fast-food restaurant. The shift leader gave her a very brief introduction to the food and cash handling procedures. Unfortunately, at the end of Sally's shift, there was a lot of food waste and the cash count was short. Detail the training Sally needs in order to perform the work successfully.

3. "Mentorship programs are a waste of time and money." Why might an employer say this? What might you say to the employer to counter the employer's thinking?

4. You have recently joined an organization as a customer service representative. The company places high value on satisfied customers. Specifically describe the type of training you ought to have in order to ensure customers receive a high level of customer satisfaction. What would be the "hard skills" and the "soft skills"?

5. What contributions can a career development program make to an organization that is forced to downsize its operations?

6. Sukh has just been promoted to a managerial role in a small auto parts company in Southern Ontario. She immediately noticed that the company had no orientation process for new employees. A decision was made to implement a new orientation process for all employees. What might be included and over what period of time?

7. You work in an organization that focuses on sales. Recently, there have been a number of complaints about a particular sales representative in terms of accuracy of orders and timeliness of work being completed. Complete the four steps in the systems approach to training and development. Specifically, (1) how will you determine if training is the answer? (2) identify a possible learning or training objective; (3) what methods would you use to implement training? (4) how would you evaluate if the training was effective?

DEVELOPING YOUR SKILLS

1. Role Playing. In class, working in pairs, determine which role each person will play from the following scenario. Play the role for 15 to 20 minutes. After the time period, the class will discuss how they felt, what worked, what could have been done better, and how they might use role play if they were a supervisor.

Scenario

ROLE 1: HOTEL MANAGER You are getting ready for a quarterly review of the performance of your front-desk supervisor. You are halfway through the performance year. You have had weekly discussions about the service levels and have reviewed results against the targets. You have also discussed specific training needs of the supervisor and the staff who report to the supervisor.

In setting objectives at the beginning of the year, you and the supervisor had agreed that the supervisor's style of management needed to change. The company is moving toward empowering frontline staff, and managers need to have a different approach and relationship with employees. It is in this area that your supervisor is struggling. Employees have complained that the supervisor tells them what to do, is very abrupt in interactions, and at times says things in a way that people feel is disrespectful. You have discussed this behaviour before, but you are not seeing the improvement you'd like to see. On the other hand, you are confident the supervisor can modify the behaviour and become the kind of leader the company wants. You want this interview to be positive and constructive and you want to find the right training program to help the supervisor.

ROLE 2: FRONT-DESK SUPERVISOR You are getting ready for the quarterly review of your performance with your boss. You are pleased with the results of service levels as targets have been exceeded every week for the last six months.

You are certain your boss will want to discuss your management style. This is an area where you are still having difficulty. You want to act differently with your employees but you aren't sure exactly what to do. You have read some articles but that doesn't seem to help when you try to put some of the suggestions into practice. You'd like to have some training but you aren't sure if the hotel will support you.

2. In groups of three to four students, develop a list of behaviours or skills that would improve your performance as a team member. For each behaviour or skill, identify one or two training methods that would be appropriate for learning that behaviour or skill.

Motorola University
www.motorola.com

www.motorola.com/
motorolauniversity.jsp

**GE's John F. Welch
Leadership Development
Center**
www.ge.com/careers

www.ge.com/company/
culture/leadership_learning.
html

Royal Bank Careers
www.rbc.com/careers/index.
html

3. Providing training to employees is a significant retention tool in a tight labour market. In groups of four to five students, discuss the benefits of training for individuals and organizations. Prepare a response to the following statement: "Employees should be required to repay the cost of any training if they leave the organization before one year."

4. In groups of three to four students, access the following websites for major corporations that use a number of different techniques for training and development. Write a one- to two-page paper describing the similarities and the differences:

   Motorola University, **www.motorola.com (www.motorola.com/motorolauniversity.jsp)**
   GE's John F. Welch Leadership Development Center, **www.ge.com/careers (www.ge.com/company/culture/leadership_learning.html)**
   Royal Bank Careers, **www.rbc.com/careers/index.html**

5. Each student will search **www.tmreview.com** and find one item that might be a valuable training resource in the future. Students are to print the description and describe in approximately one-half page why this is a useful training resource.

Training Media Review
www.tmreview.com

Case Study 1

Orientation at Bell Canada

On May 15, 2006, Bell Canada began to roll out a new orientation program with a large e-based component for new hires. The website that introduces new employees to their orientation is an upbeat and interactive design where new employees can quickly find much of the information necessary to orient themselves to their new company. The orientation process allows for a consistent message to be delivered to all employees across Canada, in either French or English, and grants the new hire's immediate supervisor more tools that can be used to help welcome the employees over the first few days and months at Bell.

It is only the starting point for a new career at Bell Canada. Bell's corporate culture promotes self-service, where much of the information relating to an individual's options regarding career growth and development is posted on the intranet. This provides each individual private access to only their information. This orientation process aligns with the culture of self-service and acquaints new employees with the knowledge of how things get done around Bell and provides links for where they can look for more information. It also encourages the new hires to ask for direction from their managers and to seek information on any items that may have been missed during their first few weeks.

While orientation is a necessary step in welcoming and guiding a new employee, it is a costly endeavour for organizations. Bell's decision to move to a large online orientation component was a conscious decision to find savings where possible. In a national company, the transportation costs of bringing all new hires to a central location may have benefits but other options such as intranet information, conference calls, and other forms of communication should be considered. The current program at Bell gives the same message and without the costs involved in a classroom-dependent process. The extra bonus in this method is that employees have access to information that aids in their education about their work environment, and permits them to begin contributing to their teams fairly soon after starting work.

Given the high cost of hiring new employees, it is important that the employee is able to start being productive as soon as possible. As part of the connecting the new employee to the organization, and allowing the transition to occur, Bell has leveraged an already established program using employees known to be Pride Builders. This program identifies employees across all levels and departments who take special pride in their work and display excellent organizational citizenship and desired behaviours. According to Randi Haimovitz, project designer of the orientation program, Pride Builders make it a priority to connect with the new hires within their first few weeks at work and when possible meet them for a coffee in order to provide valuable company information and make the new hire feel more welcomed. New hires are also introduced to other new employees outside of their immediate business units via semi-annual forums.

Questions

1. What are the advantages of the orientation program at Bell? Describe some of the limitations.
2. The goals of orientation processes are to explain the values of the organization, the culture, and expectations, not just the details of a person's own job. What elements in Bell's orientation program would be conducive to these goals? Do you think orientation should be done electronically or in person? Why or why not?
3. Do you think Bell's orientation meets the needs of the different work generations? Why or why not? Would it meet your needs?

Case Study 2

People Development Strategies at Credit Union Central of Saskatchewan

There are 128 credit unions in Saskatchewan, with assets ranging from less than $1 million to more than a billion dollars. All of these are affiliated with Credit Union Central of Saskatchewan, which facilitates cooperation among credit unions and provides consulting services, trade association functions, and liquidity management.

Credit Union Central, together with the four largest Saskatchewan credit unions, developed a plan to implement a comprehensive human resource management system to produce, first, a better alignment of employee performance to organizational objectives, and, second, more focused training to produce desired business results and an enhanced ability to retain employees through opportunities for professional development. Working with Hay Management Consultants, the first step was to develop a competency glossary, followed by performance management processes and tools, selection and staffing tools, and then succession planning.

Competencies can be defined as attitudes, skills, knowledge or behaviours that are essential to perform at work and that differentiate superior performers. The competency glossary defines core competencies, which apply to all roles within the organization, and role-specific competencies. Competency target levels indicating superior performance are set for each role.

An example of a core competency, based on the key values and strategies of the organization, is "results orientation."

When your employee tried to improve his/her own performance he/she

1. Identified areas of waste or inefficiency but didn't take any action
2. Made some changes to work methods in order to reach particular goals that had been set for him/her
3. Made specific changes in the system and his/her own work methods in order to improve performance beyond goals set
4. Set own challenging goals that were accomplished with a significant amount of planning, analysis, and effort
5. Set individual goals by thinking through the costs and benefits, and explicitly considered potential profits, risks, and return on investment, in order to make decisions that ended up having a positive organizational impact

6. Took a calculated entrepreneurial risk and committed significant organizational resources to act on an idea that ended up significantly improving performance.

A role-specific competency might be "concern for order, quality, and compliance" defined as follows:

When your employee demonstrated attention to detail in his/her work, he/she

1. Checked on the work to ensure it was accurate, complied with all relevant regulations, and followed all standard practices and procedures.
2. Monitored the accuracy and quality of his/her own work and others' work consistently and systematically and kept a detailed record of work when it was necessary.
3. During the project, monitored the progress of the project against metrics and deliverables, took action to ensure the procedures put in place were effective, and quickly corrected any weaknesses or deficiencies.
4. Established and utilized a procedure and/or system to facilitate work efficiency and ensure high-quality output; modified and improved the procedure and/or system when a weakness was identified, in order to ensure that high-quality work was being produced.

Managers work with employees to assess competency levels. The competency glossary and a competency assessment questionnaire enable managers and employees to discuss skills, abilities, and behaviours using a common framework. Training and development plans are based on gaps between target performance and actual performance. A developmental resource kit, which includes training courses, seminars, books, and work opportunities, all classified by competency, assists with building development plans.

This approach has resulted in clear direction on performance and development plans to move employees toward optimum performance levels.

Questions

1. Describe the advantages and disadvantages of the approach used to identify performance gaps.
2. Why would managers resist or support this approach? Explain your answers.

NOTES AND REFERENCES

1. Mark A. Youndt and Scott A. Snell, "Human Resource Configurations, Intellectual Capital, and Organizational Performance," *Journal of Managerial Issues* XVI, no. 3 (Fall 2004): 337–60.
2. Ibid.
3. "Training and Learning Spending Stagnant in Canada," *Conference Board of Canada,* May 1, 2007, www.newswire.ca/en/releases/archive/May2007/01/c3343.html (accessed February 2, 2009).
4. Ibid.
5. *Training Magazine,* "Training Top 125 2008: Winners," www.trainingmag.com, February 6, 2008; and Hewitt Associates, "50 Best Employers in Canada Well Positioned to Meet Economic Challenges," December 31, 2008.
6. Jeffrey M. O'Brien, "100 Best Companies to Work For: Zappos Knows How to Kick It," *Fortune,* February 2, 2009, 58.
7. Michael Laff, "Training During a Recession," ASTD, August 2008, www.astd.org/TD/Special/0808_Steady_Under_Pressure.htm (accessed February 3, 2009).
8. Matt Hurst, "Work-related Training," *Perspectives,* Statistics Canada, April 2008, 12–21,
9. Royal and Rebecca Masson, "Employee Engagement in Tough Times," *Workforce Management* Webcast, February 3, 2009.
10. Susan M. Heathfield, "Performance Development Planning," About.com, http://humanresources.about.com/cs/perfmeasurement/a/pdp.htm (accessed February 2, 2009).
11. Shannon Klie, "Do Incentives Help Change Behaviour," *Canadian HR Reporter,* April 2, 2008, www.hrreporter.com/ArticleView.aspx?l=1&articleid=5997 (accessed February 3, 2009).
12. John Eary, "Networked Interactive Video for Group Training, *British Journal of Educational Technology* 39, no. 2 (2008): 365–368.
13. "Gauges and Drivers," *Training,* 45, no. 9 (November/December 2008): 16–34.
14. "Training Needs Assessment Summary Report," Center of Excellence for Training and Research Translation, December 2006.

15. Finning (Canada) and the Caterpillar Foundation Invest $3 Million in NAIT," media release, Edmonton, Alberta, September 9, 2008.

16. S. O'Donnell, B. Beaton, and F. McKelvey, "Videoconferencing and Sustainable Development for Remote and Rural First Nations in Canada," National Research Council, Institute for Information Technology, October 2008.

17. "What to Do Now that Training is Becoming a Major HR Force," *HRFocus,* February 2005, 5–6; and Phil Britt, "E-Learning on the Rise in the Classroom: Companies Move Content Online: Cisco Systems' Employees and Partners Routinely Watch Videos on the Internet," *EContent* 27 no. 11 (November 2004): 36–41.

18. "Does E-Learning Help Companies Save Money and Improve Productivity," Canadian Training Solutions, Industry Canada, www.ic.gc.ca/eic/site/cts-scf.nsf/eng/sl00044.html (accessed February 4, 2009).

19. Marc Rosenberg, Ph.D., "Building a Learning Culture," *ELearning! Magazine,* www.elearning.b2bmediaco.com, April/ May 2008.

20. "Boosting Productivity through Virtual Collaboration," *Business Week* Webcast, February 5, 2009.

21. Peer Resources—The Mentors Corporation, www.mentors.ca (accessed November 26, 2004).

22. Virginia Galt, "The Task of Getting Workers Up to Speed," *The Globe and Mail,* April 22, 2004, B15.

23. Matthew Georghiou, "Games, Simulations Open World of Learning," *Canadian HR Reporter,* May 5, 2008, www.hrreporter.com/ArticleView.aspx?l=1&articleid=6033 (accessed February 4, 2009).

24. Dom Williams, "Measuring Training Effectiveness," ManageSmarter.com, July 30, 2007.

25. Saul Carliner, Mohamed Ally, Naxin Zhao, Leslie Bairstow, Sam Khoury, Lynn Johnston, "A Review of the State of the Field of Workplace Learning: What We Know and What We Need to Know about Competencies, Diversity, E-Learning, and Human Performance Improvement," The Canadian Society for Training and Development, June 2006.

26. Monica Belcourt, George Bohlander, and Scott Snell, *Managing Human Resources,* 5th Cdn. ed. (Toronto: Nelson Thomson, 2008), 324.

27. Allan Bailey, "Meeting Canada's Productivity Challenge," *The Canadian Learning Journal* 12, no. 2 (Fall 2008): 25–27.

28. Uyen Vu, "Numbers-Cruncher Makes Impact on Training Culture at TD," *Canadian HR Reporter,* July 12, 2004, 1.

29. Les Weisser, "Soaring to New Heights," *The Canadian Learning Journal* 12, no. 1 (Spring 2008): 33–35.

30. Anna Montesano, "Orienting New Employees for Career Success," *Canadian HR Reporter,* October 22, 2007, 23.

31. Vas Taras, "Inclusive Offices are Better for Everyone, *National Post,* December 9, 2008, FP13.

32. "Three Quick and Easy Ways to Gauge Your Training Outcomes," *IOMA's Report on Managing Training & Development,* January 2005, 4–5; and "Use This Eight-Step Process to Predict the ROI of Your Training Programs," *IOMA's Human Resource Department Management Report,* December 2004, 4–5.

33. Shannon Klie, "12 Million Adults have Low Literacy Skills," Canadian HR Reporter, August 11, 2008, www.hrreporter.com/ArticleView.aspx?l=1&articleid=6264 (accessed February 7, 2009).

34. Ibid.

35. "Want the Competitive Edge? Literacy in the Workplace," Employment Ontario, 2007.

36. "Adult Literacy Facts," ABC Canada, www.abc-canada.org/en/adult_literacy/facts (accessed February 7, 2009).

37. Tristan E. Johnson, Youngman Lee, Miyoung Lee, Debra L. O'Connor, Mohammed K. Khalil, and Xiaoxia Huang, "Measuring Sharedness of Team-Related Knowledge: Design and Validation of a Shared Mental Model Instrument," *Human Resource Development International* 10, no. 4 (December 2007): 437–454.

38. Jo Lamb-White, "Measures of Team Effectiveness," May 17, 2008, suite 101.com, http://workplaceculture.suite101.com/article.cfm/measures_of_team_effectiveness (accessed February 10, 2009).

39. Lisa Gueldenzoph Snyder, "Teaching Teams About Teamwork: Preparation, Practice and Performance Review, *Business Communications Quarterly,* March 2009, 74–79.

40. Joe Santana, "Avoid Piecemeal Pitfalls: Use a Whole System Approach to Achieve Diversity Results," HR.com, May 22, 2006.

41. Shannon Klie, "Training Important during Recession" *Canadian HR Reporter,* June 1, 2009, 1.

42. Lynn Johnston, "Employees Put High Price on Learning, Development," *Canadian HR Reporter,* November 3, 2008, 29.

43. Belle Liang and Jean Rhodes, "Guest Editorial: Cultivating the Vital Element of Youth Mentoring," *Applied Development Science* 11, no. 2 (2007): 104–107.

44. Thomas J. DeLong, John J. Gabarro, and Robert J. Lees, "Why Mentoring Matters in a Hypercompetitive World," *Harvard Business Review,* January 2008, 115–121.

45. Judy Sweeney, "Career Paths for Gen X, Gen Y," *Canadian HR Reporter,* June 16, 2008, www.hrreporter.com/ArticleView.aspx?l=1&articleid=6148 (accessed February 12, 2009).

6

MANAGING PERFORMANCE

OUTCOMES

After studying this chapter, you should be able to

1 Define a performance management system.

2 Explain the purpose of a performance management system.

3 Describe the management practices necessary for a good performance management system.

4 Identify the steps in an effective performance management system.

5 Describe the different sources of performance review information.

6 Explain the various methods used for performance reviews.

7 Outline the characteristics of an effective performance review interview.

OUTLINE

HRM CLOSE-UP

"People want to know that they're doing a good job. The feedback should therefore be ongoing and continuous."

Sandra D'Alimonte. Courtesy of Sandra D'Alimonte

As Optionelle's newly appointed president, Sandra D'Alimonte is helping the company develop its U.K. and European divisions. But even when on a special assignment near London, England, D'Alimonte stays connected with her supervisors at the home office in London, Canada. In fact, she estimates that half her daily work time is dedicated to interacting with her supervisory team.

Optionelle manufactures and markets its unique brand of Canadian fashion abroad. With the European expansion underway, there is much change to manage. And with business shifting, regular review of jobs and roles is necessary. "For our new salespeople, we are setting objectives at high but comfortable levels," explains D'Alimonte, "It's a two-way commitment necessary for growth."

The company has an annual performance management process with inputs gathered from different sources. With independent sales consultants selling directly to customers, Optionelle receives regular feedback on its operations. "We believe they have a voice and we want to hear from them," she says. "They reveal operational issues right away and this makes their feedback very valuable."

At the home office, jobs are firmly established and standards of performance are well understood. But even in the most standard roles, employees still need goals, recognition, and feedback. "People want to know that they're doing a good job," D'Alimonte explains, "The feedback should therefore be ongoing and continuous."

"Nobody likes performance reviews and it can be uncomfortable for everyone," she comments. D'Alimonte believes that coaching should be done daily and issues like absenteeism and lateness should be addressed immediately. She feels that a performance review is not the time to bring up a major concern. Rather, the review should be "a positive experience for everyone—a recap of progress to date."

How job performance is measured varies greatly depending on the role. D'Alimonte finds job performance in areas such as shipping and receiving, fairly easy to measure. "We chart and review things like shipping accuracy and then we meet to review results. It's important to find out why errors are made and get employee input into how the process can be improved."

D'Alimonte finds managing performance at the management and supervisory levels more complex and she asks staff to evaluate themselves on a number of measures first. Then, she documents her own observations before sitting down for a performance discussion with her employee.

D'Alimonte has had the benefit of using the Predictive Index program and has completed a course at the analyst level. This program identifies a person's characteristics and shows how they see themselves in their job. It has been helpful in determining the type and level of direction and coaching an individual employee needs. "When an employee is reacting in a certain way, it has to do with their needs. I coach the supervisors and help them adapt their style to meet those individual needs. For me this has been a very powerful and useful management tool."

INTRODUCTION

In the preceding chapters, we discussed how an organization hires and develops a productive workforce. In this chapter, we turn to performance management, which is one of the most critical processes that managers use to maintain and enhance productivity and facilitate progress toward strategic goals. While we will focus mainly on a formal system, the processes of managing and reviewing performance can be informal as well. All managers monitor the way employees work and assess how this matches organizational needs. Supervisors and managers form impressions about the relative value of employees to the organization and seek to maximize the contribution of every individual. Yet while these ongoing informal processes are vitally important, most organizations also have a system that includes a formal review of the person's performance once or twice a year, or on an ongoing basis. In the HRM Close-Up, Sandra D'Alimonte explains the successes of regular and continuous feedback.

The success or failure of a performance management system depends on the philosophy underlying it, its connection with business goals, the attitudes and skills of those responsible for using it, and the individual components of the system. A performance management system is more than the actual review—it is an overall approach to getting the maximum contribution from each individual.

WHAT IS A PERFORMANCE MANAGEMENT SYSTEM?

 Outcome 1

Performance management system
A set of integrated management practices

Outcome 2

A **performance management system** is a set of integrated management practices. While the formal review of employees' performance is a key component, a good performance review program does not make a good performance management system. A systems approach to performance management (1) allows the organization to integrate the management functions in order to maximize employee potential, and (2) helps increase employees' satisfaction with their work and with the organization.

Formal programs for reviewing performance are by no means new to organizations. Performance review programs are used in large and small organizations in both the public and private sectors. Advocates see these programs as among the most logical means to review, develop, and thus effectively utilize the knowledge and abilities of employees. However, many CEOs do feel that their organizations' performance management systems are useful.[1] Robert Bacal, a long-time observer of performance management systems, argues that one of the primary reasons performance management systems fail is that the organization hasn't been clear on what it wants the system to accomplish.[2] Sometimes companies want systems to communicate what work is valued; at other times, performance management systems are used to base pay decisions. For example, an organization that employs a team-based structure might have a performance management system that focuses on reviewing individual performance. This gives mixed messages about who owns the responsibility for the results.

There is no doubt that managing performance is not always easy. Managers and supervisors frequently avoid discussing employee performance—whether it is good or poor. Yet, according to a recent study, superior performance can be achieved—and consistently maintained—when supervisors and managers provide feedback and encouragement to the employee to continue practicing and improving what they do.[3]

Performance management is not an added activity in the busy supervisor's life—it is central to the everyday work of managers and managers need to be held accountable for doing the performance reviews.[4] However, supervisors and managers have struggled for years to find ways to make such an important activity more meaningful and helpful to employees.

There have been a number of different research studies in a variety of industries including engineering, health care, and education that demonstrate the strong link between performance management systems and organizational success. These studies consistently demonstrate that "what gets measured, gets done" and that ongoing feedback to the employees is critical in achieving goals.[5] With such clear evidence of the value of performance management systems, it will be useful for managers and HR practitioners to use these research findings when building a business case for the implementation of such a system.

MANAGEMENT PRACTICES

Outcome 3

The following management practices are essential for an effective performance management system:

1. Setting and communicating clear performance expectations for all work and all jobs.
2. Ensuring clear and specific performance objectives (or standards of performance) for all work.
3. Providing supportive and helpful coaching by the supervisor to enable staff to reach their objectives.
4. Focusing on the accomplishment of objectives during performance reviews.
5. Recognizing and celebrating good performance.
6. If necessary, creating action plans to improve performance.

As shown, the actual review step (item 4) is only one component of the system. However, the vast majority of performance management systems focuses primarily on the review and typically use that step for making compensation decisions.[6] The practice of "pay for performance" is found in all types of organizations. For example, the British Columbia Lottery Corporation has a combination of base pay, merit, and variable pay for all employees.[7]

Purposes of Managing Performance

There are several purposes for performance reviews, all intended to benefit both the organization and the employee and to ensure that any decisions are based on objective information.

Compensation Purposes

The most frequent use of performance management systems is to make compensation decisions. Whether or not that is what was intended, most employees believe that their pay is the major outcome of any performance review.[8] And the form of compensation can be everything from an increase in base salary to some other type of incentive—all with the intended outcome of motivating employees to achieve performance targets.[9]

Administrative Purposes

A performance management system also integrates a number of other major HR processes, such as promotion, transfer, and layoff decisions. Further, it can be used as part of HR planning—particularly when the organization has a succession plan. As well, the system provides a "paper trail" for documenting HRM processes that may result in legal action. For example, if a person were being disciplined regarding very poor customer service, the system would be able to identify what the goals were, how well the person met the goals, and the discussions and coaching sessions to improve performance in relation to customer service.

Measurement of Performance

In order to assess the overall success of the organization, it is important to be able to measure the accomplishments of the employees. Thus, you want to know how the employees performed compared to the established goals. A well-designed performance management system will be able to measure the performance of the organization and the employees. A performance management system also has the capability to influence employee behaviour, thereby leading directly to improved organizational performance.[10]

Developmental Purposes

From the standpoint of individual development, a performance system provides the feedback essential for discussing strengths and areas where performance needs improving—at both the individual and organizational levels. For example, if, through setting objectives, many supervisors identify that people have to improve their computer literacy skills, then the organization can provide a solution that meets those needs. From this information, the organization may set up a formal training program for all employees. This can be a better solution than having each supervisor deal with each person on an individual basis. Without such a step in the system, the manner in which developmental needs are identified can be hit-and-miss.

Regardless of the employee's level of performance, the system provides an opportunity to identify issues for discussion, eliminate any potential problems, and work on ways of achieving high performance. Newer approaches to performance management emphasize training as well as development and growth plans for employees. A developmental approach recognizes that the purpose of a manager is to support and help the person (or team) achieve results for good organizational performance. Having a sound basis for identifying performance goals, coaching, reviewing, and recognizing performance leads to successful organizations.

Figure 6.1 provides a summary of the purposes of managing performance.

Why Performance Management Systems Sometimes Fail

In actual practice, formal performance management systems sometimes yield disappointing results. Figure 6.2 shows that the primary reasons include keeping objectives secret (the supervisor knowing what the employee ought to achieve but not informing the employee), imposing objectives on the employee, and not having constructive feedback. For example, if a review is used to provide a written assessment for salary action and at the same time to motivate employees to improve their work, the administrative and developmental purposes may be in conflict. As a result, the actual review interview may become a discussion about salary in which the manager seeks to justify the action taken. In such cases, the discussion might have little influence on the employee's future job performance.

As with all HR processes and systems, if the support of top management is lacking, the system will not be successful. Even the best-conceived process will not work in an environment where managers are not encouraged by their superiors to take their responsibilities seriously in managing performance. To underscore the importance of this responsibility, top management should ensure that managers and supervisors are also part of the overall performance management system and that their performance will be reviewed for how well they are managing their employees' performance. At Work with HRM 6.1 describes the performance system at Mount Sinai Hospital in Ontario.

Other reasons performance management systems can fail include the following:

1. Managers feel that little or no benefit will be derived from the time and energy spent on the process.
2. Managers dislike the face-to-face discussion and performance feedback.
3. Managers are not sufficiently adept in setting goals and performance measures, in coaching and supporting, or providing performance feedback.
4. The judgmental role of a review can conflict with the helping role of developing employees.

FIGURE 6.1   Purposes for Managing Performance

Compensation
- Salary increases
- Bonuses and pay-for-performance awards

Administrative
- Promotion decisions
- Transfer decisions
- Layoff decisions
- Succession planning
- Paper trail for documenting HRM actions

Measurement of Performance
- Determine accomplishment of goals
- Influence employee behaviour
- Improve organizational performance

Developmental
- Feedback for discussing strengths and areas for improvement
- Eliminate potential problems
- Identify training needs

FIGURE 6.2   Reasons Performance Management Systems Can Fail

1. There are no plans for helping employees develop in the work period after the review.
2. There is no ongoing goal review and feedback from managers.
3. There is little or no training for managers on how to conduct a performance appraisal meeting.
4. The metrics used are questionable or unknown to the employees.
5. There are few ways of addressing and resolving poor performance.
6. Appraisal information is limited to the judgment of supervisors.
7. The PM system is not consistent across the whole organization.
8. Formal reviews only occur once a year.
9. Lack of executive commitment to the process.
10. Managers within the organization are not using the same "yardstick" to evaluate performance.
11. Lack of strong manager capability (specifically, ensuring that evaluations are "fair" and "equitable" and holding formal performance evaluation discussions with employees).

Sources: Adapted from Human Resource Institute, Canadian Management Centre, "Nine Keys to Performance Management," 2006; and *2008 Performance Management Practices Survey,* Mercer Consulting, October 10, 2008.

Performance management in many organizations is a once-a-year activity in which the review interview becomes a source of friction for both managers and employees. An important principle of performance management is that continual feedback and employee coaching must be a positive regular activity—be it daily or hourly. The annual or semiannual performance review should simply be a logical extension of the day-to-day supervision process. For example, Mead Johnson Canada, a subsidiary of Bristol-Myers Squibb, a large pharmaceutical firm, changed its performance management system so that employees received ongoing reviews. This system now has a future growth and expectations focus with immediate and specific feedback.

AT WORK **with HRM 6.1**

ONLINE PERFORMANCE MANAGEMENT

Hospitals are assessed every few years against a set of national standards. The assessors are external experts as well as internal staff. As part of a recent assessment, Mount Sinai Hospital in Toronto, Ontario, was asked to improve its performance management system. Additionally, staff had indicated in surveys that they wanted a performance review that was regular, fair, and consistent. Mount Sinai chose an automated system that would support its Balanced Scorecard measurement system, which measures efficiency and growth, safety, patient and family-centred care, learning, and innovation.

Debbie Fischer, senior VP of organizational development and strategic projects, praises the new online system. Managers now have access to previous performance appraisals and feedback from other employees, and can make comparisons by area of competency or by work group. They can generate reports about competency gaps and training plans. The system contains reminders about appraisal and training dates. Multiple raters can provide input, and may assess anecdotally or numerically or a combination of both. Trent Dark, director of organizational development at Mount Sinai, says "there are metrics and benchmarks for the different categories, and we track competencies in teamwork, leadership and change management. There are milestones for specific activities such as training."

CRITICAL THINKING QUESTIONS

1. What are the strengths and weaknesses of a balanced scorecard approach to performance review?
2. What are the advantages of an online performance management system? Can you think of some potential problems with this system?

Source: Adapted from Susan Singh, "Mount Sinai Goes Online for Performance Management," *Canadian HR Reporter,* June 20, 2005, 1–4.

One of the main concerns of employees is the fairness of the performance management system, since the process is central to so many HRM decisions. Employees who believe the system is unfair may consider the review interview a waste of time and leave the interview with feelings of anxiety or frustration. Also, they may view compliance with the system as mechanical and thus play only a passive role during the interview process. By addressing these employee concerns during the planning stage of the system, the organization will help the performance management system succeed in reaching its goals. Employees can help ensure that the review is fair by being well prepared. This can include keeping track of positive (and negative) feedback from the supervisor and keeping records of courses, workshops, and any other training activities.

Finally, managers can have biases even in a well-run system.[11] For example, managers may inflate reviews because they desire higher salaries for their employees or because higher subordinate ratings make them look good as managers. Alternatively, managers may want to get rid of troublesome employees, passing them off to another department by inflating their ratings. Supervisors and managers have to be watchful for the same types of errors in performance reviews as in selection interviews. The supervisor may make decisions about a person's performance based on recent events (recency error) or judging performance favourably or unfavourably overall by putting emphasis on only one area that is important in the supervisor's mind (halo error). Likewise, the supervisor may be unwilling to give either extremely low or extremely high assessments and decide to rate everyone as "above average" (central tendency). A supervisor can also be biased by comparing one employee's performance to another (contrast error) instead of assessing the employee against a set of standards.

STEPS IN AN EFFECTIVE PERFORMANCE MANAGEMENT SYSTEM

About.com
humanresources.about.com

Free Management Library
www.managementhelp.org/

Development Dimensions International
www.ddiworld.com/

The HR department ordinarily has the primary responsibility for overseeing and coordinating the performance management system. HR may also design or select a performance management system to use. Managers from the operating departments must also be actively involved, particularly in helping to establish the objectives for the system. Furthermore, employees are more likely to accept and be satisfied with the performance management system when they have the chance to participate in its development. Their concerns about fairness and accuracy in determining raises, promotions, and the like tend to be alleviated somewhat when they have been involved at the planning stage and have helped develop the performance standards themselves. This section describes five steps that are key to an effective performance management system. In addition, other useful information on performance management can be found at About.com (**humanresources.about. com/**), Free Management Library (**www.managementhelp.org/**), and Development Dimensions International (**www.ddiworld.com/**).

Clarifying the Work to Be Done

Before any goals can be established or any performance standards identified, it is important to clarify the work to be accomplished. And this is done by identifying the expected outcomes or results and determining how those results will be measured. For example, an expected result for a cook at a fast-food restaurant may be "no food wastage." The supervisor and cook would then decide how this will be measured. It could be measured by determining the number of kilograms of food in the garbage pail or the number of voided customer orders. Note that the clarification step is done jointly with the supervisor and the employee. The key to a good performance management system is the involvement of the employee in the entire process.

Setting Goals and Establishing a Performance Plan

Once the supervisor and employee (or team) are clear on expected results and how those results will be measured, goals must be set. And for the system to really work, these goals must be linked to overall business objectives. For example, an overall business objective for the fast-food restaurant is to reduce costs. Since food costs are a large proportion of overall costs, the restaurant may decide to focus on

reducing food costs. Therefore, for the individual employee, the ability to cut down on wasted food will reduce the overall food costs and the goal may be "to reduce food waste by 10% within the next three months." You will note that this is a very specific goal that includes a time frame.

To ensure that there is a strong link to business goals, the supervisor may also need to establish "softer measures" such as customer satisfaction or customer loyalty.[12] With the use of both financial results (e.g., cost of food) and soft measures (e.g., customer satisfaction), the results are more strongly linked to the overall restaurant outcomes. This step also involves discussion between both the supervisor and the employee, which leads to greater involvement and commitment to the specific goals.

There are other types of methods, such as trait and behavioural, in addition to goals, which can be used in establishing the performance plan. These will be discussed later in the chapter.

Regular and Frequent Coaching

Coaching sessions are designed to help employees achieve their results. Coaching should not involve fault-finding or blaming. Most people want to do a good job, and, therefore, it is important that a supervisor approach coaching in a helpful and supportive way. If the employee is having difficulty reaching a goal, the supervisor and employee can explore together the reasons why and what can be done to fix the difficulty. Coaching is also a good way to avoid costs of firing employees and hiring new employees. It is very difficult for employees to improve on mistakes if the supervisor does not take the time to help them understand what they need to do. For coaching to be effective, the supervisor needs to describe what the specific behaviours are that need to be reinforced or redirected, along with the specific situations where the behaviour was observed.[13] Providing feedback on behaviours is not just describing what the supervisor might want to see differently but also describing the positive behaviours.

Conducting a Formal Review of Performance

Most performance management systems include an annual formal review of the employee's overall performance. This allows both the supervisor and employee to consider the employee's accomplishments and to discuss development areas for the next year. It is also usually at this point that the organization uses the results of the annual performance review for salary adjustments.

Since the employee was involved in the original goal setting, and since there has been regular and frequent feedback and coaching, this step is more of a review—there shouldn't be any surprises.

Recognizing and Rewarding Performance

No system will be effective without recognition of accomplishments. Although we usually think of recognition in monetary terms, some nonfinancial rewards for the employee include the following:

1. Being considered for a promotion.
2. Being given the opportunity to work on a special project.
3. Being praised by the supervisor.
4. Being profiled in a business journal about a particular achievement or receiving an award of excellence.

These types of rewards cost little or no money. People like to know that their good work and achievements are noticed. Appropriate rewards can be a great tool in helping the organization be successful.[14] During the recent economic recession, managers were reminded that their praise is a valuable corporate resource and can be used to improve employee performance. By careful use of praise and positive feedback, the manager can energize the individual and the person's work will improve in related areas.[15]

Complying with the Law

Since performance assessments are used as a basis for HRM actions, they must meet certain legal requirements. The legality of any performance management system is measured against criteria of reliability, fairness, and validity. *Reliability* refers to whether performance is measured consistently among the employee participants. *Fairness* refers to the extent to which the system avoids bias caused by any factors unrelated to performance. *Validity* refers to the extent to which the system is job-related and accurate. Under the Charter of Rights and Freedoms, and other federal and provincial human rights requirements, performance management systems must be, above all, valid. Worker performance must be assessed on the basis of job requirements to ensure legal compliance.

Although currently there is little litigation pertaining to performance management systems in Canada, the spillover effect of litigation in the United States has prompted organizations to try to eliminate vagueness in descriptions of traits, such as attitude, cooperation, dependability, initiative, and leadership. For example, the trait "dependability" can be made much less vague if it is spelled out as employee tardiness and/or unexcused absences. In general, reducing room for subjective judgments will improve the entire performance review process.

Employers might face legal challenges to their performance management systems when reviews indicate acceptable or above-average performance but employees are later passed over for promotion, disciplined for poor performance, discharged, or laid off from the organization. In these cases, the performance reviews can undermine the legitimacy of the subsequent decision. And legal challenges can be very costly. For example, if an organization terminated someone due to a downsizing, but then subsequently said it was for poor performance, the company would not be successful in defending its action if the personnel file did not contain a poor performance review.

Therefore, performance reviews should meet the following guidelines:

- Performance ratings must be job-related, with performance standards related to the work as identified through job analysis.
- Employees must be given a written copy of their performance standards in advance of any formal performance review.
- Managers who conduct the review must be able to observe the behaviour they are assessing. This implies having a measurable standard with which to compare employee behaviour.
- Managers and supervisors should be trained to understand their role in managing performance, specifically on (1) how to set goals and performance standards; (2) how to coach and conduct a formal review session; and (3) how to write a review report or use any other written materials associated with the performance system.
- Reviews should be discussed openly with employees and coaching or corrective guidance offered to help poor performers improve their performance.
- An appeals procedure should be established to enable employees to express disagreement with the formal evaluation.

HRM and the law 6.1

LACK OF PERFORMANCE DOCUMENTATION

If someone is being disciplined for poor performance, and that it is serious enough to warrant termination, then good documentation is critical. Here are two recent court cases that reinforce the point.

The first case involved a person that had been with the organization for 17 years. The company developed a new corporate strategy and brought in several new senior managers, one that was the employee's supervisor. The new supervisor, based on information received from others, determined that there were some concerns about the person's performance and eventually demoted the employee. Along the way, the supervisor also made comments about the age of the employee. The employee didn't go along with the demotion but charged the company with age discrimination. The result: the company lost the case on the grounds that 17 years of good performance reviews

were evident and the one poor performance review relied on undocumented factors.

The second case involved an employee who had initially good performance reviews and then the performance began to slip. The supervisor met with the person on several occasions and clearly explained what was expected and made documented notes of the meetings. After some period of time, it became obvious to the supervisor, and co-workers, that the person was not able to perform all the work. Eventually the person was transferred and demoted to another role. Eventually the person stated that discrimination was occurring. However, the courts ruled in favour of the company due to the strong documentation that clearly indicated there had been an ongoing performance issue.

Do you think these were appropriate outcomes? Why or why not?

Sources: Adapted from "Supervisor's Past Ratings of Worker Lead to Trouble when Performance Suffers," and "'Grandma' Tries to Get Even When Manager Hints that She Can't Change," *Legal Alert for Supervisors,* January 5, 2009.

Employers must ensure that managers and supervisors document reviews and reasons for subsequent HRM actions. This information may prove decisive should an employee take legal action. An employer's credibility is strengthened when it can support performance results by documenting instances of poor performance. Read HRM and the Law 6.1 to get an understanding of what can happen when performance issues are not clearly documented.

Deciding Who Should Provide Performance Information

Outcome 5

For many years, the traditional approach to reviewing an employee's performance was based solely on information the supervisor gathered through first-hand knowledge of the person. However, given the complexity of today's jobs, it is often unrealistic to presume that one person can fully observe and assess an employee's performance. Also, there may be a desire to gather information directly from those who are best acquainted with the person's performance, such as a customer. Consequently, information about a person's performance may come from supervisors, the employee being reviewed, peers, team members, subordinates, and customers. The Canadian Institute of Chartered Accountants and the Ontario Ministry of Northern Development and Mines have begun using information gathered from a number of sources. Since supervisors spend much of their time on gathering data for and conducting the performance review, the remainder of this section will focus on that portion of the performance management system.

Manager and/or Supervisor Review

Manager and/or supervisor review
Performance review done by the employee's supervisor

Manager and/or supervisor review has been the traditional approach to assessing an employee's performance. In most instances, supervisors are in the best position to perform this function, although it may not always be possible for them to do so. Managers often complain that they do not have the time to fully observe the performance of employees. These managers must then rely on performance records to review an employee's performance. For example, American Express Canada uses telephone monitors to assess the quality of the communication between a service centre representative and a customer. Employees are aware that they are being monitored for developmental purposes. If such reliable and valid measures are not available, the review may be less than accurate.

Where a supervisor reviews employees independently, provision is often made for an analysis of the reviews by the supervisor's superior. Having reviews examined by a supervisor's superior reduces the chance of superficial or biased reviews. Reviews by superiors generally are more objective and provide a broader perspective of employee performance than do reviews by immediate supervisors.

Self-Review

Self-review
Performance review done by the employee being assessed, generally on a form completed by the employee prior to the performance interview

Sometimes employees are asked to assess themselves on some or all aspects of their performance. **Self-review** is beneficial when managers seek to increase an employee's involvement in the review process. Such an approach may require an employee to complete a review form prior to the performance interview. At a minimum, this gets the employee thinking about strengths and areas for improvement and may lead to discussions about barriers to effective performance. During the performance interview, the manager and the employee discuss job performance and agree on a final assessment. This approach also works well when the manager and the employee jointly establish future performance goals or employee development plans.

Critics of self-review argue that employees are more lenient than managers in their assessments and tend to present themselves in a highly favourable light. However, one of the authors has found through personal experience that people tend to underrate their overall performance. Research also suggests that people may also understate their performance as they may feel they are boasting.[16] Therefore, managers are able to build on employees' views of themselves and make employees feel better about their performance. When used as part of a review process, self-reviews can be a valuable source of information.[17]

Subordinate Review

Subordinate review
Performance review of a superior by an employee, which is more appropriate for developmental than for administrative purposes

Some organizations use **subordinate appraisal** to give managers feedback on how their subordinates view them. Subordinates are in a good position to provide feedback on their managers since they are in frequent contact with their superiors and occupy a unique position from which to observe many performance-related behaviours. Those performance dimensions judged most appropriate for subordinate input include leadership, oral communication, delegation of authority, coordination of team efforts, and interest in subordinates. However, dimensions related to managers' specific job tasks, such as planning and organizing, budgeting, creativity, and analytical ability, are not usually appropriate for subordinate feedback.

Since subordinate feedback gives employees power over their bosses, the managers themselves may be hesitant to endorse such an approach, particularly when it might be used as a basis for compensation decisions. However, when the information is used for developmental purposes, managers tend to be more open to the idea. Available evidence suggests that when managers heed the advice of their subordinates, their own performance can improve substantially. Nevertheless, to avoid potential problems, subordinate feedback should be submitted anonymously and combined across several individual raters.[18]

Peer Review

Peer review
Performance reviews done by one's fellow employees, generally on forms that are compiled into a single profile for use in the performance interview conducted by the employee's manager

Individuals of equal rank who work together are increasingly asked to assess each other. A **peer review** provides information that differs to some degree from information by a superior, since peers often see different dimensions of performance. Peers can readily identify leadership and interpersonal skills along with other strengths and weaknesses of their co-workers. A superior asked to provide input about a server in a restaurant on a dimension such as "dealing with the public" may not have had much opportunity to observe it. Fellow servers, on the other hand, have the opportunity to observe this behaviour regularly.

One advantage of peer input is the belief that these assessments furnish more accurate and valid information than assessments by superiors. The supervisor often sees employees putting their best foot forward, while those who work with their fellow employees on a regular basis may see a more realistic picture. With peer input, co-workers are asked to provide input on specific areas, usually in a structured, written format. The information is then compiled into a single profile, which is given to the supervisor for use in the final review.[19]

Despite evidence that peer reviews are possibly the most accurate method of judging employee behaviour, there are reasons why they are not used.[20] Some of the reasons commonly cited are:

1. Peer reviews are simply a popularity contest.
2. Managers are reluctant to give up control over the assessment process.
3. Those receiving low ratings might retaliate against their peers.
4. Peers rely on stereotypes in ratings.
5. Peers, through discussion, can have more extreme views of the person's performance.

When peers are in competition with one another (e.g., sales associates), peer reviews may not be advisable for administrative decisions, such as those relating to salary or bonuses. Also, employers who use peer reviews must make sure to safeguard confidentiality in handling the review forms. A breach of confidentiality can create interpersonal rivalries or hurt feelings and foster hostility among fellow employees.

Team Review

Team review
Performance review, based on TQM concepts, that recognizes team accomplishment rather than individual performance

An extension of the peer assessment is the **team review**. While peers are on equal standing with one another, they may not work closely together. In a team setting, it may be nearly impossible to separate out an individual's contribution. Advocates of team review argue that, in such cases, individual reviews can be dysfunctional since they detract from the critical issues of the team. To address this issue, organizations will occasionally use team reviews to assess the performance of the team as a whole.

A company's interest in team reviews is frequently motivated by its commitment to TQM principles and practices. At its root, TQM is a control system that involves setting standards (based on customer requirements), measuring performance against those standards, and identifying opportunities for continuous improvement. In this regard, TQM and performance reviews are perfectly complementary. However, a basic tenet of TQM is that performance is best understood at the level of the system as a whole, whereas performance reviews traditionally have focused on individual performance. Team reviews represent one way to break down barriers between individuals and encourage their collective effort.[21]

Customer Input

Customer input
Performance review that, like team review, is based on TQM concepts and seeks information from both external and internal customers

Also driven by TQM concerns, an increasing number of organizations use internal and external **customer input** as a source of performance review information. While external customers' information has been used for some time to review restaurant, hotel, and car rental company personnel, companies such as Federal Express, UPS, and Sears have begun utilizing external customers as well. For example, Sears's customers receive a coupon asking them to call a 1–800 number within the next week. In exchange for answering prerecorded questions on a touch-tone phone, they receive $5 off their next purchase. Each call can be linked to a particular transaction (and sales associate) based on the receipt number. With 468 million transactions a year, enough survey data are generated for each sales associate to provide meaningful feedback on such performance measures as service and product knowledge. Customer information can also tell an organization if employees are following procedures. Secret shoppers at the Radisson Hotel Saskatoon provided feedback to hotel management that employees were failing to provide accurate accounting on some customers' bills.

Managers establish customer service measures (CSMs) and set goals for employees that are linked to company goals. Often the CSM goals are linked to employee pay through incentive programs. Customer survey data are then incorporated into the performance evaluation. By including CSMs in their performance reviews, managers hope to produce more objective evaluations, more effective employees, more satisfied customers, and better business performance.[22]

In contrast to external customers, internal customers include anyone inside the organization who depends on an employee's work output. For example, managers who rely on the HR department for recruitment and training services would be candidates for seeking internal customer feedback of that department. For both developmental and administrative purposes, internal customers can provide extremely useful feedback about the value added by an employee or team of employees.

Putting It All Together: 360-Degree Review

As mentioned previously, many companies are combining various sources of performance appraisal information to create multi-person—or 360-degree—appraisal and feedback systems. Jobs are multifaceted, and different people see different things. As the name implies, 360-degree feedback is intended to provide employees with as accurate a view of their performance as possible by getting input from all angles: supervisors, peers, subordinates, customers, and the like. Although in the beginning, 360-degree systems were purely developmental and were restricted mainly to management and career development, they have migrated to performance appraisal and other HR purposes. Over 90% of Fortune 1000 companies have implemented some form of 360-degree feedback for career development, performance review, or both.

Because the system combines more information than a typical performance appraisal, it can become administratively complex. For that reason, organizations are using Web-based technology (Internet, intranet) to compile and aggregate the information.[23] For example, PerformancePlus and Competency Plus, developed by Exxceed, allow managers and employees to develop performance plans, goals, and objectives, and then track their progress over time. Managers can see all of an employee's goals and action steps on a single screen, and self-appraisals and multiple-rater reviews can be combined into a 360-degree format. After rating an employee's performance on each goal, raters can provide summary comments in three categories: victories and accomplishments, setbacks and frustrations, and general comments. To ensure security, a user ID and password are required and all the data are captured and saved in the employee's history file. Other types of performance management software can calculate and manage financial rewards based on how well employees perform as well as identify their performance gaps and manage their education, certification, and training.[24]

Figure 6.3 is a graphical depiction of 360-degree input sources.

FIGURE 6.3   360-Degree Review Information

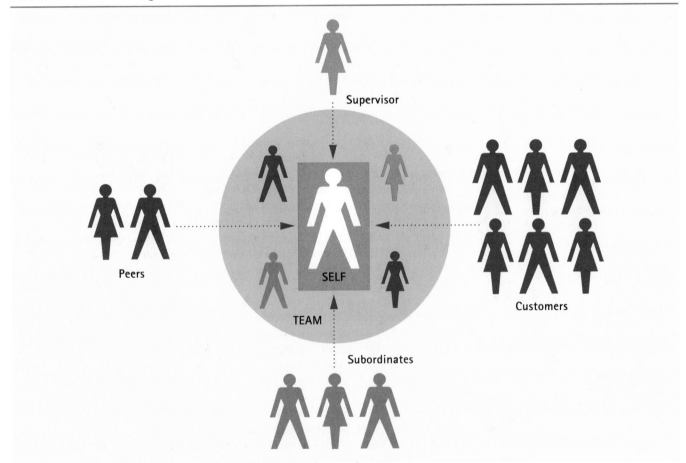

Halogen Software
www.halogensoftware.ca/

Survey Connect
www.surveyconnect.com

Software used to help prepare 360-degree feedback systems is available from a number of companies. Among these are Halogen Software (**www.halogensoftware.ca**) and Survey connect (**www.surveyconnect.com/**) that not only give a list of resources for anyone interested in using 360-degree systems but also provide information about "best practices."

Figure 6.4 lists the pros and cons of 360-degree feedback.

Although 360-degree feedback can be useful for both developmental and administrative purposes, most companies start with an exclusive focus on development. Employees may be understandably nervous about the possibility of everyone "ganging up" on them in their evaluations. If an organization starts with only developmental feedback—not tied to compensation, promotions, and the like—employees will become accustomed to the process and will likely value the input they get from various parties.

When Erik Djukastein of Contech Electronics, a Victoria, B.C.-based company introduced a 360-degree system, he made sure as CEO that he was included in the process. He knew that he could sometimes do things impulsively but was surprised when staff said that he didn't always follow through on commitments.

While it is unusual to have the CEO involved in a 360-degree process, Djukastein found that even though the feedback was scary, he appreciated the honesty of his staff. And he wasn't about to ignore the feedback. In order to make it real, he hired a coach as well as inviting his staff to "call him" on any commitments that he didn't deliver on.

FIGURE 6.4 Pros and Cons of 360-Degree Feedback

Pros

- The system is more comprehensive in that responses are gathered from multiple perspectives.
- The information may not be available through other means.
- Provides a complete picture of the employee's performance.
- It provides better data for developmental purposes.
- It complements TQM initiatives by emphasizing internal and external customers and teams.
- It may lessen bias and prejudice since feedback comes from more people, not one individual.
- It provides more consistent information on behaviours and actions.
- Feedback from peers and others may increase employee self-development.
- Can assist in strengthening employee engagement.
- A person can compare self-perceptions with others.

Cons

- The system is administratively cumbersome in combining all the responses.
- System can't improve managerial ineptness.
- Organization has to be committed and supportive of the system.
- Isn't to be used to collect and demonstrate poor performance for termination purposes.
- Feedback can be intimidating and cause resentment if the employee feels the respondents have "ganged up."
- It can be seen as a popularity contest.
- There may be conflicting opinions, though they may all be accurate from the respective standpoints.
- People can feel overwhelmed and in shock from the information.
- The system requires training to work effectively.
- System must be carefully designed to meet objectives or providing multi-rater input.
- Employees may collude or "game" the system by giving invalid evaluations of one another.

Sources: Adapted from Christina Robertson, "Getting the Information You Need Through a 360 Feedback Report," *Chemical Engineering,* April 2008, 63–66; Tracey Maylett and Juan Riboldi, "Using 360 Feedback to Predict Performance," *T & D,* September 2007, 48–52; and Manfred F.R. Kets de Vries, Pierre Vrignaud, Elizabeth Florent-Treacy, and Konstantin Korotov, "360-degree feedback instruments: An overview," INSEAD Global Leadership Centre, 2007/01.

In order to make the system effective and easy to use, Djukastein recommends:

- *Use expertise.* Retain a consultant or a firm that has expertise in implementing and administering 360 reviews.
- *Customize system to your organization.* It is important that the input documents are customized to fit the organization's competencies.
- *Include many sources of input.* The input should include all direct reports and others that work closely with the person—the more the better.
- *Make use of feedback.* It doesn't help the person, or the organization, if the feedback is not acted on.[25]

At Work with HRM 6.2 provides information about the success Canadian Tire has had with a 360-degree approach.

AT WORK **with HRM 6.2**

CANADIAN TIRE 360-DEGREE MATRIX

"Accentuate the positive; build on leadership strengths" is the principal theme of leadership performance evaluation and development conducted by the Canadian Tire Corporation as described by Janice Wismer, vice president of Human Resources. Canadian Tire is a network of interrelated businesses with retail, financial, and petroleum interests. About 45,000 employees work in 1000 retail stores across Canada.

The customized 360-degree feedback process used at Canadian Tire is research based and designed to build a cadre of great leaders. The first step in the design of the 360-degree feedback instrument was to benchmark other organizations that had effective 360-degree feedback processes. Twenty-seven key employees at Canadian Tire were interviewed to identify the attributes of their great leaders as measured by the standards of the organization. These key leadership attributes were then discussed and evaluated in workshops with important stakeholders. A total of 16 competencies were identified: seven related to "who one is"—characteristics, such as trustworthy, passionate, and curious. Nine others focused on "what one can do for the team, business, and enterprise," such as make strategic choices, motivate and celebrate, communicate authentically.

To date, about 170 managers have been assessed by an average of nine colleagues, including peers, subordinates, and bosses. Colleagues complete a self-survey, and all feedback assessment is analyzed relative to their own organization and to industry standards, which are maintained in a database. A confidential feedback report is given to each individual.

According to Ed Haltrecht, PhD, CHRP, who specializes in measurement and organizational leadership development, in most organizations when performance feedback is presented, both the employee and the manager focus on the reds—the weaknesses—and try to work out methods of development to improve this area. What is unique about Canadian Tire is that the focus is on the positive. It has found that improvements in weak areas (provided it is not a fundamental flaw) do not affect overall performance, while improvements in areas of strength bring managers from good to extraordinary. The goal is to identify and strengthen attributes so employees will distinguish and present themselves as extraordinary. Individuals first address any "fundamental flaws"—either a very weak attribute of the individual or, more importantly, elements regarded as critical to the organization.

Canadian Tire's leadership development system also recognizes two other significant research findings: first, extraordinary leaders have about three competencies that they excel at and developing a few strengths to very high performance levels has a greater impact than improving several competencies from poor to average. Second, competencies travel together and improvement in one leads to significant progress in others. Identifying these companion competencies has proven to be extremely worthwhile. In a nutshell, these are the findings: start with the right set of competencies or attributes; focus on strengths; eliminate any fundamental flaws; and pay attention to companion attributes.

The assessment feedback process at Canadian Tire is seen as a tool for dialogue and for focusing on what makes a great company and what matters in leadership. Those employees who try to improve are given a developmental opportunities guidebook. Canadian Tire has discovered that the best development methods are stretch challenging assignments, coaching and mentoring, personal feedback, talks with consultants, and training programs.

CRITICAL THINKING QUESTION

What would be your reaction to this approach if you were working for Canadian Tire? Explain your answer.

SAMPLE 360-DEGREE STATEMENTS WITH DESCRIPTORS

Based on interaction that you have had with the individual, select the level that best describes their performance in each competency area.

Level 4: Consistently demonstrates the behaviour.

Level 3: Usually demonstrates the behaviour.

Level 2: Sometimes demonstrates the behaviour.

Level 1: Rarely demonstrates the behaviour.

Competency 1: Teamwork—Works effectively with others within own department and across departments for benefit of company. Specifically, displays an openness to ideas, works collaboratively with team members, participates in development of the team, celebrates team successes, and treats team members with respect.

Competency 2: Customer service—Shows a commitment to understanding customer needs and strives to exceed their expectations. Specifically, displays knowledge of customer needs, provides exceptional service to customers, exhibits knowledge of products, shows steady gains in response time without sacrificing positive interaction.

Based on the experiences of companies like Celestica, Allstate Insurance, and Canadian Tire, it appears that 360-degree feedback can provide a valuable approach to performance review. Its success, as with any performance review method, depends on how managers use the information and how fairly employees are treated. Manager's Toolkit 6.1 provides sample competency descriptors and how they might be assessed on a 360-degree performance review.

Training Reviewers

A weakness of many performance management systems is that managers and supervisors are not adequately trained for setting performance goals or assessing performance and therefore provide little meaningful feedback to subordinates. Because they lack precise standards for reviewing subordinates' performance and have not developed the necessary observational and feedback skills, their reviews often become general, unspecific, and meaningless. Therefore, training people who will conduct performance reviews can vastly improve the overall performance management system. Thus it is important that supervisors and managers be trained in how to conduct performance reviews. The training needs to help remove the barriers of time constraints, lack of knowledge, and interpersonal conflicts. By overcoming these barriers, the performance review process will be more effective.

PERFORMANCE REVIEW METHODS

Outcome 6

Since the early years of their use by the federal government, methods of reviewing staff have evolved considerably. Old systems have been replaced by new methods that reflect technical improvements and legal requirements and are more consistent with the purposes of a performance management system. In the discussion that follows, you will be introduced to those methods that have found widespread use; methods that are used less frequently will be touched on briefly. Performance review methods can be broadly classified as measuring traits, behaviours, or results; many organizations may incorporate all three into their system.

Trait Methods

Trait approaches to performance reviews are designed to measure the extent to which an employee possesses certain characteristics—such as dependability, creativity, initiative, and leadership—that are viewed as important for the job and the organization in general. Trait methods are popular as they are easy to develop but can be notoriously biased.

When using the trait method of performance review, a customer service representative may be reviewed on being friendly and helpful.

Keith Brofsky/Photodisc Green/Getty Images

Frequently in the trait method, the supervisor is asked to numerically rate the person on the specific characteristics. For example, on the characteristic of "dependable," the supervisor might be asked to rate the person on a scale of 1 to 5, with 1 being unsatisfactory and 5 being exceptional. This is called a **graphic rating scale,** a sample of which is shown in Manager's Toolkit 6.2. The supervisor may also be asked to provide a short paragraph commentary on the person's dependability.

Graphic rating scales
A trait approach to performance review whereby each employee is rated according to a scale of characteristics

Behavioural Methods

As mentioned above, one of the potential drawbacks of a trait-oriented performance review is that traits tend to be vague and subjective. Behavioural methods have been developed to specifically describe which actions should (or should not) be exhibited on the job. Since behavioural methods are becoming more common, this section describes three approaches that use them: the behavioural checklist method, the behaviourally anchored rating scale (BARS), and the behaviour observation scales (BOS).

Behavioural Checklist Method

This method consists of having the supervisor check those statements on a list that are believed to be the characteristics of the employee's performance or behaviour. A checklist developed for computer salespeople might include a number of statements like the following:

_____   Is able to explain equipment clearly
_____   Keeps abreast of new developments in technology
_____   Tends to be a steady worker
_____   Reacts quickly to customer needs
_____   Processes orders correctly

MANAGER'S TOOLKIT **6.2**

GRAPHICS RATINGS SCALE WITH PROVISION FOR COMMENTS

Appraise employee's performance in PRESENT ASSIGNMENT. Check (✓) most appropriate square. Appraisers are *urged to freely use* the "Remarks" sections for significant comments descriptive of the individual.

1. KNOWLEDGE OF WORK: Understanding of all phases of his/her work and related matters	Needs instruction or guidance		Has required knowledge of own and related work		Has exceptional knowledge of own and related work
	☐	☐	☐	☑	☐
Remarks: *Is particularly good on gas engines.*					

2. INITIATIVE: Ability to originate or develop ideas and to get things started	Lacks imagination		Meets necessary requirements		Unusually resourceful
	☐	☑	☐	☐	☐
Remarks: *Has good ideas when asked for an opinion, but otherwise will not offer them. Somewhat lacking in self-confidence.*					

3. APPLICATION: Attention and application to his/her work	Wastes time Needs close supervision		Steady and willing worker		Exceptionally industrious
	☐	☐	☑	☐	☐
Remarks: *Accepts new jobs when assigned.*					

4. QUALITY OF WORK: Thoroughness, neatness, and accuracy of work	Needs improvement		Regularly meets recognized standards		Consistently maintains highest quality
	☐	☐	☐	☐	☑
Remarks: *The work he turns out is always of the highest possible quality.*					

5. VOLUME OF WORK: Quantity of acceptable work	Should be increased		Regularly meets recognized standards		Unusually high output
	☐	☐	☑	☐	☐
Remarks: *Would be higher if he did not spend so much time checking and rechecking his work.*					

Behaviourally Anchored Rating Scale (BARS)

Behaviourally anchored rating scale (BARS)
A behavioural approach to performance review that consists of a series of vertical scales, one for each important dimension of job performance

The **behaviourally anchored rating scale (BARS)** approach consists of a series of five to 10 vertical scales—one for each important dimension or component of performance. These components are then given a numerical scale based on critical incidents of on-the-job performance. Manager's Toolkit 6.3 displays an example of this for an employee in a service-based industry such as hospitality.

Behaviour Observation Scales (BOS)

A behaviour observation scale (BOS) is similar to a BARS in that both are based on critical incidents. The value of BOS is that it enables the reviewer to play the role of observer rather than judge. In this way, he or she can more easily provide constructive feedback to the employee.

EXAMPLE OF BARS FOR SERVICE-BASED INDUSTRY

Communications: This area of performance concerns the ability of the person to exchange information in all forms including demonstration of active listening.

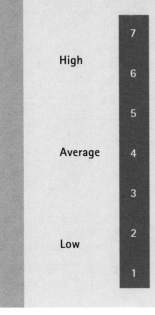

High   7

6

Consistently demonstrates exceptional verbal and written communication skills. Demonstrates exceptional sensitivity and empathy. Improves lines of communication throughout hotel.

5

Frequently demonstrates exceptional verbal and written communication skills. Correctly assesses and responds to sensitive situations.

Average   4

Facilitates the clear, concise communication of information in appropriate forms in a timely fashion. Adapts communication style to meet the needs of others.

3

Inconsistent ability to communicate effectively or in a timely manner. Does not always adapt communication style to meet the needs of others.

2

Low

Receives and imparts information inaccurately.

1

Results Methods

Rather than look at the traits of employees or the behaviours they exhibit on the job, many organizations review employee accomplishments—the results they achieve through their work. Advocates of results methods argue that they are more objective and empowering for employees. Looking at results, such as sales figures, production output, and the like, involves less subjectivity and therefore this method may be less open to bias. Furthermore, this approach often gives employees responsibility for their outcomes, while giving them discretion over the methods they use to accomplish them (within limits). This is empowerment in action.

Productivity Measures

A number of results measures are available to review performance. Salespeople are reviewed on the basis of their sales volume (both the number of units sold and the dollar amount in revenues). Production workers are reviewed on the basis of the number of units they produce and perhaps the scrap rate or number of defects that are detected. Customer service people are reviewed on the number of customers handled. Executives are frequently reviewed on the basis of company profits or growth rate. Each of these measures directly links what employees accomplish with results that benefit the organization. In this way, results reviews can directly align employee and organizational goals.

Results methods may inadvertently encourage employees to "look good" on a short-term basis, while ignoring the long-term ramifications. Line supervisors, for example, may let their equipment suffer to reduce maintenance costs. Further, in any job involving interaction with others, it is not enough to simply look at production or sales figures. Factors such as cooperation, adaptability, initiative, and concern for human relations may be important to job success. If these factors are important job standards, they should be added to the review. For productivity measures to be successful, the right things need to be measured and employees need to understand the measurement tools.[26]

Management by Objectives

One method that attempts to overcome some of the limitations of results-oriented reviews is **management by objectives (MBO).** MBO is a management philosophy, pioneered by Peter Drucker, that has employees establish objectives (e.g., production costs, sales per product, quality standards, profits), through consultation with their superiors and then uses these objectives as a basis for review.[27] MBO is a useful approach to an overall performance management system. As shown in Figure 6.5, MBO begins with setting the organization's common goals and objectives and ultimately returns to that step. For additional information on Management by Objectives, review the article on improving productivity at **www.accel-team.com**.

As the figure illustrates, a significant feature of the cycle is the establishment of specific goals by the employee. However, since those goals are based on a broad statement of employee responsibilities prepared by the supervisor, situations can arise in which unrealistic expectations can be agreed to.

To ensure success, MBO programs should be viewed as part of a total system for managing, not as merely an addition to the manager's job. Managers must be willing to empower employees to accomplish their objectives on their own, giving them discretion over the methods they use (but holding them accountable for outcomes). The following guidelines may be especially helpful:

1. Managers and employees must be willing to establish goals and objectives together.
2. Objectives should be quantifiable and measurable for the long and short term.
3. Expected results must be under the employee's control.
4. Managers and organizations must be supportive and provide necessary resources in order for employees to reach the expected outcomes.
5. Goals and objectives must be consistent for each level (top executive, manager, and employee).
6. Managers and employees must establish specific times when goals are to be reviewed and evaluated.

With the recent concern about business ethics, more and more organizations are including standards of performance related to ethics and reviewing ethical behaviour as part of the performance management system. Ethics in HRM 6.1 discusses how this might be done. Manager's Toolkit 6.4 presents a sample goal-setting worksheet used in organizations. You will note the column titled "Key Results." This is a description of what the goal will look like when it has been achieved. For example, a key result might be "Increased customer satisfaction." This would be measured by the percentage of satisfied customers and the goal might be "To increase the customer satisfaction level from 75% to 80%."

FIGURE 6.5 Performance Management Using an MBO Approach

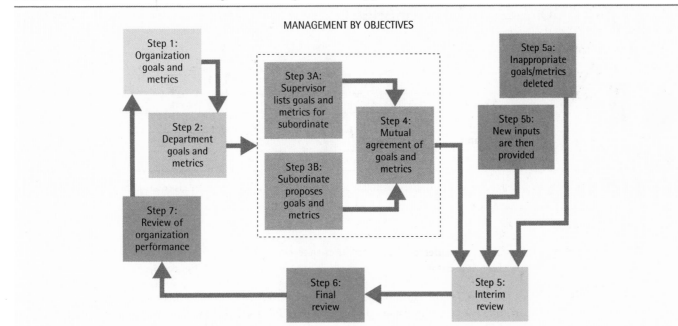

ETHICS **in HRM 6.1**

MEASURING ETHICAL PERFORMANCE

How do you distinguish between ethical and unethical behaviour and performance at work? The answer frequently is "Not easily." As there continue to be business scandals even in the recessionary times, boards of directors and senior managers are looking at ways to review and assess ethical behaviour.

Much has been written on "corporate responsibility" over the last several years—the behaviour of organizations that believe their responsibility extends beyond the shareholder to the employees, customers, and community at large. Many of the companies that take this view have also developed codes of ethics—a set of statements that indicate correct behaviour and actions in the organization. It is from this code that specific and measurable behaviours of performance can be established. For example, frequently in a code of ethics there is a statement about "being respectful to each other." Therefore, the performance measure might be "Demonstrates respect for all staff and customers." This particular measure would also

need to have very clear definitions for respect, as this word can mean different things to different people.

Just as companies wish to be seen as ethical, organizations that look at the ethics of a company and then write reports are becoming more prevalent. EthicsScan Canada Ltd. prepares profiles on organizations it then makes available to subscribers. For example, it prepared a profile on Research In Motion (RIM), the developers of the BlackBerry, that includes information about RIM's ethics policies, its management practices, and even things such as workplace accidents and the type of training that is done. Through these types of reports, investors and the general public can make conclusions about how ethical the company is.

Organizations are driven to be fair-minded and to be as transparent as possible in all their dealings. And this will work when organizations link performance to more than short-term goals. People pay attention to what they are measured on.

Sources: Adapted from "In the Game of Business, Playing Fair Can Actually Lead to Greater Profits," *Knowledge@Wharton,* March 13, 2008; and "Profile Report—Research In Motion Ltd.," EthicsScan Canada, retrieved February 16, 2009.

MANAGER'S TOOLKIT **6.4**

SAMPLE GOAL-SETTING WORKSHEET

PERFORMANCE MANAGEMENT SYSTEM

Name		Performance Period	
Key Results	Measure	Goal	By When

The Balanced Scorecard

One of the most enthusiastically adopted performance management innovations over the past decade has been the Balanced Scorecard (BSC). Developed by Harvard professors Robert Kaplan and David Norton, the BSC is a measurement framework that helps managers translate strategic goals into operational objectives. The generic model, shown in Manager's Toolkit 6.5, has four related categories: (1) financial, (2) customer, (3) processes, and (4) learning. The logic of the BSC is that learning and people management help organizations improve their internal processes. These internal processes—product development, service, and the like—are critical for creating customer satisfaction and loyalty. Customer value creation in turn is what drives financial performance and profitability.

Similar in some ways to MBO, the BSC enables managers to translate broad corporate goals into divisional, departmental, and team goals in a cascading fashion. The value of this is that each individual can see more clearly how his or her performance ties into the overall performance of the firm.

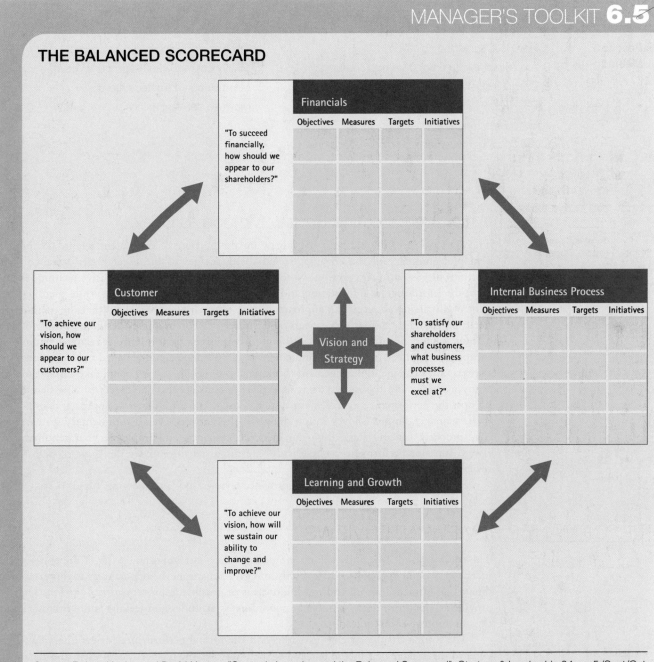

MANAGER'S TOOLKIT 6.5

THE BALANCED SCORECARD

Financials
"To succeed financially, how should we appear to our shareholders?"

Objectives	Measures	Targets	Initiatives

Customer
"To achieve our vision, how should we appear to our customers?"

Objectives	Measures	Targets	Initiatives

Vision and Strategy

Internal Business Process
"To satisfy our shareholders and customers, what business processes must we excel at?"

Objectives	Measures	Targets	Initiatives

Learning and Growth
"To achieve our vision, how will we sustain our ability to change and improve?"

Objectives	Measures	Targets	Initiatives

Source: Robert Kaplan and David Norton, "Strategic Learning and the Balanced Scorecard", *Strategy & Leadership 24,* no 5 (Sept/Oct 1996): 18-24.

FIGURE 6.6 Summary of Various Review Methods

	Advantages	Disadvantages
Trait Methods	1. Are inexpensive to develop 2. Use meaningful dimensions 3. Are easy to use	1. Have high potential for rating errors 2. Are not useful for employee counselling 3. Are not useful for allocating rewards 4. Are not useful for promotion decisions
Behavioural Methods	1. Use specific performance dimensions 2. Are acceptable to employees 3. Are useful for providing feedback 4. Are fair for reward and promotion decisions	1. Can be time-consuming to develop/use 2. Can be costly to develop 3. Have some potential for rating error
Results Method	1. Have less subjectivity bias 2. Are acceptable to employees and superiors 3. Link individual performance to organizational performance 4. Encourage mutual goal setting 5. Are good for reward and promotion decisions	1. Are time-consuming to develop/use 2. May encourage short-term perspective 3. May use contaminated criteria 4. May use deficient criteria

Which Performance Review Method to Use?

The approach used should be based largely on the purpose of the system. Figure 6.6 provides a helpful summary of the advantages and disadvantages of the specific performance review methods discussed in this section. Note that the simplest and least expensive techniques often yield the least accurate information and focus only on the actual review. While there has been a lot of discussion about which approach to use, research has determined that the method used needs to fit the organization's culture and strategy.[28] For example, designing and producing a form for supervisors to use in reviewing an employee's performance is relatively simple and inexpensive. On the other hand, implementing a 360-degree performance management system may require a change in management thinking and philosophy. This could take a long time with many meetings and the involvement of expensive consultants. The bigger picture here focuses on how the performance management system is used. Having a first-rate approach does no good if the manager simply "shoves it in a drawer." Alternatively, even a rudimentary system, when used properly, can initiate a discussion between managers and employees that genuinely gives rise to superior performance. These issues are discussed next under the topic of performance review interviews.

For additional information on performance reviews, look at Emerging Trends 6.1.

PERFORMANCE REVIEW INTERVIEWS

The coaching and review discussions are perhaps the most important parts of the entire performance management process. These discussions give a manager the opportunity to discuss a subordinate's performance record and to explore areas of possible improvement and growth. They also provide an opportunity to identify the subordinate's attitudes and feelings more thoroughly and thus to improve communication.

The format for the coaching sessions and the formal performance review interview will be determined in large part by the purpose of the interview, the type of system used, and the organization of any interview form. Most performance interviews attempt to give feedback to employees on how well they are performing their jobs and on planning for their future development.

EMERGING TRENDS **6.1**

1. ***Just-in-time feedback.*** With Gen X and Y having grown up with interactive technology, there is an expectation that there is ongoing feedback in a work environment. This is not something most supervisors are comfortable with. However, a company in Toronto has created a system where the employees choose advisers that will respond quickly and anonymously—a real time performance review.

2. ***Improving managers' skills to give feedback.*** Organizations such as SaskEnergy are using peer-mentoring programs where managers can practice giving feedback to each other. These sessions improve the skills of the managers who are then better able to give constructive and useful feedback to employees.

3. ***Web-based technology.*** As organizations get more complex and the need to evaluate performance at all levels increases, online technology will become more prevalent. Such technology will not only make it easier for managers to review previous information but will also allow the information to be kept more secure.

4. ***More emphasis on performance management as a process and not just an event.*** As managers become better equipped to coach and mentor, the focus of the review will be on continual feedback to the employee.

Sources: Adapted from "The Just-in-Time Performance Review," *The Globe and Mail,* February 13, 2009, B15; "Performance Management, Evaluation, Review Improvement," About.com: Human Resources, humanresources.about.com/od/performancemanagement/Performance_Management_Evaluation_Review_Improvement.htm (accessed February 16, 2009); and Linda Finkelstein, "Coaching SaskEnergy to Higher Performance," *Canadian HR Reporter,* December 1, 2008, www.hrreporter.com/ArticleView.aspx?l=1&articleid=6536.

Interviews should be scheduled far enough in advance to allow the interviewee, as well as the interviewer, to prepare for the discussion. Usually 10 days to two weeks is a sufficient amount of lead-time.

Conducting the Formal Performance Interview

While there are no hard-and-fast rules for how to conduct a formal review, there are some guidelines that may increase the employee's acceptance of the feedback, satisfaction with the interview, and intention to improve in the future. Many of the principles of effective interviewing discussed in Chapter 4 apply to performance review interviews as well. Here are some other guidelines that should also be considered.

1. *Ask for a self-assessment.* As noted earlier in the chapter, it is useful to have employees review their own performance prior to the interview. Recent research evidence suggests that employees are more satisfied and view the performance management system as providing more procedural justice when they have input into the process. The interview can then be used to discuss those areas where the manager and the employee have reached different conclusions—not so much to resolve the "truth," but to work toward a resolution of problems.

2. *Invite participation.* The basic purpose of a performance interview is to initiate a dialogue that will help employees improve their performance. Research evidence suggests that participation is strongly related to an employee's satisfaction with the review feedback as well as that person's intention to improve performance. It is also important to link performance to organizational goals.[29] During the conversation, it is important that the supervisor actively listens to the employee's comments and responses to questions.

3. *Express appreciation.* Praise is a powerful motivator, and in a performance interview, particularly, employees are seeking positive feedback. Start the interview by expressing appreciation for what the employee has done well. In this way, the employee may be less defensive and more likely to talk about aspects of the job that are not going so well.

4. *Minimize criticism.* If an employee has many areas in need of improvement, managers should focus on those few objective issues that are most problematic or most important to the job.

5. *Change the behaviour, not the person.* Avoid suggestions about personal traits to change; instead, suggest more acceptable ways of performing. For example, instead of focusing on a person's "unreliability," a manager might focus on the fact that the employee "has been late to work seven times this month."

6. *Focus on solving problems.* In addressing performance issues, it is frequently tempting to get into the "blame game" in which both manager and employee enter into a potentially endless discussion of why a situation has arisen. The interview should be directed at devising a solution to the problem.

7. *Be supportive.* One of the better techniques for engaging an employee in the problem-solving process is for the manager to ask: "What can I do to help?" By being open and supportive, the manager conveys to the employee that the manager will try to eliminate external roadblocks and work with the employee to achieve higher standards.

8. *Establish goals.* Since a major purpose of the performance review is to make plans for further growth and development, it is important to focus the interviewee's attention on the future rather than the past.

9. *Follow up day to day.* Ideally, coaching and ongoing feedback should be a regular part of a manager's job. Feedback is most useful when it is immediate and specific to a particular situation.

10. *Meeting set-up.* Providing feedback is better when done in private and scheduled when both people can take the time to focus on the review.

There may be times that the performance interview is very difficult—either because the manager is uncomfortable or the employee is not willing to take responsibility. Therefore, it is very important that the supervisor remain calm and is very clear on what the problem is and what specifically needs to be done differently. For further tips on handling this type of interview, view the video clip produced by trainingABC at **www.trainingabc.com/screeningroom.htm**.

trainingABC

www.trainingabc.com/
screeningroom.htm

Improving Performance

In many instances, the performance interview will provide the basis for noting deficiencies in employee performance and for making plans for improvement. Unless these deficiencies are brought to the employee's attention, they are likely to continue until they become quite serious. Sometimes underperformers do not understand exactly what is expected of them. However, once their responsibilities are clarified, they are in a position to take the corrective action needed to improve their performance.

People in retail are frequently assessed on their customer service interactions.

© 2009 Jupiterimages Corporation

Identifying Sources of Ineffective Performance

There are many reasons why an employee's performance might not meet the standards. First, each individual has a unique pattern of strengths and weaknesses that play a part. In addition, other factors—such as the work environment, the external environment (including home and community), and personal problems—have an impact on job performance. To provide a better understanding of possible sources of ineffective performance related to these environments, the comprehensive list shown in Figure 6.7 has been devised.

It is recommended that a diagnosis of poor employee performance focus on three interactive elements: skill, effort, and external conditions. For example, if an employee's performance is not up to standard, the cause could be a skill problem (knowledge, abilities, technical competencies), an effort problem (motivation to get the job done), and/or some problem in the external conditions of work (poor economy). Any one of these problem areas could cause performance to suffer.

Managing Ineffective Performance

Once the sources of performance problems are known, a course of action can be planned. This action may lie in providing training in areas that would increase the knowledge and/or skills needed for effective performance. A transfer to another job or department might give an employee a chance to become a more effective member of the organization. In other instances, greater attention may have to be focused on ways to motivate the individual.

If ineffective performance persists, it may be necessary to transfer the employee, take disciplinary action, or discharge the person from the organization. Whatever action is taken to cope with ineffective performance, it should be done with objectivity, fairness, and a recognition of the feelings of the individual involved. More information on dealing with ineffective performance is covered in Chapter 9.

FIGURE 6.7 Sources of Ineffective Performance

Organization Policies and Practices

- Ineffective placement
- Insufficient job training
- Ineffectual employment practices
- Permissiveness with enforcing policies or job standards
- Heavy-handed management
- Lack of attention to employee needs or concerns
- Inadequate communication within organization
- Unclear reporting relationships

Job Concerns

- Unclear or constantly changing work requirements
- Boredom with job
- Lack of job growth or advancement opportunities
- Management-employee conflict
- Problems with fellow employees
- Unsafe working conditions
- Unavailable or inadequate equipment or materials
- Inability to perform the job
- Excessive workload
- Lack of job skills

Personal Problems

- Marital problems
- Financial worries
- Emotional disorders (including depression, guilt, anxiety, fear)
- Conflict between work demands and family demands
- Physical limitations, including disabilities
- Low work ethic
- Other family problems
- Lack of effort
- Immaturity

External Factors

- Industry decline or extreme competition
- Legal constraints
- Conflict between ethical standards and job demands
- Union-management conflict

SUMMARY

1. Define a performance management system.
   - Set of integrated management practices.
2. Explain the purpose of a performance management system.
   - Allows the organization to get the right things done.
   - Helps increase employees' satisfaction with their work and the organization.
3. Describe the management practices necessary for a good performance management system.
   - Setting and communicating clear performance expectations.
   - Clear and specific performance objectives.
   - Supportive and helpful coaching by the supervisor.
   - Focusing on accomplishment of objectives during performance appraisals.
   - Recognizing and celebrating good performance.
4. Identify the steps in an effective performance management system.
   - Clarifying the work (job) to be done.
   - Setting goals and establishing a performance plan.
   - Regular and frequent coaching.
   - Conducting formal review of performance.
   - Recognizing and rewarding performance.
5. Describe the different sources of performance review information.
   - Manager or supervisor who is able to provide feedback on contribution.
   - Self—provides a personal review of accomplishments.
   - Subordinate—provides a perspective on certain behaviours such as leadership.
   - Peers and team members—who are able to describe how the person works with others.
   - Customers—provides input about the quality of service.
6. Explain the various methods used for performance reviews.
   - Trait approaches are designed to measure the extent to which an employee possesses certain characteristics.
   - Behavioural methods specifically describe which actions should (or should not) be exhibited on the job.
   - Productivity measures look at results or outputs.
   - Management by objectives (MBO) is a philosophy of management that has employees establish objectives (e.g., production costs, sales per product, quality standards, profits), through consultation with their superiors and then uses those objectives as a basis for appraisal.
7. Outline the characteristics of an effective performance review interview.
   - Ask the employees to review and assess their own performance prior to the interview.
   - Invite and encourage active participation by employees in the discussion of their performance.
   - Express appreciation for what the employee has done well.
   - Minimize criticism.
   - Change the behaviour, not the person.

NEED TO KNOW

- Definition of performance management system
- Purpose and reasons for introducing a performance management system
- The characteristics of an effective performance management system
- Various methods used to gather performance information
- Advantages and disadvantages of various performance review methods
- Guidelines for conducting a performance appraisal interview

NEED TO UNDERSTAND

- Link of management practices with performance management systems
- Relationship of organizational performance with performance management systems
- Role supervisor or line manager plays in the effectiveness of any system
- Relationship of methods to the overall system and the style of management
- Importance of good coaching and interviewing skills for appraising overall performance

KEY TERMS

behaviourally anchored rating scale (BARS) 183

customer input 177

graphic rating scales 182

management by objectives (MBO) 185

manager and/or supervisor review 175

peer review 176

performance management system 168

self-review 176

subordinate review 176

team review 177

REVIEW QUESTIONS

1. What are the major purposes of a performance management system?
2. Describe the relationships among performance management systems and selection, training, and development.
3. How can a performance management system be adjusted to include the principles of total-quality management (TQM)?
4. Describe the steps of an effective performance management system.
5. Discuss the guidelines that performance evaluations should meet in order to be legally defensible.
6. Who could evaluate the performance of people working in the following jobs?
   a. Sales representative
   b. Air traffic controller
   c. Room attendant in a hotel
   d. Activity coordinator in an eldercare centre
   e. Customer service representative in a financial institution
7. In many organizations, evaluators submit the reviews of their subordinates to their immediate superiors for review before discussing them with the individual employees they have evaluated. What advantages are there to this procedure?
8. What are the pros and cons of trait, behaviour, and results evaluations?
9. What are the suggested guidelines for conducting an effective performance review?

CRITICAL THINKING QUESTIONS

1. Your study group at school has been asked to develop a set of performance standards by which you could measure your performance. What would you include and why?
2. Assume you have just been hired as a customer service representative in a call centre for a bank. Your supervisor has asked that you work with a small task force to develop an appropriate performance appraisal approach. What method would you recommend and why?
3. An autopart's purchasing department is responsible for ordering and receiving all deliveries, including rush deliveries. Recently the person who checked the orders received failed to check that an urgent part had been received for a key client. When discovered by the supervisor after the client complained, the person confirmed that this was not checked. This was not the first time that a shipment had not been properly checked. The supervisor was also aware that during the employee's vacation the replacement worker had been able to perform all the duties without any difficulty. Explain how a performance management system might have prevented such a situation.
4. Discuss how you would diagnose poor performance in an accounting clerk's job. List several factors to consider.
5. Do you think students ought to be able to provide input into their instructor's performance? Why or why not? Explain your reasoning.

DEVELOPING YOUR SKILLS

1. On an individual basis, use the worksheet shown in Manager's Toolkit 6.4 to establish goals in relation to either this course or a job you are currently doing. After completing the worksheet, pair up with another student. Review and critique each other's work. In particular, look for realistic measurements and dates of completion.

2. Working in pairs, identify three to four performance characteristics on which your instructor ought to be reviewed. Share your responses with the entire class. Develop a single list of three to four performance characteristics. Discuss as an entire class. Determine whether the instructor agrees with your list; if not, enquire as to what ought to be on the list.

3. Working in groups of three to four students, review the following descriptions of three different employees. Describe the potential causes of poor performance in each case. And for each potential cause, identify appropriate solutions to enhance performance.
   a. *Carl Spackler* is the assistant greenskeeper at Bushwood Country Club. Over the past few months, members have been complaining that gophers are destroying the course and digging holes in the greens. Although Carl has been working evenings and weekends to address the situation, the problem persists. Unfortunately, his boss is interested only in results, and because the gophers are still there, he contends that Carl is not doing his job. He has accused Carl of "slacking off" and threatened his job.
   b. *Sandeep Dhillon* works in research and development for a chemical company that makes non-nutritive food additives. His most recent assignment has been the development of a nonstick aerosol cooking spray, but the project is way behind schedule and seems to be going nowhere. CEO Frank Shirley is decidedly upset and has threatened that if things don't improve, he will suspend bonuses again this year like he did last year. Sandeep feels dejected, because without the bonus he won't be able to take his family on vacation.
   c. *Soon Tan* is the host of a local television talk show called *Morning Winnipeg*. Although she is a talented performer and comedian, Soon has an unacceptable record of tardiness. The show's producer, David Bellows, is frustrated, because the problem has affected the quality of the show. On several occasions, Soon was unprepared when the show went on the air. Bellows has concluded that Soon is not a morning person and has thought about replacing her with a different host.

4. Access **www.panoramicfeedback.com**. Click the link "Demo" and develop a 360-degree feedback survey, respond to it, and receive the report. Print the report. In groups of four to five students, compare the survey instrument and the reports.

5. Access the following two websites:
   • www.performance-appraisal.com/anpas.htm
   • www.hrtools.com
   Each of these sites has a sample performance assessment tool. Try each tool, using information about yourself. As you go through the samples, identify features that are useful for the supervisor and ones that might not be as useful. Write a one-page summary of the tools, explaining which you would use and why.

6. Access the Government of Canada's website for small business (**www.employers.gc.ca**) and click the link titled "HR for Employers." Follow the link to "Managing Employees" and then to "Performance Appraisals." Review one of the documents and prepare a one-page summary explaining how the information would help a small business owner deal with performance management.

Panoramic Feedback
www.panoramicfeedback.com

Archer North's Performance Appraisal
www.performance-appraisal.com/anpas.htm

HR Tools
www.hrtools.com

Government of Canada
www.employers.gc.ca

Case Study  1

Workload Worries

A hotel's receiving department is responsible for checking deliveries of food and beverages, checking what has been received against what has been ordered, and verifying the quality of the merchandise received. In May 2009 an employee of a Winnipeg hotel failed to check a case of vegetables, which had started to rot. The receiver, who had been with the hotel for 17 years, admitted that he had not checked the vegetables. As a result, his supervisor gave him a written warning. The employee grieved, stating that he was too busy because the workload was excessive.

There was an investigation, which indicated that the grievor had not worked any overtime, nor had he requested permission to work any overtime. It was also noted that during the receiver's vacation period, the replacement worker had been able to perform the job without any difficulty. There was also evidence that the receiver was taking excessive breaks.

As a result of this investigation, the grievance was denied. In addition, the employee was sent a letter reminding him of his job responsibilities and of the need to restrict himself to the scheduled breaks. As a last step he was given a procedure to follow if he believed that the work was becoming excessive.

Questions

1. Discuss how a performance appraisal system might have prevented this grievance.
2. Which performance appraisal method would you recommend for this type of job?

Case Study 2

A Performance Appraisal Snafu

Research has shown that the performance appraisal process, and particularly the interaction between employees and managers, is a key determinant affecting employee motivation and productivity. Understandably, managers can view the appraisal of employee performance as a "Catch-22" in which the slightest mistake can cause employee resentment, as this case illustrates.

Marcus Singh, a research economist, has worked for a medium size municipality for the past 10 years. During that time, his supervisors have perceived Singh as an above-average performer. However, due to the small size of the department and the close working relationship between employees and management, a formal evaluation of employees was considered unnecessary. About 10 months ago, Singh and the other employees were assigned to another department as part of the municipal reorganization.

Shortly after the reorganization, the new department director issued a directive to all unit heads to formally evaluate the performance of their subordinates. Attached to his memorandum was a copy of a new performance appraisal form to be used in conducting the evaluations. These were done by the various supervisors and submitted to the director.

On examination of the completed appraisal forms from the various departments, the director had noticed that not one employee was appraised in either the "fair" or "satisfactory" category. In fact, most employees were rated as "outstanding" in every category. The director felt that his unit heads were too lenient and asked them to redo the evaluations in a more objective and critical manner. Furthermore, because the department's compensation budget for salary increases was largely based on a distribution of employee ratings, evaluating all employees as outstanding exceeded budget limits.

Singh's supervisor explained the director's request to his subordinates and asked them to redo their appraisals with the idea of being more objective this time. To his astonishment, the new appraisals were not much different from the first ones. Believing he had no choice in the matter, he unilaterally formulated his own ratings and discussed them with each employee.

Marcus Singh was not pleased when he found out that his supervisor had rated him one level lower on each category. Although he signed the second appraisal form, he indicated on the form that he did not agree with the evaluation. This new appraisal was forwarded to the director and was eventually added to the employees' permanent files. When pay raises were awarded in the department three weeks later, Marcus Singh did not receive a merit raise. He was told that it was due to his less-than-outstanding appraisal. He did, however, receive the general increase of $1,200 given to all employees regardless of their performance appraisal. This increase matched the increase in the CPI.

Singh has lost all motivation and complains bitterly to his colleagues about his unfair ratings. While he reports to work at 8 a.m. sharp and does not leave until 5 p.m. each day, he has been observed to spend a lot of time reading newspapers and books while at work.

Source: This case was adapted from a case prepared by James G. Pesek and Joseph P. Grunenwald of Clarion University of Pennsylvania.

Questions

1. What do you see as the problems in this case? Explain.
2. Could these problems have been avoided? How?
3. What can be done to correct the problem with Marcus Singh?

NOTES AND REFERENCES

1. David Brown, "Performance Management Systems Need Fixing: Survey," *Canadian HR Reporter*, April 11, 2005, www.hrreporter.com/ArticleView.aspx?l=1&articleid=3780 (accessed February 13, 2009).

2. Robert Bacal, "Why Improving Performance Management Systems Is So Difficult—Part 1," www.work911.com/cgi-bin/links/jump.cgi?ID=2002 (accessed February 13, 2009).

3. K. Anders Ericsson, Michael J. Prietula, and Edward T. Cokely, "The Making of an Expert," *Harvard Business Review*, July-August, 2007, 114–121.

4. "How Do We Teach New Supervisors to Judge Employee Performance?" *Workforce Management*, February 4, 2009, www.workforce.com/archive/feature/26/15/14/index.php?ht= (accessed February 13, 2009).

5. Adrian Furnham, "Performance Management Systems," *European Business Journal*, 2004, 83–94.

6. Uyen Vu, "Holt Renfrew Goes After the Unique; B.C. Lottery Focuses on Work Environment," *Canadian HR Reporter*, January 29, 2007, www.hrreporter.com/ArticleView.aspx?l=1&articleid=4955 (accessed February 13, 2009).

7. Adrian Furnham, "Performance Management Systems."

8. Roy Saunderson, "Telling the Truth About Rewards Programs," *Workforce Management*, www.workforce.com/archive/feature/26/17/43/index.php?ht= (accessed February 12, 2009).

9. Kit Fai Pun and Anthony Sydney White, "A Performance Measurement Paradigm for Integrating Strategy Formulation: A Review of Systems and Frameworks," *International Journal of Management Reviews* 7, no. 1 (2005): 49–71.

10. Deborah Wilson, Bronwyn Croxson and Adele Atkinson, "What Gets Measured Gets Done," *Policy Studies* 27, no. 2 (2006): 153–171; Lisa Norcross, "Building on Success," *IET Manufacturing Engineer*, June/July 2006, 42–45; and Susan Heathfield, "Performance Appraisals Don't Work—What Does?" *The Journal for Quality & Participation*, Spring 2007, 6–9.

11. "How to Conduct Annual Employee Reviews," *Inc. Guidebook* 1, no. 9 (2008).

12. Accenture Business Services, *The Point* 3, no. 5 (2004), www.accenture.com/fs (accessed December 4, 2004).

13. Jay Forte, "Give Feedback, Get Performance," *Supervision* 70, no. 3 (March 2009): 3–4.

14. Scott Cohen and Nidhi Verma, "Rethinking Performance Management as a Business Tool to Spark a High-Performance Culture," Hewitt Associates, 2008.

15. Timothy R. Hinkin and Chester A. Schriesheim, "Performance Incentives for Tough Times," *Harvard Business Review,* March 2009, 26.

16. Adrienne Fox, "Curing What Ails Performance Reviews," *HR Magazine,* January 2009, 52–56.

17. Ibid.

18. Francie Dalton, "360-Degree Feedback Mechanisms," *MRO Today,* www.mrotoday.com/mro/archives/exclusives/360Degree.htm (accessed February 14, 2009).

19. Tracy Gallagher, "360-Degree Performance Reviews Offer Valuable Perspectives," *Financial Executive,* December 2008, 61.

20. Jerry K. Palmer and James M. Loveland, "The Influence of Group Discussion on Performance Judgments: Rating Accuracy, Contrast Effects, and Halo," *The Journal of Psychology* 142 (s) (2008): 117–130.

21. David Wayne, "Team Deming," *Industrial Engineer,* October 2008, 26–30.

22. Dick Grote, "Passing Judgment," *The Conference Board Review,* September/October 2008, 35–43.

23. Paul Loucks, "Plugging Into Performance Management," *Canadian HR Reporter,* February 26, 2007, www.hrreporter.com/ArticleView.aspx?l=1&articleid=5016 (accessed February 15, 2009).

24. Douglas P. Shuit, "Huddling with the Coach—Part 2," *Workforce Management* 84, no. 2 (February 1, 2005): 5; and "Ceridian and Softscape Announce an Agreement to Deliver Employee Performance and Development Solutions," *Payroll Manager's Report,* May 2004, 13.

25. Susan Bowness, "Full-Circle Feedback: 360-Degree Performance Reviews," *Canadian Business-Profit,* April 2006, www.canadian-business.com/entrepreneur/managing/article.jsp?content=20060406_150353_1772 (accessed February 16, 2009).

26. Patty Kujawa, "You Get What You Pay For," *Workforce Management,* January 30, 2008, www.workforce.com/archive/feature/25/33/83/index.php?ht= (accessed February 16, 2009).

27. "Management by Objectives (MBO)," www.1000ventures.com/business_guide/mgmt_mbo_main.html (accessed February 16, 2009).

28. Kit Fai Pun and Anthony Sydney White, "A Performance Measurement Paradigm for Integrating Strategy Formulation: A Review of Systems and Frameworks."

29. "Make Staff Reviews Count," *Credit Union Magazine,* January 2009, 12.

CHAPTER 7

RECOGNIZING AND REWARDING EMPLOYEES

OUTCOMES

After studying this chapter, you should be able to

1. Explain an organization's concerns in developing a strategic rewards program.

2. Identify the various factors that influence the setting of pay levels.

3. Describe the major job evaluation systems.

4. Describe the compensation structure.

5. List the types of incentive plans.

6. Explain the employee benefits that are required by law.

7. Describe voluntary benefits.

OUTLINE

HRM CLOSE-UP

Dave Taillefer (third from left) with members of his Code Shoppe [Icona Inc.] team. Courtesy of Dave Taillefer, The Code Shoppe

"We are focused today on staying profitable during difficult economic times. But one day, I want our staff to benefit more directly from our profits."

Schooled in biology, Dave Taillefer chose a completely different field when he began his business in the late 1990s. He pursued a website development and hosting business because he saw a lot of demand for the service. In those early years, Taillefer focused on application development, programming, and the technical aspects of building interactive websites. For the creative side, he relied on hiring designers and graphic artists on a freelance basis. But as business grew, this approach became difficult to manage.

Taillefer set out in search of a suitable business partner and found a small design shop whose owner shared his desire for growth. The companies merged and became Icona Inc. They decided to use the design shop's logo but with Taillefer's company colours. With this merger, everything changed from administration to client relationship practices. Of course managing human resources changed greatly too.

After reviewing their options, the partners decided to put each member of the team on salary with health benefits and even an employee code of conduct. "It mattered greatly who was working for us. Gone are the days of leveraged labour for a piece of the pie," reflected Taillefer. "Today, we have salaried employees with clear duties and responsibilities."

Taillefer seeks people who are highly competent and self-starters. He expects them to manage themselves and manage their time. He hires on a "50% skill and 50% personality" basis because the shop is fairly small and being a team player is paramount. "It has to be a good fit, someone who meshes with everyone else and can share the vision we have."

When setting salaries, Taillefer used his experience of working as an independent Web designer. "I set salaries based on instinct and with the knowledge of what it would take to do it myself," Taillefer comments. He regularly shares revenue and expense numbers with staff and feels it establishes trust and ensures that everyone continues to have common goals as the company grows. "I'm confident that everyone understands the vibe," he explains.

Salaries may be slightly below what the market pays at Icona, but Taillefer offers another form of compensation he describes as "lifestyle benefits." The office space is funky, in a two-storey loft with lots of natural light and no cubicles. To make the space even more inspirational, he hired local artists to paint a graffiti mural on the wall. At Icona, there is no dress code and the staff is encouraged to use the lounge to rest and relax. Hours of work aren't regimented either. "If you want to work 8 til 4, that's fine with me. If you choose to work a day on the weekend, you can take a day off during the regular work week." Of course, client work comes first and there's an expectation that deadlines and clients' expectations are consistently met.

If business goes well, Taillefer will reward staff with a year-end bonus. The bonus will be tied to performance and related to hours worked. One day, Taillefer would like to implement profit sharing or other forms of ownership for staff but admits that he is not there yet. "We are focused today on staying profitable during difficult economic times. But one day, I want our staff to benefit more directly from our profits."

INTRODUCTION

You will note from the HRM Close-Up that compensation is a big issue not just for employees but also for the managers of those employees and the owner of the company. Although companies may set guidelines about how much each position or job is worth, it is the manager who has to implement those guidelines. It is the manager who will make decisions about who gets paid what. Therefore, it is important for the manager and supervisor to have an understanding of compensation and its link to the success of the organization. It is also important for the manager to understand how compensation is derived, and what factors influence the setting of the wage and benefits structure.

Literature and research indicates that important work-related variables leading to job satisfaction include challenging work, interesting job assignments, equitable rewards, competent supervision, and rewarding careers.[1] It is doubtful, however, that many employees would continue working were it not for the money they earn. Employees want compensation systems that are fair and commensurate with their skills and expectations. Pay, therefore, is a major consideration in HRM because it provides employees with a tangible reward for their services, as well as a source of recognition and livelihood. As mentioned earlier, the effectiveness of the manager has a large impact on the employee's job satisfaction and it is usually the manager who is the first one to deal with any concerns or issues regarding compensation. While an HR professional in the organization may be responsible for gathering compensation information and developing approaches to how compensation is managed, it is the manager who typically makes decisions on how much a person is compensated. Further, with the economic downturn, a recent study conducted by Towers Perrin, a global management consulting firm, reinforces that while organizations may not do any compensation changes in 2009, there was still some monies available to ensure that companies kept their key staff.[2]

It is important to know that employee rewards and recognition includes all forms of pay and rewards received by employees for the performance of their jobs. **Direct compensation** encompasses employee wages and salaries, incentives, bonuses, and commissions. **Indirect compensation** comprises the many benefits supplied by employers, such as dental plans, life insurance coverage, and *nonfinancial compensation* includes employee recognition programs, rewarding jobs, and flexible work hours to accommodate personal needs. Direct and indirect compensation are referred to as "total compensation" or "total rewards approach." This latter phrase helps communicate to employees that their compensation doesn't have just a monetary value but that it includes other forms of recognition and reward.

Both managers and scholars agree that the way compensation is allocated among employees sends a message about what management believes is important and the types of activities it encourages. Furthermore, for an employer, total compensation constitutes a sizable operating cost. In manufacturing firms, compensation is seldom as low as 20% of total expenditures, and in service enterprises it often exceeds 80%. A strategic compensation program, therefore, is essential so that pay can serve to motivate employee production sufficiently to keep labour costs at an acceptable level.

While the focus of this chapter is on salary and benefits, it is important to state that more organizations are beginning to think about and create "reward strategies." The thrust of this approach is to develop an organizational mind-set to recognize and reward people based on performance.[3] Further, it is important to ensure that the recognition and rewards are seen as valuable to the employees and helps in the retention of employees.[4] In doing so, organizations will tend to have components of direct compensation that are tied to the success of the organization and to the contributions of that success through individual (or team) performance.

Towers Perrin
www.towersperrin.com

Direct compensation
Employee wages and salaries, incentives, bonuses, and commissions

Indirect compensation
Benefits, such as dental plans and life insurance, supplied by employers

REWARDS AS PART OF COMPANY STRATEGY

Outcome 1

Companies structure their compensation in ways that enhance employee motivation and growth while aligning the employees' efforts with the objectives, philosophies, and culture of the organization. Designing the compensation system goes beyond determining what market rates to pay employees—although market rates are one element of compensation planning. Research has shown that companies that make the rewards strategy a part of the overall motivational framework have higher organizational performance than those companies that don't.[5] This makes a compelling argument to ensure that the organization takes into consideration what employees see as important in the reward equation.

Looking at the compensation system in a strategic fashion serves to mesh the monetary payments made to employees with specific HR, and, therefore, business objectives. For example, in the recruitment of new employees, the rate of pay for jobs can increase or limit the supply of applicants. Employers have adopted special pay strategies to attract job applicants with highly marketable skills, such as high-tech workers, and engineers and scientists with financial knowledge and good people skills. Organizations also use compensation to retain scarce skills. According to a Conference Board of Canada survey of 395 Canadian companies, there was still concern about retaining critical skills even in recessionary times.[6] Of the organizations surveyed, 95% expect to continue with their variable pay plans as part of their overall retention strategy.

If rates of pay are high, creating a large applicant pool, then organizations may choose to raise their selection standards and hire better-qualified employees. This in turn can reduce employer training costs. When employees perform at exceptional levels, their performance assessments may justify an increased pay rate. For these reasons and others, an organization should ensure it has a systematic way to manage employee compensation and that it is linked to business performance. For example, a recent survey conducted by Watson Wyatt, a large consulting firm in Canada and the rest of the world, has demonstrated that there is a link between an integrated approach to rewards and achieving strong business results.[7] A summary of this and other similar compensation reports can be found at Watson Wyatt's website (**www.watsonwyatt.com**).

It is important to remember that the concept of "total rewards" is a broader set of elements and includes the tangible rewards of pay, benefits, etc. but also includes factors such as career development, work climate/culture, and work-life balance.[8] Other items in total rewards include peer-to-peer recognition programs, an extra day off to spend time with family, or organizing some type of fun event. For example, Dimension Data Canada Inc., a specialty IT firm, has created a "chief fun officer" role that promotes excitement, energy, and team building at work.[9] At Work with HRM 7.1 discusses the importance of creating an overall rewards approach.

Watson Wyatt
www.watsonwyatt.com

AT WORK **with HRM 7.1**

TOTAL REWARDS

"It is important to take a holistic approach to maximize your attraction and retention strategy," says Michael D'Amico, senior vice president of HR at Iogen, a small biotech firm in Ottawa. While the company only has about 320 employees, it is making sure that it stays competitive, even in a difficult economic climate.

D'Amico goes on to say, "It's so easy to put out programs and spend money on them but if employees aren't valuing them to the same extent, you're splitting your total rewards pie and you're certainly not optimizing how you're using your resources."

With a relatively small number of employees in a highly competitive environment, losing a couple of key people in any one area could impact successful business outcomes. So, without the depth of bench strength, it is important to have a total rewards approach when looking at retaining people. The issue is slightly more difficult since the company is in Ottawa. Potential employees will frequently compare their overall rewards package to the government. It is necessary, therefore, for employees know the tradeoffs between more vacation and bonuses and stock options.

Since the total rewards approach is relatively new, D'Amico conducted focus group sessions with different employee groups as well as undertaking an employee survey.

In addition, the company will analyze the existing programs and compare to how competitive the rewards are externally. For example, vacation is one of several offerings that Iogen is looking at critically as there are currently inconsistencies in how and how much vacation is allocated. However, "rather than going in and doing it independently, we want to make sure we fit it into a total review perspective," stated D'Amico. There is no desire to do a quick fix or without looking at the whole.

As changes occur, Iogen will ensure that the metrics are there to gauge the success of its overall approach. Currently some of its benefits include a group RRSP, flexible work arrangements, and a strong focus on personal and career development. It is important that as changes are made, employees feel that the overall rewards package is still valuable to each of them.

CRITICAL THINKING QUESTIONS

1. If you are working, do you know the value of your total rewards? Would you think differently about the organization if you did?
2. Providing information about the value of compensation does take resources that could be used differently. Would you want to know the total value of your compensation? Why or why not?

Source: Adapted from Sarah Dobson, "Total Rewards Overhaul," *Canadian HR Reporter*, November 3, 2008, 21.

Linking Compensation to Organizational Objectives

Compensation has been revolutionized by heightened domestic competition, globalization, increased employee skill requirements, and new technology. Therefore, an outcome of today's dynamic business environment is that managers have needed to change their pay philosophies from paying for a specific position or job title to rewarding employees on the basis of their individual competencies or group contributions to organizational success. A recent study showed that 81% of responding organizations listed *improving employee's focus on achieving business goals* as a significant objective influencing reward changes (see Figure 7.1). A compensation program, therefore, must be tailored to the needs of the organization and its employees. And in doing so, it is important to ensure that employees feel they are being rewarded. A study in early 2009 determined that employees would find ways of rewarding themselves (such as taking a sick day, longer breaks, etc.) if they felt that their employer was not acknowledging extra efforts during times of reduced staffing levels and longer hours.[10]

It is not uncommon for organizations to establish specific goals for aligning their organizational objectives with their compensation program.[11] Formalized compensation goals serve as guidelines for managers to ensure that wage and benefit policies achieve their intended purpose. Some of the more common goals are the following:

1. To reward employees' past performance.
2. To remain competitive in the labour market.
3. To maintain salary equity among employees.
4. To mesh employees' future performance with organizational goals.
5. To control the compensation budget.
6. To retain key staff.[12]
7. To influence employee behaviours and attitudes.[13]

To achieve these goals, specific actions or steps must be taken. Three areas of action are discussed below.

The Pay-for-Performance Standard

Pay-for-performance standard
Standard by which managers tie compensation to employee effort and performance

A **pay-for-performance standard** serves to raise productivity and lower labour costs in today's economic environment. It is agreed that managers must tie at least some reward to employee effort and performance. Without this standard, employees will not clearly see the link between performance and rewards.[14]

The term "pay for performance" refers to a wide range of direct compensation options, including merit-based pay, bonuses, salary commissions, job and pay banding, team or group incentives, and gainsharing programs.[15] Each of these compensation systems seeks to differentiate

FIGURE 7.1   Significant Goals Driving Pay and Reward Changes

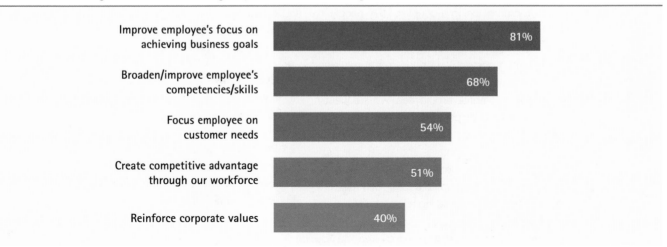

between the pay of average performers and that of outstanding performers. For example, ACS, a worldwide company with operations in Canada, specializes in providing business processing outsourcing, including call centres. It uses four to five employee measures, such as quality and quantity of work, to link pay-to-performance. When a particular group at ACS saved 23% more than was projected, the employees involved saw the results of their efforts in their compensation package.[16] Interestingly, productivity studies show that employees will increase their output by 15 to 35% when an organization installs a pay-for-performance program.

Unfortunately, designing a sound pay-for-performance system is not easy. Considerations must be given to how employee performance will be measured, what monies will be allocated for compensation increases, which employees will be covered, what payout method will be used, and when payments will be made. A critical issue concerns the size of the monetary increase and its perceived value to employees, as a pay-for-performance program will lack its full potential when pay increases only approximate the rises in the cost of living. Figure 7.2 provides a summary of the advantages and disadvantages of different pay-for-performance systems.

The Motivating Value of Compensation

Pay is a quantitative measure of an employee's relative worth. For most employees, pay has a direct bearing not only on their standard of living, but also on the status and recognition they may be able to achieve both on and off the job. Since pay represents a reward received in exchange for an employee's contributions, it is essential that the pay be equitable in relation to those contributions. It is also important that an employee's pay be equitable in relation to what other employees are receiving for their contributions.

Equity can be defined as anything of value earned through the investment of something of value. Equity theory is a motivation theory that explains how employees respond to situations in which they feel they have received less (or more) than they deserve.[17] Central to the theory is the role of perception in motivation and the fact that individuals make comparisons. It states that individuals form a ratio of their inputs (abilities, skills, experiences) in a situation to their outcomes (salary, benefits) in that situation. They then compare the value of that ratio with the value of the input/output ratio for other individuals in a similar class of jobs either internal or external to the organization. If the value of their ratio equals the value of another's, they perceive

FIGURE 7.2 Advantages and Disadvantages of Pay-for-Performance Systems

Type of System	Advantages	Disadvantages
Individual	• Simple to compute • Clearly links pay to organizational outcomes • Motivates employees • Are variable costs • Employees focus on clear performance targets • Distributes success among those responsible for producing success	• Standards of performance may be difficult to establish • May not be an effective motivator • Difficult to deal with missed performance targets • Available money may be inadequate • Employees may be unable to distinguish merit pay from other types of pay increases
Team	• Support group planning • Builds team culture • Can broaden scope of contribution that employees are motivated to make • Tends to reduce jealousies and complaints • Encourage cross-training	• Individuals may perceive efforts contribute little to group success • Intergroup social problems can limit performance • Can be difficult to compute and therefore difficult to understand
Organization	• Creates effective employee participation • Can increase pride in organization • Can be structured to provide tax advantages • Are variable costs	• Difficult to handle if organization's performance is low • Can be difficult to compute and therefore difficult to understand • More difficult for individual effort to be linked to organizational success

the situation as equitable and no tension exists. However, if they perceive their input/output ratio as inequitable relative to others', this creates tension and motivates them to eliminate or reduce the inequity. The strength of their motivation is proportional to the magnitude of the perceived inequity. If a person feels that someone is getting more compensation for similar work, this can negatively affect that employee's view of the value of the employee's own work. HR practitioners who specialize in compensation systems are particularly concerned not only that employees are paid fairly for the work they do but also that they are paid equitably relative to other people in the organization.

Equitable pay
Compensation received is perceived to be equal to the value of the work performed

For employees, pay is **equitable** when the compensation given is perceived to be equal to the value of the work performed. Research clearly demonstrates that employees' perceptions of equity, or inequity, can have dramatic effects on their work behaviour and productivity.[18] Although line managers do not design compensation systems, they do have to respond to employee concerns about being paid equitably. Compensation policies are internally equitable when employees believe that the wage rates for their jobs approximate the job's worth to the organization. Perceptions of external equity exist when the organization is paying wages and benefits that are relatively equal to what other employers are paying for similar types of work. At Work with HRM 7.2 provides an interesting perspective on pay-for-performance and equity.

The Bases for Compensation

Hourly work
Work paid on an hourly basis

Piecework
Work paid according to the number of units produced

Work performed in most private, public, and not-for-profit organizations has traditionally been compensated on an hourly basis. This is referred to as **hourly work**, in contrast to **piecework**, in which employees are paid according to the number of units they produce. Hourly work, however, is far more prevalent than piecework as a basis for compensating employees.

AT WORK **with HRM 7.2**

INCENTIVE COMPENSATION

Yvonne Blaszczyk, FCHRP, publisher of *Strategic Human Resources Compensation News*, suggests that when the economy is unstable, organizations look to control basic compensation and motivate employees through incentive compensation. Because markets are fragile, organizations are not achieving the profit performances that were expected, and so incentive compensation payouts for individual performers are variable and declining. How can incentive plans be structured so that not only employee results and organizational outcomes are rewarded, but so are contribution and efforts? These softer and less objective measures of contribution and effort can be measured and are important to the survival and ultimate success of organizations. For example, one company that deals with the financing and leasing of equipment has to work closely with another company that is selling the equipment. The first company cannot influence sales and therefore cannot be rewarded on the sales results. However, the company does have to service the leases and ensure customer retention. The incentive program for this company recognizes the importance of maintaining good relations with the sales company and so rewards

employees based on the number of contacts, number of successfully resolved conflicts, and success in renewal of difficult contracts.

The other major change is that of the decline of merit compensation. A fixed pool of money usually distributed at the rate of 3 to 4% per employee is not motivating. The most common complaint heard by Blaszczyk is from high-producing employees who receive the same salary increases as average-performing employees. So companies are taking the merit money and distributing it at larger rates to only the top performers. In the next decade we can expect to see companies bravely embarking on heavily weighted incentive pay, with lower base compensation. The base salary pays for day-to-day work; the incentives pay for making sure the company stays in business and is profitable. But there may be legal issues. Current employees may perceive this as a change in the implicit agreement about how they are paid.

CRITICAL THINKING QUESTION

Would you like to have your pay tied directly to your performance? Why or why not?

Employees compensated on an hourly basis are classified as *hourly employees*, or wage earners. Those whose compensation is computed on the basis of weekly, biweekly, or monthly pay periods are classified as *salaried employees*. Hourly employees are normally paid only for the time they work. Salaried employees, by contrast, are generally paid the same for each pay period, even though they occasionally may work more hours or fewer than the regular number of hours in a period. They also usually receive certain benefits not provided to hourly employees.

DETERMINING COMPENSATION

Outcome 2

A combination of *internal* and *external* factors can influence, directly or indirectly, the rates at which employees are paid, as shown in Figure 7.3.

Internal Factors

The internal factors that influence wage rates are the employer's compensation policy, the worth of a job, an employee's relative worth in meeting job requirements, and an employer's ability and willingness to pay.

Employer's Compensation Strategy

Organizations will usually state objectives regarding compensation for their employees. For example, a public-sector employer may wish to pay fairly and at the market average. (Remember: "market" means the geographical area in which the organization typically finds qualified candidates for work.) On the other hand, a software development company may wish to pay fairly but be the industry leader to attract and retain high-calibre staff.

Usually both large and small employers set pay policies reflecting (1) the internal wage relationship among jobs and skill levels, (2) the external competition or an employer's pay position relative to what competitors are paying, (3) a policy of rewarding employee performance, and (4) administrative decisions concerning elements of the pay system, such as overtime premiums, payment periods, and short- or long-term incentives.

Worth of a Job

Organizations without a formal compensation program generally base the worth of jobs on the subjective opinions of people familiar with the jobs. In such instances, pay rates may be influenced heavily by the labour market or, in the case of unionized employees, by collective bargaining.

FIGURE 7.3 Factors Affecting the Wage Mix

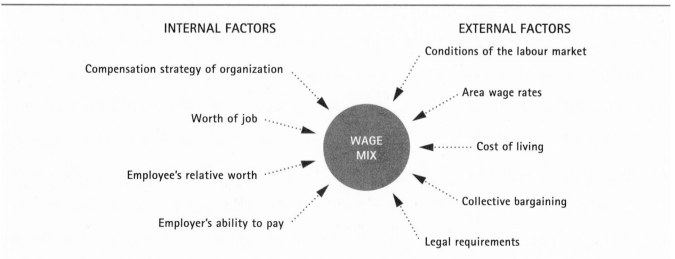

INTERNAL FACTORS

Compensation strategy of organization

Worth of job

Employee's relative worth

Employer's ability to pay

WAGE MIX

EXTERNAL FACTORS

Conditions of the labour market

Area wage rates

Cost of living

Collective bargaining

Legal requirements

Organizations with formal compensation programs, however, are more likely to rely on a system of job evaluation to aid in rate determination. Even when rates are subject to collective bargaining, job evaluation can assist the organization in maintaining some degree of control over its wage structure.

Job evaluation

Systematic process of determining the relative worth of jobs in order to establish which jobs should be paid more than others within an organization

Job evaluation is the systematic process of determining the *relative* worth of jobs in order to establish which jobs should be paid more than others within the organization. Job evaluation helps to establish internal equity between various jobs. Job worth is usually measured by the following criteria: level of skill, effort, responsibility, and working conditions of the job, no matter which particular formal system is used. The relative worth of a job is then determined by comparing it with others within the organization using these criteria. Furthermore, each method of comparison may be made on the basis of the jobs as a whole or on the basis of the parts that constitute the jobs. Refer to the four methods of comparison explored at "Job Evaluation Systems" starting on page 209.

Employee's Relative Worth

In both hourly and salaried jobs, employee performance can be recognized and rewarded through promotion and with various incentive systems. Superior performance can also be rewarded by granting merit raises on the basis of steps within a rate range established for a job class. If merit raises are to have their intended value, however, they must be determined by an effective performance appraisal system that differentiates between those employees who deserve the raises and those who do not. This system, moreover, must provide a visible and credible relationship between performance and any raises received. Unfortunately, too many so-called merit systems provide for raises to be granted automatically. As a result, employees tend to be rewarded more for merely being present than for being productive on the job.

In some situations, supervisors will also compare the performance of one employee to another. While proponents of performance stress that a person is to be assessed against standards of performance, there is a tendency to compare employees against each other. This is particularly true in the absence of any performance management system.

Employer's Ability and Willingness to Pay

In the public sector, the amount of compensation (pay and benefits) employees can receive is limited by the funds budgeted for this purpose and by the willingness of taxpayers to provide them. Federal government employees had their pay frozen for six years, in response to the drive to balance the budget and because of the public's perception of highly paid government workers. In the private sector, profits and other financial resources available to employers often limit pay levels. Economic conditions and competition faced by employers can also significantly affect the rates they are willing to pay. Competition and recessions can force prices down and reduce the income from which compensation payments are derived. In such situations, employers may have little choice but to reduce wages and/or lay off employees, or, even worse, to go out of business.

External Factors

The major external factors that influence wage rates include overall economy, labour market conditions, area wage rates, cost of living, collective bargaining if the employer is unionized, and legal requirements.

Hewitt Associates
www.hewittassociates.com

Economy

With the current economic recession, many organizations have re-examined their compensation approach to ensure that it is appropriate. A study done in mid-2009 by Hewitt Associates (**www. hewittassociates.com**) identified the following actions by companies:

- Differentiating between average and high performers when making compensation adjustments;
- Reducing bonuses;

- Creating unpaid vacations;
- Managing overall workforce costs through a combination of hiring freezes and terminating poor performers.[19]

Labour Market Conditions

The labour market reflects the forces of supply and demand for qualified labour within an area. These forces help to influence the wage rates required to recruit or retain competent employees. It must be recognized, however, that counterforces can reduce the full impact of supply and demand on the labour market. The economic power of unions, for example, may prevent employers from lowering wage rates even when unemployment is high among union members. Employment laws also may prevent an employer from paying at a market rate less than an established minimum.

Area Wage Rates

A formal wage structure should provide rates that are in line with those being paid by other employers for comparable jobs within the area. Data pertaining to area wage rates may be obtained at minimal cost from local area wage surveys. Wage-survey data also may be obtained from consulting firms, such as Towers Perrin and Watson Wyatt. Smaller employers use government or local board of trade surveys to establish rates of pay. Many organizations conduct their own surveys. Others engage in a cooperative exchange of wage information or rely on various professional associations, such as the Professional Engineering Association of Ontario or British Columbia, for these data.

Cost of Living

Because of inflation, compensation rates tend to be adjusted upward periodically to help employees maintain their purchasing power. To do this, organizations frequently use the **consumer price index (CPI)**. The CPI is a measure of the average change in prices over time in a large "basket" of goods and services purchased by Canadians.[20] The index is based on prices of food, clothing, shelter, and fuels; transportation fares; charges for medical services; and prices of other goods and services that people buy for day-to-day living. Statistics Canada collects price information on a

Statistics Canada
www.statcan.gc.ca

Consumer price index (CPI)
Measure of the average change in prices over time in a fixed "market basket" of goods and services

An employee's contribution to the organization (relative worth) is often considered when making salary decisions.

© Royalty-Free/Corbis

FIGURE 7.4   Inflation and Wage Increases (1993–2009)

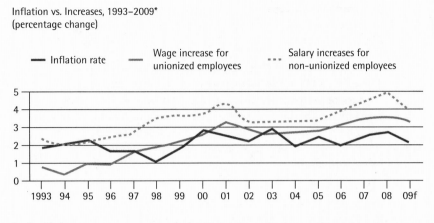

Inflation vs. Increases, 1993–2009*
(percentage change)

f = forecast
*Wage increases for unionized employees during 1993-2007 are actuals as reported by
Human Resources and Skills Development Canada, Workplace Information Directorate.
Wage increases for unionized employees for 2008 and 2009 projected are from the
Compensation Outlook 2009 survey.
Sources: The Conference Board of Canada; Human Resources and Skills Development
Canada, Workplace Information Directorate.

Source: Compensation Planning Outlook 2009, The Conference Board of Canada, Ottawa, 2009. Reproduced with permission from the Conference Board of Canada.
Note: Figures given for 2009 are forecasts.

monthly basis and calculates the CPI for Canada as a whole and various Canadian city averages. Figure 7.4 illustrates wage increases for unionized and nonunionized employees, compared with the inflation rate.

Using the CPI to determine changes in pay rates can also compress pay rates within a pay structure, thereby creating inequities among those who receive the wage increase. For example, an increase of 50 cents an hour represents a 10% increase for an employee earning $5 an hour, but only a 5% increase for someone earning $10 per hour.

Collective Bargaining

Real wages
Wage increases larger than rises in the consumer price index; that is, the real earning power of wages

As you will see in Chapter 10, one of the primary functions of a labour union is to bargain collectively over conditions of employment, the most important of which is compensation. The union's goal in each new agreement is to achieve increases in **real wages**—wage increases larger than the increase in the CPI—thereby improving the purchasing power and standard of living of its members. This goal includes gaining wage settlements that equal if not exceed the pattern established by other unions within the area.

The agreements negotiated by unions tend to establish rate patterns within the labour market. As a result, wages are generally higher in areas where organized labour is strong. To recruit and retain competent personnel and avoid unionization, nonunion employers must either meet or exceed these rates. The "union scale" also becomes the prevailing rate that all employers must pay for work performed under government contract. The impact of collective bargaining therefore extends beyond that segment of the labour force that is unionized.

Legal Requirements

As discussed in Chapter 2, legislation is in place that either influences or requires certain pay rates. For example, most provinces have a legislated minimum hourly wage. This means that an employer cannot pay any worker less than the per-hour rate. In addition, pay equity legislation obliges certain companies to pay the same wage rate for jobs of a dissimilar nature and is based on comparing jobs performed mostly by men to jobs performed mostly by women. Under pay equity, a company must use a "gender-neutral" system, comparing jobs based on the amount and type of skill, effort, and responsibility needed to perform the job and on the working conditions in which the job is performed. Some provinces also consider male–female pay rates under human rights legislation. Read HRM and the Law 7.1 for a recent human rights decision that involved what a person was paid.

Job Evaluation Systems

As mentioned earlier in this chapter, job evaluation is a way to determine the relative worth of jobs in an organization. The most typical job evaluation systems are described below.

Job Ranking System

Outcome 3

The simplest and oldest system of job evaluation is the job ranking system, which arrays jobs on the basis of their relative worth. Job ranking can be done by a single individual knowledgeable about all jobs or by a committee composed of management and employee representatives. The basic weakness of the job ranking system is that it does not provide a very refined measure of each job's worth and therefore is not used frequently except in smaller organizations.

Job Classification System

In the job classification system, jobs that are sufficiently alike with respect to duties and responsibilities are grouped and will have a common name and common pay. Jobs that require increasing amounts of job responsibility, skill, knowledge, ability, or other factors selected to compare jobs would then be grouped together, with a different common name and a different common pay. For example, within the Public Service Agency of the federal government, the "Border Services" classification uses 10 different factors, including "risk to health," to group positions together.[21]

The descriptions of each of the job classes constitute the scale against which the specifications for the various jobs are compared. Managers then evaluate jobs by comparing job descriptions with

HRM and the law 7.1

PAY RATES CAN CAUSE COMPLAINTS OF DISCRIMINATION

In a recent case in Saskatchewan, a female administrator claimed that she was paid less than the previous incumbent (male) even though she had higher qualifications. The law in Saskatchewan forbids an employer from discriminating "between his male and female employees by paying a female employee at a rate of pay less than the rate of pay paid to a male employee, or vice versa, where such employees are employed by him for similar work which is performed in the same establishment under similar working conditions and the performance of which requires similar skill, effort and responsibility, except where such payment is made pursuant to a seniority system or merit system." However, companies may pay employees different rates of pay if the skills are not similar. In this case, the complainant was saying that she was being dis-criminated against as she had superior qualifications and therefore ought to have been paid the same as the male.

Through an investigation of the complaint, it was determined that the complainant had "not shown that there was a significant differential between the salary of the male administrator and her salary, when we take into account the inflationary impact on their salaries. It would seem that the RM paid both administrators similar salaries, except that for the first few years, the complainant was paid marginally more than her male predecessor." The Saskatchewan Human Rights Tribunal concluded that even though the administrator was initially paid more than the male predecessor, she was paid appropriately and that she had not been discriminated against.

What do you think?

Sources: Adapted from *Cruise-Pratchler v. Govan* and *Cruise-Pratchler v. RM of Last Mountain Valley*, Tribunal Panel Decisions, Saskatchewan Human Rights Tribunal, www.saskhrt.ca/forms/index/Descisions/02262008a.htm (retrieved February 22, 2009).

the different wage grades in order to "slot" the job into the appropriate grade. While this system has the advantage of simplicity, it is less precise than the point and factor comparison systems (discussed in the next sections) because the job is evaluated as a whole.

Point System

The point system is a quantitative job evaluation procedure that determines a job's relative value by calculating the total points assigned to it. It has been successfully used by high-visibility organizations, such as Boeing and Honeywell, and by many other public and private organizations, both large and small. Although point systems are rather complicated to establish, once in place they are relatively simple to understand and use. The principal advantage of the point system is that it provides a more refined basis for making judgments than either the ranking or classification systems and thereby can produce results that are more valid and less easy to manipulate.

The point system permits jobs to be evaluated quantitatively on the basis of factors or elements—commonly called *compensable factors*—that constitute the job. The skills, efforts, responsibilities, and working conditions that a job usually entails are the more common major compensable factors that serve to evaluate the worth of a job as more or less important than another.

Factor Comparison System

The factor comparison system, like the point system, permits the job evaluation process to be accomplished on a factor-by-factor basis. A factor comparison system is typically used for legislated pay equity purposes. It differs from the point system, however, in that the compensable factors of the jobs to be evaluated are compared against the compensable factors of key jobs within the organization that serve as the job evaluation scale.

Key jobs are evaluated against five compensable factors—skill, mental effort, physical effort, responsibility, and working conditions—resulting in a ranking of the different factors for each key job. An example of a factor comparison system can be found on the University of British Columbia website (**www.hr.ubc.ca**), where the HR unit has posted its job evaluation program. You will note that things such as the type and amount of independent decision-making are sub-factors of responsibility.

Regardless of the methodology used, it is important to remember that all job evaluation methods require varying amounts of judgment made by individuals. Supervisors or managers make decisions on the components of any job. Also, supervisors will make decisions on how much

w(w)w

University of British Columbia

www.hr.ubc.ca

What system would you use to determine the worth of a rescue worker's job?

Donovan Reese/Photodisc Green/Getty Images

MAKING GOOD USE OF AN HRMS IN JOB EVALUATION

Organizations that have an HRMS sometimes only have minimal information with which to make decisions. In many cases, the HRMS may only store the final decision while manual systems are used for decision-making. The outcome of this is a sense of secrecy around the entire process. However, with careful planning and attention, an HRMS can provide valuable assistance in the overall job evaluation process. Here are some key things to consider:

• Job evaluation plays a supportive role to rewards management—not controlling pay levels.

• A good HRMS with job evaluation capabilities provides a foundation for talent management.

• The job is a function of business needs and doesn't just exist.

• Using technology can generate faster results.

• It becomes a system that is owned by the managers and employees and is not just in the "black box of HR."

Source: Duncan Brown and Brian Dive, "Level Pegging," *People Management*, January 15, 2009, 26–28.

responsibility and authority any particular job may have. Therefore, as careful an organization is in having objective ways of measuring the value of a job, subjective decisions are made regarding the content of the job. As mentioned previously, organizations frequently use a committee or panel for job evaluation assessments to help ensure objectivity in the process.

Whatever system a company uses, it will frequently make use of the companies HRMS to actually collect the data, assess the data, and to record the final decision. This is particularly true if the organization is medium to large and is using either a point or factor comparison system. Manager's Toolkit 7.1 describes what needs to be considered if an HRMS is used to administer the job evaluation system in any organization.

THE COMPENSATION STRUCTURE

Wage and salary survey
Survey of the wages paid to employees of other employers in the surveying organization's relevant labour market

Watson Wyatt
www.watsonwyatt.com

Hewitt Associates
www.hewittassociates.com

Mercer
www.mercer.ca

Hay Group
www.haygroup.com

Job evaluation systems provide for internal equity and serve as the basis for wage-rate determination. *They do not in themselves determine the wage rate.* The evaluated worth of each job based on its rank, class, points, or monetary worth must be converted into an hourly, daily, weekly, or monthly wage rate. The compensation tool used to help set wages is the wage and salary survey.

Wage and Salary Surveys

The **wage and salary survey** is a survey of the wages paid by employers in an organization's relevant labour market—local, regional, or national, depending on the job. The labour market is frequently defined as that area from which employers obtain certain types of workers. The labour market for office personnel would be local, whereas the labour market for engineers would be national. It is the wage and salary survey that permits an organization to maintain external equity—that is, to pay its employees wages equivalent to the wages similar employees earn in other establishments.

Collecting Survey Data

Although many organizations conduct their own wage and salary surveys, a variety of "pre-conducted" pay surveys are available to satisfy the requirements of most public, not-for-profit, or private organizations. For example, you might want to see what the average hourly rate is for an accounting clerk in the Toronto area. Or you might want to know the average hourly rate for a Web designer anywhere in Canada. Companies such as Watson Wyatt (**www.watsonwyatt.com**), Hewitt Associates (**www.hewittassociates.com**) Mercer (**www.mercer.ca**), and Hay Group (**www.haygroup.com**) conduct annual surveys.

The Wage Curve

The relationship between the relative worth of jobs and their wage rates can be represented by means of a wage curve. This curve may indicate the rates currently paid for jobs within an organization, the new rates resulting from job evaluation, or the rates for similar jobs currently being paid by other organizations within the labour market. Figure 7.5 provides an example of a wage curve.

Pay Grades

Pay grades
Groups of jobs within a particular class that are paid the same rate or rate range

From an administrative standpoint, it is generally preferable to group jobs into **pay grades** and to pay all jobs within a particular grade the same rate or rate range. When the classification system of job evaluation is used, jobs are grouped into grades as part of the evaluation process. When the point and factor comparison systems are used, however, pay grades must be established at selected intervals that represent either the point or the evaluated monetary value of these jobs.

Rate Ranges

Although a single rate may be created for each pay grade, it is more common to provide a range of rates for each pay grade. The rate ranges may be the same for each grade or proportionately greater for each successive grade, as shown in Figure 7.6. Rate ranges constructed on the latter basis provide a greater incentive for employees to accept a promotion to a job in a higher grade.

FIGURE 7.5 Wage Curve

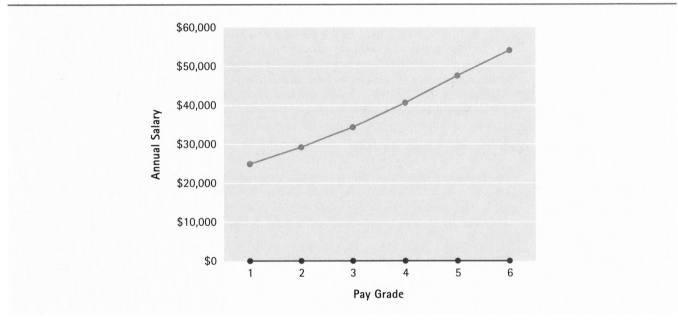

FIGURE 7.6 Salary Structure with Increasing Rate Ranges

Pay Grade	Minimum	Mid-Point	Maximum
6	$49,120	$53,970	$58,830
5	43,220	47,500	51,770
4	36,750	40,375	44,000
3	31,250	34,320	37,400
2	26,600	29,200	31,800
1	22,600	24,820	27,050

Other Ways to Determine Wages

The predominant approach to employee compensation is still the job-based system. Unfortunately, such a system often fails to reward employees for their skills or the knowledge they possess or to encourage them to learn a new job-related skill. Additionally, job-based pay systems may not reinforce an organizational culture stressing employee involvement or provide increased employee flexibility to meet overall production or service requirements. Therefore, many organizations have introduced competency-based or skill-based pay plans.

Competency-based pay
Pay based on how many capabilities employees have or how many jobs they can perform

Competency-based pay—also referred to as knowledge-based pay, skill-based pay, pay-for-knowledge, or multiskilled-based pay—compensates employees for the different skills or increased knowledge they possess or the collective behaviours or characteristics that they demonstrate rather than for the job they hold in a designated job category.[22] Regardless of the name, these pay plans encourage employees to earn higher base wages by learning and performing a wider variety of skills (or jobs) or displaying an array of competencies that can be applied to a variety of organizational requirements. For example, in a manufacturing setting, new tasks might include various assembly activities carried out in a particular production system or a variety of maintenance functions.

Competency-based pay systems represent a fundamental change in the attitude of management regarding how work should be organized and how employees should be paid for their work efforts. The most frequently cited benefits of competence-based pay include greater productivity, increased employee learning and commitment to work, improved staffing flexibility to meet production or service demands, and the reduced effects of absenteeism and turnover, since managers can assign employees where and when needed. Competency-based pay also encourages employees to acquire training when new or updated skills are needed by an organization. Therefore, when considering the introduction of competency-based pay, it is important to:

- identify competencies that demonstrably affect performance;
- devise methods to measure achievement of each competency;
- compensate each competency; and
- provide learning opportunities.[23]

For example, the Treasury Board of Canada uses a competency-based approach where it defines competency as "the knowledge, skills, abilities and behaviours that an employee applies in performing his/her work and that are the key employee-related levers for achieving results that are relevant to the organization/s business strategies."[24]

BROADBANDING Organizations that adopt a skill-based pay system frequently use broadbanding to structure their compensation payments to employees. Broadbanding simply collapses many traditional salary grades into a few wide salary bands. Broadbands may have midpoints and quartiles or they may have extremely wide salary ranges or no ranges at all. Banding encourages lateral skill building while addressing the need to pay employees performing several jobs with different skill-level requirements. Additionally, broadbands help eliminate the obsession with grades and, instead, encourage employees to move to jobs where they can develop in their careers and add value to the organization. Paying employees through broadbands enables organizations to consider job responsibilities, individual skills and competencies, and career mobility patterns in assigning employees to bands.

INCENTIVE PLANS

Outcome 5

For the last several years, a clear trend in compensation management has been the growth of incentive plans, also called variable pay programs, for employees throughout the organization. However, with the economic downturn, many companies are re-examining whether or not these are appropriate in the current circumstances. A recent study by Deloitte Consulting indicated that almost 60% of the companies would be reducing the value of the cash incentives and 11% were eliminating the incentives altogether.[25]

A further study in late 2008 indicated that many incentive plans were focusing more on the attainment of business unit and group goals instead of focusing on individual achievement.[26]

Incentive plans create an operating environment that champions a philosophy of shared commitment through the belief that every individual contributes to organizational performance and success.

By linking compensation with organizational objectives, managers believe that employees will assume "ownership" of their jobs, thereby improving their effort and overall job performance. Incentives are designed to encourage employees to put out more effort to complete their job tasks—effort they might not be motivated to expend under hourly and/or seniority-based compensation systems. Financial incentives are therefore offered to improve or maintain high levels of productivity and quality, which in turn improves the market for Canadian goods and services in a global economy.

Do incentive plans work? Various studies have demonstrated a measurable relationship between incentive plans and improved organizational performance. A recent study also indicated that a well-designed plan needed to recognize that the person closest to the work or the customer was in the best position to know what needed to be done and how to do it.[27]

A variety of individual and group incentive plans exists for both hourly and salaried employees. These include the following:

1. *Individual bonus*—an incentive payment that supplements the basic pay. It has the advantage of providing employees with more pay for exerting greater effort, while at the same time giving employees the security of a basic wage. Bonuses are common among managerial employees but as indicated earlier, organizations are increasingly providing bonuses to frontline staff.
2. *Team or group-based incentive*—a plan that rewards team members with an incentive bonus when agreed-upon performance standards are exceeded. Figure 7.7 provides the pros and cons of team incentive plans.
3. *Merit raises*—an incentive, used most commonly for salaried employees, based on achievement of performance standards. One of the problems with merit raises is that they may be perpetuated year after year even when performance declines.
4. *Gainsharing*—a plan in which both employees and the organization share the financial gains according to a predetermined formula that reflects improved productivity and/or decreased labour costs.[28]
5. *Profit-sharing*—any plan by which an employer pays special sums based on the profits of the organization.
6. *Employee stock ownership plans (ESOPs)*—stock plans in which an organization contributes shares of its stock to an established trust for the purpose of stock purchases by its employees. With the recent economic turmoil, stock and stock options have not been as popular. And where options were previously granted, there has been a desire by some companies, such as Intel Corp. to seek permission from its shareholders to revalue stock options in an effort to retain key staff.[29]

But do incentive plans work? Read At Work with HRM 7.3, which provides some insights.

FIGURE 7.7   The Pros and Cons of Team Incentive Plans

Pros	Cons
• Team incentives support group planning and problem solving, thereby building a team culture.	• Individual team members may perceive that "their" efforts contribute little to team success or to the attainment of the incentive bonus.
• The contributions of individual employees depend on group cooperation.	• Intergroup social problems-pressure to limit performance (for example, team members are afraid one individual may make the others look bad) and the "free-ride" effect (one individual puts in less effort than others but shares equally in team rewards)–may arise
• Unlike incentive plans based solely on output, team incentives can broaden the scope of the contribution that employees are motivated to make	• Complex payout formulas can be difficult for team members to understand.
• Team bonuses tend to reduce employee jealousies and complaints over "tight" or "loose" individual standards.	
• Team incentives encourage cross-training and the acquiring of new interpersonal competencies.	

AT WORK **with HRM 7.3**

ORGANIZATIONAL BENEFITS OF INCENTIVE PLANS

Incentive pay is a strategic tool used most often to attract and retain employees and to improve organizational outcomes. Organizations may spend as much as 17% of salary costs on variable compensation programs. Is this money well spent?

1. Almost 90% of organizations report that incentive compensation is an effective tool for attracting and retaining employees.

2. Four out of five organizations are using incentives for employees outside the sales force.

3. Incentives can be a powerful motivator if there is clarity on performance expectations.

4. About 20% of Canadian organizations offer profit-sharing as part of their performance incentives.

5. To be effective, the incentive must help support corporate goals, such as increased customer retention.

   WestJet is proud to provide a profit-sharing program for its employees. It feels that this type of recognition and reward has enabled it to be the most profitable North American airline.

Sources: Mary de Reus, "Bonuses Spreading, But Do They Work?" *Canadian HR Reporter*, November 19, 2007, www.hrreporter.com/ArticleView.aspx?l=1&articleid=5622 (retrieved February 23, 2009); Ann Bares, "Incentive Plan Design Begins With Good Questions," *Workforce Management*, www.workforce.com/archive/feature/25/83/07/index.php?ht= (accessed February 23, 2009); Ann Macaulay, "Walking the Line in Incentive Programs," *Canadian HR Reporter*, April 23, 2007, www.hrreporter.com/ArticleView.aspx?l=1&articleid=5147 (accessed February 23, 2009); and "Vision and Values Help WestJet Soar," *National Post*, January 21, 2009, FP11.

EMPLOYEE BENEFITS

 Outcome 6

Employee benefits constitute an indirect form of compensation intended to improve the quality of the work and personal lives of employees. The cost of benefits can be as high as 40% when you include premiums for health and welfare, government-mandated coverage such as WCB, vacation, and paid sick leave. In return, employers generally expect employees to be supportive of the organization and to be productive. Since employees have come to expect an increasing number of benefits, the motivational value of these benefits depends on how the benefits program is designed and communicated. Once viewed as a gift from the employer, benefits are now considered rights to which all employees are entitled.

Too often a particular benefit is provided because other employers are doing it, because someone in authority believes it is a good idea, or because there is union pressure. However, the contributions that benefits will make to the compensation package (and therefore to organizational performance) depend on how much attention is paid to certain basic considerations.

Linking Benefits to the Overall Compensation Program

Like any other component of the compensation plan, an employee benefits program should be based on specific objectives. The objectives an organization establishes will depend on many factors, including the size of the firm, its profitability, its location, the degree of unionization, and industry patterns. Most important, these objectives must be compatible with the organization's strategic rewards and recognition plan, including its philosophy and policies.

The chief objectives of most benefits programs are to

- Improve employee work satisfaction
- Meet employee health and security requirements
- Attract and motivate employees
- Retain top performing employees
- Maintain a favourable competitive position

For example, Jacques Whitford, an environmental consulting firm in Halifax, recognizes that the individual components of any benefits program needs to change over time to meet the needs of employees. It is this desire to change that enabled the company to be listed in Canada's Top 100

Employers in 2008.[30] Further, Hewitt Associates conducted a survey in 2007 that indicated that benefits are becoming more important when people decide to join and stay with a company.[31] And, as with other good HR practices, it is a good idea to consult with employees when a new benefit is being considered. Many organizations establish committees made up of managers and employees to administer, interpret, and oversee their benefits policies. Opinion surveys are also used to obtain employee input. Having employees participate in designing benefits programs helps to ensure that management is satisfying employee wants.

Cost Concerns

Organizations can typically spend about 35 to 45% of their annual payroll costs on benefits such as group health plans, pension contributions, EI premiums, CPP premiums, and WCB premiums. The increasing costs, particularly of health-care provisions, have made more and more organizations strive to manage those costs.

Since many benefits represent a fixed rather than a variable cost, management must decide whether it can afford this cost under less favourable economic conditions. As managers can readily attest, if an organization is forced to discontinue a benefit, the negative effects of cutting it may outweigh any positive effects that accrued from providing it.

To minimize negative effects and avoid unnecessary expense, many employers enlist the cooperation of employees in evaluating the importance of particular benefits. For example, the TD Bank Financial Group asks employees on a regular basis what tangible benefits are of value. Recently, it moved to a philosophy of providing opportunities to employees to create a personal benefits package that met their needs and that could change over time as needs changed. Employees are provided with "benefit credits," which can be used as they wish from a number of options.[32] Increasingly, employers are requiring employees to pay part of the costs of certain benefits (e.g., through co-payments or higher deductibles). At all times, benefit plan administrators are expected to select benefit service vendors who have the most to offer for the best cost.

The escalating cost of health-care benefits is a major concern to employers, who must strike an appropriate balance between offering quality benefits and keeping costs under control. Some employers have even considered reducing health care premiums for employees with healthy lifestyles (exercise, not smoking, etc.) as a way to reduce costs and encourage healthier choices.[33] At Work with HRM 7.4 describes what a company in Toronto has done to manage costs and help employees plan for the future. For additional articles on managing the cost of health care, check out the website of Benefits Canada (**www.benefitscanada.com**).

Benefits Canada

www.benefitscanada.com

Providing medical benefits will be a growing burden on employers in years to come.

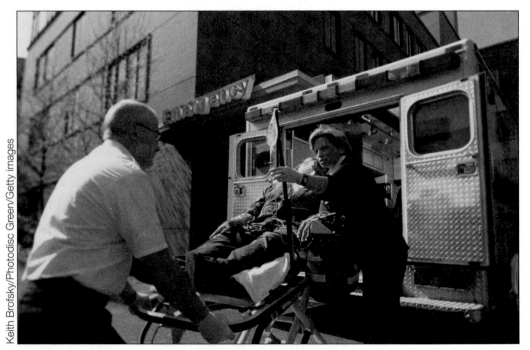

Keith Brofsky/Photodisc Green/Getty images

AT WORK with **HRM 7.4**

MANAGING COSTS AND PREPARING FOR THE FUTURE

Fuller Landau, an accounting firm in Toronto, recently decided to change one of their benefits offerings in a way to enable employees to save for their retirement.

For a number of years, the 50-year-old firm had spent a fair amount of money on its annual Christmas party for staff. However, the company decided to take the same money and provide a holiday party for students at a local public school. By doing so, the company felt it was investing in the future.

In addition, the company determined that it was also important for its employees to be saving towards their retirement and developed a voluntary group RRSP program. While it did consider a pension plan, eventually Fuller Landau decided that this wasn't feasible for such a

small organization. Further, a pension plan wasn't portable whereas the group RRSP was as employees moved onto other careers. The company particularly wanted something that would be meaningful to the Gen X and Y staff.

Currently, only about 30% of small businesses offer any type of pension plan. Most cite that the costs of administering a plan, with the amount of government regulation, make it quite prohibitive. On the other hand, these same organizations do want to encourage people to plan for their retirement and want people to start at an earlier age.

CRITICAL THINKING QUESTION

Do you think it is important to save for your retirement? Provide reasons for your answer.

Source: Brooke Smith, "Small World … at a Cost," *Benefits Canada*, March 1, 2008, www.benefitscanada.com/benefit/health/article.jsp?content=200 80328_114716_1948 (accessed February 23, 2009).

BENEFITS REQUIRED BY LAW

Legally required employee benefits cost over 12% of an organization's annual payroll.[34] These benefits include employer contributions to Canada/Quebec pension plans, unemployment insurance, workers' compensation insurance (covered in Chapter 8), and, in some provinces, provincial medicare.

Canada and Quebec Pension Plans (CPP/QPP)

The Canada and Quebec pension plans cover almost all Canadian employees between the ages of 18 and 70. Both plans require employers to match the contributions made by employees. The revenues generated by these contributions are used to pay three main types of benefits: retirement pensions, disability benefits, and survivors' benefits. With Canada's population aging, funds from the CPP will not be able to meet the needs of retirees unless those currently working, and their employers, significantly increase their contributions.

Employment Insurance (EI)

Employment insurance (EI) benefits have been available for over 50 years and were provided as income protection to employees who were between jobs. Employees and employers both contribute to the Employment Insurance fund. The amount of benefit paid is a formula (which can change) based on the number of hours of employment in the past year and the regional unemployment rate. With the economic upheaval starting in 2008, the federal government changed some of the EI programs, including the provision of extended benefits if the recipient is in a long-term training program.[35] Further, in early 2009, the EI benefits were extended by five weeks so that benefits could be received for a minimum of 19 weeks and a maximum of 50 weeks. As well, the federal government offered to pay for a few weeks of severance if companies go bankrupt.[36]

Provincial Hospital and Medical Services

Most provinces fund health-care costs from general tax revenue and federal cost sharing. Ontario, Quebec, and Newfoundland also levy a payroll tax, while other provinces, such as Alberta and

British Columbia, charge premiums that are payable by the resident or an agent, usually the employer (subsidies for low-income residents are provided).

The cost of providing health care has escalated to the point where major reform in Canada's health-care system is occurring. As of 2008, 25% of the Canadian population is over 55 with those over 80 comprising 4%.[37] As has been discussed by policy makers, politicians, and journalists, the increasing longevity of people and the major health problems that do occur mean that our health-care system will need significant redesign to be sustainable in the future.[38]

Leaves Without Pay

Most employers grant leaves of absence to employees who request them for personal reasons. In some provinces, legislation mandates that these types of leaves must be granted. These leaves are usually taken without pay, but also without loss of seniority or benefits.

Other Required Benefits

In addition to the ones described, through provisions in employment standards legislation, provinces do require employers to pay for statutory holidays, minimum vacation pay, premiums when people work overtime, and in some provinces a severance payment when employees are terminated.

VOLUNTARY EMPLOYEE BENEFITS

**International Foundation
of Employee Benefit Plans**
www.ifebp.org

In addition to the benefits that are required by legislation, employers can choose to provide additional benefits as part of the overall compensation package. Organizations do this to ensure that they are able to attract and retain the kind of employees they want. These benefits are called "voluntary benefits." While there can be many of these types of benefits, we will look at the more typical ones. You can review some of the other voluntary benefits at the International Foundation of Employee Benefit Plans website (**www.ifebp.org**).

Health and Welfare Benefits

The benefits that receive the most attention from employers today, due to sharply rising costs and employee concern, are health-care benefits. In the past, health insurance plans covered only medical, surgical, and hospital expenses. Today, employers include prescription drugs as well as dental, optical, and mental health-care benefits in the package they offer their workers. As mentioned earlier in this chapter, employers are attempting to ensure that the benefit provided will be of value to the person. Listed below is a brief description of typical health and welfare benefits.

Dental Coverage

Dental plans are designed to help pay for dental-care costs and to encourage employees to receive regular dental attention. Typically, the insurance pays a portion of the charges and the employee pays the remainder.

Extended Health Coverage

This benefit provides for additional payments beyond the basic provincial medical coverage. It typically provides such things as semi-private or private hospital rooms, prescription drugs, private nursing, ambulance services, out-of-country medical expenses that exceed provincial limits, and vision care. In an effort to better manage these costs, a number of larger employers, such as Caterpillar, have formed an employers' association to negotiate lower drug prices directly with the manufacturers instead of through the companies that manage the extended health coverage. In doing so, they are hoping to reduce their yearly prescription drug costs of $4 billion.[39]

Many employers offer additional health benefits, such as dental coverage.

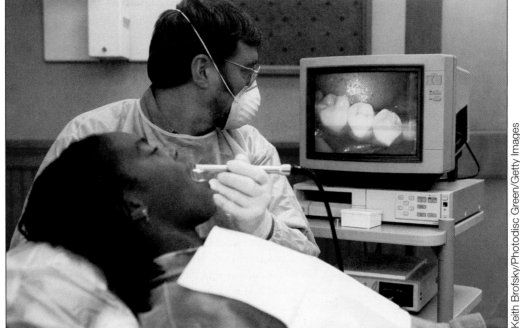

Keith Brofsky/Photodisc Green/Getty Images

It should be noted that there can be duplication of coverage if both partners in a relationship have access to health coverage. In some cases, if there is better coverage in one plan than in another, the partner with the better coverage will enroll and include the partner.

One of the aspects of extended health coverage that is increasing greatly is the cost of prescription drugs. To counter this increase, many plans make use of generic drugs but this only goes so far. According to a recent study conducted by the University of Toronto, there is little competition in Canada and therefore the costs can be much higher than in the U.S. The study noted that 60% of the market for generic drugs is supplied by only two producers.[40] Other ways to reduce the cost of prescription drugs is to encourage the use of mail order for refills (which can reduce the cost by 33%) and to encourage employees to have a healthy life style that eliminates the need for increased prescriptions.[41]

Life Insurance

One of the oldest and most popular employee benefits is group term life insurance, which provides death benefits to beneficiaries and may also provide accidental death and dismemberment benefits.

Retirement and Pension Plans

Retirement is an important part of life and requires sufficient and careful preparation. In convincing job applicants that theirs is a good organization to work for, employers usually emphasize the retirement benefits that can be expected after a certain number of years of employment.

Pension plans are classified into two primary categories: (1) defined benefit, and (2) defined contribution. In a *defined benefit plan*, a person receiving benefits receives a specific amount (usually based on years of service and average earnings), regardless of the amount of contributions. On the other hand, a *defined contribution plan* provides to the recipient an amount that is based on the amount of accumulated funds and how much those funds can purchase (at the time of retirement) for retirement benefits.

Since defined benefit plans have to provide the specific payment whether or not the employee has made sufficient contributions, the organization becomes liable for the difference. With the aging workforce, more and more organizations and employees are expressing concern about whether their plan will be able to fund what has been promised. The recent economic turmoil has created many problems for pension plans. For example, both BCE and Bombardier have had the value of the pension plans reduced considerably due to the stock market meltdown. BCE's pension plan deficit grew by over 275% in 2008 to an estimated $3.2 billion.[42] Likewise, Bombardier's pension deficit doubled in 2008 to an estimated $2.4 billion.

Unfortunately, the concerns about the value of pension plans are not new. For some time, Canadian organizations have been faced with the dilemma of potentially having insufficient resources in the future to pay pensions to the number of people that will be retiring in the future. These concerns have led some employers to consider changing pension plan design from defined benefit to defined contribution. There is also concern from various levels of government that the overall pension system needs to improve and hence a number of reports recently have called for new models that are more flexible and appealing to employers.[43] In early 2009, Quebec passed legislation allowing the government take over private pension plans if a company goes bankrupt. The government says that it is a short-term measure to protect workers and pensioners.[44] Both the B.C. and Alberta governments are also considering creating a new occupational pension plan for both provinces, geared primarily to small and medium-sized businesses. The Alberta/B.C. (ABC) defined contribution plan, operated at arm's length from government but regulated under the pension standards, would be available at a reasonable cost and feature automatic enrolment for employers and employees, who could opt out.[45]

Given the current volatility of the stock market and the concern about future payments from pension plans, it is no wonder that there is a push from existing retirees to lobby to fold private pension plans into the Canada Pension Plan.[46] Ethics in HRM 7.1 discusses the dilemma of pensions as stock markets plunge.

ETHICS in HRM 7.1

PENSIONS IN A DYNAMIC MARKET

When newspaper headlines in late 2008 were full of stories about the significant decline in stock market prices, did anyone think about the impact of that on pension plans? The answer is probably "no." Most people were more concerned about their own investments or what was happening to their employment.

However, one of the significant results of the decrease in the stock market was the impact on pension plans. Pension plans function by having sufficient assets to pay for pensions to the retirees. But with the stock market decline, about 70% of the defined pension plans in Canada didn't have sufficient resources to pay for all the pensions necessary in the future. And it is important to remember that a defined benefit plan is one where the pension value is a fixed amount promised in the future. Therefore, for those types of plans, it is necessary to have sufficient growth in the assets over time to be able to make good on that promise.

Fortunately, the government regulators understand the severity of the stock market turbulence and are allowing under-funded pension plans to take up to five years to get the pension plan on a solid footing. However, this relief may not help pensions at Nortel Networks. The company may break itself up and sell the parts—which is good news for existing employees. But in doing so the pensioners that are in an old defined benefit plan may find that there will be no way to keep the plan solvent and that pensions may lose as much as 40% of their pension.

Some pension plans are reluctant to invest very much in the stock market simply because of the potential volatility. On the other hand, it is through prudent purchases in the stock market that pension plan assets grow at a reasonable level in order to pay future benefits.

CRITICAL THINKING QUESTION

Was it ethical for pension plans to invest in the stock market? Why or why not?

Sources: Adapted from Tom Ford, "Pension Problems Brewing," *Winnipeg Free Press*, August 12, 2008, www.winnipegfreepress.com/opinion/westview/Pension_problems_brewing.html (accessed February 23, 2009); and Karen Mazurkewich, "Nortel Breakup May Not Be Good for Pensioners," *Financial Post*, March 13, 2009, FP5.

Pay for Time Not Worked

The "pay for time not worked" category of benefits includes statutory holiday pay, vacation pay (above any legislated minimum), bereavement, rest periods, coffee breaks, sick leave, and parenting benefits (salary continuance). These benefits typically account for a large portion of overall benefit costs.

Vacations with Pay

It is generally agreed that vacations are essential to the well-being of an employee. Eligibility for vacations varies by industry, locale, and organization size. To qualify for longer vacations of three, four, or five weeks, one may expect to work for seven, 15, and 20 years, respectively.

Paid Holidays

Both hourly and salaried workers can expect to be paid for statutory holidays as designated in each province. The standard statutory holidays in Canada are New Year's Day, Good Friday, Canada Day (Memorial Day in Newfoundland), Labour Day, and Christmas Day. Other holidays that are recognized by various provinces are Victoria Day, Thanksgiving Day, Remembrance Day, and Family Day. Additionally, each province may designate special holidays important to that province only. Many employers give workers an additional one to three personal days off. With the increasing diversity in culture and religions in the workforce, there may be situations where the governments may need to change the number and type of statutory holidays so that there are more general types of observations and not tied to any one particular faith. For example, York University had a longstanding practice of cancelling classes for Jewish holidays. However, in 2008, it ceased this practice as a consequence of a human rights complaint that determined this practice discriminated against students of other religions.[47]

Sick Leave

Employees may be compensated in several ways during periods when they are unable to work because of illness or injury. Most public employees, as well as many in private firms (particularly in white-collar jobs), receive a set number of sick-leave days each year to cover such absences. Where permitted, sick leave that employees do not use can be accumulated to cover prolonged absences. Accumulated vacation leave may sometimes be used as a source of income when sick-leave benefits have been exhausted. Group insurance that provides income protection during a long-term disability is also becoming more common. As discussed earlier in the chapter, income lost during absences resulting from job-related injuries may be reimbursed, at least partially, through workers' compensation insurance.

According to a recent Statistics Canada report, sick-leave absences have risen over the last several years. In 2007, an average of 8.3 work days (approximately 3%) were lost due to illness.[48] Much of this amount is due to the aging workforce. Workers aged 55 to 64 missed 13 days of work on average each year, while workers aged 35 to 44 missed only 10.1 days.[49]

Wellness Programs

In recent years, new types of services have been offered to make life at work more rewarding and to enhance employee well-being. The Industrial Accident Prevention Association in Mississauga won a National Quality Institute award for its approach to wellness. "When it comes to healthy workplaces, we are Canada's leading health and safety organization and we've got to walk the talk," says Colin Appleby, vice president of corporate services. "We believe a healthy workplace is critical to the success of any organization." Employees have had ergonomic work stations built at their new headquarters as well as an on-site fitness centre, lunch sessions on fitness, nutrition and mental health.[50] Recent research suggests that for every $1 spent on wellness programs, the return in terms of increased production, fewer absences, more satisfied employees is close to $6.[51]

Employee Assistance Programs

To help workers cope with a wide variety of problems that interfere with the way they perform their jobs, organizations have developed employee assistance programs (EAPs). An employee assistance program typically provides diagnosis, limited counselling, and referral for advice or treatment when necessary for problems related to substance (alcohol, drug) abuse, emotional difficulties, and financial or family difficulties. (EAPs will be discussed in detail in Chapter 8.) Approximately 80% of Canadian employers have an EAP for their employees and families.[52] The main intent of these programs is to help employees solve their personal problems or at least to prevent problems from turning into crises that affect their ability to work productively.

Educational Assistance Plans

One of the benefits most frequently mentioned in literature for employees is the educational assistance plan. The primary purpose of this plan is to help employees keep up to date with advances in their fields and to help them get ahead in the organization. Usually the employer covers—in part or totally—costs of tuition, books, and related fees, while the employee is required to pay for meals, transportation, and other expenses. And depending on the organization, some companies are willing to pay for courses that are not directly related to a specific job. For example, the Metro Vancouver Port Authority will pay for a variety of different courses that invigorate and rejuvenate the workforce.[53]

Childcare and Eldercare

Consider these statistics:

- Over 13% of the Canadian population is 65 or older.
- 70% of caregivers to the elderly are employed.[54]
- Five million (approximately 15% of the overall population) Canadians are caring for a loved one with long-term health problems.[55]

In the past, working parents had to make their own arrangements with sitters or with nursery schools for pre-school children. Today, benefits may include financial assistance, alternative work schedules, and family leave. For many employees, on-site or near-site childcare centres are the most visible, prestigious, and desired solutions.

A growing benefit offered employees with children experiencing a short illness is called mildly ill childcare. Medical supervision is the primary difference between these facilities and traditional day care arrangements. See At Work with HRM 7.5 for the benefits of these arrangements as cited by CIBC.

Eldercare

Care provided to an elderly relative by an employee who remains actively at work

Responsibility for the care of aging parents and other relatives is another fact of life for more and more employees. The term **eldercare**, as used in the context of employment, refers to situations where an employee provides care to an elderly relative while remaining actively at work. Most caregivers are women. According to the most recent census (2006), 4.3 million Canadians were 65 or older, of which close to 30% were over 80.[56] By 2026, it is estimated that approximately 7.8 million Canadians, or approximately 20%, will be 65 and older.[57] One-fifth of this number will have some type of disability. As a consequence of the expected shortfall in eldercare facilities, the responsibility for the care of these seniors will be borne by their children and other relatives. The majority of caregivers are women.

To reduce the negative effects of caregiving on productivity, organizations may offer eldercare counselling, educational fairs and seminars, printed resource material, support groups, and special flexible schedules and leaves of absence.

Interest in and demand for eldercare programs is increasing dramatically as the Canadian population ages and lives longer. Approximately 30% of people aged 45 to 64 had unmarried children and were also caring for a senior.[58] One of the authors of this text (Stewart) found herself in just this situation: raising a young child and having to care for aging parents at a distance.

AT WORK **with HRM 7.5**

CIBC CARES

CIBC was the first Canadian corporation to open an employer-sponsored centre dedicated to backup childcare. Every parent has faced the hardship of finding emergency care, when regular childcare arrangements break down due to a caretaker's illness, or when schools are closed for professional development days or snow days. The CIBC Children's Centre offers special play areas for children of different ages and is licensed under the Day Nurseries Act. Since it first opened in 2002, more than 6800 employee days representing close to $1.4 million in productivity savings has been achieved. These savings were projected over five years and were realized within three years. The intangible benefits include increased attraction and retention of employees and allowing them to achieve better work-life family balance. Full- and part-time employees with children aged three months to 12 years can use the childcare centres up to a total of 20 days per year. CIBC pays all the costs for the program. CIBC is so pleased with the results that it has created similar centres in 14 other cities, including Calgary, Ottawa, Vancouver, and Waterloo. As Joyce Phillips, CIBC executive vice president human resources, states, "I am delighted that we are now going to be able to expand the program from coast to coast."

Source: "CIBC Expands Child Care Program for Employees," *Canadian HR Reporter*, February 23, 2005, www.hrreporter.com/ArticleView. aspx?l=1&articleid=3681 (accessed February 24, 2009).

Many organizations recognize the needs of working parents and ensure appropriate childcare is available.

Nelson Education

Other Services

The variety of benefits and services that employers offer today could not have been imagined a few years ago. Some are fairly standard, and we will cover them briefly. Some are unique and obviously grew out of specific concerns, needs, and interests. Some of the more creative and unusual benefits are group insurance for employee pets, free baseball tickets for families and friends, summer boat cruises, and subsidized haircuts for MPs. At Work with HRM 7.6 describes the special benefits at SAS Canada.

There are many emerging trends in relation to rewards and recognition. See Emerging Trends 7.1 for some of the more prominent ones.

AT WORK **with HRM 7.6**

PERKS AT SAS CANADA

SAS Canada, which develops business software, employs about 220 employees across Canada and is rated one of Canada's top employers. The benefits it offers employees is one of the reasons for its success. First, employees receive $1,000 in subsidies aimed at fitness. Second, it serves fresh fruit on Mondays, M&Ms on Wednesdays, as well as breakfast on Fridays. Occasionally, there is also a BBQ at the Toronto office. Third, it has on-site daycare and provides yoga classes. In addition, employees are encouraged to not work hard, but to work smart. As John

Quinn says, "We want to keep employees healthy and happy, mentally and physically.

Research suggests that top employers outperform from a financial perspective. And when staff are not healthy, there is more stress and employees are less engaged.

CRITICAL THINKING QUESTION

Do you think these special benefits are reasonable? Why or why not?

Sources: Tavia Grant, "To Consider at the Next Staff Pajama Party," *The Globe and Mail*, February 7, 2009, B15; and SAS Canada, "Who We Are," www. sas.com/offices/NA/canada/8-canada_en.html (accessed February 24, 2009).

EMERGING TRENDS **7.1**

1. ***Rising employee expectations for state-of-art health care.*** As employees' expectations rise, there is a direct conflict with the employers concerns about rising costs. With an aging population, new technologies, and pharmaceuticals, demand is ever-increasing.

2. ***Individual differences.*** Depending on the age of the employee, there is a different mix of the rewards and recognition program that is attractive to employees. Therefore, it is important to shape the benefits portion to meet the individual needs.

3. ***Life style diseases are on the rise.*** Whether it is diabetes, stress, or obesity, all of these are on the rise that puts a strain on the costs to both employers and governments.

4. ***Phased retirement.*** Despite the economic problems, organizations are still concerned about losing the knowledge base from workers retiring. Therefore, some organizations are looking at ways and means to allow their employees to partially retire. Employees would receive a combination of pay for work plus

receive some portion of their company pension. Another area that is being explored is how to access partial pension benefits while the person is doing partial work in preparation for full retirement.

5. ***Range of voluntary options.*** Primarily to deal with the changing demographics, employers will be looking at ways to provide a range of options from which to select. These can be handled through health spending accounts (HAS—which is a fixed sum of money that is used to purchase benefits) or flexible benefit plans.

6. ***Creative benefit choices.*** Despite the recession, many companies are still concerned about retaining their staff. Therefore, some of the new benefits being considered are tax-free savings accounts, rewarding employees for good health, preventative care benefits, paying for professional membership fees, and individualized voluntary options such as homeowner insurance.

7. ***Cost of retiree benefits.*** Many organizations in better economic times provided retirees access to benefit plans—either at little or no cost. However, with

the escalating cost of health care premiums, organizations are looking at whether or not it should continue to subsidize retiree benefits. While the organization may wish to continue with the benefit provision, it would be the responsibility of the retiree to pay the full cost of the premiums. This is also true of arrangements around pension plans that have an automatic adjustment for cost-of-living. There is a suggestion that this be eliminated and thereby save billions of dollars.

8. ***Examination of executive compensation, particularly CEOs.*** There is no doubt that with the economic recession and some of the compensation packages for executives, shareholders and the general public have asked a number of questions about the pay and performance link. There is a trend to move to more discretionary pay but ensuring that there is a better link between compensation and the overall performance of the organization. While companies want to hire the best talent for their executive group, there is also a need to ensure that the company is meeting its performance targets, even in difficult economic times, and not just paying to compete in the employment market.

Sources: Jody White, "The Top 10 Global Benefit Challenges," *Benefits Canada*, February 4, 2009; Dean Taylor, "Retaining Older Workers: Is Phased Retirement the Answer," *Canadian HR Reporter*, February 9, 2009, 14; "Employee Benefits Menu Boosted by Mix of Voluntary Options," *Workforce Management*, February 12, 2008, www.workforce.com/archive/article/25/36/01.php?ht= (accessed February 23, 2009); Laura Hirsh, "Non-monetary Rewards Gaining Traction," *Canadian HR Reporter*, November 3, 2008, 24; John Partridge, "Employee Benefits: Up Next: Tax-free Savings Accounts?" *The Globe and Mail*, July 4, 2008, C1; Danielle Harder, "Debate Rages Over Post-65 Benefits," *Canadian HR Reporter*, March 24, 2008, 1; John Greenwood, "COLA Freeze on Pensions Can Help Save Billions," *Financial Post*, March 10, 2009, FP4; Dave Guilmette and Ron Fontanetta, "Moving Boldly to Stem Health-Care Spending," *Financial Executive*, January/February 2009, 1–4; and Fiona Anderson, "Performance and Pay Don't Always Match," *The Vancouver Sun*, June 3, 3009, D1.

SUMMARY

1. Explain an organization's concerns in developing a strategic rewards program.
   - Companies structure compensation in ways that enhance employee motivation and growth.
   - Compensation must be tailored to fit the needs of the company and its employees.
   - Companies are concerned that employees believe the compensation to be equitable.

2. Identify the various factors that influence the setting of pay levels.
   - There are internal and external factors.
   - Internal factors include the organization's compensation policy, the perceived worth of the job, the performance of the employee, and the employer's willingness to pay.
   - The external factors include labour market conditions, cost of living, collective bargaining, and legal considerations.

3. Describe the major job evaluation systems.
   - Job ranking system, which groups jobs on the basis of their relative worth.
   - Job classification system, where jobs are grouped according to a series of predetermined grades based on a number of factors.
   - Point system, which determines a job's relative worth by using a quantitative system of points.
   - Factor comparison system, where a job is evaluated on a factor-by-factor basis; this type of system is typically used for legislated pay equity purposes.

4. Describe the compensation structure.
   - Wage and salary survey, which provides information about average wage rates external to the organization.
   - Developing a wage curve, which indicates the rates currently paid for jobs within the organization.
   - Development of pay rates for paying individuals based on the job.

5. List the types of incentive plans.
   - Individual bonus.
   - Team- or group-based.
   - Merit raises.

- Gainsharing.
- Profit-sharing.
- Employee stock ownership plan.

6. Explain the employee benefits that are required by law.
   - Canada and Quebec pension plans, which provide for a pension for all employees working in Canada.
   - Employment insurance, which provides income protection to employees who are between jobs.
   - Workers' compensation insurance, which pays people for work-related accidents or illnesses.

7. Describe voluntary benefits.
   - Benefits that are considered indirect compensation.
   - Benefits an organization chooses to provide.
   - Can include health and welfare coverage, pay for time not worked (vacation, sick leave), wellness programs, and childcare assistance.

NEED TO KNOW	**NEED TO UNDERSTAND**
• Definition of compensation and compensation management • Internal and external factors that affect compensation • Types of incentive plans • Types of voluntary and mandatory benefits	• Relationship of compensation and organizational objectives • Complexity of factors in relation to compensation decisions • Role of line manager in making individual employee pay decisions • Impact of benefits costs on costs of running business

KEY TERMS

competency-based pay 213

consumer price index (CPI) 207

direct compensation 200

eldercare 222

equitable pay 204

hourly work 204

indirect compensation 200

job evaluation 206

pay grades 212

pay-for-performance standard 202

piecework 204

real wages 208

wage and salary survey 211

REVIEW QUESTIONS

1. List the common goals of a compensation strategy.
2. Explain the motivational value of pay.
3. What are the internal and external factors used in determining compensation levels?
4. What is job evaluation? Describe the various methods of job evaluation.
5. Explain incentive plans.
6. What are some of the problems of developing a pay system based on equal pay for comparable value?
7. What are some of the advantages of team-based pay? The disadvantages?
8. List the benefits required by law.
9. Describe some of the types of benefits that employers voluntarily provide for employees.

CRITICAL THINKING QUESTIONS

1. You work for a retail store in your community that is part of a large national chain of retail stores. The store manager has approached you about your thoughts on introducing a bonus based on the sales each person generates. How would you respond and why?
2. A fast-food restaurant in your community has a large number of part-time employees, primarily in the 16- to 18-year age range. The owner of the restaurant knows that you are taking an

introductory course in human resource management and has approached you to give some ideas about the restaurant's benefits package. What items would you suggest be included and why?

3. You have recently been promoted to supervisor. Your company is in the hardware business and has a policy that supervisors are paid on a salary instead of an hourly wage basis. Why would the company do this? What are the advantages and disadvantages to you and your company?

4. One of the objections to granting wage increases on a percentage basis is that the lowest-paid employees, who are having the most trouble making ends meet, get the smallest increase, while the highest-paid employees get the largest increase. Is this objection a valid one? Explain.

5. Because of competitive forces within your industry, you have decided to implement a profit-sharing plan for your employees. Discuss the advantages of profit-sharing and identify specific characteristics that will assure success for your plan.

6. Many organizations are concerned about the rising cost of employee benefits and question their value to the organization and to the employees.
   a. In your opinion, what benefits are of greatest value to employees? To the organization? Why?
   b. What can management do to increase the value to the organization of the benefits provided to employees?

7. Do you think that compensation is the only way of rewarding employees? What other methods can organizations use that will prove effective motivators for employees?

8. Access your province's employment standards legislation and determine the current minimum wage.

9. You are a small employer wishing to establish a benefits program for your employees. What things should you consider to ensure that the program is a success for your employees?

10. You are the general manager of a 100-person manufacturing firm with an aging workforce. The company no longer has a mandatory retirement policy and you are concerned about retaining key workers while at the same time ensuring that the benefits' costs of older workers do not become prohibitive. What factors would you consider and why?

DEVELOPING YOUR SKILLS

1. Since pay-for-performance is an important factor governing salary increases, managers must be able to defend the compensation recommendations they make for their employees. Merit raises granted under a pay-for-performance policy must be based on objective appraisals if they are to achieve their intended purposes of rewarding outstanding employee performance. As managers know, however, other factors that can affect salary recommendations must be dealt with. These may include the opinions of the employee's peers or extenuating circumstances, such as illness or family responsibilities. The purpose of this exercise is to provide you with the experience of granting salary increases to employees based on their work performance and other information.

ASSIGNMENT

1. Following are the work records of five employees. As their supervisor, you have just completed their annual appraisal reviews, and it is now time to make recommendations for their future salaries. Your department budget has $8,000 allocated for salary increases. Distribute the $8,000 among your employees based on the descriptions for each subordinate.
   a. Janet Jenkins currently earns $35,000. Her performance appraisal rating was very high. She is respected by her peers and is felt to be an asset to the work group. She is divorced and has three young children to support.
   b. Russell Watts earns a salary of $32,000. His annual performance appraisal was average. Several members of the work group have spoken to you about the difficulty involved in Russell's job. They feel that it is a tough and demanding job and that he is doing his best.
   c. Jack Perkins earns $33,000. His performance appraisal was below average and he seems to have difficulty adjusting to his co-workers. Jack has had a difficult time this past year. His wife passed away early in the year and his father has recently been diagnosed as terminally ill.

     d. Rick Jacobson earns $32,000. His performance appraisal was above average. He is respected by his peers and is generally considered to be a "good guy."

     e. Paula Merrill earns $32,000. Her performance appraisal was very high. Her peers are upset because they feel that she is working only to provide a second income. Moreover, her peers see her as trying to "show them up."

Share your results with other class members. Be prepared to explain your allocation of money.

2. Working in groups of four to five students, pick an organization that is relatively familiar to all students in the group—this could even be the college/university in which you are taking this course. Develop two to three compensation objectives for the organization and decide whether you would include an incentive program and give your reasons. Share your results with the class, including an explanation of your results.

3. Working in teams of three or four, list and discuss the various benefits offered by your employer (or former employer). How were the costs of these benefits paid for?

4. Assume your team has been hired as a benefits consultant by a small business with 50 to 60 employees. What benefits do you believe this employer should offer given its limited resources? Explain why you would offer these benefits.

5. On an individual basis, search **www.workforce.com** (Workforce Management). Find a link that references or deals with "compensation" and/or "benefits." Pick two to three specific online resource sites that would be useful to you as a line manager. Print the first page of the site; bring it to class and share the information with your fellow students—including a description of why the site is valuable to you.

6. In pairs, access the Employee Benefit Research Institute at **www.ebri.org**. Select one of its current press releases. Review the contents and do a comparison with materials presented in this chapter. Share the results of your comparison with others in the class.

Workforce Management
www.workforce.com

**Employee Benefit
Research Institute**
www.ebri.org

Case Study

Pay-for-Performance: The Merit Question

In January 2005, Central Hospital implemented a formal performance review program for its 127 staff nurses. The program originally met with some resistance from a few nurses and supervisors, but generally the system was welcomed as an objective way to appraise nursing performance. Complaints centred on the increase in time it took to complete the appraisal review process and the fact that supervisors disliked having to confront nurses who disagreed with their performance review. Nursing supervisors are required to appraise employee performance annually and to forward to the HR department a copy of each appraisal form.

In July 2009, Thomas Chen, HR manager for the hospital, reviewed all nurses' assessments on file since the beginning of the program. From this study he concluded that the large majority (82%) of nurses were assessed as performing at an "average" level, as indicated by a global rating at the bottom of the form. Approximately 10% were rated "above average" or "superior," and the remainder received "below standard" performance reviews. As a response to these findings, Chen decided to base the annual raise for all nurses on the consumer price index for the hospital's metropolitan area. This, he concluded, would allow the nurses to maintain their standard of living while guaranteeing all nurses a yearly raise.

As part of the hospital's employee involvement program, Chen holds quarterly meetings with groups of employees to solicit their feelings regarding hospital policy and their jobs. Both positive and negative opinions are expressed at these gatherings. These opinions are used to modify hospital policy. At meetings in the past year, a number of both junior and senior nurses have expressed dissatisfaction with the across-the-board pay policy for annual raises. The biggest complaint concerns the lack of motivation to increase output, since all nurses are paid the same regardless of individual performance. These comments have been numerous enough that Chen has considered changing the nurses' compensation policy. During the past seven months, nine of the better nurses have quit to take jobs with area hospitals that award annual increases on a merit or pay-for-performance basis.

Questions

1. What are the advantages of adopting a merit pay plan for hospital nurses? Are there any disadvantages to starting a merit pay program?
2. What problems might arise with a supervisor's assessment of nurses?
3. Develop a merit pay guideline chart based on the following levels of performance evaluation: superior, above average, average, below average, and poor. Use current cost-of-living figures for your area or salary survey data available to you to guide your merit percentage increases.
4. It is not uncommon for hospital nurses to work in teams. Explain how a team-based incentive program for nurses might be developed. What criteria might be used to evaluate team performance?
5. Should the hospital give higher starting salaries for nurses with unique skill sets that are in high demand (such as operating room nurses) where such salaries may be higher than more senior nurses? Why or why not?

Case Study 2

Team-Based Incentive Rewards: It's Not All Roses

Network Cable, Inc., operates in an area described as a "high-growth market." With approximately 45,000 subscribers, the company is a service provider for cable TV and high-speed Internet.

In June 2008, Tara Kennedy, vice president of human resources, convinced the company president that restructuring the organization workforce into teams would benefit both Network Cable and its employees. Cost savings, improved engagement, and team synergy were cited as inherent benefits of teams. Based on these assessments, in January 2009, a select group of three senior managers, plus Tara and the company's financial officer, implemented teams within the company's installation department. Here, 40 service installers were formed into eight teams of five installers each. Management set performance goals for the installation teams linked to attractive incentive rewards—cash bonuses—when performance goals were reached. Performance measures included indices for improved installation time, customer satisfaction scores, additional sales, equipment maintenance, and repair/callback problems. Each team could earn incentive bonuses up to a maximum of $20,000 annually with cash bonuses shared equally by each team member—a possible cash bonus of $4,000 for each installer. Team bonuses after the first year were as follows: two teams, $20,000; one team $15,000; one team $12,500; one team $7,500; and one team, $3,500.

During July 2009 Tara sent to all installers and their supervisors a survey requesting feedback on the satisfaction with teams, and specifically, the incentive rewards. While survey results were generally positive, not all was rosy. Problems could be grouped into the following categories:

1. Some installers believed that various team members did not "buy into" the team concept and were simply "free riders."
2. There was a general feeling that several teams were routinely assigned difficult installations that prevented them from achieving higher performance goals.
3. Teams did not always display the motivation and synergy expected, as bickering was prevalent between average performers and superior performers. Average performers complained that high performers made them look bad.
4. Some survey respondents (29%) felt the incentive rewards program was unfair and asked for a return to fixed across-the-board salary increases.

Questions

1. Do results from the survey illustrate typical complaints about teams and specifically about team incentive rewards? Explain.
2. If appropriate, what changes would you recommend to improve the incentive reward program? Be specific.
3. Would management have benefited from employee involvement in the initial design and implementation of the program? Explain.

Video Feature

PART 3—IN VIEW

1. "COUNTRY KIDS" (04:08)

This segment considers the situation of daycare throughout Canada.

2. "PENSION PROMISE" (14:17)

This excerpt from *The National* tells the story of what happens when a company goes bankrupt and employees lose not only their jobs but also their pension plans.

QUESTIONS

1. Should employers provide day care? Why or why not?

2. Do you think universal childcare ought to be a national policy and funded by the federal government? Why or why not?

3. If employers have the financial responsibility of pension plans, should they be allowed sole discretion on how the funds are invested? Why?

4. Should provincial governments provide more time-off for childrearing responsibilities? Why or why not?

5. What role does education play in ensuring that employees have sufficient resources for their retirement?

6. What might be the risks with a company pension plan?

NOTES AND REFERENCES

1. Don Hellriegel and John W. Slocum, Jr., *Organizational Behaviour,* 10th ed., (Mason, OH: South-Western, 2004), 51.
2. "Companies Step Up Employee Pay Cuts," February 2009, Towers Perrin, www.towersperrin.com/tp/showdctmdoc.jsp?country=global&url=Master_Brand_2/USA/News/Spotlights/2009/Feb/2009_02_12_spotlight_employee_paycuts.htm (accessed February 17, 2009).
3. Allison Cowan, *Compensation Planning Outlook 2009: Economic Uncertainty Spells Caution Ahead,* The Conference Board of Canada, October 2008.
4. James Kalamas, Paul D. Mango, and Drew Ungerman, "Linking Employee Benefits to Talent Management," *The McKinsey Quarterly,* www.mckinseyquarterly.com/Linking_employee_benefits_to_talent_management_2219 (accessed February 17, 2009).
5. Nitin Mohria, Boris Groysberg, and Linda-Eling Lee, "Employee Motivation: A Powerful New Model," *Harvard Business Review,* July–August 2008, 78–84.
6. *Compensation Planning Outlook 2009—Winter Update,* Conference Board of Canada, February 2009.
7. *The Power of Integrated Reward and Talent Management— 2008/2009 Global Strategic Rewards Report And Canadian Findings,* Watson Wyatt, 2008, www.watsonwyatt.com/research/resrender.asp?id=2008-US-0248&page=1 (accessed February 20, 2009).
8. "What Makes the Most Admired Companies Great," seminar sponsored by Hay Group, Vancouver, June 2008.
9. Tavia Grant, "Thanking Staff Without a Fistful of Dollars," *The Globe and Mail,* March 21, 2009, B15.
10. Misty Harris, "Employees Finding Ways to 'Reward' Themselves," *The Vancouver Sun,* March 12, 2009, B1.
11. Sarah Dobson, "Offering Employees What They Want," *Canadian HR Reporter,* October 22, 2007, 15.
12. Alex Shevelenko and Erik Berggren, "Winning Through Talent in Uncertain Times: Five Strategies to Get Ahead," Success Factor Research, Mercer Consulting, 2008.
13. *The Future of Work: Total Reward Strategies and Canada's Aging Workforce,* Total Benefits, Sun Life Financial, 2008.
14. Nitin Mohria, Boris Groysberg, and Linda-Eling Lee, "Employee Motivation: A Powerful New Model."

15. Ann Macaulay, "Walking the Line in Incentive Programs," *Canadian HR Reporter,* April 23, 2007, www.hrreporter.com/ArticleView.aspx?l=1&articleid=5147 (accessed February 20, 2009).

16. Patty Kujawa, "You Get What You Pay For," *Workforce Management,* January 30, 2008, www.workforce.com/archive/feature/25/33/83/index.php?ht= (accessed February 20, 2009).

17. Steven J. McShane, *Canadian Organizational Behaviour,* 6th ed. (Toronto: McGraw-Hill Ryerson, 2006), 148–151.

18. Steven J. McShane, *Canadian Organizational Behaviour,* 6th ed., 149–150.

19. "Impact of Global Economic Conditions on Non-U.S. Compensation and HR Programs," Hewitt Associates Web conference, April 9, 2009.

20. *The Consumer Price Index (CPI) and You,* StatsCan, May 20, 2008, www.statcan.gc.ca/pub/62-560-x/62-560-x2004001-eng.htm (accessed February 22, 2009).

21. "Public Service Human Resources Management Agency of Canada, Classification Standard: Border Services Group," August 26, 2005, Canada Public Service Agency, www.psagency.gc.ca/ (accessed February 22, 2009).

22. Richard Long, "Paying for Knowledge: Does It Pay?" *Canadian HR Reporter,* March 28, 2005, www.hrreporter.com/ArticleView.aspx?l=1&articleid=3737 (accessed February 22, 2009).

23. Richard Long, "Pay for Knowledge for Managers Too Complex to Put to Use," *Canadian HR Reporter,* March 11, 2005, www.hrreporter.com/ArticleView.aspx?l=1&articleid=3707 (accessed February 22, 2009).

24. "Framework for Competency-based Management," Human Resource Systems Group, 2007.

25. Alex Palmer, "Incentive Cash Concerns," *Incentive* 183, no. 1 (January 2009): 5.

26. "Salary Increases Holding Stable for 2009; Pay for Performance Increasing, Survey Finds," *PA Times,* American Society for Public Administration, January 2009, 22.

27. Michael Raith, "Specific Knowledge and Performance Measurement," *RAND Journal of Economics* 39, no. 4 (Winter 2008): 1059–1079.

28. Fay Hansen," The Toughest HR Job in America," *Workforce Management,* February 28, 2008, www.workforce.com/archive/feature/25/38/85/index.php?ht= (accessed February 23, 2009).

29. Franklin Paul, "Intel Pushing to Give Staff Stock Break," *Financial Post,* March 24, 2009, FP12.

30. Sarah Dobson, "A Rolling Stone Gathers No Moss," *Canadian HR Reporter,* March 24, 2008, 13.

31. Roma Luciw, "Workers Want More Than Gold Watch," *Globe and Mail Online,* June 8, 2007.

32. Danielle Harder, "TD Takes Family-friendly Benefits to the Bank," *Canadian HR Reporter,* February 23, 2009, 20.

33. Brooke Smith, "Paying Less for Benefits?" *Benefits Canada,* May 15, 2008, www.benefitscanada.com/benefit/health/article.jsp?content=20080515_144632_3580 (accessed February 23, 2009).

34. Jacqueline Taggart, "No Easy Answer for Cost Conundrum," *Canadian HR Reporter,* April 19, 2004, 11.

35. C. Ian Genno and James Pierlot, "2009 Federal Budget Contains Several HR-related Measures for Employers," *Canadian HR Reporter,* February 23, 2009, www.hrreporter.com/ArticleView.aspx?l=1&articleid=6682.

36. Juliet O'Neill, "EI Benefits Extended by Five Weeks, Several Protections Introduced," *The Vancouver Sun,* January 29, 2009, B2.

37. Statistics Canada, "Population by Sex and Age Group, www40.statcan.gc.ca/l01/cst01/demo10a-eng.htm (accessed February 23, 2009).

38. Information gathered by the current author on a consulting assignment to Vancouver Coastal Health Authority, 2007–2008.

39. Milt Freudenheim, "Big Employers Join Forces in Effort to Negotiate Lower Drug Prices," *The New York Times,* June 12, 2004, B1.

40. Danielle Harder, "Generic Drugs Cheaper South of the Border," *Canadian HR Reporter,* February 9, 2009, 17.

41. "Finding the Right Prescription," *Fortune,* May 25, 2009, 42.

42. Brent Jang, "BCE, Bombardier Pension Plan Shortfalls Grow," *The Globe and Mail,* October 31, 2008, B3.

43. Janet McFarland, "Ontario Must Make Pension Plans 'Attractive,'" *The Globe and Mail,* November 21, 2008, B2.

44. Danielle Harder, "Quebec Backs Private Pension Plans," *Canadian HR Reporter,* February 9, 2009, 1.

45. Sarah Dobson, "Joint Effort by B.C., Alberta to Improve Pensions," *Canadian HR Reporter,* January 12, 2009, www.hrreporter.com/ArticleView.aspx?l=1&articleid=6608 (accessed February 23, 2009).

46. Bruce Cheadle, "Wrap Up Private Plans in Favour of Better CPP, Retirees Tell Ottawa," *The Globe and Mail,* March 14, 2009, A5.

47. "Work Absence Rates 2007," Statistics Canada, Catalogue no. 71-211-X, 30.

48. Louise Brown, "University Loses Round on Holiday Policy," thestar.com, March 31, 2008, www.thestar.com/article/407447 (accessed June 17, 2009).

49. "Work Absence Rates 2007," 116 and 118.

50. Shannon Klie, "Awards Recognize Quality, Health," *Canadian HR Reporter,* October 6, 2008, www.hrreporter.com/ArticleView.aspx?l=1&articleid=6402 (accessed February 24, 2009).

51. Joanne Wojcik, "Employer Data Quantifies the Value of Wellness Programs, *Workforce Management,* April 1, 2008, www.workforce.com/archive/feature/25/45/03/254507.php?ht= (accessed February 24, 2009).

52. "A Brief History of the Employee Assistance Program," Manulife Financial, http://groupbenefits.manulife.com/canada/GB_V2.nsf/LookupFiles/EBNQ305EAPHistory/$File/EAPHistory.htm (accessed February 24, 2009).

53. Danielle Harder, "Tuition Reimbursement Can Put Employees at the Top," *Canadian HR Reporter,* March 24, 2008, 17.

54. Shannon Klie, "Employers Can Help With the 'Long Goodbye,'" *Canadian HR Reporter,* www.hrreporter.com/ArticleView.aspx?l=1&articleid=5357 (accessed February 24, 2009).

55. Shannon Proudfoot, "Millions of Canadian Caregivers Burning the Candle at Both Ends," *The Vancouver Sun,* April 16, 2009, B3.

56. 2006 Census, Statistics Canada, "Age and Sex," www12.statcan.gc.ca/english/census06/data/highlights/agesex/pages/Page.cfm?Lang=E&Geo=PR&Code=01&Table=1&Data=Count&Sex=1&StartRec=1&Sort=2&Display=Page (accessed February 24, 2009).

57. Erin Pooley "House Work," *Canadian Business,* June 19–July 16, 2006.

58. Heather Lynch, "Think City, Dream Vancouver: Policy Brief Eldercare and the Sandwich Generation" *Working Our Way Towards Stability in Senior Care,* February 2008.

PART 4

Employee Relations

CREATING A SAFE AND HEALTHY WORK ENVIRONMENT

OUTCOMES

After studying this chapter, you should be able to

1 Describe what supervisors and managers can do to create a safe and healthy work environment.

2 Cite the measures that should be taken to control and eliminate health and safety hazards.

3 List the current workplace health and safety issues.

4 Describe the organizational services and programs for building better health.

5 Explain the role of employee assistance programs.

6 Explain the impact of substance abuse and stress in the workplace.

OUTLINE

HRM CLOSE-UP

Holly O'Rourke with her staff at Saint Andrews Physiotherapy Clinic. Courtesy of Holly O'Rourke, Saint Andrews Physiotherapy Clinic

"Because we all work in the same area, it's in our best interest to keep the work area safe."

When your business is physiotherapy, you're about as close as possible to the real reason for health and safety programs in the workplace. "We've been in business since 1992 without accidents or injuries," explains Holly O'Rourke, owner of the Saint Andrews Physiotherapy Clinic in Saint Andrews, New Brunswick. "I attribute that to the nature of our work and our knowledge of proper body mechanics."

O'Rourke works as a physiotherapist in addition to being the business owner. About half the clients she treats have workplace injuries, and most of those injuries are related to over-use and repetitive strain. Sometimes the remedy is a simple change in habit, O'Rourke explained. "I had one client who worked in a laundromat and twisted to the left hundreds of times each day. Simply unloading the entire basket on a table has improved her situation immensely." Treating these types of injuries makes O'Rourke keenly aware of the repetition her own staff do during the course of a day.

When she first set up the business, she realized that her staff needed ergonomically correct computers and chairs. She was also concerned about how staff moves large pieces of equipment from cubicle to cubicle. O'Rourke introduced rolling carts to move equipment around in order to ease the strain. She placed outlets at waist height to limit the amount of bending required to plug in and unplug equipment, and she organized supply shelves at waist height in order to reduce the amount of reaching required.

When it comes to safety, O'Rourke continually seeks feedback and ideas from staff. Most problems are solved with common sense and creativity. "Because we all work in the same area, it's in our best interest to keep the work area safe."

Many of the clinic's orthopaedic patients use the exercise stations and equipment to do their physiotherapy programs.

Because the clinic is quite busy, O'Rourke is watchful that a clear pathway for staff and patients is always maintained. For example, she placed different exercise stations along the periphery of the clinic allowing a central passage. There are also many electric machines in the clinic, so O'Rourke installed extra electrical outlets to avoid having cords run across the floor. She also built plastic rings to hold the clinic's large exercise balls to prevent them from rolling around on the floor.

As the business owner, O'Rourke feels personally responsible for keeping the workplace a safe and happy environment. Putting the right physical safeguards in place is one thing; keeping the staff happy and content with their jobs is another concern. "Because we are such a small business, we become like family. Not only is it a cost benefit to keep all staff happy and healthy, but it would be upsetting to me if a staff member was injured on the job, especially if the injury could have been prevented," explains O'Rourke. "I have a direct and personal interest in the health and safety of my staff."

And for O'Rourke, mental health is as important in the workplace as physical health. As a mother of three children, she respects parents who may need to receive or make phone calls pertaining to important family matters. She also recently discovered the practice of yoga and will accommodate staff schedules so that others can attend classes. "Yoga helps compensate for imbalances, so not only do I recommend it to clients, but I try to find ways to help my staff participate as well."

INTRODUCTION

You will note from the HRM Close-Up that health and safety concerns have a significant impact on managers. Occupational health and safety accidents are both numerous, costly to employers, and can even result in criminal charges. For example, in 2008, a Quebec company was charged with criminal negligence causing death. The circumstances related to an employee being crushed to death by a machine that stacks bricks. The company had been previously instructed by the workers' compensation board to repair the faulty machine—which they did not do.[1] To prevent accidents such as these, employers are required by law to provide working conditions that do not impair the safety or health of their employees.

Although the laws safeguarding employees' physical and emotional well-being are certainly an incentive to provide desirable working conditions, many employers are motivated to comply by virtue of their sensitivity to human needs and rights. The more cost-oriented employer recognizes the importance of avoiding accidents and illnesses wherever possible. Costs associated with sick leave, disability payments, replacement of employees who are injured or killed, and workers' compensation far exceed the costs of maintaining a safe and healthy workplace. Accidents and illnesses attributable to the workplace may also have pronounced effects on employee morale and on the goodwill that the organization enjoys in the community and in the business world.

While managers at all levels are expected to know and enforce health and safety standards throughout the organization, in reality it is the supervisor who has the biggest role. The supervisor must ensure a work environment that protects employees from physical hazards, unhealthy conditions, and unsafe acts of other personnel. Through effective safety and health practices, the physical and emotional well-being of employees may be preserved and even enhanced. This chapter will discuss health and safety in the workplace, including the responsibilities of employers, supervisors, and workers. You will also be presented with information about how to create a safe and healthy work environment and culture.

HEALTH AND SAFETY: THE LAW

Consider these facts (most recent statistics available):

- In 2007, approximately 975,000 workplace incidents occurred.
- In 2007, 1055 employees died in work-related accidents.
- Workers' compensation boards throughout Canada pay out close to $5 billion in benefits each year.
- In 2007, over 317,000 work-related injuries were reported.
- In 2007, close to 14,500 young adults between the ages of 15 and 19 were injured.[2]

The burden on the country's commerce as a result of lost productivity and wages, medical expenses, and disability compensation is staggering. It is estimated that more than 16 billion days are lost each year to accidents and injuries, costing the Canadian economy over $10 billion.[3] And there is no way to calculate the human suffering involved.

The federal, provincial, and territorial governments regulate occupational health and safety. While statutes and standards differ slightly from jurisdiction to jurisdiction, attempts have been made to harmonize the various acts and regulations. Health and safety legislation has had an impact on workplace injuries and illnesses. The number of workplace accidents in Canada has declined even though there has been an increase in the number of workers.

Occupational injury
Any cut, fracture, sprain, or amputation resulting from a workplace accident

Occupational illness
Abnormal condition or disorder resulting from exposure to environmental factors in the workplace

An **occupational injury** is any cut, fracture, sprain, or amputation resulting from a workplace accident or from an exposure involving an accident in the work environment. An **occupational illness** is any abnormal condition or disorder, other than one resulting from an occupational injury, caused by exposure to environmental factors associated with employment. It includes acute and chronic illnesses or diseases that may be caused by inhalation, absorption, ingestion, or direct contact. With regard to parts of the body affected by accidents, injuries to the back occur most frequently, followed by leg, arm, and finger injuries.

Acts and Regulations

All supervisors, managers, and HR professionals should become familiar with the occupational health and safety legislation governing the jurisdiction under which their organization operates. The applicable legislation for each jurisdiction, the Web addresses, and the agency that administers the legislation are shown in Manager's Toolkit 8.1.

Duties and Responsibilities

The fundamental duty of every employer is to take every reasonable precaution to ensure employee safety. The motivating forces behind workplace legislation were effectively articulated in the landmark case *Regina v. Wholesale Travel Group*, which dealt with the legal liability and obligation of employers to behave in accordance with legislation:

> Regulatory legislation is essential to the operation of our complex industrial society; it plays a legitimate and vital role in protecting those who are most vulnerable and least able to protect themselves. The extent and importance of that role have increased continuously since the onset of the Industrial Revolution. Before effective workplace legislation was enacted, labourers—including children—worked unconscionably long hours in dangerous and unhealthy surroundings that evoke visions of Dante's inferno. It was regulatory legislation with its enforcement provisions that brought to an end the shameful situations that existed in mines, factories and workshops in the nineteenth century.

Duties of Employers

Outcome 1

In addition to providing a hazard-free workplace and complying with the applicable statutes and regulations, employers must inform their employees about safety and health requirements. Employers are also required to keep certain records, to compile an annual summary of work-related injuries and illnesses, and to ensure that supervisors are familiar with the work and its associated hazards (the supervisor, in turn, must ensure that workers are aware of those hazards). And in most jurisdictions, employers are required to ensure that the employees are knowledgeable about workplace health and safety. Organizations with large numbers of employees may have a full-time health and safety officer. In At Work with HRM 8.1, the training, safety, & recruitment VP at the B.C. Maritime Employers Association talks about the health and safety issues that apply to any waterfront workplace.

MANAGER'S TOOLKIT **8.1**

WORKERS' COMPENSATION REFERENCE CHART

Jurisdiction	Body of Legislation	Administration Agency	Website
Canada			www.canoshweb.org
Alberta	Occupational Health and Safety Act	Workers' Compensation Board of Alberta	www.wcb.ab.ca
British Columbia	Workers' Compensation Act	WorkSafeBC	www.worksafebc.ca
Manitoba	The Workers' Compensation Act	Workers Compensation Board of Manitoba	www.wcb.mb.ca
New Brunswick	Occupational Health and Safety Act	WorkSafeNB	www.worksafenb.ca
Newfoundland and Labrador	Occupational Health and Safety Act	Workplace Health, Safety and Compensation Commission (Newfoundland)	www.whscc.nf.ca
Northwest Territories	Workers' Compensation Act	Workers' Safety and Compensation Commission	www.wcb.nt.ca/

(Continued)

Jurisdiction	Body of Legislation	Administration Agency	Website
Nova Scotia	Occupational Health and Safety Act	Workers' Compensation Board of Nova Scotia	www.wcb.ns.ca
Nunavut	Workers' Compensation Act	Workers' Safety and Compensation Commission	www.wcb.nt.ca/
Ontario	Occupational Health and Safety Act/Workplace Safety and Insurance Act	Workplace Safety and Insurance Board (Ontario)	www.wsib.on.ca
Prince Edward Island	Occupational Health and Safety Act/Workers' Compensation Act	Workers' Compensation Board of Prince Edward Island	www.wcb.pe.ca
Quebec	Act Respecting Occupational Health and Safety	Commission de la santé et de la sécurité du travail of Quebec	www.csst.qc.ca
Saskatchewan	The Workers' Compensation Act	Saskatchewan Workers' Compensation Board	www.wcbsask.com
Yukon	Workers' Compensation Act/ Occupation Health and Safety Act	Yukon Workers' Compensation Health and Safety Board	www.wcb.yk.ca

AT WORK **with HRM 8.1**

SAFETY AND SECURITY ON THE COAST

John Beckett, vice president, training, safety, & recruitment at the B.C. Maritime Employers Association, describes a very complex health and safety environment. The B.C. Maritime Employers Association, while not directly an employer, provides a variety of services to waterfront employers along Vancouver's coast. Its members include shipping companies that regularly use the Vancouver waterfront for movement of goods and the stevedoring companies that move the goods to and from the ship. The environment is complex as the BCMEA functions as the face-of-the-industry to many regulators, particularly at the federal level. All the regulators, such as Transport Canada Rail or Transport Canada Marine, are concerned about the safety and security of operations at the coast. In addition, BCMEA members are covered for workers' compensation through WorkSafeBC.

It is important to remember that the BCMEA works with what is called a "dispatch" workforce—a workforce that might work for multiple employers over a very short period of time. The BCMEA is responsible for dispatching the workers to the various docks to unload and load cargo.

Recently, the BCMEA developed an overall health and safety strategy to reduce accidents and create a healthy and safe work environment, which through a number of different actions has reduced its yearly accident rate from 22 to six. It has accomplished this by providing comprehensive training for waterfront workers. When a worker shows up to unload cargo, they are expected to know the safety protocols for each employer. Since this could be quite confusing with different employers, the BCMEA has developed consistent safety protocols across all shipping lines. By using a risk-mitigation approach, workers only learn one set of safety standards.

Since WorkSafeBC covers the BCMEA for insurance purposes only, the association decided that it would advance its health and safety strategy by participating in the Certificate of Recognition Program. This program, which is voluntary, is designed to recognize organizations that implement health and safety systems and return-to-work programs, which exceed legislative requirements. The certificate is granted after a comprehensive audit has occurred, where the audit focuses on ensuring that there is an integrated health and safety management system. With such recognition, the BCMEA has also been providing similar health and safety services to other waterfront employers, such as tugboat operators.

As Beckett says, "Achieving the WorkSafeBC certificate demonstrates that with careful planning and execution, safe work practices can be achieved in any type of industry."

CRITICAL THINKING QUESTION

Can you identify some of the safety issues at your place of work or your school?

Source: Interview with John Beckett, March 2009.

WSIB-Young Worker Awareness Program

www.youngworker.ca

In all jurisdictions, employers are required to report any accidents that cause injuries and diseases to the Workers' Compensation Board. Accidents resulting in death or critical injuries must be reported immediately; the accident must then be investigated and a written report submitted. Finally, employers must provide safety training and be prepared to discipline employees for failing to comply with safety rules. The high incidence of youth injuries is attributable to lack of work experience and insufficient training. To help build the awareness of safety at work in young people, the Ontario agency has created a separate website as a resource for young people (**www.youngworker.ca**). Its objective is to help younger workers protect themselves and others in the workplace. The poster in Manager's Toolkit 8.2 is targeted towards young people—making them aware of workplace risks.

Duties of Workers

Employees are required to comply with all applicable acts and regulations, to report hazardous conditions or defective equipment, and to follow all employer safety and health rules and regulations, including those prescribing the use of protective equipment, such as wearing hard hats or steel-toed boots at a construction site or protective eyewear in a laboratory.

Workers have many rights that pertain to requesting and receiving information about safety and health conditions. They also have the right to refuse unsafe work without fear of reprisal. (Some professionals, such as police, firefighters, teachers, and health-care workers have only a limited right of refusal in the sense that their work is inherently dangerous.) For example, in Ontario, an employee who suspects hazardous work conditions may refuse to do the work but must immediately report this concern to the supervisor, triggering an investigation by the supervisor and a worker representative.

A work-refusal investigation can result in either the employee's return to work in a safer environment or the employee's continued refusal. In the latter case, the appropriate ministry is notified and an investigator is dispatched to the job site to provide a written decision. If a replacement worker is used, that individual must be notified of the previous employee's refusal to work. Employees cannot be suspended, fired, or docked pay for refusing unsafe work and can continue to refuse the work until the situation is corrected.[4] For more information on the standards in Ontario, check out the province's agency responsible for workplace safety (**www.wsib.on.ca**).

Workplace Safety and Insurance Board

www.wsib.on.ca

Duties of Supervisors

A *supervisor* is generally defined as a person (with or without a title) who has charge of a workplace and authority over a worker. Occupational health and safety laws require supervisors to advise employees of potential workplace hazards; ensure that workers use or wear safety equipment, devices, or clothing; provide written instructions where applicable; and take every reasonable precaution to guarantee the safety of workers. As you will read later in this chapter, the supervisor is key in creating a healthy and safe work environment. It is the supervisor who is the

MAKING YOU THINK ABOUT SAFETY

LESSON 3:
Major Causes of Workplace Injury

Student Handout 7:
Young Workers: Be a Survivor

Young workers, be on guard

Take care on the job.
Your workplace can be dangerous.

Count on some risk

Young workers have more injuries than any other age group in B.C. This is roughly how it adds up:

- 34 young workers injured every working day
- 5 permanently disabled each week
- About 5 die each year at work

Hardest hit are young male workers. They are 70 percent more likely to be injured than any other group of workers.

Your top seven dangers

Here are the top seven dangers for young workers in B.C.:

1. Lifting objects as retail clerks, shipper-receivers, labourers, material handlers
2. Working on ladders, stairs, scaffolding, other raised areas
3. Using knives in food service, retail sales, supermarkets
4. Working with hot substances or equipment in restaurants
5. Driving or riding in vehicles and operating or working near mobile equipment
6. Operating food slicers in restaurants, supermarkets
7. Working near running equipment or machinery in a variety of jobs

Tips for your best defence

- Always ask. Never assume you can do something you've never done before. Always have your supervisor show you how to do it safely.
- Use safety gear and protective clothing when your job calls for them.
- Always follow safe work procedures and get co-workers to do the same.
- Fix anything unsafe or report it to your supervisor — right away.
- Know how to handle any hazardous material you use on the job.
- Tell your supervisor if you feel at all unsafe.

STUDENT WorkSafe Planning 10
WORKERS' COMPENSATION BOARD OF BC
- 30 -

Source: © WorkSafeBC. Used with permission. The image "Young worker, be on guard" on page 240 is © WorkSafeBC, from Student WorkSafe Planning 10, and is available free of charge at WorkSafeBC.com.

point-of-contact for almost every question regarding health and safety. Further, it is the supervisor who will reinforce safety and health training and it will be the supervisor who is the person held accountable for the employees' understanding and behaviour regarding health and safety in the workplace.

The more complex and diverse your workplace, the more difficult managing safety can be.

Comstock Images

Duties of Joint Health and Safety Committees

Most jurisdictions require the formation of health and safety committees operated jointly by employee and management representatives. This arrangement is intended to create a nonadversarial climate in which labour and management work together to create a safe and healthy workplace. In Ontario, at least one management committee member and one worker representative must be certified. The certification program provides training in such subjects as safety laws, sanitation, general safety, rights and duties, and indoor air quality.

In addition, the legislation in British Columbia requires that a joint worker–employer committee must be formed in a company with 20 or more employees. Further, the employer is obligated to provide at least eight hours of annual educational leave for training and upgrading on health and safety issues.[5]

Figure 8.1 summarizes the legally required duties and responsibilities of those directly involved in health and safety issues.

Penalties for Employer Noncompliance

Penalties for violations of occupational health and safety regulations vary across provinces and territories. The Ontario Health and Safety Act provides for fines of up to $500,000, and offenders can be sent to jail. For example, in 2008, Ontario-based National Steel Car Ltd. was fined a total of $250,000 in connection with two separate incidents in which one worker died.[6] Also, that same year Golden Triangle Partnership and Chamberlain Construction Services were fined a total of $56,000 for safety violations.[7] And lastly, Bondfield Construction Company in Toronto was fined $85,000 in total for multiple safety violations.[8]

The federal government was so concerned about employers' responsibilities for workplace health and safety that the Criminal Code was changed to make it easier to bring criminal charges against co-workers, supervisors, executives, and employers when a worker is killed or injured on the job. The first conviction under this law occurred in 2008 when Transpavé, a Quebec company, was ordered to pay $110,000 in the death of a worker.[9] The legislation was a direct result of a public inquiry into the Westray Mine disaster in 1992 that killed 26 workers. Numerous safety infractions occurred at Westray, and it was determined that senior managers and executives knew of the infractions but did nothing to fix them. There is no doubt that violations of health and safety laws can have significant consequences. Look at some other examples in HRM and the Law 8.1.

FIGURE 8.1   Health and Safety Duties and Responsibilities

Employers

- Provide a hazard-free workplace
- Comply with laws and regulations
- Inform employees about safety and health requirements
- Keep records
- Compile annual summary of work-related injuries and illnesses
- Ensure supervisors are familiar with work and associated hazards
- Report accidents to WCB
- Provide safety training

Workers

- Comply with all laws and regulations
- Report hazardous conditions or defective equipment
- Follow employer safety and health rules
- Refuse unsafe work

Supervisors

- Advise employees of potential workplace hazards
- Ensure workers use or wear safety equipment
- Provide written instructions
- Take every reasonable precaution to guarantee safety of workers

Joint Health and Safety Committees

- Advise employer on health and safety matters
- Create nonadversarial climate to create safe and healthy work environment
- Investigate accidents
- Train others in safety obligations

HRM and the law 8.1

CHARGES UNDER HEALTH AND SAFETY ACT

A commercial pilot, and former employee of Keystone Air Service in Manitoba, was sentenced to two years of house arrest for his role in a crash that killed a man. The judge in the Manitoba Court of Queen's Bench case said, "the decision is a signal to pilots and small commercial airline owners and operators that a corporate culture of bending or ignoring aeronautics regulations to get the job done at the cost of reduced safety is criminal behaviour." However, the company indicated that the incident was unusual, as the plane had run out of fuel, not that there was something wrong with the aircraft or its maintenance. During the hearing, several pilots indicated that there was intense pressure on young pilots who were anxious to accumulate hours, and therefore might have a tendency to bend the rules. Pilots said that there was little if any support or guidance from various small airlines to encourage them to fly a plane safely.

In early 2009, Sunshine Village Corporation, a ski resort in Alberta, was found guilty under the Occupational Health and Safety Act in Alberta. The company was convicted on the primary charge of failing to ensure health and safety. The charge was the result of a young person who was killed on the first day of work.

Sources: Adapted from Joe Friesen, "Linking Corporate Culture, Plane Crash Called Unfair," *The Globe and Mail,* March 22, 2008, A12; and Peter Cheney, "Company Found Guilty in Ski Resort Death," *The Globe and Mail,* January 31, 2009, A8.

Workers' Compensation

Under workers' compensation, injured workers or workers who become ill as a result of their work environment can receive benefits in the form of a cash payout (if the disability is permanent) or wage-loss payments (if the worker can no longer earn the same amount of money). Unlimited medical aid is also provided, along with vocational rehabilitation, which includes physical, social, and psychological services. The goal is to return the employee to the original job (or some modification thereof) as soon as possible. Sun Life Assurance Company of Canada has a return-to-work awards program, which will give premium credits to employers that allow injured workers to change jobs or duties to enable these employees to return to work. A person who has been off work for six months has a 50% chance of returning; after 12 months, a 20% chance; and after two years, a 10% chance. A recent study in Ontario demonstrated that carefully designed return-to-work programs can shorten work absences by providing early assessment and graduated transitional programs.[10]

Equally problematic is compensation for stress, which is discussed in more detail later in the chapter. Stress-related disabilities are usually divided into three groups: physical injuries leading to mental disabilities (e.g., clinical depression after a serious accident); mental stress resulting in a physical disability (ulcers or migraines); and mental stress resulting in a mental condition (anxiety over work load or downsizing leading to depression). Most claims, it should be pointed out, result from accidents or injuries.

In some industrial sectors, employers are working together to establish rules and training programs to further the cause of accident prevention. For further information on the specific objectives of each provincial and territorial workers' compensation agency, visit the websites listed in Manager's Toolkit 8.1.

Compensation has become a complex issue. Workers are now able to receive payment if they have contracted an **industrial disease**. An industrial disease is a disease resulting from exposure to a substance relating to a particular process, trade, or occupation in industry. Cause and effect can be difficult to determine. Consider, for example, the case of a mine worker who has contracted a lung disease, but who also smokes heavily.

Industrial disease
A disease resulting from exposure relating to a particular process, trade, or occupation in industry

While the number of Canadians injured at work every year is decreasing, there are still close to 1,000,000 people injured and the cost of these injuries is over $5.5 billion in compensation claims.[11] This has left workers' compensation boards with a huge deficit to pay existing claims. To encourage employers to introduce better prevention and claims management practices, the emphasis on workers' compensation has been shifting from assessments and payments to the creation of a safety-conscious environment intended to reduce the number of work-related accidents, disabilities, and diseases. Figure 8.2 lists some ways in which employers can reduce their workers' compensation costs.

CREATING A SAFE WORK ENVIRONMENT

Outcome 2

We have seen that employers are required by law to provide healthy and safe working conditions for their employees. To achieve this objective, the majority of employers have a formal safety program. The success of a safety program depends largely on managers and supervisors of operating departments, even though an HR department may have responsibility for coordinating the safety

FIGURE 8.2   Ways to Reduce Workers' Compensation Costs

1. Perform an audit to assess high-risk areas within a workplace.
2. Prevent injuries by proper ergonomic design of the job (such as position of keyboard) and effective assessment of job candidates.
3. Provide quality medical care to injured employees by physicians with experience and preferably with training in occupational health.
4. Reduce litigation by effective communication between the employer and the injured worker.
5. Manage the care of an injured worker from the injury until return to work. Keep a partially recovered employee at the work site.
6. Provide extensive worker training in all related health and safety areas.

communication and training programs, and maintaining safety records required by occupational health and safety regulations. And above all else, it is the CEOs and other senior leaders that set the tone for safe and healthy work practices. A recent Conference Board of Canada study confirmed that the CEO is in a unique position of influence for how the organization views and responds to a safety culture.[12]

Organizations with formal safety programs generally have an employee-management safety committee that includes members from management, each department or manufacturing or service unit, and the pool of employees. Committees are typically involved in investigating accidents and helping to publicize the importance of safety rules and their enforcement.

The Canada Safety Council website (**www.safety-council.org**) provides resources to assist in the development of a safe work environment.

Canada Safety Council

www.safety-council.org

Promoting Safety Awareness

Probably the most important role of a safety program is motivating managers, supervisors, and subordinates to be aware of safety considerations. While there is a requirement by law to do this, success comes when a manager/supervisor willingly promotes a safe work environment. If managers and supervisors fail to demonstrate awareness, their subordinates can hardly be expected to do so. Unfortunately, most managers and supervisors wear their "safety hats" far less often than their "production, quality control, and methods improvement hats."

While discipline may force employees to work safely, the most effective enforcement of safety expectations occurs when employees willingly obey and "champion" safety rules and procedures. This can be achieved when management actively encourages employees to participate in all aspects of the organization's safety program and the organization provides incentives to do so. Hydro One in Ontario determined that it needed to not only have management encourage employees but that it also needed to recognize that there were four generational cohorts that thought about the workplace differently. With the expected retirements and the hiring of younger people, Hydro One determined that it was important through the orientation process to instill the importance of having a safe and healthy work environment. This was then reinforced through mentoring where different generations used different approaches to meet the needs of the mentee in relation to

In certain workplaces, safety standards require the use of protective clothing.

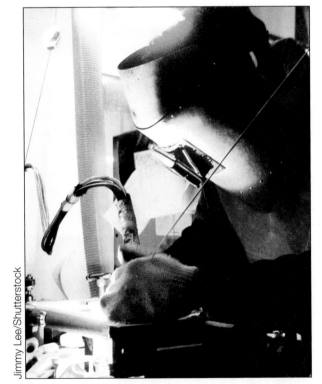

Jimmy Lee/Shutterstock

MANAGER'S TOOLKIT 8.3

STEPS TO A SUCCESSFUL SAFETY INCENTIVE PROGRAM

- Obtain the full support and involvement of management by providing cost benefits.

- Review current injury and health statistics to determine where change is needed.

- Decide on a program of action and set an appropriate budget.

- Select a realistic safety goal, such as reducing accidents by a set percentage, improving safety suggestions, or achieving a length of time without a lost-time injury. Communicate your objectives to everyone involved.

- Select incentive rewards on the basis of their attractiveness to employees and their fit with your budget.

- Develop a program that is both interesting and fun. Use kickoff meetings, posters, banners, quizzes, and/or games to spark employee interest. Give all employees a chance to win.

- Communicate continually the success of your program. Provide specific examples of positive changes in behaviour.

- Reward safety gains immediately. Providing rewards shortly after improvements reinforces changed behaviour and encourages additional support for the safety program.

health and safety. And of course, there was the ongoing leadership from the senior team in demonstrating their commitment to health and safety. It was important that they modelled the type of behaviour that they were expecting from the rest of the employees. With this approach, Hydro One feels as if it is creating a culture of safety awareness.[13] Manager's Toolkit 8.3 provides some steps in setting up a safety incentive program.

Safety Awareness Programs

Most organizations have a safety awareness program that entails the use of several different media. Safety lectures, commercially produced films, specially developed videocassettes, and other media, such as pamphlets, are useful for teaching and motivating employees to follow safe work procedures. Posters have been found to be very effective because they can be displayed in strategic locations where workers will be sure to see them. For example, a shipyard found that placing posters at the work site helped reduce accidents by making employees more conscious of the hazards of using scaffolds.

The Key Role of the Supervisor

One of a supervisor's major responsibilities is to communicate to an employee the need to work safely. Beginning with new employee orientation, safety should be emphasized continually. Proper work procedures, the use of protective clothing and devices, and potential hazards should be explained thoroughly. Furthermore, employees' understanding of all these considerations needs to be verified during training sessions, and employees encouraged to take some initiative in maintaining a concern for safety. Since training by itself does not ensure continual adherence to safe work practices, supervisors must observe employees at work and reinforce safe practices. Where unsafe acts are detected, supervisors should take immediate action to find the cause. Supervisors need to foster a team spirit of safety among the work group. Again, it is important to identify that while this is a legal requirement, the success of any safety awareness depends on the willingness of the supervisor to actively support the employees in creating a safe work environment.

Proactive Safety Training Program

What are the most popular subjects in safety training programs? The most frequent topics are (1) first aid, (2) accident investigation, (3) accident prevention techniques, (4) hazardous materials, and (5) emergency procedures.[14]

Most programs emphasize the use of emergency first-aid equipment and personal safety equipment. Furthermore, many organizations provide training in off-the-job safety—at home, on the highway, and so on—as well as in first aid. Injuries and fatalities away from the job occur much more frequently than do those on the job and are reflected in employer costs for insurance premiums, wage continuation, and interrupted production.

HR professionals and safety directors, in particular, advocate employee involvement when designing and implementing safety programs.[15] Employees can offer valuable ideas regarding specific safety and health topics to cover, instructional methods, and proper teaching techniques. Furthermore, acceptance for safety training is heightened when employees feel a sense of ownership in the instructional program. The Industrial Accident Prevention Association (IAPA) offers six diploma programs for workers, supervisors, managers, and health and safety representatives. Course topics include health and safety legislation, hazard identification, and workplace inspection. Visit the website of the IAPA (**www.iapa.on.ca**).

**Industrial Accident
Prevention Association
(IAPA)**
www.iapa.on.ca

Information Technology and Safety Awareness and Training

Several reasons are advanced for the use of the Internet and information technology in safety and health training. First, enhanced delivery modes enhance the learner's experience.[16] Videos, PowerPoint presentations, and interactive CD-ROM training are ideal methods for standardized safety, environmental, and health instruction. Second, information technology allows organizations to customize their safety and health training needs.[17] The City of Toronto used interactive videos as part of its training program to retrain 10,000 Toronto cab drivers on new safety equipment.[18]

Enforcement of Safety Rules

Specific expectations and standards concerning safety are communicated through supervisors, bulletin-board notices, employee handbooks, and signs attached to equipment. Safety rules are also emphasized in regular safety meetings, at new employee orientations, and in manuals of standard operating procedures. Such rules typically refer to the following types of employee behaviours:

- Using proper safety devices
- Using proper work procedures
- Following good housekeeping practices
- Complying with accident and injury reporting procedures
- Wearing required safety clothing and equipment
- Avoiding carelessness or horseplay

Penalties for violation of safety rules are usually stated in the employee handbook. In a large percentage of organizations, the penalties imposed on violators are the same as those imposed for violations of other standards and expectations. They include an oral or written warning for the first violation, suspension or disciplinary layoff for repeated violations, and, as a last resort, dismissal. However, for serious violations—such as smoking around volatile substances—even the first offence may be cause for termination.

Sometimes the consequences of poor safety behaviours result in serious injuries. For example, an employee died after being struck by a reversing truck while working on the construction site; the employee had not been alerted to the site being dangerous. The company was fined $75,000 in Ontario.[19]

Accident Investigations and Records

Every accident, even those considered minor, should be investigated by the supervisor and a member of the safety committee. Such an investigation may determine the factors contributing to the accident and may reveal what corrections are needed to prevent it from happening

Safety begins with preparedness, as these employees demonstrate in a practice situation.

Photodisc Collection/Getty Images

again. Correction may require rearranging workstations, installing safety guards or controls, or, more often, giving employees additional safety training and ensuring that they understand the importance of safe work practices.

Employers are also required to keep certain records and to compile and post an annual summary of work-related injuries and illnesses. From these records, organizations can compute their *incidence rate*, the number of injuries and illnesses per 100 full-time employees during a given year. The standard formula for computing the incidence rate is shown by the following equation, where 200,000 equals the base for 100 full-time workers who work 40 hours a week, 50 weeks a year:

$$\text{Incidence rate} = \frac{\text{Number of injuries and illnesses} \times 200{,}000}{\text{Total hours worked by all employees during period covered}}$$

It should be noted that the same formula can be used to compute incidence rates for (1) the number of workdays lost because of injuries and illnesses, (2) the number of nonfatal injuries and illnesses without lost workdays, and (3) cases involving only injuries or only illnesses.

Incidence rates are useful for making comparisons between work groups, between departments, and between similar units within an organization. They also provide a basis for making comparisons with other organizations doing similar work. Occupational health and safety departments in each province and Human Resources and Skills Development Canada compile data that an organization can use as a basis for comparing its safety record with those of other organizations. Progressive organizations can also use this information to benchmark "best practices." As Ethics in HRM 8.1 indicates, reporting and investigating accidents can make an organization subject to more inspections, higher insurance premiums, and possible lawsuits.

ETHICS **in HRM 8.1**

SUPERVISOR AND EMPLOYEES BURY THE RECORD

A supervisor was instructing a group of new recruits in the cleaning of metal parts in an assembly plant. She was attempting to demonstrate the cleaning technique to two employees at one workstation, while at another workstation another new employee was trying to clean the parts himself. The cleaning liquid was highly toxic. The employee felt restricted by his safety gloves and so removed them. His eyes started to water, and instinctively he rubbed them with his solution-soaked hands. The pain was overwhelming, and no water was immediately available with which he could rinse his eyes. The employee suffered some temporary vision loss.

Who is to blame? The worker who started to clean without receiving full instructions and without using the issued gloves? The supervisor who could have forbidden the worker to start work until she explained the safety aspects? Or the company that failed to post warning signs about the hazardous nature of the cleaning solvent and to have an eye-washing facility available?

Because workplace accidents increase workers' compensation premiums and the number of inspections, the company had an interest in not reporting the accident. Furthermore, because the company had instituted a reward program that provided incentives to employees for accident-free days, even the employees did not want to report the accident. Thus the supervisor and the employees agreed to "bury the record." What are the consequences of this decision?

CREATING A HEALTHY WORK ENVIRONMENT

Occupational health and safety legislation was clearly designed to protect the health, as well as the safety, of employees. Because of the dramatic impact of workplace accidents, however, managers and employees alike may pay more attention to these kinds of immediate safety concerns than to job conditions or work environments that may be dangerous to their health. It is essential, therefore, that health hazards be identified and controlled. Attention should also be given to nonwork-related illnesses and injuries and their impact on the organization and its members. Special health programs may also be developed to provide assistance to employees with health problems.

Largely because of the growing public awareness of the efforts of environmentalists, factors in the work environment affecting health are receiving greater attention. Unprecedented air and water pollution throughout the world has made everyone more conscious of the immediate environment in which they live and work. Articles about workers who have been exposed to potential dangers at work can frequently be found in the newspapers. Pressure from the federal government and unions, as well as increased public concern, has given employers a definite incentive to provide the safest and healthiest work environment possible.

As part of "Developing Your Skills" at the end of this chapter, you will be asked to explore the website for the Canadian Centre for Occupational Health and Safety (**www.ccohs.ca**).

Canadian Centre for Occupational Health and Safety

www.ccohs.ca

Health Hazards and Issues

At one time health hazards were associated primarily with jobs found in industrial processing operations, such as coal mining. In recent years, however, hazards in jobs outside the plant, such as in offices, health-care facilities, and airports, have been recognized and preventive methods adopted. Substituting materials, altering processes, enclosing or isolating a process, issuing protective equipment, and improving ventilation are some of the common methods to prevent problems. General conditions of health with respect to sanitation, housekeeping, cleanliness, ventilation, water supply, pest control, and food handling are also important to monitor.

Workplace Hazardous Materials Information Systems

Believing that workers have the right to know about potential workplace hazards, industry, labour, and government joined forces several years ago to develop a common information system for labelling hazardous substances. The Workplace Hazardous Materials Information Systems (WHMIS) is based on three elements:

1. *Labels.* Labels are designed to alert the worker that the container holds a potentially hazardous substance. The two types of labels (supplier labels and workplace labels) must contain specified and regulated information, including product identifiers and data on safe handling and material safety. WHMIS class symbols and subclass designations are shown in Figure 8.3.

Material Safety Data Sheet (MSDS)
Documents that contain vital information about hazardous substances

2. *Material Safety Data Sheet (MSDS).* The **MSDS** identifies the product and its potentially hazardous ingredients, and suggests procedures for the safe handling of the product. The MSDS information must be comprehensive, current, and available in English and French.

FIGURE 8.3 WHMIS Class Symbols and Subclass Designations

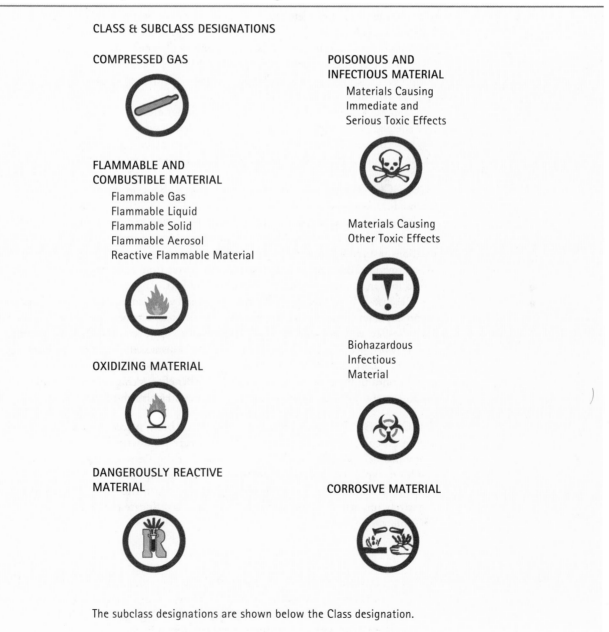

CLASS & SUBCLASS DESIGNATIONS

COMPRESSED GAS

POISONOUS AND INFECTIOUS MATERIAL
Materials Causing Immediate and Serious Toxic Effects

FLAMMABLE AND COMBUSTIBLE MATERIAL
Flammable Gas
Flammable Liquid
Flammable Solid
Flammable Aerosol
Reactive Flammable Material

Materials Causing Other Toxic Effects

OXIDIZING MATERIAL

Biohazardous Infectious Material

DANGEROUSLY REACTIVE MATERIAL

CORROSIVE MATERIAL

The subclass designations are shown below the Class designation.

Source:Solvents in the Workplace, Cat. No. B01230 (Toronto Industrial Accident Prevention Association, March 1990).

3. *Training*. Workers must be trained to check for labels and to follow specific procedures for handling spills. Training workers is part of the due diligence required of employers; it also becomes an important factor in the event of a lawsuit. The Peel Board of Education in Ontario has developed a computer-based program to train workers in WHMIS, allowing illiterate workers to respond to audio commands by touching the screen, thus giving the right response.

Recently, Canada has been working with other countries to develop a standardized global system. This new system, Globally Harmonized System of Classification and Labelling of Chemicals (GHS) is intended to ensure that the symbols used by many countries, such as Japan, the U.S., and some countries in the EU, are more universal. Through this joint effort workers throughout the world handling hazardous materials will have common education and training.[20]

Indoor Air Quality

As a consequence of energy concerns, commercial and residential construction techniques have been changed to increase energy efficiency of heating, ventilating, and air-conditioning systems. This has included sealing windows, reducing outside air intake, and in general "buttoning up" buildings—thus resulting in the "sick building syndrome" (SBS) and "building related illnesses" (BRI) that give rise to such employee complaints as headaches and nausea, etc. Popular office equipment, including photocopying machines, computer terminals, fax machines, and laser printers, contributes to these health complaints.

Four basic ways to overcome polluted buildings are to (1) eliminate tobacco smoke, (2) provide adequate ventilation, (3) maintain the ventilating system, and (4) remove sources of pollution. It is now common practice in both office and industrial settings, as well as public facilities (airports, hotels, schools, and so on), to monitor and manage the quality of indoor air.

TOBACCO SMOKE Probably the most talked-about workplace health issue in recent years is smoking. Nonsmokers, fuelled by studies linking "passive smoking" (inhaling other people's smoke) with disease and death and irritated by smoke getting in their eyes, noses, throats, and clothes, have been extremely vocal in demanding a smoke-free environment. The number of organizations restricting smoking in the workplace has risen dramatically, motivated by legislation in most provinces. Banning smoking releases employers from concerns about future lawsuits or being forced into installing ventilating systems for smokers.

Because of health research over the last several years, smokers have been banned from lighting up on airplanes, at work, and in restaurants and hotels. Furthermore, nonsmokers have demanded a smoke-free environment that will also benefit employers. Smokers on average miss over six days of work per year, nearly double the rate of nonsmokers.[21] It has also been documented that health-care costs are higher for smokers; for this reason, some employers are charging smokers more for health insurance or are reducing their benefits. However, many employers prefer positive reinforcement through wellness programs to encourage employees to stop smoking.

FRAGRANCES Recently more attention has been placed on keeping fragrances such as perfumes, colognes, oils, and other personal care product with scents clear of the workplace. Many people can suffer painful reactions even if the scent is a very low concentration.[22] If an employee expresses concern about fragrances, it is important for the organization to treat the concern seriously, openly, and honestly. Depending on the number of employees that may be negatively impacted, the organization may need to educate the employees and develop a scent-free policy.

Technology

Initially, the concerns about the effects of technology on workers' health focused on computer monitors, or video display terminals (VDTs). However, many fears about computer terminals have proved to be unfounded. Although employers are learning ways to minimize the negative effects of desktop computers, serious health concerns remain an issue.

Cumulative Trauma Disorders

Cumulative trauma disorders
Injuries involving tendons of the fingers, hands, and arms that become inflamed from repeated stresses and strains

Meat cutters, cooks, dental hygienists, textile workers, violinists, flight attendants, office workers at computer terminals, and others whose jobs require repetitive motion of the fingers, hands, or arms are reporting injuries in growing percentages. Known as **cumulative trauma disorders** or repetitive motion injuries, these musculoskeletal disorders (MSDs) are injuries of the muscles, nerves, tendons, ligaments, joints, and spinal discs caused by repeated stresses and strains. One of the more common conditions is *carpal tunnel syndrome*, which is characterized by tingling or numbness in the fingers occurring when a tunnel of bones and ligaments in the wrist narrows and pinches nerves that reach the fingers and base of the thumb. While this condition was more prevalent in the early 2000s, the incidence has been dropping—probably due to more awareness and better workplace equipment.[23]

Ergonomics attempts to design equipment and systems that can be easily and efficiently used by people. As a result, ergonomics techniques are also successfully used to improve or correct workplace conditions that cause or aggravate cumulative trauma disorders.[24] Continuous developments in office furniture, video display terminals, tool design, computer keyboards, and adjustable workstations are all attempts to make the work setting more comfortable—and, hopefully, more productive—but also to lessen musculoskeletal disorders. Mini-breaks involving exercise and the changing of work positions have been found helpful. Importantly, these kinds of injuries often go away if they are caught early. If they are not, they may require months or years of treatment or even surgical correction. Also, when cumulative trauma disorders result from work activities, they can be as high as 40% of the workers' compensation claims.[25]

Communicable Diseases

Communicable diseases, such as herpes simplex (cold sores), influenza, and athlete's foot, and AIDS (acquired immune deficiency syndrome), are covered in public health legislation, not occupational health and safety legislation. In recent years, no issue has received as much attention as SARS (severe acute respiratory syndrome). SARS is a pneumonia-like and potentially fatal illness that infected areas such

Many employers were unprepared to deal with SARS issues, such as employee quarantines.

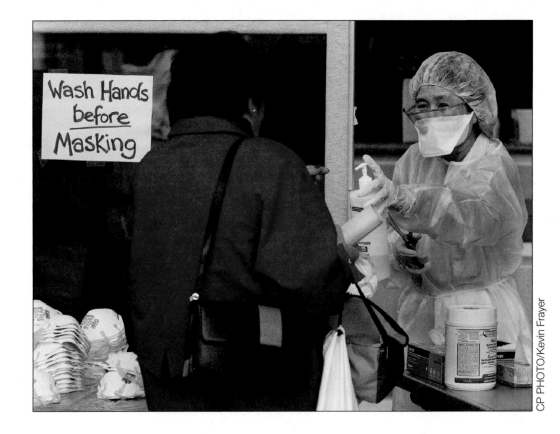

CP PHOTO/Kevin Frayer

as Hong Kong, Taiwan, Singapore, and Toronto earlier this decade. The Centres for Disease Control advised business travellers to avoid these areas. Employers in Canada had to make decisions about travel bans, quarantines, the right to refuse work, and what constituted a safe work environment.

Since the SARS issue, public health officials, and therefore employers, have become concerned about pandemics, particularly those caused by the avian flu virus. As a result, organizations such as Telus, have prepared emergency health plans to both take care of its employees as well as ensure that the increase in telecommunications traffic is handled.[26] At Work with HRM 8.2 describes how some employers cope with pandemics.

AT WORK **with HRM 8.2**

ARE YOU READY?

The last decade will be remembered for the necessity to develop disaster recovery planning and business continuing planning. Events that disrupted business included ice storms, Y2K, 9/11, strikes, and blackouts. The greatest fear is a pandemic, where it is estimated that absenteeism will run at 20–60% for a period of two to four weeks. Companies like UPS and FedEx would be seriously affected by a pandemic, and have contingency plans in place. But a true pandemic would cross all business sectors.

Human resource professionals, particularly those working in hospitals, faced a crisis in the spring of 2003 that none had seen in their working lifetimes. For the first time in the memory of most hospital employees at Sunnybrook and Women's College Health Sciences Centre in Toronto and London Health Sciences Centre in London, Ontario, there was a code orange crisis—in other words, the most serious level. People looked to the HR team to initiate action plans to deal with sick employees, quarantined employees, and scared employees. Unlike crises such as the events of September 11, 2001, where there is one dramatic event, SARS was an escalating event, with every day creating new problems. At Sunnybrook, the HR director took every decision with the thought "What are the repercussions? Long after SARS ends, the employees and the unions will remember how they were treated." The escalating pace was difficult. HR people had to train employees to screen 12,000 people a day and had just one weekend to design the process and hire and train staff. Communication had to be objective and immediate, not only with employees but with their worried families. For the first time, health-care workers could not leave their work behind, with most having to wear masks at home and avoid contact with their families. To deal with these concerns, staff forums were held (employees had a need to talk about their concerns). The managers learned a lot and now crisis planning has become an ongoing activity in the organization.

The London Health Sciences Centre faced similar issues. Both vice presidents of HR emphasized the need for visible leadership. One immediate problem that was soon evident was the folly of any absenteeism program that motivated employees to come to work sick, which of course increased the risk of communicable diseases spreading throughout the workforce. Some employees continued to come to work even when they weren't feeling well because they were worried they would lose income, so a policy that had to be developed immediately was a commitment to maintain the wages of workers in quarantine. Another unusual problem was that certain categories of workers, such as nurses, have limited rights to refuse work. When Mount Sinai Hospital in Toronto asked employees to staff screening stations, a librarian refused to do this work as she deemed it to be unsafe. A lesson learned is the importance of preparing for an emergency by stockpiling personal protective equipment and training all staff in its use.

It is not just hospitals that have to be prepared for outbreaks of communicable diseases. Hewlett-Packard has a workforce of 8000 employees, with 3200 of them at 10 sites in the Greater Toronto Area. Two HP employees were hospitalized with SARS, and one site was forced to close. Fortunately, because the site had always required employees and visitors to sign in, and access was controlled with a pass card, all those known to have been at the site were easy to trace and all pass cards were revoked. Also, because HP is a high-tech company, with all employees online all the time, communication with employees was not difficult. However, the nature of the highly mobile workforce posed problems for health-care officials. The public health department required lists of all employees who were absent, but HR does not track absences because most HP employees work from home or off site.

Avian flu may be the next pandemic, with an estimate of up to 58,000 deaths and 138,000 hospitalizations in Canada. Experts suggest that senior management drive the emergency preparedness program, and that a program team be established that would create a plan to protect human life, eliminate or minimize risk and injury, protect physical assets, minimize losses, and resume operations as quickly as possible. The plan must be communicated in advance and every employee needs to know what to do. There must be a test and practice phase, with emergency drills.

CRITICAL THINKING QUESTIONS

1. What are the potential problems when a hospital does not have enough skilled employees available to handle a public health crisis such as SARS?
2. What would be some of the impacts if many businesses in one city had to close down for a limited period of time due to a similar crisis?

Sources: B. Orr, "SARS Outbreak Teaches Valuable Lessons on a New 'Normal' State for HR Management," *Canadian HR Reporter* June 2, 2003, 5; Ministry of Labour, "Workplace Laws and SARS," www.gov.on.ca/LAB; A. Picard, "Mommy Are You Going to Die?" *The Globe and Mail*, April 5, 2003; David Brown "One Year Later—The Invaluable Lessons of SARS," *Canadian HR Reporter*, March 8, 2004, 1; Michael Bennet, "Are You Ready," *HR Professional,* October/November 2005, 21–26; and Phillip Quinn, "Plan for Pandemic," *The National Post,* March 29, 2006, WK1 and 5.

Workplace Security

Perhaps the most significant event that has affected workplace security has been the events that occurred on September 11, 2001. From that day forward, organizations throughout Canada have placed renewed emphasis on personal safety and security at work. On a recent study tour, one author of this book was acutely aware of the heightened security measures to get into certain government buildings. In some cases, unless you were employed there, you could not enter. Further, if you were an employee, you had to go through substantive security checks, including metal detectors, prior to being authorized to enter.

Once largely confined to foreign countries, terrorism is now a major concern to many Canadian employers, such as airlines, sporting facilities, energy plants, high-tech companies, and financial institutions. The heightened security procedures at these facilities show the importance employers place on the prevention of terrorist attacks. Some of the steps taken to have more secure facilities are increased video surveillance, blast-resistant glass, tightened garage security, and off-site emergency offices.

And the concerns of employees are not restricted to those from terrorism or bomb threats. In fact, changes to the Canadian Labour Code have provided an expanded definition of the reasons that employees can refuse work that they perceive as dangerous. Employees can now refuse on the basis of any "potential" condition that could reasonably be expected to cause injury or illness.[27] The legislation was tested recently when a group of maximum security prison guards in British Columbia challenged a prohibition from carrying handcuffs as a routine practice. The prison officials had banned the practice to remove an overt symbol of authority in daily dealings with prisoners, but the guards felt that a potential danger was created by doing so.[28]

Workplace Violence

Many people think of workplace violence as a physical assault. But there are many forms including:

- Threatening behaviour such as shaking fists or throwing objects.
- Verbal or written threats.
- Harassment—any behaviour that demeans, embarrasses, or humiliates.
- Verbal abuse including swearing, insults, or condescending language.
- Physical attacks including hitting, shoving, pushing, or kicking.[29]

Several provinces, including Alberta, British Columbia, Saskatchewan, Manitoba, Nova Scotia, and Prince Edward Island, have implemented regulations dealing with workplace violence as part of their Occupational Health and Safety Regulations. Among the requirements of these regulations are a risk assessment, development of policies and procedures to handle the risks identified, instruction and training of workers in handling violence, and a requirement that incidents be reported.[30] A recent case in Alberta where an employee at Garda Security was sexually assaulted resulted in the government charging the company with failing to ensure the health and safety of workers. While the legislation requires employers to conduct a hazard assessment, implement safety measures to reduce risks, and ensure workers have an effective way of communicating with other employees, the government feels that there was a failure on the part of the employer to do what was expected given the nature of the business. Some observers suggest that the legislation ought to have a total ban on working alone.[31]

Exposure to workplace violence results in employees fearing more incidents of violence, leading to personal strains (such as stress) and organizational strains (such as reduced commitment). To implement some preventative measures, the Canadian Centre for Occupational Health and Safety suggests:

- Workplace design, such as locks or physical barriers, lighting and electronic surveillance.
- Administrative practices such as keeping cash register funds to a minimum, varying the time of day that cash is emptied, and using a security firm to deliver cash.
- Work practices (particularly for those working alone or away from an office) that include having a designated contact, checking the credentials of a client, and having an emergency telephone source.[32]

Even without legislated requirements, employers can take specific actions to reduce workplace violence. For example, organizations can screen job applicants for histories showing a propensity to violence. Additionally, managers and employees can be trained to recognize violence indicators, such as those given in Figure 8.4. Proper training and reinforcement of security measures can help reduce the potential of workplace incidents, whether in Canada or abroad.[33]

FIGURE 8.4   Warning Signs of Violence in the Workplace

Workplace violence can start as small incidents involving negative remarks and inappropriate behaviour. It may escalate to physical or psychological violence. It is much easier to prevent violence by stopping small incidents than trying to deal with the aftermath of a major crisis.

It is extremely important to understand that the following behaviours do not mean a person will become violent, but they may indicate that the person is experiencing high levels of stress. Each situation is unique and professional judgment or outside assistance may be necessary to determine if intervention is necessary.

Always take particular note if:

- There is a change in their behaviour patterns.
- The frequency and intensity of the behaviours are disruptive to the work environment.
- The person is exhibiting many of these behaviours, rather than just a few.

Warning signs include:

- Crying, sulking or temper tantrums
- Excessive absenteeism or lateness
- Disregard for the health and safety of others
- Disrespect for authority
- Increased mistakes or errors, or unsatisfactory work quality
- Refusal to acknowledge job performance problems
- Faulty decision making
- Testing the limits to see what they can get away with
- Swearing or emotional language
- Overreacting to criticism
- Making inappropriate statements
- Forgetfulness, confusion, and/or distraction
- Inability to focus
- Blaming others for mistakes
- Complaints of unfair treatment

FIGURE 8.4 *(Continued)*

- Talking about the same problems repeatedly without resolving them
- Insistence that he or she is always right
- Misinterpretation of communications from supervisors or co-workers
- Social isolation
- Personal hygiene is poor or ignored
- Sudden and/or unpredictable change in energy level
- Complaints of unusual and/or non-specific illnesses

Source: "What Are the Warning Signs of A Troubled Person or Employee?" Canadian Centre for Occupational Health and Safety, www.ccohs.ca (accessed February 26, 2009).

Awareness of these threatening behaviours can provide an opportunity to intervene and prevent disruptive, abusive, or violent acts. It is also critical that any violent behaviour is challenged and confronted. Employees need to know that violent behaviour is not acceptable. Finally, organizations can establish formalized workplace prevention policies, informing employees that aggressive employee behaviour will not be tolerated. Manager's Toolkit 8.4 lists violence-prevention measures that organizations can take.

Organizations are also using a number of different ways to inform employees about security issues. For example, Seneca College in Ontario uses its intranet as a communication tool to inform employees of internal security as well as external security issues in the surrounding geographic area of the college. In another example, the province of Manitoba was so concerned that workplace violence can occur as a result of domestic violence that it recently committed $100,000 to develop domestic violence awareness training for employers.[34] Another innovative approach to learning

---

MANAGER'S TOOLKIT **8.4**

WORKPLACE SECURITY MEASURES

Everyone in the workplace must be committed to, and involved in creating, a workplace violence prevention program: employers, workers, the joint health and safety committee, and unions.

Follow these steps to prevent workplace violence:

1. Establish violence prevention policy and standards.

2. Conduct a risk assessment.

3. Control violence hazards through workplace design and work practices.

4. Regularly inspect your workplace and review your program to ensure standards are maintained.

5. Include domestic violence issues in workplace violence prevention policies and programs.

6. Educate employees on these policies and programs, appropriate actions to take, signs of domestic violence, how to prevent violence, and resources for victims of domestic violence.

7. Develop a safety plan, if an employee reports domestic violence, to ensure the victim is protected while at the workplace.

8. Ensure all employees are aware the employee assistance provider is available.

9. Encourage the victim to contact a professional.

10. Screen for the abuser (with the victim's permission) by providing a photo or description to reception and security.

11. Inform all workplace parties they must report any abuse or violent behaviour.

12. Act upon any reports immediately.

Sources: "Violence in the Workplace" WSIB Ontario, www.wsib.on.ca/wsib/wsibsite.nsf/public/WorkplaceViolence (accessed February 26, 2009); and Sarah Dobson, "Tackling Domestic Violence at Work," *Canadian HR Reporter*, December 1, 2008, www.hrreporter.com/ArticleView.aspx?l=1&articleid=6523 (accessed February 26, 2009).

more about preventing workplace violence is the Canadian Initiative on Workplace Violence (**www.workplaceviolence.ca**). It is a research firm with partners from universities, unions, and employers who research the impact of workplace violence and provides educational resources to help organizations eliminate such violence. For example, it has available on its website a very informative article by Glenn French and Paul Morgan on "Addressing Workplace Violence." This article provides helpful ideas for an appropriate policy for employers.

Crisis Management Teams

Some organizations have formal crisis management teams. Home Depot has a crisis management team that arrives within one hour of an incident. These teams, composed of both hourly and managerial employees, conduct initial risk assessment surveys, develop action plans to respond to violent situations, and, importantly, perform crisis intervention during violent, or potentially violent, encounters.[35] For example, a crisis management team would investigate a threat reported by an employee. The team's mandate would be to gather facts about the threat, decide if the organization should intervene, and, if so, to determine the most appropriate method of doing so. RBC, as part of its corporate social responsibility, created an emergency telephone line for employees and families in the event of an RBC-wide crisis such as blackouts or severe weather conditions.[36]

When violent incidents, such as the death of a co-worker, happen at work, employees can experience anxiety, shock, guilt, grief, apathy, resentment, cynicism, isolation, and a host of other emotions.[37] Such incidents may require the violence response team to perform crisis intervention through positive counselling techniques.

Building Better Health

Outcome 4

Along with improving working conditions that are hazardous to employee health, many employers provide health services and have programs that encourage employees to improve their health habits. It is recognized that better health benefits not only the individual but also the organization in reduced absenteeism, increased efficiency, and better morale. An understanding of the close relationship between physical and emotional health and job performance has made broad health-building programs attractive to employers as well as to employees. Further, recent surveys are suggesting that 50% of employers are committed to building and maintaining a culture of health for employees and that a multidimensional approach (physical, psychological, and social) is being used.[38]

Effective handling of workplace violence involves intervention from specialists trained in handling workplace traumas.

Bruce Ayres/Stone/Getty Images

Health Services

The type of health services employers provide is primarily related to the size of the organization and the importance of such services. Small organizations have only limited facilities, such as those needed to handle first-aid cases, while many larger firms offer complete diagnostic, treatment, and emergency medical services. Since employers are required to provide medical services after an injury, the larger firms may have nurses and physicians on full-time duty or certainly have arrangements with local physicians for preferred attention. Medium-sized and smaller organizations have one or more physicians on call.

Alternative Approaches

In a discussion of health services as well as health benefits, it should be emphasized that there are many nontraditional approaches to better health. These are typically referred to as alternative approaches. Many of the approaches differ from traditional medicine in that they are less invasive and they empower the patient by enlisting patient participation in health-care decisions.

Relaxation techniques, chiropractic, therapeutic massage, acupuncture, homeopathy, megavitamin and herbal therapy, special diets, and many other alternative approaches are used to treat a wide variety of health problems.

Similarly, changes to the physical structure of the work environment can also improve the overall effectiveness of employees. This is especially true if the organization is part of the information-age economy where there are many cross-functional interactions and creative approaches to the business. Also, there have been studies that demonstrated a strong link between high-performance work systems and occupational safety. In such a system, employees are the primary source of the company's competitive advantage, are treated accordingly, and therefore are motivated to perform at high levels. With such an approach, employees who are treated respectfully tended to be more committed and participated more fully in workplace safety.[39]

Wellness Programs

Many organizations have developed programs that emphasize regular exercise, proper nutrition, weight control, and avoidance of substances harmful to health. For example, the employee health management program at Xerox includes cardiovascular fitness through aerobic exercises, such as jogging, skipping rope, and racquet sports.

Wellness programs are not only popular, but they can produce measurable cost savings. Wellness efforts are particularly effective when organizations target their wellness initiatives at specific health risks, such as high cholesterol or blood pressure counts, high body-fat levels, or smoking. Every dollar invested in a wellness program produces a return of $1.95 to $3.75 per employee.[40] For example, Husky Oil believes that its program has enabled its absenteeism rate in its Canadian operations to be less than one-half of the manufacturing industry average (3.7 days per year versus 9.1).[41] Even in difficult economic situations, a modest approach to wellness in the workplace can occur with things such as encouraging employees to get some amount of exercise each day and encouraging staff to take breaks to rebuild their energies during the day.[42] Other success stories can be found in At Work with HRM 8.3.

However, not everyone is convinced of the effectiveness of wellness programs. Unions, such as CUPE and the Canadian Union of Postal Workers (CUPW), express concern that too much attention is focused on a person's unhealthy lifestyle and that in doing so, potential workplace issues that are creating unhealthy employees are being ignored. There is also some evidence that suggests it is difficult to identify a wellness program being the variable in reducing absenteeism.[43]

Disability Management

Disability management
Integrated approach to managing disability-related benefits

More and more organizations are taking an integrated approach to dealing with short- and long-term absences. Initially, **disability management** programs were linked to workplace injuries as a way to get employees back to work as soon as possible. These programs have now evolved to an

AT WORK **with HRM 8.3**

INVESTING IN EMPLOYEE HEALTH

For the 1600 employees at Aviva Canada, the idea of a fitness facility at its Toronto headquarters was beyond their expectations. Aviva is in the property and casualty insurance business and as such many of the employees spend a lot of time doing sedentary work. In order to convince the decision-makers, the company developed a business case that included architectural drawings, specifications for fitness equipment, financial projections, liability guidelines, and operational guidelines. Part of the financial framework was an employee-paid fee of $25 per month that is deducted from paycheques. The success of the endeavour—where 25% of the employees were participating after only 10 months encouraged Aviva to coordinate similar offerings at its other Canadian worksites.

Visa Canada for a number of years has provided a fitness-subsidy program to its employees that work in downtown Toronto. It has paid gym membership fees up to a maximum of $500 per year. To better reflect the company's commitment to employee wellness, it redesigned this subsidy to a "health and wellness allowance," which now includes reimbursement for such expenses as home fitness equipment, vitamins, and expenses related to recreational sports and activities. Since this change, there has been a 10% increase in employee participation.

Overall, studies of wellness programs document an ROI of 300–500%, or $3–$5 for every dollar spent. Organizations have indicated that lost time decreases as well as an increase in employee engagement with appropriately designed wellness programs.

CRITICAL THINKING QUESTION

If wellness programs can save a company money, why don't more organizations have them? Explain your answer.

Sources: Shannon Klie, "Employers Aren't Analyzing Health Risks," *Canadian HR Reporter,* November 20, 2006, www.hrreporter.com/ArticleView.aspx?l=1&articleid=4837 (accessed February 27, 2009); Sue Pridham, "Whipping Workplace Fitness Into Shape," *Canadian HR Reporter,* June 4, 2007, www.hrreporter.com/ArticleView.aspx?l=1&articleid=5222 (accessed February 27, 2009); and "Wellness Programs Benefit From Management Support," *Workforce Management,* January 12, 2009.

approach that combines a strong organizational commitment centred on line supervisors, overseen by expert internal resources, and supported by clinical case management.[44] This means that the focus is also on creating a work environment where employees are wanting to return to work as soon as they are medically able. Part of an effective disability management program includes a graduated-return-to-work where the employee works fewer hours and in some situations, accommodating the employee by having a different shift.[45] Even in difficult economic times, a carefully designed and well-managed program can be effective in getting capable staff back to work while knowing that the employer is interested in their well-being.[46]

Employee Assistance Programs

Employee assistance program (EAP)
Program to provide short-term counselling and referrals to appropriate professionals

EAP Directory
www.eap-sap.com

A broad view of health includes the emotional as well as the physical aspects of one's life. While emotional problems, personal crises, alcoholism, and drug abuse are considered to be personal matters, they become organizational problems when they affect behaviour at work and interfere with job performance. It is estimated that psychological problems, including depression, anxiety, and stress, in the workplace cost Canadian companies approximately $35 billion each year.[47] **Employee assistance programs (EAPs)** can provide a useful way to deal with problems, such as stress and depression, which could lead to more serious mental health problems. Supervisors are often given training and policy guidance in the type of help they can offer their subordinates. To be able to handle such problems, organizations such as Purolator in Mississauga and Chrysler Canada offer an employee assistance program.[48] Figure 8.5 outlines the types of EAP services offered to employees in Canada. While many companies do not offer programs due to concerns over the cost/benefits of such initiatives research has shown that 80% of mental health problems can be successfully treated with early detection and treatment.

For additional information on EAP service providers, access **www.eap-sap.com**.

FIGURE 8.5   Employee Assistance Programs

Listed below are some of the usual services in EAPs

- personal issues
- job stress
- relationship issues
- eldercare, childcare, parenting issues
- harassment
- substance abuse
- separation and loss
- balancing work and family
- financial or legal
- family violence

In addition, and depending on the wishes of the company, there may also be services on smoking cessation, counselling for crisis situations, and specific advice to managers/supervisors dealing with difficult situations.

Source: Employee Assistance Programs, Canadian Centre for Occupational Health and Safety, www.ccohs.ca/oshanswers/hsprograms/eap.html (accessed February 27, 2009).

Personal Crises

The most prevalent problems among employees are personal crises involving marital, family, financial, or legal matters. Such problems often come to a supervisor's attention. In most instances, the supervisor can usually provide the best help simply by being understanding and supportive and by helping the individual find the type of assistance needed. In many cases, the person is referred to the EAP program. Many organizations that have an EAP also have operations and offices that are in many different locations yet want to use the same EAP provider. Therefore, in recent years, many EAP providers have offered 24/7 telephone access to bilingual expert counsellors, telephonic counselling sessions, and online assistance.[49]

Emotional Problems

Mental health claims are the fastest-growing reason for days lost to disability.[50] People have emotional upsets from time-to-time and this is quite normal. While personal crises are typically fraught with emotion, most of them are resolved in a reasonable period of time, and the troubled individual's life reaches balance. There will, however, be a small percentage of employees—roughly 3% on average—who have emotional problems serious enough to require professional treatment. However, depression and other forms of mental illness are rising. It is estimated that more than 35 million workdays in Canada are lost each year due to mental illness.[51] Depression alone is responsible for 30% to 40% of disability claims.[52] However, approximately 79% of employees will attempt to hide the fact that they are suffering from depression for fear of hurting potential career advances.[53] Whether such individuals will be able to perform their jobs must be determined on an individual basis. In reviewing such cases, the organization should pay particular attention to workplace safety factors, since there is general agreement that emotional disturbances are primary or secondary factors in a large proportion of industrial accidents and violence.

Substance Abuse

Business and industry lose billions each year because of substance abuse. According to the most recent study by the Canadian Centre on Substance Abuse, the total cost is close to $40 billion on a yearly basis, or $1,267 for every Canadian. In addition, legal substances such as tobacco and alcohol account for 80% of the abuse. Specifically, the following losses occur:

- $14.6 billion from alcohol abuse
- $8.2 billion from illicit drugs
- $17 billion from tobacco[54]

In confronting the problem, employers must recognize that substance abuse is now considered a disease that follows a rather predictable course. Thus, they can take specific actions to deal with employees showing symptoms of the disease at particular stages of its progression. Substance abuse typically begins with social drinking or drug taking that gets out of control. As the disease progresses, the person loses control over how much to use and when to use. The person uses denial to avoid facing the problems created by the substance abuse and often blames others for these problems. The first step in helping the substance abuser is to awaken the person to the reality of the situation.

To identify substance abuse as early as possible, it is essential that supervisors monitor the performance, attendance, and behaviour of all employees regularly and systematically. A supervisor should carefully document evidence of declining performance, behaviour, and/or attendance and then bring the matter to the attention of the employee with evidence that the individual's work is suffering. The employee should be assured that help will be made available without penalty. In fact, through decisions of the court concerning substance abuse, the courts have confirmed that substance abuse is a disability, and employers are legally obliged to deal with the problem. This means that the employer can no longer terminate a person's employment simply because they have an abuse problem. Specifically, a supervisor needs to set clear expectations, be consistent, act, and follow any other health and safety regulations. Since the assessments are made solely with regard to poor job performance, attendance, or behaviour, a supervisor can avoid any mention of the abuse and allow such employees to seek aid as they would for any other problem. A supervisor cannot discipline an employee because a person is suspected of abusing a substance: discipline is dependent on the degree of problem with job performance, attendance, or behaviour. Between 70 and 80% of employees accept the offer to get help and resolve their problems. Therefore, it is important for supervisors and managers to recognize that any discipline, whether it is a verbal warning or a termination, has to be related to the job. Further, as mentioned in previous chapters, there are many constraints on employers to legally test to see if an employee is using any substance that might impair the work performance.

Job-Related Stress

Outcome 6

Stress
Any adjustive demand caused by physical, mental, or emotional factors that requires coping behaviour

Many people use EAPs to help them deal with **stress**. But what is stress? People frequently talk about being stressed at work, yet they are often unable to explain what they mean. Stress is simply any demand on the physical or emotional self that requires a person to cope with that demand. For example, while running five kilometres an individual may become short-winded after three kilometres. Thus the body is "stressed" as the individual deals with being short of breath. Likewise, a student may have just received a special award at school and be excited about the recognition. Again, the student has to cope with this. Stress can be either positive or negative, and each person handles stress differently.

Causes of workplace stress are many; however, high workloads, excessive job pressures, precarious employment, such as temporary or part-time, and concerns about level of income are identified as the primary causes of employee stress.[55] Additionally, disagreements with managers or fellow employees are a common cause of stress, along with little or no say about how a job is performed, lack of communication on the job, and lack of recognition for a job well done. Even minor irritations, such as lack of privacy, unappealing music, excessive noise, or other conditions, can be stressful to one person or another. Whatever the causes of workplace stress, the condition is now costing the Canadian economy more than $33 billion annually in lost productivity and billions more in health-care costs.[56]

Burnout is the most severe stage of distress. Career burnout generally occurs when a person begins questioning his or her own personal values. Quite simply, one no longer feels that what he or she is doing is important. Depression, frustration, and a loss of productivity are all symptoms of burnout. Burnout is due primarily to a lack of personal fulfillment in the job or a lack of positive feedback about performance. In organizations that have downsized, remaining employees can experience burnout since they must perform more work with fewer co-workers.

And burnout isn't just a phenomenon of more established workers. Young people can experience burnout when their high expectations about their work don't match the work or the organization that they're in.[57]

Coping with organizational stress begins by having managers recognize the universal symptoms of work stress as well as the stressful situations particular to their work unit. Major stressors include the following:

- Long hours of work.
- Accessibility during off hours (either through pagers or cellphones).
- Lack of resources.
- Organizational changes.
- Inability to balance work-life demands.
- Poor communication.[58]

Many employers have developed stress management programs to teach employees how to minimize the negative effects of job-related stress. A typical program might include instruction in relaxation techniques, coping skills, listening skills, methods of dealing with difficult people, time management, and assertiveness. Organizational techniques, such as flexible work hours, learning opportunities, and regular feedback on job performance, should not be overlooked in the process of teaching employees how to handle stress.[59]

Even though the number and severity of organizational stressors can be reduced, everyone encounters situations that may be described as distressful. Those in good physical health are generally better able to cope with the stressors they encounter. Figure 8.6 describes several ways to reduce job-related stress.

Before concluding this discussion, we should observe that stress that is harmful to some employees may be healthy for others. Most managers learn to handle distress effectively and find that it actually stimulates better performance. However, there will always be those who are unable to handle stress and need assistance in learning to cope with it. The increased interest of young and old alike in developing habits that will enable them to lead happier and more productive lives will undoubtedly be beneficial to them as individuals, to the organizations where they work, and to a society where people are becoming more and more interdependent. Progressive companies such as Telus, Canada Post, and Dofasco are also discovering that other interventions, such as rewarding employees for exhibiting appropriate behaviours, encouraging employees to be innovative, and taking a holistic approach to wellness is also reducing stressors for employees.[60] Further, organizations that focus on having an engaged workforce (as discussed in Chapter 3) have shown a direct correlation between engagement and reduced stress.[61] Overall employee well-being and health is more likely in organizations with highly engaged staff. Therefore, there is additional rationale to ensure work stressors are kept to a minimum.

Consider Emerging Trends 8.1 for information about what is on the horizon for workplace health and safety.

FIGURE 8.6 Tips for Reducing Job-Related Stress

- Build rewarding relationships with co-workers.
- Talk openly with managers or employees about job or personal concerns.
- Prepare for the future by keeping abreast of likely changes in job demands.
- Don't greatly exceed your skills and abilities.
- Set realistic deadlines; negotiate reasonable deadlines with managers.
- Act now on problems or concerns of importance.
- Designate dedicated work periods during which time interruptions are avoided.
- When feeling stressed, find time for detachment or relaxation.
- Don't let trivial items take on importance: handle them quickly or assign them to others.
- Take short breaks from your work area as a change of pace.

EMERGING TRENDS **8.1**

1. ***Enhanced EAP services.*** With the economic upheaval, more employees have had higher levels of anxiety. To help employees through these difficult times, EAP services have expanded to include financial counselling as well as services dealing with bankruptcy and divorce.

2. ***Increased fines for workplace health/safety infractions.*** With the increase in fatalities in the workplace, the various workers' compensation boards are increasing penalties. For example, EnCana Corp. was fined $150,000 for the death of a tree faller. The total penalties in B.C. for 2008 were more than $2.7 million.

3. ***Dealing with "presenteeism."*** In many situations, employees who are ill still come to work, creating a situation where the person is present but not very productive or engaged. Sometimes employees do this because they have irrational expectations of themselves or in some workplaces, such as education and health care, there are not enough people to do the work. However, employers are now realizing that an unwell employee is not only unproductive but could possibly spread the illness to healthy workers. As a result, employers are supporting employees to stay home and take care of themselves.

4. ***Understanding role of literacy for health and safety in the workplace.*** Through a number of studies it has been demonstrated that there is strong link between workplace literacy and good health and safety. By investing in building literacy skills in the workplace, organizations can raise health and safety standards and ensure that they are maintained.

5. ***Ensuring harassment and bullying are not present in the work environment.*** Although harassment and bullying were discussed in Chapter 2 in relation to human rights legislation, many organizations consider these elements as a form of workplace violence and are taking more proactive steps to eliminate them from the work environment. Recent research has indicated that in North America, bullying is more harmful in the workplace than harassment.

Sources: Tavia Grant, "High Anxiety, Low Productivity," *The Globe and Mail,* February 27, 2009, B16; Marke Andrews, "Safety Agency Fines EnCana $150,000 Over Death," *The Vancouver Sun,* February 6, 2009, D3; Caitlin Crawshaw, "Under the Weather? Better to Stay in Bed," *The Vancouver Sun,* January 10, 2009, I1; Alison Campbell, *All Signs Point to Yes: Literacy's Impact on Workplace Health and Safety,* The Conference Board of Canada, 2008; and "Bullying More Harmful than Sexual Harassment On the Job, Say Researchers," APA Online, March 8, 2008, www.apa.org/releases/bullying0308.html (accessed June 18, 2009).

SUMMARY

1. Describe what supervisors and managers can do to create a safe and healthy work environment.
   - Become familiar with the occupational health and safety legislation governing their operation.
   - Enforce health and safety standards throughout the organization.
   - Protect employees from physical hazards, unhealthy conditions, and unsafe acts of other employees.

2. Cite the measures that should be taken to control and eliminate health and safety hazards.
   - Take every reasonable precaution to ensure employee safety.
   - Inform and train employees about safety and health requirements in the organization.
   - Keep records and investigate any accidents.
   - Involve employees in identifying and eliminating health and safety problems.
   - Provide safety training programs and emphasize the importance of health and safety in the workplace.
   - Enforce safety procedures.

3. List the current workplace health and safety issues.
   - Indoor air quality, including second-hand smoke.
   - Cumulative trauma disorders.
   - Communicable diseases.
   - Workplace violence.

4. Describe the organizational services and programs for building better health.
   - Wellness programs that emphasize regular exercise, proper nutrition, weight control, and avoidance of substances harmful to health.
   - Employee assistance programs.
   - Programs that deal with substance abuse.
   - Stress management programs.

5. Explain the role of employee assistance programs.
   - Organizations recognize that personal problems can create organizational problems.
   - EAPs provide employees in need with appropriate resources.
   - EAPs typically cover financial, family, and emotional issues.

6. Explain the impact of substance abuse and stress in the workplace.
   - Results in lost productivity.
   - Creates safety and health issues.
   - Increases costs of disability.
   - Creates social costs in the health-care system.

NEED TO KNOW

- Definition of WHMIS
- Types of health and safety concerns and issues in the workplace, such as air quality, technology
- Definition of employee assistance programs and what they handle

NEED TO UNDERSTAND

- Role of legislation in occupational health and safety
- Duties and responsibilities of employer, supervisor, and employee regarding health and safety
- Role supervisor plays in creating a healthy and safe work environment
- Prevention and control of workplace violence
- Role supervisor can play in preventing burnout

KEY TERMS

cumulative trauma disorders 251

disability management 257

employee assistance program (EAP) 258

industrial disease 243

Material Safety Data Sheet (MSDS) 249

occupational illness 236

occupational injury 236

stress 260

REVIEW QUESTIONS

1. List the primary duties and responsibilities in relation to health and safety for each of the following:
   employers
   workers
   supervisors
2. What is the purpose of workers' compensation legislation?
3. What can employers do to reduce the cost of workers' compensation?
4. Identify some specific ways that an employer can create a safe work environment.
5. List the warning signs of violence in the workplace.
6. Explain the purpose of an employee assistance program and list some of the problems handled.
7. What is stress and what are the specific causes of workplace stress?

CRITICAL THINKING QUESTIONS

1. An unhealthy work environment can lower productivity, contribute to low morale, and increase medical and workers' compensation costs. Working individually or in teams, list specific ways managers can
   a. Improve indoor air quality.
   b. Reduce the harmful effects of technology.
   c. Reduce risks of violence in the workplace.
   d. Accommodate the desires of smokers and nonsmokers.
2. You've just been hired by ABC Auto Parts as a management trainee. Part of your responsibilities includes introducing a "Safety First" mindset. How would you approach this task and what elements would you want in the mindset?
3. Samir has recently joined a well-known retail clothing store in his community. On his first full shift he noticed a number of safety and health violations. What advice would you give him and why?
4. You work in the medical equipment and pharmaceutical department at a local hospital. Your department is responsible for dispensing medical supplies and prescriptions to patients. There have been some recent incidents in which patients have been quite vocal and threatening in their behaviour toward staff. As a consequence, you and four other staff have been appointed to a task group to undertake a workplace violence audit and then develop appropriate procedures. What steps could you take to do the audit and what might be some of the procedures you could use to minimize the possibility of workplace violence?

DEVELOPING YOUR SKILLS

1. Working in pairs, identify health and safety concerns at your school or work. Suggest ways in which these concerns could be addressed and how you would go about solving them. Share your responses with the rest of the class.
2. Access your provincial workers' compensation website. Identify five companies that violated health and safety regulations in your province. Prepare a one- to two-page summary describing the losses to the organizations in work (hours) and the dollar penalties.
3. Individually, think about a situation where employees follow the safety rules when the supervisor is watching yet violate the rules when the supervisor isn't watching. How would you motivate these employees to follow the rules when the supervisor isn't there? In groups of four to five students, develop a plan to improve safety under these conditions. Share your information with the rest of the class and identify any common approaches.
4. Access the following websites:
   - **www.safety-council.org** (Canada Safety Council)
   - **www.ccohs.ca** (Canadian Centre for Occupational Health and Safety)
   - **www.awcbc.org** (Association of Workers' Compensation Boards of Canada)
   Compare the home page of each site. If you were an employee and needed information, which home page would appear to meet that need? If you were a supervisor? Select the one topic that is the same from each site. Compare the information from the supervisor's perspective. Which information is similar? Which information is different? Prepare a one- to two-page report outlining the similarities and differences.
5. Many of the concerns with workplace health and safety focuses on the lack of experience of young workers. As a result several workers' compensation boards have created special websites to provide information and resources for young workers. Access the following sites:
   www2.worksafebc.com/Topics/YoungWorker/Home.asp (WorkSafeBC)
   www.youngworker.ca/en/ (WSIB Ontario)
   Explore each site. Compare the information (including how presented) at each. Which of these sites are more appealing to young people? Why? Prepare a one- to two-page report explaining which site you would use and why.

Canada Safety Council
www.safety-council.org

Canadian Centre for Occupational Health and Safety
www.ccohs.ca

Association of Workers' Compensation Boards of Canada
www.awcbc.org

Case Study 1

UPS: Empowering Employees to Be Safe

Confronted with unacceptably high injury rates, UPS Inc. took a chance and flipped its traditional top-down management approach to a ground-up safety program fashioned by drivers and parcel handlers. It worked.

Today, injury rates among the company's 327,600 employees are tumbling, turnover is down, and UPS reports that company-wide attitudes toward safety have improved significantly. Committees of drivers and parcel handlers have broad powers to design and implement safety strategies under a company-wide initiative called the Comprehensive Health and Safety Process.

Keith Jones, director of health and safety for UPS, says the goal of the CHSP program was to make safety a personal value of every UPS employee. "We challenged our employees," Jones says. "They rose to the occasion."

When the program began, UPS workers were reporting injuries—mostly sprains and strains—at a rate of 27.2 injuries per 200,000 hours worked. By the end of 2004, UPS got the injury rate down to 10.2 for every 200,000 hours worked and by 2007, the company wants the injury rate down to 3.2.

The company's 2400 CHSP committees are driving the improved numbers. Each group has at least five members, composed of both management and non-management employees. The committees investigate accidents, conduct facility and equipment audits, counsel employees on how they can perform their jobs more safely, and make a full report on every accident.

Activities like loading and unloading packages and getting into and out of trucks seem like fairly straightforward jobs. But UPS' safety program breaks down the mechanics of such things as bending the knees properly when picking up a parcel or backing up a delivery truck. Then it empowers safety committee members to make sure the jobs are done the right way.

Non-management employees on the safety committees are schooled in health and safety issues such as eating properly, stretching, and getting enough rest. One manual alone has a checklist of 60 safety items. If committee members see someone engaged in an unsafe activity, such as bending from the waist rather than the knees, they are required to approach the employee immediately or face a reprimand themselves. Initially, management was reluctant to give up the reins. "We are talking about 90 years of culture," Jones says. "It was really a challenge for us culturally to give up some of our authority to non-management folks."

At the same time, workers on the loading docks wondered whether the non-management safety committee members, with their distinctive T-shirts, were representatives of management. Committee members say they are now widely accepted, even among workers who have to be retrained in the proper way to do a job.

Source: Douglas P. Shuit, "A Left Turn for Safety," *Workforce Management* 84, no. 3 (March 1, 2005): 49. Reprinted by permission.

Questions

1. Why was it a good idea for UPS to put its employees in charge of their own safety?
2. Should all companies make employees responsible for their own safety? What drawbacks do you see to such a plan?
3. Do you think UPS could empower its employees to improve their performance in other areas of the business? What might those areas be?

Case Study 2

Safety Concerns at Majestic Hotel

Majestic Hotel has received many awards for its customer service approach. It has over 5000 people staying at its hotel every year. Part of the success of the hotel has been its focus on training its staff to provide an exceptional experience for the hotel guest.

Recently the hotel general manager has noticed an increase in the number of reported accidents and workplace injuries. A hotel worker was so concerned about the number of back injuries and wrist strains that the worker contacted the local WCB officer and asked that there be a safety audit. However, the audit did not uncover anything unusual for the hotel industry.

Majestic Hotel has the following Health and Safety Policy:

Majestic Hotel is committed to the prevention of illness and injury through the creation of a healthy and safe work environment. The hotel endeavours to provide an environment that promotes health and safety practices that go beyond the minimum required by law. The hotel expects that health and safety, of both employees and guests, is primary in every area of operation.

New employees receive training on how to do their work safely with a special emphasis on lifting, carrying, and using items such as sheets and trash cans. Employees also receive reminders about safe work practices at monthly staff meetings. As new methods are identified to minimize the physical impact of the work, all employees receive training. To do anything more would mean more dollar resources than are currently allocated for all health and safety initiatives.

Last week the general manager received notification from the provincial agency that the hotel's workers' compensation premiums would be increased in the following calendar year as a result of the increased claims.

Questions

1. Why might the accident and injury claims be increasing?
2. By law, workplace safety is the responsibility of the employer and employee. What else can Majestic Hotel do to ensure that employees are doing their work in a safe and healthy way?
3. Develop a new health and safety approach that will improve the hotel's safety and health performance.
4. Suggest some ergonomic solutions, even at a cost, that might be considered.

NOTES AND REFERENCES

1. "Quebec Employer First to be Criminally Convicted in Death of Worker," *Canadian HR Reporter*, February 7, 2008, www.hrreporter.com/ArticleView.aspx?l=1&articleid=5814 (accessed February 25, 2009).
2. "Key Statistical Measures for 2007," Association of Workers' Compensation Boards of Canada; "Number of Accepted Time-loss Injuries, by Age and Jurisdiction, 2005–2007," Association of Workers' Compensation Boards of Canada; "Number of Accepted Time-loss Injuries, by Jurisdiction, 1982–2007," Association of Workers' Compensation Boards of Canada.
3. National Union of Public and General Employees, "NUPGE Poster Marks Day of Mourning for Canadian Workers," www.nupge.ca/news_2007/n11ap07c.htm (accessed February 28, 2009).
4. "Your Health and Safety Rights and Responsibilities," Workplace Safety and Insurance Board, www.wsib.on.ca/wsib/wsibsite.nsf/public/PreventionYHSRR#Worker (accessed February 25, 2009).
5. "Workers Compensation Act (British Columbia)," www.bclaws.ca/Recon/document/freesideW-/Workers Compensation Act RSBC 1996 c. 492/00_Act/96492_03.xml#part3_division4 (accessed February 25, 2009).
6. "Quarter-Million-Dollar Fine in Death," *OHS Canada*, www.ohscanada.com/web-exclusive/2009/01/quarter-million-dollar-fine-in-death.asp (accessed February 25, 2009).
7. "Two Companies Fined for Repeat Violations," *OHS Canada*, www.ohscanada.com/web-exclusive/2009/01/two-companies-fined-for-repeat-violations.asp (accessed February 25, 2009).
8. "Separate Incidents Bring $85,000 in Fines," *OHS Canada*, www.ohscanada.com/web-exclusive/2009/01/separate-incidents-bring-85000-in-fines.asp (accessed February 25, 2009).
9. Danielle Harder, "'Corporate killing' law scrutinized," *Canadian HR Reporter*, April 21, 2008, www.hrreporter.com/ArticleView.aspx?l=1&articleid=6014 (accessed February 26, 2009).
10. R-L Franche, C. Severin, S Hogg-Johnson, P Cote, M Vidmar, and H Lee, "Two Key Strategies are Critical for Return-to-Work Programs," *Journal of Occupational and Environmental Medicine* 49, no.9 (2007 September): 960–974; Institute for Work and Health, www.iwh.on.ca/highlights/two-key-strategies-are-critical-to-return-to-work-programs (accessed February 26, 2009).
11. "Key Statistical Measures for 2007," Association of Workers' Compensation Boards of Canada.
12. Trefor Munn-Venn and Bjorn Rutten, "From Commitment to Action: How CEOs Can Transform Health and Safety, The Conference Board of Canada, November 2008.
13. Trefor Munn-Venn and Bjorn Rutten, "Workforce Renewal: New Opportunities to Transform Health and Safety Culture, The Conference Board of Canada, July 2008.
14. Carola Hicks, "Due Diligence Competency," *Monthly News e-Letter*, Workplace Safety Group, June 2008.
15. "Basic OH & S Program Elements," Canadian Centre Occupational Health and Safety, www.ccohs.ca/oshanswers/hsprograms/basic.html (accessed February 26, 2009).
16. "Petroleum Industry Embraces Technology 'Just in Time' for Training and Recruitment," March 2, 2006.

17. "Innovation Reaps Rewards," *Canadian HR Reporter,* December 4, 2007, www.hrreporter.com/ArticleView.aspx?l=1&articleid=5684 (accessed February 26, 2009).

18. Ibid.

19. David Hamilton, "Safety First Pays Off," *National Post,* May 7, 2008, FP9.

20. Andy Shaw, "Slow Evolution from WHMIS to GHS," *Canadian HR Reporter,* March 10, 2008, 11.

21. Todd Humber, "Snuffing Out Smoking," *Canadian HR Reporter,* April 11, 2005, 19.

22. Laurie Harada and Mario Longo, "Protecting Workers from Deadly Allergies," *Canadian HR Reporter,* June 5, 2006, www.hrreporter.com/ArticleView.aspx?l=1&articleid=4495 (accessed February 26, 2009).

23. Sun Media, "Experts Debate Why Workplace Cases of RSI have Plummeted Since They Reached Epidemic Proportions," *North American Occupational Safety and Health Weekly,* May 1, 2008, 1.

24. Helen McRobbie, "Applying Ergonomics to Reduce Repetitive Strain Injuries," Occupational Health Clinics for Ontario Workers Inc., February 28, 2006.

25. "Prevent Musculoskeletal Disorders (MSD)," WSIB Ontario, www.wsib.on.ca/wsib/wsibsite.nsf/Public/PreventMSD (accessed February 26, 2009).

26. Presentation by Michael T. Kelly and Kasey Reese to the HRMA Leadership Forum, September 26, 2006.

27. Uyen Vu, "Right to Refuse Dangerous Work Expands," *Canadian HR Reporter*, August 9, 2004, 1.

28. "Working Without Cuffs Unsafe: Guards," *Canadian HR Reporter*, August 9, 2004, 2.

29. Canadian Centre for Occupational Health and Safety, www.ccohs.ca (accessed February 26, 2009).

30. Ibid.

31. Sarah Dobson, "Sexual Assault Prompts OHS Charge," *Canadian HR Reporter,* December 15, 2008, 1.

32. Canadian Centre for Occupational Health and Safety, www.ccohs.ca (accessed February 26, 2009).

33. Alex Elson, "Security in an Insecure World," *Canadian HR Reporter,* January 29, 2007, www.hrreporter.com/ArticleView.aspx?l=1&articleid=4961 (accessed February 27, 2009).

34. Sarah Dobson, "Tackling Domestic Violence at Work," *Canadian HR Reporter,* December 1, 2008, www.hrreporter.com/ArticleView.aspx?l=1&articleid=6523 (accessed February 27, 2009).

35. "Crisis Management," DestinEducation, www.destineducation.ca/health-safety/4-3_e.htm (accessed February 27, 2009).

36. RBC, "Corporate Responsibility—Governance and Ethics—Business and Crisis Management," www.rbc.com/responsibility/governance/crisis.html (accessed February 27, 2009).

37. "Common Responses to Stress During a Community Crisis," Waterloo Region, Pandemic Influenza Planning (accessed February 27, 2009).

38. Dan Eisner, "Workplace Wellbeing: The Path to Enhance Productivity," Workshop presented by Towers Perrin, February 19, 2009.

39. Anthea Zacharatos and Julian Barling, "High-Performance Work Systems and Occupational Safety," *Journal of Applied Psychology* 90, no. 1 (2005): 77–93.

40. "Wellness for a Healthy Bottom Line," *Canadian Business,* January 17–30, 2005.

41. Ibid.

42. Antonio Zivanovic, "Wellness Offers ROI in Tight Times," *Peopletalk,* Summer 2009, 21.

43. Anthony Pizzino, "Show Us the Link to OH&S," *Canadian HR Reporter,* May 9, 2005, 8.

44. "Disability Case Management," BC Public Service, www.bcpublicservice.ca/dismgmt/ (accessed June 18, 2009).

45. Hugh Secord, "Easing a Worker Back on the Job," *Canadian HR Reporter,* February 5, 2009, www.hrreporter.com/ArticleView.aspx?l=1&articleid=6664 (accessed June 18, 2009).

46. Mike Schwartz, "Return to Work in Progress," *Benefits Canada,* March 1, 2009, www.benefitscanada.com/benefit/disability/article.jsp?content=20090323_174547_7024 (accessed June 18, 2009).

47. Jean-Pierre Brun, "Assessing the Costs of Work Stress," January 2006, 3.

48. Shannon Klie, "Don't Play Psychologist," *Canadian HR Reporter,* August 13, 2007, 11.

49. "Employee Assistance," Ceridian Canada, www.ceridian.ca (accessed February 27, 2009).

50. John Morrissy, "Study Finds Stress, Depression on Rise Among Canadian Workers," *The Vancouver Sun,* May 2, 2008, H2.

51. Helen Morris, "Mental Illness Cited as Significant Cost to Employers," *The Vancouver Sun,* July 16, 2008, C7.

52. Lesley Young, "Employers Help Fight Depression," *Canadian HR Reporter,* October 22, 2007, 1.

53. Ibid.

54. "The Costs of Substance Abuse in Canada," Canadian Centre on Substance Abuse, www.ccsa.ca/Eng/Priorities/Research/CostStudy/Pages/default.aspx (accessed February 27, 2009).

55. "Is Your Job Making You Sick?" *Canadian HR Reporter,* September 17, 2008, www.hrreporter.com/ArticleView.aspx?l=1&articleid=6339 (accessed February 27, 2009); and "Low Income Leads to Anxiety and Depression: StatsCan," *Canadian HR Reporter,* January 22, 2009, www.hrreporter.com/ArticleView.aspx?l=1&articleid=6644 (accessed February 27, 2009).

56. Ken MacQueen, Martin Patriquinn, and John Intini, "Workplace Stress Costs the Economy Billions," *Maclean's Magazine,* October 15, 2007.

57. Caitlin Crawshaw, "Burnout: A Disconnect Between Expectations and Reality of the Job," Canwest News Service, January 27, 2008.

58. Karen Pallarito, "Employers Take Steps to Relieve Workers' Stress," *Workforce Management,* August 5, 2008, www.workforce.com/archive/feature/25/69/08/index.php?ht= (accessed February 27, 2009).

59. Katy Kamkar, "High Cost of Anxiety," *Canadian HR Reporter,* December 15, 2008, www.hrreporter.com/ArticleView.aspx?l=1&articleid=6575 (accessed February 27, 2009).

60. 2006 Business and Economic Plan for Mental Health and Productivity, Global Business and Economic Roundtable on Addiction and Mental Health.

61. Sarah Dobson, "Higher Engagement Equals Better Health: Study," *Canadian HR Reporter,* April 6, 2009, 3.

CHAPTER

9

MANAGEMENT RIGHTS, EMPLOYEE RIGHTS, AND DISCIPLINE

OUTCOMES

After studying this chapter, you should be able to

1 Explain statutory rights, contractual rights, due process, and legal implications of those rights.

2 Identify the job expectancy rights of employees.

3 Explain the process of establishing disciplinary practices, including the proper implementation of organizational rules.

4 Discuss the meaning of discipline and how to investigate a disciplinary problem.

5 Explain the differences between progressive and positive discipline.

6 Identify the different types of alternative dispute-resolution procedures.

7 Discuss the role of ethics in the management of human resources.

OUTLINE

HRM CLOSE-UP

"We discuss the new policy or procedure and we get input from staff as well. This gives us good buy-in and prevents issues from arising down the road."

For warehouse supervisor Mike Brooks, the most important right his employees have is the right to refuse work that is unsafe. "I want to make sure everyone goes home safely at night," he says. "We take a lot of pride in the safety of our warehouse and my staff knows that I want them to come to me with any issues they have."

Brooks has responsibility for all shipping, receiving, fulfillment, and inventory control at Amway Global's Canadian distribution warehouse. His team is small but mighty. Together they load, unload, lift, stack, pack, and ship thousands of items daily for one of the world's largest direct-selling organizations.

Working at Amway in the summer during high school and college, Brooks worked his way up from an entry-level loader, to receiver, team leader to his current position as supervisor. With his first-hand knowledge of many of the jobs he now supervises, he has an excellent rapport with staff and feels they work well as a team. "They know my role and responsibilities and I know theirs," he says, "This gives us mutual respect and allows us all to get the job done."

Each employee has a handbook describing company policies and procedures. The information is duplicated on the company's intranet site where standard operating procedures are there for all to view. Brooks has department-specific operating procedures and when new procedures are introduced, communication is done face-to-face.

"We discuss the new policy or procedure and we get input from staff as well," explains Brooks. "This gives us good buy-in and prevents issues from arising down the road." After five business days, employees sign a document saying that they have read and that they understand the new policy or procedure. Then, annually, operating procedures are reviewed during team meetings.

The company recently implemented a new procedure related to heat stress. The warehouse environment is not climate-controlled and management wanted to protect workers from the ill effects of high heat and humidity. "We bring in fluids like water and provide heat breaks," says Brooks. "We also monitor workloads so that when we have a particularly heavy volume in the warehouse, these precautions kick in even before the heat reaches our guideline levels."

Mike Brooks, supervisor, Amway Global. Courtesy of Mike Brooks.

In the area of employee discipline, it's ironic that many correction actions taken are around safety issues—violations of policies and procedures that are in place to ensure a worker's safety. If this happens, Amway has a corrective action program that begins with a verbal discussion. "If I have to discuss something with an employee, it usually ends there," says Brooks. "Once something is pointed out, the employee considers what has happened and is usually successful at correcting the issue."

If the action isn't corrected, the supervisor has a second meeting with the employee. If the situation escalates, Brooks seeks assistance from human resources and a written formal warning is issued. Following that, suspensions without pay, ranging from one day through to 10 days can be levied on the employee. This can ultimately lead to dismissal, which Brooks says has only happened with very serious issues.

As a supervisor, Brooks aims to understand his employees' skills, abilities and environment so that they can work effectively together. "In the end, we all have a job to do and if it's done right, it's good for customers and good for business."

INTRODUCTION

In this chapter, employee rights, management rights, workplace privacy, and employee discipline are discussed. Managers note that these topics have a major influence on the activities of both employees and supervisors. Managers are discovering that the right to discipline and discharge employees—a traditional responsibility of management—is more difficult to exercise in light of the growing attention to employee rights. In addition, disciplining employees is a difficult and unpleasant task for most managers and supervisors; many of them report that taking disciplinary action against an employee is the most stressful duty they perform. Balancing employee rights and employee discipline may not be easy, but it is a universal requirement and a critical aspect of good management. As Mike Brooks expressed in the HRM Close-Up, the role of the supervisor is to help employees understand their rights as well as the company's expectations.

Because the growth of employee rights issues may lead to an increase in the number of lawsuits filed by employees, this chapter includes a discussion of alternative dispute resolution as a way to foster a less legalistic approach to solving disagreements. As managers are the people who take disciplinary actions that are subject to challenge and possible reversal through governmental agencies or the courts, managers should make a positive effort to prevent the need for such action. Further, managers often avoid difficult performance reviews and thus may create a situation where disciplinary action is considered. When disciplinary action becomes impossible to avoid, however, that action should be taken in accordance with carefully developed HR policies and practices. Since ethics is an important element of good managerial practice, the chapter concludes with a discussion of organizational ethics in employee relations. The vast majority of this chapter applies to both nonunionized and unionized workplaces. Where a concept applies only to a nonunion workplace, this will be identified.

MANAGEMENT RIGHTS AND RESPONSIBILITIES

All companies have people, usually called "managers" that make fundamental decisions such as how the business is run or how much the company should charge for its products or services. In making these decisions, they have both rights and responsibilities. One of the more basic rights is that the company has the right to hire or terminate whomever it wants.

However, as discussed in both this chapter and in Chapter 10, those rights now have to be exercised in certain ways and managers have increased responsibilities in how those rights are exercised. Managers function as the representative of the organization and therefore have the legal responsibilities and liabilities that go with the managerial role. One illustration of this is "negligent hiring." Negligent hiring refers to a situation where a person is hired and then involved in job-related misconduct that could have been determined if the person's previous work background and behaviours were referenced.[1] While any claim would be against the employer, it is the action (or lack of action) of the manager that creates the situation. Think about a situation in a long-term residential care facility where a resident is physically assaulted by an employee who has a long (and verifiable) history of physical violence. Negligent hiring would occur if the manager did not do a thorough enough background check to identify the history or did and still hired the person.

In addition, supervisors and managers are expected to behave and act in ways that acknowledge that employees also have certain rights. Managers are no longer able to make decisions or take actions without being aware of their obligations as to how an employee must be treated in today's workplace.

EMPLOYEE RIGHTS

Various human rights laws, wage and hour regulations, and safety and health legislation have secured basic employee rights and brought numerous job improvements to the workplace. Now employee rights litigation has shifted to such workplace issues as employees' rights to protest unfair disciplinary action, to refuse to take drug tests, to have access to their personnel files, to challenge employer searches and surveillance, and to how much information an employer may acquire on a potential employee.[2] All these things make it very important that managers act and behave in fair and objective ways.

The current emphasis on employee rights is a natural result of the evolution of societal, business, and employee interests. **Employee rights** refers to the expectation of fair treatment from employers in the employment relationship. These expectations become rights when they are granted to employees by the courts, legislatures, or employers. Employee rights frequently involve an employer's alleged invasion of an employee's right to privacy. Unfortunately, the difference between an employee's legal right to privacy and the moral or personal right to privacy is not always clear. The confusion is due to the lack of a comprehensive and consistent body of privacy protection, whether from laws or from court decisions.

There can be perceived invasion of privacy when the employer uses electronic monitoring or surveillance to observe or monitor employees while they are doing their work. Although such action is not illegal, employers are well advised to let employees know when and why they are doing it. For example, companies that have a call-centre operation frequently will use electronic means to monitor customer calls. However, employees are provided full information about the purpose and in some situations given guarantees that the data will be used only to help the employees learn and improve their customer-service skills.

Balanced against employee rights is the employer's responsibility to provide a safe workplace for employees while guaranteeing safe, high-quality goods and services to consumers. An employee who uses drugs may exercise a privacy right and refuse to submit to a drug test. But should that employee produce a faulty product as a result of drug impairment, the employer can be held liable for any harm caused by that product. Employers must therefore exercise *reasonable care* in the hiring, training, and assignment of employees to jobs. As mentioned earlier, without the exercise of reasonable care, employers can be held negligent by outside parties or other employees injured by a dishonest, unfit, or violent employee.[3] In law, **negligence** is the failure to use a reasonable amount of care where such failure results in injury to another person. For example, an Ontario court case dealing with the behaviour of an employee toward children in a residential home determined that the employer was liable for the conduct of the employee and that it had not taken sufficient care in the hiring of a person who had had previous criminal charges of inappropriate behaviours and relationships with children.[4]

It is here that employee rights and employer responsibilities can come most pointedly into conflict. The failure of employers to honour employee rights can result in costly lawsuits, damage the organization's reputation, and hurt employee morale. But failure to protect the safety and welfare of employees or consumer interests can invite litigation from both groups. At Work with HRM 9.1 discusses the practical implications for managers of the balance between employee rights and employer responsibilities. The remainder of this section will discuss various rights employees have come to expect from their employers.

Employee rights
Expectations of fair treatment from employers

Negligence
Failure to provide reasonable care where such failure results in injury to consumers or other employees

---

AT WORK **with HRM 9.1**

EMPLOYEE RIGHTS LITIGATION

For a number of years, two court cases[5] demonstrated the special recognition to the employer–employee relationship given through decisions of the Supreme Court of Canada (SCC). These decisions focused on the fair and individual treatment of each person. This meant that the manager must pay greater attention to the particular individual before, during, and at the conclusion of employment.

One of the cases, *Wallace v. United Grain Growers*, pointed to the need for employers to pay more attention to the way in which people are terminated. Besides compensation for lack of notice, employees were seeking damages if they felt they were poorly treated during the actual termination. This meant that the manager's behaviour during the process could have a bearing on how much the termination would cost the employer.

(Continued)

However, a significant case decided by the SCC in mid-2008 changed this. In *Honda Canada Inc. v. Keays,* the court determined that earlier decisions had been inappropriate. In lower court decisions, the employee had been awarded $100,000 in punitive damages for the manner in which Honda conducted itself in the termination. The employee had been diagnosed with chronic fatigue syndrome resulting in his eventually being placed in Honda's disability program. That program required that employees provide Honda with medical information from the physician that absences were due to the medical condition. What the employee's physician provided was insufficient and Honda requested that the employee meet with an occupational medical specialist—to which he refused. Honda then terminated him. The employee sued for wrongful dismissal stating that Honda had demonstrated bad faith. The court disagreed saying that he had not been treated poorly—either in terms of compensation or behaviour.

This case eliminated a number of principles established through the *Wallace* case, the most significant being that employees were not entitled to additional severance or punitive damages—employees are only entitled to receive compensation for "actual" damages—i.e., loss of wages. But the case maintained that employers must act in good faith when dismissing employees and the employees must be treated respectfully.

In another SCC case, the court again confirmed how far "duty to accommodate" needs to go in relation to absenteeism. The case involved Hydro-Quebec and the termination of an employee who had missed an average of 128 workings days a year for 7 1/2 years. During the court hearings, Hydro-Quebec demonstrated that it had been tolerant, flexible, and willing to try any number of ways to solve the chronic absenteeism before it decided to terminate the employee. Duty to accommodate only required the duty up to "undue hardship" but some court decisions expected the employer to demonstrate that it was impossible to accommodate. Of course, the larger the employer, the more easily (according to the courts) the employer could accommodate the needs of the employee.

These cases have both demonstrated that there needs to be a balance between the employment contract and the expectations an employer can have of an employee, and the needs of the individual employee.

CRITICAL THINKING QUESTIONS

1. Do you believe that employees have too many rights? Why or why not?
2. What would you have decided in these cases and why?

Sources: Kathryn Leger, "Top Court Verdict on Chronic-Absentee Case," *National Post,* Wednesday, August 13, 2008, FP11; Jim Middlemiss, "Court Upholds Honda's Role in Dismissal," *National Post,* June 28, 2008, FP 6; Kirk Makin, "Court Sides with Honda on Chronic Fatigue Firing," *The Globe and Mail*, June 28, 2008, A7; Graeme McFarlane, "Cyber-Sacking and Severance Liability," *PeopleTalk,* Spring 2009, 30–31; and M.J. O'Brien, "Recent Changes in Employment Law," Presentation to BCHRMA Leadership Forum, March 24, 2009.

Employment Protection Rights

It is not surprising that employees should regard their jobs as an established right—a right that should not be taken away lightly. Without the opportunity to hold a job, our personal well-being would be greatly curtailed. This line of reasoning has led to the emergence of three legal considerations regarding the security of one's job: statutory rights, contractual rights, and due process.

Statutory Rights

Outcome 1

Statutory rights
Rights that derive from legislation

Statutory rights are rights that derive from legislation. As we saw in Chapter 2, human rights legislation protects employees from discrimination on the basis of such grounds as age, sex, and race. For example, in Ontario a woman was terminated for making a race-based comment in the workplace. As a social worker, she was a frontline counsellor at a women's shelter. She stated that during her employment she felt harassed by management. She was Caucasian but her bosses were all women-of-colour and she expressed at one point that she was concerned about working only with women-of-colour. Eventually, she was terminated because of alleged discriminatory behaviour. During the court case, the judge determined that while the shelter's zero-tolerance policy was understandable, the termination was thoughtless and ill-conceived. The Ontario Superior Court ordered the employer to pay $30,000 in legal feels as well as approximately $28,000 for severance pay.[6]

Provincial employment standards acts establish basic rights for such things as overtime pay and minimum vacation pay. One of the more interesting cases dealing with statutory rights is the class-action suit against CIBC in relation to unpaid overtime. Specifically in both 2007 and 2008, lawsuits were started where workers claimed that they were expected to work overtime on a regular basis but that the employers were discouraged from reporting or claiming the overtime. And some of the employees were in white-collar jobs such as stock analysts, investment bankers, and financial advisors. The focus of the lawsuit revolves around whether any of the employees were considered exempt from overtime provisions. Specifically, overtime refers to "employees." There are people in certain occupations, such as accountants and engineers that are exempt. Likewise, positions such as "manager" also are exempt. So, if a person isn't a manager or in a profession, then they are entitled to overtime. However, for many years, organizations have considered employees that are paid a salary exempt from overtime. This is not correct according to the law. The lawsuits are claiming close to $1 billion in unpaid overtime.[7] While one class action suit was dismissed in June 2009, it did not rule out the possibility of individuals launching independent cases.[8]

Occupational health and safety legislation attempts to ensure safe and healthy working conditions while labour relations laws (discussed in Chapter 10) give employees the right to form and belong to unions, and to bargain for better working conditions. All these laws are "statutory" and grant certain rights to people.

Contractual Rights

Contractual rights

Rights that derive from contracts

While law establishes statutory rights, **contractual rights** are derived from contracts. A contract is a legally binding agreement; if one party breaches the contract, a remedy can be sought through an appeal to the courts. Although formal contracts between employers and full-time employees are rare, they are standard practice when it comes to contingent workers, a growing segment of the Canadian labour force. Such a contract is referred to as the "employment contract" and will contain such items as the type of work, length of work, the amount of pay for the work, including any benefits, and whether or not there is any obligation on the employer if the employee is terminated.

Not all contracts are written. An implied contract can occur when an employer extends to an employee a promise of some form of job security. Implied contractual rights can be based on either oral or written statements made during the pre-employment process or subsequent to hiring. Promises of job security are sometimes contained in employee handbooks, HR manuals, or employment applications. Whether explicit or implicit, promises of job security are generally ruled by the courts to be binding. A recent case of an employee's contractual rights revolved around an employer's attempt to order an employee to hide a tattoo on the employee's shoulders. The case involved a daycare worker in Quebec who had a dragon tattoo on the shoulder. The employer had not allowed the employee to show the tattoo while at work. This went on for five years before a judge in the Quebec Superior Court ruled that forcing the cover-up violated the employee's rights.[9]

The following are circumstances in which an implied contract may become binding:

- Telling employees their jobs are secure as long as they perform satisfactorily and are loyal to the organization.
- Stating in the employee handbook that employees will not be terminated without the right of defence or access to an appeal procedure (that is, due process).
- Urging an employee to leave another organization by promising higher wages and benefits, and then reneging after the person has been hired.

To lessen their vulnerability to implied-contract lawsuits, employers can do the following:

1. Train supervisors and managers not to imply contract benefits in conversations with new or current employees.
2. Include in employment offers a statement that an employee may voluntarily terminate employment with proper notice, and the employee may be dismissed by the employer at any time and for a justified reason (just cause). The language in this statement must be appropriate, clear, and easily understood while conveying a tone of welcome to the company.

3. Explain the nature of the employment relationship in documents—for example, employee handbooks, employment applications, and letters of employment.
4. Have written proof that employees have read all documents pertaining to the employment relationship. This can be in the form of an offer-of-employment letter that the person signs or another type of sign-off document.

It is important that in a contractual situation employees also have obligations and responsibilities. For example, RBC was successful in an action against a former employee who had helped a competitor recruit staff from a branch where the former employee had been the manager. Specifically, the former employee was ordered to pay $1.5 million to compensate for lost profits. The Supreme Court found that the employees recruited away had breached the implied terms of their employment contracts by not giving reasonable notice. The court indicated that the manager had an implied term in his employment contract with RBC that expected him to retain the employees under his supervision and that encouraging them to leave and join him at another employer was a serious breach.[10]

Due Process

Management has traditionally had the right to direct employees and to take corrective action when needed. Nevertheless, many individuals also believe that a job is the property right of an employee and that the loss of employment has such serious consequences that an employee should not lose their job without the protection of due process. Managers normally define **due process** as the employee's right to a fair treatment in the handling of an employment matter.[11] However, proactive employers will additionally incorporate the following principles—or rights—in their interpretation of due process:

1. The right to know job expectations and the consequences of not fulfilling those expectations.
2. The right to consistent and predictable management action for the violation of rules.
3. The right to fair discipline based on facts, the right to question those facts, and the right to present a defence.
4. The right to appeal disciplinary action.
5. The right to progressive discipline—to be informed about an incident and be given a chance to improve.

Employment Rights Not a Guarantee

It should be understood that although employees might have cause to regard their jobs as an established right, there is no legal protection affording employees a permanent or continuous job. Furthermore, in general, the concept of due process does not guarantee employees any assurance of employment. However, the concepts of due process and of job as a right do obligate management to act in a consistent and fair manner.

Employees *do* have the right to expect sound employment practices and to be treated respectfully as individuals. In Canada, in absence of a formal contract specifying the duration of employment, the employment relationship can be construed as ongoing. While employment is not considered necessarily to be permanent, the employer must provide reasonable notice and grounds for termination. Thus, Canada functions under statutory and common (contract) law.[12]

Outcome 2

Job Expectancy Rights

Once hired, employees expect certain rights associated with fair and equitable employment. Employee rights on the job include those regarding substance abuse and drug testing, privacy, plant closing notification, and just-cause disciplinary and discharge procedures.

Canadian Centre on Substance Abuse

www.ccsa.ca

Substance Abuse and Drug Testing

The social costs, including lost productivity and health-care costs in Canada due to substance abuse have been estimated at $17 billion for alcohol, $14.6 billion for tobacco, and $8.2 billion for illicit drugs. Taken together, all forms of substance abuse account for $39 billion or $1,267 per capita.[13] Most human rights legislation considers substance abuse as a disability and therefore needs to be accommodated.[14]

Due process
Employee's right to a fair process in making a decision related to employment relationship

According to a recent survey by Statistics Canada, 20% of men and 8% of women aged 19 to 70 reported consuming more than two alcoholic drinks per day.[15] The trend in the general population continues to find daily and heavy drinking significantly higher for males than females, that the highest marijuana use levels are in the 18 to 39 age group, and approximately twice as many males are current marijuana users as females. Since illicit drugs are available and increasingly available in high quality throughout Canada, studies are finding cannabis use is up among Canadian adults, and recent student surveys in Ontario find use patterns increasing for most drug categories. Various studies have credited alcohol and other drug use with contributing to increased turnover, accidents, absenteeism, workers' compensation, sick benefits and insurance claims, loss of productivity and human potential, low-quality products and services, theft and trafficking.[16]

As mentioned earlier in this chapter, the failure of an employer to ensure a safe and drug-free workplace can result in astronomical liability claims when consumers are injured because of a negligent employee or faulty product. Because of this, Canadian companies are ensuring that their occupational health and safety programs include policies on alcohol and other drugs.[17] Although the Canadian government has not introduced legislation on drug testing, such legislation exists south of the border. Companies with drug-testing policies report reductions in absenteeism, sick days, and accidents. Some of the issues surrounding drug testing are discussed in At Work with HRM 9.2.

Employee Searches and Electronic Monitoring

Consider these:

- General Electric employs tiny fish-eye lenses installed behind pinholes in walls and ceilings to observe employee suspected of crimes.
- DuPont uses long-distance cameras to monitor its loading docks.
- An Alberta IDA drugstore requires cashiers to place their fingers on a pad that scans their fingerprints and allows them access to the system.

While these examples may seem a violation of privacy rights, it is not uncommon for employers to monitor employee conduct through surveillance techniques. Most retailers use some form of monitoring. Because employees forget passwords, Holt Renfrew, for example, uses the fingerprint scans as protection against others using passwords or cards. Indeed, the scans are now used to track time and attendance.[18]

AT WORK **with HRM 9.2**

WHEN IS DRUG AND/OR ALCOHOL TESTING DISCRIMINATORY?

Many employers express concern about the impact of an employee being impaired at work. The concerns range from loss of productivity to safety for customers and employees. While legislation exists in the United States to allow random and regular drug testing, there is no legislation in Canada that allows this. Further, since most human rights tribunals see drug or alcohol abuse as a disability, any testing for these substances can be a form of discrimination.

So what can an employer do? A recent arbitration case in B.C. may not have clarified that question. The case, *Canadian National Railway Company v. U.S.W.A.*

(Local 2004) 2008, challenged CNR's policy on drug and alcohol testing. Specifically, the employee was involved in a physical altercation that led to the employee being required to undergo a drug test. The outcome of the test was that the employee tested positive for marijuana. Through the follow-up investigation on both the incident and the drug test, CNR determined that the employee had broken its drug and alcohol policy and as a consequence was fired.

The union grieved the termination, staying that the discipline was unjust as the drug test didn't prove that the employee was impaired, only that the employee had

(Continued)

used marijuana in the past and that there were some traces left. CNR argued that the policy didn't allow for any presence of drugs in an employee's system while at work. The arbitrator ruled that a positive drug test is not sufficient in itself to be grounds for termination and CNR was ordered to reinstate the employee with full back wages.

CRITICAL THINKING QUESTIONS

1. Do you think employers ought to have the right to test for drug or alcohol use? Why or why not?
2. Do you agree that drug and/or alcohol abuse ought to be considered a disability? Why or why not?
3. How would you feel if your employer did random drug and alcohol tests? Explain your answer.

Sources: Adapted from Jeffrey R. Smith, "Positive Drug Test Not Cause for Dismissal," *Canadian HR Reporter*, November 3, 2008, 5; and "Drug and Alcohol Dependencies in Alberta Workplaces," Alberta Human Rights and Citizenship Commission Information Sheet, February 2009.

Employees have no reasonable expectation of privacy in places where work rules that provide for inspections have been put into effect. They must comply with probable-cause searches by employers. And they can be appropriately disciplined, normally for insubordination, for refusing to comply with search requests. It is advisable that employers inform new employees through either the final employment interview or an orientation session that mandatory or random searches are done. See Figure 9.1 for the range of employee monitoring practices.

Managers must be diligent when conducting employee searches. Improper searches can lead to employee complaints under various privacy legislations (see Chapter 2) and possible lawsuits claiming defamation of character and negligent infliction of emotional distress.

It is not uncommon for employers to monitor the conduct of employees through surveillance techniques. One of the most common means of electronic surveillance by employers is telephone surveillance to ensure that customer requests are handled properly or to prevent theft. With the Personal Information Protection and Electronic Documents Act (PIPEDA), there is an expectation

FIGURE 9.1   Employee Monitoring Practices

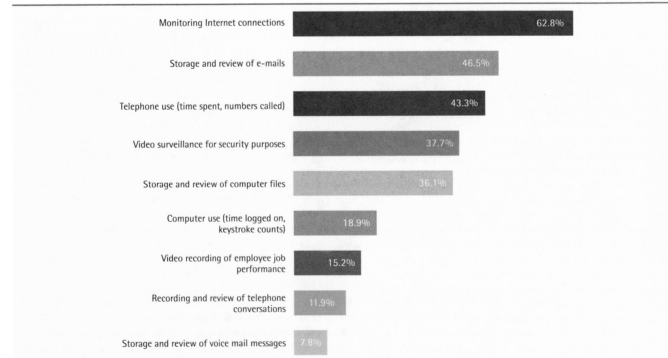

Source: Uyen Vu, "Employee Resistant to Any Form of Computer Video Monitoring, Study Says," *Canadian HR Reporter,* March 8, 2004, 2.

Video monitoring is frequently used in retail operations.

UpperCut Images/Getty Images

that employers are reasonable in their use of any type of surveillance technique. When an employer is considering using surveillance, it is suggested that the employer:[19]

1. Get legal advice as even with good intentions, mistakes can be made.
2. Explain to employees why this is necessary and be sure advance notice is given to employees.
3. Be clear on what type of equipment/instruments will be monitored such as text messages on cellphones.
4. Be consistent in follow-up and follow through.

Employers have the right to monitor employees, and to disclose certain information to another agency. Specifically, the Alberta Information and Privacy Commissioner determined that an employer was able to provide information to the Alberta Drive Fitness and Monitoring Branch relating to an accident the employee had and the employee's ability to drive.[20] As technology continues to change, privacy commissioners are requested to examine the appropriateness of the technology. Recently, the Canadian Privacy Commissioner was asked to consider whether radio frequency identification (RFID) systems used in the workplace for productivity and security enhancements could also be used as a surveillance tool and thus undermine the autonomy and dignity of workers.[21] Ethics in HRM 9.1 highlights some of these issues.

Access to Employee Files

The information kept in an employee's official employment record or employee file can have a significant impact—positive or negative—on career development. The personnel file, typically kept by the HR department, can contain performance reviews, salary information, investigatory reports, credit checks, criminal records, test scores, and family data.

In compliance with legislation, most employers give their employees access to their employment files. There is virtually no organization that is exempt from privacy legislation. PIPEDA also entitles employees to examine their own personnel file—including any information that is stored

ETHICS **in HRM 9.1**

WHEN DOES EMPLOYEE MONITORING BECOME AN INVASION OF PRIVACY?

More and more employers are using a variety of electronic surveillance techniques to monitor employee activities in the workplace—everything from attendance reporting to controlling employee access to certain areas of work. Organizations with off-site assets use GPS (global positioning systems) to monitor the use of company vehicles. And of course, there is the monitoring of a person's profile on any of the social networking websites such as Facebook or LinkedIn. But when does this become an invasion of one's privacy?

The Canadian privacy commissioner investigated the use of a GPS for a company that used the technology to track the location of its vehicles, as well as its dispatch and route employees, to job sites. While the commissioner did accept the company's arguments, the commissioner also cautioned employers and managers about making assumptions about the employees' activities from that type of information. As part of the decision, the commissioner asked the company to clearly explain to the employees how the GPS would be used.

And the concern isn't just about tracking what employees do during work. Companies are also concerned about theft of company property as well as fraud.

It is estimated that as much as 7% of company revenues are lost to some type of internal fraud. Therefore, sophisticated technology can determine the flow of information both internal and external to the organization. And it would seem that during the economic downturn starting in 2007, companies were using surveillance techniques more and more frequently.

Then, of course, there is the issue of companies looking at their employees' profiles and information on social networking sites. Sites such as Facebook have been described as the "virtual water cooler." While many people might not consider a social network site a potential workplace issue, think about these: 1) What if there is defamatory content about the company or customers? 2) What if the content breaches privacy? 3) What about publication of confidential corporate information? and 4) What if the content brings the employer's reputation into disrepute? There have been longstanding legal decisions that say an employee has a duty of loyalty to the employer and therefore a person's "free speech" can be constrained.

Would you work differently if you knew that your performance was continually monitored? Is it ethical for employers to do this?

Sources: Adapted from Dan Fallows "Technology Paves the Way for Big Brother," *Canadian HR Reporter,* April 9, 2007, www.hrreporter.com/ArticleView. aspx?l=1&articleid=5118 (accessed March 2, 2009); Uyen Vu, "Privacy Law Working Well: Commissioner," *Canadian HR Reporter,* December 18, 2006, www.hrreporter.com/ArticleView.aspx?l=1&articleid=4884 (accessed March 2, 2009); 2007 Labour, Employment & Human Rights Seminar, Fasken Martinau, Vancouver, October 26, 2007; Michelle Conlin, "To Catch a Corporate Thief," *Business Week,* February 12, 2009; and "Staff Surveillance at a Tipping Point?" *Computer Weekly,* September 16, 2008, 3.

in an electronic format. In addition, any personal information cannot be used or disclosed without the prior knowledge and consent of the employee. For example, if you are seeking a car loan and the company wants confirmation of your employment, only you can authorize release of that information from your employer. The most important legal principle with regard to data privacy is the concept of consent—ahead of time from the employee. Under PIPEDA, the person must be notified of the following before any information can be provided:

- That he or she is about to provide personal data.
- The purposes for which the information is to be processed.
- The people or bodies to whom the information might be disclosed.
- The proposed transfer of information to other countries.
- The security measures protecting the information.

For example, if there is a need to collect and retain medical information on an employee, it is important for the company to ensure the confidentiality of the information besides just paying attention to the legal requirements.[22]

It is also important to ensure that appropriate items do reside in the employee file. Recently, a Saskatchewan employer terminated the employment of its senior director for not acquiring documentation or placing the documentation in the employee file as directed by its board. The director was terminated for breach of trust and conduct unbefitting a director. The Saskatchewan Provincial Court ruled that while the director had failed to disclose certain information about the new employee, it was not dishonest enough to warrant termination. The courts awarded severance and legal costs.[23] Employment professionals recommend that organizations develop a policy on employee files that includes, as a minimum, the points noted in Manager's Toolkit 9.1.

Electronic Privacy

The benefits of e-mail and voice mail are many: they encourage openness and sharing of information; they diffuse power throughout the organization; and they allow more employees to participate in decision-making.[24] Unfortunately, the growth of management and financial information systems can create privacy problems by making personnel information more accessible to those with prying eyes, or "hackers," who might use the information inappropriately. Messages can be read or heard, and deleted messages can be accessed. Further, without separate software or making use of online resources, there is no way to verify that the "from" is really from the person listed.[25] Further, there is the issue of an employee bad-mouthing co-workers in more public forms, such as blogs. Recently, an Albertan government employee was terminated for calling people names and insulting co-workers on the employee's blog. When the government discovered this, the employee was spoken with about the conduct. The employee was not apologetic and did not see that there was any harm. Through an arbitration board, the termination was upheld and it did confirm that while a person was entitled to a personal blog and own opinions, it was inappropriate in an employment relationship to publicly display those opinions.[26] Moreover, messages can be forwarded, replicated, and printed with ease. In addition, e-mail that exposes employees to inappropriate materials by co-workers can make for a hostile work environment, which creates a liability for organizations under human rights legislation.[27]

Technology creates the need for a critical balance between employee privacy and the employer's need to know. Although employees may assume that their right to privacy extends to e-mail and voice-mail messages, it does not. The Freedom of Information and Protection of Privacy Act (federal legislation) applies only to records in the custody or control of public bodies, such as a Crown corporation, a school board, or a government ministry. This act does not apply to the employment relationship in many organizations. This means employers have the right to monitor materials

---

MANAGER'S TOOLKIT **9.1**

POLICY GUIDELINES ON HANDLING PERSONNEL FILES

- Ensure compliance with legislation.
- Define exactly what information is to be kept in employee files.
- Ensure informed consent has been received from employees regarding types of information that will be collected and stored.
- Develop different categories of personnel information, depending on legal requirements and organizational needs.
- Specify where, when, how, and under what circumstances employees may review or copy their files.

- Ensure appropriate security measures are in place to safeguard information.
- Identify company individuals allowed to view personnel files.
- Prohibit the collection of information that could be viewed as discriminatory or could form the basis for an invasion-of-privacy suit.
- Audit employment records on a regular basis to remove irrelevant, outdated, or inaccurate information.

Employees often assume that they have a right to privacy on the company's telephone.

© ThinkStock/SuperStock

created, received, or sent for business-related reasons.[28] Employers are strongly encouraged to develop clear policies and guidelines that explain to employees how any form of electronic communication is to be used, including when and under what conditions employees can be monitored (see Manager's Toolkit 9.2). In addition, employees should be reminded of their responsibilities under the company's policy every time they log on to the company's computer system. More and more decisions by courts and arbitrators are reaffirming the organization's right to monitor e-mail or any other electronic transmission on the company-owned computers. This is also true for a company that monitors the Internet use of its employees. For example, if an employee subjects co-workers to inappropriate materials from a website (such as racial jokes or graphic sexual pictures), the employer has an obligation to protect the co-workers.[29]

Therefore, it is important for managers and supervisors, as well as employees, to understand that employers have the right to monitor any and all electronic transmissions at work. Where e-mail and voice-mail policies do exist, employees should be required to sign a form indicating that they have read and understand the policy. In most cases, courts will find disciplining an employee for Internet abuse to be a reasonable action.[30]

Employee Conduct Outside the Workplace

Consider the following case. On Monday morning the owner of ABC Corporation reads in the newspaper that a company employee has been charged with robbery and assault on a local convenience store owner. The employee has been released pending trial. A phone call to the employee's supervisor reveals that the employee has reported to work. What should the owner do?

New technologies enable employers to monitor staff very closely, even on their personal time. While most courts uphold the right of the employer to monitor employees at the workplace, particularly if there is a justifiable reason to collect evidence, the monitoring of employees outside the workplace is more complex. For example, a spa employee in Kelowna, B.C., was fired via Facebook for failing to attend a meeting—which she announced on her Facebook profile. While this might

MANAGER'S TOOLKIT **9.2**

E-MAIL, INTERNET, AND VOICE-MAIL POLICY GUIDELINES

- Ensure compliance with any federal and provincial legislation.

- Specify that anything sent through the company's computer systems is the property of the employer, including any files and documents.

- Expressly prohibit accessing certain Internet sites, including storage of certain types of materials or posting on electronic bulletin boards.

- Expressly prohibit use of pirated software or any other potential copyright violations.

- Specify who has access and how it is acquired.

- Specify the circumstances, if any, under which the system can be used for personal use.

- Specify that confidential information is not to be sent electronically.

- Inform employees that the employer reserves the right to monitor and that employees must agree to the monitoring.

- Specify that electronic information be sent only to users who need it for business purposes.

- Prohibit use of any electronic means to harass others or send any inappropriate content to anyone.

- Advise employees that e-mail and computer use is not private and therefore may be reviewed by others.

- Specify that employees who violate the policy are subject to discipline, including dismissal.

Sources: Adapted from materials presented at workshop sponsored by Fasken Martineau, October 26, 2007; and Stuart Rudner, "The High Cost of Internet, E-mail Abuse," *Canadian HR Reporter: Report on Employment Law*, January 31, 2005, R5.

---

sound unusual, the employee was also hired via Facebook.[31] In another case, an employee was fired for blog postings that were critical of the company and revealed critical information about when the company would be releasing new software.[32] Organizations that want to discipline employees for off-duty misconduct must establish a clear relationship between the misconduct and its negative effect on other employees or the organization. This might be established, for example, in cases where off-duty criminal misconduct (e.g., child molestation) creates a disruptive impact on the

With the Internet increasingly becoming a place where people's movements are tracked, logged, and bought and sold, a Montreal-based company, ZeroKnowledge Systems Inc., has launched a product that will prevent unauthorized users from tracking your usage.

Zero Knowledge Systems Co-founders Hammie, Austin and Hamnett Hill

Canada Law Book
www.canadalawbook.com

workplace. Another example might be where the public nature of the employee's job (e.g., police or fire department personnel) creates an image problem for the organization. Ultimately whether an employer can terminate someone for activities outside the work will depend on the profession, the profession's code of conduct, and the role the profession plays in our society.[33]

Further legal resources on the topics discussed in this chapter can be found on the website of Canada Law Book (**www.canadalawbook.com**).

DISCIPLINARY POLICIES AND PROCEDURES

The rights of managers to discipline and discharge employees are increasingly limited. There is thus a great need for managers at all levels to understand discipline procedures. Disciplinary action taken against an employee must be for justifiable reasons, and there must be effective policies and procedures to govern its use. Such policies and procedures serve to assist those responsible for taking disciplinary action and help to ensure that employees receive fair and constructive treatment. Equally important, these guidelines help to prevent disciplinary action from being voided or from being reversed through the appeal system.

If an organization has an HR department, it will have a major responsibility in developing the disciplinary policies and procedures. While the HR department will get top-management approval, it is also critical that supervisors and managers be involved in the development of the policies and procedures. It will be the supervisors and managers who carry out the policies, and therefore any of their experiences can contribute to more effective coordination and consistency in the use of disciplinary action throughout the organization. As part of the manager–HR partnership, the HR department will work with the manager to ensure that any actions taken against employees are consistent with any collective agreements and conform to current law.

The primary responsibility for preventing or correcting disciplinary problems rests with an employee's immediate supervisor. This person is best able to observe evidence of unsatisfactory behaviour or performance and to discuss the matter with the employee. Discussion is frequently all that is needed to correct the problem, and disciplinary action becomes unnecessary. However, when disciplinary action is needed, the supervisor should strive to use a problem-solving attitude. Causes underlying the problem are as important as the problem itself, and any attempt to prevent recurrence will require an understanding of them.

Admittedly, it is often difficult for supervisors to maintain an objective attitude toward employee infractions. But if supervisors can maintain a problem-solving stance, they are likely to come up with a diagnosis that is nearer the truth than would be possible were they to use the approach of a trial lawyer. For example, if an employee is late for work several days in a row, the supervisor needs to discuss the situation with the employee and try to determine the reasons for the lateness. The supervisor needs to remember that the objective is to get the employee to get to work on time—not to discipline the individual for being late. Therefore, by attempting to find out the reasons for the lateness, the supervisor is in a better position to work with the employee to find an acceptable solution. For additional resources in disciplining employees, see Office Depot (**www.officedepot.com**; access the link Business Resource Centre and then link to Small Business Handbook) and Business Owner's Toolkit (**www.toolkit.com** and access the Business Tools link).

Office Depot Business Tools
www.officedepot.com

Business Owner's Toolkit
www.toolkit.com

Setting Organizational Rules

Clearly stating expectations of performance and behaviour is the foundation for an effective disciplinary system. These expectations govern the type of behaviour expected of employees. Since employee behaviour standards are established through the setting and communicating of organizational procedures and rules, the following suggestions may help reduce problems in this area:

1. Information about rules should be widely distributed and known to all employees. It should not be assumed that employees know what is expected of them.
2. Rules should be reviewed periodically—perhaps annually—especially those critical to work success.
3. The reasons for rules concerning performance and behaviour should always be explained. Acceptance is greater when employees understand the reasons behind rules.

4. Organization policies and rules should always be written. Ambiguity should be avoided, since this can result in different interpretations by different supervisors.
5. Rules must be reasonable and relate to the safe and efficient operation of the organization. These should not be made simply because of personal likes or dislikes.
6. If management has been lax in the enforcement of a policy or rule, it must be restated, along with the consequences for its violation, before disciplinary action can begin.
7. Have employees sign that they have read and understand the organizational rules regarding their behaviour and performance in that organization.

When seeking reasons for unsatisfactory performance, supervisors must keep in mind that employees may not be aware of certain expectations. Before initiating any disciplinary action, therefore, it is essential that supervisors determine whether they have given their employees careful and thorough orientation in what is expected of them in relation to their jobs.

Defining Discipline

Outcome 4

Discipline
(1) Treatment that punishes;
(2) Orderly behaviour in an organizational setting; or (3) Training that moulds and strengthens desirable conduct—or corrects undesirable conduct—and develops self-control

In dictionaries, **discipline** normally has three meanings:

1. Treatment that punishes;
2. Orderly behaviour in an organizational setting; or
3. Training that moulds and strengthens desirable conduct—or corrects undesirable conduct—and develops self-control.

To some managers, discipline is synonymous with force. They equate the term with the punishment of employees who violate rules or regulations. Other managers think of discipline as a general state of affairs—a condition of orderliness where employees conduct themselves according to standards of acceptable behaviour. Discipline viewed in this manner can be considered positive when employees willingly practice self-control and respect organizational values and expectations.

The third definition considers discipline a management tool used to correct undesirable employee performance or behaviour. Discipline is applied as a constructive means of getting employees to conform to acceptable standards of behaviour and performance. Figure 9.2 provides examples of common disciplinary problems.

FIGURE 9.2 Common Disciplinary Problems

Attendance Problems

- Unexcused absence
- Chronic absenteeism
- Unexcused or excessive tardiness
- Leaving without permission

Dishonesty and Related Problems

- Theft
- Falsifying employment application
- Willfully damaging organizational property
- Punching another employee's time card
- Falsifying work records

Work Performance Problems

- Failure to complete work assignments
- Producing substandard products or services
- Failure to meet established production requirements

On-the-Job Behaviour Problems

- Intoxication at work
- Insubordination
- Horseplay
- Smoking in unauthorized places
- Fighting
- Gambling
- Failure to use safety devices
- Failure to report injuries
- Carelessness
- Sleeping on the job
- Using abusive or threatening language with supervisors
- Possession of narcotics or alcohol
- Possession of firearms or other weapons
- All forms of harassment, such as sexual innuendo or actions, teasing, racial slurs, inappropriate jokes, and bullying

FIGURE 9.3   A Disciplinary Model

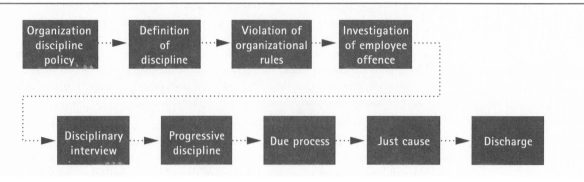

Many organizations, such as Goodyear Aerospace, define the term "discipline" in their policy manuals as training that "corrects, moulds, or perfects knowledge, attitudes, behaviour, or conduct." Discipline is thus viewed as a way to correct poor employee performance rather than simply as punishment for an offence. As these organizations emphasize, discipline should be seen as a method of training employees to perform better or to improve their job attitudes or work behaviour. It is also interesting to note that the word "discipline" is derived from the word "disciple," which means follower or pupil. Figure 9.3 shows one disciplinary model, which consists of several steps that must be carried out to ensure that the termination is justifiable.

Investigating the Disciplinary Problem

It's a rare manager who has a good, intuitive sense of how to investigate employee misconduct. Too frequently, investigations are conducted in a haphazard manner; worse, they overlook one or more investigative concerns. In conducting an employee investigation, it is important to be objective and to avoid the assumptions, suppositions, and biases that often surround discipline cases. Manager's Toolkit 9.3 lists seven questions to consider in investigating an employee offence. Attending to each question will help ensure a full and fair investigation while providing reliable information free from personal prejudice.

When preparing documentation, it is important for a manager to record the incident immediately after the infraction takes place, when the memory of it is still fresh, and to ensure that the record is complete and accurate. It is critical that the documentation be complete, including any information about whether there had been any previous warnings with an opportunity to improve. These documents are necessary to prove that the employer had the right to discipline.[34]

The Investigative Interview

Before any disciplinary action is initiated, an investigative interview should be conducted to make sure employees are fully aware of the offence. This interview is necessary because the supervisor's perceptions of the employee's behaviour may not be entirely accurate. The interview should concentrate on how the offence violated the performance standards of the job. It should avoid getting into personalities or areas unrelated to job performance. Most important, the employee must be given a full opportunity to explain so that any deficiencies for which the organization may be responsible are revealed. In fact, it is critical to the outcome of any discipline to conduct a careful investigation as quickly as possible and ensure that the investigation is approached with care and professionalism.[35]

Approaches to Disciplinary Action

When taken against employees, disciplinary action should never be thought of as punishment. Discipline can embody a penalty as a means of obtaining a desired result; however, punishment should not be the intent of disciplinary action. Rather, discipline must have as its goal the improvement of the employee's future behaviour. To apply discipline in any other way—as punishment or as a way of getting even with employees—can only invite problems for management, including possible wrongful-dismissal suits. If a thorough investigation shows that an employee has violated some organization rule, disciplinary action must be imposed. Two approaches to disciplinary action are progressive discipline and positive discipline.

Progressive Discipline

Progressive discipline
Application of corrective measures by increasing degrees

Generally, discipline is imposed in a progressive manner. By definition, **progressive discipline** is the application of corrective measures by increasing degrees. Progressive discipline is designed to motivate employees to correct their misconduct voluntarily. The technique is aimed at correcting unacceptable behaviour as soon as it starts, using only enough corrective action to remedy the shortcoming. However, the sequence and severity of the disciplinary action vary with the type of offence and the circumstances surrounding it. Since each situation is unique, a number of factors must be considered in determining how severe a disciplinary action should be. Some of the factors to consider were listed in Manager's Toolkit 9.3.

The typical progressive discipline procedure includes four steps: (1) an oral warning (or counselling) that subsequent unsatisfactory behaviour or performance will not be tolerated, (2) the action may progress to a written warning, (3) to a suspension without pay, and (4) ultimately to termination.

The corrective discipline used by several organizations is described in At Work with HRM 9.3. The "capital punishment" of discharge is utilized only as a last resort. Organizations normally use lower forms of disciplinary action for less severe performance problems. It is important for organizations to follow "best practices" when documenting discipline:

1. Use an employee discipline form—this helps in ensuring that there is a uniform process and all the important information is gathered.
2. Conduct a fair and full investigation.

MANAGER'S TOOLKIT 9.3

CONSIDERATIONS IN DISCIPLINARY INVESTIGATIONS

1. In very specific terms, what is the offence charged?
   - Is management sure it fully understands the charge against the employee?
   - Was the employee really terminated for insubordination, or did the employee merely refuse a request by management?
2. Did the employee know he or she was doing something wrong?
   - What rule or provision was violated?
   - How would the employee know of the existence of the rule?
   - Was the employee warned of the consequence?
3. Is the employee guilty?
   - What are the sources of facts?
   - Is there direct or only indirect evidence of guilt?
   - Has anyone talked to the employee to hear his or her side of the situation?
4. Are there extenuating circumstances?
   - Were conflicting orders given by different supervisors?

- Does anybody have reason to want to "get" this employee?
- Was the employee provoked by a manager or another employee?
5. Has the rule been uniformly enforced?
   - Have all managers applied the rule consistently?
   - What punishment have previous offenders received?
   - Were any other employees involved in this offence?
6. Is the offence related to the workplace?
   - Is there evidence that the offence hurt the organization?
   - Is management making a moral judgment or a business judgment?
7. What is the employee's past work record?
   - How many years of service has the employee given the organization?
   - How many years or months has the employee held the current job?
   - What is the employee's personnel record as a whole, especially his or her disciplinary record?

AT WORK **with HRM 9.3**

CORRECTIVE DISCIPLINE APPROACHES

A number of organizations have readily available guidelines aimed at changing unwanted employee behaviour. Before discipline begins, it is expected that the supervisor can show that the employee is aware of desired behaviour and that he or she is choosing to act otherwise. Frequently all that is needed is to let employees know that a particular behaviour is not appropriate. Employees usually react positively to this. It definitely is not used as a way of punishing an employee. Typical steps in a discipline process are the following:

Step 1: Oral or verbal warning. This is a private discussion between the employee and the supervisor that takes place immediately after the incident. The supervisor describes the incident and ensures that all sides of the story are heard. Human Resources and Skills Development Canada's verbal warning step also states that the supervisor needs to be very clear on outlining the consequences if expectations are not met.

Step 2: Written warning. If the employee's behaviour continues, a meeting is held with the supervisor and the employee. At the meeting the supervisor describes the events, reviews expectations as discussed in Step 1, seeks solutions from the employee, and indicates what will happen if unacceptable behaviour continues. The meeting is summarized in writing and placed in the employee's personnel file. It is also helpful if the written warning includes a plan to ensure that the employee has sufficient time to improve.

Step 3: Suspension. If the inappropriate behaviour continues, the supervisor will next consider suspension. A meeting is held, similar to the meeting in Step 2. At the conclusion of the meeting, a suspension may be imposed with a length that is linked to the nature of the problem. It can be for one day or for several days. A letter of suspension is written and placed in the employee's file.

Step 4: Dismissal. This is a very serious step and is taken only when all other options have been exhausted. Again, a meeting is held to review facts and expectations and to summarize previous meetings and actions. Even at this meeting it is important to provide an opportunity for the employee to explain. At the end of the meeting, a letter of dismissal is presented, which is also placed in the employee's file with a copy given to the employee.

CRITICAL THINKING QUESTION

Are there any other steps that ought to be taken in corrective discipline? Describe and explain.

Sources: Adapted from "Progressive Discipline," www.hrsdc.gc.ca/eng/labour/publications/employment_standards/discipline.shtml (accessed March 3, 2009); and Natalie C. MacDonald, "Progressing Towards Just Cause," *Canadian HR Reporter*, September 22, 2008, www.hrreporter.com/ArticleView.aspx?l=1&articleid=6350 (accessed March 3, 2009).

3. Get the facts.
4. Be objective.
5. Be clear and specific.
6. Complete the form while the information is fresh.
7. Get the employee's acknowledgment.
8. Allow the employee to explain the actions.
9. Be fair.
10. To the degree possible, use the discipline process as a positive experience.[36]

Positive Discipline

Although progressive discipline is the most popular approach to correcting employee misconduct, recently some managers have questioned its logic. They have noted that it has certain flaws, including its intimidating and adversarial nature, which prevent it from achieving the intended purpose. For these reasons, some organizations are using an approach called **positive**, or **nonpunitive, discipline**. Positive discipline is based on the concept that employees must assume responsibility for their personal conduct and job performance.[37]

Positive discipline requires a cooperative environment in which the employee and supervisor engage in joint discussion and problem solving to resolve incidents of employee irresponsibility. The approach focuses on the early correction of misconduct, with the employee taking total

Positive, or nonpunitive, discipline

System of discipline that focuses on the early correction of employee misconduct, with the employee taking total responsibility for correcting the problem

responsibility for resolving the problem. Management imposes nothing; all solutions and affirmations are jointly reached. While positive discipline appears similar to progressive discipline, its emphasis is on giving employees reminders rather than reprimands as a way to improve performance. Figure 9.4 illustrates the procedure for implementing the three-step positive discipline procedure.

Compiling a Disciplinary Record

In applying either progressive or positive discipline, it is important for managers to maintain complete records of each step of the procedure. When employees fail to meet the obligation of a disciplinary step, they should be given a warning, and their manager should document the warning. A copy of this warning is usually placed in the employee's personnel file. After an established period—frequently six months—the warning is usually removed, provided that it has served its purpose. Otherwise it remains in the file to serve as evidence should a more severe penalty become necessary later.

An employee's personnel file contains the employee's complete work history. It serves as a basis for determining and supporting disciplinary action and for evaluating the organization's disciplinary policies and procedures. Maintenance of proper records also provides management with valuable information about the soundness of its rules and regulations. Those rules that are violated most frequently should receive particular attention, because the need for them may no longer exist or some change might be required to facilitate their enforcement. If the rule is shown to have little or no value, it should be revised or rescinded. Otherwise employees are likely to feel they are being restricted unnecessarily.

Documentation of Employee Misconduct

"It's too complicated." "I just didn't take time to do it." "I have more important things to do." These are some of the frequent excuses used by managers who have failed to document cases of employee misconduct. The most significant cause of inadequate documentation, however, is

FIGURE 9.4 Positive Discipline Procedures

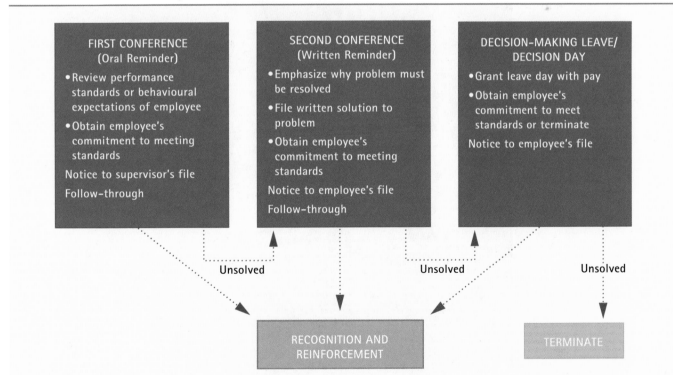

that managers have no idea what constitutes good documentation. Unfortunately, the failure of managers to record employee misconduct accurately can result in the reversal of any subsequent disciplinary action. Written records are key in discipline.[38] For documentation to be complete, the following eight items should be included:

1. Date, time, and location of the incident(s).
2. Negative performance or behaviour exhibited by the employee—the problem.
3. Consequences of that action or behaviour on the employee's overall work performance and/ or the operation of the employee's work unit.
4. Prior discussion(s) with the employee about the problem.
5. Disciplinary action to be taken and specific improvement expected.
6. Consequences if improvement is not made, and a follow-up date.
7. The employee's reaction to the supervisor's attempt to change behaviour.
8. The names of witnesses to the incident (if appropriate).

About Human Resources
humanresources.about.com

It is critical that managers at all levels understand the guidelines for appropriate discipline. For additional resources on discipline, do a search on "discipline" at **humanresources.about.com**.

Grounds for Dismissal

No matter how helpful and positive a supervisor is with an employee who is not abiding by the organization's policies and rules, there may come a time when the employee must be dismissed. Since dismissal has such serious consequences for the employee—and possibly for the organization—it should be undertaken only after a deliberate and thoughtful review of the case.

Wrongful Dismissal

When an employer dismisses or terminates an employee for not performing as expected or not following the company's rules, this is called dismissal for "just cause." To do this, the employer must document and prove serious misconduct or incompetence on the part of the employee. In recent

The final stage of discipline is termination.

Ariel Skelley/Photographer's Choice/Getty Images

Wrongful dismissal
Terminating an employee's employment without just cause

years, a growing number of employees have sued their former employers for "**wrongful dismissal**," claiming the termination was "without just or sufficient cause," implying a lack of fair treatment by management or insufficient reasons for the termination. Termination for cause also expects that the employee could do something different and had been informed of this prior to termination. This means that a termination resulting from a job redefinition/redesign, downsizing, restructuring, or lack of organizational fit is not just cause. However, poor performance, poor interpersonal relationships, and technical incompetence might be just cause if the employee had been informed of expectations and had been given a chance to improve but failed to conform. Figure 9.5 lists some "just-cause" reasons.

Many managers are faced with having to terminate someone when there are sufficient and legitimate grounds for doing so. Some companies may suggest that just cause includes the organization's financial difficulties. It is important for managers and supervisors to know that the economic hardship of the company is not a justifiable reason to terminate someone's employment. HRM and the Law 9.1 gives two examples of unsuccessful wrongful dismissal cases. For additional information on wrongful dismissals, see **www.duhaime.org**.

Duhaime Law
www.duhaime.org

FIGURE 9.5   Sample "Just-Cause" Reasons

- Excessive lateness or absenteeism
- Theft from the company
- Improper or wrong conduct, such as fighting with a co-worker

Depending on the seriousness of the wrongdoing, the individual may be terminated immediately, bypassing the steps of progressive discipline. For example, a hotel concierge who makes threatening statements to a guest could be terminated right away.

HRM and the law 9.1

EMPLOYERS DID NOT HAVE CAUSE TO TERMINATE

A recent Federal Court of Canada decision dealt with an employee who was terminated after being with the employer for over 20 years. The employer fired the employee due to the employee's incompetence after being promoted to a new job—a job that the employee didn't have the training to do and the employer could not provide the training required prior to the deadline for meeting performance objectives. The employee sued for wrongful dismissal. The court ruled in favour of the employee, saying that the employee's impeccable performance before the promotion was not considered. Further, the court stated that promoting and then firing sends inappropriate messages to other employees. The court again acknowledged that in these types of circumstances, it would be understandable if few employees would take the risk of applying for a promotion if dismissal could follow if they were not up to the situation.

In another case, a Canada Labour Code adjudicator determined that a trucking company in New Brunswick did not have sufficient reason to terminate one of its truck drivers. The adjudicator did acknowledge that there was misconduct and that discipline was warranted but that termination was too harsh. The driver got into a heated argument with the president of the company and called the president an idiot. The driver was then fired for insubordination. Prior to this situation, there had been two other disciplinary incidents with the driver—one where the driver had fallen asleep at the wheel, causing an accident that resulted in the loss of the company truck and trailer, and another one where the driver took two weeks of unauthorized leave. In both cases there had been written warnings but there was no mention of possible termination for inappropriate behaviour.

How would you have ruled?

Sources: Adapted from Wallace Immen, "Peter Principle Meets Legal Principles," *The Globe and Mail*, April 18, 2008, C2; and Jeffrey R. Smith, "Truck Driver Fired After Calling Boss 'Idiot,'" *Canadian HR Reporter*, September 22, 2008, www.hrreporter.com/ArticleView.aspx?l=1&articleid=6347 (accessed March 3, 2009).

Managers must be able to document that any performance problems have been brought to the attention of the employee and that sufficient time, training, and assistance have been given to improve the weak performance. If the organization has an HR professional, the line manager needs to work closely with the HR person to ensure that the appropriate type of documentation occurs. Other tips to prevent a challenge by a terminated employee are discussed later in the chapter.

If an employee termination is to be upheld for good cause, what constitutes fair employee treatment and valid reasons? This question is not easily answered, but standards governing just-cause dismissal have evolved from the field of labour arbitration. These standards are applied by arbitrators in dismissal cases to determine if management had just cause for the termination. These guidelines are normally set forth in the form of questions, provided in the Manager's Toolkit 9.4. For example, before dismissing an employee, did the manager warn the person of possible disciplinary action in the past? A "no" answer to any of the seven questions generally means that just cause was not established and that management's decision to terminate was arbitrary, capricious, or discriminatory. These guidelines are being applied not only by arbitrators in dismissal cases but also by judges in wrongful-dismissal suits. For example, the B.C. Supreme Court recently assessed damages against Dams Ford Lincoln Sales for having been untruthful about why a person was terminated.[39] Therefore, it is important for an employer to represent itself truthfully regarding the reasons for termination.

Constructive Dismissal

Constructive dismissal
Changing an employee's working conditions such that compensation, status, or prestige is reduced

Another type of dismissal is constructive. **Constructive dismissal** occurs when an employer changes an employee's working conditions such that compensation, status, or prestige is reduced. Even if the employee agrees to the changed conditions (the only other option might be unemployment) or resigns, the court may consider the employee to have been dismissed.[40]

Two cases illustrate the concept. One involved VoiceGenie and its software quality assurance manager. The manager considered that he had been constructively dismissed when his supervisor indicated that he and a major client hadn't gotten off to a very good start. Because the employee reacted to this, the employee chose not to show-up for work. After two days' absence, the supervisor sent an e-mail complimenting the employee on his skills but asked that he be more cooperative. The manager responded by e-mail, making a number of demands, and stating that he would not return to work until expectations were clarified in writing. More e-mails went back-and-forth with the tone of the notes getting more demanding; he also refused to meet with his supervisor. Eventually, the manager did return to work but discovered that his security card and access card had been cut-off. When this occurred, the manager did agree to meet with his supervisor who outlined expectations, including a performance improvement plan that dealt with the absenteeism and customer relations. Again, the manager refused to return to work until his demands were

---

MANAGER'S TOOLKIT **9.4**

"JUST-CAUSE" DISMISSAL GUIDELINES

1. Did the organization forewarn the employee of the possible disciplinary consequences of his or her action?

2. Were management's requirements of the employee reasonable in relation to the orderly, efficient, and safe operation of the organization's business?

3. Did management, before changing the working conditions or discharging the employee, make a reasonable effort to establish that the employee's performance was unsatisfactory?

4. Was the organization's investigation conducted in a fair and objective manner?

5. Did the investigation produce sufficient evidence or proof of guilt as charged?

6. Has management treated this employee under its rules, orders, and penalties as it has other employees in similar circumstances?

7. Did the discharge fit the misconduct, considering the seriousness of the proven offence, the employee's service record, and any mitigating circumstances?

met or that he would quit in three days. The company indicated that the performance plan was non-negotiable and was not subject to the employee's approval. At that point the manager was ordered to either resign or return to work; when he didn't do either, he was fired. Somehow the fired manager accessed the company's computer system and downloaded a variety of documents. The case eventually was heard in court where a judge determined that the manager had not been constructively dismissed and that he had an obligation to return and keep working. The fired manager was ordered to pay court and legal costs in the amount of $61,000 to the company.[41]

The second one involved an account manager at Bell Mobility. A senior manager started treating one of his direct-reports in a blunt and forceful way when describing expectations, including yelling and swearing at her. The employee began feeling vulnerable because of her age, sex, and the highly competitive work environment at Bell. At one point, he ordered her out of his office, pushing her on the shoulder. The employee was so shaken that she left and didn't return until the following week. When she returned, she was presented a performance improvement plan with a notation saying that if the performance didn't improve she would be terminated. No one in the company was prepared to listen to her concerns about her supervisor, so she decided to sue for constructive dismissal. The company responded by saying that she had orchestrated the constructive dismissal. The judge ruled in favour of the employee, indicating that the employer had an obligation to be civil in its behaviour toward employees. Bell Mobility was ordered to pay $500,000 in damages.[42]

These are two different cases dealing with performance improvement plans and yet have different outcomes. To access the latest information on constructive dismissals, *The Wrongful Dismissal Handbook*, 4th ed.(Carswell) is a helpful resource.

In a nonunion setting, employers can give notice of future changes in compensation (wages and benefits), working hours, location, and other similar items so long as they provide actual notice equivalent to that given for dismissal. For example, if the company wished to reduce the amount of paid sick leave, they could do so with sufficient notice.

Dismissing Employees

Regardless of the reasons for a dismissal, it should be done with personal consideration for the employee affected. Every effort should be made to ease the trauma a dismissal creates. The employee must be informed honestly, yet tactfully, of the exact reasons for the action. Such candour can help the employee face the problem and adjust to it in a constructive manner.

Managers need to discuss, and even rehearse, with their peers the upcoming termination meeting. This practice can ensure that all important points are covered while giving confidence to the manager. Although managers agree that there is no single right way to conduct the dismissal meeting, the following guidelines will help to make the discussion more effective:

1. Hold the meeting early in the week and in a neutral meeting place.
2. Come to the point within the first two or three minutes, and list in a logical order all reasons for the termination.
3. Be straightforward and firm, yet tactful, and remain resolute in the decision; avoid debating reasons and decisions.
4. Make the discussion private, businesslike, and fairly brief; make notes of the meeting.
5. Avoid making accusations against the employee and injecting personal feelings into the discussion; be courteous and respectful at all times.
6. Avoid bringing up any personality differences.
7. Provide any information concerning severance pay and the status of benefits and coverage.
8. Explain how employment inquiries from future employers will be handled.
9. Arrange a mutually agreed upon time for the employee to clear out personal belongings and for the return of any company property.
10. Have another manager present as a witness.

Termination meetings should be held in a neutral location, such as a conference room, so that the manager can leave if the meeting gets out of control. The prudent manager will also have determined, prior to the termination decision, that the dismissal does not violate any legal rights the employee may have.

Finally, when terminated employees are escorted off the premises, the removal must not serve to defame the employee. Managers should not give peers the impression that the terminated employee was dishonest or untrustworthy. Furthermore, managers are advised never to discuss the discharge with other employees, customers, or any other individual.

Providing Career Transition Assistance

Employers often use career transition or outplacement services to assist employees who are being dismissed. This assistance is especially likely to be provided for employees of long tenure. And recently it is occurring more frequently due to the large number of layoffs in all industries in North America due to the recession.[43] Many organizations are seeing this as a good return on investment, particularly when the economy begins to rebound and employers may want these same individuals back. One company has called returning employees "boomerangs" and even provides the person with a wooden boomerang with their name, leaving date, and returning date.[44] These agencies not only provide job search technique help but also emotional support. While terminations do not have the negative stigma they once did, they are still traumatic for the employee.

Managers cite the following reasons for providing outplacement services: concern for the well-being of the employees, protection against potential lawsuits, and the psychological effect on remaining employees. Outplacement consultants assist employees being terminated by reducing their anger and grief and helping them regain self-confidence as they begin searching in earnest for a new job. Since many terminated workers have been out of the job market for some time, they may lack the knowledge and skills needed to look for a new job. Outplacement specialists can coach them in how to develop contacts, probe for job openings through systematic letter and telephone campaigns, and handle employment interviews and salary negotiations.

The Results of Inaction

Failure to act implies that the performance or behaviour of the employee concerned is acceptable. If disciplinary action is eventually taken, the delay will make it more difficult to justify the action if appealed. In defending against such an appeal, the employer is likely to be asked why an employee who had not been performing or behaving satisfactorily was kept on the payroll. Or an even more probing question might be "Why did that employee continue to receive pay adjustments if there was a question about the performance?"

Such contradictions in practice can only aid employees in successfully challenging management's corrective actions. Unfortunately, some supervisors try to build a case to justify their corrective

Job-site learning joins the electronic age. Nova Scotia's virtual apprenticeship program is a case in point: it allows those wanting to learn a certified trade to complete the classroom portions of their training via the Internet.

Reprinted by permission of Maclean's Magazine.

actions only after they have decided that a particular employee should be dismissed. The following are common reasons given by supervisors for their failure to impose a disciplinary penalty:

1. The supervisor had failed to document earlier actions, so no record existed on which to base subsequent disciplinary action.
2. Supervisors believed they would receive little or no support from higher management for the disciplinary action.
3. The supervisor was uncertain of the facts underlying the situation requiring disciplinary action.
4. Failure by the supervisor to discipline employees in the past for a certain infraction caused the supervisor to forgo current disciplinary action in order to appear consistent.
5. The supervisor wanted to be seen as a likable person.

It is critical to remember that any grounds for discipline must be well-documented. Failure to do so can result in the disciplinary action being invalid.

APPEALING DISCIPLINARY ACTIONS

With growing frequency, organizations are taking steps to protect employees from arbitrary and inequitable treatment by their supervisors. A particular emphasis is placed on creating a climate in which employees are assured that they can voice their dissatisfaction with their superiors without fear of reprisal. This safeguard can be provided through the implementation of a formal procedure for appealing disciplinary actions.

Alternative Dispute-Resolution Procedures

Outcome 6

Alternative dispute resolution (ADR)
Term applied to different types of employee complaint or dispute-resolution procedures

ADR Institute of Canada
www.amic.org

In unionized workplaces, grievance procedures are stated in virtually all collective agreements. In nonunion organizations, however, **alternative dispute resolution (ADR)** processes are increasingly being used to keep employers out of court—in fact 90–95% of cases settle before any trial.[45] The employer's interest stems from the desire to meet employees' expectations for fair treatment in the workplace while guaranteeing them due process—in the hope of minimizing discrimination claims or wrongful-dismissal suits.

Some organizations prefer these procedures as an avenue for upward communication for employees and as a way to gauge the mood of the workforce. Others view these systems as a way to resolve minor problems before they mushroom into major issues, thus leading to improved employee morale and productivity.

The appeal procedures described in this chapter are mediation, the step-review system, the use of a hearing officer, the open-door policy, the use of an ombudsperson, and arbitration. A helpful resource for additional information on ADR can be found at **www.amic.org**.

Mediation

Mediation
The use of an impartial third party to help facilitate a resolution to employment disputes

Mediation is fast becoming a popular way to resolve employee complaints and is discussed in detail in Chapter 10. The essence of mediation is facilitating face-to-face meetings so that the employee and manager can reach an agreement. Mediation is a flexible process that is shaped to deal with the particular conflict between the parties.[46] Also, it can be used to resolve a wide range of employee complaints, including discrimination claims or traditional workplace disputes.[47] Employees like the process because of its informality. According to one authority, "Mediation is a useful way to solve workplace disputes."[48] Settlements fashioned through mediation are readily accepted by the parties, thus promoting a favourable working relationship.

Step-Review Systems

Step-review system
System for reviewing employee complaints and disputes by successively higher levels of management

As Figure 9.6 illustrates, a **step-review system** is based on a pre-established set of steps—normally four—for the review of an employee complaint by successively higher levels of management. These procedures are patterned after the union grievance systems, which will be discussed in Chapter 10.

FIGURE 9.6   Step-Review Appeal Procedure

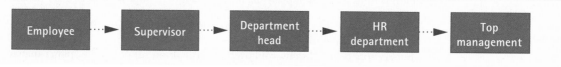

For example, they normally require that the employee's complaint be formalized as a written statement. Managers at each step are required to provide a full response to the complaint within a specified time period, perhaps three to five working days.

Use of a Hearing Officer

This procedure is ordinarily confined to large organizations, where unions may represent employees. The **hearing officer** holds a full-time position with the organization but assumes a neutral role when deciding cases between an aggrieved employee and management. Hearing officers are employed by the organization; however, they function independently from other managers and occupy a special place in the organizational hierarchy. Their success rests on being perceived as neutral, highly competent, and completely unbiased in handling employee complaints. They hear cases upon request, almost always made by the employee. After considering the evidence and facts presented, they render decisions or awards that are normally final and binding on both sides.

> **Hearing officer**
> Person who holds a full-time position with an organization but assumes a neutral role when deciding cases between management and the aggrieved employees

Open-Door Policy

The open-door policy is an old standby for settling employee complaints. In fact, most managers, regardless of whether their organization has adopted a formal open-door policy, profess to maintain one for their employees. The traditional **open-door policy** identifies various levels of management above the immediate supervisor that an aggrieved employee may contact; the levels may extend as high as a vice president, president, or chief executive officer. Typically, the person who acts as "the court of last resort" is the HR director or a senior staff official.

> **Open-door policy**
> Policy of settling grievances that identifies various levels of management above the immediate supervisor for employee contact

Ombudsperson System

An **ombudsperson** is a designated individual from whom employees may seek counsel for the resolution of their complaints. The ombudsperson listens to an employee's complaint and attempts to resolve it by mediating a solution between the employee and the supervisor. This individual works cooperatively with both sides to reach a settlement, often employing a clinical approach to problem solving. Since the ombudsperson has no authority to finalize a solution to the problem, compromises are highly possible and all concerned tend to feel satisfied with the outcome. To function successfully, ombudspersons must be able to operate in an atmosphere of confidentiality that does not threaten the security of the managers or subordinates who are involved in a complaint.

> **Ombudsperson**
> Designated individual from whom employees may seek counsel for the resolution of their complaints

Arbitration

Private employers may require that employees submit their employment disputes for a binding resolution through arbitration. (Arbitration is fully explained in Chapter 10.) Arbitration can save court costs and voice time delays and unfavourable publicity.

ORGANIZATIONAL ETHICS IN EMPLOYEE RELATIONS

 Outcome **7**

Throughout this textbook the legal requirements of HRM are emphasized. Laws and court decisions affect all aspects of the employment process—recruitment, selection, performance appraisal, safety and health, labour relations, and testing. Managers must comply with governmental regulations to promote an environment free from litigation.

Ethics

Set of standards of conduct and moral judgments that help to determine right and wrong behaviour

However, beyond what is required by the law is the question of organizational ethics and the ethical—or unethical—behaviour engaged in by managers. **Ethics** can be defined as a set of standards of acceptable conduct and moral judgment. Ethics provides cultural guidelines—organizational or societal—that help decide between proper and improper conduct. Therefore, ethics, like the legal aspects of HR, permeates all aspects of the employment relationship. For example, managers may adhere to the organization's objective of hiring more members of designated groups, but how those employees are supervised and treated once employed gets to the issue of managerial ethics. Compliance with laws and the behavioural treatment of employees are two completely different aspects of the manager's job. While ethical dilemmas will always occur in the supervision of employees, it is how employees are treated that largely distinguishes the ethical organization from the unethical one. An ethical organization recognizes and values the contributions of employees and respects their personal rights. And certainly the court cases mentioned earlier in this chapter are reinforcing this belief.

Many organizations have their own codes of ethics that govern relations with employees and the public at large. These codes are formal written statements of the organization's primary values and provide a basis for the organization, and individual managers, for behaviours and actions. In Canada, 90% of companies with revenues over $1 billion (all of which are operating on a world-wide basis) have a stated code of ethics.[49] Organizations now have ethics committees and ethics ombudspersons to provide training in ethics to employees. In addition, the Government of Canada has an ethics commissioner, reporting directly to the prime minister. As part of the work, there has been new legislation for elected politicians regarding ethics and accountability, as well as overseeing and monitoring the code of ethics for public servants.[50] The ultimate goal of ethics training is to avoid unethical behaviour and adverse publicity; to gain a strategic advantage; but most of all, to treat employees in a fair and equitable manner, recognizing them as productive members of the organization.

However, even with codes of ethics and ethics committees, people do not always behave ethically. When this happens, employees will sometimes report an organization's unethical practices outside the organization. This is referred to as "whistle-blowing." A recent court case in Richmond, B.C., reaffirmed that even if an employee is covered by a collective agreement, the employee has the right to use civil courts to defend allegations of whistle-blowing. The employee went public with allegations that private asphalt contractors were delivering less material than had been contracted and that other city employees knew of this and benefited from it. The employee testified that he had been threatened and harassed. However, the City of Richmond management stated that this was a labour relations issue and ought to be handled through other challenges. The judge ruled that given how the person was treated, the employee had a right to be heard in civil court.[51]

As demonstrated above, organizations have frequently attempted to discipline or punish an employee for whistle-blowing. But with the renewed interest in business ethics, more and more companies are taking steps to ensure that any unethical behaviour or action by an employee is punished and that people are encouraged to report unethical actions. In order to ensure that employees understand the importance of dealing with unethical behaviour, top management needs to visibly support ethical actions by behaving ethically themselves, have a whistleblower policy, and that whistleblowing issues are handled quickly.[52]

For trends in the areas covered in this chapter, see Emerging Trends 9.1.

EMERGING TRENDS 9.1

1. ***More checks on the use of "contract workers."*** As companies reduce the need for on-going employees, as well as to eliminate exposure to wrongful dismissals, there is a tendency to want to use more "contract workers." However, in many cases the person is really an employee and the company can face tax and other consequences of such an arrangement. Whether the person is a contractor or an employee is a function of how much control the organization has over the person's time and the way in which the work gets done.

(Continued)

2. ***Better systems to validate overtime.*** With the number of lawsuits concerning overtime, employers will be putting terms of employment, including overtime, in written documents, will have more tracking/recording of overtime, and will have written policies regarding overtime.

3. ***Increased monitoring of employee activities.*** Companies have legitimate rights to protect their products and their employees. They also are obliged to protect their reputations. With technology becoming increasingly more sophisticated, it can be easier to both monitor and protect.

Sources: Howard Levitt, "Are You Really Hiring a Contract Worker," *Financial Post,* August 13, 2008, FP18; Howard Levitt, "Put Double-Check System in Play for Payroll," *The Vancouver Sun,* December 10, 2008, D6; Jeffrey R. Smith, "Worker Wins Overtime Suit, Gets a Loonie," *Canadian HR Reporter,* December 15, 2008, 5; and David Halpern, Patrick J. Reville, and Donald Grunewald, "Management and Legal Issues Regarding Electronic Surveillance of Employees in the Workplace," *Journal of Business Ethics* 80, no. 2 (June 2008): 175–180.

SUMMARY

1. Explain statutory rights, contractual rights, due process, and legal implications of those rights.
   * Statutory rights derive from legislation, such as human rights legislation.
   * Contractual rights are derived from contracts, such as an employment contract.
   * Due process is the employee's right to be heard through a complaint process.
   * Legal implications flow from how the employee is treated.

2. Identify the job expectancy rights of employees.
   * Fair and equitable treatment.
   * Ensuring that the workplace is safe and drug-free.
   * Reasonable treatment regarding privacy.
   * Access to employee's own personnel file.
   * Not being subject to discipline for off-duty behaviour.
   * Being notified of any plant closings.

3. Explain the process of establishing disciplinary practices, including the proper implementation of organizational rules.
   * The primary purpose of having disciplinary procedures is to prevent or correct discipline problems.
   * Failure to take disciplinary action only serves to aggravate a problem that eventually must be resolved.
   * Organizations need to clearly outline rules and expectations regarding performance and behaviour.

4. Discuss the meaning of discipline and how to investigate a disciplinary problem.
   * Discipline is action that results in desirable conduct or performance.
   * If a problem occurs, the supervisor needs to determine when the situation occurred and to have a full discussion with the employee to get the employee's view of the situation.

5. Explain the differences between progressive and positive discipline.
   * Progressive discipline is the application of corrective measures by increasing degrees.
   * Progressive discipline is designed to motivate an employee to correct misconduct.
   * Positive discipline is based on the concept that the employee must assume responsibility for personal conduct and job performance.
   * Positive discipline requires a co-operative environment for joint discussion and problem solving between the supervisor and the employee.

6. Identify the different types of alternative dispute-resolution procedures.
   * Step-review systems.
   * Peer-review systems.
   * Use of hearing officers.

- Open-door system.
- Ombudsperson system.
- Arbitration.

7. Discuss the role of ethics in the management of human resources.
    - Ethics in HRM extends beyond the legal requirements of managing employees.
    - Managers engage in ethical behaviour when employees are treated in a fair and objective way and when an employee's personal and work-related rights are respected and valued.

NEED TO KNOW	NEED TO UNDERSTAND
• Definition of termination with cause, and wrongful dismissal • Types of disciplinary approaches • Types of discipline appeal mechanisms for nonunion staff • Definition of ethics	• How employee rights are protected • How to conduct a discipline investigation • How to dismiss an employee • Factors used to determine if termination was for cause • Relationship of organizational ethics to employee rights and expectations

KEY TERMS

alternative dispute resolution (ADR) 293

constructive dismissal 290

contractual rights 273

discipline 283

due process 274

employee rights 271

ethics 295

hearing officer 294

mediation 293

negligence 271

ombudsperson 294

open-door policy 294

positive, or nonpunitive, discipline 286

progressive discipline 285

statutory rights 272

step-review system 293

wrongful dismissal 289

REVIEW QUESTIONS

1. What is meant by management rights? Employee rights?
2. Define statutory rights and contractual rights.
3. What are some of the guidelines for developing a policy on employee searches?
4. List several guidelines for inclusion in an employer's policy manual for e-mail, Internet, and voice-mail usage.
5. Why is documentation so important to the disciplinary process? What constitutes correct documentation?
6. Describe progressive and positive discipline, noting the differences between these two approaches.
7. Define "just-cause" dismissal and "wrongful" dismissal.
8. Explain mediation.
9. What is a code of ethics?

CRITICAL THINKING QUESTIONS

1. Sara has recently been asked to develop a voice-mail and e-mail protocol for the home improvement company for which she is working. What specific items would she want in the protocol?
2. Pardeep works as a millwright in a sawmill. The company is considering redesigning its discipline procedures to be oriented toward positive discipline. What would be the advantages and disadvantages of this change? What would the company want to include in the new procedure?
3. You have recently been promoted to a supervisory position. One of your first tasks is to discipline one of your staff for an ongoing tardiness problem. What information do you need prior to the discipline meeting and how would you conduct the meeting?

4. Your professor is dealing with a case where a student was alleged to have cheated on a final exam. Would documentation be important? If so, what type of documentation would be necessary?

5. A new manager has recently joined a large financial institution. She has noticed that some staff are not following the code of ethics. What advice would you give her in dealing with this?

DEVELOPING YOUR SKILLS

Privacy Commissioner of Canada
www.privcom.gc.ca

Privacy Rights Clearinghouse
www.privacyrights.org

Electronic Frontier Foundation
www.eff.org/issues/privacy

Fair Measures Inc.
www.fairmeasures.com

ADR Resources
www.adrr.com

ADR Institute of Ontario
www.adrontario.ca

Conflict Resolution Network
www.crnhq.org

1. Working in a group of four to five students, identify the ethical dilemmas that could arise in the areas of selection, performance reviews, health and safety, privacy rights, and compensation.

2. Individually read the following scenarios. Then in groups of four to five students, determine if the situations are or are not fair. Explain your reasons. Be prepared to share your information with the rest of the class.

   a. Jane was using the company network system to locate childcare facilities in her local community. Her supervisor observed this and then sought confirmation from the IT unit. Jane was given a written reprimand. Meanwhile, John used his desk telephone to do his personal banking and bill paying. John was not reprimanded.

   b. Sonita spent her lunch hour at the gym; she is following a strenuous workout program as she prepares for a triathlon event in the next several weeks. Meanwhile, Anthony met his friends for lunch, sharing several beers at the local pub. Both employees felt fatigued in the afternoon, and their work performance decreased, which was noted by their supervisor. Anthony was asked to meet with his supervisor to review performance expectations and received a verbal warning. Sonita did not.

3. Access the following websites, which discuss employee privacy rights in the workplace. Prepare a one- to two-page report summarizing what each site has to offer. Indicate if there are any areas of the site that might be more helpful to an employee rather than an employer.
   - **www.privcom.gc.ca**
   - **www.privacyrights.org**
   - **www.eff.org/issues/privacy**
   - **www.fairmeasures.com/issues/privacy/default.asp**

4. Access the following websites on alternative dispute resolution:
   - **www.adrr.com**
   - **www.adrontario.ca**
   - **www.crnhq.org**

In addition, conduct your own Internet search, using any search engine, under the heading of "alternative dispute resolution." Share with your classmates what you learned about alternative dispute resolution.

Case Study 1

Improving Performance through a Progressive Discipline Policy

Jennifer started her new job as vice president, human resources at ABC Manufacturing—a manufacturer of state-of-the-art furniture products in Southern Ontario. She started in mid-2007. One of the first issues she faced was an unacceptable absenteeism rate. There were about 250 employees on the three assembly lines, operating two shifts a day. The average employee was absent 14 days a year. The benchmark for other manufacturing sites was nine days. Jennifer calculated that the company was employing between 30 and 35 extra people to cover absences. This hurt the bottom line.

A related problem was punctuality. Employees were habitually five or 10 minutes late for their shifts. In a white-collar environment with flextime, this would not have been as critical. But tardiness in this situation meant that the assembly line could not operate, and that the other employees on the three lines were forced to remain idle.

The solution was to develop a system of progressive discipline. Jennifer prepared a simple two-page policy. Page one dealt with behaviour in the control of employees, such as arriving late, leaving work without permission, calling in sick but playing golf, and so on. Page two dealt with legitimate absences, such as food poisoning, stomach flu, etc. Jennifer met with the unions and notified them that this policy would come into effect as of December 2007. All employees started with zero absences at this time.

The policy assumed that all absences were innocent. However, if an employee was absent five times in a 12-month period, the supervisor met with that employee to express concern over the absences and to identify any need for counselling or assistance. The goal of the meeting was to express legitimate concerns, reinforce that the employee was needed, and ensure that the employee accepted responsibility for managing his or her own attendance. Following this meeting, if the employee had fewer than two absences in the ensuing six months, the employee was no longer part of the program. However, if the pattern of absence continued, the employee was counselled a second and third time. If no improvements resulted, a level 4 employment status review was conducted. This was done on a case-by-case basis. For example, a frequently absent employee with 28 years of good service would be treated differently from another employee with the same absenteeism record but only two years of employment.

The results were impressive. About 70 employees entered the program. Of these, eight to 10 advanced to step 2, two to step 3, and none to step 4. The absenteeism rate dropped to an average of less than 10 days, and punctuality was no longer an issue. Labour costs were reduced, because it meant that 20 fewer employees were needed.

Questions

1. "The policy assumed that all absences were innocent." What do you think this means?
2. The policy was active as of December 2007, and all employees were treated equally from that date, regardless of their previous absenteeism records. Was this fair? Why or why not?
3. Do you think that this policy will continue to get the results being sought? Why or why not?

Case Study 2

Whistle-Blowing and the Environment

Chantale Leroux works as a clerk for Avco Environmental Services, a small toxic-waste disposal company.

The company has a contract to dispose of medical waste from a local hospital. During the course of her work, Chantale comes across documents that suggest that Avco has actually been disposing of some of this medical waste in a local municipal landfill. Chantale is shocked. She knows this practice is illegal. And even though only a small portion of the medical waste that Avco handles is being disposed of this way, any amount at all seems a worrisome threat to public health.

Chantale gathers together the appropriate documents and takes them to her immediate superior, Dave Lamb. Dave says, "Look, I don't think that sort of thing is your concern, or mine. We're in charge of record-keeping, not making decisions about where this stuff gets dumped. I suggest you drop it."

The next day, Chantale decides to go one step further, and talk to Angela van Wilgenburg, the company's operations manager. Angela is clearly irritated. Angela says, "This isn't your concern. Look, these are the sorts of cost-cutting moves that let a little company like ours compete with our giant competitors. Besides, everyone knows that the regulations in this area are overly cautious. There's no real danger to anyone from the tiny amount of medical waste that 'slips' into the municipal dump. I consider this matter closed."

Chantale considers her situation. The message from her superiors was loud and clear. She strongly suspects that making further noises about this issue could jeopardize her job. Further, she generally has faith in the company's management. They've always seemed like honest, trustworthy people. But she was troubled by this apparent disregard for public safety. On the other hand, she asks herself whether maybe Angela was right in arguing that the danger was minimal. Chantale looks up the phone number of an old friend who worked for the local newspaper.

Source: Chris MacDonald, Businessethics.ca. Reprinted with permission through www.businessethics.ca.

Questions

1. What should Chantale do?
2. What are the reasonable limits on loyalty to one's employer?
3. Would it make a difference if Chantale had a position of greater authority?
4. Would it make a difference if Chantale had scientific expertise?

NOTES AND REFERENCES

1. "Pre-Employment Screening Services," www.dataresearch.com/services.htm (accessed February 28, 2009).
2. Anthony Moffatt, "The Danger of Digging Too Deep," *Canadian HR Reporter,* August 11, 2008, www.hrreporter.com/ArticleView.aspx?l=1&articleid=6261 (accessed February 28, 2009).
3. Lisa De Plante, "Watch Out for Dangerous Employees," *Canadian HR Reporter,* October 22, 2007, hrreporter.com/ArticleView.aspx?l=1&articleid=5528 (accessed February 28, 2009).
4. Ibid.
5. *Wallace v. United Grain Growers* (1997), 152 DLR (4th) 1 (SCC); *BC(PSERC) v. BCGEU* (1999), SCJ No. 46 (SCC).
6. Craig Offman, "Fired Shelter Worker Wins $68K," *National Post,* October 19, 2007, A9.
7. Shannon Klie, "CIBC Hit with $600-Million Lawsuit," *Canadian HR Reporter,* July 16, 2007, 1; and Jim Middlemiss, "Lawsuit Seeks OT for Bankers: CIBC Targeted," *National Post,* October 29, 2008, 1.
8. Jacquie McNish and Tara Perkins, "CIBC Overtime Lawsuit Dismissed," *The Globe and Mail,* June 19, 2009, B3.
9. Ingrid Peritz, "Visible Tattoos Okay on the Job, Quebec Judge Rules," *The Globe and Mail,* June 11, 2009, A10.
10. Jeffrey R. Smith, "Worker Ordered to Pay $1.5 Million," *Canadian HR Reporter,* December 1, 2008, 8.
11. *The Online Ethics Center Glossary,* www.onlineethics.org/CMS/glossary.aspx?letter=D (accessed March 1, 2009).
12. Peter Kovessy "The Pitfalls of Employment Law," *Ottawa Business Journal,* July 9, 2008, www.ottawabusinessjournal.com/292115414746991.php (accessed March 1, 2009).
13. "The Costs of Substance Abuse in Canada," Canadian Centre on Substance Abuse, April 2006, www.ccsa.ca/Eng/Priorities/Research/CostStudy/Pages/default.aspx (accessed March 2, 2009).
14. "Drug or Alcohol Dependency and Abuse as a Disability," Ontario Human Rights Commission, www.ohrc.on.ca/en/resources/Policies/PolicyDrugAlch?page=PolicyDrugAlch-DRUG.html (accessed March 2, 2009).
15. Didier Garriguet, "Beverage Consumption of Canadian Adults," *Statistics Canada,* November 2008, 25.
16. Barbara Butler & Associates, "Brief Analysis of Current Workplace Substance Abuse Issues and Activities in Canada," 2007, Canadian Centre on Substance Abuse.
17. Ibid.
18. Marina Straus, "Print Scans: Retail Tool or Invasion of Privacy?" *The Globe and Mail,* December 8, 2004, B1 and 7.
19. Keith Burkhardt, "Privacy vs. Policy: Personal Use of Company Equipment," *Canadian HR Reporter,* November 20, 2008, www.hrreporter.com/ArticleView.aspx?l=1&articleid=6514 (accessed March 2, 2009); and *"Personal Information Protection Act,"* November 4, 2003, seminar sponsored by Fasken Martineau.
20. Jeffrey R. Smith, "Safety Concerns Outweigh Employee's Privacy Rights in Disclosure of Medical Information," *Canadian HR Reporter,* October 4, 2007, www.hrreporter.com/ArticleView.aspx?l=1&articleid=5505 (accessed March 2, 2009).
21. "Privacy Commissioner Looking at RFID Technology," *Canadian HR Reporter,* March 11, 2008, www.hrreporter.com/ArticleView.aspx?l=1&articleid=5896 (accessed March 2, 2009).
22. Estelle Morrison, "Breaching Privacy More than Legal Concern," *Canadian HR Reporter,* April 21, 2008, www.hrreporter.com/ArticleView.aspx?l=1&articleid=5996 (accessed March 2, 2009).

23. Howard Levitt, "When does a Lie Warrant Firing?" *National Post,* May 28, 2008, WK1 and 4.

24. "Las Vegas Hotel Improves Decision Making and Guest Satisfaction with In-House Portal," TechRepublic, April 2007, www.whitepapers.techrepublic.com.com/abstract. aspx?docid=344389 (accessed March 2, 2009).

25. "How to Verify any Email Address," *Technology Magazine,* October 19, 2007, techmagazine.ws/how-to-verify-any-email-address/ (accessed March 2, 2009).

26. Lorna Harris, "Staffer Fired After Bad-Mouthing Colleagues, Management in Blog," *Canadian HR Reporter,* September 8, 2008, www.hrreporter.com/ArticleView.aspx?l=1&articleid=6313 (accessed March 2, 2009).

27. 2007 Labour, Employment & Human Rights Seminar, Fasken Martineau, Vancouver, October 26, 2007.

28. Ibid.

29. Ibid.

30. Jim Rapoza, "Unintended Consequences," *eWeek,* December 15, 2008, 40.

31. Janice Tibbetts, "Fired through Facebook," *The Vancouver Sun,* January 5, 2009, B2.

32. Stephen E. Fox and Elizabeth M. Bedell, "Reaching Employee Conduct Beyond the Workplace," Fish & Richardson P.C., 2007, 2.

33. Shannon Klie, "Teacher Loses Licence for Off-Duty Racist Conduct," *Canadian HR Reporter,* December 17, 2007, www. hrreporter.com/ArticleView.aspx?l=1&articleid=5709 (accessed March 2, 2009).

34. Natalie C. MacDonald, "Progressing Towards Just Cause," *Canadian HR Reporter,* September 22, 2008, www.hrreporter. com/ArticleView.aspx?l=1&articleid=6350 (accessed March 2, 2009).

35. Todd Hunter, "Return of the Bad Employee," *Canadian HR Reporter,* January 16, 2006, www.hrreporter.com/ ArticleView.aspx?l=1&articleid=4201 (accessed March 2, 2009).

36. Thadford A. Felton, "Best Practices in Documenting Employee Discipline," *Workforce Management,* January 15, 2009, www. workforce.com/archive/feature/26/10/10/index.php? ht= (accessed March 3, 2009).

37. Readers interested in the pioneering work on positive discipline should see James R. Redeker, "Discipline, Part 1: Progressive Systems Work Only by Accident," *Personnel* 62, no. 10 (October 1985): 8–12; James R. Redeker, "Discipline, Part 2: The Nonpunitive Approach Works by Design," *Personnel* 62, no. 11 (November 1985): 7–14. See also Alan W. Bryant, "Replacing Punitive Discipline with a Positive Approach," *Personnel Administrator* 29, no. 2 (February 1984): 79–87.

38. Natalie C. MacDonald, "Progressing Towards Just Cause."

39. Howard Levitt, "Take Fear Out of Firing," *National Post,* June 17, 2009, FP12.

40. "Constructive Dismissal," www.duhaime.org/ LegalDictionary/C/Constructivedismissal.aspx (accessed March 3, 2009).

41. Howard Levitt, "Worker's Demands Got Him Fired," *National Post,* February 4, 2009, FP15.

42. Howard Levitt, "'Hands-On' Manager Who Went Too Far," *The Vancouver Sun,* December 17, 2008, C6.

43. Jessica Marquez, "Outplacement Becomes a Coveted Benefit in Hard Times," *Workforce Management,* March 1, 2009, www.workforce.com/archive/feature/26/19/34/index.php? ht= (accessed March 4, 2009).

44. L. M. Sixel, "Can I Get My Old Desk Back, Too?" *The Globe and Mail,* March 22, 2008, B15.

45. "Why Include Negotiation in ADR," ADR Institute of Canada, www.amic.org (accessed March 4, 2009).

46. Cinnie Noble, "The 'Evilution' of Workplace Conflict," *Canadian HR Reporter,* March 10, 2008, www.hrreporter.com/ ArticleView.aspx?l=1&articleid=5879 (accessed March 4, 2009).

47. Ibid.

48. Carolin Carter, "Limited Future for Workplace Mediation," *Personnel Today,* November 25, 2008, 9.

49. Stephen P. Robbins, David A. DeCenzo, Robin Stuart-Kotze, Eileen B. Stewart, *Fundamentals of Management* (Toronto: Pearson Education Canada Inc., 2005): 38.

50. "Strengthening the Role of the Ethics Commissioner," Federal Accountability Act, www.faa-lfi.gc.ca/fs-fi/03fs-fi-eng.asp (accessed March 4, 2009).

51. Gerry Bellett, "Appeal Court to Hear Case of 'Whistle-Blower' City Employee," *The Vancouver Sun,* February 12, 2005, B11.

52. David Craik, "Whistling While at Work," *Employers Law,* September 2008, 14–15; and Lori Holder-Webb, Jeffrey Cohen, Leda Nath, and David Wood, "A Survey of Governance Disclosures Among U.S. Firms," *Journal of Business Ethics* 83, no. 3 (December 2008): 543–563.

CHAPTER 10

LABOUR RELATIONS AND COLLECTIVE BARGAINING

OUTCOMES

After studying this chapter, you should be able to

1 Explain the federal and provincial legislation that provides the framework for labour relations.

2 Cite the reasons employees join unions.

3 Describe the process by which unions organize employees and gain recognition as their bargaining agent.

4 Describe the functions labour unions perform at the national and local levels.

5 Describe the bargaining process and the bargaining goals and strategies of a union and an employer.

6 Describe the forms of bargaining power that a union and an employer may utilize to enforce their bargaining demands.

7 Identify the major provisions of a collective agreement, including the issue of management rights.

8 Describe a typical grievance procedure and explain the basis for arbitration awards.

OUTLINE

HRM CLOSE-UP

"We share a common goal and that is to serve our customers. If the company is successful, the unions will also be successful."

Eric Poirier remembers his first union meeting in the mid 1990s. He was a university student studying electrical engineering and felt fortunate to have a great job as a technician with a telephone company in New Brunswick. He recalls his union membership as being an important part of his work. But he didn't really appreciate the importance of good management–labour relations until he began to manage his own team years later.

In his first role as a manager for Bell Aliant, a telecommunications company with customers throughout Atlantic Canada and rural areas in Ontario and Quebec, Poirier spent time getting to know what each employee did. He also wanted to show his support for staff by being available when they needed him. "When the phone rang, I answered it. If I received a voice mail, I responded as soon as I could," he said. "It was an effort to build relationships and develop trust and respect."

In a subsequent position, Poirier managed people who did maintenance and provisioning of more advanced inter-networking technology. "Those jobs were new to me, and it was important for me to understand more about the employees' work," he recalls. "When I learned that some maintenance activities had to be done between the hours of 2:00 a.m. and 6:00 a.m., I came in at that time to learn first-hand from them." According to Poirier, working on strengthening the manager-employee relationship helps the manager when there's a business issue that needs attention.

Managing a unionized group has its benefits says Poirier. "There are rules of engagement and when it comes to making decisions about things like vacation and sick time, being able to refer to the collective agreement makes it easier." He feels some managers may be nervous the first time they have to deal with a grievance, for example. "But really, the grievance process just gives us a way to have a discussion. It's a process that's laid out for us and enables us to talk through an issue and find a resolution."

Eric Poirier. Courtesy of Eric Poirier

Recently, Bell Aliant began monthly meetings between senior executive leaders from both the union and the company. The goal of this "Common Interest Forum" is to get both parties together to discuss business strategy. "We share a common goal and that is to serve our customers. If the company is successful, the unions will also be successful," Poirier explains.

Perhaps the greatest challenge for Poirier is how to recognize and reward employees who do outstanding work. In an environment where all employees must be treated fairly and equally, and everyone is compensated in the same way, he must find creative ways to recognize performance excellence. Sometimes assigning a special project allows Poirier to provide additional job satisfaction to top performers. "I've had staff getting involved in test installations when we do a trial for a new service offering. This kind of thing becomes a source of pride for staff and lets them become role models for others who are developing their skills."

Building great relationships with staff is Poirier's secret. "If you've built a solid foundation, you can drive improvements and introduce change that will strengthen the business. It's a win-win."

INTRODUCTION

Mention the word "union" and most people will have some opinion, positive or negative. To some, the word evokes images of labour–management unrest—grievances, strikes, picketing, boycotts. To others, the word represents fairness, opportunity, equal representation, and someone who will look after them. Many think of unions as simply creating an adversarial relationship between employees and managers, while others feel that unions are necessary to counterbalance the power employers have.

Regardless of how people feel about them, unions have been an important force shaping organizational practices, legislation, and political thought in Canada since the mid-1800s. Consider Eric Poirier's statements in the HRM Close-Up. Some people might say that fears about unionization have helped employers become better at managing people. Today, unions remain of interest because of their influence on organizational productivity and competitiveness, the development of labour law, and HR policies and practices. Like business organizations themselves, unions are undergoing changes in both operation and philosophy. Labour–management co-operative programs, company buyouts by unions, and labour's increased interest in global trade are examples of labour's new role in society.

In spite of the long history of unions, the intricacies of labour relations are unfamiliar to many individuals. Therefore, this chapter describes government regulation of labour relations, the labour relations process, the reasons workers join labour organizations, the structure and leadership of labour unions, contemporary challenges to labour organizations, and the role a supervisor or manager plays in labour relations.

Unions and other labour organizations can significantly affect the ability of managers to direct and control the various HR processes. For example, union seniority provisions in the labour contract may influence who is selected for job promotions or training programs. Pay rates may be determined through union negotiations, or unions may impose restrictions on management's employee evaluation methods. Therefore, it is essential that managers understand how unions operate and familiarize themselves with the growing body of laws governing labour relations. It is also important for the supervisor to understand how unionization affects the actions of the union and those of the HR professional.

THE LAWS GOVERNING LABOUR RELATIONS

Unions have a long history in North America, and the regulations governing labour relations have evolved over time. Initially, employers strongly opposed union growth, using court injunctions (e.g., court orders forbidding various union activities, such as picketing and strikes) and devices, such as the "yellow-dog contract." A yellow-dog contract was an employer's anti-union tactic by which employees had to agree not to join a union while working for the employer's organization. Using strikebreakers, blacklisting employees (e.g., circulating the names of union supporters to other employers), and discriminating against those who favoured unionization were other anti-union tactics.

Today, the laws governing labour relations seek to create an environment in which both unions and employers can exercise their respective rights and responsibilities. Chapter 2 provided an overview of the various employment laws, including those governing labour relations. This chapter now looks at the laws in more detail.

Labour Relations Legislation

 Outcome **1**

The first labour relations legislation, the Trades Unions Act, was passed by the federal Parliament in 1872. This act exempted unions from charges of criminal conspiracy, allowed them to pursue goals of collective bargaining without persecution, and gave them the ability to strike. Between 1872 and 1900, legislation to settle industrial disputes was enacted in a number of provinces, including Quebec, Ontario, British Columbia, and Nova Scotia. Although these acts are no longer in effect, they did mark Canada's early recognition of the rights of unions.

Several different laws at the federal and provincial levels currently regulate labour relations. These laws make up a labour relations "system" consisting of government, unions, and employers. The government makes the laws that regulate how unions and employers behave with each other.[1] In making laws, the government will determine who can unionize and where they can unionize. There are specific laws, or acts, for different sectors, industries, and workers. Canada's labour relations system is highly decentralized, whereas the U.S. system is highly centralized. For example, in Canada, the federal law governs interprovincial transportation and communications, while provincial legislation governs manufacturing and mining. However, 90% of the workforce is governed by provincial legislation. As mentioned earlier in this book, federally regulated companies such as Bell, Rogers, Sprint, and Telus are governed by the Canada Labour Code, whereas companies such as Molson Breweries are governed by the province in which they operate. Labour legislation, whether federal or provincial, has certain features in common:

- The right of people to join unions.
- The requirement that employers recognize a certified union as the rightful and exclusive bargaining agent for that group of employees.
- The identification of unfair labour practices.
- The right of unions to strike and right of employers to lock out workers.[2]

The Canada Industrial Relations Board (CIRB) was established to administer and enforce the Canada Labour Code. Similarly, each province has a labour relations board (LRB) whose members are appointed by the provincial government and who administer the labour law. (The exception is Quebec, which has a labour court and commissioners.) The LRB is generally separate from the government and is composed of representatives from labour and management. The duties of the LRB include, but are not limited to

- processing union applications to represent employees;
- processing applications to terminate union bargaining rights;
- hearing unfair labour practice complaints; and
- hearing complaints and issuing decisions regarding strikes, lockouts and picketing.[3]

It is important to remember that the administrative regulations are greatly influenced by the politics of any provincial government. Therefore, the legislation can be relatively similar, but the interpretation of the law can vary greatly from one province to another. The law typically gets interpreted by the decisions made by the respective labour boards that then influence the actions a union or company can take in the future. To learn more about the administration of labour relations, Manager's Toolkit 10.1 lists the websites of the labour relations boards.

MANAGER'S TOOLKIT 10.1

LABOUR RELATIONS BOARDS

Labour relations boards are making it easier for employers and employees to access information. The following websites are a valuable resource for the supervisor and HR professional.

Jurisdiction	Name	Website
Federal government	Canada Industrial Relations Board	www.cirb-ccri.gc.ca
Alberta	Alberta Labour Relations Board	www.alrb.gov.ab.ca/
British Columbia	Labour Relations Board	www.lrb.bc.ca
Manitoba	Manitoba Labour Board	www.gov.mb.ca/labour/labbrd
New Brunswick	Industrial Relations Branch	www.gnb.ca/0110/index-e.asp
Newfoundland and Labrador	Labour Relations Board	www.hrle.gov.nl.ca/lrb/
Nova Scotia	Labour Relations Board	www.gov.ns.ca/lwd/
Ontario	Ontario Labour Relations Board	www.olrb.gov.on.ca
Prince Edward Island	Labour Relations Board	www.gov.pe.ca/cca/index.php3?number=1006679&lang=E
Quebec	The Labour Code is administered through investigations and commissions created at the time of a complaint.	
Saskatchewan	Labour Relations Board	www.sasklabourrelationsboard.com

WHY EMPLOYEES UNIONIZE

Outcome 2

Employees frequently feel that individually they will be unable to exercise power regarding their employment conditions at any particular employer. The treatment and benefits they receive depend in large part on how their employers view their worth to the organization. Of course, if they believe they are not being treated fairly, they have the choice of quitting. However, another way to correct the situation is to organize and bargain with the employer collectively. When employees pursue this direction, the labour relations process begins. As Figure 10.1 illustrates, the **labour relations process** consists of a logical sequence of four events: (1) employees desire collective representation, (2) union organizers or employees begin the organizing campaign, (3) collective negotiations lead to a collective agreement, and (4) the collective agreement is administered. Laws and administrative rulings influence each of the separate events by granting special privileges to, or imposing defined constraints on, employees, employers, and union officials.[4]

Labour relations process
Logical sequence of four events: (1) workers desire collective representation, (2) union begins its organizing campaign, (3) collective negotiations lead to a contract, and (4) the contract is administered

The majority of research on why employees unionize comes from the study of blue-collar employees in the private sector. These studies generally conclude that employees unionize as a result of

1. economic need;
2. general dissatisfaction with managerial practices; and/or
3. a desire to fulfill social and status needs.

Union shop
Provision of the collective agreement that requires employees to join the union as a condition of their employment

It should be pointed out that some employees join unions because of the **union shop** provisions of the collective agreement that require employees to join as a condition of their employment. Others join because it is a **closed shop**—only members of a union will be hired or because they choose to under an **open shop** provision. Even when forced to join, many employees eventually accept the concept of unionism. The sections that follow look at some of the more specific reasons people unionize and what role the supervisor and/or organization plays in the unionization process.

Closed shop
Provision of the collective agreement that requires employers to hire only union members

Pay, Benefits, and Working Conditions

Open shop
Provision of the collective agreement that allows employees to join or not join the union

Whether or not a union can become the bargaining agent for a group of employees will be influenced by the employees' degree of dissatisfaction, if any, with their overall employment conditions. For example, employees may feel their concerns about health and safety are ignored or they may be required to wear uniforms without being reimbursed for the cost. It will also depend on whether

FIGURE 10.1   Labour Relations Process

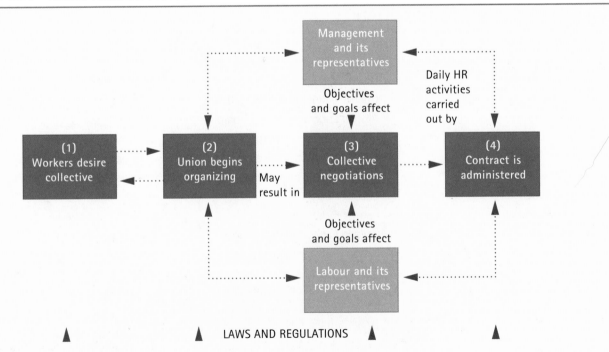

Winnipeg Strike of 1919, showing a group of strikers lining a downtown street in Winnipeg. In the centre of the photo is a burning streetcar. Metal workers started the strike to force their employers to improve their working conditions.

CP PHOTO/fls

the employees perceive the union as likely to be effective in improving these conditions. However, unhappiness with wages, benefits, and working conditions appear to be the strongest reasons to join a union. Unions will generally try to convince potential members that they can deliver pay increases and benefits. Other issues that have concerned unions include changes in business practices, outsourcing, and corporate mergers.[5]

Dissatisfaction with Supervisors and Managers

Employees may seek unionization when they perceive that managerial practices regarding promotion, transfer, shift assignment, or other job-related policies are decided unfairly. Employees cite favouritism shown by managers as a major reason for joining unions. This is particularly true when the favouritism concerns discipline, promotion, and wage increases. Unions will describe the structured complaint process in the collective agreement (the grievance or arbitration process) as a formal way in which employees can have their complaints heard and acted on.

This book has noted that today's employees are better educated than those of the past and often express a desire to be more involved in decisions affecting their jobs. Chapter 3 discussed the concept of employee empowerment and highlighted various employee involvement techniques. The failure of employers to give employees an opportunity to participate in decisions affecting their welfare may encourage union membership. It is widely believed that one reason managers begin employee involvement programs and seek to empower their employees is to avoid collective action by employees. For example, a unionization attempt by the United Steelworkers at Dofasco Steel in Hamilton, Ontario, was eventually abandoned when it didn't have enough signed union cards. The plant has operated for almost 100 years without a unionized workforce. The plant has a long track-record of offering a comprehensive compensation package and good relationships with its managers.[6]

Social and Status Concerns

Employees whose needs for status and recognition are being frustrated may join unions as a means of satisfying these needs. Through their union, they have an opportunity to fraternize with other employees who have similar desires, interests, and problems. Joining the union also enables them to put to use any leadership talents they may have. In the final analysis, the deciding factor is likely to be whether employees perceive that the benefits of joining a union outweigh the costs associated with membership.

HOW EMPLOYEES ORGANIZE

Once employees desire to unionize, a formal organizing campaign may be started either by a union organizer or by employees acting on their own behalf. Contrary to popular belief, most organizing campaigns are begun by employees rather than by union organizers. Large national unions like the Canadian Auto Workers, the United Brotherhood of Carpenters, the United Steelworkers, and the Teamsters, however, have formal organizing departments whose purpose is to identify organizing opportunities and launch organizing campaigns. It has been no secret that the labour movement has targeted certain types of employers. Larger unions have moved out of their traditional industries into other areas. This has been due to changes from a goods-producing society to a service-based society as well as a decline in union membership in industries such as mining and forestry.[7]

One of the more prominent campaigns has been to organize employees at Walmart stores. However, to date, the only success in North America has been in the province of Quebec.[8] While it is difficult to determine exactly why Walmart has not been unionized, some of the reasons appear to be the typical age of the workers (teenagers), the type of employment (part-time), and the difficulty unions have had in organizing the service sector.

Since organizing campaigns can be expensive, union leaders carefully evaluate their chances of success and the possible benefits to be gained from their efforts. Important in this evaluation is the employer's vulnerability to unionization. Union leaders also consider the effect that allowing an employer to remain nonunion may have on the strength of their union within the area. A nonunion employer can impair a union's efforts to standardize employment conditions within an industry or geographic area, as well as weaken the union's bargaining power with employers it has unionized. Unions will also assess whether there is a possibility that future employees may wish to decertify. Just as the costs of unionizing can be high, so can the challenges coming from employees wanting to cease having the union represent them.

Employees will frequently consider a union if there is dissatisfaction with how they are treated.

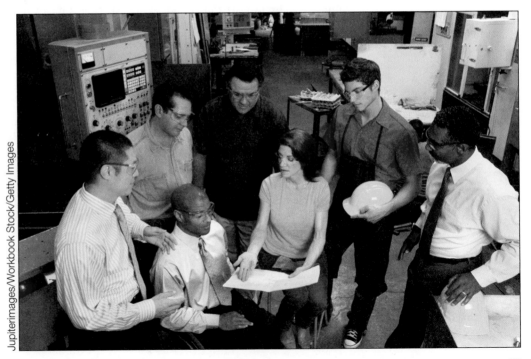

Jupiterimages/Workbook Stock/Getty Images

Organizing Steps

 Outcome 3

The typical organizing campaign follows a series of progressive steps that can lead to employee representation. The organizing process normally includes the following steps:

1. Employee–union contact.
2. Initial organizational meeting.
3. Formation of in-house organizing committee.
4. Application to labour relations board.
5. Issuance of certificate by labour relations board.
6. Election of bargaining committee and contract negotiations.

STEP 1 The first step begins when employees and union officials make contact to explore the possibility of unionization. During these discussions, employees will investigate the advantages of representation, and union officials will begin to gather information on employee needs, problems, and complaints as well as information on the employer's financial health and supervisory styles. To win employee support, union organizers must build a case against the employer and for the union.

Supervisors and managers can become familiar with the questions unions ask employees during organizing drives and therefore better assess the effectiveness of their management practices. Manager's Toolkit 10.2 presents these questions.

STEP 2 As an organizing campaign gathers momentum, the organizer will schedule an initial union meeting to attract more supporters. The organizer will use the information gathered in Step 1 to address employee needs and explain how the union can secure these goals.

STEP 3 The third important step in the organizing drive is to form an in-house organizing committee composed of employees willing to provide leadership to the campaign. The committee's role is to interest other employees in joining the union and in supporting its campaign. An important task of the committee is to have employees sign a **membership card** (or authorization card) indicating their willingness to be represented by a labour union in collective bargaining with their employer.

Membership card
A statement signed by an employee authorizing a union to act as a representative of the employee for purposes of collective bargaining

---

MANAGER'S TOOLKIT **10.2**

FREQUENTLY ASKED QUESTIONS

Many organizations find themselves unionized and are surprised that it has happened. There is also a mistaken belief that unions do not actively recruit new members. The following are the questions union organizers usually ask employees:

1. Do you think people get paid more in other organizations? (Unions will know how much people are paid in the industry and geographic area.)

2. Are decisions about how much employees are paid based on logic or favouritism? (Unions will have usually received information that supervisors make decisions in an arbitrary fashion.)

3. Are decisions about promotions based on merit or favouritism? (Unions usually have information about a particular individual that was promoted for reasons other than merit.)

4. If something happens that you feel is unfair, do you have recourse? Can you get your complaint heard?

Who will hear it? Can they fix it? (Many small companies do not have a way to handle employee complaints. Unions will talk about the formal grievance procedure and the protections that can be provided to employees who feel helpless in dealing with a problem.)

5. How are shift schedules determined? (Unions will say that shifts ought to be determined by seniority.)

6. How are performance problems handled? (Unions will convince potential members that a union can ensure that people are treated fairly if there are performance issues.)

7. Do you feel that your manager criticizes you unfairly? (Unions will describe the processes that can be used if employees feel that they have not been treated fairly.)

8. Does your boss treat you with respect? (Unions will indicate that the power of a collective group of people will make the employer treat everyone respectfully.)

The number of signed membership cards demonstrates the potential strength of the labour union. Legislation across Canada states that unions must have a majority of employees as members in a bargaining unit before they can apply for certification election. However, most jurisdictions now interpret this to mean that at least 50% of those voting constitute a majority. In other words, those who do not cast ballots are not assumed to be voting against the certification of the union. The union membership card, once signed, is confidential, and only the labour relations board has access to the cards.

STEP 4 Application is made to the appropriate labour relations board. In Canada, a majority of unions are certified without a vote if the labour relations board finds that the union has the support of the majority of the employees, based on the number of signed cards. However, in Ontario, if 40% or more of the employees sign membership cards, then a vote can be requested.

STEP 5 The labour relations board reviews the application and initially informs both the employer and the employees about the application. This application is posted so that either employees or the employer have an opportunity to challenge.

STEP 6 Once the labour relations board determines that the union is certified, a bargaining committee is put in place to start negotiating a collective agreement. If the union is a national union, such as the Canadian Auto Workers, usually a national representative works with the bargaining committee to negotiate the collective agreement with the company.

Canadian Auto Workers
www.caw.ca

Employer Tactics

Employers must not interfere with the certification process. They are prohibited by law from dismissing, disciplining, or threatening employees for exercising their rights to form a union. Employers cannot promise better conditions, such as increased vacation days, if the employees vote for no union or choose one union over another. They cannot unilaterally change wages and working conditions during certification proceedings or during collective bargaining. Like unions, they must bargain in good faith, meaning that they must demonstrate a commitment to bargain seriously and fairly. In addition, they cannot participate in the formation, selection, or support of unions representing employees.

None of these prohibitions prevents an employer from making the case that the employees have a right not to join a union or that they can deal directly with the employer on any issue. Employer resistance to unionization is the norm in Canada; however, employers need to recognize that employees must be free from threats, intimidation, pressure, or coercion.[9]

Attempts by employers to influence employees are scrutinized closely by officials of the organizing unions and the labour relations board. In one recent case, the International Association of Machinists and Aerospace Workers (IAMAW) accused Toyota Canada of unfair labour practices in relation to a unionization drive at its Cambridge, Ontario, plant. Specifically, Toyota is charged with intimidating and unduly influencing employees to vote against the union.[10] This case was never heard by the Ontario Labour Relations Board, nor was there a certification vote, as the IAMAW withdrew its entire application for certification in April 2008.[11]

Union Tactics

Unions also have a duty to act in accordance with labour legislation. Unions are prohibited from interfering with the operation of an employer's organization. They cannot intimidate or coerce employees to become or remain members of a union. Nor can they force employers to dismiss, discipline, or discriminate against nonunion employees. They must provide fair representation for all employees in the **bargaining unit**, whether in collective bargaining or in grievance procedure cases. Unions cannot engage in activities such as strikes before the expiration of the union contract.

Any of the prohibited activities discussed above for both employers and unions are considered **unfair labour practices**. Charges of unfair labour practices are made to the labour relations board, whose duty is to enforce the applicable labour laws and decide if an unfair labour practice occurred. An example of an unfair labour practice by an employer would be to threaten to fire people who wanted to join a union. Similarly, a union cannot threaten harm to employees if they

Bargaining unit
Group of two or more employees who share common employment interests and conditions and may reasonably be grouped together for purposes of collective bargaining

Unfair labour practices
Specific employer and union illegal practices that operate to deny employees their rights and benefits under labour law

FIGURE 10.2   Unfair Labour Practices

Unfair labour practices by employers include the following.

- Helping to establish or administer a union.
- Altering the working conditions of the employees while a union is applying for certification without the union's consent.
- Using intimidation, coercion, threats, promises, or exercising undue influence while a union is being organized.
- Failing to recognize or bargain with the certified union.
- Hiring professional strike breakers.

Unfair labour practices by unions include the following.

- Contributing financial or other support to an employee's organization.
- Not representing fairly the employees in the bargaining unit.
- Bargaining or negotiating a collective agreement with an employer while another union represents the employees in the bargaining unit.
- Calling or authorizing an unlawful strike, or threatening to do so.

don't join the union. Figure 10.2 provides a list of unfair labour practices on both the union and the management side.

CERTIFICATION PROCEDURES

Certification
Acquisition of exclusive rights by union to represent the employees

The procedures for union **certification** vary across Canadian jurisdictions. As mentioned earlier, if an applicant union can present documentation that it has sufficient support in the proposed bargaining unit, labour boards will grant certification to the union or grant a vote. The labour relations board must certify a union before it can act as a bargaining unit for a group of employees. The union normally provides evidence by submitting signed authorization cards and proof that initiation dues or fees have been paid.[12] Recognition of a union may be obtained through voluntary recognition, regular certification, or a prehearing vote.

However, there can be a situation whereby the legal framework of labour relations forces a person to join a particular union if the person wants to work. For example, the government of Quebec has legislation that forces all construction workers to belong to one of five unions. This also means that any construction company must hire only unionized workers.

Voluntary Recognition

All employers, except those in the province of Quebec, may voluntarily recognize and accept a union. This rarely happens, except in the construction industry where there is a great reliance on union hiring halls. However, attempting to provide voluntary recognition can create problems with the employees. For example, 400 non-union employees at the Johnson Controls International plant in Orangeville, Ontario, have consistently resisted attempts by the Canadian Autoworkers Union (CAW) to be unionized. However, when a nearby plant of Johnson became unionized earlier in the same year, the owners of Johnson Controls invited the CAW into its Orangeville operation to speak to its employees. The non-union employees objected to this tactic and the company decided to take a different approach.[13]

Regular Certification

The regular certification process begins with the union submitting the required minimum membership evidence to the labour relations board. Generally, if an applicant union can demonstrate that it has sufficient support in the proposed bargaining unit, labour boards may grant certification on that basis. (However, with changes in government, labour relations legislation is often reformed. Therefore, requirements for granting certification may change.) The labour relations board may order a representative vote if a sizable minority of workers have indicated either support for or opposition to the unionization.

The CAW is Canada's largest private-sector union.

Courtesy of CAW Local 195

Prehearing Votes

If there is evidence of irregularities, such as unfair labour practices taking place during the organizing drive, a prehearing vote may be taken. The purpose of this vote is to establish the level of support among the workers. Depending on the particular labour relations legislation, votes can be called if less than 50% of the employees indicate support for a union.

Once a union has been certified, employees are part of a collective and can no longer individually make special arrangements on pay, hours of work, and so on. Likewise, this means that the manager and supervisor can no longer treat individuals differently—that is, they can't make individual deals.

Contract Negotiations

Once a bargaining unit has been certified by the labour relations board, the employer and the union are legally obliged to bargain in good faith over the terms and conditions of a collective agreement. The collective agreement is for at least one year. As the contract expiry date approaches, either party must notify the other of its intention to bargain for a renewal collective agreement or contract negotiation.

Decertification

All legislation allows for decertification of unions under certain conditions. If the majority of employees indicate that they do not want to be represented by the union or that they want to be represented by another union, or if the union has failed to bargain, an application for decertification can be made to the labour relations board. If a collective agreement has been reached with the employer, this application can be made only at specified times, such as a few months before the agreement expires. The application for decertification can be initiated by either employees or the employer if the union fails to bargain.

Impact of Unionization on Managers

The unionization of employees can affect managers in many ways. Perhaps most significant is the effect it can have on the ability of managers to make decisions about employees. A union can assist employees if they believe they haven't been treated in accordance with the agreed-to employment conditions. As an example, if a company doesn't have a formal complaint mechanism, there is now a structured grievance procedure. And the decisions of a structured grievance procedure can be enforced through the courts (as will be discussed later in this chapter). Unionization also restricts the freedom of management to formulate HR policy and practices unilaterally.

Challenges to Management Decisions

Management rights
Decisions regarding organizational operations over which management claims exclusive rights

Unions typically attempt to achieve greater participation in management decisions that affect their members. Specifically, these decisions may often involve such issues as the subcontracting of work, productivity standards, and job content. Employers quite naturally seek to claim many of these decisions as their exclusive **management rights.** However, these rights are subject to challenge and erosion by the union. They may be challenged at the bargaining table, through the grievance procedure, and through strikes. In difficult economic times, challenges can include preventing equipment from being moved from one location to another. That occurred in early 2009 when laid-off workers at Aradco, an auto parts manufacturer in Windsor, occupied its buildings that prevented Chrysler from removing equipment that was necessary for its auto production. Chrysler had initially agreed to pay the workers severance but the union members rejected the offer. Eventually the CAW and Chrysler reached a deal that allowed Chrysler to remove the equipment. The plant had been closed due to a dispute the owners had with Chrysler.[14]

Loss of Supervisory Flexibility

At a recent labour–management conference a union official commented, "Contract terms covering wages, benefits, job security, and working hours are of major importance to our membership." However, for managers and supervisors, the focal point of the union's impact is at the operating level (the shop floor or office facility), where the terms of the collective agreement are implemented on a daily basis. For example, these terms can determine what corrective action is to be taken in directing and disciplining employees. When disciplining employees, supervisors must be certain they can demonstrate just cause (see Chapter 9) for their actions, because these actions can be challenged by the union and the supervisor can be called as defendant during a grievance hearing. If the challenge is upheld, the supervisor's effectiveness in coping with subsequent disciplinary problems may be impaired. Specific contract language can also reduce the supervisor's flexibility to manage in such areas as scheduling, training, performance evaluation, and promotions, to name a few.

The list provided in Manager's Toolkit 10.3 offers guidelines to help managers and supervisors understand what they can do to create a work environment where there is no need to unionize.

MANAGER'S TOOLKIT 10.3

CREATING A POSITIVE WORK ENVIRONMENT

1. If you have something to say to one of your employees, say it directly—and soon.

2. Praise employees publicly; criticize in private.

3. Remember: actions speak louder than words. Be sure your actions "say" what you want them to.

4. Be respectful of all your employees—even the poor performers.

5. Set up a file system for employee information where you can keep documentation on pay raises, performance reviews, and the like. Allow employees access to their files and encourage them to review their files.

6. Create performance goals with each employee— goals that are challenging but attainable; monitor performance and provide feedback.

7. Share business information.

8. Seek input from employees when making changes that will affect them.

9. Ask employees for suggestions on how to improve business operations.

HOW UNIONS OPERATE

International Brotherhood of Electrical Workers

www.ibew.org/

Brotherhood of Boilermakers

www.boilermakers.org/

Canadian Union of Postal Workers

www.cupw.ca

Ontario Secondary School Teachers' Federation

www.osstf.on.ca/

Canadian Labour Congress

www.clc-ctc.ca

Unions that represent skilled craft workers, such as carpenters or masons, are called craft unions, such as the International Brotherhood of Electrical Workers (IBEW) and the Brotherhood of Boilermakers. Unions that represent unskilled and semiskilled workers employed along industry lines are known as industrial unions, for example, the Canadian Union of Postal Workers and the Ontario Secondary School Teachers' Federation. While the distinction between craft and industrial unions still exists, technological changes and competition among unions for members have helped to reduce it. Today, skilled and unskilled workers, white-collar and blue-collar workers, and professional groups are being represented by both types of union.

Besides unions, there are also employee associations representing various groups of professional and white-collar employees. Examples of employee associations include the Federation of Quebec Nurses and the Alberta Teachers' Association. In competing with unions, these associations may function as unions and become just as aggressive as unions in representing members. These associations are nonunion; however, if the employee association met the necessary criteria under labour legislation, the association could become certified as a union.

Regardless of their type, labour organizations are diverse organizations, each with its own method of governance and objectives. And it is important to remember that unions are primarily political organizations. That is, they have elected leaders who can be voted out of office if the wishes of the members are not met.

Because of the political nature of unions, many unions have come together under an umbrella organization called the Canadian Labour Congress (CLC). Through this organization, the CLC attempts to influence government policy by commenting on economic conditions, such as the unemployment rate. Also, since most of the major unions in Canada are members of the CLC, it helps to referee between unions if they are seeking to organize the same group of workers. Because of its size and resources, the CLC is a very influential organization in Canada, and globally. For example, the CLC, along with other international labour leaders in late 2008 met with the G-20 heads of governments to discuss coordinated action to prevent a global job crisis and to encourage reform of the global financial system.[15] On the other hand, the head of the CLC, Ken Georgetti, publicly said in early 2009 that the Canadian government was not doing enough in the economic stimulus package to address the problems faced by working families during the recession.[16] For further information on the CLC, go to its website at **www.clc-ctc.ca**.

Structure, Functions, and Leadership of International and National Unions

International unions tend to be affiliates of American unions, with headquarters in the United States. In Canada, there are 39 international unions (with membership of about 1.2 million workers) and 175 national unions (with membership of close to 3 million).[17] There are fewer international and national unions than five years ago as mergers within unions occur for a number of reasons. The merger of three international unions—the United Steelworkers, the United Auto Workers, and the International Association of Machinists—into the largest industrial union in North America results in a strike fund of $1 billion.[18]

Outcome **4**

Both international and national unions are made up of local unions. The objectives of these unions are to help organize local unions, to provide strike support, and to assist local unions with negotiations, grievance procedures, and the like. These unions also represent membership interest with internal and external constituents. By ensuring that all employers pay similar wages to their unionized workers, they serve the additional role of removing higher wages as a competitive disadvantage.

Structure and Functions of Local Unions

Employees of any organization can form their own union, with no affiliation to a national or international union. In this case, the local is the union. However, most local unions are members of national or international unions or the Canadian Labour Congress, which make available to them financial resources and advice. There are approximately 15,000 locals in Canada.[19]

Canadian Auto Workers
www.caw.ca

Unionized employees pay union dues that finance the operation of the local union. The officers of a local union are usually responsible for negotiating the local collective agreement, for ensuring the agreement is adhered to, and for investigating and processing member grievances. At Work with HRM 10.1 describes how the Canadian Auto Workers union operates (see also **www.caw.ca**).

AT WORK **with HRM 10.1**

THE CANADIAN AUTO WORKERS

Ken Lewenza, president of the Canadian Auto Workers (CAW), oversees the operations of Canada's largest private-sector union. The CAW was established in 1985 after breaking away from its American affiliate, the United Auto Workers. Membership has since increased from 118,000 to 255,000 through mergers with other unions, including Mine Mill Workers, the Canadian Brotherhood of Railway Transportation, and General Workers. The CAW represents employees in all major sectors of the Canadian economy, including aerospace, health care, hospitality, in addition to the auto industry.

The CAW describes itself as being a democratic structure and as such, its 2008 Collective Bargaining Conference and Political Action Convention brought people together to discuss a number of issues, some of which had to do with the poor economic climate. The outcome of the conference identified the economic challenges for the auto industry, the growth of the use of temporary workers, and the need to find new ways to organize younger workers. It also specifically identified it would agree to freezing base wages. This is a very different agenda from three years ago when the focus was on improved wages and benefits, shorter work time, greater job security.

About the same time, the CAW agreed to a wage freeze for three years plus a severance package for the GM Canada Windsor plant that is scheduled to shut down in 2010. However, this was before the stock market meltdown in October 2008, which has created a variety of economic stimulus programs from both the Canadian and U.S. governments that is designed to help the auto industry. In January 2009, the CAW agreed to negotiate with the Canadian units of GM, Ford, and Chrysler to reduce labour costs. Lewenza stated, "There's a demand on the union to be part of the solution or the consequences could be horrible." In March 2009, exploratory talks were started with GM to assist it

through the restructuring—which is part of the government demand for any more financial assistance. The focus for GM is on paid time off and health- care/benefits costs.

Earlier in 2009, the unionized employees at an auto parts factory in Windsor were faced with a tough choice: vote "yes," to keep their jobs but with reduced wages or vote "no," and the company would shut down. The workers agreed to the reduced wages even though the CAW recommended that the employees reject the proposal. A labour relations expert expressed that there was a return to concessionary bargaining—something that happened in the early 1980s during the last significant recession.

At the same time in March 2009 that talks were commencing with GM, Chrysler announced the elimination of its third shift at the minivan assembly plant in Windsor, Ontario, which would result in the layoff of 1200 workers. The president of Local 444 stated, "This news is devastating for the Windsor community which already has the highest unemployment rate of any city across the country. There are 40 parts plants in the Windsor area directly associated with the minivan plant, all of which will be in jeopardy of losing more jobs."

The membership of the CAW had remained relatively static for the last several years. However, with the significant decline in the auto industry, there is a possibility that the CAW could find itself faced with an eroding membership base. Much like other organizations in difficult economic times, the CAW may have to consider how it responds to declining revenues.

CRITICAL THINKING QUESTIONS

1. What do think the future of the CAW looks like? What has happened to the CAW since 2009?
2. Do you think unions ought to be able to organize workers in any industry, like retail or fast food? Why?

Sources: Adapted from "CAW Beats Back Two-Tier Wages, Wins Reprieve for St. Thomas Plant," *CAW News*, April 28, 2008,"Taking the Challenge," *CAW Newsletter* 38, no. 23 (June 16, 2008) www.caw.ca (accessed March 5, 2009); Chris Vander Doelen, "CAW Settles with Both Chrysler and GM," *National Post*, May 16, 2008; FP1; Greg Keenan, "Auto Deal's Fate Rides on CAW Concessions," *The Globe and Mail*, January 30, 2009, B1;"CAW to Open Exploratory Talks with General Motors," www.caw.ca/en/5656.htm (accessed March 5, 2009); Nicolas Van Praet and Paul Vieira, "Workers Faced with Toughest Choice," *Financial Post*, February 11, 2009, FP1; and "Canadian Auto Industry Suffers Further Blow as Economy Continues to Struggle," www.caw.ca/en/5657.htm (accessed March 5, 2009).

Role of the Union (Shop) Steward

Union (shop) steward
Employee who, as a nonpaid union official, represents the interests of members in their relations with management

The **union (shop) steward** represents the interests of union members in their relations with their immediate supervisors and other members of management. Union stewards are employees of the company and are normally selected by union members within their department and serve without union pay.

A union steward can be viewed as a "person in the middle," caught between conflicting interests and groups. It cannot be assumed that stewards will always champion union members and routinely oppose managerial objectives. Union stewards are often insightful individuals working for the betterment of employees and the organization. Therefore supervisors and managers at all levels are encouraged to develop a positive working relationship with stewards and all union officials. This relationship can have an important bearing on union–management cooperation and on the efficiency and morale of the workers.

Role of the Business Agent

Business agent
Normally a paid labour official responsible for negotiating and administering the collective agreement and working to resolve union members' problems

Negotiating and administering the collective agreement and working to resolve problems arising in connection with it are major responsibilities of the **business agent.** In performing these duties, business agents must be all things to all people within their unions. They frequently are required to assume the role of counsellor in helping union members with both personal and job-related problems. They are also expected to satisfactorily resolve grievances that cannot be settled by the union stewards. Administering the daily affairs of the local union is another significant part of the business agent's job.

Union Leadership Approaches and Philosophies

To evaluate the role of union leaders accurately, one must understand the nature of their backgrounds and ambitions and recognize the political nature of the offices they occupy. The leaders of many national unions have been able to develop political machines that enable them to defeat opposition and to perpetuate themselves in office. Tenure for the leaders of a local union, however, is less secure. If they are to remain in office, they must be able to convince a majority of the members that they are serving them effectively.

Although it is true that union leaders occupy positions of power within their organizations, rank-and-file members can and often do exercise a strong influence over these leaders, particularly with respect to the negotiation and administration of the collective agreement. It is important for managers to understand that union officials are elected to office and, like any political officials, must be responsive to the views of their constituency. The union leader who ignores the demands of union members may risk (1) being voted out of office, (2) having members vote the union out as their bargaining agent, (3) having members refuse to ratify the union agreement, or (4) having members engage in wildcat strikes or work stoppages.

To be effective leaders, union officials must also pay constant attention to the general goals and philosophies of the labour movement. Currently, with the recession in Canada, the focus is on job security and less on wage increases.[20] Unions also have historically been very politically active, backing such parties as the NDP. However, there are times that a union will comment on government policy. For example, the Canadian Auto Workers and United Steel Workers jointly criticized the federal government in February 2009 for not making a "buy Canadian" policy a part of the economic stimulus package.[21]

As mentioned earlier, unions are expanding their memberships by organizing employees in a number of different sectors in the economy. To get a fuller appreciation of the range of different unions in different industries, review At Work with HRM 10.2

One of the success stories of union philosophy is the worker-owned pulp mill in British Columbia. The Harmac mill, located in Nanaimo, had been one of the assets of Pope & Talbot that was declared insolvent in 2008 and then placed into receivership. A group of employees, including members of the Pulp, Paper and Woodworkers of Canada, with the help of investors, put together an offer to take over the operation. The employees also agreed to buy into the mill at $25,000 per person. And the results? Six months after the close of the deal and the re-start of the mill, it has reduced its production costs by $100/tonne and is competing in the world markets. The employees

Canadian Union of Public Employees
cupe.ca/

National Union of Public and General Employees
www.nupge.ca

Public Service Alliance of Canada
www.psac.com

AT WORK **with HRM 10.2**

DIFFERENT UNIONS IN DIFFERENT INDUSTRIES

Service Employees International Union (SEIU)

- Impact Cleaning Services
- Red Cross
- Windsor Raceway
- Casino Nova Scotia
- Melville Gardens

Canadian Auto Workers (CAW)

- Boeing
- Coca Cola
- Alcan
- Loblaws
- The Bay
- Via Rail
- Great Blue Heron Casino

Communication, Energy, and Paperworkers' Union of Canada (CEP)

- Winnipeg Free Press
- Catalyst Paper
- Bell Canada
- CTV
- Nova Scotia Government

CRITICAL THINKING QUESTION

Do you think unions can effectively represent the interests of its members in such diverse industries? Why or why not?

Sources: Information accessed on union websites: www.seiu.ca/; www.caw.ca; www.cep.ca (accessed March 6, 2009).

on the shop floor now feel that their contributions and work makes a difference—and it does. They are confident that once the recession is over that they will see their investment continue to grow and that the mill now has a future.[22]

Labour Relations in the Public Sector

Collective bargaining among federal, provincial, and municipal government employees, and among employees in parapublic agencies (private agencies or branches of the government acting as extensions of government programs) has increased dramatically since the 1960s. About 71% of all public employees are now unionized.[23] The three largest unions in Canada represent public-sector employees. The Canadian Union of Public Employees (CUPE) is the largest union in Canada, representing 590,000 members. The second-largest union, with 340,000 members, is the National Union of Provincial Government Employees (NUPGE), which represents employees at the provincial level. The largest union representing employees at the federal level is the Public Service Alliance of Canada (PSAC), with 167,000 members.[24] Growth in these unions is threatened by increased cost-cutting efforts of governments at all levels, resulting in employee reductions.

While public- and private-sector collective bargaining have many features in common, a number of factors differentiate the two sectors. However, two key distinctions are the political nature of the labour–management relationship and public-sector strikes.

Political Nature of the Labour–Management Relationship

Government employees are not able to negotiate with their employers on the same basis as their counterparts in private organizations. It is doubtful that they will ever be able to do so because of inherent differences between the public and private sectors.

One of the significant differences is that labour relations in the private sector have an economic foundation, whereas in government their foundation tends to be political. Since private employers must stay in business in order to sell their goods or services, their employees are not likely to make demands that could bankrupt them. Governments, on the other hand, must stay in business because alternative services are usually not available. For example, in the fall of 2008

Public-sector workers picket to publicize their disputes and discourage people from entering the premises.

Public-sector workers picket to publicize their disputes and discourage people from entering the premises.

when the federal government was beginning to deal with the recession, extreme political pressure was put on the Public Service Alliance of Canada to agree to a very reduced wage offer. The union indicated that given the tough economy, it was responsible on behalf of PSAC to agree to the government's demands.[25]

Strikes in the Public Sector

Strikes by government employees create a problem for lawmakers and for the general public. Because the services that government employees provide, such as police work and firefighting, are often considered essential to the well-being of the public, public policy is opposed to such strikes. However, various provincial legislatures have granted public employees the right to strike. Where striking is permitted, the right is limited to specific groups of employees—those performing nonessential services—and the strike cannot endanger the public's health, safety, or welfare. Public-sector unions contend, however, that denying them the same right to strike as employees in the private sector greatly reduces their power during collective bargaining.

Public employees who perform essential services do, in fact, strike. Teachers, sanitation employees, police, transit employees, firefighters, and postal employees have all engaged in strike action. To avoid a potentially critical situation, various arbitration methods are used for resolving collective-bargaining deadlocks in the public sector. One is compulsory binding arbitration for employees such as police officers, firefighters, and others in jobs where strikes cannot be tolerated. Another method is final-offer arbitration, under which the arbitrator must select one or the other of the final offers submitted by the disputing parties. With this method, the arbitrator's award is more likely to go to the party whose final bargaining offer has moved the closest to a reasonable settlement. The government can also enact back-to-work legislation, an option being used with increasing frequency when there are concerns about public health or safety.

THE COLLECTIVE BARGAINING PROCESS

Outcome 5

Once a union wins bargaining rights for employees, its two primary functions are to negotiate the collective agreement and resolve member complaints, usually through the grievance-arbitration process. Interestingly, according to labour law, once the union is certified to negotiate for bargaining-unit members, it must represent everyone in the unit equally, regardless of whether employees subsequently join the union or elect to remain nonmembers. The collective agreement that is ultimately negotiated establishes the wages, hours, employee benefits, job security, and other conditions under which represented employees agree to work.

Those unfamiliar with contract negotiations often view the collective bargaining process as an emotional conflict between labour and management, complete with marathon sessions and fist pounding. In reality, negotiating a collective agreement entails long hours of extensive preparation combined with diplomatic manoeuvring and the development of bargaining strategies. Furthermore, negotiation is only one part of the collective bargaining process. Collective bargaining may also include the use of economic pressures in the form of strikes and boycotts by a union. Lockouts, plant closures, and the replacement of strikers are similar pressures used by an employer. In addition, either or both parties may seek support from the general public or from the courts as a means of pressuring the opposing side. To help you understand the collective bargaining process, review Figure 10.3.

Good-Faith Bargaining

Once a union has been recognized as the representative for employees, an employer is obligated to negotiate in good faith with the union's representatives over conditions of employment. Good faith requires the employer's negotiators to meet with their union counterparts at a reasonable time and place to discuss these conditions. In discussing the other party's proposals, each side will put forward their demands and attempt to justify their position.[26] Finally, at the conclusion of negotiations, a written document—the collective agreement—is produced, which governs the day-to-day employment relationship.[27] Furthermore, an employer cannot override the bargaining process by making an offer directly to the employees. Figure 10.4 illustrates several common examples of bad-faith employer bargaining.

Preparing for Negotiations

Preparing for negotiations includes planning the strategy and assembling data to support bargaining proposals. This will permit collective bargaining to be conducted in an orderly fashion and on a factual and positive basis with a greater likelihood of achieving desired goals. Negotiators often develop a bargaining book that serves as a cross-reference file to determine which contract

FIGURE 10.3 The Collective Bargaining Process

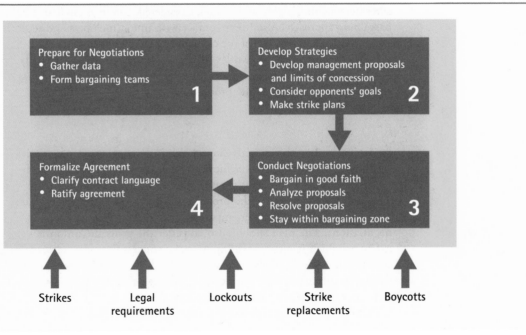

FIGURE 10.4   Examples of Bad-Faith Bargaining

Employer

- Using delaying tactics, such as frequent postponements of bargaining sessions
- Insisting that the union stop striking before resuming negotiations
- Unilaterally changing bargaining topics
- Negotiating with individual employees other than authorized union representatives
- Going through the motions of bargaining rather than conducting honest negotiations
- Refusing to meet with authorized union representatives

Union

- Using delaying tactics such as frequent postponements of bargaining sessions
- Withdrawing concessions previously granted
- Unilaterally changing bargaining topics
- Going through the motions of bargaining rather than conducting honest negotiations
- Refusing to meet with authorized employer representatives

clauses would be affected by a demand. Assuming that the collective agreement is not the first to be negotiated by the parties, preparation for negotiations ideally should start soon after the current agreement has been signed. This practice will allow negotiators to review and diagnose weaknesses and mistakes made during the previous negotiations while the experience is still current in their minds.

Gathering Bargaining Data

Internal data relating to grievances, disciplinary actions, transfers and promotions, layoffs, overtime, former arbitration awards, and wage payments are useful in formulating and supporting the employer's bargaining position. In addition, information can be obtained from other collective agreements negotiated in the company's industry. These agreements are usually available through the labour relations boards.

The supervisors and managers who must live with and administer the collective agreement are the key sources of ideas and suggestions concerning changes that are needed in the next agreement. It is important that any concerns supervisors and managers might have with the collective agreement are thoroughly understood, considered, and incorporated as appropriate into the overall bargaining approach. Also, their contact with union members and representatives provides them with a firsthand knowledge of the changes that union negotiators are likely to propose. And since it is the supervisor who has to work with the collective agreement on a daily basis, it is important that the supervisors and managers be involved in the data collection process so that they understand and feel part of the bargaining process.

Developing Bargaining Strategies

It is critical that the organization develop a strategy for negotiations. Without adequately planning what it wants to achieve, a company could end up with an unwanted outcome. Negotiators for an employer should develop a written plan covering their bargaining strategy. The plan should consider the proposals that the union is likely to submit, based on the most recent agreements with other employers and the demands that remain unsatisfied from previous negotiations. The plan should also consider the goals the union is striving to achieve and the extent to which it may be willing to make concessions or to resort to strike action in order to achieve these goals. Likewise, it is essential that the company identify the point at which it is willing to let the employees strike or to lock out the employees. Not knowing the organization's limits can create difficulties at negotiations and perhaps incur job action that could have been avoided.

At a minimum, the employer's bargaining strategy must address these points:

- Identify the likely union objectives, including specific proposals and management responses to them.
- Develop a list of organizational objectives, including management demands, limits of concessions, and anticipated union responses.
- Identify the nature of the union–management relationship and the relationship the union has with its members.
- Determine if the company is prepared to lock out or take a strike.
- Develop a database to support management bargaining proposals and to counteract union demands.
- Determine whether the company will operate if employees strike and prepare a contingency operating plan.

Certain elements of strategy are common to both the employer and the union. Generally, the initial demands presented by each side are greater than those it actually may hope to achieve. This is done in order to provide room for compromise. Moreover, each party will usually avoid giving up the maximum it is capable of conceding in order to allow for further compromise that may be needed to break a bargaining deadlock.

Forms of Collective Bargaining

Traditionally, the collective bargaining relationship between an employer and a union has been an adversarial one. The union has held the position that, while the employer has the responsibility for managing the organization, the union has the right to challenge certain actions of management. Unions also have taken the position that the employer has an obligation to operate the organization in a manner that will provide adequate compensation to employees. Moreover, unions maintain that their members should not be expected to subsidize poor management by accepting less than their full entitlement.

With adversarial bargaining, negotiators start with defined positions and through deferral, persuasion, trade, or power, the parties work toward resolving individual bargaining demands. In traditional bargaining, with its give-and-take philosophy, the results may or may not be to the complete satisfaction of one or both parties. In fact, when one side feels it has received "the short end of the stick," bitter feelings may persist for the life of the agreement.

To overcome these negative feelings, labour and management practitioners may follow a nonadversarial approach. **Interest-based bargaining** (IBB) or interest-based negotiations is based on the identification and resolution of mutual interests rather than the resolve of specific bargaining demands. IBB is "a rational approach to problem solving that helps management and labour reduce conflict that occurs during negotiations and during the life of the collective agreement."[28] The focus of bargaining strategy is to discover mutual bargaining interests with the intent of formulating options and solutions for mutual gain.

Interest-based bargaining is novel in both its philosophy and process. Also distinct are the bargaining tools used to expedite a successful nonadversarial negotiating experience. Rather than using proposals and counterproposals to reach agreement (as with adversarial negotiations), participants use brainstorming, consensus decision making, active listening, process checking, and matrix building to settle issues. This style of negotiations was pioneered by Roger Fisher and William Ury, two professors at the Harvard Business School and published in their highly successful book, *Getting to Yes*. They stressed the need to focus on the problem (not the positions of the parties); to separate the people from the problem; and to create options for mutual benefit. In this fashion, the parties strive to find solutions to problems and thus improve their overall relationship.[29]

Conducting the Negotiations

Among the factors that tend to make each bargaining situation unique are the economic conditions under which negotiations take place, the experience and personalities of the negotiators on each side, the goals they are seeking to achieve, and the strength of the relative positions. Some collective

Interest-based bargaining
Problem-solving bargaining based on a win-win philosophy and the development of a positive long-term relationship

agreements can be negotiated informally in a few hours, particularly if the contract is short and the terms are not overly complex. Other agreements, such as those negotiated with large organizations, such as Air Canada and Stelco, require months before settlements are reached. Given the global recession that started in 2008, the Conference Board of Canada predicts that there will be more labour peace for the next few years and that unions will be more concerned about the survival of the firms and maintenance of union membership rather than other demands.[30]

Bargaining Teams

The composition and size of bargaining teams are often a reflection of the desires and practices of the parties. Normally, each side will have four to six representatives at the negotiating table. The chief negotiator for management is usually the senior HR person; the chief negotiator for the union is usually the local union president or union business agent. Others making up management's team may include representatives from accounting or finance, operations, and other HR staff. The local union president is likely to be supported by the chief steward, various local union vice presidents, and a representative from the national union. In some cases the representative from the national union will be the chief negotiator for the local union.

Labour negotiations have become increasingly complex and legalistic. Therefore, it is advisable that the parties have an experienced negotiator.

The initial meeting of the bargaining teams is a particularly important one because it establishes the climate that will prevail during the negotiations that follow. A cordial attitude, with perhaps the injection of a little humour, can contribute much to a relaxation of tensions and help the negotiations to begin smoothly.

Analyzing the Proposals

The negotiation of a collective agreement can have some of the characteristics of a poker game, with each side attempting to determine its opponent's position while not revealing its own. Each party will normally try to avoid disclosing the relative importance that it attaches to a proposal so that it will not be forced to pay a higher price than is necessary to have the proposal accepted. As with sellers who will try to get a higher price for their products if they think the prospective buyer strongly desires them, negotiators will try to get greater concessions in return for granting those their opponents want most.

As they develop their collective bargaining proposals, astute negotiators know that some demands are more important to their side than others—either for economic or for political reasons. Therefore the proposals that each side submits generally may be divided into those it feels it must achieve, those it would like to achieve, and those it is submitting primarily for trading purposes. As bargainers discuss the proposals from each side, they are constantly trying to determine the intensity with which each side is committed to its demands. The ability to accurately gauge "commitment" to various proposals can spell the difference between an agreement and a bargaining impasse.

Resolving the Proposals

For each bargaining issue to be resolved satisfactorily, the point at which agreement is reached must be within limits that the union and the employer are willing to accept. The area within these two limits is called the bargaining zone. In some bargaining situations, the solution desired by one party may exceed the limits of the other party. Thus that solution is outside the bargaining zone. If that party refuses to modify its demands sufficiently to bring them within the bargaining zone, or if the opposing party refuses to extend its limit to accommodate the demands of the other party, a bargaining deadlock will result.[31] For example, when bargaining a wage increase for employees, if the union's lowest limit is a 2% increase and management's top limit is 3%, an acceptable range—the bargaining zone—is available to both parties. If management's top limit is only 1%, however, a bargaining zone is not available to either side and a deadlock is likely to occur.

The Union's Power in Collective Bargaining

Outcome 6

During negotiations, it is necessary for each party to retreat sufficiently from its original position to permit an agreement to be achieved. If this does not occur, the negotiations will become deadlocked, and the union may resort to the use of economic power to achieve its demands. Otherwise its only alternative will be to have members continue working without a collective agreement once the old one has expired. The economic power of the union may be exercised by striking, picketing, or boycotting the employer's products and encouraging others to do likewise. As managers know well, the ability to engage or even threaten to engage in such activities also can serve as a form of pressure. And in some cases, employees do not actually strike, but slow down their work and create pressure on the company. Or the employees will "work to rule"—strictly following the terms of the collective agreement. This means that if the collective agreement specifies that employees will have a 45-minute lunch break, yet most employees take only 30 and work the other 15 minutes, in a work-to-rule, the employees would take the full 45 minutes.

Striking

Strike
A situation in which unionized workers refuse to perform their work during labour negotiations

A **strike** is the refusal of a group of employees to perform their jobs. This is only legal during negotiations after the collective agreement has expired. Employees cannot strike during the collective agreement as proscribed by labour legislation. Although strikes account for only a small portion of total workdays lost in industry each year, they are a costly and emotional event for all concerned. For example, in late 2008, the teaching assistants at York University, who are represented by CUPE, went on strike to pressure the university to agree to a short contract. The strike lasted for almost 30 months and prevented 50,000 students from attending class.[32] Unions usually will seek strike authorization from their members to use as a bargaining ploy to gain concessions that will make a strike unnecessary. A strike vote by the members does not mean they actually want or expect to go out on strike. Rather, it is intended as a vote of confidence to strengthen the position of their leaders at the bargaining table. And the threat of a strike creates as much of a problem as an actual strike.

Since a strike can have serious effects on the union and its members, the prospects for its success must be analyzed carefully by the union. For example, gold mine operators in Prince George, B.C., were attempting to forestall a lengthy shutdown that would cause hardship in a fragile economy. However, the workers also knew at the time that gold prices were at an all-time high and therefore believed that the companies had the financial means to meet their demands.[33]

There had been a downward trend in Canada during the 1980s and 1990s for the number of strikes. However, starting in the early 2000s, strikes began to increase—and the number of workers involved and days lost increased by 300%.[34] Strikes can be disruptive and challenging to the organizations struck. Of critical importance is whether the employer will be able to continue operating using supervisory and nonstriking personnel and replacement workers. In organizations with high levels of technology and automation, and consequently fewer employees, continuing service with supervisors and managers is more likely. For example, among the highly automated telephone companies, supervisors can maintain most services during a strike. The greater the ability of the employer to continue operating the company's services, the smaller the union's chances of achieving its demands through a strike.

To understand more about the issues over which unions will strike, check out the websites of the International Association of Machinists and Aerospace Workers (**www.iamaw.ca**), Canadian Union of Public Employees (**cupe.ca**), and the International Brotherhood of Electrical Workers (IBEW) (**www.ibew.org**).

International Association of Machinists and Aerospace Workers
www.iamaw.ca

Canadian Union of Public Employees
cupe.ca

International Brotherhood of Electrical Workers
www.ibew.org

Picketing

When a union goes on strike, it will picket the employer by placing persons at business entrances to advertise the dispute and to discourage people from entering the premises. Even when the strikers represent only a small proportion of the employees within the organization, they can cause

ANDY CLARK/Reuters /Landov

the shutdown of an entire organization if a sufficient number of the organization's remaining employees (i.e., sympathy strikers) refuse to cross their picket line. Also, because unions often refuse to cross another union's picket line, the pickets may serve to prevent trucks and railcars from entering the business to deliver and pick up goods.

If a strike fails to stop an employer's operations, the picket line may serve as more than a passive weapon. Employees who attempt to cross the line may be subjected to verbal insults and even physical violence. Mass picketing, in which large groups of pickets try to block the path of people attempting to enter an organization, may also be used. However, the use of picket lines to exert physical pressure and incite violence is illegal and may harm more than help the union cause.

Boycotting

Another economic weapon of unions is the boycott, which is a refusal to patronize the employer. For, example, production employees on strike against a hand-tool manufacturer might picket a retail store that sells the tools made by the struck employer. Unions will also use handbills, radio announcements, and notices in newspapers to discourage purchase of the employer's product or service.

The Employer's Power in Collective Bargaining

The employer's power in collective bargaining largely rests in being able to shut down the organization or certain operations within it. The employer can transfer these operations to other locations or can subcontract them to other employers through outsourcing. General Motors outsources to foreign manufacturers many parts used in the assembly of North American cars. In exercising their economic freedom, however, employers must be careful that their actions are not interpreted by the provincial labour relations board to be an attempt to avoid bargaining with the union.

Operating During Strikes

When negotiations become deadlocked, typically it is the union that initiates action and the employer that reacts. In reacting, employers must balance the cost of taking a strike against the long- and short-term costs of agreeing to union demands. They must also consider how long operations might be suspended and the length of time that they and the unions will be able to endure a strike. An employer who chooses to accept a strike must then decide whether to continue operating if it is possible to do so.

Should employees strike the organization, employers in certain jurisdictions are limited in their ability to hire replacement workers. Quebec and British Columbia have passed "anti-scab" laws, forbidding the use of replacement workers during a strike. Employers have the right to dismiss workers who engage in sabotage or violence during a strike.

Workers are entitled to return to their jobs, but not necessarily their previous position, once a strike is settled. The right to return to work is often an issue to be negotiated. Although laws vary, in many cases employees must submit, in writing, their intention to return to their job once a strike is finalized.

Using the Lockout

Lockout

Strategy by which the employer denies employees the opportunity to work by closing its operations

Although not often used, a **lockout** occurs when an employer takes the initiative to close its operations. Besides being used in bargaining impasses, lockouts may be used by employers to combat union slowdowns, damage to their property, or violence within the organization that may occur in connection with a labour dispute.

Under Labour Relations Board provisions, an employer cannot enforce a lockout within a prescribed number of hours (48 to 72) of a strike vote. Lockouts affect nonstriking workers. For example, when miners at Inco are locked out, administrative work ceases and office staff are locked out or laid off. Employers may be reluctant to resort to a lockout, however, because of their concern that denying work to regular employees might hurt the organization's image.

Resolving Bargaining Deadlocks

When a strike or a lockout occurs, both parties are soon affected by it. The employer will suffer a loss of profits and customers, and possibly of public goodwill. The union members suffer a loss of income that is likely to be only partially offset by strike benefits or outside income.

Walmart has made headlines by closing unionized stores in Quebec.

JIM GRAHAM/Bloomberg News /Landov

The union's leaders risk the possibility of losing members, of being voted out of office, of losing public support, or of having the members vote to decertify the union as their bargaining agent. As the losses to each side mount, the disputing parties usually feel more pressure to achieve a settlement.

Mediation and Arbitration

When the disputing parties are unable to resolve a deadlock, a third party serving in the capacity of a conciliator, a mediator, or an arbitrator may be called on to provide assistance. In many jurisdictions, conciliation is compulsory before a legal strike or lockout. The conciliator, appointed by the provincial ministry of labour, helps the parties reconcile their differences in an attempt to reach a workable agreement. If the conciliation effort is unsuccessful, a report is filed with the ministry of labour, which in rare instances may appoint a conciliation board that accepts presentations from both parties and makes nonbinding formal recommendations. If a settlement cannot be reached at this stage, a strike is permitted, except in Manitoba, Alberta, Saskatchewan, and Quebec, where strikes are permissible during conciliation. This two-stage conciliation process is normally reserved for high-profile cases in which significant social and economic consequences would result from a strike.

Mediation is similar to conciliation except that it is voluntary (the two parties contract a neutral third party to help them), and the mediator assumes a more active role as a negotiator. A **mediator** serves primarily as a fact finder and someone to open up a channel of communication between the parties. Typically the mediator meets with one party and then the other in order to suggest compromise solutions or to recommend concessions from each side that will lead to an agreement without causing either to lose face. Mediators have no power or authority to force either side toward an agreement. They must have exceptional communication skills, a variety of assessment skills, and the ability to determine the power imbalance.[35]

One of the newer forms of mediation is online mediation. Through using Internet-based help, ways can be found to use experts in helping solve the dispute without actually having the expert present. Check out some of these resources by visiting the following websites: Mediate.com (**www.mediate.com/odr/**), ADR Resources (**www.adrr.com**), and ADR Institute of Canada (**www.adrcanada.ca**).

Arbitration is the only third-party resolution form that results in binding decisions. An **arbitrator** assumes the role of a decision maker and determines what the settlement between the two parties will be. In other words, arbitrators write a final contract that the parties must accept. Compared with mediation, arbitration is not often used to settle private-sector bargaining disputes. In those essential-service areas within the public sector where strikes are prohibited, the use of **interest arbitration** is a common method to resolve bargaining deadlocks. Because one or both parties are generally reluctant to give a third party the power to make the settlement for them, a mediator typically is used to break a deadlock and assist the parties in reaching an agreement. Once an agreement is concluded, an arbitrator may be called on to resolve disputes arising in connection with the administration of the agreement. This type of arbitration is called grievance arbitration or **rights arbitration**.

Sidebar definitions

Mediator
Third party in a labour dispute who meets with one party and then the other in order to suggest compromise solutions or to recommend concessions from each side that will lead to an agreement

Mediate.com
www.mediate.com/odr/

ADR Resources
www.adrr.com

ADR Institute of Canada
www.adrcanada.ca

Arbitrator
Third-party neutral who resolves a labour dispute by issuing a final and binding decision in an agreement

Interest arbitration
A mechanism to renew or establish a new collective agreement for parties

Rights arbitration
A mechanism to resolve disputes about the interpretation and application of a collective agreement during the term of that collective agreement

THE COLLECTIVE AGREEMENT

 Outcome **7**

At the conclusion of negotiations, a collective agreement is put in writing and ratified by the union membership. The union typically does this by asking that the members vote on the new terms. The representatives of both parties then sign the agreement. This is a legal, binding contract. The scope of the agreement (and the length of the written document) will vary with the size of the employer and the length of the bargaining relationship. Manager's Toolkit 10.4 shows some of the major articles in a collective agreement and also provides examples of some new and progressive contract clauses.

Two important items in any collective agreement pertain to the issue of management rights and the forms of security afforded the union.

MANAGER'S TOOLKIT **10.4**

TYPICAL ITEMS IN A COLLECTIVE AGREEMENT

Typical clauses will cover

- Wages
- Vacations
- Holidays
- Work schedules
- Management rights
- Union security
- Transfers
- Discipline
- Grievance procedures
- No strike/no lockout clause
- Overtime
- Safety procedures
- Severance pay
- Seniority
- Pensions and benefits

Progressive clauses will cover

- Employee access to records
- Limitations on use of performance evaluation
- Eldercare leave
- Flexible medical spending accounts
- Protection against hazards of technology (repetitive strain injuries or chemicals, such as PCBs)
- Limitations against electronic monitoring
- Procedures governing drug testing (or other substances)
- Bilingual stipends
- Domestic partnership benefits (same-sex benefits)

The Issue of Management Rights

Management rights have to do with conditions of employment over which management is able to exercise exclusive jurisdiction. Since virtually every management right can and has been challenged successfully by unions, the ultimate determination of these rights will depend on the relative bargaining power of the two parties. Furthermore, to achieve union cooperation or concessions, employers have had to relinquish some of these time-honoured rights.

Residual Rights

Residual rights
Concept that management's authority is supreme in all matters except those it has expressly conceded to the union in the collective agreement

In the collective agreement, management rights may be treated as **residual rights** or as defined rights. The residual rights concept holds that

> management's authority is supreme in all matters except those it has expressly conceded in the collective agreement, or in those areas where its authority is restricted by law. Put another way, management does not look to the collective agreement to ascertain its rights; it looks to the agreement to find out which and how much of its rights and powers it has conceded outright or agreed to share with the union.[36]

Residual rights might include the right of management to determine the product to produce or to select production equipment and procedures. Employers who subscribe to the residual rights concept prefer not to mention management rights in the collective agreement on the grounds that they possess such rights already. To mention them might create an issue with the union.

Defined Rights

Defined rights
Concept that management's authority should be expressly defined and clarified in the collective agreement

The **defined rights** concept, on the other hand, is intended to reinforce and clarify which rights are exclusively those of management. This concept means that the employer only has those rights that are written into the collective agreement. It serves to reduce confusion and misunderstanding and to remind union officers, union stewards, and employees that management never relinquishes its right to operate the organization. For example, a defined right would include the right of management to take disciplinary action against problem employees.

The great majority of collective agreements contain provisions covering management rights. The following is an example of a general statement defining management rights in one collective agreement:

> It is agreed that the company possesses all of the rights, powers, privileges, and authority it had prior to the execution of this agreement; and nothing in this agreement shall be construed to limit the company in any way in the exercise of the regular and customary functions of management and the operation of its business, except as it may be specifically relinquished or modified herein by an express provision of this agreement.[37]

Forms of Union Security

When a labour organization is certified by a labour relations board as the exclusive bargaining representative of all employees in a bargaining unit, it must, by law, represent all employees in the unit, nonunion and union members alike. In exchange for its obligation to represent all employees equally, union officials will seek to negotiate some form of compulsory membership as a condition of employment. Union officials argue that compulsory membership prevents the possibility that some employees will receive the benefits of unionization without paying their share of the costs. A standard union security provision is dues checkoff, which gives the employer the responsibility of withholding union dues from the paycheques of union members who agree to such a deduction.

The more common forms of union security found in collective agreements are the following:

1. The *closed shop* states that employers will hire only union members.
2. The *union shop* provides that any employee not a union member upon employment must join the union within 30 days or be terminated.
3. The *agency shop* states that union membership is voluntary yet all bargaining unit members must pay union dues and fees.
4. The *open shop* allows employees to join the union or not. Nonmembers do not pay union dues. This is the rarest form of union security.

Few issues in collective bargaining are more controversial than the negotiation of these agreements. Though rare, closed-shop clauses are perhaps the most adversarial because they require employers to recruit employees from a union hiring hall.

Working in conjunction with the union-shop clause are the various seniority provisions of the collective agreement. Unions prefer that many personnel decisions (promotions, job transfers, shift assignments, vacations) be based on seniority, a criterion that limits the discretion of managers to make such decisions on the basis of merit. However, depending on the words of the seniority clause, not all employees are totally protected. For example, Telus recently decided that it would move 50 full-time positions in western Canada to one of its international call centres in the Philippines. To achieve this, approximately 300 employees were being offered a choice of severance or transfer to another job. So even though only 50 positions are impacted, 300 people will be affected.[38]

Administration of the Collective Agreement

Negotiation of the collective agreement, as mentioned earlier, is usually the most publicized and critical aspect of labour relations. Strike deadlines, press conferences, and employee picketing help create this image. Nevertheless, as managers in unionized organizations know, the bulk of labour relations activity comes from the day-to-day administration of the agreement. Once the collective agreement is signed, each party frequently will interpret clauses differently. These differences are traditionally resolved through the grievance procedure.

Manager's Toolkit 10.5 provides some examples of clauses from collective agreements.

CLAUSES FROM COLLECTIVE AGREEMENTS

1. PAID EDUCATION LEAVE

The Company agrees to pay into a special fund two cents (2¢) per hour per employee for all compensated hours for the purpose of providing paid education leave. Such leave shall be for upgrading the employee's skills in all aspects of trade union functions. Payments should be made on a quarterly basis into a trust fund established by the National Union, CAW, effective from date of ratification. Cheques shall be made payable to....

The Company further agrees that members of the bargaining unit, selected by the Union to attend such courses, shall be granted a leave of absence without pay for twenty (20) days class time, plus travel time where necessary, said leave of absence to be intermittent over a twelve (12) month period from the first day of leave. Employees on said leave of absence shall continue to accrue seniority and benefits during such leave.

[Between The Eight (8) Rinks Hockey Complex and National Automobile, Aerospace, Transportation and General Workers Union (CAW-Canada) Local 3000]

2. LAYOFFS

a. When there is a reduction in the workforce of the Employer, the most junior employee shall be laid off first.

b. When an employee requests a layoff, for any reason, the said employee will not be allowed to bump a junior person upon return to work.

c. Maternity Leave—Maternity leave shall be granted in accordance with Part 7 of the Employment Standards Act.

[Between Pacific Coast Traffic Control and Local Union 258 of the International Brotherhood Of Electrical Workers]

3. PAY FOR OVERTIME WORKED

Overtime shall be compensated at the following rates:

a. up to eight (8) hours in a regularly scheduled workday be paid at the regular rate of pay;

b. time and one-half (1 1/2) for the next three (3) hours of overtime on a regularly scheduled workday;

c. double time for hours worked in excess of (b).

[Between Young Women's Christian Association of Vancouver (YWCA) and B.C. Government and Service Employees' Union (BCGEU)]

GRIEVANCE PROCEDURES

Grievance procedure
Formal procedure that provides for the union to represent members and nonmembers in processing a grievance

The **grievance procedure** typically provides for the union to represent the interests of its members (and nonmembers as well) in processing a complaint that something in the collective agreement has been violated. It is considered by some authorities to be the heart of the bargaining agreement—the safety valve that gives flexibility to the whole system of collective bargaining.[39] When negotiating a grievance procedure, one important concern for both sides is how effectively the system will serve the needs of employees and management. A well-written grievance procedure will allow grievances to be processed quickly and with as little red tape as possible. Furthermore, it should serve to foster cooperation, not conflict, between the employer and the union.

The operation of a grievance procedure is unique to each individual collective bargaining relationship but is required under Canadian labour relations codes. Grievance procedures are negotiated to address the organization's structure and labour–management philosophy and the specific desires of the parties. Although each procedure is unique, there are common elements among systems. For example, grievance procedures normally specify how the grievance procedure is to be initiated, the number and timing of steps that are to compose the procedure, and the identity of representatives from each side who are to be involved in the hearings at each step (see Figure 10.5). The purpose of this multi-step process is to allow higher levels of union and management representatives to look at the issue from different perspectives. When a grievance cannot be

FIGURE 10.5 Grievance Procedure

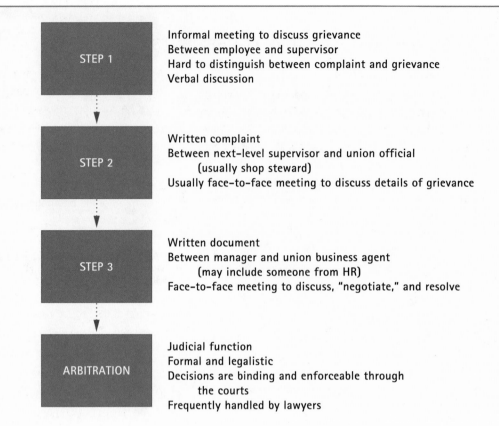

STEP 1
Informal meeting to discuss grievance
Between employee and supervisor
Hard to distinguish between complaint and grievance
Verbal discussion

STEP 2
Written complaint
Between next-level supervisor and union official
    (usually shop steward)
Usually face-to-face meeting to discuss details of grievance

STEP 3
Written document
Between manager and union business agent
    (may include someone from HR)
Face-to-face meeting to discuss, "negotiate," and resolve

ARBITRATION
Judicial function
Formal and legalistic
Decisions are binding and enforceable through
    the courts
Frequently handled by lawyers

resolved at one of the specified steps, most agreements provide for the grievance to be submitted to a third party—usually an arbitrator—whose decision is final and binding. It is not the function of an arbitrator to help the two parties reach a compromise solution. Rather, it is the arbitrator's job to mandate how the grievance is to be resolved.

Initiating the Formal Grievance

In order for an employee's grievance to be considered formally, it must be expressed orally and/or in writing, ideally to the employee's immediate supervisor. If the employee feels unable to communicate effectively with the supervisor, the grievance may be taken to the union steward, who will discuss it with the supervisor. Since grievances are often the result of an oversight or a misunderstanding, many of them can be resolved at this point. Whether or not it is possible to resolve a grievance at the initial step will depend on the supervisor's ability and willingness to discuss the problem with the employee and the steward. Supervisors should be trained formally in resolving grievances. This training should include familiarization with the terms of the collective agreement and the development of counselling skills to facilitate a problem-solving approach.

In some instances, a satisfactory solution may not be possible at the first step because there are legitimate differences of opinion between the employee and the supervisor or because the supervisor does not have the authority to take the action required to satisfy the grievor. Personality conflicts, prejudices, emotionalism, stubbornness, or other factors may also be barriers to a satisfactory solution at this step.

One of the more entertaining grievances occurred in June 2009 when Molson Canada decided to eliminate the supply of free beer to its 2400 retirees. Molson determined that it could save about $1 million per year and that by doing this, it would not have to cut employees or reduce pensions. The union representing the retirees launched the grievance.[40]

Grievance Resolution

If a grievance is to be resolved successfully, representatives of both management and the union must be able to discuss the problem in a rational and objective manner. A grievance should not be viewed as something to be won or lost. Rather, both sides must view the situation as an attempt to solve a problem. Throughout the process, both parties will try to resolve the issue. However, if the conflict cannot be resolved through discussion and compromise, all collective agreements in Canadian jurisdictions contain a provision for arbitration, or **grievance resolution.** An arbitrator (usually a lawyer or professional skilled in the arbitration process) or a board or panel (consisting of a union nominee, a management nominee, and a neutral chair) hears the case and submits a decision, including the rationale. The decision is final and the parties are legally bound to accept the decision unless there is a serious concern over the arbitrator's competence or integrity.

Grievance resolution
Process in which a neutral third party assists in the resolution of an employee grievance

One criticism of the arbitration process is that it is slow (up to two years) and costly. One solution is expedited arbitration, which is an agreement to bypass some steps in the grievance process when the issue is particularly important or urgent, as in the case of employee dismissals. The United Steelworkers of America and the International Nickel Company of Canada Ltd. use expedited arbitration in their Sudbury and Port Colborne operations.

Rights Arbitration

The function of rights (or grievance) arbitration is to provide the solution to a grievance that a union and an employer have been unable to resolve by themselves. As mentioned earlier, arbitration is performed by a neutral third party (an arbitrator or impartial umpire). This third party's decision dictates how the grievance is to be settled. Both parties are obligated to comply with the decision. Even if one of the parties believes the arbitrator's award is unfair, unwise, or inconsistent with the collective agreement, that party may have no alternative but to comply with the decision. Read HRM and the Law 10.1 for what might be considered an unusual decision.

The Decision to Arbitrate

If a grievance cannot be resolved through the grievance procedure, each disputing party must decide whether to use arbitration to resolve the case. The alternatives would be for the union to withdraw the grievance or for the employer to agree to union demands.

In deciding whether to use arbitration, each party must weigh the costs involved against the importance of the case and the prospects of gaining a favourable award. It would seem logical that

HRM and the law 10.1

BUT WAS IT A FUNERAL?

When an employee's mother-in-law died, the family decided to have an informal gathering rather than a formal service at a church or funeral home. The informal gathering was done several days later at the deceased's home, with family and friends in attendance. Everyone gathered around the urn containing the ashes, telling stories and sharing a meal in her honour.

The employee took three days off work as bereavement leave expecting to be paid even though the language of the collective agreement stated that a funeral had to be attended. The company stated that the gathering was not a funeral as it interpreted the collective agreement. The employee insisted that the event was equivalent to a funeral and the union launched a grievance.

The case was determined by an arbitrator who ruled in favour of the grievor. In doing so the arbitrator said that the company had been too literal given Canada's pluralistic society where there are many different religious and spiritual practices. While the arbitrator noted that the arrangements were perhaps a bit unconventional, it was the only family event commemorating the death.

What do you think about this decision?

Source: Adapted from Lorna Harris, "Arguing Over 'Funeral' Offends Common Sense, Arbitrator Rules," *Canadian HR Reporter*, June 6, 2005, 5.

neither party would allow a weak case to go to arbitration if there were little possibility of gaining a favourable award. But there may be other reasons for advancing a grievance. For example, it is not unusual for a union to take a weak case to arbitration in order to demonstrate to the members that the union is willing to exhaust every remedy in looking out for their interests. Union officers also are not likely to refuse to take to arbitration the grievances of members who are popular or politically powerful in the union, even though their cases are weak. Moreover, unions have a legal obligation to provide assistance to members who are pursuing grievances. Because members can bring suit against their unions for failing to process their grievances adequately, many union officers are reluctant to refuse taking even weak grievances to arbitration.

Management, on the other hand, may allow a weak case to go to arbitration to demonstrate to the union officers that management "cannot be pushed around." Also, managers at lower levels may be reluctant to risk the displeasure of top management by stating that a certain HR policy is unworkable or unsound. Stubbornness and mutual antagonism also may force many grievances into arbitration because neither party is willing to make concessions to reach an agreement, even when it may recognize that it is in the wrong.

The Arbitration Process

The issues to be resolved through arbitration may be described formally in a statement. Each party makes a joint submission to the arbitrator indicating the rationale for the grievance. The submission to arbitrate must state the nature of the dispute with reference to the section of the collective agreement that has allegedly been breached. Such a statement might read: "Was the three-day suspension of Alex Hayden for just cause? If not, what is the appropriate remedy?" However, the two parties at the beginning of the hearing also present grievable issues orally to the arbitrator. The purpose of an arbitration hearing is to provide a full and fair hearing of the matter in dispute. If minutes and memoranda covering the meetings held at earlier stages of the grievance procedure have been prepared, these are sometimes submitted prior to the formal hearing to acquaint the arbitrator with the issues.

In arbitrating a dispute, it is the responsibility of the arbitrator to ensure that each side receives a fair hearing, during which it may present all the facts it considers pertinent to the case. The procedures for conducting arbitration hearings and the restrictions governing the evidence that may be introduced during these hearings are more flexible than those permitted in a court of law. Hearsay evidence, for example, may be introduced, provided it is considered as such when evaluated with the other evidence presented. The primary purpose of the hearing is to assist the arbitrator in obtaining the facts necessary to resolve a human resources problem rather than a legal one. The arbitrator, therefore, has a right to question witnesses or to request additional facts from either party.

Depending on the importance of the case, the hearings may be conducted in an informal way or in a very formal manner not unlike that of a court trial. If the proceedings have witnesses who will testify, the witnesses are sworn in. After conducting the hearing and receiving all written evidence, or any other submissions allowed, the arbitrator customarily has 30 days in which to consider the evidence and to prepare a decision. In the majority of labour contracts, the parties share the costs of arbitration equally. In all grievance arbitrations except those involving any form of discipline, the "burden of proof" rests with the union. This means that the union must prove that the employer violated the written collective agreement.

The Arbitration Award

Arbitration award
Final and binding award issued by an arbitrator in a labour–management dispute

The **arbitration award** should include not only the arbitrator's decision but also the rationale for it. The reasoning behind the decision can help provide guidance concerning the interpretation of the collective agreement and the resolution of future disputes arising from its administration. In pointing out the merits of each party's position, the reasoning that underlies the award can help lessen the disappointment and protect the self-esteem of those representing the unsuccessful party. In short, tact and objective reasoning can help to reduce disappointment and hard feelings.

The foundation for an arbitrator's decision is the collective agreement and the rights it establishes for each party. In many instances, the decision may hinge on whether management's actions were justified under the terms of this agreement. Sometimes it may depend on the arbitrator's interpretation of the wording of a particular provision. Established HR policies and past practices can also provide the basis for determining the award. And it must be remembered that an arbitration decision, if need be, is enforceable through the courts.

In many grievances, such as those involving employee performance or behaviour on the job, the arbitrator must determine whether the evidence supports the employer's action against the grievor. The evidence must also indicate whether the employee was accorded the right of due process, which is the employee's right to be informed of unsatisfactory performance and to have an opportunity to respond to these charges. Under most collective agreements an employer is required to have just cause (i.e., a good reason) for the action it has taken, and such action should be confirmed by the evidence presented.

If the arbitration hearing indicates that an employee was accorded due process and the disciplinary action was for just cause, the severity of the penalty must then be assessed. Where the evidence supports the discipline imposed by the employer, the arbitrator will probably let the discipline stand intact. However, it is within the arbitrator's power, unless denied by the submission agreement, to reduce the penalty. It is not uncommon, for example, for an arbitrator to reduce a discharge to a suspension without pay for the period the grievor has been off the payroll.

Because of the importance and magnitude of arbitration in grievance resolution, the process by which arbitrators make decisions and the factors that influence those decisions are of continuing interest to managers. Typically, arbitrators use four factors when deciding cases:

1. The wording of the collective agreement.
2. The submission agreement as presented to the arbitrator.
3. Testimony and evidence offered during the hearing about how the collective agreement provisions have been interpreted.
4. Arbitration criteria or standards (i.e., similar to standards of common law) against which cases are judged.

When deciding the case of an employee discharged for absenteeism, for example, the arbitrator would consider these factors separately and/or jointly. Arbitrators are essentially constrained to decide cases on the basis of the wording of the collective agreement and the facts, testimony, and evidence presented at the hearing. For example, in a termination case, the employee (a nurse) was

Arbitration is a formal process to solve a grievance.

dismissed for unacceptable conduct with a patient. The arbitration panel determined through the facts, testimony, and evidence presented that the person had been terminated with cause.[41]

Given the current economic climate, changes continue to impact labour relations and collective bargaining. See Emerging Trends 10.1 for some of the more important ones.

EMERGING TRENDS 10.1

1. *Longer strikes.* Even though the Canadian economy is going through some challenges, when strikes do occur they are longer in duration. For example, in 2008, the Ottawa transit strike was 51 days, the Fairmont Hotel in Montreal was 77 days, and the Government of New Brunswick was 39 days. Some of the reasons suggested for this occurring is the merger of unions, which is producing bigger strike funds and new technologies that are allowing employers to run bare-bones operations without certain staff.

2. *Union mergers.* Just as businesses merge and/or are acquired, so too with unions. Unions are faced with the same business issues: declining revenues (dues collected from fewer members), competition (from other unions), and economic impacts where there might be significant layoffs in an industry. For example, at one point, the Industrial Wood and Allied Workers of Canada (IWA) had over 55,000 members in the forestry sector across Canada. With the significant restructuring that has occurred, it continued to lose members. Eventually in 2004 it merged with the United Steelworkers.

3. *Change in labour-management relations.* As organizations use new and innovative work practices to increase organizational performance and improve employee satisfaction, companies have also been developing new relationships with their unions. And as organizations continue to change and evolve, unions can be helpful in providing the employer with insights about how the employees are feeling. However, for these positive relations to occur, it is important for the company to also treat the union as a partner in the overall enterprise.

4. *Different bargaining demands.* With the increased use of BlackBerries, and other similar wireless devices, more and more employees are using them for work purposes. And this means that the person might be accessible 24/7. While most jobs don't need that degree of availability, unions feel that if a person has one, the employer ought to pay for the time the person is using it. However, some labour relations experts suggest that this could backfire as employers may then require people to use them, thus intruding on the person's own time.

Also, as companies are faced with economic challenges, employers will continue to press for greater flexibility in assigning work and therefore may become slightly more militant in bargaining. Or companies may be able to extract certain concessions such as what occurred between GM and the CAW in early 2009 where they agreed to freezing wages and pensions until 2012 in order to reduce labour costs and hopefully help GM survive. And by mid-2009, more companies were looking for union concessions to help them stay in business. For example, Air Canada and its unions reached an agreement that allowed Air Canada to suspend contributing to pension plans for a period of 21 months, and GM-CAW agreed to reducing the benefits received by retirees, thus saving up to $1 billion.

Where the industry is heavily unionized, such as auto makers, forestry, and airlines, the labour costs can become a barrier to the company surviving the current economic situation. Therefore, more and more companies are demanding concessions on the costs of labour in order to stay in business.

Lastly, both employers and unions are using another bargaining technique of "doing nothing." There is a desire to not run the risk of a confrontation and therefore both parties let the existing collective agreement continue without beginning any contract negotations.

5. *Demographics.* Union density in Canada continues to decline—currently at about 30%. Much of the decline is due to the shift from an industrial economy to one of service and knowledge. People in these sectors are usually more educated and therefore tend to resist collective action. Also, Gen X and Y, and the Millennials have different expectations and views of their role in the workplace. These younger workers see themselves as more independent, able to make their own way, and expect to be encouraged to contribute. They also see the unionized workplace as

adversarial and thus do not want to be associated with that type of environment.

6. ***Increasing pressures to unionize service sector.*** As the work environment changes from industrial to knowledge and service-based, unions are increasing their efforts to unionize other sectors (see At Work with HRM 10.2). The result is that companies such as Walmart have been targeted for union organizing campaigns; however the only Walmart store in North America that is unionized is in Quebec. As mentioned previously in this chapter, unions continue to look at other sectors to increase their influence and unionization rates.

Sources: David Akin, "Duration of Canadian Work Stoppages Growing," *The Vancouver Sun*, January 31, 2009, G5; "About District Three: The Steelworkers in Western Canada," www.usw.ca/program/content/3195.php (accessed March 7, 2009); Blaine Donais, "Making Unions Partners in Change," *Canadian HR Reporter*, August 13, 2007, 17; Vito Pilieci, "BlackBerry Becoming a Union Issue," *National Post*, April 29, 2008; A5; Christopher Hallamore, *Industrial Relations Outlook 2006*, The Conference Board of Canada; Pradeep Kumar, "Whither Unionism: Current State and Future Prospects of Union Renewal in Canada," presented to Canadian Industrial Relations Association, Vancouver, June 2008; Craig Offman, "The Fate of the Unions," *National Post*, December 20, 2008, A5; Ken Kaiser, "Will the Unionized Workplace Attract and Retain New Talent?" Queen's University Industrial Relations Centre, June 2008; Garry Marr, "GM Deal Freezes Wages, Pensions," *National Post*, March 9, 2009, A1; Andy Georgiades, "Contract Imposed on Walmart Store," *Financial Post*, April 9, 2009, FP12; John Greenwood, "Labour Showdowns," *National Post*, April 4, 2009, FP3; and Brent Jang, "Air Canada, Unions Reach Deal on Pension Funding," *The Globe and Mail*, June 9, 3009, A7; Nicolas Van Praet, "GM-CAW Deal to Cut Key Legacy Costs," *Financial Post*, March 24, 2009, FP2; and Tavia Grant, "Downturn Brings New Bargaining Tactic: Do Nothing," *Report on Business*, July 8, 2009, B1.

SUMMARY

1. Explain the federal and provincial legislation that provides the framework for labour relations.
   - Laws determine who can unionize.
   - Laws require that unions and employers bargain in good faith.
   - Laws provide for unions to strike and for employers to lock out.

2. Cite the reasons employees join unions.
   - Dissatisfaction with pay and benefits.
   - Dissatisfaction with managerial practices.
   - Desire for recognition and status.

3. Describe the process by which unions organize employees and gain recognition as their bargaining agent.
   - Employees make contact with a union representative.
   - Union schedules meeting with other employees.
   - Application is made to labour relations board.
   - Labour relations board grants bargaining rights.

4. Describe the functions labour unions perform at the national and local levels.
   - National unions help organize local unions.
   - National unions help train and educate local unions.
   - Local unions negotiate collective agreement and process member grievances.

5. Describe the bargaining process and the bargaining goals and strategies of a union and an employer.
   - Each side will prepare a list of goals it wishes to achieve while additionally trying to anticipate the goals desired by the other side.
   - Both employer and union negotiators will be sensitive to current bargaining patterns within the industry, general cost-of-living trends, and geographical wage differentials.
   - The collective bargaining process includes not only the actual negotiations but also the power tactics used to support negotiating demands.

6. Describe the forms of bargaining power that a union and an employer may utilize to enforce their bargaining demands.
   - The union's power in collective bargaining comes from its ability to picket, strike, or boycott the employer.
   - The employer's power during negotiations comes from its ability to lock out employees or to operate during a strike by using managerial or replacement employees.

7. Identify the major provisions of a collective agreement, including the issue of management rights.
   - Typical collective agreements will contain numerous provisions governing the labour–management employment relationship.
   - Major areas of interest concern wages (rates of pay, overtime differentials, holiday pay), hours (shift times, days of work), and working conditions (safety issues, performance standards, retraining).
   - Management rights refers to the supremacy of management's authority in all issues except those shared with the union through the collective agreement.

8. Describe a typical grievance procedure and explain the basis for arbitration awards.
   - The procedure will consist of three to five steps—each step having specific filing and reply times.
   - Higher-level managers and union officials will become involved in disputes at the higher steps of the grievance procedure.
   - The final step of the grievance procedure may be arbitration.
   - Arbitrators render a final decision for problems not resolved at lower grievance steps.
   - Arbitrators consider the wording of the collective agreement, testimony, and evidence offered during the hearing, including how the parties have interpreted the collective agreement.

NEED TO KNOW

- Legislation in your province governing labour relations
- Steps employees go through to unionize
- Definition of collective bargaining
- Definition of grievance
- Difference between mediation and arbitration
- Definition of define rights and residual rights

NEED TO UNDERSTAND

- Relationship of supervisory actions and behaviours in employees unionizing
- Expected behaviours from employers and unions during organizing drive
- Impact of unionization on supervisory actions
- Steps and importance of preparation for negotiations
- Steps in grievance process

KEY TERMS

arbitration award 332
arbitrator 326
bargaining unit 310
business agent 316
certification 311
closed shop 306
defined rights 327
grievance procedure 329

grievance resolution 331
interest arbitration 326
interest-based bargaining 321
labour relations process 306
lockout 325
management rights 313
mediator 326
membership card 309

open shop 306
residual rights 327
rights arbitration 326
strike 323
unfair labour practices 310
union (shop) steward 316
union shop 306

REVIEW QUESTIONS

1. Describe how labour relations are regulated at the federal and provincial levels.
2. Which unfair labour practices apply to (1) unions and (2) employers?
3. Describe the impact on supervisory actions after employees have become unionized.
4. What is the role of a business agent? A shop steward?
5. Describe the bargaining process.
6. What is a strike? A lockout?
7. What is the difference and similarities between mediation and arbitration?
8. What are some of the working conditions covered in a collective agreement?
9. What is a rights (or grievance) arbitration?

CRITICAL THINKING QUESTIONS

1. You have recently been appointed as a shop steward for your work unit. The supervisor of the unit tends to be fairly autocratic and directive in his approach to staff. However, you feel that the supervisor has always been fair in dealing with members of the bargaining unit. What type of relationship would you want to develop with the supervisor? Why?
2. Contrast the arguments concerning union membership that are likely to be presented by a union with those likely to be presented by an employer.
3. Provincial labour laws typically do not cover individuals who are self-employed. What arguments might you give for stating that the government ought to change its labour laws to protect self-employed individuals?
4. One of your friends is a supervisor in a fast-food restaurant. The restaurant has just become unionized and your friend is not sure how to treat his staff. What advice would you give?
5. You are on the bargaining team representing all the workers in a small manufacturing firm. Many of your fellow workers are in the age bracket 18 to 27. What are some items these workers might want in relation to hours of work and benefits?
6. The negotiations between Data Services International and its union have become deadlocked. What form of bargaining power does each side possess to enforce its bargaining demands? What are the advantages and disadvantages of each form of bargaining power for both the union and the employer?
7. A friend of yours was recently terminated due to poor work performance. The union business agent has grieved the action and a meeting has been scheduled between the union and the senior manager of the company. What type of evidence would you expect the company to put forward to prove that this termination was with cause?

DEVELOPING YOUR SKILLS

1. There has been a substantial increase (some estimate 40%) in the number of individuals who are self-employed. Some see this as a positive sign (i.e., of an increase in entrepreneurial activity); others see it as a response to the lack of permanent employment opportunities. The labour laws in each province effectively ignore independent workers. For many of them, wages (i.e., contract rates) are low, working conditions are difficult, and income security does not exist. Prepare to debate solutions to this issue, taking one of two sides: "Governments should change labour laws to recognize and protect self-employed workers," or "Unions should organize these independent contractors and fight for better treatment."
2. During a union organizing drive, labour and management will develop a plan to present their positions to employees. A goal of each side will be to collect information on the other that can be used to build a case for or against the union. Additionally, each side will seek to avoid committing unfair labour practices. Working in teams of union and management representatives, answer the following questions and be prepared to present your findings during a discussion period.

Canadian Union of Public Employees

cupe.ca

Canadian Auto Workers

www.caw.ca

Ontario Teachers' Federation

www.otffeo.on.ca/

Canadian Industrial Relations Board

www.cirb-ccri.gc.ca/
decisions/index_eng.asp

a. What methods might the union use to contact employees?

b. What information might the union collect on management in order to obtain employee support?

c. What information might management want to collect on the union?

d. What methods might unions and management use to tell their story to employees? What illegal actions will the union and management want to guard against?

e. Access the following union websites:

- **www.cupe.ca**
- **www.caw.ca**
- **www.otffeo.on.ca/**

3. A group of students wants a health food restaurant on their college campus. College administrators want a Burger King fast-food franchise. Resources allow for only one food outlet. Divide the class into bargaining teams, with one team representing the students, and the other team representing the college administrators. The objective is for each side to negotiate from that perspective and reach an agreement. (If there is another issue on your campus use the real and current issue instead.)

Review the profile of the union and the current issues it supports. Compare each union with regard to membership and issues. Bring your information to class and share it in groups of four to five. Identify at least one aspect of the website that surprised you and one thing that impressed you.

4, Using any search engine, conduct a search using the phrase "collective bargaining." Review at least 10 sites and determine if they would be useful for getting additional information about collective bargaining or collective agreements. Identify the sites you searched, pick one site, and prepare a one-page summary describing what the site is about and how you could use it if you were involved in collective bargaining.

5. Access the Canadian Industrial Relations Board website (**www.cirb-ccri.gc.ca/decisions/index_eng.asp**) where summaries of cases can be found. Also, access the website of your provincial labour relations board (see Manager's Toolkit 10.1 on page 305 of this chapter) and access the link to decisions. Retrieve two or three decisions from each site. Prepare a two- to three-page report comparing the decisions.

Case Study ❶

Walmart Stores in Canada

In 2009, Walmart has 7200 stores with over 2 million employees around the world. In the early 1990s Walmart Stores Inc. expanded into Canada, with the purchase of 122 stores from the failing Woolco chain. Walmart had refused to purchase nine Woolco stores, which were unionized.

Walmart tries to distinguish itself from other retailers by its culture. For example, it calls its workers "associates," not employees. Every day at 8:45 a.m., a compulsory meeting is held at each store during which company managers share financial information and performance targets and respond to questions. The meeting ends with the Walmart cheer. The company operates an open-door policy, whereby any employee can talk to any member of management about issues, and receive answers, without being threatened with reprisal. The sundown rule ensures that management responds to the questions before sundown the same day.

The first Walmart store ever to be unionized was in Windsor, Ontario, where the United Steelworkers (Retail and Wholesale Division) was certified by the Ontario Labour Relations Board. On April 14, 1997, the United Steelworkers began its organizing drive. On April 26, the store manager became aware that associates were being approached to sign unionization cards. The district manager was told of the organizing drive and the next morning attended the morning meeting. The district manager asked the associates why they would want to join a union and spent the day circulating through the store to discuss their problems or concerns. By April 27, 84 associates had signed cards. On April 29, an associate asked to speak at the morning meeting, and there expressed her opposition to the union, ending with the statement, "A union will only cause discontentment in our store, and I assure you as I am standing here, Walmart will not put up with it." (Management did not ask, nor did the associate reveal, why she wanted to speak.) An inside organizer was prevented from responding because it was 9 a.m. and customers were waiting to enter the store.

Between May 4 and May 9, Walmart managers—including managers from outside the store—responded to questions placed in a question-and-answer box, and to those raised while they wandered about the store. Most of the questions focused on compensation and hours of work. However, one associate testified that one manager said that things would change if the employees were unionized—for example, the profit-sharing plan would be revoked. During one meeting, the managers were asked if the store would close; they replied, "It would be inappropriate for your company to comment on what it will or will not do if the store is unionized." On May 9, the union lost the vote, with 151 employees voting against it, and 43 voting for it.

The Ontario Labour Relations Board nonetheless certified the union, because the employer violated the Labour Relations Act by not disassociating itself from the remarks made by the associate at the meeting; by not allowing the inside organizer to respond; by subtly threatening job security; and by allowing outside managers in the store from May 4 to 9. The OLRB stated that the union had 84 cards signed before the managers' visits, and a week later, this support had dropped. A second vote would not change the outcome, because the threat to job security could not be erased from employees' minds. The legislation that allows the OLRB to overturn a certification board has now been changed.

Despite numerous organizing drives, Walmart has successfully prevented unionization, and most of their 318 Canadian stores remain union-free. In late 2008, Walmart closed its Tire and Lube Express (TLE) in Gatineau, Quebec. This occurred two months after an arbitrated collective agreement was imposed. Even though the store has 250 employees, only six were employed in the TLE and these six were represented by the United Food and Commercial Workers (UFCW) Canada. The union stated that this was a blatant example of Walmart's regard for employees and the rights employees have.

However, in December 2008, another Walmart store in Gatineau was unionized by the UFCW. The union was hopeful that Walmart would take the opportunity to demonstrate it does believe in employee rights by sitting down and negotiating a fair collective agreement.

To date, this one store in Quebec is the only Walmart in North America with a unionized workforce.

Sources: Adapted from V. Galt, "Walmart Must Give Union Access," *The Globe and Mail*, May 13, 2003; "Employer Interference: The Walmart Case," *Worklife Report* 11, no. 2: 1–4. Walmart Canada, Company profile, www.walmart.ca/wps-portal/storelocator/Canada-About_Walmart.jsp (accessed March 7, 2009); "Corporate Facts: Walmart by the Numbers," July 17, 2008; Shannon Klie, "Walmart Closes Union Shop in Quebec," *Canadian HR Reporter*, November 3, 2008, 3; and Bert Hill, "Another Walmart Unionized," *Financial Post*, December 8, 2008, FP6.

Questions

1. What were the rights of Walmart, the employer, during these two organizing drives?
2. The certification of the first Walmart was hailed by labour as a milestone event. Why?
3. In your opinion, can Walmart remain union-free indefinitely? Why or why not?

Case Study 2

The Arbitration Case of Jesse Stansky

At the arbitration hearing, both parties were adamant in their positions. Nancy Huang, HR manager of Phoenix Semiconductor, argued that the grievor, Jesse Stansky, was justly terminated for arguing and hitting a co-worker—a direct violation of company policy and the employee handbook. Stansky argued that he had been a good employee during his eight years of employment.

The submission agreement governing the case read, "It is the employer's position that just cause existed for the discharge of Mr. Jesse Stansky and the penalty was appropriate for the offence committed." Additionally, the employer introduced into evidence the labour agreement, which defined just cause termination as follows:

Just cause shall serve as the basis for disciplinary action and includes, but is not limited to: dishonesty, inefficiency, unprofessional conduct, failure to report absences, falsification of records, violation of company policy, destruction of property, or possession or being under the influence of alcohol or narcotics.

Stansky was hired as a systems technician on November 20, 2000, a position he held until his termination on October 25, 2008. According to the testimony of Huang, Phoenix Semiconductor strived to maintain a positive and cordial work environment among its employees. Fighting on the job was strictly prohibited. Stansky's performance evaluation showed him to be an average employee, although he had received several disciplinary warnings for poor attendance and one three-day suspension for a "systems control error." Stansky was generally liked by his co-workers, and several testified on his behalf at the arbitration hearing.

The termination of Stansky concerned an altercation between himself and Gary Lindekin, another systems technician. According to witnesses to the incident, both Stansky and Lindekin became visibly upset over the correct way to calibrate a sensitive piece of production equipment. The argument—one witness called it no more than a heated disagreement—lasted approximately three minutes and concluded when Stansky was seen forcefully placing his hand on Lindekin's shoulder. Lindekin took extreme exception to Stansky's behaviour and immediately reported the incident to management. After interviews with both Stansky and Lindekin, and those who observed the incident, Huang, Samantha Lowry, the employee's immediate supervisor, and Grant Ginn, department manager, decided that Stansky should be terminated for unprofessional conduct and violation of company policy.

Source: Adapted from an arbitration heard by George W. Bohlander. All names are fictitious.

Questions

1. Which arguments should be given more weight: those based on company policy, the employee handbook, and the collective agreement, or mitigating factors given by the grievant and his witnesses? Explain.
2. How might unprofessional conduct be defined? Explain.
3. If you were the arbitrator, how would you rule in this case? Explain fully the reasons for your decision.

NOTES AND REFERENCES

1. For a more complete understanding of the labour relations system, refer to J. T. Dunlop, *Industrial Relations Systems*, rev. ed. (Boston: Harvard Business School Press, 1993); and Alton W. J. Craig and Norma A. Solomon, *The System of Industrial Relations in Canada*, 5th ed. (Scarborough, Ont.: Prentice Hall Canada Inc., 1996).

2. "Labour Law," Labour Canada, www.hrsdc.gc.ca/eng/labour/labour_law/index.shtml (accessed March 4, 2009).

3. Larry Suffield, *Labour Relations* (Toronto: Pearson Education, 2005), 82.

4. To read more about the labour relations process, consult John Pierce, *Canadian Industrial Relations*, 2nd ed. (Toronto: Pearson Education, 2003); Suffield, *Labour Relations*; Robert R. Sinclair and Lois E. Tetrick, "Social Exchange and Union Commitment: A Comparison of Union Instrumentality and Union Support Perceptions," *Journal of Organizational Behavior* 16, no. 6 (November 1995): 669–79.

5. Ernest B. Akyeampong, "Collective Bargaining Priorities," *Perspectives on Labour and Income,* Statistics Canada, August 2005, 5–10.

6. Tavia Grant and Greg Keenan, "Steelworkers Suffer Setback," *The Globe and Mail,* March 28, 2008, B5; and "Steelworkers Drop Dofasco Union Bid," *National Post,* March 28, 2008, FP6.

7. Larry Suffield, *Labour Relations*, 24.

8. Jean-Francois Bertrand, "Eight Quebec Walmart Employees Become First in North America with a Union Contract," *The Vancouver Sun,* August 16, 2008, G4.

9. John Lewis, "Avoiding Unions All About Being Proactive," *Canadian HR Reporter,* October 22, 2007, 5.

10. Nicolas Van Praet, "IAMAW Files Labour Charges Against Toyota," *National Post,* March 18, 2008, FP7.

11. Nicolas Van Praet, "Vote to Unionize Will be Held at Toyota," *National Post,* March 15, 2008, FP8; and *International Association of Machinists and Aerospace Workers v. Toyota Motor Manufacturing Canada Inc.*, 2008 CanLII 14775 (ON L.R.B.)—2008-04-02.

12. Canada Industrial Relations Board Regulations and Ontario Labour Relations Act.

13. Mark Milke, "Top-Down Unionism," *National Post,* June 8, 2006, FP3.

14. Donald McArthur, "Laid-off Auto Workers End Standoff," *The Vancouver Sun,* March 19, 2009, C5.

15. Canadian Labour Congress, "CLC Analysis of the G-20 Summit," November 18, 2008, http://canadianlabour.ca/en/clc-analysis-g-20-summit (accessed March 5, 2009).

16. Canadian Labour Congress, "Labour Mobilizing for Change," February 10, 2009, http://canadianlabour.ca/en/labour-mobilizing-change (accessed March 5, 2009).

17. Workplace Information Directorate, Labour Program, Human Resources and Social Development Canada, *Union Membership in Canada—2007*, 6.

18. Workplace Information Directorate, Labour Program, Human Resources and Social Development Canada, *Union Membership in Canada—2006*.

19. *Union Membership in Canada—2007*, 7.

20. Shannon Klie, "Economic Crisis Changes Union Priorities," *Canadian HR Reporter,* December 1, 2008, 3.

21. "CAW and USW Leaders Make Joint Call for Buy Canadian Policy," February 10, 2009, www.caw.ca (accessed March 6, 2009).

22. Gordon Hamilton, "Worker-Owned Pulp Mill Dodges the Scrap Heap," *The Vancouver Sun,* February 27, 2009, F2.

23. "Trends in Union Density Across Canada," *Industrial Relations Bulletin* 39, no. 10 (October 19, 2007).

24. Visit these websites: www.cupe.ca; www.nupge.ca; www.psac.com; and *Union Membership in Canada—2007*, 3.

25. Bill Curry, "Federal Employees Agree to 'Tough Times' Wage Deal," *The Globe and Mail,* November 25, 2008, A4.

26. Larry Suffield, *Labour Relations*, 201–18.

27. Morley Gunderson, Allen Ponak, and Daphne G. Tars, *Union-Management Relations in Canada*, 5th ed. (Toronto: Pearson Education, 2005), 294–300.

28. Government of Newfoundland and Labrador, "Interest Based Negotiations," www.hrle.gov.nl.ca/lra/labourrelations/interestbased.htm (accessed June 22, 2009).

29. Roger Fisher and William Ury, *Getting to Yes* (Toronto: Penguin Books, 1991).

30. Derek Abma, "Bad Economy Promotes Labour Peace, Conference Board Says," *The Vancouver Sun,* February 6, 2009, D5.

31. Ross Stagner and Hjalmar Rosen, *Psychology of Union–Management Relations* (Belmont, Calif.: Wadsworth, 1965), 95–97. This is another classic in the field of labour–management relations.

32. Elizabeth Church, "CUPE Working to Gain Student Support to Increase Its Clout," *The Globe and Mail,* November 8, 2008, A7; Elizabeth Church, "High Stakes for Higher Learning," *The Globe and Mail,* December 27, 2008, A8; and "York President Welcomes End of Strike," York University, www.yorku.ca/mediar/archive/Release.php?Release=1599 (accessed March 6, 2009).

33. Scott Simpson, "Gold Mine Faces Shutdown," *The Vancouver Sun*, February 23, 2005, D1; and Scott Simpson, "High Metal Prices Benefit Canadian Firms," *The Vancouver Sun*, February 23, 2005, D1.

34. Ernest B. Akyeampong, "Increased Work Stoppages," *Perspectives on Labour and Income,* Statistics Canada, August 2006, 5–9.

35. Ontario Ministry of Justice, www.attorneygeneral.jus.gov.on.ca/english/family/appendixa.asp (accessed March 6, 2009).

36. For an expanded discussion of management's residual rights, termed "reserved rights" in the United States, see Paul Prasow and Edward Peters, *Arbitration and Collective Bargaining*, 2nd ed. (New York: McGraw-Hill, 1983): 33–34. This book is considered an authority on management rights issues.

37. Labour agreement, Wabash Fibre Box Company and Paperworkers.

38. Brian Morton, "Telus Union Protests Job Shift to Philippines," *The Vancouver Sun,* February 6, 2009, D5.

39. *Grievance Guide,* 12th ed., Bureau of National Affairs, July 2008.

40. "Union Grieves the Demise of Free Beer for Old Guys," *The Vancouver Sun,* June 10, 2009, D5.

41. Natalie MacDonald, "Innocent Until Proven Guilty—Mostly," *Canadian HR Reporter,* August 13, 2007, 5.

11

INTERNATIONAL HUMAN RESOURCES MANAGEMENT

OUTCOMES

After studying this chapter, you should be able to

1. Identify the types of organizational forms used for competing internationally.

2. Explain the economic, political-legal, and cultural factors in different countries that need to be considered from an HR perspective.

3. Explain how Canadian and international HRM differ.

4. Describe the staffing process for individuals working internationally.

5. Identify the unique training needs for employees that work internationally.

6. Identify the characteristics of a good international recognition and rewards program.

7. Reconcile the difficulties of home- and host-country performance management systems.

8. Explain how labour relations differ around the world.

OUTLINE

HRM CLOSE-UP

"As an executive walking into an operation in another country, you have to think carefully about how things will be perceived.

"Everything you do or say, communicates." This is one of the most important conclusions John Sheppard has made from his vast experience managing employees internationally.

Sheppard is chief executive officer of Icelandic Glacial Waters, a premium water bottling company with operations in the U.S., U.K., and Iceland. When he was first exposed to labour rules in Iceland, some of the differences surprised him. "As an example, a first-year employee earns five weeks vacation and 21 days for national holidays in Iceland. In the U.S., one week vacation and about 10 statutory holidays is the standard for a new employee."

Besides vacation policies, hiring practices were another area of great difference abroad. "In Europe, you can ask pretty well anything in an employment interview," Sheppard comments. "And in England, the process for firing an employee is again very different. Even for someone who has been in a position a relatively short period of time, you must grade their work performance using a matrix and spend significant time reviewing it with the employee." This must happen before a termination discussion begins, he adds.

As a former chief executive for CocaCola, Sheppard has been in charge of employees in 29 countries. "As an executive walking into an operation in another country, you have to think carefully about how things will be perceived. You need to be aware that employees are looking at how you dress, how you manage, how you behave." And, he adds "you sometimes learn **more** from knowing what **not** to do."

And while it may be straightforward to learn about employment law in another country, understanding the more subtle aspects of lifestyle and cultural differences is key. Sheppard recalls a colleague who learned the hard way after circulating a memo giving employees direction on personal hygiene. "He had to retract the memo and in hindsight, it's a rather funny example,

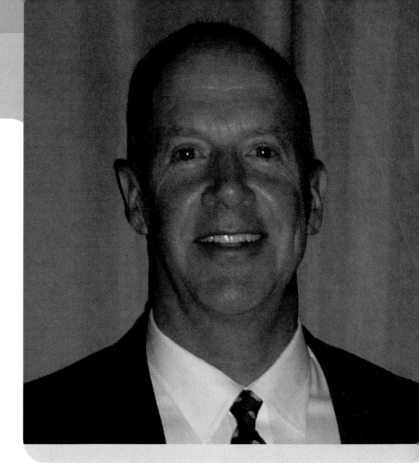

John Sheppard, CEO, Icelandic Glacial Waters.
Courtesy of John Sheppard

but you cannot presume people place the same value as you do on washing and using deodorant!"

For new managers working internationally, Sheppard's advice includes speaking to employees directly and asking them for input. "This management practice is often new to employees in other cultures," he explains, "and they love to meet the new executive. They like to be recognized as an important part of the business."

Between Canada and the United States, Sheppard observes that labour practices and managing human resources are generally more similar than different. He does note the tendency for unions to be stronger in the U.S. and that handling the processes associated with employment contracts can become very labour intensive.

One aspect of labour practice that Sheppard does value in Canada is that he feels Canadians tend to respect the time away from the office a little more. "It's much easier here to take a holiday and not be expected to check in. As a manager in the U.S., taking a two-week vacation and really being away is a challenge."

INTRODUCTION

Even with the recession and a political suggestion to "buy Canadian," there are still stories of companies trying to compete in a global environment. These stories might include mergers of international companies, such as Stelco and US Steel in 2008. Or they might highlight companies expanding into other markets, such as Bombardier in Asia or BMO in the United States or Icelandic Glacial Waters as described in HRM Close-up. Or the stories might focus on international companies gaining dominance here in Canada, such as Starbucks or Walmart.

Whatever the angle, we see clearly that globalization is a chief factor driving Canadian business. Nearly all organizations today are influenced by international competition. Some handle the challenge well, while others fail miserably when they try to manage across borders. More often than not, the difference boils down to how people are managed, the adaptability of cultures, and the flexibility of organizations. Because of this, many organizations are reassessing their approaches to human resources management.[1]

The importance of globalization notwithstanding, we have—for the most part—emphasized HRM practices and systems as they exist in Canada. This is not so much an oversight on our part as it is a deliberate decision to explain the HR practices in the most fundamental way. However, the topic of international HRM is so important that we wanted to dedicate an entire chapter to its discussion. Our thinking is that now after you have read (and, we hope, discussed) some of the best practices for managing people at work, it may be appropriate to see how some of these HRM practices may change as we begin to manage people in an international arena.

MANAGING ACROSS BORDERS

International business operations can take several different forms. A large percentage of them carry on their international business with only limited facilities and minimal representation in foreign countries. Others, particularly Fortune 500 corporations, have extensive facilities and personnel in various countries of the world. For example, Dell employs more people outside the United States than within it. Managing these resources effectively, and integrating their activities to achieve global advantage, is a challenge to the leadership of these companies.

Figure 11.1 shows four basic types of organizations and how they differ in the degree to which international activities are separated to respond to the local regions and integrated to achieve global efficiencies. The **international corporation** is essentially a domestic firm that builds on its existing capabilities to penetrate overseas markets. Companies such as Honda, General Electric, and Procter & Gamble used this approach to gain access to Europe—they essentially adapted existing products for overseas markets without changing much else about their normal operations. One such adaptation, for example, was P&G's extremely successful introduction of a detergent brick used on washboards in India.

A **multinational corporation (MNC)** is a more complex form that usually has fully autonomous units operating in several countries. Shell, Philips, and ITT are three typical MNCs. These companies have traditionally given their foreign subsidiaries a great deal of latitude to address local issues such as consumer preferences, political pressures, and economic trends in different regions of the world. Tata Communications, a part of the Mumbai-based Tata Group, purchased the Canadian Crown corporation, Teleglobe Inc., and then entered into an agreement with the British Telecom Group to be the primary supplier of international direct dial outside the U.K. and other European countries served by BT.[2] Another company within the Tata Group, Tata Motors, has just produced the cheapest car on the road. At a selling price of US$2,000, it has moved into the global auto market.[3] Frequently, these subsidiaries are run as independent companies, without much integration. The **global corporation,** on the other hand, can be viewed as a multinational firm that maintains control of operations back in the home office. Japanese companies such as Matsushita and NEC, for example, tend to treat the world market as a unified whole and try to combine activities in each country to maximize efficiency on a global scale. These companies operate much like a domestic firm, except that they view the whole world as their marketplace.

International corporation
Domestic firm that uses its existing capabilities to move into overseas markets

Multinational corporation (MNC)
Firm with independent business units operating in several countries

Global corporation
Firm that has integrated worldwide operations through a centralized home office

FIGURE 11.1 Types of Organizations

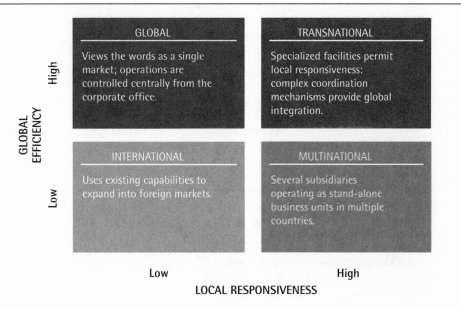

Transnational corporation
Firm that attempts to balance local responsiveness and global scale via a network of specialized operating units

Finally, a **transnational corporation** attempts to achieve the local responsiveness of an MNC while also achieving the efficiencies of a global firm. To balance this "global/local" dilemma, a transnational uses a network structure that coordinates specialized facilities positioned around the world. By using this flexible structure, a transnational provides autonomy to independent country operations but brings these separate activities together into an integrated whole. For most companies, the transnational form represents an ideal, rather than a reality. However, Manpower, one of the largest suppliers of staffing resources—both temporary and on-going—has evolved its global operations into a transnational model.[4]

Although various forms of organization exist, in this chapter we will generally refer to any company that conducts business outside its home country as an international business. Canada, of course, has no monopoly on international business. International enterprises are found throughout the world. In fact, some European and Pacific Rim companies have been conducting business on an international basis much longer than their Canadian counterparts. The close proximity of European countries, for example, makes them likely candidates for international trade. Figure 11.2 shows a list of some of the top international companies, measured in a number of ways. You will note significant changes in the composition of the lists between 2008 and 2009 as a result of the worldwide market crisis.

These companies are in a strong position to affect the world economy in the following ways:

1. Production and distribution extend beyond national boundaries, making it easier to transfer technology.
2. They have direct investments in many countries, affecting the balance of payments.
3. They have a political impact that leads to cooperation among countries and to the breaking down of barriers of nationalism.

Although Figure 11.2 is showing financial measures to demonstrate "top" or "best," Figure 11.3 lists the world's "Most Admired Companies" done by surveying executives, directors, and industry analysts in a methodological "peer review" of reputation. Conducted jointly by *Fortune* and Hay Group, it is done in this way as there is a belief that a company's reputation is positively related to measurable (i.e., financial) outcomes.[5] And in the 2009 list, further observations were made about the importance of company reputation during economic downturns and that certain elements created a positive reputation. These are: 1) strong, stable strategy; 2) stable structures; 3) focus on identifying and developing talent on a global scale; and 4) orderly succession plans for the senior staff.[6]

FIGURE 11.2   Top International Companies—2008 and 2009

2009 Rank	2008 Rank	Company (overall ranking)	Headquarters	2009 Market Value (Billions US$)	2008 Market Value (Billions US$)
1	2	General Electric	United States	85.04	180.81
2	6	Royal Dutch Shell	Netherlands	135.10	221.09
3	8	Toyota Motor	Japan	102.35	175.08
4	5	ExxonMobil	United States	335.54	465.51
5	7	BP	United Kingdom	119.70	204.94
6	1	HSBC Holdings	United Kingdom	85.04	180.81
7	12	AT&T	United States	140.08	210.22
8	16	Wal-Mart Stores	United States	193.15	198.60
9	21	Banco Santander	Spain	49.75	113.27
9	17	Chevron	United States	121.70	179.97
	3	Bank of America	United States		176.53
	4	JP Morgan Chase	United States		136.88
	9	ING Group	Netherlands		75.78
19	10	Berkshire Hathaway	United States	122.11	216.65

2009 Rank	2008 Rank	Company	Headquarters	2009 Sales (Billions US$)	2008 Sales (Billions US$)
1	3	Royal Dutch Shell	Netherlands	458.36	355.78
2	2	ExxonMobil	United States	425.70	358.60
3	1	Wal-Mart Stores	United States	405.61	378.80
4	4	BP	United Kingdom	361.14	281.03
5	6	Toyota Motor	Japan	263.42	203.80
6	5	Chevron	United States	255.11	203.97
7	12	ConocoPhillips	United States	225.42	171.50
8	7	Total	France	235.15	199.74
9	8	ING Group	Netherlands	213.99	197.93
10	10	General Electric	United States	182.52	172.74
17	9	General Motors	United States	149.98	181.12

2009 Rank	2008 Rank	Company	Headquarters	2009 Profits (Billions US$)	2008 Profits (Billions US$)
1	1	ExxonMobil	United States	45.22	40.61
2	3	Gazprom	Russia	26.78	23.30
3	2	Royal Dutch Shell	Netherlands	26.28	31.33
4	8	Chevron	United States	23.93	18.69
5	5	BP	United Kingdom	21.16	20.60
6	9	PetroChina	China	19.94	18.21
7	4	General Electric	United States	17.41	22.21
8	10	Microsoft	United States	17.23	16.96
9	14	Toyota Motor	Japan	17.21	13.99
10	37	Nestlé	Switzerland	16.91	9.38
12	6	Total	France	14.74	19.24
67	7	HSBC Holdings	United Kingdom	5.73	19.13

Source: "The World's Biggest Companies," *Forbes,* April 2, 2008 and April 9, 2009, www.forbes.com/lists/2008/18/biz_2000global08_The-Global-2000_Prof.html and www.forbes.com/lists/2009/18/global-09_The-Global-2000_Prof.html (accessed June 25, 2009).

FIGURE 11.3 Most Admired Companies

Company	Headquarters
1. Apple	U.S.
2. Berkshire Hathaway	U.S.
3. Toyota Motor	Japan
4. Google	U.S.
5. Johnson & Johnson	U.S.
6. Procter & Gamble	U.S.
7. FedEx	U.S.
8. Southwest Airlines	U.S.
9. General Electric	U.S.
10. Microsoft	U.S.

Source: Geoff Colvin, "The World's Most Admired Companies 2009," *Fortune,* March 16, 2009, 76. ©2009 Time Inc. All rights reserved.

Another more recent list measures the world's most sustainable organizations—those that are equipped to prosper in the long-term because of their approach to relationship-building with all the various stakeholders. This list had the following five Canadian companies: Encana Corporation, Royal Bank of Canada, Telus Corp., TD Bank, and Transcanada Corp.[7] It is important to remember that Canada is an export nation and therefore most of our major companies do business outside Canada. For example, 96% of the sales of both the Potash Corporation of Saskatchewan and Bombardier Inc. are outside Canada as are 95% of the sales of Onex Corporation (based in Toronto). These three corporations are included in Canada's list of 500 largest corporations.[8]

So how do Canadian companies compare to those on the world lists? Figure 11.4 lists the top 10 publicly traded companies for 2009.

Are there any companies that are on all the lists? If so, which ones? What changes do you notice, particularly in Figure 11.2 from 2008 to 2009?

FIGURE 11.4 Top 10 Canadian Companies

Rank	Company	2009 Profits (Billions US$)	2009 Revenues (Billions US$)
1	EnCana Corp.	5.944	30,280
2	Canadian Natural Resources	4.985	16,173
3	Royal Bank of Canada	4.555	37,566
4	Imperial Oil	3.878	30,167
5	Toronto Dominion Bank	3.833	25,721
6	Husky Energy	3.754	25,256
7	Potash Corp. of Saskatchewan	3.495	10,012
8	Talisman Energy	3.519	13,726
9	Bank of Nova Scotia	3.140	26,628
10	Petro-Canada	3.134	27,785

Source: "Rankings by Profit," *Report on Business,* July/August 2009, 64.

**Society for Human
Resource Management**
www.shrm.org

The Society for Human Resources Management provides current news updates on issues concerning HRM from around the world. Currently, the information can be found at "Global HR" under its HR Disciplines category.

How Does the Global Environment Influence Management?

In Chapter 1, we highlighted some of the challenges facing business and therefore affecting human resources management. One of the major economic issues we discussed was the creation of free trade zones within Europe, North America, and the Pacific Rim. As of March 2009, there were 27 member countries within the European Union (EU), whose goal is to have a single market for the movement of goods, services, people and money across certain national borders.[9] A similar transition has been occurring within North America after 15 years since the passage of NAFTA (discussed in Chapter 1). While there had been fears that NAFTA would lead to a loss of jobs for companies in the three countries, just the opposite has occurred. A recent study indicated that trade totalled over $900 billion annually and that employment has risen sharply in all three countries.[10] Further, in early 2009, Canada and the EU began discussions on an "economic agreement" for certain sectors such as trade in goods and intellectual property. The EU is Canada's second largest economic partner; the U.S. is Canada's largest partner.[11]

Like NAFTA, numerous trade agreements, including the Association of Southeast Asian Nations (ASEAN), East Asia Economic Group, and Asia-Pacific Economic Cooperation (APEC) have significantly facilitated trade among Asian countries, making Asia the fastest-growing region in the world. China—its fastest-growing country—has emerged as a dominant trade leader since instituting trade reforms in the late 1970s. In the last 15 years, China's economy has grown fourfold, drastically altering political and trading relations among nations. Some industry analysts estimate that the country now produces 50% of the world's cameras, 30% of air conditioners and televisions, 25% of washing machines, and 20% of refrigerators worldwide. In addition, China's 1.3 billion people represent a massive, largely untapped consumer market for global companies. Even with the worldwide recession that started in 2008, China's GDP still expanded by almost 12%.[12] Today more cars are sold in China than in Europe. Driving this trend are big multinational corporations such as General Electric, Toyota, and Intel, which are building or expanding their manufacturing units in the country. But many smaller firms are heading to China as well. For example, in mid-2008 Fruits & Passion, the Canadian personal care product company, opened its fourth boutique store in Shanghai—which is its 13th store in China.[13] Also, Quebec-based Roctest Ltd. was awarded a contract to supply numerous instruments for a new dam on the Yalong River in China. Roctest designs, manufactures, and markets high-precision measuring instruments.[14] One of the more interesting changes due to the decline of the North American auto industry is the purchase of the Hummer brand from GM. Sichuan Tengzhong Heavy Industry Machinery Co. purchased Hummer one day after GM declared bankruptcy. Currently Tengzhong makes special-use vehicles, construction and energy equipment, and structural components for bridges and highways. However, while the company has said it will continue to manufacture the Hummer in the existing GM plants, it has also stated it intends to move the manufacturing operation to China in the next several years.[15]

In addition to China, other key countries for trade are Brazil, Russia, and India. With China, these countries are called BRIC and are considered to have fast-growing economies. In the midst of the worldwide recession, sales of automobiles in BRIC were strong and India was projecting a 10.7% growth in its service industry.[16]

Outcome 2

The fact that international corporations can choose the countries in which they do business or relocate operations generally results in the selection of countries that have the most to offer. In addition to economic factors, political-legal factors are a huge consideration. In many countries, particularly those in Africa, property rights are poorly protected by governments. Whoever has the political power or authority can seize others' property with few or no consequences. Civil unrest can also lead to the poor enforcement of property rights. This gives companies less incentive to locate factories or invest there. Another issue relates to intellectual property rights—rights related to patents, trademarks, and so forth. Despite the fact that private property rights are now generally enforced in China, intellectual property rights have seen little protection. For example, when General Motors formed a joint venture with a Chinese company to produce and sell a new automobile in the country, a knockoff version of the car could be seen on China's streets even before GM and its partner were able to manufacture their first car. Environmental restrictions also make some countries more attractive to do business in than others.

Cultural environment
Communications, religion, values and ideologies, education, and social structure of a country

Beyond the economic and political-legal issues just mentioned, a country's **cultural environment** (communications, religion, values and ideologies, education, and social structure) also has important implications when it comes to a company's decision about when and how to do business in another country. Because of language and culture similarities, many Canadian companies are finding the U.S., Ireland, and the U.K. attractive places to locate their facilities, particularly call centres. Eastern Europe has also begun to attract interest because citizens there are well educated and largely possess English-speaking skills. Figure 11.5 summarizes the complexity of the cultural environment in which HR must be managed. Culture is an integrated phenomenon. By recognizing and accommodating taboos, rituals, attitudes toward time, social stratification, kinship systems, and the many other components listed in Figure 11.5, managers stand a better chance of understanding the culture of a **host country**–a country in which an international business operates. Different cultural environments require different approaches to human resources management. At Work with HRM 11.1 presents the stories of people who made changes and what were some of the things they encountered.

Host country
Country in which an international corporation operates

FIGURE 11.5 The Cultural Environment of International Business

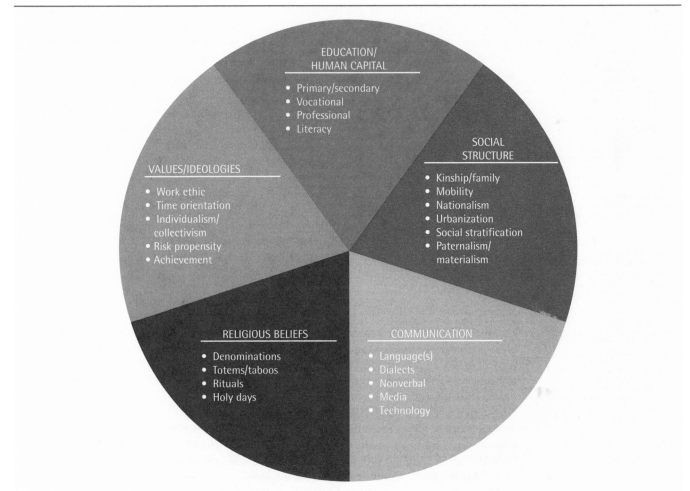

AT WORK with HRM 11.1

ADVENTURES IN WORKING IN OTHER COUNTRIES

People find unusual things occur when they relocate for work to other countries. Take the first story of a person from Toronto who moved to Auckland, New Zealand. The language wasn't a problem—except for the accent. However, the pay was less and the person didn't have a credit rating in order to get a mortgage. Also, the person found out that over-the-counter drugs were very expensive and could not be purchased in large sizes.

Another individual, also from Toronto, moved to Singapore in the mid-1990s. At the time there was huge economic and business growth, as well as a change to a democratic form of government. In terms of language, English is prevalent so the person was able to get by. However, he did say it is important to have an open mind and be prepared for the unexpected.

The third person transferred to Switzerland with a global pharmaceutical firm. He eventually learned German as he discovered that it was the most prominent language and also that language was extremely important in everyday life. He said a key learning was the high cost of living—particularly in relation to accommodation and health insurance. Since the family lived in a small, rural village, getting around became a challenge and an adventure. It was in the village that being able to speak one of the local languages became very important.

CRITICAL THINKING QUESTIONS

1. Would you like to work in another country? Why or why not?
2. If you did work in another country, which country would it be? What would you need to learn about the cultural environment before moving to that country?

Source: Adapted from Sarah Dobson, "Relocation Postcards," *Canadian HR Reporter*, December 1, 2008, www.hrreporter.com/ArticleView.aspx?l=1&articleid=6532 (accessed March 9, 2009).

NAFTA

www.nafta-sec-alena.org/

Europa

europa.eu/

ASEAN

www.aseansec.org/

Foreign Affairs and International Trade Canada

international.gc.ca/

Outcome **3**

Strategies, structures, and management styles that are appropriate in one cultural setting may lead to failure in another. Even in countries that have close language or cultural links, HR practices can be dramatically different. In some countries night shifts are taboo. In other countries employers are expected to provide employees with meals and transportation between home and work. In India, workers generally receive cash bonuses on their wedding anniversaries with which to buy gifts for their spouses, and dating allowances are provided to unmarried employees. Also in India, promotional opportunities are more highly valued than compensation. And in France, work-life balance is critical.[17] These are practices that would probably never occur to Canadian managers.[18]

For more information on the various trade agreements and doing business in other countries, check out NAFTA (**www.nafta-sec-alena.org/**), Europa (**europa.eu/**), ASEAN (**www.aseansec.org/**), and Foreign Affairs and International Trade Canada (**international.gc.ca/**)

Canadian vs. International HRM

International HRM differs from domestic HRM in several ways. In the first place, it necessarily places a greater emphasis on functions and activities such as relocation, orientation, and translation services to help employees adapt to new and different environments outside their own countries and to help newly hired employees in foreign countries adapt to working for companies headquartered outside their borders. Because of the complexity of HR when doing business in other countries, larger companies will have HR professionals devoted solely to assisting with the globalization process. Further, some companies will also hire international staffing firms such as Boston Global Consulting. These firms have expertise when it comes to relocating employees, establishing operations abroad, and helping with import/export and foreign tax issues.

HR information systems have also come a long way in terms of helping firms improve their international coordination. A good HR information system can facilitate communication, record keeping, and a host of other activities worldwide. Some HRISs are designed to track the whereabouts of employees travelling or on assignment. This can be important in the event of a transportation accident, a natural disaster such as a tsunami, a terrorist attack, or civil strife if evacuation plans must be implemented. Occasionally, however, even the seemingly simplest of cultural differences can be difficult to overcome when a company attempts to set up a global HRIS. When Lucent Technologies rolled out a PeopleSoft system to more than 90 countries, the company's managers found that the order of employees' names was so important—and so varied—that it took two months to settle on a name format allowing employees to be entered into the system. As you can see, even small differences such as format of name, can create problems for international companies.

International Staffing

Outcome 4

Expatriates, or home-country nationals
Employees from the home country who are on international assignment

Host-country nationals
Employees who are natives of the host country

Third-country nationals
Employees who are natives of a country other than the home country or the host country

International management poses many problems in addition to those faced by a domestic operation. Because of geographic distance and a lack of close, day-to-day relationships with headquarters in the home country, problems must often be resolved with little or no counsel or assistance from others. It is essential, therefore, that special attention be given to the staffing practices of overseas units.

There are three sources of employees with whom to staff international operations. First, the company can send people from its home country. These employees are often referred to as **expatriates,** or **home-country nationals.** Second, it can hire **host-country nationals,** natives of the host country, to do the managing. Third, it can hire **third-country nationals,** natives of a country other than the home country or the host country.

Each of these three sources of overseas workers provides certain advantages and certain disadvantages. Most corporations, such as the Four Seasons Hotel (described in At Work with HRM 11.2), use all three sources for staffing their multinational operations.

AT WORK **with HRM 11.2**

SELECTING FOR SERVICE

Four Seasons Hotels, with a staff of over 25,000, manages 50 hotels and luxury resorts around the world, from Bali to Boston. The Four Seasons brand is synonymous with luxury and first-class service standards. The execution of the strategy of being the best in the world starts with leaders who are passionate about the corporation's customer service and employee relations values. These leaders can take a concept such as "We will deliver exceptional personal service" and paint a picture for employees that is clear and motivational and that results in the delivery of that exceptional personal service.

Does the perception of service excellence depend on the country or culture in which Four Seasons operates? John Young, executive vice president of human resources, states that the Four Seasons guest is typically a sophisticated global traveller who has acquired a sensitivity to differences in culture without negative preconceptions. Nevertheless, Four Seasons trains service staff to be sensitive to guests' needs and to minimize or avoid culture and language problems. For example, in Asia, when an

English-speaking guest gives a food or beverage order, the service staff are trained to repeat the order. This is done not only to prevent a potential service error, but also to avoid loss of face for the employee. In North America, a repetition of the order would be seen as redundant.

So that employees can meet these high performance expectations, Four Seasons selects employees based on their service attitudes. Candidates for employment must undergo four behaviourally based interviews (including one with the general manager) to determine their service attitudes and current skills and knowledge. As Young says, "Customer service is the heart and soul of our business, and we need to assess if a candidate has sensitivity to the needs and wants of others. Of course, we also look at high levels of knowledge, skill, and experience, but these can be trained. We continuously adapt our service to match guest needs. For example, many years ago, in our Seattle hotel, one of the valet parking attendants noted that on weekends our guests were disproportionately families with children. On his own initiative, he put chocolate chip cookies

(Continued)

and milk in cars that he was returning to these departing guests. They loved it. This practice has now become one of Four Seasons' standards."

Four Seasons does not have a rigid formula for selecting home country nationals or expatriates for any given country. The ratios depend on three factors: regulations, economics, and corporate management development needs. Young continues, "For example, Indonesia used to have a rule that no more than three expatriates could be employed per hotel. So we set expatriate reduction targets to meet this regulation. Economically it made sense for us, since an expatriate general manager could cost us as much as 75 or 80 local employees. And finally, we will choose candidates based on their need for global exposure and professional development, to match our targeted needs for international expansion.

"Our biggest challenge in international HR now is management development in the context of our growth plans. We need to develop culturally appropriate leadership in preparation for specific new locations on a defined time line. If we cannot find managers who can speak the language, and understand the culture, then our ability to grow is limited. Recently we opened a hotel in Puerto Vallarta. We found a Spanish-speaking general manager from Colombia who, over time, was able to integrate the Four Seasons way of doing business with the Mexican culture. Business culture in Mexico tends to be very rule and policy driven. Employees continuously asked, 'What is the policy ...' in HR, sales, everything." Over time, the general manager learned to deal with the questions by no longer looking to home office for all the rules, but by asking himself and his team, "What should the rule be in our situation?"

"We cannot just hire the management talent we want from other sectors or hotel chains on short lead time, because of differences in operating standards and corporate culture. For example, we were opening a hotel with a general manager recruited from Hilton International. As he toured the new facility with Issy Sharp, our founder and CEO, the general manager said that the lounge facilities ought to be larger. He explained that this would make guests more comfortable while waiting for their dinner reservations. Issy replied, 'At Four Seasons our guests do not wait for their reservations.' These cultural differences, across countries, across sectors, and across competitors, underline the importance of our investing the time and effort in developing our own management talent, which is culturally and linguistically fluent, mobile, and imbued with our service culture."

This attention to the selection and development of high-performance employees has resulted in Four Seasons being named by *Fortune* magazine one of the 100 best employers continuously for 10 years since 1998. Consequently, Four Seasons is now able to attract more and better applicants. Four Seasons is also widely recognized as the best luxury hotel chain in the world. Furthermore, the turnover rate at Four Seasons is one of the lowest in the hospitality sector. Even those employees who have left are often recaptured as they elect to return to the kind of culture that treats them as they treat the guests.

As shown in Figure 11.6, at early stages of international expansion, organizations often send home-country expatriates to establish activities (particularly in less-developed countries) and to work with local governments. This is generally very costly. Expatriate assignments cost companies, on average, $1 million over a three-year period. This can be three to five times what a domestic assignment costs. As a result, many companies are taking greater pains to more clearly outline the overall goal of the foreign assignment and its timetable for completion. Some companies to reduce the costs are considering short-terms assignments and/or "commuter" assignments. A short-term assignment is 6–12 months, with the employee remaining under a home-country employment contract. A "commuter" assignment is up to three months and the compensation package remains with the home-country. In both cases, there is either a per-day or monthly living allowance, or an expense account.[19]

Nearly 70,000 Canadians are working abroad, mainly in the U.S. (44%), followed by Europe (33%), then Asia/Pacific (15%), and Central and South America (8%). Most employees now consider foreign work credentials essential or extremely useful.[20]

At later stages of internationalization, there is typically a steady shift toward the use of host-country nationals. This has three main advantages:

1. Hiring local citizens is less costly than relocating expatriates.
2. Since local governments usually want good jobs for their citizens, foreign employers may be required to hire them.
3. Most customers want to do business with companies (and people) they perceive to be local versus foreign.

FIGURE 11.6   Changes in International Staffing Over Time

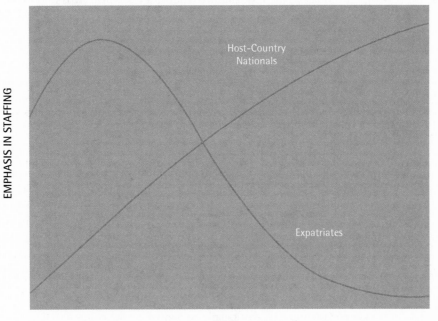

Because Canadian companies want to be viewed as true international citizens, there has also been a trend away from hiring expatriates to head up operations in foreign countries, particularly European countries. Bombardier and Four Seasons, which have strong regional organizations, tend to replace their expatriate managers with local managers as quickly as possible. At Work with HRM 11.3 describes some of the issues in checking references of locals. In addition to hiring local managers to head their foreign divisions and plants, more companies are using third-country nationals. Third-country nationals are often multilingual and already acclimated to the host country's culture—perhaps because they live in a nearby region. Thus, they are also less costly to relocate and sometimes better able to cope culturally with the foreign environment.

AT WORK **with HRM 11.3**

REFERENCING CHECKING

An American company was very impressed with the 20-page résumé of a candidate for a management position for its new Japanese office. The promising candidate had worked on a wide variety of deals. However, upon checking his references, the company learned that indeed he had been involved in all these deals—as the interpreter!

Those checking references in foreign countries have to be aware of privacy regulations. For example, in Canada and the United States, there are privacy laws that govern what data is and is not allowed to be accessed and used by potential employers. An employee working in the Indian office of a Canadian company is covered by the laws of India, not Canada.

There are also cultural differences in the ways references are checked. If you wanted to know if a candidate had a criminal history in Latin America, you would need to know the name of the applicant's mother. It is also helpful to understand the political context in which reference checking is done. One candidate who had worked in a country that had just recently become a democracy supplied the name of his former supervisor as a reference. However, when the supervisor was contacted, he claimed to have never known the candidate. After the call, the supervisor phoned the applicant and said, "A company called asking about you, but don't worry. I told them that I don't know you and that you never worked for us." Based on the practices of the former government, the supervisor was sensitive to any kinds of investigative questions.

Source: Adapted from Traci Canning, "Hiring Global," *HR Professional,* June/July 2006, 34.

Companies tend to continue to use expatriates only when a specific set of skills is needed or when individuals in the host country require development. It is important to note, however, that while top managers may prefer one source of employees to another, the host country may place pressure on them that restricts their choices. Such pressure takes the form of sophisticated government persuasion through administrative or legislative decrees designed to employ host-country individuals. Tax incentives, tariffs, and quotas are frequently implemented by the host country to encourage local hiring.

World Education Services
www.wes.org/ca

Canadian employers wishing to assess thousands of academic credentials for foreign-born employees can consult the not-for-profit World Education Services at **www.wes.org/ca.**

Recruiting Internationally

Improved telecommunications and travel have made it easier to match up employers and employees of all kinds worldwide. Rolls-Royce, headquartered in the United Kingdom, hires 25% of its 25,000 employees abroad. Because its customers come from around the globe, Rolls-Royce figures its workforce should as well. Airbus, the European commercial jet maker, recruits engineers from universities and colleges all over Europe. American-based Boeing's need for engineers is so great that it also recruits internationally and has even opened a design centre in Moscow. The trend is likely to continue as the populations in developed countries age and companies search for talent elsewhere. Even China, despite its massive population, will face labour shortages because laws there prohibit couples from having more than one child.

Companies must be particularly responsive to the cultural, political, and legal environments both domestically and abroad when recruiting internationally. For example, companies such as Starbucks and Honeywell have made a special effort to create codes of conduct for employees throughout the world to ensure that standards of ethical and legal behaviour are known and understood. PepsiCo has taken a similar approach to ensuring that company values are reinforced (even while recognizing the need for adapting to local cultures). The company has four core criteria that are viewed as essential in worldwide recruiting efforts: (1) personal integrity, (2) a drive for results, (3) respect for others, and (4) capability. However, it is important to recognize local cultures in relation to implementing ethical codes in other countries. Read At Work With HRM 11.4 to learn of the difficulties Wal-Mart had in Germany.

In general, however, employee recruitment in other countries is subject to more government regulation than it is in Canada. Regulations range from those that cover procedures for recruiting employees to those that govern the employment of foreign workers or require the employment of the physically disabled, war veterans, or displaced persons. Many Central

---

AT WORK **with HRM 11.4**

CODES OF ETHICS IN OTHER COUNTRIES

Is a code of ethics or a code of conduct ever a problem? They can be if the culture of the country isn't taken into account.

Walmart Stores Inc., which has a number of stores in Germany, discovered that doing business in Germany isn't the same as in the U.S. It has a code of conduct that bans relationships at work as well as a hotline for employees to report misdeeds by co-workers. In doing so, it neglected to consult with workers' representatives—which is fundamental to the business environment in Germany.

North American firms have become quite focused on business ethics and therefore are applying such codes in response to the expectation of enhanced corporate governance. However, attempting to export to other countries may not work; or if the code is to work, there may be certain expectations to how it is to be introduced. As commented by the representative of the German services union, "This is a case of an overly simplistic attempt to transpose U.S. regulations into Germany."

Source: Adapted from Bettina Wassener, "Walmart Runs Afoul of German Law," *Financial Post*, June 17, 2005, FP8.

American countries, for example, have stringent regulations about the number of foreigners that can be employed as a percentage of the total workforce. Virtually all countries have work-permit or visa restrictions that apply to foreigners. A **work permit**, or **visa**, is a document issued by a government granting authority to a foreign individual to seek employment in that government's country.

Work permit, or visa
A government document granting a foreign individual the right to seek employment

Multinational companies (MNCs) tend to use the same kinds of internal and external recruitment sources as are used in their home countries. At the executive level, companies use search firms such as Korn/Ferry in Canada or Spencer Stuart in the United Kingdom. At lower levels, more informal approaches tend to be useful. While unskilled labour may be readily available in a developing country, recruitment of skilled workers may be more difficult. Many employers have learned that the best way to find workers in these countries is through referrals and radio announcements because many people lack sufficient reading or writing skills. Other firms use international recruiting firms to find skilled labour abroad. Some countries, in fact, require the employment of locals if adequate numbers of skilled people are available. Specific exceptions are sometimes granted (officially or unofficially) for difficult situations such as farm workers from Mexico in Canada or for Italian, Spanish, Greek, and Turkish workers in Germany and the Benelux countries (Belgium, the Netherlands, and Luxembourg). Foreign workers invited to come to perform needed labour are usually referred to as **guest workers.** Although hiring non-nationals may result in lower direct labour costs for a company, the indirect costs—those related to housing, language training, health services, recruitment, transportation, and so—can be substantial. Some organizations, such as health authorities recruiting nursing staff, are nonetheless finding the expenditures worthwhile.[21]

Guest workers
Foreign workers invited to perform needed labour

The worldwide recession that started in 2008 has created some interesting recruitment situations in other countries. For example, emerging companies in India were using the services of executive search firms such as Korn/Ferry to source skilled talent in mid-2008 in what was a very tight labour market.[22] By the end of 2008, these same companies were finding that there was a surplus of skilled talent as Indian firms began to downsize, particularly in the IT and financial sectors.[23] And there were fewer opportunities for people to move to Western countries to take on roles of nannies and cleaners as households cut back on domestic help. It created a particularly difficult situation for the Philippines where 12% of its economy is driven by funds coming in from other countries that employ Filipino workers.[24]

On the other hand, there is still a concern that emerging markets will grow and that finding talent will be a challenge, particularly as world markets recover from the recession. A recent study suggested that for attracting and retaining talent in new countries, organizations will need to focus on:

1. Brand—having a reputation for excellence, being a global leader, and having leadership that inspires others;
2. Purpose—demonstrating a commitment to the local region and being a global citizen;
3. Opportunity—providing challenge work with competitive pay and continual development;
4. Culture—being authentic and transparent.[25]

Apprenticeships

A major source of trained labour in European nations is apprenticeship-training programs (described in Chapter 5). On the whole, apprenticeship training in Europe is superior to that in Canada. In Europe, a dual-track system of education directs a large number of youths into vocational training. The German system of apprenticeship training, one of the best in Europe, provides training for office and top jobs under a three-way responsibility contract between the apprentice, the parents, and the organization. At the conclusion of their training, apprentices can work for any employer but generally receive seniority credit with the training firm if they remain in it. France has been able to draw on its "Grandes Écoles" for centuries. Created during the Renaissance to fulfill a need that universities weren't meeting at the time, the Grandes Écoles educate prospective engineers up to the equivalent level of Master of Engineering. It is said that France is run by people who have graduated from the various institutions in the Grandes Écoles—even the former French president.[26]

Staffing Transnational Teams

Transnational teams
Teams composed of members of multiple nationalities working on projects that span multiple countries

In addition to focusing on individuals, it is also important to note that companies are increasingly using transnational teams to conduct international business. **Transnational teams** are composed of members of multiple nationalities working on projects that span multiple countries. For example, Accenture, a global technology services and outsourcing firm, has teams all over the world working on a number of different projects. It feels that one of the successes of transnational teams is the support received from colleagues.[27]

Sometimes companies send employees on temporary assignments abroad as part of transnational teams lasting a few months. This might be done to break down cultural barriers between international divisions or disseminate new ideas and technology to other regions. Accenture, for example, had a team that was demonstrating the aspects of a particular software program to five different executives in France. One of the team members wasn't sure about the software capabilities and was able to quickly get information from the other team members.[28]

The fundamental task in forming a transnational team is assembling the right group of people who can work together effectively to accomplish the goals of the team. Many companies try to build variety into their teams in order to maximize responsiveness to the special needs of different countries. For example, when Heineken formed a transnational team to consolidate its production facilities, it ensured that team members were drawn from each major region within Europe. Team members tended to have specialized skills, and members were added only if they offered some unique skill that added value to the team.

Selecting Employees Internationally

As you might imagine, selection practices vary around the world. In Canada, managers tend to emphasize merit, with the best-qualified person getting the job. In other countries, however, firms tend to hire on the basis of family ties, social status, language, and common origin. The candidate who satisfies these criteria may get the job even if otherwise unqualified. Much of this is changing—there has been a growing realization among organizations in other nations that greater attention must be given to hiring those most qualified. In addition to a person's qualifications, various other hiring laws are enforced around the world. Labour union restrictions, which will be discussed later in this chapter, can also have an impact on hiring.

The Selection Process

The selection process for international assignments should emphasize different employment factors, depending on the extent of contact that one would have with the local culture and the degree to which the foreign environment differs from the home environment. For example, if the job involves extensive contacts with the community, as with a chief executive officer, this factor should be given appropriate weight. In addition, other factors that might be different in a foreign environment include the physical remoteness, the transportation routes, housing, pollution, disease, and sanitation.[29]

If a candidate for expatriation is willing to live and work in a foreign environment, an indication of the person's tolerance of cultural differences should be obtained. On the other hand, if local nationals have the technical competence to carry out the job successfully, they should be carefully considered for the job before the firm launches a search (at home) for a candidate to fill the job. As stated previously, most corporations realize the advantages to be gained by staffing international operations with host-country nationals wherever possible. Read At Work with HRM 11.5 to see why a Canadian company hired foreign nationals.

Selecting home-country and third-country nationals requires that more factors be considered than in selecting host-country nationals. While the latter must of course possess managerial abilities and the necessary technical skills, they have the advantage of familiarity with the physical and cultural environment and the language of the host country. And depending on the country, certain factors in the environment may be key whether or not the person is an expat. For example, people who are leaders in China require an understanding of how complex China is and that there is a

AT WORK **with HRM 11.5**

IMPORTING CULTURE

The Inn at Manitou in Ontario's Muskoka District has a staff of about 70, half of whom are not Canadian. The decision to recruit outside Canada for this Relais et Chateux luxury hotel and spa was made after years of trying to find Canadian workers and train them to offer the type of service that a luxury inn must offer.

Ben Wise, the inn's owner, gives several reasons for employing non-Canadians. The first is culture: "We hire Europeans, who have a culture of hospitality. To serve people is not perceived by Europeans to be denigrating. Canadians berate the job of a waiter, saying that they are not waiters, but on their way to be stockbrokers. Being a waiter is a profession in Europe. Chefs are celebrities in Europe."

In Europe, jobs in the hospitality sector are seen as professions for which extensive training is necessary. Europeans arrive at Wise's inn with four to five years of training and experience at some of the best hotels. Canadian candidates cannot compete. Wise tried to train

Canadians, but four weeks of on-the-job training could not match the extensive training Europeans receive. Besides, he didn't think it was fair to ask the inn's clients to put up with the mistakes and deficiencies of workers in training.

Another reason was the seasonal nature of the hospitality industry in Muskoka District: "Canadians have a summer job mentality to these positions. Consequently, a report on their performance is of no value to them. There is little we can do to motivate them to meet our service expectations. Europeans are serious. Their future employment depends on our performance evaluations and our references." So each year The Inn at Manitou places ads in trade magazines, screens hundreds of applicants, interviews and selects those with training and experience at the best resorts and hotels, and finally arranges work permits for the lucky 30. Why lucky? "Canada has a fascinating appeal for Europeans, especially the French, who must have all read books about a charming little cabin in the woods, with mountains, space, and fresh water."

balance required when the culture of intense hierarchy clashes with a global idea of flat structures with open management.[30] The discussion that follows will focus on the selection of expatriate managers from the home country.

Selecting Expatriate Managers

One of the toughest jobs facing many organizations is finding employees who can meet the demands of working in a foreign environment. There are several steps involved in selecting individuals for an international assignment. And the sequencing of these activities can make a big difference.

STEP 1: BEGIN WITH SELF-SELECTION. Employees should begin the process years in advance by thinking about their career goals and interest in international work. By beginning with self-selection, companies can more easily avoid the problems of forcing otherwise promising employees into international assignments where they would be unhappy and unsuccessful. In cases where individuals have families, the decisions about relocation are more complicated. Employees should seek out information to help them predict their chances of success in living abroad. Companies such as EDS and Deloitte & Touche give the self-selection instruments to their employees to help them think through the pros and cons of international assignments.

STEP 2: CREATE A CANDIDATE POOL. After employees have self-selected, organizations can put together a database of candidates for international assignments. Information on the database might include availability, languages, country preferences, and skills.

STEP 3: ASSESS CORE SKILLS. From the shortlist of potential candidates, managers can assess each candidate on technical and managerial readiness relative to the needs of the assignment. Although there are many factors that determine success abroad, the initial focus should be on the requirements of the job.

FIGURE 11.7   Expatriate Selection Criteria

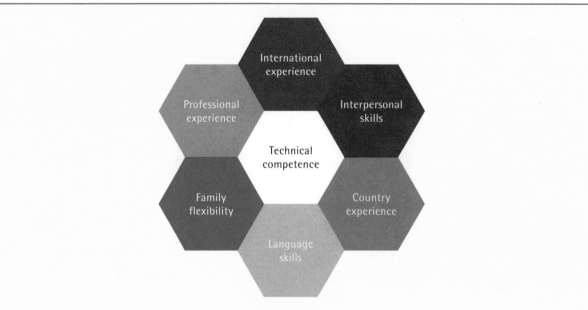

STEP 4: ASSESS AUGMENTED SKILLS AND ATTRIBUTES. As shown in Figure 11.7, expatriate selection decisions are typically driven by technical competence as well as professional and international experience. In addition, however, an increasing number of organizations have also begun considering an individual's ability to adapt to different environments. Satisfactory adjustment on things such as understanding the local culture and educational system, being able to "think locally," and understanding what a person has learned and what is instinctive to that person.[31]

To be more specific, companies such as Colgate-Palmolive, Whirlpool, and Dow Chemical have identified a set of **core skills** that they view as critical for success abroad and a set of **augmented skills** that help facilitate the efforts of expatriate managers. For example, decision-making, team building, and adaptability are some of the core skills; negotiation skills and change management are two of the augmented skills. It is worth noting that many of these skills are not significantly different from those required for managerial success at home.

Even companies that believe they have selected the best candidates frequently experience high expatriate **failure rates.** The primary reason for an assignment failure is the person's family—spouse and children. In studies on this topic, it was determined that inadequate attention was paid to ensuring that the family could adapt to the new conditions. Besides family issues, failures also occurred due to the person not being open-minded; not having respect for the belief of others; unrealistic expectations; unable to adapt to a different social setting, and not trusting in the new environment.[32] It is estimated that the financial costs associated with failed global assignments is $2–$2.5 billion annually.[33]

There are a number of ways to improve the success of expatriate assignments. One important step is to involve spouses early in the process. In addition, training and development (which will be discussed next) for both expatriates and their families can have a big impact. As an example of how companies can prepare employees and their families, Shell has created an online information centre called the Outpost Expatriate Network (**www.outpostexpat.nl/**)

Core skills
Skills considered critical to an employee's success abroad

Augmented skills
Skills helpful in facilitating the efforts of expatriate managers

Failure rate
Percentage of expatriates who do not perform satisfactorily

Outpost Expatriate Network
www.outpostexpat.nl/

TRAINING AND DEVELOPMENT

Outcome 5

Although companies try to recruit and select the very best people for international work, it is usually necessary to provide some type of training. Not only is this type of training important to expatriate managers, it is also important for the foreign employees they will ultimately supervise. To know and understand how the Japanese or Chinese negotiate contracts or how businesspeople from Latin America view the enforcement of meeting times, for example, can help expatriate managers and their employees deal with each other more successfully. To illustrate this latter point, Finning International in its desire to provide global exposure to its key staff, have had to ensure that the Canadian managers understand that the concept of time is very relaxed in the operations in Chile.[34] The biggest mistake managers can make is to assume that people are the same everywhere. Corporations that are serious about succeeding in global business are tacking these problems head-on by providing intensive training.

Content of Training Programs

Lack of training is one of the principal causes of failure among employees working internationally. Those working internationally need to know as much as possible about (1) the country where they are going, (2) that country's culture, and (3) the history, values, and dynamics of their own organizations. Figure 11.8 gives an overview of what one needs to study for an international assignment. In many cases, the employee and the family can obtain a great deal of general information about the host country, including its culture, geography, social and political history, climate, food, and so on, through the Internet, books, lectures, and DVDs. The knowledge gained will at least help the participants have a better understanding in their assignments. Sensitivity training can also help expatriates overcome ethnic prejudices they might harbour. Expatriates can simulate a field experience in sensitivity training by visiting a nearby subculture in their native countries or by actually visiting a foreign country prior to relocating there. Key elements of training and development programs that prepare employees for working internationally include language training; social and cultural training (including values and codes of conduct); and training and information on the practical aspects (e.g., housing, health care, education).[35]

Language Training

Communication with individuals who have a different language and a different cultural orientation is extremely difficult. Most executives agree that it is among the biggest problems for the foreign business traveller. Students who plan careers in international business should start instruction in one or more foreign languages as early as possible. The top-ranked China Europe International Business School (CEIBS), jointly founded by the Chinese government and the European Union, also offers language training. Some companies do their own language training. Multinational companies as well as businesses that outsource work abroad stand to benefit from this type of training.

Fortunately for most Canadians, English is almost universally accepted as the primary language for international business. Particularly when many people from different countries are working together, English is usually the designated language for meetings and formal discussions. Proctor and Gamble has created its "P&G College," which is attended also by families to acquire both language and cultural skills.[36] Many companies also provide instruction in English for those who are required to use English in their jobs.

FIGURE 11.8   Preparing for an International Assignment

To prepare for an international assignment, one should become acquainted with the following aspects of the host country:

1. Social and business etiquette
2. History and folklore
3. Current affairs, including relations between the host country and Canada
4. Cultural values and priorities
5. Geography, especially its major cities
6. Sources of pride and great achievements of the culture
7. Religion and the role of religion in daily life
8. Political structure and current players
9. Practical matters such as currency, transportation, time zones, hours of business
10. The language

International assignments provide an employee with a set of experiences that are uniquely beneficial to both the individual and the firm.

Pankaj & Insy Shah/Gulfimages/Getty Images

Learning the language is only part of communicating in another culture, though. The following list illustrates the complexities of the communication process in international business.

1. In England, to "table" a subject means to put it on the table for current discussion. In Canada, it means to postpone discussion of a subject, perhaps indefinitely.
2. In Canada, information flows to a manager. In cultures where authority is centralized (such as Europe and South America), the manager must take the initiative to seek out the information.
3. Getting straight to the point is uniquely North American. Many Europeans, Arabs, and others resent this directness in communication.
4. In Japan, there are 16 ways to avoid saying "no."
5. When something is "inconvenient" to the Chinese, it is most likely downright impossible.
6. In most foreign countries, expressions of anger are unacceptable; in some places, public display of anger is taboo.
7. The typical North American must learn to treat silences as "communication spaces" and not interrupt them.
8. In general, North Americans must learn to avoid gesturing with the hand. Nonverbal communication training can help businesspeople avoid some of these communication pitfalls.[37]

Cultural Training

Cross-cultural differences represent one of the most elusive aspects of international business. Brazilians tend to perceive North Americans as always in a hurry, serious, reserved, and methodical, whereas the Japanese view North Americans as relaxed, friendly, and impulsive. Why do these different perceptions exist and how do they affect the way we do business across borders?

Managerial attitudes and behaviours are influenced, in large part, by the society in which managers have received their education and training. Similarly, reactions of employees are the result of cultural conditioning. Each culture has its expectations for the roles of managers and employees. On her first day on the job abroad, one expatriate manager recalls her boss ordering a bottle of wine to split between the two of them at lunch. Although this is a common practice in Britain, the expatriate manager was initially taken aback. Being successful as a manager depends on one's ability to understand the way things are normally done and to recognize that changes cannot be made abruptly without considerable resistance, and possibly antagonism, on the part of local nationals. A senior manager from Toronto for ADP, a firm that specializes in business outsourcing such as payroll, tax and benefits administration, confirms that in a global assignment in France, he did not ask nearly enough questions prior to the assignment. He didn't appreciate the amount of resentment from the local people: they perceived he was relatively young for such a senior position and didn't understand why someone from oversees had been relocated.[38] Being successful depends on one's ability to understand the way things are normally done and to recognize that changes cannot be made abruptly without considerable resistance, and possibly antagonism, on the part of local nationals.

Studying cultural differences can help managers identify and understand work attitudes and motivation in other cultures. When compared with the Japanese, North Americans may feel little loyalty to their organization. In Japan, for example, employees are more likely to feel a strong loyalty to their company, although recent reports show that this may be changing. Japanese companies no longer universally guarantee an employee a job for life, and layoff decisions are increasingly being made based on merit, not seniority—a practice unthinkable in the country in the past. For example, at the beginning of the global recession in late 2008, Nissan eliminated 2500 jobs in both the U.S. and Europe, and also laid-off 1000 temporary workers in Japan.[39] Latin Americans tend to view themselves as working not only for a particular company but also for an individual manager. Thus managers in Latin American countries can encourage performance only by using personal influence and working through individual members of a group.

One of the important dimensions of leadership, whether we are talking about international or domestic situations, is the degree to which managers invite employee participation in decision making. While it is difficult to find hard data on employee participation across different countries, careful observers report that Canadian managers are about in the middle on a continuum of autocratic to democratic decision-making styles. Scandinavian and Australian managers also appear to be in the middle. South American and European managers, especially those from France, Germany, and Italy, are toward the autocratic end of the continuum; Japanese managers are at the most participatory end. Additional information about living, relocating and working globally, as well as daily news, can be found at EscapeArtist.com (**www.escapeartist.com**).

EscapeArtist.com
www.escapeartist.com

Assessing and Tracking Career Development

International assignments provide some definite developmental and career advantages. For example, working abroad tends to increase a person's responsibilities and influence within the corporation. In addition, it provides a person with a set of experiences that are uniquely beneficial to both the individual and the firm. In this way, international assignments enhance a person's understanding of the global operations.[40]

To maximize the career benefits of a global assignment, a candidate should ask two key questions before accepting an international position:

1. Do the organization's senior executives view the firm's international business as a critical part of its operation? Research shows that expatriates with clear goals that truly need to be accomplished are likely to find their assignments more rewarding. Realizing this, fewer companies are sending expatriates abroad for career development purposes only.
2. Within top management, how many executives have a foreign-service assignment in their background, and do they feel it important for one to have overseas experience? Colgate-Palmolive sees a foreign assignment as part of an extended career track rather than as a one-off assignment. A successful international assignment tends to lead to another and another. "Our top priority is to identify, develop, and retain the next two to three generations of leaders," said one Colgate-Palmolive manager. Part of that strategy includes directly using the knowledge of the company's current and former expatriates.

Managing Personal and Family Life

As noted previously, one of the most frequent causes of an employee's failure to complete an international assignment is personal and family stress. **Culture shock**—a disorientation that causes perpetual stress—is experienced by people who settle overseas for extended periods. The stress is caused by hundreds of jarring and disorienting incidents such as being unable to communicate,

Culture shock
Perpetual stress experienced by people who settle overseas

having trouble getting the telephone to work, being unable to read the street signs, and a myriad of other everyday matters that are no problem at home. Soon minor frustrations become catastrophic events, and one feels helpless and drained, emotionally and physically.

In Chapter 4, it was noted that more and more employers are assisting two-career couples in finding suitable employment in the same location. To accommodate dual-career partnerships, some employers are providing informal help finding jobs for the spouses of international transferees. In a recent survey, it was estimated that approximately 40% of international assignments are impacted by the spouse's career.[41] To facilitate this, some companies are establishing more formal programs to assist expatriate couples. These include career- and life-planning counselling, continuing education, intercompany networks to identify job openings in other companies, and job-hunting/fact-finding trips. In some cases, a company may even create a job for the spouse— though this is not widely practised.

Repatriation

Repatriation
Process of employee transition home from an international assignment

An increasing number of companies such as Enbridge are developing programs specifically designed to facilitate **repatriation**—that is, helping employees make the transition back home. Coming back is often difficult. An employee recently repatriated from Columbia walked outside his Edmonton office and waited for his driver, not remembering that he had driven his own car to work. Another family, repatriated from Kazakhstan, had to be restrained from purchasing all the fresh vegetables at the supermarket, because over there, if there was fresh produce, you hoarded it because it might not be there next week. Repatriation programs are designed to prepare employees for adjusting to life at home (which at times can be more difficult than adjusting to a foreign assignment). ExxonMobil employees are given a general idea of what they can expect following a foreign assignment even before they leave home. Unfortunately, not all companies have career development programs designed for repatriating employees. Several studies have found that the majority of companies do not do an effective job of repatriation. Here are some general findings:

1. Slightly over one-third of Canadian companies have a repatriation plan.
2. Another third typically have programs to facilitate appropriate career positions upon repatriation.
3. Over two-thirds provide career planning assistance toward the end of assignment.
4. About one-fifth of companies start planning for repatriation even before the candidate leaves.[42]

Employees often lament that their organizations are vague about repatriation, about their new roles within the company, and about their career progression. In many cases, employees abroad have learned how to run an entire international operation—or at least significant parts of it. When they return home, however, their responsibilities are often significantly diminished. In fact, the evidence suggests that only a fraction of them are actually promoted. It is also not at all uncommon for employees to return home after a few years to find that there is *no* position for them in the firm and that they no longer know anyone who can help them. Employees often feel their firms disregard their difficulties in adjusting to life back in Canada.

Even where employees are successfully repatriated, their companies often do not fully utilize the knowledge, understanding, and skills developed on these global assignments. This hurts the employee, of course, but it may hurt equally the firm's chances of using that employee's expertise to gain competitive advantage. Not surprisingly, expatriates sometimes leave their company within a year or two of coming home. Since as many of 50% of returning employees leave the company soon after their return, one global expert suggests that the key to making the repatriation successful is communication—constantly so that the employees have good information about what can be expected on the return. And it is important to give the employees sufficient time to also reinstall their families.[43]

At companies with good repatriation processes, employees are given guidance about how much the expatriate experience may have changed them and their families. Some firms introduce former expatriates and their spouses to other former expatriates at special social events. And more companies are making an effort to keep in touch with expatriates while they are abroad, which has been made easier by e-mail, instant messaging, and videoconferencing. Colgate's division executives and other corporate staff members frequently visit international transferees. Dow appoints a high-level manager who serves as a home-country contact for information about organization changes, job opportunities, and anything related to compensation.

Given the economic climate, it is important that people have good information as to what is expected after a global assignment. It has been suggested that an international assignment letter be developed that includes the following items:

- Location and duration of assignment;
- Total compensation including base salary, incentives and benefits, pension plans and currency of payment;
- Information on tax issues such as equalization, tax reporting, and tax advice;
- Information on host country such as housing, any allowances for goods and services including any differentials;
- Relocation program including home and automobile sale, family allowances (if family does not relocate), house hunting, moving, schooling, eldercare, language training, and cultural programs;
- Information on vacation and home leave including number of trips, compensation, emergency and compassionate travel provisions; and
- Assignment conclusion, including employment opportunities upon the employee's return or resignation/dismissal.[44]

REWARDS AND RECOGNITION

Outcome 6

One of the most complex areas of international HRM is compensation. Different countries have different norms for employee compensation. Managers should consider carefully the motivational use of incentives and rewards in foreign countries. For North Americans, while nonfinancial incentives such as prestige, independence, and influence may be motivators, money is likely to be the driving force. Other cultures are more likely to emphasize respect, family, job security, a satisfying personal life, social acceptance, advancement, or power. Since there are many alternatives to money, the rule is to match the reward with the values of the culture. In individualistic cultures, such as Canada, pay plans often focus on individual performance and achievement. However, in collectively oriented cultures such as Italy and Portugal, people may value pay less than group relationships.[45]

In general, a guiding philosophy for designing pay systems might be "think globally and act locally." That is, executives should normally try to create a pay plan that supports the overall strategic intent of the organization but provides enough flexibility to customize particular policies and programs to meet the needs of employees in specific locations. For example, Hewitt Associates determined that with the economic upheaval in 2008 and 2009, global companies were changing the eligibility criteria, size of compensation adjustments, and differentiating long-term compensation to align more with the local markets.[46] After a brief discussion of compensation practices for host-country employees and managers, the focus will be on the problems of compensating expatriates.

Compensation of Host-Country Employees

As shown in Figure 11.9, hourly compensation can vary dramatically from country to country, from more than $40 in Norway to $6 in Taiwan and Hungary. Host-country employees are generally paid on the basis of productivity, time spent on the job, or a combination of these factors. In industrialized countries, pay is generally by the hour; in developing countries, by the day. The piece-rate method is quite common. In some countries, including Japan, seniority is an important element in determining employees' pay rates. When companies commence operations in a foreign country, they usually set their wage rates at or slightly higher than the prevailing wage for local companies. Eventually, though, they are urged to conform to local practices to avoid "upsetting" local compensation practices.

Employee benefits can range dramatically from country to country as well. In France, for example, benefits are about 70% compared with around 30% in Canada. Whereas in North America, most benefits are awarded to employees by employers, in other industrialized countries most of them are legislated or ordered by governments. For example, in India the focus is on benefits and other perks rather than salaries; employee stock option plans were one of the key extras that employees wanted.[47]

FIGURE 11.9   Hourly Compensation Costs in Different Countries for Production Workers in Manufacturing

Country	$/Hour (U.S. Dollars)
Norway	41.05
Germany	34.21
Belgium	31.85
Sweden	31.80
Switzerland	30.67
United Kingdom	27.10
Australia	26.14
Canada	25.74
Italy	25.07
France	24.90
United States	23.82
Japan	20.20
Spain	18.83
Korea	14.72
Israel	12.98
Portugal	7.65
Taiwan	6.43
Hungary	6.29
Hong Kong	5.78
Brazil	4.91
Mexico	2.75

Source: U.S. Department of Labor, Bureau of Labor Statistics, "International Comparisons of Hourly Compensation Costs in Manufacturing," January 25, 2008.

Labour costs are one of the biggest motivators for international expansion, but there are many managerial and administrative issues that must be addressed when an organization establishes operations overseas. For example, bad press can be generated for charging hundreds of dollars for individual products while the people who make them—sometimes children in developing countries working under poor conditions—early only a few cents. Or the bad press can also be generated when a company does something during economic troubling times. See Ethics in HRM 11.1 for the story of Wells Fargo in the U.S.

ETHICS **in HRM 11.1**

EMPLOYEE RECOGNITION IN DIFFICULT TIMES

Financial services firm, Wells Fargo, took out full-page ads in February 2009 to refute allegations that it was misusing taxpayer money after it had received a $25-billion bailout from the U.S. government. Wells Fargo had originally planned an employee recognition event over several days in Las Vegas. Rooms had been booked in the most expensive hotels. Media had criticized the company for doing something so extravagant in the midst of one of the largest economic downturns. Subsequently, Wells Fargo cancelled all events for 2009.

CRITICAL THINKING QUESTION

Do you think companies ought to eliminate employee recognition events during tough financial times? Why or why not?

Source: "Wells Fargo Blasts Media Outlets for Criticizing Employee Recognition Events," *National Post,* February 10, 2009, FP3. Material reprinted with the express permission of: "The National Post Company," a Canwest Partnership.

Compensation of Host-Country Managers

In the past, remuneration of host-country managers has been ruled by local salary levels. However, increased competition among different companies with subsidiaries in the same country has led to a gradual upgrading of host-country managers' salaries. Overall, international firms are moving toward a narrowing of the salary gap between the host-country manager and the expatriate. For example, a recent survey conducted in China indicated that multinational corporations increased their total compensation packages in China, some by as much as 53% in the space of one year—and these increases were for Chinese nationals.[48] There is a recognition that talent is scarce and that there is intense competition.

The global economic recession in 2008 created new pressures for companies. UBS AG, the large Swiss bank, cancelled its bonuses in 2008 and introduced a new model for future compensation. This new model is tied to longer-term profit and is intended to ensure that pay-for-performance compensation really takes in consideration the financial health of a company over a longer period.[49]

Compensation of Expatriate Managers

If the assignment is going to be successful, the expatriate's compensation plan must be competitive, cost-effective, motivating, fair, easy to understand, consistent with international financial management, easy to administer, and simple to communicate.

For short-term assignments, usually those that are project-based, expatriates are frequently given per-diem (per day) compensation. These managers might reside in hotels and service apartments instead of leasing houses. They are also less likely to bring their family members with them. The assignment becomes more like a commuting assignment in which the expatriate spends the week in the host country and returns home on the weekend.

For longer-term assignments, there are two basic types of compensation systems. The first is home-based pay where the pay is based on the expatriate's home country's compensation practices. The second type of compensation system is host-based pay. Companies are under pressure to move expatriates to host-based pay because it is generally less costly. Host-based pay is compensation that is equivalent to that earned by employees in the country where the expatriate is assignment. When host-country pay is used, decisions also need to be made about pension plans. For example, Argentina nationalized all private pension plans in late 2008. As a result, the Chilean government had to give assurances to its many multinational companies that it would not do the same thing.[50]

Whether a company uses home-based or host-based pay depends on whether the employee will ultimately remain abroad or return home. In a recent study by KPMG, it was identified that more and more organizations are splitting pay between the home and host currencies—allowing the employee to handle financial obligations at home while making purchases locally.[51]

A serious issue related to expatriate compensation is medical care. Employees are unlikely to consent to a global assignment if they cannot get healthcare comparable to what's available in their home countries. Often Canadian-based plans can't cover expatriate employees or efficiently deal with claims that need to be reimbursed in foreign currency. One solution is to transfer the employee to a global employment company that can provide these types of benefits. Another issue is the need to provide expatriates and employees who travel abroad with security. If the company operates in a "high risk market," such as oil and gas exploration in some countries in South America, expatriates will go through specialized training on "how not to be a kidnap magnet."[52]

PERFORMANCE MANAGEMENT

Outcome 7

As we noted earlier, individuals frequently accept international assignments because they know that they can acquire skills and experiences that will make them more valuable to their companies. Frequently, however, it can be difficult for the home office to assess the performance of employees working abroad. Even the notion of performance assessment is indicative of a North American management style that focuses on the individual, which can cause problems in Asian countries such as China, Japan, and Korea and eastern European countries such as Hungary and the Czech Republic.

Who Should Be Involved?

In many cases, an individual working internationally has at least two allegiances: one to his or her home country (the office that made the assignment) and the other to the host country in which the employee is currently working. Superiors in each location frequently have different information about the employee's performance and may also have very different expectations about what constitutes good performance. For these reasons, the multirater (360-degree) appraisal discussed in Chapter 6 is gaining favour among global firms.

Home- vs. Host-Country Reviews

Domestic managers are frequently unable to understand expatriate experiences, value them, or accurately measure their contribution to the organization. Geographical distances create communication problems for expatriates and home-country managers even with the use of technology such as e-mail and instant messaging. However, local managers with daily contact with expatriates are more likely to have an accurate understanding of their performance. But there can still be problems with this. First, local cultures may influence one's perception of how well an individual is performing. As noted earlier in the chapter, participative decision making may be viewed either positively or negatively, depending on the culture. Such cultural biases may not have any bearing on an individual's true level of effectiveness. In addition, local management frequently does not have enough perspective on the entire organization to know how well an individual is truly contributing to the firm as a whole.

Given the pros and cons of home-country and host-country reviews, most observers agree that performance reviews should try to balance the two sources of performance information. Although host-country employees are in a good position to view day-to-day activities, in many cases the individual is still formally tied to the home office. Promotions, pay, and other administrative decisions are connected there, and as a consequence, the written evaluation is usually handled by the home-country manager. Nevertheless, the review should be completed only after vital input has been gained from the host-country manager.

Video conferencing is one way for remote employees to stay in close contact with their home office.

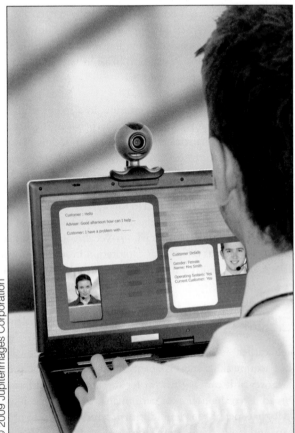

© 2009 Jupiterimages Corporation

Performance Criteria

Because expatriate assignments are so costly, organizations are increasingly under pressure to calculate the return on investment of these assignments. What did the firm get for the $1 million it spent to send an expatriate abroad? Has the expatriate achieved the goals set forth in the assignment in the appropriate time frame? Obviously, the goals and responsibilities inherent in the job assignment are among the most important criteria used to assess an individual's performance, and different goals necessitate measuring different criteria. Using a return-on-investment (ROI) approach, similar as to what was discussed in Chapter 5 for determining the value of training and development, can be lacking. Productivity, profits, and market share, while valid, may not capture the full range of an expatriate's responsibility. Leadership development, for example, involves a much longer-term value proposition. In many cases, an expatriate is an ambassador for the company, and a significant part of the job is cultivating relationships with citizens of the host country. As discussed at the beginning of this chapter, an individual's success or failure is affected by a host of technical and personal factors. For example, as one might guess, it is much easier to adjust to similar cultures than to dissimilar ones. A Canadian can usually travel to the United Kingdom or Australia and work with locals almost immediately. Send the same individual to Hungary or Malaysia and the learning curve is steeper.

Providing Feedback

Performance feedback in an international setting is clearly a two-way street. Although the home-country and host-country superiors may tell expatriates how well they are doing, it is also important for expatriates to provide feedback regarding the support they are receiving, the obstacles they face, and the suggestions they have about the assignment. More than in most any other job, expatriates are in the very best position to evaluate their own performance.

In providing feedback and other ways to keep the expatriates motivated, here are some tips:

1. Use differences in time zones to your advantage, such as a daily teleconference.
2. Bring the team together, face-to-face on a regular basis.
3. Be sensitive to cultural differences such as alternating weekly conference calls between different geographic locations so that the same people are not inconvenienced all the time.
4. Provide the feedback on a regular basis and recognize accomplishments.
5. Make use of videoconferencing so that people can actually see each other.[53]

If the performance is not successful after review and coaching, careful attention needs to be paid to the local environment before terminating employees. In some cases, such as China, there are restrictions as to when workers can be terminated; in other cases, the process is critical as is the case of Germany where employers are required to notify the local employment office if more than a certain percentage of the workforce is to be terminated.[54]

THE LABOUR ENVIRONMENT WORLDWIDE

Outcome 8

Labour relations in countries outside Canada differ significantly from those in Canada. Differences exist not only in the collective bargaining process but also in the political and legal conditions. For example, the EU prohibits discrimination against workers in unions, but in many countries, labour unions are illegal. China has only one union, the All-China Federation of Trade Unions, controlled by the Communist Party but more closely aligned to employers than to the employees.[55] Further, in 2008 China enacted the Labour Contract Law that was designed to protect workers as well as clarifying the rights of employers.[56] Read HRM and the Law 11.1 to understand some of the impacts of labour laws in other countries. To get a basic idea about labour-management relations in an international setting, we will look at four primary areas: (1) the role of unions in different countries, (2) collective bargaining in other countries, (3) international labour organizations, and (4) the extent of labour participation in management.

HRM and the law 11.1

FIRED FOR SINGING AT WORK

What might seem unusual in a Canadian setting may make perfect sense in another country. Take for example the woman in Italy who was fired for singing at work. She had worked for 20 years in a metalworking shop without any other problem. The union challenged the termination, saying that it was ridiculous given that her work of hammering metal meant that she couldn't be heard unless someone was really close to her. The union felt that it was the employer's attempt to deal with a poor economic climate. She was awarded six months' wages by the tribunal.

And is there a situation where being drunk on the job doesn't result in termination? Yes, according the Peru's top court. While the person was intoxicated at work, the court stated that the firing was excessive as the person could still speak and write and that he didn't hurt anyone. The Peruvian Labour Ministry was quite concerned that this might set a precedent with companies relaxing certain expectations at work.

CRITICAL THINKING QUESTION

Do you think these decisions were fair? Why or why not?

Sources: "Woman Fired for Singing at Work Wins Six Months' Compensation," *National Post,* February 27, 2009, A12; and "Employees Cannot be Fired for Being Drunk on the Job, Peru's Top Court Rules," *National Post,* January 15, 2009, A9.

The Role of Unions

The role of unions varies from country to country and depends on many factors, such as the level of employee participation, per capita labour income, mobility between management and labour, homogeneity of labour (racial, religious, social class), and unemployment levels. These and other factors determine whether the union will have the strength it needs to represent labour effectively. Nearly all of Sweden's workers are organized, giving the unions in this country considerable strength and autonomy. By contrast, in countries with relatively high unemployment, low pay levels, and no union funds with which to support social welfare systems, unions are driven into alliance with other organizations: political party, church, or government. This is in marked contrast to Canada, where the union selected by the majority of employees bargains only with the employer, not with other institutions. And as mentioned earlier in this section, China has a central union that is more aligned with employers than the employees. This has led Nike Inc. to find other ways to ensure that its Chinese suppliers are not falsifying documents or using underage workers, and that effective grievance systems are in place.[57]

There are several other examples of how government action can create a reaction from unions. For example, public opinion in France became divided in 2007 over the support of unions when unions launched a strike that paralyzed the transportation system.[58] This was in reaction to changes that the newly elected President Sarkozy wanted to make to the pension system. And a year later in early 2009, unions called for a one-day strike in all industries that effectively brought business to a standstill.[59] Again, this was to protest the president's decision to not include workers in the government's recovery plan for its recession. Likewise, Mexican miners staged a nationwide strike over the re-election of one of its own union leaders. The government would not confirm the re-election of the leader as it was getting ready to arrest him on charges of corruption.[60] Traffic in Mumbai, India, came to a halt when the government announced it was phasing out the autorickshaw (three-wheeled taxis) businesses, affecting over 50,000 drivers.[61] Lastly, with the new administration in the U.S., aircraft unions are lobbying to eliminate the outsourcing that has occurred for years in aircraft maintenance that has been done in Asia, Mexico, and Central America.[62]

Collective Bargaining in Other Countries

In Chapter 10, you studied the collective bargaining process as it is typically carried out in companies operating in Canada. When you look at other countries, you find that the whole process can vary widely, especially with regard to the role of government. In Australia and New Zealand, for most of the 20th century, labour courts had the authority to impose wages and other employment conditions on a broad range of firms. In the United Kingdom and France, the government intervenes in all aspects of collective bargaining. Government involvement is only natural where parts of industry are nationalized. Also, in countries where there is heavy nationalization, government involvement is more likely to be accepted, even in the non-nationalized companies.

International Labour Organizations

The most active of the international union organizations has been the International Confederation of Free Trade Unions (ICFTU, **www.icftu.org**), which has its headquarters in Brussels. Cooperating with the ICFTU are numerous International Trade Secretariats (ITSs), which are really international federations of national trade unions operating in the same or related industries. In addition to the ITSs, the ICFTU also cooperates with the European Trade Union Confederation (ETUC, **www. etuc.org**) that represents over 60 million trade unionists in the EU and is recognized by the EU as a social partner.[63] Another active and influential organization is the International Labor Organization (ILO, **www.ilo.org**), a specialized agency of the United Nations. The ILO perhaps has had the greatest impact on the rights of workers throughout the world. It promotes the rights of worker to organize, the eradication of forced and child labour, and the elimination of discrimination.

Labour Participation in Management

In many European countries, law establishes provisions for employee representation. An employer may be legally required to provide for employee representation on safety and hygiene committees, worker councils, or even on boards of directors. While their responsibilities vary from country to country, worker councils basically provide a communication channel between employers and workers. The legal codes that set forth the functions of worker councils in France are very detailed. Councils are generally concerned with grievances, problems of individual employees, internal regulations, and matters affecting employee welfare.

A higher form of worker participation in management is found in Germany, where law requires representation of labour on the board of directors of a company. This arrangement is known as **codetermination** and often by its German word, *Mitbestimmung*. While sometimes puzzling to outsiders, the system is fairly simple: Company shareholders and employees are required to be represented in equal numbers on the supervisory boards of all corporations with more than 2000 employees.

Concluding Comments

Each of these differences makes managing human resources in an international context more challenging. But the crux of the issue in designing HRM systems is not choosing one approach that will meet all the demands of international business. Instead, organizations facing global competition must balance several approaches and make their policies flexible enough to accommodate differences across national borders. Throughout this book we have noted that different situations call for different approaches to managing people, and nowhere is this point more clearly evident than in international HRM.

As the discussion on international HRM draws to a close, it is important to remember that even with a global economic upheaval, today's organizations will need to be vigilant about employee engagement in a global context. There is, and will continue to be, competition for global talent—particularly as companies move into countries that are low in labour costs and fast-growing, such as BRIC (Brazil, Russia, India, and China).[64] And as has already been demonstrated, multinational companies will relocate operations that provide a competitive advantage—whether it is in terms of natural resources, cost-of-labour, or inducements by governments.

Are the factors in employee engagement different for global assignments than domestic ones? The top two factors are rewards/recognition and customer focus that are the same whether a person is working on a global assignment or not.[65] After that, the expat is more concerned about respect in the workplace and what the relationship is with the supervisor.

Moving forward out of a global recession, organizations will have to continue with its emphasis on talent management in order to succeed in what is now a solid global economy. Consider the other areas to watch in Emerging Trends 11.1.

International Confederation of Free Trade Unions

www.icftu.org/

European Trade Union Confederation

www.etuc.org/

International Labor Organization

www.ilo.org

Codetermination
Representation of labour on the board of directors of a company

EMERGING TRENDS **11.1**

1. *Shorter international assignments.* A recent study of 200 multinational organizations in Europe, North America, Latin America, and Asia indicated that 84% were using short-term global assignments. These organizations found that there was less disruption to the family and from an overall career perspective, employees found the assignments more attractive. And 77% of the same survey indicated they were increasing the use of short-term international assignments.

2. *Increase in women undertaking global assignments.* As women move into more significant roles in organizations, more women are being provided with opportunities to work in other countries. It is possible that this is also facilitated due to the trend in shorter global assignments.

3. *Global recession will see shifts in compensation and benefits, as well as type of assignments.* More and more organizations are assessing in a much more critical way the pay expatriates receive as well as the number and length of global assignments. Many individuals have already been recalled to their home country in an effort to reduce operating costs.

Sources: Margaret Sim and Liam Dixon, "Number of Women Expats Increasing," *Canadian HR Reporter,* May 21, 2007, www.hrreporter.com/ArticleView. aspx?l=1&articleid=5202 (accessed March 11, 2009); Liam Dixon and Margaret Sim, "Short-Term Assignments Growing in Popularity," *Canadian HR Reporter,* March 10, 2008, www.hrreporter.com/ArticleView.aspx?l=1&articleid=5875 (accessed March 13, 2009); Laura Bianchi, "Relocated—Just for a Few Months," *Workforce Management,* May 7, 2008, www.workforce.com/archive/feature/25/51/78/index.php?ht= (accessed March 13, 2009); and "Expats Hearing Call From Their Companies to Come Home," *Workforce Management,* March 5, 2009, www.workforce.com/archive/article/26/22/57. php?ht= (accessed March 15, 2009).

SUMMARY

1. Identify the types of organizational forms used for competing internationally.
   - International—domestic firm that uses existing capabilities to move into global markets
   - Multinational—fully autonomous units operating in multiple countries.
   - Global—multinational firm that maintains control back in the home office.
   - Transnational—a firm that attempts to balance local responsiveness with efficiencies of global firm.

2. Explain the economic, political-legal, and cultural factors in different countries that need to be considered from an HR perspective.
   - Trade agreements can shift jobs from one location to another.
   - Companies will move or expand operations depending on which country provides best economic return.
   - Property rights and intellectual property rights will determine which countries companies do business in.
   - Cultural factors include language, religion, values, education, and social structure.

3. Explain how Canadian and international HRM differ.
   - Functions such as relocation, orientation and translation services become more important for global assignments.
   - Decisions need to be made regarding the currency of compensation.
   - More attention is paid to the security of international staff, particularly if the geographic area is high-risk.

4. Describe the staffing process for individuals working internationally.
   - Companies can send people from the home-country (expatriates).
   - Firms can hire employees who are natives to the host country.
   - Employee recruitment in other countries is subject to more government regulation than in Canada.

5. Identify the unique training needs for employees that work internationally.
   - Content needs to have information about the country and the country's culture.
   - Language training may be necessary.

- Special attention needs to be paid to helping the employees manage personal and family life.
- Some development programs are designed to facilitate repatriation.

6. Identify the characteristics of a good international recognition and rewards program.
   - Different cultures value recognition and rewards differently.
   - Need to determine if employee will be paid through the policies of home or host-country and in what currency.

7. Reconcile the difficulties of home- and host-country performance management systems.
   - Decisions need to be made on who will be involved in performance process.
   - Domestic managers may not fully understand the expatriate experiences and therefore it is a good idea to involve host-country manager.
   - Performance criteria need to include more than just financial goals.
   - It is important to provide feedback on a regular basis to the expatriate.

8. Explain how labour relations differ around the world.
   - Labour laws are different from one country to another.
   - Government may be more involved in determining wage rates even with unionized staff.
   - Some countries, such as Germany, have a high degree of worker participation.

NEED TO KNOW

- Definition of international, multinational, global, and transnational corporation
- Definition of expatriate
- Definition of culture shock

NEED TO UNDERSTAND

- Role of economic, political-legal, and cultural issues in global assignments
- Advantages of using home- or host-country nationals
- Contents of training program when someone is taking on global assignment
- Different components of recognition and reward in an international assignment
- Role home-country manager plays in supporting expatriate
- Differences in international labour relations

KEY TERMS

augmented skills 358

codetermination 369

core skills 358

cultural environment 349

culture shock 361

expatriates, or home-country nationals 351

failure rate 358

global corporation 344

guest workers 355

host country 349

host-country nationals 351

international corporation 344

multinational corporation (MNC) 344

repatriation 362

third-country nationals 351

transnational corporation 345

transnational teams 356

work permit, or visa 355

REVIEW QUESTIONS

1. Describe how a company goes from an international form to a multinational, to a global, and to a transnational form.
2. Describe the cultural environment of international business.
3. Explain what a home-country national and host-country national is.
4. Identify some of the training components in planning for international assignments.
5. Explain the difference between home-based and host-based pay.
6. Explain codetermination.

CRITICAL THINKING QUESTIONS

1. Pizza Hut is opening new restaurants in Europe every day, it seems. If you were in charge, would you use expatriate managers or host-country nationals in staffing the new facilities? Explain your thinking.
2. In what ways are North American managers likely to experience difficulties in their relationships with employees in foreign operations? How can these difficulties be minimized?
3. Talk with an international student on your campus; ask about his or her experience with culture shock on first arriving in Canada. What did you learn from your discussion?
4. If learning (individual and organizational) is an important outcome of an overseas assignment, how can this be worked into a performance appraisal system? How would a manager assess individual and organizational learning?
5. If the cost of living is lower in a foreign country than in North America, should expatriates be paid less than they would be at home? Explain your position.
6. Do you believe that codetermination will ever become popular in Canada? Explain your position.

DEVELOPING YOUR SKILLS

Department of Foreign Affairs

www.voyage.gc.ca

Living in Indonesia

www.expat.or.id

1. Identify a Canadian company attempting to open offices in Asia. Interview one of the decision-making managers to determine the kinds of problems that they will face, and the preparations they are undergoing to deal with these. Prepare a one- to two-page summary and share with your classmates.
2. Many young Canadians (18 to 30 years of age) have found international work through the Department of Foreign Affairs youth program. Having international experience is a very useful credential. Think about a country in which you would like to acquire work or educational experiences. Access the Foreign Affairs website (**www.voyage.gc.ca**) and determine what documentation you would need to work or study in your country of choice. Click on "Country Profiles" and prepare a list of cultural differences between Canada and your chosen country.
3. The most common reason for failure of an expatriate assignment is the spouse. Go to Living in Indonesia (**www.expat.or.id**) and click on "Practical Information" and then on "Myths of Expatriate Life." Summarize the information. Determine what HR practices would help reduce the magnitude of the problems.

Case Study 1

Economic Downturn and Foreign Workers

What do companies do about foreign workers—home or host-country—when the economy begins to slow? Do all countries experience recession the same? These are questions that many managers in many companies have never had to ask. However, with the recession that started in late 2007 in the U.S., and eventually spread worldwide in 2008, companies all over the world are asking these questions. And the answers will have a direct impact on global assignments.

Brazil, Russia, India, and China (BRIC) have for some years been viewed as the growth opportunities for both North American and EU companies. But the worldwide recession has created differences as to which might be the better choice. According to a number of analysts, China is looking more promising than Russia, although Russia is cheaper even if riskier. And part of any of the risk has to do with the international banking system—still in jeopardy.

As a result of the global economic turmoil, the World Bank estimated that poverty will become more prevalent and emerging economies will suffer, thereby eroding any increasing consumer base that impacts global business.

What has this meant for foreign workers? Well, for one thing, more countries are revoking work visas and/or making it more difficult for people to go from one country to another to work. For example, the Czech Republic government was paying for plane tickets and a bonus for non-EU workers to return to their home countries. Similarly, in early 2009 the U.S., which had for years relied upon global talent, particularly in the IT sector, to increase the capacity and competiveness of U.S. firms, began to reduce the number of foreign work visas. And in the U.K., KPMG asked its 11,000 workers to reduce their hours as a way to weather the economic storm. However, under new labour laws in China, some companies were finding it more difficult to reduce its workforce as layoffs is not something that occurs in Asian countries.

It isn't just the issue of whether there are foreign workers or not. Companies are also reducing or changing the compensation package. British Steel, for example, changed its pension plan for any new employee. It had a defined-benefit plan that applied to its 41,000 global workforce and it wanted to reduce its future liabilities. Companies in India were planning salary increases—but only single digit. This may sound unusual, but India for a number of years had double-digit salary increases. Even though there may be salary increases, other companies in India, such as Siemens, were reducing the number of days worked in a month.

Sources: "Employers in China Have Issues Shedding Workers," *Workforce Management,* December 28, 2008, www.workforce.com/section/00/article/26/05/57.php, (accessed March 16, 2009); Levi Folk, "Not all BRICS Created Equal," *National Post,* March 14, 2009, FP9; Peter Goodspeed, "Global Mess Gives Birth to New Era," *National Post,* March 14, 2009, A13; "Czech Republic Gives Foreign Workers Ticket, Money to Get Home," *Canadian HR Reporter,* March 5, 2009, www.hrreporter.com/ArticleView. aspx?l=1&articleid=6734 (accessed March 16, 2009); "Deep Corporate Staff Cuts Heat Up H-1B Visa Debate," *Workforce Management,* February 5, 2009, www.workforce.com/section/00/article/26/15/70.php (accessed March 16, 2009); "KPMG Asks U.K. Staff to Cut Hours," www.hrreporter.com/ArticleView. aspx?l=1&articleid=6636 (accessed March 16, 2009); "British Steel Closes DB Plan to New Employees," *Workforce Management,* January 26, 2009, www.workforce.com/section/00/article/26/13/46.php (accessed March 16, 2009); and "Salary Increments in India Inc to Dip in 2009," March 16, 2009, http://econom-ictimes.indiatimes.com/News/News-By-Industry/Jobs/Salary-increments-in-India-Inc-to-dip-in-2009/ articleshow/4270265.cms (accessed March 16, 2009).

Questions

1. If you were on a global assignment and there was a significant change in the world economy, what would you expect the company to do in relation to your work?
2. What kinds of hardships do you think foreign workers have in a global recession?
3. Do you think it is appropriate for a global company to unilaterally change its compensation program? Why or why not?

Case Study 2

Recruiting and Retaining International Staff

New York Life International, the global arm of New York Life Insurance, offers life insurance and other similar products throughout the world. It has operations in Latin America and Asia, being the third largest private insurance company in India and having a rapid expansion in major population centres in China. With intense competition in a global industry, it is using a number of new ways to attract talent. Among these were employee referrals as well as ensuring that any advertising is done in the right places.

As an international company, it has a number of different markets with different levels of maturity. Some are growing quickly while others are growing at a slower pace. However, in all cases, the company wants people to move from one market to another as well as making sure business goals and individual goals are aligned. It sees that the ability for people to move from one global operation to another is a key factor in attracting the people. And with the rapid growth, there is also emphasis being placed on leadership development. This is achieved partially by having learning programs that are flexible and evolve quickly.

It also provides ongoing support to its field staff, as well as boosting its recruitment efforts, in a number of different cultural markets, such as Asian-Indian, Korean, and Vietnamese. For example, the company recently took a group of 15 youths to India to learn about its economy, education, culture, and environment. Likewise, there are websites that use the local language instead of being in English. In this way, New York Life supports and encourages understanding of cultural differences throughout its global operations.

Source: Adapted from Jessica Marquez, "The Global Talent Battle," *Workforce Management,* June 20, 2008, www.workforce.com/archive/feature/25/60/91/index.php?ht= (accessed March 16, 2009).

Questions

1. In general, what should a candidate for an international assignment do to prepare for a job, in the absence of company orientation and training?
2. Do you think having a website for employees in their native language is helpful? Does this help or hinder understanding of cultural differences?

Video Feature

PART 4—IN VIEW

1. "YOUNG BLOOD" (2:24)

This excerpt from *Venture* describes the need for unions to recruit younger talent.

2. "YOUNG INJURIES" (2:15)

The Government of Ontario has developed a controversial campaign to raise awareness of workplace safety hazards amongst young people. Using disturbingly violent cartoons depicting young people losing limbs and inflicting other injuries on the job, the government hopes youth will take safety seriously.

3. "HOW BAD IS YOUR BOSS" (21:36)

This segment describes how some managers behave and what the consequences are for employees and the work environment.

QUESTIONS

1. Do you think there should be more or less government regulation of safe and healthy work practices? Why or why not?

2. Have you had a "bad boss"? How did you handle your boss?

3. What are other ways employees can deal with poor bosses?

4. Will unions have continued difficulty in unionizing the service sector? Why? Why not?

5. Are unions still relevant in Canada? Why or why not?

NOTES AND REFERENCES

1. Brian J. Glade, "Be Intentional About Globalization," *Canadian HR Reporter,* March 9, 2009, www.hrreporter.com/ArticleView.aspx?l=1&articleid=6717 (accessed March 8, 2009); and Stephen Cyrne, "Homeward Bound," *Canadian HR Reporter,* March 9, 2009, www.hrreporter.com/ArticleView.aspx?l=1&articleid=6721 (accessed March 9, 2009).

2. "Tata's Pact with British Telecom Could be Worth US$1-Billion," *Financial Post,* June 26, 2009, FP 3.

3. Natalie Alcoba, "Economic Engine," *Financial Post,* March 28, 2009, FW1.

4. Betsy Massar, "Manpower Poised to Further Extend its Broad Global Reach," *Workforce Management,* August 1, 2006, www.workforce.com/archive/feature/24/45/26/index.php?ht= (accessed March 8, 2008).

5. Hay Group brochure as part of briefing materials for seminar in March 2008, Vancouver, B.C.

6. Geoff Colvin, "The World's Most Admired Companies 2009," *Fortune,* March 16, 2009, 77-78.

7. "Global 100 Most Sustainable Corporations Announced in Davos," www.global100.org, January 28, 2009.

8. "Canada's 500 Largest Corporations—2009," *Financial Post Magazine,* June 2009, 42.

9. "A Europe Without Frontiers," and "A Decade of Further Expansion," http://europa.eu/abc/history/index_en.htm (accessed March 8, 2009).

10. Gary Clyde Hufbauer and Jeffrey J. Schott, "NAFTA's Bad Rap," *The International Economy,* Summer 2008, 19–23.

11. "Canada, EU to Start Talks on 'Economic Agreement,'" ReportonBusines.com, March 6, 2009, www.theglobeandmail.com/servlet/story/LAC.20090306.RTICKERA06-5/TPStory/Business (accessed March 8, 2009).

12. Don Lee, "China Feels the Crunch," *The Vancouver Sun,* November 8, 2008, B9.

13. "Fruits & Passion New Boutique in Shanghai," Government of Canada, http://geo.international.gc.ca/asia/china/media/news_releases-en.aspx?id=13128 (accessed March 8, 2009).

14. "Canada-China Success Stories," Government of Canada, http://geo.international.gc.ca/asia/china/media/success_stories-en.aspx (accessed March 8, 2009).

15. Fan Yan and Edmund Klamann, "Can Hummer Survive?" *Financial Post,* June 5, 2009, FP9.

16. "Slumdog Suburbia," *Fortune,* March 16, 2009, 18; and "BRIC Countries See Improving February Auto Sales," *Platinum Today,* March 10, 2009, www.platinum.matthey.com/media_room/bric_countries_see_improving_february_auto_sales_19066124.html (accessed March 12, 2009).

17. Lesley Young, "Attracting, Keeping Employees Overseas," *Canadian HR Reporter,* April 7, 2008, www.hrreporter.com/ArticleView.aspx?l=1&articleid=5957 (accessed March 9, 2009).

18. For more information on culture and organizations, interested readers can access the journal *Culture and Organization* published by Routledge, in affiliation with the Centre for Innovative Management at Athabasca University, Alberta.

19. Liam Dixon and Margaret Sim, "Short-Term Assignments Growing in Popularity," *Canadian HR Reporter,* March 10, 2008, 17.

20. Wallace Immen, "Going Abroad to Get Ahead," *The Globe and Mail,* February 22, 2006, C1.

21. Interview with Anne Harvey, vice president, Employee Engagement, Vancouver Coastal Health Authority, March, 2009.

22. Vikas Kumar, "Emerging Cos Knock at Headhunters for Top Talent," *The Economic Times (Mumbai),* October 6, 2008, 10.

23. Shobhana Chadha & Lisa Mary Thomson, "Now, Cos Helping Bench Staff Find New Jobs," *The Economic Times on Sunday (Mumbai),* October 19, 2008, 6.

24. Duncan Mavin, "Cutbacks Hit Nannies, Cleaners," *Financial Post,* November 12, 2008, FP1.

25. Douglas A. Ready, Linda A. Hill, and Jay A. Conger, "Winning the Race for Talent in Emerging Markets," *Harvard Business Review,* November 2008, 63-79.

26. "Education in France: Understanding the Grandes Écoles," www.understandfrance.org/France/Education.html (accessed March 9, 2009).

27. Jessica Marquez, "A Culture of Colleague Support," *Workforce Management,* September 26, 2008, www.workforce.com/archive/feature/25/78/76/257878.php?ht= (accessed March 9, 2009).

28. Ibid.

29. Tim Berbic, "Improving the Odds on Risky Moves," *Canadian HR Reporter,* September 24, 2007, www.hrreporter.com/ArticleView.aspx?l=1&articleid=5459 (accessed March 11, 2009).

30. Ed Frauenheim, "The Right Profile for Leading in China," *Workforce Management,* March 16, 2007, www.workforce.com/archive/feature/24/80/98/248101.php?ht= (accessed March 11, 2009).

31. Jennifer McAdams, "Casting Call," *Computerworld,* February 20, 2006, 36-37.

32. "How Do We Determine Which Employees Are Best Suited for Expatriate Assignments," *Workforce Management,* June 29, 2007, www.workforce.com/archive/article/24/99/01.php?ht= (accessed March 11, 2009).

33. Semere Haile, Marcus D. Jones, Tsegai Emmanuel, "Challenges Facing Expatriate Performance Abroad," *International Journal of Business Research* VII (November 5, 2007): 100-105.

34. Information supplied to current author by chair of the board of birectors, Doug Whitehead, December 2008.

35. Semere Haile, Marcus D. Jones, Tsegai Emmanuel, "Challenges Facing Expatriate Performance Abroad."

36. Ibid.

37. Managers who are interested in setting up a language-training program or who wish to evaluate commercially available language-training programs should consult the "Standard Guide for Use-Oriented Foreign Language Instruction." The guide is put out by the American Society for Testing and Materials (ASTM) www.astm.org/. Other useful resources are Rosetta Stone, www.rosettastone.com/ and Laird Technologies University, www.lairdtech.com.

38. Sarah Dobson, "Overseas Relocations Well Worth the Trip," *Canadian HR Reporter,* September 22, 2008, www.hrreporter.com/ArticleView.aspx?l=1&articleid=6353 (accessed March 13, 2009).

39. Marcus Gee, "Pillars of Japan Showing Some Cracks," *The Globe and Mail,* November 7, 2008, B5.

40. Mark Larson, "More Employees Go Abroad as International Operations Grow," *Workforce Management,* June 21, 2006, www.workforce.com/archive/feature/24/41/22/index.php?ht= (accessed March 13, 2009).

41. "Spousal Issues in Relocation," *Workforce Management,* August 11, 2008, 36.

42. Virginia Galt, "It's Not Easy to Come Home Again," *The Globe and Mail*, February 22, 2006, C6.

43. Stephen Cryne, "Homeward Bound," *Canadian HR Reporter,* March 9, 2009, www.hrreporter.com/ArticleView. aspx?l=1&articleid=6721 (accessed March 14, 2009).

44. Joyce Head, "How Paper can Protect International Relocations," *Canadian HR Reporter,* March 13, 2006, www.hrreporter.com/ ArticleView.aspx?l=1&articleid=4307 (accessed March 14, 2009).

45. Steve McShane, *Canadian Organizational Behaviour* (Toronto: McGraw-Hill Ryerson, 2006), 42.

46. "Impact of Global Economic Conditions on Non-U.S. Compensation and HR Programs," Hewitt Associates Web conference, April 9, 2009.

47. Shikha Sharma & Vivek Sinha, "Your Salary Benefits Now Lie in the Fringes," *The Economic Times Mumbai,* October 6, 2008, 1.

48. Tony Dickel and Chris Watkins, "Hiring and Compensation Trends," *China Business Review,* July-August 2008, 20-23.

49. Helen Popper, "Argentina Nationalizes Private Pension Plans," and "Chile Says Retirement Funds are Secure; has No Plans to Nationalize Them," *National Post*, October 22, 2008, FP3.

50. Janet McFarland, "UBS Leads Way on Pay Reforms," *The Globe and Mail,* November 18, 2008, B4.

51. "Global Compensation Strategies: Managing and Administering Split Pay for an Expatriate Workforce," *Benefits Quarterly,* Third Quarter 2008, 76.

52. Craig Malcolm, "Protecting Employees in Danger Zones," *Canadian HR Reporter,* September 24, 2007, www.hrreporter. com/ArticleView.aspx?l=1&articleid=5460 (accessed March 15, 2009).

53. Monica Ginsburg, "Overseeing Overseas," *Workforce Management,* December 31, 2008, www.workforce.com/ section/search_results.php?account=1005&account=1005& Go=Search&q=expatriate%20feedback&page=10 (accessed March 15, 2009).

54. George Avraam, Adrian Ishak, and Trish Appleyard, "Terminating Employees Around the World," *Canadian HR Reporter,* April 6, 2009, 12.

55. William C. Bruce, "The Union-Free Good Times May be Over in China," *Workforce Management,* July 12, 2007, www. workforce.com/archive/feature/24/99/99/index.php?ht= (accessed March 15, 2009).

56. Duncan Mavin, "China's New Labour Laws Losing Edge," *National Post,* February 3, 2009, FP3.

57. John Ruwitch, "Nike's Chinese Suppliers Defy Labour Laws," *Financial Post,* March 15, 2008, FP16.

58. Peter O'Neil, "Anti-Sarkozy Strike Cripples Travel in France," *National Post,* October 19, 2007, A16.

59. Henry Samuel, "Angry Unions Bring France to Standstill," *National Post,* January 30, 2009, A7.

60. "Mexican Miners Strike Nationwide Over Union Leader's Re-election," *Financial Post,* May 27, 2008, FP18.

61. "Auto-Taxi Union to Go on Strike on October 16," *The Economic Times (Mumbai),* October 15, 2008, 3.

62. Marilyn Geewax, "U.S. Unions Want End to Outsourcing Aircraft Maintenance," *Financial Post,* November 14, 2008, FP17.

63. The European Trade Union Confederation, www.etuc.org/ (accessed March 15, 2009).

64. Lesley Young, "Attracting, Keeping Employees Overseas."

65. Richa Gulati, "Engaging the expatriate Workforce in Asia-Pacific," February 2008, Watson Wyatt.

GLOSSARY

Achievement tests Measures of what a person knows or can do right now

Alternative dispute resolution (ADR) Term applied to different types of employee complaint or dispute-resolution procedures

Apprenticeship training System of training in which a worker entering the skilled trades is given thorough instruction and experience, both on and off the job, in the practical and theoretical aspects of the work

Aptitude tests Measures of a person's capacity to learn or acquire skills

Arbitration award Final and binding award issued by an arbitrator in a labour–management dispute

Arbitrator Third-party neutral who resolves a labour dispute by issuing a final and binding decision in an agreement

Augmented skills Skills helpful in facilitating the efforts of expatriate managers

Bargaining unit Group of two or more employees who share common employment interests and conditions and may reasonably be grouped together for purposes of collective bargaining

Behaviour modification Technique that if behaviour is rewarded it will be exhibited more frequently in the future

Behavioural description interview (BDI) Question about what a person actually did in a given situation

Behaviourally anchored rating scale (BARS) A behavioural approach to performance review that consists of a series of vertical scales, one for each important dimension of job performance

Benchmarking Finding the best practices in other organizations that can be brought into a company to enhance performance

Benchmarking Process of measuring one's own services and practices against the recognized leaders in order to identify areas for improvement

Bona fide occupational qualification (BFOQ) A justifiable reason for discrimination based on business reasons of safety or effectiveness

Business agent Normally a paid labour official responsible for negotiating and administering the collective agreement and working to resolve union members' problems

Certification Acquisition of exclusive rights by union to represent the employees

Closed shop Provision of the collective agreement that requires employers to hire only union members

Codetermination Representation of labour on the board of directors of a company

Competency-based pay Pay based on how many capabilities employees have or how many jobs they can perform

Constructive dismissal Changing an employee's working conditions such that compensation, status, or prestige is reduced

Consumer price index (CPI) Measure of the average change in prices over time in a fixed "market basket" of goods and services

Contractual rights Rights that derive from contracts

Cooperative training Training program that combines practical on-the-job experience with formal education

Core competencies A combination of knowledge, skills, and characteristics needed to effectively perform a role in an organization

Core skills Skills considered critical to an employee's success abroad

Cultural environment Communications, religion, values and ideologies, education, and social structure of a country

Culture shock Perpetual stress experienced by people who settle overseas

Cumulative trauma disorders Injuries involving tendons of the fingers, hands, and arms that become inflamed from repeated stresses and strains

Customer input Performance review that, like team review, is based on TQM concepts and seeks information from both external and internal customers

Defined rights Concept that management's authority should be expressly defined and clarified in the collective agreement

Designated groups Women, visible minorities, First Nations peoples, and persons with disabilities who have been disadvantaged in employment

Development The acquisition of skills, behaviours, and abilities to perform future work or to solve an organizational problem

Direct compensation Employee wages and salaries, incentives, bonuses, and commissions

Disability management Integrated approach to managing disability-related benefits

Discipline (1) Treatment that punishes; (2) Orderly behaviour in an organizational setting; or (3) Training that moulds and strengthens desirable conduct—or corrects undesirable conduct—and develops self-control

Diversity management The optimization of an organization's multicultural workforce in order to reach business objectives

Downsizing The planned elimination of jobs

Due process Employee's right to a fair process in making a decision related to employment relationship

Eldercare Care provided to an elderly relative by an employee who remains actively at work

E-learning Learning that takes place through electronic media

Employee assistance program (EAP) Program to provide short-term counselling and referrals to appropriate professionals

Employee empowerment Granting employees power to initiate change, thereby encouraging them to take charge of what they do

Employee rights Expectations of fair treatment from employers

Employee teams An employee-contributions technique in which work functions are structured for groups rather than for individuals, and team members are given discretion in matters traditionally considered management prerogatives, such as process improvements, product or service development, and individual work assignments

Employment equity A distinct Canadian process for achieving equality in all aspects of employment

Equitable pay Compensation received is perceived to be equal to the value of the work performed

Ethics Set of standards of conduct and moral judgments that help to determine right and wrong behaviour

Expatriates, or home-country nationals Employees from the home country who are on international assignment

Failure rate Percentage of expatriates who do not perform satisfactorily

Global corporation Firm that has integrated worldwide operations through a centralized home office

Globalization Moving local or regional business into global marketplace

Graphic rating scales A trait approach to performance review whereby each employee is rated according to a scale of characteristics

Grievance procedure Formal procedure that provides for the union to represent members and nonmembers in processing a grievance

Grievance resolution Process in which a neutral third party assists in the resolution of an employee grievance

Guest workers Foreign workers invited to perform needed labour

Harassment Any unwanted physical or verbal conduct that offends or humiliates the individual

Hearing officer Person who holds a full-time position with an organization but assumes a neutral role when deciding cases between management and the aggrieved employees

Host country Country in which an international corporation operates

Host-country nationals Employees who are natives of the host country

Hourly work Work paid on an hourly basis

Human capital The individual's knowledge, skills, and abilities that have economic value to an organization

Human resource planning Process that the people required to run the company are being used as effectively as possible, where and when they are needed, in order to accomplish the organization's goals

Human resources information system (HRIS) A technology system that provides data for purposes of control and decision making

Human resources management (HRM) An integrated set of processes, programs, and systems in an organization that focuses on the effective deployment and development of its employees

Indirect compensation Benefits, such as dental plans and life insurance, supplied by employers

Industrial disease A disease resulting from exposure relating to a particular process, trade, or occupation in industry

Instructional objectives Desired outcomes of a training program

Interest arbitration A mechanism to renew or establish a new collective agreement for parties

Interest-based bargaining Problem-solving bargaining based on a win-win philosophy and the development of a positive long-term relationship

Internal job posting Method of communicating information about job openings

International corporation Domestic firm that uses its existing capabilities to move into overseas markets

Internship programs Programs jointly sponsored by colleges, universities, and other organizations that offer students the opportunity to gain real-life experience while allowing them to find out how they will perform in work organizations

ISO 9000 Worldwide quality standards program

Job A group of related activities and duties

Job analysis Process of obtaining information about jobs by determining the duties, tasks, or activities and the skills, knowledge, and abilities associated with the jobs

Job characteristics model An approach to job design that recognizes the link between motivational factors and components of the job to achieve improved work performance and job satisfaction

Job description A document that lists the tasks, duties, and responsibilities of a job to be performed along with the skills, knowledge, and abilities, or competencies needed to successfully perform the work

Job design Process of defining and organizing tasks, roles, and other processes to achieve employee goals and organizational effectiveness

Job evaluation Systematic process of determining the relative worth of jobs in order to establish which jobs should be paid more than others within an organization

Job specifications Statement of the needed knowledge, skills, and abilities of the person who is to perform the position. The different duties and responsibilities performed by only one employee

Labour market Area from which applicants are recruited

Labour relations process Logical sequence of four events: (1) workers desire collective representation, (2) union begins its organizing campaign, (3) collective negotiations lead to a contract, and (4) the contract is administered

Lockout Strategy by which the employer denies employees the opportunity to work by closing its operations

Management by objectives (MBO) Philosophy of management that rates performance on the basis of employee achievement of goals

Management forecasts Opinions and judgments of supervisors or managers and others that are knowledgeable about the organization's future employment needs

Management rights Decisions regarding organizational operations over which management claims exclusive rights

Manager and/or supervisor review Performance review done by the employee's supervisor

Markov analysis Method for tracking the pattern of employee movements through various jobs

Material Safety Data Sheet (MSDS) Documents that contain vital information about hazardous substances

Mediation The use of an impartial third party to help facilitate a resolution to employment disputes

Mediator Third party in a labour dispute who meets with one party and then the other in order to suggest compromise solutions or to recommend concessions from each side that will lead to an agreement

Membership card A statement signed by an employee authorizing a union to act as a representative of the employee for purposes of collective bargaining

Mentors Managers who coach, advise, and encourage less experienced employees

Multinational corporation (MNC) Firm with independent business units operating in several countries

Negligence Failure to provide reasonable care where such failure results in injury to consumers or other employees

Occupational illness Abnormal condition or disorder resulting from exposure to environmental factors in the workplace

Occupational injury Any cut, fracture, sprain, or amputation resulting from a workplace accident

Ombudsperson Designated individual from whom employees may seek counsel for the resolution of their complaints

On-the-job training (OJT) Method by which employees are given hands-on experience with instructions from their supervisor or other trainer

Open shop Provision of the collective agreement that allows employees to join or not join the union

Open-door policy Policy of settling grievances that identifies various levels of management above the immediate supervisor for employee contact

Orientation Formal process of familiarizing new employees with the organization, their jobs, and their work unit and embedding organizational values, beliefs, and accepted behaviours

Outsourcing Contracting outside the organization for work that was formerly done by internal employees. The small-business owner saves money, time, and resources by outsourcing tasks such as accounting and payroll.

Panel interview An interview in which a board of interviewers questions and observes a single candidate

Pay equity The practice of equal pay for work of equal value

Pay grades Groups of jobs within a particular class that are paid the same rate or rate range

Pay-for-performance standard Standard by which managers tie compensation to employee effort and performance

Peer review Performance reviews done by one's fellow employees, generally on forms that are compiled into a single profile for use in the performance interview conducted by the employee's manager

Performance management system A set of integrated management practices

Piecework Work paid according to the number of units produced

Position Specific duties and responsibilities performed by only one employee

Positive, or nonpunitive, discipline System of discipline that focuses on the early correction of employee misconduct, with the employee taking total responsibility for correcting the problem

Progressive discipline Application of corrective measures by increasing degrees

Promotion Change of assignment to a job at a higher level in the organization

Real wages Wage increases larger than rises in the consumer price index; that is, the real earning power of wages

Reasonable accommodation Attempt by employers to adjust the working conditions and employment practices of employees to prevent discrimination

Recruitment The process of locating and encouraging potential applicants to apply for jobs

Reliability The degree to which interviews, tests, and other selection procedures yield comparable data over time and alternative measures

Repatriation Process of employee transition home from an international assignment

Residual rights Concept that management's authority is supreme in all matters except those it has expressly conceded to the union in the collective agreement

Reverse discrimination Giving preference to members of certain groups such that others feel they are the subjects of discrimination

Rights arbitration A mechanism to resolve disputes about the interpretation and application of a collective agreement during the term of that collective agreement

Selection The process of choosing individuals who have relevant qualifications and who will best perform on the job to fill existing or projected job openings

Self-review Performance review done by the employee being assessed, generally on a form completed by the employee prior to the performance interview

Situational question Question in which an applicant is given a hypothetical incident and asked how he or she would respond to it

Six Sigma A process used to translate customer needs into a set of optimal tasks that are performed in concert with one another

Skills inventory Information about the education, experiences, skills, etc. of staff

Staffing table Graphic representations of organizational jobs along with the numbers of employees currently occupying those jobs and future employment needs

Standards of performance Set out the expected results of the job

Statutory rights Rights that derive from legislation

Step-review system System for reviewing employee complaints and disputes by successively higher levels of management

Strategic human resources management Identifying key HR processes and linking those to the overall business strategy

Stress Any adjustive demand caused by physical, mental, or emotional factors that requires coping behaviour

Strike A situation in which unionized workers refuse to perform their work during labour negotiations

Subordinate review Performance review of a superior by an employee, which is more appropriate for developmental than for administrative purposes

Systemic discrimination The exclusion of members of certain groups through the application of employment policies or practices based on criteria that are not job-related

Talent management Leveraging competencies to achieve high organizational performance

Team review Performance review, based on TQM concepts, that recognizes team accomplishment rather than individual performance

Third-country nationals Employees who are natives of a country other than the home country or the host country

Trainee readiness The consideration of a trainee's maturity and experience when assessing him or her

Training The acquisition of skills, behaviours, and abilities to perform current work

Transfer Placement of an individual in another job for which the duties, responsibilities, status, and remuneration are approximately equal to those of the previous job

Transfer of training Effective application of principles learned to what is required on the job

Transnational corporation Firm that attempts to balance local responsiveness and global scale via a network of specialized operating units

Transnational teams Teams composed of members of multiple nationalities working on projects that span multiple countries

Trend analysis Quantitative approach to forecasting labour demand on an organizational index

Unfair labour practices Specific employer and union illegal practices that operate to deny employees their rights and benefits under labour law

Union shop Provision of the collective agreement that requires employees to join the union as a condition of their employment

Union (shop) steward Employee who, as a nonpaid union official, represents the interests of members in their relations with management

Validity How well a test or selection procedure measures a person's attributes

Virtual teams A team with widely dispersed members linked together through computer and telecommunications technology

Wage and salary survey Survey of the wages paid to employees of other employers in the surveying organization's relevant labour market

Work Tasks or activities that need to be completed

Work permit, or visa A government document granting a foreign individual the right to seek employment

Wrongful dismissal Terminating an employee's employment without just cause

NAME AND ORGANIZATION INDEX

SUBJECT INDEX